Essential Public Affairs for Journalists

# Essential Public Affairs for Journalists

SECOND EDITION

James Morrison

OXFORD
UNIVERSITY PRESS

# OXFORD
UNIVERSITY PRESS

Great Clarendon Street, Oxford OX2 6DP

Oxford University Press is a department of the University of Oxford.
It furthers the University's objective of excellence in research, scholarship,
and education by publishing worldwide in

Oxford New York

Auckland Cape Town Dar es Salaam Hong Kong Karachi
Kuala Lumpur Madrid Melbourne Mexico City Nairobi
New Delhi Shanghai Taipei Toronto

With offices in

Argentina Austria Brazil Chile Czech Republic France Greece
Guatemala Hungary Italy Japan Poland Portugal Singapore
South Korea Switzerland Thailand Turkey Ukraine Vietnam

Oxford is a registered trade mark of Oxford University Press
in the UK and in certain other countries

Published in the United States
by Oxford University Press Inc., New York

© James Morrison and the NCTJ 2011

British Library Cataloguing in Publication Data
Data available

Library of Congress Cataloging in Publication Data
Data available

Typeset by Laserwords Private Ltd, Chennai, India
Printed in Great Britain
on acid-free paper by
Clays Ltd, St Ives plc

ISBN 978-0-19-959200-5

10 9 8 7 6 5 4 3 2

For my beloved Annalise, Scarlet, and Rosella

# Preface—the changing face of public affairs

There can never be an ideal time to update a textbook on contemporary public affairs. If in Harold Wilson's era a week was 'a long time in politics', in this age of 24-hour rolling news and multimedia global communications the same could just as easily be said of a day, or even an hour. In Britain, even at the height of the parliamentary Summer Recess, any given week is liable to throw up a consistent drip-drip of policy announcements and controversies—some trivial, others all too material.

But while the capricious nature of policymaking means that some of the revisions in this volume were always doomed to be hostages to fortune, nothing could have prepared the author for the political earthquake of the May 2010 election. Shortly after the first edition of *Public Affairs for Journalists* 'went to bed' (to borrow a journalistic metaphor) the global financial sector was hit by the biggest banking collapse since the 1930s—necessitating a hasty post-deadline rewrite of Chapter 8 (on the Treasury and economy). If that caused me something of a headache, imagine the scale of the migraine engendered by the fact that the week I sat down to begin work on this second edition witnessed not only a change of UK government but also the emergence of the country's first ruling coalition since the Second World War.

Leaving aside the necessity to hastily amplify the book's previous mention of coalitions and hung Parliaments (which, as several of my students amusedly pointed out, earned little more than a paragraph in the original book), the sheer scale and pace of change since the Cameron–Clegg double act stepped out to greet reporters in that first, sun-dappled, Downing Street press conference has been extraordinary. The early weeks of any new government produce scenes of ministerial hyperactivity, as newly installed administrations seek to stamp their marks symbolically on the policy agenda. But the three months between the signing of the coalition agreement and my end-of-August copy deadline saw (among myriad other schemes and initiatives): the passage of an education Bill giving parents the right to set up their own schools and allowing all existing ones to become academies; a seismic emergency Budget that hiked VAT, froze, capped, and cut a raft of benefits, and signalled impending public spending cut-backs of up to 40 per cent; the announcement of fixed-term parliaments and a referendum on electoral reform; and a root-and-branch reinvention (or break-up, depending on your perspective) of the National Health Service.

Any one of these reforms would have merited a sizeable chapter revision but, taken together, the sustained and significant nature of so many of the coalition's announcements has forced me to substantially rewrite large sections of this textbook. This has been particularly true of chapters focusing on the White-hall spending departments that look to be the target of their most far-reaching reforms, such as Chapters 6 (the NHS), 8 (home affairs and welfare), and 15 (education).

And the changes introduced by the coalition government are only the half of it. Long before Messrs Cameron and Clegg thrashed out the details of their coalition agreement, the interval between editions had already witnessed: the beginning and end (one hopes) of the deepest recession since the Great Depression; an unprecedented scandal over parliamentary expenses culminating in countless MP resignations, the toppling of the Commons Speaker, and several criminal prosecutions; the ratification of the Lisbon Treaty and the appointment of the first European Council president; the withdrawal of British combat troops from Iraq; and at least two attempted coups against Gordon Brown by Labour plotters desperate to save their party from electoral oblivion. All of this, and more, is documented on the Online Resource Centre accompanying the book, but none of it (until now) has made it into these pages.

So what else is new about this second edition of *Essential Public Affairs for Journalists*? Well, just as the past two years have witnessed a succession of momentous developments in British (and, indeed, global) politics, so too have they seen their fair share of changes in the NCTJ programme of study. From September 2011, the two separate exams in Public Affairs Local Government and Public Affairs Central Government will be scrapped, to be replaced by a single paper covering the whole syllabus. Like the redrawn study programme, this will be christened 'Essential Public Affairs'. At the same time, a new PA-related assessment will be introduced into trainees' Multimedia Portfolio, in the form of a real-life feature article or audio or video package based on a relevant issue.

We've responded to these developments in several ways. Taking the latter first, at the close of each chapter you will now find additional pedagogic material providing pointers towards potential news angles relevant to the portfolio assessment. To make these 'topical feature' scenarios as authentic as possible, a mix of approaches has been used—with several chapters incorporating full-text reproductions or extracts from genuine newspaper articles, and others copies of real-life council agendas, financial reports, and background papers. As a reflection of the new PA exam's emphasis on issue-based questions—including ones that straddle the domains of both local and central (not to mention European Union-level) government—each chapter also ends with a list of 'current issues' that, at time of writing, were making headlines. In addition, a range of new icons have been introduced into the text itself to signpost readers to connections between interrelated central and local government topics, and to highlight all mentions of devolution (which, as before, is discussed in several chapters, rather than a discrete one of its own) and issues or controversies that received significant media coverage at the time they arose.

It's not all flux and change, though. While the NCTJ may be abandoning its long-standing dual local and central government exams, after much discussion it was decided that the overall structure of the book should remain the same—that is, with the first half focusing on the origins of the UK constitution, parliamentary democracy, and the present-day balance of powers at national level, and the second on councils and local service delivery. Anecdotal feedback from lecturers in the field (not least my fellow members of the NCTJ's PA examining board) indicates that, in practice, most centres will continue to deliver the programme in these two distinct 'phases'. Likewise, although the new-look Essential PA syllabus contains no mention of 'key terms'—the bête noire of many a past NCTJ trainee (and trainer)—and candidates will no longer be required to answer discrete key terms exam questions, the Glossary of Key Terms proved a popular feature of the first edition of PAFJ. While all mention of 'key terms' per se has therefore been excised from the book, it was decided that some form of glossary should remain, at least for this edition. Given that, when this book hits the shelves, a number of accredited centres will still be running the 'old' programme (until the end of the 2010–11 academic year), the contents of our latest glossary has been adapted to match the interim list of key terms that they will be using.

All that remains, then, is for me to issue my customary disclaimer: despite making every effort to ensure that the book was accurate and up to date at time of going to press, it was only possible to do precisely that. Even as the pages were being proofread and typeset, prior to being shunted off to the printers, a new Labour leader was preparing to take on the coalition, a host of commissions and review bodies were poised to publish their recommendations (for everything from changing the child welfare system to reforming the House of Lords), and Chancellor George Osborne was finalizing the full details of his October Comprehensive Spending Review. Whatever transpires between now (September 2010) and Spring 2011, when this book is due out, some sections of it will inevitably seem outdated or incomplete. I am confident, however, that in the main—and read in conjunction with the regularly updated Online Resource Centre it will offer you a worthy roadmap through the ever-more-labyrinthine landscape of twenty-first century British public affairs.

JM

# More praise for *Essential Public Affairs for Journalists*

'Journalists need to know what they need to know. Government, at every level, and public bodies are where they will find the stories that really affect their readers, listeners, and the viewers. This is a practical guide to help cut through the bureaucracy, jargon, smoke-screens, and secrecy.'

Bob Satchwell, Executive Director, Society of Editors

'Accurate reporting of the ever-changing political landscape is at the heart of thorough and trustworthy journalism. James Morrison delivers a definitive account of how national and local government works, packed with all the detail every journalist needs. This book is vital for anyone serious about responsible news reporting.'

Janet Jones, NCTJ Chief Examiner in Public Affairs

'This is a wonderfully thorough, clear, and up-to-date guide to the political mechanics of the country. James Morrison takes readers by the hand and leads them expertly through the twisty byways of British public life and its multi-farious institutions.'

Roger Alton, former Editor, *The Independent*

# Acknowledgements

I would like to thank my colleagues on the NCTJ's public affairs board, and particularly the inestimable Mandy Ball whose recent departure from the chair will be greatly missed by us all, for their support and encouragement as I wrote this book. Thanks, too, are due to the various other lecturers and journalists who reviewed the chapters as I wrote them, for their invariably salient advice. Special mention must go to Ron Fenney, and to David Kett—the nearest Britain has, surely, to a PA guru—for the huge amount of legwork they both did before me to make sense of the tangle of legislation and 'officialese' that bedevils local and central government today. I would also like to thank the Department for Communities and Local Government (DCLG), the National Archive, and the Economic and Social Research Council (ESRC) for their prompt responses to requests for data, and their willingness for us to reproduce tables and charts (which we have credited where this is the case). Finally, thanks to the various other government departments, executive agencies, and quangos that have helped with enquiries in one way or other both in relation to this and the previous edition: HM Treasury; the Department for Work and Pensions (DWP); the Foreign and Commonwealth Office's Europe Delivery Group; the School Improvement Division of the erstwhile Department for Children, Schools, and Families; the Commission for Social Care Inspection; the Department of Health; the United Nations Department of Public Information; the Directorate General for Budget of the European Commission; and the Institute of Fiscal Studies.

For permission to reproduce articles and documents in the topical feature ideas we are grateful to the *Manchester Evening News* (MEN Media), Guardian News and Media Ltd 2010, *Birmingham Mail*, *Western Morning News*, *Oxford Mail*, *Computer Weekly*, Tamworth Borough Council, Nottingham City Council, the Audit Commission, and Cambridgeshire County Council.

Every effort has been made to trace and contact copyright holders but this has not always been possible. If notified, the publisher will undertake to rectify any errors or omissions at the earliest opportunity.

# Brief contents

# Detailed contents

# Guide to the book's features

Each chapter in *Essential Public Affairs for Journalists* contains a selection of features to help you navigate your way through the book, and direct you to sources of further information.

Magna Carta (the Great Charter), si
as the foundation stone of Britain's
ciple of *rule of law*. This embodied tl
of a criminal offence to a free and f

## Glossary terms

Key terms are emboldened in the text and are defined in a glossary at the end of the book.

---

**☰ Topical feature idea**

The article in Figure 6.3 is taken from the *Manchester Evening News* of 23 June 2010. It concerns an announcement by Health Secretary Andrew Lansley that two maternity units earmarked for closure since 2006 might now be saved. His intervention came as part of a nationwide review of Labour's controversial moves to rationalize the NHS by closing or merging some hospitals and centralizing core services like accident and emergency in major ones in towns and cities. The proposed closure of the two units made national headlines when announced because Salford MP Hazel Blears joined a protest march despite being a minister in Mr Blair's government. How would you follow up this story to develop it into a background feature for the paper? Who would you approach for interviews, and what questions would you ask them?

## Topical feature ideas

Topical feature ideas at the end of chapters suggest possible sources of a story on each subject.

---

**✳ Current issues**

- **Electoral reform:** in the horse-trading between Mr Clegg and Mr Cameron's Conservatives which led to the formation of the Lib-Con coalition, the Tories eventually made the 'final offer' of a referendum on the Alternative Vote (AV)—a system used in Australia which Labour had already pledged to explore in its manifesto. It remains to be seen how actively Tory MPs will be permitted to campaign for a 'no' vote in the referendum, due to be held in May 2011, and whether the Lib Dem grass roots will continue to support its leadership remaining in the coalition if AV is rejected.
- **Fixed-term parliaments:** the Lib-Con coalition is introducing fixed-term parliaments in the mould of France, America, and other countries—ending the age-old

## Current issues

For each chapter some of the most interesting and relevant issues have been picked out, into which you may wish to look further.

---

**? Review questions**

1. Which is the oldest UK political party—Conservative, Labour, or Liberal Democrat?
2. To what extent has Labour stayed true to its democratic socialist roots, and are traditional labels such as 'left-wing', 'right-wing', and 'centrist' still relevant today?
3. Outline the similarities and differences between the role of the 1922 Committee in the Conservative Party and the Parliamentary Labour Party.
4. What is the difference between a political donation and loan in UK law?
5. What are the arguments for and against state funding of political parties in Britain?

## Review questions

A set of questions at the end of each chapter allows you to test your knowledge of what has been covered.

## Further reading

Take your learning further by using the reading lists at the end of each chapter to find more detailed information on a specific topic.

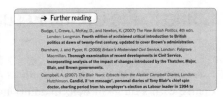

→ Further reading

Budge, I., Crewe, I., McKay, D., and Newton, K. (2007) *The New British Politics*, 4th edn, London: Longman. **Fourth edition of acclaimed critical introduction to British politics at dawn of twenty-first century, updated to cover Brown's administration.**

Burnham, J. and Pyper, R. (2008) *Britain's Modernised Civil Service*, London: Palgrave Macmillan. **Thorough examination of recent developments in Civil Service, incorporating analysis of the impact of changes introduced by the Thatcher, Major, Blair, and Brown governments.**

Campbell, A. (2007) *The Blair Years: Extracts from the Alastair Campbell Diaries*, London: Hutchinson. **Candid, if 'on message', personal diaries of Tony Blair's chief spin doctor, charting period from his employer's election as Labour leader in 1994 to**

In the margin you will also find a number of icons with the following meanings.

This icon indicates an issue is being discussed, which is concerned with **devolution** in the United Kingdom. It allows you to see at a glance where devolved subjects are dealt with in the book.

This icon occurs where there is discussion of public affairs **reporting in practice**. The icon is used to highlight mention of debates and issues that led to major news stories in the British media, and examples of resources that are available to assist journalists in reporting on aspects of public affairs.

Certain subjects are matters for both central and local government. In those cases the **central/local cross-references** direct you to the appropriate coverage elsewhere in the book.

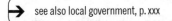

→ see also local government, p. xxx

The **Online Resource Centre** icon appears to remind you when additional or updated material can be found on the book's accompanying Online Resource Centre.

# Guide to the Online Resource Centre

*Essential Public Affairs for Journalists* is accompanied by an Online Resource Centre with a range of helpful additional materials. These resources are free of charge and designed to accompany the book. The Online Resource Centre can be found at:

www.oxfordtextbooks.co.uk/orc/morrison2e/

## Regular updates

Key new developments in public affairs are succinctly summarised so that you can always keep up to date.

## News feeds

Real life articles from various news sites are linked to via RSS.

## Audio podcast with the author

A recording of the author discussing the practicalities of reporting public affairs is available to listen to online or download.

## Additional and updated tables

Tables with information that changes regularly can be found in an updated form online, alongside additional tables that do not appear in the book.

Table 4.2 Distribution of seats in the House of Commons following the May 2010 election

| Party | Seats | Gains | Losses | Net gain/loss | Votes (%) | Votes | Swing |
|---|---|---|---|---|---|---|---|
| Conservative | 307 | 101 | 3 | +97 | 36.1 | 10,706,647 | +3.8% |
| Labour | 258 | 3 | 94 | -91 | 29.0 | 8,604,358 | -6.2% |
| Liberal Democrat | 57 | 8 | 13 | -5 | 23.0 | 6,827,938 | +1.0% |

## Topical feature ideas

To help you consider where to find a story or to prepare for the NCTJ portfolio assessment further topical feature ideas are provided.

## Web links

Useful websites relating to the topics in each chapter are listed to allow you to find further information.

Chapter 6

www.dh.gov.uk
Official website of Department of Health in England and Wales. A hugely comprehensive website with links other resources, plus detailed breakdowns on individual areas of responsibility, including National Service Frameworks, NHS trusts, and foundation hospitals.

www.nice.org.uk/aboutnice/
Website of the National Institute for Health and Clinical Excellent (NICE). Includes an overview of its remit and powers and details of recent rulings on medication and treatment.

www.ombudsman.org.uk/about_us/our_history/index.html
Official website of the Health Service Ombudsman, including details of the types of complaints investigated and the procedure for complaining.

www.healthcarecommission.org.uk
Website of the Healthcare Commission, which monitors NHS and private healthcare standards in England.

# Introduction

## ▶ Confessions of a local council reporter

I'll always remember the name 'Mervyn Lane'. From the moment I arrived as a naive raw recruit on the *North Devon Journal* in Barnstaple—bristling with high ideas, most of them hugely unrealistic and some more than a little 'conspiracy theorist'—Mervyn and I were destined to clash. I'd been taken on as a junior reporter without a car (or, for that matter, driving licence) and was only hired on condition I passed my test within six months of starting. Logically enough, I was immediately posted to Bideford—the area's 'second town', some ten miles west of the paper's Barnstaple headquarters—but still expected to soldier into head office each day, and cover a sprawling patch of rustic terrain into the bargain.

To top it all, I was required to generate a district edition single-handedly each week, filling three pages of news and finding at least one front-page lead without fail. Bideford being Bideford, there were few obvious sources of scoops: the edgiest events tended to be an annual Easter fair, known dubiously (but all too descriptively) as 'Cow Pat Fun Day', and the occasional drugs raid on a pint-sized sink estate at East-the-Water, the town's ungrammatically named answer to Moss Side.

Unsurprisingly, it wasn't long before I was turning to the local authority for inspiration (or, more accurately, out of desperation). Little did I know how fruitful this would be. Those wintry evenings spent pinching myself awake through meetings of Torridge District Council's planning committee invariably threw up a last-minute gem that, with a bit of creative editing (and barring news of an international sheep-rustling scam), would generate enough ire to merit a splash.

From the humdrum ('Supermarket Threat to Town Centre') to the absurd ('Ships in Our Back Garden'), Torridge seldom failed to deliver the goods. Inevitably, it was only a matter of time before I crossed swords with the venerable Mr Lane—at that time leader of the district council's ruling Liberal Democrat group, chairman of its powerful *policy and resources committee,* and both a Bideford town councillor and Devon county councillor to boot.

The first of our many run-ins was sparked by a front-page story I wrote about a decision to award free parking permits to all Torridge councillors and 92 senior officers (dubbed 'essential users' by the council) for use in council car parks in central Bideford whenever they were on local authority business. As controversies go, this may sound small beer—there was nothing illegal or improper about the policy—but boy did it upset the locals. To understand the scale of the furore among residents and businesses, a little context is needed. Parking and the wider subject of transport were perhaps the most toxic issues facing Bidefordians. For various reasons, driving was pretty much the only way most people had of gaining access to the town for shopping or tourism, thanks to a train line that was (literally) a museum piece (take a bow, Dr Beeching), and an antediluvian bus service. The notoriously perilous North Devon Link Road and a winding, hazardous 'coastal route' were all that connected it to civilization (or Barnstaple, at any rate)—providing lifelines for those living in outlying villages. Yet, in central Bideford—in the words of one councillor, 'a medieval town with a twentieth-century traffic problem'—any street wide enough to admit vehicles seemed to have been daubed with double-yellow lines, putting the limited car park spaces available at a premium. Hence the reaction.

My parking story was one of many to irritate Mr Lane during my 18-month tenure as Bideford district reporter. But he wasn't the only local dignitary to be in the focus of a splash on the *Journal* during this time. . .

Let's not forget George Moss, the Bideford mayor who arrived in full regalia to turn on the town's Christmas lights one November only to find that a timer switch had done so automatically several hours earlier, at the moment at which dusk had descended. He didn't fare any better a year later, when the precautions that council engineers took to avoid a similar fiasco proved so watertight that the lights couldn't be switched on at all.

Of course, council stories don't need to emanate from committee meetings—or, for that matter, councillors. Take the example of Les Garland, a community activist from Northam—a strip of suburban housing, pockmarked with scrappy golf courses, which runs along the Torridge Estuary to the east of Bideford. Armed with little more than a tape measure, he led a one-man campaign to rid the whole of Devon of the peril of 'hazardously placed' A-boards. (To the uninitiated, A-boards are the signs one finds outside newsagents bearing misspelt headlines from papers such as the *Journal.*)

Insisting they posed a hazard to pedestrians, by blocking pavements and tripping people up, Les set about scouring the small print of Devon County Council's highways regulations—not to mention various Acts of Parliament—in search of a clause that would back his assertion that they contravened health and safety legislation. I clearly remember a conversation with an apoplectic county councillor, who stormed into the *Journal's* Bideford office to inform me that the county could be faced with rewriting its entire highways policy, at a cost of tens of thousands of pounds, if Les were to force the issue.

Perhaps inevitably, Les had the last laugh. When I last visited North Devon, in 2003, I picked up a copy of that hallowed Bideford edition of the *Journal*. Turning to the district pages, I was greeted by a familiar visage, grinning at me over a caption about a good citizenship award he'd received for serving the local community. As I wandered down Bideford high street later that day, I couldn't help noticing several shops still had A-boards placed perilously distant from their doorways. But the memory of Les's beaming face reminded me that, in one way or other, his dogged devotion to civic duty had paid off.

My purpose in highlighting these anecdotal examples is to illustrate a simple point: that knowledge of public affairs (and, for the rookie journalist, local government especially) *matters*. Whether it be protests by angry parents over changes to school catchment areas, demands from worried residents for 'speed bumps' to prevent accidents on dangerous roads, or controversies about New Age traveller camps, waste disposal sites, or parasitical out-of-town superstores, local newspapers are chock-full of council-related stories on a daily and weekly basis. And to identify, research, and write up these stories in a way that is comprehensible and meaningful to their readers, journalists first need to grasp the basics of how government works and the parameters within which it operates. This book aims to make that process easier.

# 1

# The British constitution and monarchy

## ▶ What is a 'constitution'?

For any state to achieve a sense of order and identity it requires a shared set of values to be recognized and accepted by its subjects. Such values tend to be instilled by a system of fundamental laws and principles, and upheld by parliaments, courts, and other institutions established to maintain and reinforce them.

This notion of shared membership, of collective rights and responsibilities—as common to commercial companies and supranational organizations like the European Union (EU) as to organs of individual governments—is known as a 'constitution'.

Constitutions come in all shapes and sizes. They can be formal or informal, long or short, absolute or merely advisory. Most significant, though, is the difference between the two broad types of constitution adopted by individual states: *written* and *unwritten*. Naturally, for any set of ideas related to one's citizenship of a state to be communicated and sustained effectively some kind of written record will need to exist. Yet there is an important distinction between constitutions described as 'written' and ones that are not. All constitutions of any worth comprise elements that have been written in a literal sense—for example, laws or decrees set down in documentary form. But this does not make them 'written constitutions' per se. Written constitutions are, rather, *codified* frameworks: single manuscripts summarizing the rights, values, and responsibilities attached to membership of the states to which they relate.

For historical reasons some states have adopted written constitutions while others have not. In general, written constitutions have tended to emerge in countries where there has been a sudden change in the entire system of government caused by a political upheaval like a war, invasion, or revolution. This was certainly the case for two nations with which the term is perhaps most closely associated: France and the USA.

France's Constitution derives from the *Declaration of the Rights of Man and of the Citizen*, adopted on 26 August 1789 by the National Constituent Assembly convened in the aftermath of the French Revolution, and later amended to enshrine the three abiding principles of 'liberty, equality, and fraternity'. The USA adopted its equivalent a decade after declaring independence from Britain, on 17 September 1787, at a landmark constitutional convention in Philadelphia, Pennsylvania, addressed by Enlightenment philosopher Benjamin Franklin.

## The origins and sources of the British constitution

Britain—or more accurately the 'United Kingdom of Great Britain and Northern Ireland'—is a different case entirely. The story of the UK's constitutional evolution is of, first, the gradual unification of disparate kingdoms under one national sovereign (monarch), then, in due course, the struggle for supremacy between the sovereign and the Christian Church, and ultimately between the sovereign and Parliament.

As these various power struggles have been played out, at several points in its history the UK has come close to adopting a formal framework specifying the rights and responsibilities of its citizenry. Up to now however, it has stopped short of producing a definitive statement. Despite the fact that documents of one kind or another form a huge part of the constitutional framework governing the lives of its citizens, there exists no single statement of principles. Therefore, in defiance of campaigns by pressure groups ranging from the Chartists of 1848 to the coalition of liberal thinkers who put their names to Charter 88 a century and a half later, to all intents and purposes Britain still has an unwritten constitution.

As such, the British constitution has clear advantages: it is *flexible* enough to be amended, added to, or subtracted from according to the will of the elected Parliament of the day, without any of the tortuous procedures required in the USA and elsewhere whenever the slightest break with tradition is sought in the interests of political progress. Conversely, it has the disadvantage of provoking as much wrangling among lawyers, politicians, and historians as it can ever claim to circumvent, by leaving layers of ambiguity around sometimes crucial issues relating to its subjects' liberties and entitlements. The controversy surrounding Gordon Brown's decision to sign the EU's 2007 Lisbon Treaty—seen by some as a 'European constitution' in all but name—is one example of how easily the UK can adopt potentially significant changes to its constitutional fabric without any of the debate rendered necessary by the *rigid* rule systems of other countries. Meanwhile, the perceived 'Big Brother' assault on individuals' civil liberties represented by the rash of anti-terror legislation since the attacks on the Twin Towers on 11 September 2001, not to mention the launch of a national DNA database and the recently abandoned identity card scheme, was viewed by human rights campaigners as an example of the dangers of failing to enshrine core principles in a solid constitutional statement.

So what are the primary sources of the UK's constitution? The main constituent components fall into the following five broad categories:

- *statute*—that is, individual laws, known as 'Acts of Parliament';
- *common law*—sometimes known as 'judge-made' or 'case' law;
- *conventions*—that is, customs, traditions, and long-standing practices;
- *treatises*—historical works of legal and/or constitutional authority;
- *treaties*—that is, EU and other international agreements.

## Statute

Magna Carta (the Great Charter), signed by King John in 1215, is often cited as the foundation stone of Britain's constitution, invoking as it does the principle of **rule of law.** This embodied the inalienable right of any citizen accused of a criminal offence to a free and fair trial before their peers and, crucially, enshrined the principle that no one—not even the reigning sovereign—is 'above the law'. Of course, the idea that not even the sovereign is immune to prosecution is (like many constitutional concepts) a little problematic. In practice, because criminal prosecutions are instigated in the name of the Crown, if the king or queen were accused of a crime and brought before a court of law, this would provoke a constitutional crisis.

Perhaps more significant even than Magna Carta was the 1689 Bill of Rights, passed in the wake of the extraordinarily turbulent period stemming from the execution forty years earlier of the Anglican King Charles I, and the 11-year 'interregnum' that followed under his vanquisher, the Puritan 'Lord Protector' Oliver Cromwell. Although the titular head of the Church of England, Charles was felt by many to be too sympathetic to Roman Catholicism, having married the Catholic princess Henrietta Maria of France. There was also deep unease about his invocation of the loose constitutional principle (popular among medieval monarchs) known as the 'Divine Right of Kings'—a notion that the authority of the sovereign derived from his or her relationship to God and was thus immutable. In the event, the Parliamentarians secured victory over Charles's Royalist supporters in the ensuing English Civil War (1642–51), ending centuries of rule under this premise.

The Bill of Rights itself arose out of the alliance between the Protestant-dominated Parliament and William of Orange, the Dutch king whom it helped to depose Charles's younger son, James II, during the 'Glorious Revolution' of 1688. Having worked in an uneasy stalemate with James's elder brother, Charles II, after his return from exile in France following Cromwell's death in 1660, Parliament used the ascension of his uncompromising sibling (a devout Catholic) as a pretext to cement its newly asserted authority as the supreme seat of power in Britain.

To this end it identified James's Protestant daughter, Mary, as the rightful heir to the throne, prompting her father's flight to France. Together with her husband, William, Mary effectively deposed James as monarch. In exchange for Parliament's loyalty to the couple, they permitted the passage of the Bill, which formalized for the first time the transfer of constitutional supremacy from Crown to elected Parliament. Its central tenet was to ratify the principle that the sovereign could only in future rule *through* Parliament—rather than tell it what to do, as in the past. In other words, monarchs would henceforth have to seek the official consent of members of Parliament (MPs)—and, more particularly, government ministers—before passing legislation (Acts), declaring war, or invoking any of the other sovereign powers they had traditionally wielded. In this way the Bill effectively ended centuries of 'royal sovereignty' and ushered in the concept (even today a fundamental cornerstone of Britain's democracy) of **parliamentary sovereignty.**

This core constitutional principle is the one that, above all others, most symbolizes the oft-cited flexibility of an unwritten constitution. The term 'sovereignty'—or **political sovereignty**—refers to the notion of an individual or institution exercising supreme control over an area, people, or themselves. The concept of parliamentary sovereignty flows from this: as well as asserting the hegemony of the *institution* of Parliament over British subjects, it confers on *each individual UK Parliament*—the body of MPs elected at a given general election—the authority to make its own laws and to repeal any of those passed by previous Parliaments. To this extent it prevents any one Parliament being 'bound by the actions of a predecessor'.

Many constitutional experts argue that this idea is incompatible with that of a conventional written constitution because, if we were to have such a document, one Parliament could theoretically use its sovereignty to repeal the Act that introduced it. Advocates of a codified document dismiss this as a bogus argument, contending that many countries with written constitutions manage to maintain them alongside their own versions of parliamentary sovereignty without encountering such conflicts. One way of embedding written constitutions into the political fabric of a state is to compose them out of webs of interlocking legislation, rather than a single Act—making them harder to repeal. Another might be to set up an independent superior court with the power to adjudicate in constitutional disputes. Britain's new US-style **Supreme Court** (see p. 63) could conceivably fulfil this role.

In addition to formalizing the notion of parliamentary sovereignty, the Bill of Rights granted a number of privileges to all 'Englishmen'—with the exception, in certain cases, of Roman Catholics. Its main tenets are listed in Table 1.1.

The Bill also specified conditions governing the future succession of the monarchy, in light of the coronation of William and Mary over the dethroned James II:

**Table 1.1** Main entitlements listed in the Bill of Rights 1689

| Freedoms for all 'Englishmen' | Sanctions for Roman Catholics |
| --- | --- |
| Freedom from royal interference with the law—sovereigns forbidden from establishing their own courts, or acting as judge themselves | Ban on Catholics succeeding to English throne—reflecting the supposed fact that '*it hath been found by experience that it is inconsistent with the safety and welfare of this protestant kingdom to be governed by a papist prince*' |
| Freedom from being taxed without Parliament's agreement | Obligation on newly crowned sovereigns to swear oaths of allegiance to Church of England |
| Freedom to petition reigning monarch | |
| Freedom *for Protestants only* to possess 'arms for defence' | Bar on carrying weapons |
| Freedom from drafting into peacetime army without Parliament's consent | |
| Freedom to elect MPs without sovereign's interference | |
| Freedom from cruel and unusual punishments and excessive bail | |
| Freedom from fines and forfeitures without trial | |

- James's flight from England was defined as an 'abdication';
- William and Mary were officially declared James's successors;
- the throne should subsequently pass to Mary's heirs, then her sister, Princess Anne of Denmark, and her heirs, then to heirs of William by later marriage.

Finally, the Bill also introduced a further constitutional principle that remains fundamental to the workings of Parliament. Often incorrectly described as a 'convention' (rather than a product of statute, which it is), this is **parliamentary privilege**. In brief, the primary role of parliamentary privilege is to enable any elected MP sitting in the House of Commons or peer in the House of Lords to make accusations about individuals or companies in open debate in the chambers without fear of prosecution for defamation.

Recent years have seen several high-profile examples of parliamentary privilege being used by members to 'name and shame' private individuals in ways that would be considered defamatory (and which might invite legal action) if repeated outside Parliament. In 2000 Peter Hain (then Foreign Office Minister for Africa) invoked privilege to identify brothers Maurice and David Zollman as the owners of an Antwerp diamond trading business that he said was breaking **United Nations (UN)** sanctions by helping to bankroll the civil war in Angola. A year later Peter Robinson (then deputy leader of the Democratic

Unionist Party) used it to 'out' Brian Keenan and Brian Gillen as members of the Provisional Irish Republican Army (IRA) ruling army council.

A flipside of the legal protection afforded by parliamentary privilege is the fact that certain words and phrases are construed as 'unparliamentary language' and therefore unacceptable if directed at fellow members in either the Commons or Lords chambers. Most notorious is the word 'liar', which is seen to conflict constitutionally with the freedom given to members under parliamentary privilege to speak their minds. In November 1993 the Reverend Ian Paisley (then leader of the Democratic Unionists) was suspended from the Commons for five days for accusing then Prime Minister John Major of lying after it emerged that, despite previously insisting the idea of negotiating with Northern Irish Republicans (whom he dubbed 'terrorists') would 'turn his stomach', he'd actually been holding secret talks for more than a year with Sinn Féin, the main Republican party.

Just as parliamentary privilege protects MPs and peers from being sued through the courts for defamatory statements made in Parliament, it also safeguards the media and public from action arising out of repeating those claims. By way of further complicating explanations of this privilege, however, according to a literal interpretation of the Bill of Rights it also protects the press from proceedings arising from *a report alleging wrongdoing in Parliament by an MP*. This legal argument was used to enable *The Guardian* to defend a libel action brought in 1996 by former Conservative minister Neil Hamilton over its allegations two years earlier that he had accepted cash from Mohamed Al Fayed for asking parliamentary questions designed to further the Harrods owner's business interests. To muddy the constitutional waters further, as a sitting MP Mr Hamilton had to obtain formal permission to sue the newspaper in the first place. In the event, a new clause was inserted into the 1996 Defamation Act (s. 13) enabling him to waive his right to parliamentary privilege by suing *The Guardian* as a private citizen (an action that, in any case, failed).

In November 2008 a major political row erupted about a more obscure aspect of parliamentary privilege, when it emerged that the Conservatives' immigration spokesman, Damian Green, had been arrested and questioned by police over allegations that he unlawfully solicited leaks about government policy from a sympathetic civil servant in the Home Office. Both Opposition and government MPs united in criticizing the police action. Many saw it as an abuse of the long-established constitutional right of members to conduct free and open conversations with officials in the Palace of Westminster—and a throwback to Charles I's challenge to the freedoms of Parliament in the seventeenth century. MPs on all sides of the House turned their fire on the Commons *Speaker,* Michael Martin, who, as its overall custodian, was accused of having given his permission to officers to search Mr Green's office—potentially jeopardizing the confidentiality of sensitive information relating to his constituents. It later transpired that Mr Martin had in fact delegated the decision to the Sergeant-at-Arms.

Perhaps the most contentious attempt to use parliamentary privilege as a protection was the interpretation cited by three Labour MPs—Elliot Morley, Jim Devine, and David Chaytor—and Tory peer Lord Hanningfield after they were each charged with false accounting over their Commons expenses claims (see pp. 57–8). They invoked Article Nine of the 1689 Bill of Rights to argue that, as any alleged wrongdoing had been committed by them while carrying out official duties, it was for Parliament alone to try (if necessary) to punish them. In the event, their argument was overruled by the courts.

Of the UK's other key constitutional statutes, the most historically significant are the 1701 Act of Settlement and the 1706–07 Acts of Union. The former built on the newly introduced rules relating to monarchical succession in the Bill of Rights, by setting out the conditions for future sovereigns outlined in Table 1.2.

The Acts of Union, meanwhile, were twin laws passed first in England then Scotland, in 1706 and 1707 respectively, formalizing the Treaty of Union—the agreement that unified the countries as one United Kingdom under a single sovereign and Parliament. Key Acts absorbed into UK law more recently include those listed in Table 1.3.

**Table 1.2** The rules governing monarchical succession in the Act of Settlement 1701

| | Details |
|---|---|
| Protestants only | The Crown should pass to the Protestant descendants of the Electress Sophie of Hanover (a first cousin once removed of Queen Anne, who had inherited the throne after the death of Mary and William) |
| No marriages to Catholics | Monarchs '*shall join in communion with the Church of England*' and not marry Roman Catholics |
| England for the English | If a person not native to England comes to the throne, England will not wage war for '*any dominions or territories which do not belong to the Crown of England without the consent of Parliament*' |
| Loyalty from the Crown | No monarch may leave the 'British Isles' without Parliament's consent (repealed by George I in 1716) |
| Openness before Parliament | All government matters within the **Privy Council's** jurisdiction (see p. 20) should be transacted there and all such resolutions must be signed, so that Parliament knows who has taken such decisions |
| Constitutional privileges for English only | No foreigner, even if naturalized (unless born of English parents), shall be allowed to be a privy councillor or member of either House of Parliament, or to hold '*any office or place of trust, either civil or military, or to have any grant of lands, tenements or hereditaments from the Crown, to himself or to any other or others in trust for him*' (repealed by later citizenship laws) |
| Ban on election for Crown servants | No person working for the monarch or receiving a Crown pension may be an MP, to avoid 'unwelcome' royal interference in Parliament's work |
| Judiciary answerable to Parliament | Judges' commissions are valid *quamdiu se bene gesserint* (during good behaviour) and can be removed only by both Houses of Parliament |
| Parliament has ultimate sanction | No royal pardon (see p. 21) can save a person from impeachment by the Commons |

**Table 1.3** Key statutes absorbed into the UK constitution in the twentieth century

| Statute | Effect |
|---------|--------|
| Race Relations Acts 1965, 1968, and 1976 | Outlawed discrimination on racial grounds |
| Government of Scotland and Government of Wales Acts 1998 | Paved the way for national *referenda* to establish devolved power in Scotland and Wales |
| Human Rights Act (HRA) 1998 | Incorporated into British law the *Convention on the Protection of Human Rights and Fundamental Freedoms* (European Convention on Human Rights), signed by the **Council of Europe** in 1950 (see p. 306) |
| House of Lords Act 1999 | Removed all but 92 hereditary peers then remaining and created a 'transitional' Lords to remain until decisive reform was agreed by both Houses (see p. 59) |

The penultimate Act listed in Table 1.3—the Human Rights Act (HRA) 1998—justifies some discussion here, given the growing contention by many lawyers, human rights campaigners, and constitutional experts that it conflicts with the British constitution as it previously stood. For this and other reasons, the Conservatives entered the May 2010 general election with a manifesto commitment to repeal the Act, in favour of a new Bill of Rights tailored specifically to UK citizens. But with its coalition partners, the Liberal Democrats, committed to the HRA, in the short term it settled for a wide-ranging  inquiry by an independent commission. At time of writing the Act remained in place.

Although it received **royal assent** in November 1998, the HRA only came into force in October 2000. Among its stipulations was that every future Bill put before Parliament must now include a preface confirming that the relevant **secretary of state** is happy that it conforms with the convention. The principal rights safeguarded by the Convention are as outlined in Table 1.4.

In addition, the UK has accepted the First and Sixth (now 13th) Protocols to the *European Convention on Human Rights* (ECHR), of which there are 14 altogether. The First Protocol includes additional rights for property (Art. 1), education (Art. 2), and free and fair elections (Art. 3).

The 13th Protocol formally abolishes the death penalty (previously, the Sixth Protocol prohibited it in peacetime only).

The Act has, in theory, strengthened the ability of ordinary people to challenge the actions of governments, public bodies, and private companies in the UK and EU courts, by if necessary taking legal action through the **European Court of Human Rights (ECtHR)** in Strasbourg. There are, however, some notable restrictions to its pre-eminence, and it remains a moot point as to how far it takes absolute precedence over national laws and conventions. By general consensus, for example, the principle of parliamentary privilege remains unaffected by the Act. In addition, British judges—although required by it to take

**Table 1.4** The Articles of the European Convention on Human Rights (ECHR)

| Article | Right enshrined |
| --- | --- |
| 1 | Obligation to respect human rights |
| 2 | Life |
| 3 | Protection from torture and inhuman or degrading treatment |
| 4 | Protection from slavery and forced or compulsory labour |
| 5 | Right to liberty and security of person |
| 6 | Right to a fair trial |
| 7 | Protection from retrospective criminalization of acts or omissions |
| 8 | Protection of private and family life |
| 9 | Freedom of thought, conscience, and religion |
| 10 | Freedom of expression |
| 11 | Freedom of association and assembly |
| 12 | Right to marry and found a family |
| 13 | Freedom from discrimination |
| 14 | Prohibition of discrimination |
| 15 | Derogations |
| 16 | Exemption for political activities of aliens |
| 17 | Prohibition of abuse of rights |
| 18 | Limitations on permitted restrictions of rights |

account of judgments in Strasbourg when making rulings in British courts—are not permitted simply to override extant parliamentary legislation that appears to contravene the Convention.

In addition, the following formal qualifications exist in relation to the Act's implementation and enforcement:

- claims must be brought against the offending state or public body 'within one year of the action about which the complaint is being made';
- some rights can theoretically be breached if not 'in accordance with the laws of the country' that is a signatory;
- breaches are tolerated 'in the interests of national security, public safety, or the country's economic wellbeing; for the prevention of crime and disorder, the protection of health or morals, or to protect the freedom and rights of others . . .'.

In the UK the HRA has arguably been repeatedly breached by successive home secretaries. The Anti-terrorism, Crime, and Security Act 2001, passed after the 11 September attacks on New York, allowed the detention and deportation without trial of people suspected of terrorist links, and Tony Blair repeatedly threatened to amend the Act to prevent judges blocking further proposed crackdowns—particularly on the activities of extremist Islamist preachers—following the 2005 London bombings.

In Scotland the Act came into force in 1998—two years ahead of England. By November 1999 the High Court had already declared unlawful the appointment of 129 temporary sheriffs (judges in the Scottish criminal courts) because they had been hired by the Lord Advocate, the member of the *Scottish Executive* responsible for prosecutions—a clear conflict with one of the constitution's fundamental guiding principles, the **separation of powers** (see pp. 15–17).

One potential outcome of the Act's adoption in the longer term could be the abolition of the Act of Settlement, which might be argued to infringe human rights by preventing non-Protestants acceding to the British throne and maintaining a system whereby the succession passes through the male line (see below). For some time *The Guardian* has argued that the very *existence* of a  monarchy is incompatible with the HRA and that the 1701 Act should therefore be repealed. Because it is still technically illegal (under the Treason Felony Act 1848) to advocate the monarchy's abolition, the paper once even went so far as to apply for a High Court declaration that the 1848 Act was incompatible with art. 10 of the HRA. Its attempt failed, due to a loophole, because the Court ruled that the Attorney General's refusal to grant immunity to its editor was not an 'act of the state'—meaning it fell outside the HRA's remit.

The most recent twist in the newspaper's long-standing campaign for the abolition of the Act came in September 2008, when it reported that Labour MP Chris Bryant—charged by Gordon Brown during his first year as prime minister with reviewing the constitution—had recommended ending the bar on Catholics succeeding to the throne and abolishing the principle of 'eldest male primogeniture'. In the event, Mr Brown left government without taking further action.

Besides the showpiece constitutional Acts listed in Table 1.3, a number of others have contained key clauses with serious implications for the workings of the British constitution. Among these are the myriad Parliament Acts passed in the first half of the twentieth century (discussed in more detail in Chapter 2). Perhaps the single most significant constitutional reform introduced by any of these Acts was the stipulation, in the Parliament Act 1911, that a general election must be held *a maximum of five years after the previous Parliament was convened* (in other words, a little over five years after the previous polling day). Until then parliaments could theoretically last up to seven years, under the terms of the Septennial Act 1715. It would be another century, however, before fixed-term parliaments in the more widely understood sense were introduced, by the Liberal Democrat-Conservative coalition (see p. 115).

## Common law

For several centuries before the emergence of parliamentary democracy many laws passed in England were decided, on a case-by-case basis, by judges.

When this system began emerging in the eleventh and twelfth centuries judicial decisions were often taken in an ad hoc way, at a very local level, leading to significant disparities from one area of the kingdom to another—in terms of what was and was not perceived as a criminal offence, and the range and severity of punishments meted out when laws were broken.

In 1166, however, the first Plantagenet king, Henry II, began the process of institutionalizing a unified national framework of common law derived from what he saw as the more reasoned judgments made in local hearings over previous decades. This new framework—which came to apply throughout England and Wales, although not Scotland—elevated some local laws to a national level, sought to eliminate arbitrary or eccentric rulings, and established a great enduring constitutional right of citizens charged with criminal offences: a jury system, which would enshrine defendants' entitlement to be tried by '12 good men and true' from among their fellow citizens. To ensure that these new practices were implemented consistently and fairly throughout the land, Henry appointed judges at his own central court and sent them around the country to adjudicate on local disputes.

Many statutes passed—and constitutional conventions that have evolved—in subsequent centuries have their roots in common law. Even now common law is occasionally 'created': judges often have to make rulings based on their interpretations of ambiguously worded Acts or apparent conflicts between domestic and international laws. Such 'test cases' are, in their way, common law hearings.

## Conventions

Other than from formal statutes and court judgments, perhaps the single most characteristic feature of Britain's unwritten constitution is its incorporation of all manner of idiosyncratic, quaint, and occasionally absurd traditions and customs. These well-worn practices have become accepted as part of Britain's constitutional framework through little more than endless repetition.

Many of the principal conventions operating in Parliament and government today are discussed in detail elsewhere in this book. These include the doctrines of **collective responsibility** and **individual ministerial responsibility,** and the tradition that the sovereign accepts the will of Parliament by rubber-stamping new legislation with the royal assent. More amusing conventions include the fact that the Speaker in the House of Lords (until recently the *Lord Chancellor,* but now an elected **Lord Speaker**) sits on a woolsack and wears a wig. The annual State Opening of Parliament by the reigning monarch is heralded by a procession led by a ceremonial officer known as 'The Gentleman Usher of the Black Rod'. It is the task of Black Rod—as he is commonly known—to lead MPs (or 'strangers') from the Commons to the Lords to hear the *Queen's Speech.* On arriving at the Commons to summon MPs, he has the door slammed in his face, and is forced to gain entry by rapping on it three times with (naturally) a black staff. This ritual is derived from a confrontation between Parliament and the sovereign in 1642, when King Charles I tried to arrest five MPs, in what the Commons regarded as a breach of parliamentary privilege. Within Parliament today, a former of light 'class warfare' between the chambers remains: MPs only refer to the Lords as 'another place'.

### Treatises

Just as judges often have to disentangle apparently contradictory elements of Britain's unwritten constitution when making court rulings, so, too, historians, philosophers, and constitutional theorists have long struggled to make sense of it.

Of the myriad books and theses written about the UK constitution over the centuries, a handful have become so revered that they are now seen to qualify as constitutional documents themselves. Some are considered so indispensable that they are effectively used as 'handbooks' (albeit unwieldy ones) by everyone from the **Speaker** of the House of Commons to High Court barristers and judges. Many of today's new laws and court judgments are framed in reference to the wisdom imparted in such tomes, the most celebrated of which are listed in Table 1.5.

### Treaties

Over recent decades Britain has signed many international treaties. Of these only a handful are arguably 'constitutional'—that is, legally binding. Most—such as the 1945 Charter of the United Nations and the North Atlantic Treaty, which established the **North Atlantic Treaty Organization (NATO)** in 1949—are really little more than membership agreements and, as such, could theoretically be 'opted out of' at any time.

However, some—such as the ECHR, ratified by Labour in 1998—have effectively been incorporated into the UK constitution and would therefore require legislation to 'remove' the obligations they impose on the state. There has also been considerable debate about the growing powers of the EU, which Britain joined (amid some controversy) in 1973, when it was still known as the European Economic Community (EEC). Recent treaties—in particular, the 2007 Lisbon Treaty—have solidified the relationship between member states and the EU's governing institutions, leading so-called 'Euro-sceptics' to claim the UK has signed up to an 'EU constitution' by the back door and is now part of a 'European super-state' governed from Brussels, rather than an independent sovereign nation. This is discussed further in Chapter 9.

# The separation of powers in the UK

Perhaps the most fundamental guiding principle underlying the British constitution is the 'separation of powers'. Based on the theories of French political

**Table 1.5** Seminal British constitutional treatises

| Treatise | Author | Significance |
|---|---|---|
| A Practical Treatise on the Law, Privileges, Proceedings and Usage of Parliament (Parliamentary Practice) | Erskine May (1844) | Sir Thomas Erskine May (1815–86), first Baron Farnborough and a distinguished parliamentary officer, became Chief Librarian of the House of Commons Library and Clerk to the House of Commons. His most famous work remains the seminal examination of the role, rights, and responsibilities of Parliament. |
| The English Constitution | Walter Bagehot (1867) | A maths graduate from University College, London, Bagehot (1826–77) was called to the Bar, but rejected it for a career in banking and shipping. He later edited The Economist (the last column of which still bears his name in tribute), before writing his most esteemed work: a rumination on the relationship between Parliament and monarchy, and the contrast between the UK and US constitutions. |
| An Introduction to the Study of the Law of the Constitution | A. V. Dicey (1885) | Albert Venn Dicey (1835–1922) was an accomplished scholar, appointed to the Vinerian Chair of English Law at the University of Oxford in 1882, later becoming professor of law at the London School of Economics. Of all great constitutional treatises, Dicey's is considered the most authoritative and far-reaching. Its central thesis was that the 'freedom' of British subjects was under attack by an increasingly aggressive rule of law. He saw the impartiality of the courts (which he believed essential to preserving this freedom) as even then under attack from governments intent on limiting fundamental civil liberties. |

thinker Baron de Montesquieu (1689–1755), the *Trias Politica* is a notional model that splits the state into three branches:

- 'executive' (the government);
- 'legislature' (Parliament);
- 'judiciary' (the courts).

The idea is that, to avoid arbitrary or dictatorial government, a constitutional framework is needed that does not confer too much power on a single individual (or small group of individuals). In theory, if the executive is wholly 'separated' from the legislature, and in turn judiciary, each acts as a 'check and balance' on the other.

Montesquieu purportedly formulated his theory based on the workings of the UK system, although Britain's democracy arguably adheres far less strictly to this model than many that have emerged since. In practice numerous overlaps have emerged down the centuries between the roles, powers, and even membership of the key institutions charged with preserving the separation of powers, including that:

- constitutionally, the reigning monarch (as 'head of state') is titular head of all three branches of the constitution;
- until 2007, when the post was reformed (see pp. 71–2), the Lord Chancellor was a member of all three institutions, as Speaker of the House of Lords (legislature), 'manager' of the legal profession (judiciary), and a minister in the **Cabinet** (executive);
- the prime minister and most other ministers are members of the government (executive) and Parliament (legislature);
- prior to the establishment of an independent Supreme Court in October 2009, the Law Lords collectively constituted Britain's highest court of appeal (judiciary), as well as being members of the Lords (legislature).

Such constitutional overlaps are not confined to Britain. Many other parliamentary democracies—particularly those directly modelled on the UK's, as in many Commonwealth countries—display a similar fusion of powers, rather than the 'separation' to which they aspire. Constitutional historians are increasingly drawing a distinction in this regard between countries that practice 'presidential government' and those characterized by 'parliamentary government'. In the former (which include the USA, France, South Africa, and Australia) separation is felt to be both more practised and practicable than in countries like Britain, where the most senior politician (the prime minister) is today drawn from among the ranks of ordinary MPs and, as such, represents a **constituency** in the same way as his or her peers.

In the UK, executive decisions are taken primarily by prime ministers and their ministers, before being presented for approval to Parliament (where most of them are also present, this time as voting MPs and peers). In the USA and other states, in contrast, the most senior elected politician is the president— who, in the absence of a reigning monarch, is also head of state. Crucially, unlike in Britain and other parliamentary states, presidents are usually elected on different timetables to their national parliaments. The separation of powers in the USA is more pronounced than in Britain because Congress (comprising the Senate and House of Representatives—the US equivalent of Britain's Parliament) is elected in large part on a different date, and in a different manner, from the president. More crucially, the president (unlike the British prime minister) is not a member of either House; so while he or she may present policies to Congress for approval, he or she does not preside over the ensuing debates within the chambers in the way prime ministers do in the Commons.

Another feature of the separation of powers enjoyed by presidential states is the fact that, historically, they tend to have developed a more provably independent judicial system than in many prime ministerial ones. The USA has long had a Supreme Court that (in theory at least) is entirely separate from the political process. Notwithstanding controversies over the president's ability to nominate judges to replace those who retire (President Bush was castigated in 2005 for choosing Harriet Miers, his former adviser and a long-time conserva tive ally, who later withdrew her own candidacy), this system is felt to be more appropriate than one in which judges straddle the divide between legislature and judiciary by serving in both a legal and lawmaking capacity. To this end, in 2007 Jack Straw, as inaugural Secretary of State for Justice (and de facto Lord Chancellor), announced the Law Lords would be effectively removed from Parliament in 2009, to sit in the new Supreme Court.

Further reforms, including a written constitution and a Bill to give Parliament the final say over any future decision to take Britain to war, were floated by Gordon Brown at various points in his tenure, and in his 2010 Labour election manifesto, but in the event he never got to implement them.

# ▌ The monarchy

The British sovereign is the head of a 'constitutional monarchy'. This means that, while he or she remains UK head of state, with the notional prerogative to govern and take major constitutional decisions, in practice she does not do so. Unlike in presidential countries, Britain's head of state is a figurehead with little real power. Instead, day-to-day decisions regarding domestic and foreign policy are left to Parliament and, more specifically, the government, led by the 'First Lord of the Treasury' or prime minister.

The authority invested in successive prime ministers to choose their own ministers, devise and draft legislation, and decide whether to take the state to war is derived from another of those key constitutional principles: the **royal prerogative**. In essence, this is the body of customary privileges and powers historically acquired by reigning monarchs (predominantly in the Middle Ages). Today, the majority of so-called 'prerogative powers' derived from this principle are exercised not by the Crown itself but by Parliament.

## Origins of the modern British monarchy

Although the present monarchy is also descended from several powerful families with roots outside the UK, Queen Elizabeth II can reputedly trace her line on one side directly to King Egbert, the ruler who united England under one throne in AD 829. The position she occupies is that of Britain's longest standing secular institution (its only interruption being the previously mentioned interregnum from 1649 to 1660).

Although short-lived, this period—sometimes referred to as the 'English Revolution'—marked a symbolic break with the past that was to change the role of the monarchy forever. Beforehand, the prevailing 'rationale' for the existence of the sovereign derived from the 'Divine Right of Kings'. By propagating the idea that they should not be answerable to 'man-made' institutions like mere parliaments, European medieval monarchs sought to reign with the minimum of outside interference—with the possible exception of that of the Church, which, in some notable instances (such as Henry VIII's inability to obtain permission from the Pope to divorce his first wife, Catherine of Aragon) directly challenged their pre-eminence. Parliaments were generally regarded as tools to enable kings and queens to raise taxes, pass edicts, and declare wars with impunity.

In England all of this changed after the execution of Charles I. While his eldest son, Charles II, ultimately succeeded him following Cromwell's death, the concept that any monarch had a divine right to rule unchallenged had by then been all but rescinded. Through a succession of landmark constitutional statutes—most notably the Bill of Rights and Act of Settlement (see pp. 7–10)—a newly liberated Parliament stamped its authority on the nation, and (in all but name) the monarch.

## The role of the monarchy today

In *The English Constitution,* Bagehot (1826–77) argued it was incumbent on monarchs to embody the following qualities:

❝ The right to be consulted, the right to encourage, the right to warn. ❞

Specifically, the role and powers of the monarch are best explained by splitting them into two broad categories: *actual* and *notional*.

### Actual prerogative powers—those exercised by the monarch

Despite the huge upheavals of recent centuries the reigning sovereign still holds the following key constitutional offices:

- head of state;
- head of the executive, legislature, and judiciary;
- commander-in-chief of the Armed Forces;
- supreme governor of the established Church of England;
- head of the Commonwealth (and head of state of 15 of its 53 members);
- the authority from which the Royal Mint derives its licence to coin and print money (at present, in his or her image).

But so much for their official titles: what do monarchs actually *do*? And, more specifically, which prerogative powers do monarchs personally still exercise in an age when governments hold sway over most key political decisions?

The core roles and duties of the monarch—many largely ceremonial—include:

- reading Her Majesty's Most Gracious Speech, or the 'Gracious Address'— better known as the **Queen's Speech**—at the State Opening of Parliament each October or November, or shortly after a general election;
- governing the Church of England;
- 'creating' peers, and conferring knighthoods and honours in person;
- meeting the prime minister once a week (usually on Tuesdays) to discuss Cabinet business and offer advice on affairs of state;
- entertaining visiting heads of state at Buckingham Palace;
- touring other nations on official state visits—including those of the Commonwealth—as Britain's premier overseas ambassador;
- chairing meetings of the **Privy Council** (a body of advisers made up of members of the current and previous Cabinets, plus other distinguished individuals, which issues Royal Charters and Orders in Council—see p. 67);
- attending 'Trooping the Colour' (the monarch's annual birthday parade, led by regiments of HM Armed Forces).

Although this list of 'powers' may appear feeble in the scheme of things, there is considerable anecdotal evidence to suggest that recent monarchs have discharged their duties with rigour. In her first audience with then newly elected Labour Prime Minister Harold Wilson, in 1964, Queen Elizabeth II famously wrong-footed him by expressing interest in proposals for a 'new town' near Bletchley. Having not yet read his Cabinet papers, he knew nothing of them. In his 1975 resignation speech, Wilson made a joke of the episode, saying he would advise his successors to 'do their homework' before meeting the Queen.

In addition to the above prerogative powers retained by the monarch and his or her immediate family, the sovereign has traditionally been called on to fulfil a unifying role as a national figurehead at times of crisis. The late HM Queen Elizabeth the Queen Mother famously toured bombsites in London's East End to provide comfort to dispossessed families during the Blitz, while the Queen's  annual televised Christmas Day address is designed as much to 'sum up' the year past and look to the one ahead on behalf of the whole nation as to update her subjects on her own regal affairs. Such is the onus placed on the sovereign to 'speak for the nation' at times of tragedy or disaster that the Queen's initial silence following the death of Diana, Princess of Wales and her lover Dodi Fayed in a Paris car crash in 1997 became a cause célèbre among her critics— allegedly prompting newly elected premier Tony Blair to appeal to her to make a statement in tribute to her daughter-in-law.

### Notional prerogative powers—those deferred to government

Most sovereign powers are exercised 'on the advice of ministers', which means it is ministers—and the prime minister mostly—who take the decisions. In practice, then, it is the monarch who offers the 'advice' to prime ministers, rather than the other way around, and prime ministers who discharge the following functions:

- dissolving and summoning Parliament—calling elections and forming new parliaments after the results are in;
- giving the royal assent to Bills passed by Parliament;
- appointing ministers and other senior public officials, including judges, diplomats, governors, officers in the Armed Forces, police *chief constables*, and Church of England bishops and archbishops;
- devising the legislative agenda for each parliamentary session (year of Parliament) and writing the Queen's Speech, which outlines the legislative agenda for a parliamentary session and is read out by the sovereign at the State Opening of Parliament—the ceremony heralding the start of each session;
- declaring war and peace;
- the **prorogation** of Parliament—suspension of its activities over holiday periods, such as the summer recess and the annual Christmas and Easter breaks;
- drawing up lists of nominations—in consultation with the leaders of opposition parties—for peerages, knighthoods, and other honours in the New Year **Honours List** and the Queen's Birthday Honours List.

In addition, the monarch may occasionally issue a 'royal pardon'—known formally as the 'royal prerogative of mercy'—to convicted criminals. This tends to happen either when an individual convicted of a crime is subsequently pardoned in light of new evidence or (very rarely) when the actions and/or behaviour of a prisoner are deemed to warrant their early release from a sentence. Unlike all other sovereign powers exercised by the government on the monarch's behalf, pardons are issued on the advice not of the prime minister but of the Justice Secretary in England and Wales, the Scottish First Minister (Scotland), or the Northern Ireland Secretary (Northern Ireland), following the introduction of **devolution**. A recent example of a royal pardon was the posthumous forgiveness offered to families of all British soldiers executed for cowardice during the Second World War.

## How the monarchy is funded

The income of the reigning monarch and his or her immediate family—the 'Royal Household'—derives from four principal sources:

- the **Civil List**;

- grants-in-aid;
- the Privy Purse;
- personal income.

## The Civil List

Often used by those who favour abolishing the monarchy as shorthand for the Royal Family as a whole, this core fund, financed by British taxpayers, originated in the Bill of Rights.

With the accession of William and Mary, Parliament voted to give the Royal Household £600,000 to aid it in 'civil government'. The Civil List in its present form was established in 1760, during George III's reign. In return for the king's surrender to Parliament of his 'hereditary revenues'—the income generated by the Crown Lands (estates owned traditionally by the monarch)—MPs agreed to pledge a fixed annual income to the Royal Household. In practice this exchange has reaped huge dividends for Parliament: in 2008–09, the income generated for the Treasury by the Crown Lands (as administered by the Crown Estate Commissioners) was £226.5m, compared to £40m paid to the monarch.

In 2001 the Civil List itself was fixed at £7.9m a year for the Queen until at least 2011, with her husband, the Duke of Edinburgh (Prince Philip), receiving a separate annuity of £359,000. In a deal struck with former Chancellor Gordon Brown, the Queen agreed to finance any increases in her outgoings from a 'reserve fund' worth up to £30m accumulated over the previous decade. In return, her own and her husband's 'fixed' incomes would rise by 7.5 per cent a year to keep them abreast of **inflation** (which, at 3 per cent in 2001, was less than half as high). As a result, by the end of 2009–10, the Civil List had actually swelled to £14.2m. In common with many households, though, the royals emerged from the *recession* rather less solvent than beforehand: when the 2009–10 Buckingham Palace accounts were published in July 2010 they revealed the Queen had been forced to supplement the official Civil List pot by a record £6.5m during that year, reducing her reserve fund to £15.2m. With an expected drawdown of £7.2m in 2010–11 she appeared to be facing the prospect of running out of reserves by 2012—her Diamond Jubilee year. And as if this was not enough, coalition Chancellor George Osborne announced in his June 2010 Budget that future Civil List settlements would be subject to the same scrutiny as government departments, at the hands of, in turn, the National Audit Office and the influential Public Accounts Committee of MPs. In his subsequent **Comprehensive Spending Review (CSR)** he revealed that the Queen had agreed to shoulder her share of the burden of his swingeing £81bn package of spending cuts by consenting to a two-year freeze in its grant funding, in 2011–12 and 2012–13, which would necessitate a 14 per cent reduction in Royal Household spending.

But so much for the accounting: for what does the Civil List actually *pay*? In broad terms, it funds the following expenses for both the reigning monarch and his or her spouse:

- 70 per cent pays the salaries of the 645 servants, butlers, and other Royal Household employees;
- most of the remaining 30 per cent covers the costs of royal garden parties (attended by some 48,000 people each year) and hospitality during state visits.

In addition, a number of annual parliamentary allowances are issued annually to individual members of the Royal Family, including the Duke of York (Prince Andrew) and the Princess Royal (Princess Anne), under the auspices of the Civil List Acts. These amount to £2.5m extra. Since April 1993, however, the Queen has in practice refunded £1.5m of this money to Parliament, using her personal pot of money, the Privy Purse (see p. 25). The remaining £1m has been retained annually as income for the Duke of Edinburgh and, until her death in 2002, the Queen Mother (who received £643,000 a year). All other senior royals performing official duties now receive annuities from the Privy Purse, rather than the Civil List.

Perhaps surprisingly, one of the few key members of the Royal Household who benefits from no such annuity is the present heir, the Prince of Wales (Prince Charles), who as Duke of Cornwall earns substantial income from his sprawling 130,000-acre Duchy of Cornwall estate. Originally bestowed on the Black Prince in 1337, despite its name the Duchy extends over 23 counties. According to the Prince's official website, in 2009–10, it generated an income of £17.1m—a year-on-year increase of £1m, or 4 per cent. However, the grants-in-aid money and other, more minor, allowances he received from taxpayers almost halved, falling to £1.6m.

## Grants-in-aid

Awarded to the Crown by the Department of Culture, Media, and Sport (DCMS), grants totalling £15.3m a year (fixed until at least 2011) are bestowed on the 'occupied royal palaces'. These are those in which members of the Royal Family still live, as distinct from the likes of Hampton Court Palace and the Tower of London, both of which are overseen by a separate organization, Historic Royal Palaces (also funded by DCMS).

The occupied palaces include the following:

- Buckingham Palace (home of the Queen and Prince Philip);
- St James's Palace (home of Prince Charles);
- Kensington Palace;
- Windsor Castle (the Queen's second home).

In addition to grants-in-aid, Buckingham Palace and Windsor Castle also help to maintain themselves by means of their summer public openings. Grants may not be used for the upkeep of the two royal estates—Sandringham in Norfolk and Balmoral in Scotland—which are the Queen's private property and not her legacy as head of state.

A further set of grants are awarded by the Department for Transport (DfT), to the tune of £6.2m in 2007–08. These cover the cost of transporting members of the Royal Family to and from their 3,000 annual engagements in the UK and overseas. Until she was decommissioned in 1997, the biggest grant was used to maintain the *Royal Yacht Britannia*, the Queen's official ship, which was launched in 1953. Now that she is little more than a visitor attraction, royal transport consists of:

- the Royal Air Force (RAF) aircraft of the No. 32 (The Royal) Squadron;
- the Royal Train;
- other chartered and scheduled flights on official visits.

In recent years, disclosures of the Royal Family's movements in the preceding 12 months have included some eyebrow-raising details. In 2007–08 the Queen and her husband—occasionally accompanied by one or two fellow family members—made journeys totalling £200,000 on the Royal Train, including one from Windsor to Euston via (of all places) Liverpool to attend the Royal Variety Performance. This convoluted trip cost £23,750. But while £200,000 may sound a lot of money, it is half as much as the £400,000 the royal couple spent on 11 train trips in 2006–07—including a return visit to Brighton, which set them back £19,271.

No such restraint was visible, however, in the royals' flying habits: security concerns have seen family members avoiding scheduled flights in certain parts of the world more than ever, with the result that they spent £275,506 between them on chartered flights in 2007–08—£203,007 on helicopter trips. A further £143,461 went on scheduled flights and £692,790 on flights on various smaller commercial aircraft, including helicopters, light aeroplanes, and corporate  jets. The Duke of York—dubbed 'Air Miles Andy' by the media—had become so notorious for his globe-trotting by 2009 (notching up flights totalling £640,987 in the previous year) that he commissioned PricewaterhouseCoopers to audit the travel expenses he accrued while discharging his duties as Britain's trade envoy. He also announced he would be voluntarily publishing an annual report detailing these costs on his website.

A growing public backlash against extravagant royal transport costs, combined with the new mood of frugality that greeted the recent recession, encouraged the Royal Household to rein back significantly on travel spending, particularly its use of commercial flights, in 2008–09 and 2009–10. In 2008–09, total grants-in-aid for travel amounted to £6.5m, whereas in 2009–10 they fell sharply to £3.9m.

The remaining portion of the grants-in-aid budget (amounting to £400,000 in 2009–10—down from £600,000 a year earlier) is spent on royal 'communications': letters, telephone bills, and other correspondences, including invitations to garden parties.

### The Privy Purse

Dating back to 1399, the Privy Purse is derived largely from the income generated by the Duchy of Lancaster—a huge expanse of land covering 19,268 acres and the sole surviving Crown estate to remain in the monarch's possession. It is kept under lock and key by her personal accountant and administered by the Chancellor of the Duchy of Lancaster—today almost always a senior Cabinet minister.

### Personal income

Like anyone else, senior members of the Royal Family, despite deriving significant income from the state, are free to generate their own earnings—provided that they pay Income Tax on them, like their subjects. Examples of the personal incomes earned by individual members of the Royal Household include the military salaries drawn by Prince Charles, who served for a time in the Royal Navy, Prince Andrew, who saw action during the Falklands War, and Prince Harry, currently in the Household Cavalry (Blues and Royals). Other examples include the income earned by Prince Charles from his Duchy of Cornwall estate, in the form of land rent and the proceeds from goods produced there—for example, his 'Duchy Originals' products. His youngest brother, Prince Edward, Duke of Wessex, owned a film and television company, Ardent Productions, until its liquidation in 2009.

More sporadic sources of income might include everything from share dividends to windfalls from betting on the races (the Queen Mother famously liked a flutter).

## Taxation and the monarchy

Like everyone the Queen has always paid **indirect taxes**—value added tax (VAT) and other tariffs levied on consumer goods and services. She has also long paid, on a voluntary basis, local taxation—**Council Tax** and, before that, the Community Charge (or 'Poll Tax') and rates. It was not until 1993, however, that she agreed to pay **direct taxes**—principally Income Tax. This decision was taken in the wake of a mounting backlash over the revelation that much of the £60m cost of repairing Windsor Castle following a devastating fire in 1992 was funded by taxpayers, despite the fact they already hugely subsidized the Royal Household.

The monarch and certain members of her immediate family do, however, continue to enjoy substantial tax breaks not granted to her subjects. In particular, while the Privy Purse pays tax and the Queen's personal estate is subject to

Inheritance Tax, grants-in-aid are not regarded as taxable, and neither is any transfer of property 'from sovereign to sovereign'—that is, between the Queen and her successor.

## The succession

For many centuries, as is commonly the case in other European nation states, the monarchy has tended to pass from father to son in Britain, through a process known as 'eldest male primogeniture'. Only when a male line (going through the eldest son) has been exhausted does the crown pass to the next eldest male sibling of the originator of that line, and only after that will it ever go to a female sibling. Therefore, as things stand, Prince Charles will inherit the throne from his mother on her death and, after he dies, it will pass to his eldest son, William, and from him to the eldest of his own sons. If William were to die without leaving a male heir but have a daughter, it would eventually pass to her, but if he were to have no children and die before his brother, Harry, the crown would finally pass to him.

The other key 'rules' governing the succession—between them derived from the Bill of Rights and Act of Settlement—are listed in Table 1.2.

## Monarchy versus presidency—which way forward?

Although Britain has had a monarchy for the best part of 1,500 years, today it is one of the few 'developed' nations to retain one—let alone to boast an extended Royal Family, funded largely by the taxpayer. Perhaps unsurprisingly, recent years have witnessed growing calls for the monarchy to be replaced by an elected head of state. These calls have been fuelled by a succession of controversies surrounding the Royal Household and, in particular, that relating to  Prince Charles's divorce from the late Diana, Princess of Wales, and revelations about his long-standing relationship with Camilla Parker-Bowles (now his second wife and the Duchess of Cornwall). Further succour was given to those arguing for Britain's hereditary figurehead to be replaced by an elected one by the Australian electorate's narrow decision to retain the Queen as its head of state in November 1999. In 2007 the country's newly elected Labour Prime Minister, Kevin Rudd, pledged to hold a further **referendum**, but left office in 2010 (after being deposed by his deputy, Julie Gillard) before doing so.

The argument for an elected head of state is self-explanatory: in a modern democracy, so the republican case goes, it is surely only right that the state's ultimate ambassador—the individual who publicly represents its interests on the international stage—should gain a 'mandate' to do so from their subjects. But what of the arguments for retaining a monarch? Opinions differ among constitutional historians about the merits of the institution, but an oft-cited argument in favour of the hereditary principle is that it produces heads of state who have the luxury of being able to maintain an objective, independent-minded *distance* from the day-to-day workings of the political process—rather than being hidebound by the narrow, short-term thinking that constrains politicians reliant on the votes of a fickle electorate. In addition, the presence of Queen Elizabeth II through fifty years of changing governments and shifting political priorities has provided, argue some, a degree of continuity absent from presidential states.

# ▶ Devolution—from union to government in the nations

Most of this chapter has focused on outlining the process by which the modern British state came into being, and the rules, customs, and laws that have evolved to determine the balance of powers between Parliament, the monarchy, and citizens.

The UK is a 'representative democracy'—a state the power of which is exercised through democratically elected representatives (in Britain's case, MPs in the Commons). Broadly speaking, there are two main types of democracy: *federal* and *unitary*. In federal democracies, countries are divided into separate political units, each with considerable autonomy over its own affairs. The USA is an example of a federal democracy: major foreign and domestic policy decisions are taken by the national government (president and Congress) but many day-to-day matters are decided on a state-by-state basis. The most oft-cited example of **federalism** in action relates to the manner in which different states punish felons convicted of serious crimes like murder and rape: while 14 of the states making up the USA favour custodial sentences, the remaining 36 still practise capital punishment.

Britain, in contrast to the USA, is a *unitary* democracy. This means the bulk of power remains in the hand of central government and the Westminster Parliament. But while the constitutional story of Britain since the late medieval period has mostly been one of the gradual consolidation of a single UK run from the centre, in recent years this has been compromised by moves towards a more decentralized form of government, taking power closer to the people from whom it derives.

The story of the emergence of local government—elected local authorities, funded by local taxpayers, which run local services—is told in detail in the second half of this book. But, at a higher level than the strictly 'local', there now exists in Scotland, Wales, and Northern Ireland a further tier of government to which significant powers have been devolved by Westminster. This statutory transfer of power from central government to the constituent nations that, alongside England, make up the UK is known as 'devolution'.

Before proceeding further it is worth explaining the distinction between 'devolution' and 'independence'. Although the parties most enthusiastically embracing devolution in Scotland, Wales, and Northern Ireland tend to be 'nationalist' ones—those that would ultimately like to break away from the UK to become independent states—the policy does not amount to any form of independence in itself. Neither does it inevitably follow that, having gained devolution, a country will one day become independent. Indeed, one of the principal arguments used by Labour to justify devolution was that, in granting it, the party was safeguarding the union of Britain, by permitting a limited degree of autonomy that made practical sense and would answer many of the frustrations expressed by dissatisfied, but otherwise loyal, British subjects in those countries. Conversely, those in favour of independence have argued that, in the long term, it makes little sense for national assemblies in Scotland or Wales that take most of their own day-to-day decisions without needing formal permission from Westminster to remain its vassals and that full self-government is the logical next step. Although an Act would have to be passed at Westminster to pave the way for independence in practice, the clamour for a breakaway government became even more acute when Alex Salmond, leader of the Scottish Nationalist Party, was elected First Minister in May 2007, eradicating Labour's majority share of the vote in Scotland for the first time in fifty years.

Mr Salmond's repeated pledges to hold a referendum on independence were addressed decisively in a draft Bill in February 2010, in which he outlined proposals for two separate ballots of Scottish voters. The first would ask them if they supported the *Scottish Parliament* being granted more devolved autonomy, with two alternative models proposed: one, dubbed 'devolution max', involving the handover of all remaining powers from Westminster to Holyrood, apart from defence policy, foreign affairs, and financial regulation, and the other envisaging a more limited extension of devolution, along the lines of changes suggested in June 2009 by Sir Kenneth Calman. He also proposed asking voters separately if they wanted Holyrood's powers extended to enable  full-blooded independence to be achieved. But even under these plans, the Queen would remain, at least for now, Scotland's head of state. Mr Salmond's speech had a mixed reception, with opinion polls suggesting Scots remained sceptical about the wisdom of independence, and critics stressing that the near-collapse of both Halifax Bank of Scotland (HBOS) and the Royal Bank of Scotland (RBS) during the 2008–09 financial crisis, and their subsequent bailouts by HM Treasury (see pp. 207–10), had emphasized the economic security provided by the union.

In the event Mr Salmond was gazumped by the Lib-Con government. The coalition used its first Queen's Speech on 25 May 2010 to confirm plans for a Scotland Bill that would implement many of the Calman Commission's recommendations. Set up in 2007 to review the progress of Scottish devolution ten years on, the Commission had made a number of recommendations, including that 10p should be top-sliced from the basic and higher rates of income tax in Scotland, with the Scottish Parliament left to decide whether to make up the difference by levying its own top-up tax. Sir Kenneth had also recommended transferring legislative authority from Westminster to Holyrood in areas as wide-ranging as airgun control, drink-driving, speed limits, and the running of elections.

# The unification of Great Britain

## Wales

Like much of the UK's constitutional heritage, the concept of devolution originated in the Middle Ages, when Wales and Scotland first began demanding the right to rule themselves independently of the English sovereign. Of the two countries, Wales has the longest formal association with England. The main stages in its moves towards incorporation into the UK are outlined in Table 1.6.

## Scotland

Scotland's progress towards integration in the UK was a more complex one—due, in part, to the fact it was never formally absorbed into the Roman Empire. It took centuries of conflict during the medieval period for it finally to succumb to the authority of the English Crown, a timeline of which is outlined in Table 1.7.

## Northern Ireland

Northern Ireland's incorporation into the UK was more problematic, encompassing as it did its split from Southern Ireland (Eire). The early stages of the process are outlined in Table 1.8.

**Table 1.6** Timeline for the incorporation of Wales into the UK

| Date | Event |
| --- | --- |
| Fifth century | Departure of Romans and rise of Anglo-Saxon hegemony over much of Britain, despite attempts by several Welsh kingdoms—including Gwynedd, Powys, Dyfed, and Gwent—to unite to defy latest invasion |
| Late thirteenth century | Norman Conquest finally reaches south Wales |
| 1093 | All of Wales finally subsumed under English rule |
| 1707 | Acts of Union passed, fusing England, Scotland, and Wales into single 'United Kingdom of Great Britain' |
| 1536 and 1543 | Two Acts of Parliament formally incorporate Wales into a new Realm of England. Although English is new official language, Wales continues to exert its distinctive Celtic heritage—leading to the bilingualism of modern times |
| 1925 | Welsh Nationalist Party, Plaid Cymru, formed, with its first MPs elected to Parliament in 1960s |

**Table 1.7** Timeline for the incorporation of Scotland into the UK

| Date | Event |
|------|-------|
| Fifth century | Romans leave Britain, having failed to conquer Scotland fully |
| Ninth century | Individual Scottish kingdoms unite under single Celtic monarchy, which rules for several hundred years |
| 1296 | Edward I tries to impose English rule; William Wallace leads Scots revolt |
| 1328 | Edward III forced to recognize Robert Bruce as Robert I of Scotland—first king of the House of Stuart, which went on initially to establish strong links with France, rather than England |
| 1567 | English force Mary, Queen of Scots, to abdicate and hand throne to her infant son, James VI (later James I of England); Presbyterian Church usurps Catholicism to become established church of Scotland |
| 1603 | James VI succeeds childless Elizabeth I to English throne |
| 1707 | Acts of Union passed; Scotland subsequently dissolves its Parliament and sends its MPs to Westminster |

**Table 1.8** Timeline for the incorporation of Northern Ireland into the UK

| Date | Event |
|------|-------|
| 1171 | Henry II invades Ireland, proclaiming himself overlord of five extant Irish provinces (each governed by 300-year-old clans) |
| Sixteenth and seventeenth centuries | Catholics flee Ireland, leaving land around Ulster to Protestant Scottish and English migrants |
| 1692 | Protestants assume control of Ireland, spurred on by the victory of William of Orange (the first of the 'Orangemen') over deposed James II at the Battle of the Boyne a year earlier |
| Eighteenth century | Growing pressure for greater self-determination from England by controlling Protestant Irish minority |
| 1886, 1893, and 1912–14 | Successive Home Rule Bills introduced, unsuccessfully, to give Ireland limited self-government |
| 1916 | Ireland declared a republic at Dublin's General Post Office after the Easter Rising by Irish Volunteer rebels (forerunners of the IRA); they surrender five days later |
| 1918 | Sinn Féin (meaning 'Ourselves Alone'), the IRA's political wing, wins 73 Irish seats at the general election—more than twice as many as the Unionist parties combined |
| 1920 | The IRA effectively rules large areas of Ireland as the country slips into civil disobedience; Parliament passes the Government Act of Ireland, which sets up two Home Rule parliaments: one in Belfast, covering six of Ulster's nine counties; the other in Dublin, covering the remaining 23 (the 'Republic of Ireland') |
| December 1921 | Anglo-Irish Treaty passed, formalizing Northern Ireland's status as a sectarian society |
| 1949 | Republic names itself 'Eire' and withdraws from the Commonwealth |

# The path to devolution in Scotland

The workings of the governing institutions established under devolution in Scotland, Wales, and Northern Ireland are explored in more detail in the next chapter. What follows here is an outline of the process by which these institutions were created following the 1997 referenda and the levels of devolution granted in each case.

Of the three countries, Scotland has the most extensive degree of devolved government, following the enabling legislation passed to formalize devolution in 1998. In part this is a reflection of the fact that, for complex historical reasons, the country has long had certain devolved functions—most notably its distinctive legal system. More significantly, however, it reflected the growing calls north of the border after 18 years of Conservative rule at Westminster for a greater degree of autonomy from a national Parliament that seemed increasingly remote—both politically and geographically—from Scottish interests.

The path to Scottish devolution began in the 1960s, when the then Labour government established a Royal Commission to examine the arguments for some form of home rule. The sequence of events leading to eventual devolution was as outlined in Table 1.9.

Unlike Wales and Northern Ireland where (at present) the powers devolved are much the same, the **Scottish Parliament** has considerable authority, with only foreign affairs, defence policy, the welfare system, and the introduction of new taxes outside its remit. Its powers therefore include determining

**Table 1.9** Timeline for the introduction of devolution in Scotland

| Date | Event |
| --- | --- |
| 1973 | Royal Commission on Constitution, set up by Wilson's Labour government in late 1960s, recommends devolution to Edward Heath's Conservatives |
| 1978 | Re-elected Labour government passes Scotland Act, paving way for referendum on Scottish self-government: 40 per cent of Scottish electorate must vote for devolution for it to be granted |
| March 1979 | Devolution put on hold indefinitely because, although 52 per cent of those who voted supported it, this is equivalent to only 32 per cent of those *entitled* to vote |
| July 1997 | Newly re-elected Labour government publishes Scotland's Parliament, a **White Paper** advocating devolution |
| 11 September 1997 | This time, referendum attracts 60 per cent turnout, with 74 per cent of voters backing devolution and 64 per cent voting 'yes' in answer to second question, asking if they want Scottish Parliament to have *tax-varying* powers |
| 1998 | Government of Scotland Act passed, conferring devolution |
| 12 May 1999 | Queen opens new Scottish Parliament after its precise powers confirmed by consultative steering group |
| 7 September 2004 | Grand opening of £420m purpose-built Scottish Parliament at Holyrood, by foot of Edinburgh's Royal Mile |

education, health, environment, and transport policy in Scotland, and being able to 'vary'—that is, raise or lower—Income Tax by up to 3p in the pound (the so-called 'Tartan Tax' option). In July 2010, a commission set up by the *Welsh Assembly Government* recommended that Wales be given similar authority to vary Income Tax levels, but it was unclear whether such a change would be approved by Mr Cameron's Westminster coalition.

### The 'West Lothian Question'

The growing assertiveness of the Scottish Parliament in light of its powers—for example, it voted to reject foundation hospitals and undergraduate top-up fees, two deeply unpopular Blair policies adopted south of the border—has raised significant constitutional questions. None is more explosive than the 'West Lothian Question': the argument that it is unfair for Scottish MPs to be allowed to continue voting on issues that have no bearing on their own country, but directly affect England and Wales, while English and Welsh members have no power to vote on issues specific to Scotland. Although devolution was only introduced relatively recently, this quandary was first raised in debate in the Commons by Labour **backbencher** Tam Dalyell in the 1970s. It was dubbed the 'West Lothian Question' by then Tory MP Enoch Powell after the name of Dalyell's constituency.

Today the West Lothian Question rages more than ever—not least because, on more than one occasion, Mr Blair managed to bolster shaky Commons majorities in votes on controversial legislation with the help of Scottish MPs who had let it be known they did not support the same policies in their own country (see p. 73). The fact that his successor, Mr Brown, was a Scot himself, representing a Scottish constituency, did little to dampen the issue on his departure.

## The path to devolution in Wales

Welsh devolution was introduced as outlined in Table 1.10.

**Table 1.10** Timeline for the introduction of devolution in Wales

| Date | Event |
| --- | --- |
| July 1997 | White Paper entitled *A Voice for Wales* introduced by new government, outlining proposals for Welsh devolution |
| 18 September 1997 | Referendum attracts low turnout of around 50 per cent, but 50.3 per cent vote in favour of devolution |
| 1998 | Government of Wales Act passed to lay out framework |
| 1999 | National Assembly for Wales (Transfer of Functions) Order introduced, providing legal and constitutional framework |
| 6 May 1999 | First election for *National Assembly for Wales* |
| 12 May 1999 | National Assembly for Wales meets for first time |
| 1 March 2006 | Queen officially opens new purpose-built £67m Welsh Assembly building in Cardiff |

# The rocky road to devolution in Northern Ireland

Due to the fallout from 'The Troubles', the devolution process in Northern Ireland was more drawn out, with the various parties unable to agree a workable framework for devolved government until very recently. A landmark agreement signed in 2007 appeared finally, however, to have buried the hatchet between the main Republican and Unionist parties, with the ruling Democratic Unionists accepting that the IRA had decommissioned its weapons, as it had long claimed. The Northern Ireland Assembly has since been restored.

The saga that led to the granting of meaningful devolution to Northern Ireland lasted decades, so it would be impractical to list all of the twists and turns during that time, but the most significant are outlined in Table 1.11.

**Table 1.11** Timeline for the introduction of devolution in Northern Ireland

| Date | Event |
| --- | --- |
| 1968 | Civil Rights Movement starts in Ulster; street violence erupts between Protestants and Catholics (dawn of 'The Troubles') |
| 1972 | Most notorious explosion of violence in history of The Troubles, 'Bloody Sunday', occurs in Londonderry, culminating at the Bogside, a Catholic ghetto |
| 1972 | Northern Ireland constitution, prime minister, and Parliament suspended for a year due to escalating violence |
| November 1985 | Anglo-Irish Agreement (officially, 'The Hillsborough Agreement') signed by Britain and Ireland recognizes that any constitutional change in Northern Ireland can only come about with agreement of population through referendum |
| November 1992 | Inconclusive end to talks flowing from Anglo-Irish Agreement |
| December 1993 | UK Prime Minister John Major and Irish Taoiseach Albert Reynolds issue Joint Declaration from 10 Downing Street ('The Downing Street Declaration'), stipulating that future participation in discussions about the government of Northern Ireland should be restricted to parties committed to 'exclusively peaceful means' |
| August 1994 | IRA announces ceasefire, described as 'complete cessation of military operations'; the Combined Loyalist Military Command swiftly does likewise |
| February 1995 | British and Irish governments launch *A New Framework for Accountable Government in Northern Ireland*, outlining proposals for new democratic institutions |
| February 1996 | Docklands bomb brings to end IRA ceasefire |
| June 1996 | Former US Senator George Mitchell convenes Northern Ireland Forum, outlining six 'Mitchell Principles' for moves towards peace; Sinn Féin excluded until IRA formally readopts its ceasefire; two further IRA bomb blasts follow, in Manchester and County Antrim |

| Date | Event |
|------|-------|
| July 1997 | Sinn Féin president Gerry Adams and vice-president Martin McGuinness elected as Westminster MPs, and IRA resumes its ceasefire; International Commission on Decommissioning set up under Canadian general John de Chastelain to oversee process |
| September 1997 | Sinn Féin signs up to Mitchell Principles and multiparty talks start at Stormont; after being switched to Lancaster House in London, a deadline of 9 April 1998 is set for agreement |
| 10 April 1998 | 'Good Friday Agreement' (Belfast Agreement) published as basis for dual referenda on devolution in Northern and Southern Ireland; constitutionally, way is paved with passage of Northern Ireland (Elections) Act 1998 and 19th Amendment to the Irish Constitution (renouncing Eire's claim on the north) |
| 22 May 1998 | Referendum of whole of Ireland produces 94 per cent majority in favour of devolution among residents of Eire and 71 per cent 'yes' vote in Northern Ireland |
| 25 June 1998 | First elections for Northern Ireland Assembly see Ulster Unionist Party gaining most seats (28), with Social Democratic and Labour Party coming second (24) |
| 1 July 1998 | New assembly meets for first time, with Lord Alderdice as first Presiding Officer and David Trimble, Ulster Unionist Party leader, as First Minister Designate; at least three Nationalist and three designated Unionists meant to be included in government under devolution deal (known as the 'd'Hondt procedure'—a formula named after Belgian Victor d'Hondt, whereby each party is allocated seats on a 'largest average' basis relating to number of votes it receives) |
| 15 August 1998 | Twenty-nine people die in Omagh bomb planted by IRA splinter group, the 'Real IRA' |
| 1 December 1999 | Direct rule of Northern Ireland from Westminster ends with Queen's signing of Northern Ireland Act 1998 |
| 2 December 1999 | Anglo-Irish Agreement replaced by a British-Irish Agreement formally creating North-South Ministerial Council and British-Irish Ministerial Council envisaged in Good Friday Agreement; on same day, Irish Parliament replaces arts 2 and 3 of Irish Constitution—formally abandoning Eire's historic claim to hegemony over Northern Ireland |
| 11 February 2000 | Assembly suspended over continuing disagreement about pace of terrorists' decommissioning of weapons; a prolonged period of intermittent direct rule resumes while General de Chasterlain continues trying to extract firm evidence from IRA that it has put its arms beyond use |
| December 2003 | Assembly elections give largest number of seats (30) to Reverend Ian Paisley's Democratic Unionist Party, followed by the Ulster Unionist Party (27), Sinn Féin (24), and the moderate nationalist Social Democratic and Labour Party (18) |
| March 2007 | After further elections in Northern Ireland and power-sharing talks, agreement finally struck to restore devolution |
| April 2007 | Loyalist Volunteer Force follows IRA's declaration of 'final cessation of hostilities' in August 2005 with announcement that it is winding up |
| May 2007 | Power-sharing resumes in the Assembly |

Ironically, the *level of* power devolved to the province is much more limited than that of Scotland. As in Wales, Northern Ireland was until recently restricted to:

- determining some budgetary priorities in education, health, etc.;
- funding, directing, and appointing managers of its National Health Service (NHS) bodies;
- administering any EU structural funds;
- determining the content of its version of the **National Curriculum**.

However, in a highly significant and symbolic development recognizing the unique historical and geographical factors distinguishing Northern Ireland from Scotland and Wales, April 2010 saw the devolution of policing and justice powers to the Stormont assembly (see pp. 77–8). Defying trenchant opposition from the Ulster Unionists (who voted against the proposal, despite last-minute entreaties from then UK Opposition leader David Cameron, US Secretary of State Hillary Clinton, and former President George W Bush), the ruling DUP-Sinn Féin coalition won sufficient cross-community approval to drive the process to its next, decisive stage: the appointment of a Justice Minister. The vote was won by 88 to 17, receiving the backing of all 44 nationalist members and 35 out of the 52 unionists. David Ford, leader of the Alliance Party, was duly elected to the post of Justice Minister on 13 May.

A month later another watershed was reached, with the long-awaited publication of the final report by an official inquiry set up by Mr Blair into the events of 'Bloody Sunday'—after some 12 years of hearings costing £200m. The 5,000-page report concluded that when, on 30 January 1972, British paratroopers fired on a civil rights march in Londonderry, killing 13 civilians, none of the dead had been armed, the paras had shot first and without warning, and some had subsequently lied about their actions. In a Commons statement, Mr Cameron apologized to the bereaved families on behalf of the UK government, describing the shootings as 'unjustified and unjustifiable'.

## Devolution in England—the end of the road?

The increasing autonomy given to Scotland, Wales, and Northern Ireland has led to growing demands from some quarters for the major English regions outside London to be given similar powers to determine their own affairs.

Tentative moves towards an embryonic English regional devolution actually emerged under the Tories, when John Major set up regional offices manned by civil servants seconded from the main spending departments at Whitehall. As befitted these nine 'Government Offices of the Regions', however, their role was largely administrative and there were no moves to extend the remit of this 'devolved' power to embrace any form of elected government.

When Labour returned to power in 1997, however, steps were taken to intro-duce the idea of some form of elected regional authorities by then Deputy Prime Minister John Prescott's short-lived 'super-ministry': the Department for the Environment, Local Government, and the Regions. The first development was the creation of *regional development agencies (RDAs)* to drive sustainable development/regeneration and job creation in the eight English regions: East Midlands, East of England, North East, North West, South East, South West, West Midlands, and Yorkshire and Humber (see p. 464). Each region was also given a *regional chamber*, intended to pave the way, in time, for elected assem-blies à la Scotland, Wales, and Northern Ireland's. Despite their title, mem-bership of these 'shadow' bodies was initially composed of a combination of seconded civil servants (70 per cent) and members of other interested par-ties like the Confederation of British Industry (CBI), Trades Union Congress (TUC), and various statutory agencies (30 per cent).

After a lengthy but (many argued) poorly publicized consultation process, DETRA went on to pass a series of Bills designed to enable referenda to be held simultaneously in each of the eight regions in November 2004. But in the event, the North East Regional Assembly was the only one actually to hold its vote on the designated date—a postal-only ballot that proved hugely controversial, in the wake of allegations of corruption in similar-style votes for Birmingham City Council in the months preceding it. The region voted decisively against the introduction of an elected assembly—by 78 to 22 per cent—kicking regional devolution into touch for the foreseeable future. Local people appeared not to want yet another tier of government, and to be unclear about the tangible benefits that would have derived from such a body. Although chastened at the time, Mr Prescott vowed to resurrect the regional plan at a later date, but it was not to be. The Lib Dems have a long-standing leaning towards regionalism and localism both in the UK and Europe, but at time of writing there was little sign that 'English devolution' would be on the priority list any time soon for the Lib-Con *coalition government*. They have made one decisive gesture on regional devolution, though: abolishing RDAs from 2012.

## ☰ Topical feature idea

Figures released in February 2010 revealed the number of UK court cases revolving around the Human Rights Act 1998 increased for the first time in seven years in the 12 months to October 2009—rising to 348 from 327. One of the biggest contributing factors was its use in asylum and immigration cases (up from 38 to 51). This has further fuelled calls from some quarters, including the Conservative Party, for the HRA to be scrapped, and replaced with a distinctively British Bill of Rights. How widely, if at all, has the HRA been used in court cases in your area? In what kinds of case? What do local people know about the HRA and the protections it contains—and, now that a commission has been established to consider its future, what do they feel about the alternative options?

## ✳ Current issues

- **Future of the unwritten constitution:** the question of whether Britain should adopt a codified written constitution as in France and the USA returned to the fore when Mr Brown first succeeded Mr Blair as Prime Minister, and was alluded to as an aspiration in Labour's 2010 manifesto. The Liberal Democrats are long-time advocates of constitutional reform, so watch this space for developments . . .

- **Fixed-term parliaments:** the coalition is legislating to introduce fixed-term parliaments to prevent future prime ministers 'cutting and running' to call general elections at times when it suits their own political fortunes, rather than the interests of the country. Assuming the two parties can win the approval of the Houses of Commons and Lords, five-year fixed-term parliaments are due to be introduced from the next election, meaning that poll should be held on Thursday 7 May 2015.

- **The Human Rights Act 1998:** the Conservatives have long been vocal critics of the European Convention on Human Rights, particularly the precedence it takes over UK law (following the passage of the HRA). In Opposition, they were committed to reviewing, if not repealing, it, but with the Lib Dems determined to keep it, the issue is currently the subject of a review by an independent commission. Watch this space . . .

## ? Review questions

1. Outline the main sources and principles of the British constitution. What are the advantages and disadvantages of an unwritten constitution?

2. What is meant by the principle of 'separation of powers' and to what extent does it work in practice in the UK?

3. What are the main roles and powers of the British monarch—notional and actual— and how is the Royal Family funded?

4. Given that royal sovereignty has been superseded by parliamentary sovereignty, what are the arguments for retaining the British monarchy?

5. Is there an 'answer' to the West Lothian Question?

## → Further reading

Cannon, J. and Griffiths, R. (1998) *The Oxford Illustrated History of the British Monarchy*, Oxford: Oxford Paperbacks. **Full-colour history of British monarchy, from King Egbert to Elizabeth Windsor, including evaluation of its role in modern Britain.**

Hardman, R. (2007) *Monarchy: The Royal Family at Work*, London: Ebury Press. **Populist but informative companion book to BBC series of the same name, giving insights into the day-to-day reality of how the monarchy works.**

Harrison, K. and Boyd, T. (2006) *The Changing Constitution*, Edinburgh: Edinburgh University Press. **Comprehensive examination of the origins and history of the British constitution, with emphasis placed on recent reforms, including devolution and the introduction of the new Supreme Court.**

Hazell, R. and Rawlings, R. (2007) *Devolution, Law Making and the Constitution*, Exeter: Imprint Academic. **Detailed look at the mechanics of lawmaking through the devolved administrations in Scotland, Wales, and Northern Ireland.**

Leach, R., Coxall, B., and Robins, L. (2006) *British Politics*, London: Palgrave Macmillan. **Excellent guide to the nuts and bolts of contemporary British political institutions and processes at local, regional, national, and international levels.**

Moran, M. (2006) *Politics and Governance in the UK*, London: Palgrave Macmillan. **Forward-looking textbook focusing on the new and evolving forces at work in local, regional, national, and international governance in an increasingly globalized world.**

 **Online Resource Centre**

www.oxfordtextbooks.co.uk/orc/Morrison2e/

Visit the Online Resource Centre that accompanies this book for web links and regular updates.

# 2

# Parliamentary democracy in the UK

## ▌The origins of the British Parliament

As Chapter 1 explained, the reins of power in Britain no longer lie with the sovereign. Rather, they are vested primarily in the Houses of Parliament, and specifically in the members of Parliament (MPs) elected to the primary legislative chamber: the House of Commons.

But how did today's 'bicameral legislature'—a Parliament comprising twin chambers, each with its own distinct constitutional role—originate? How does it discharge its functions, and exercise the prerogative powers vested in it by the Crown? And what are the implications of recent moves towards *devolution* in the provinces?

The UK Parliament has its roots in a succession of bodies that emerged in the medieval period—initially to bolster, but ultimately to counteract, the power of the monarch. The most significant of these institutions originated in Norman times, in the era of root-and-branch constitutional upheaval that also witnessed the publication of the Domesday Book—England's first great population census—for William I in 1086. To provide mechanisms through which the sovereign could tax and rule over his subjects on a practical basis, a succession of bodies was established, one or two of which survive, notionally, to this day. These included the *Privy Council*, a group of personal confidantes of the sovereign at whose meetings they continue to officiate (see p. 20), and two other bodies—the *Magnum Concilium* and the *Curia Regis*—the history, roles, and composition of which are outlined in Table 2.1.

### Parliament today

Parliament long ago took precedence over the sovereign in the day-to-day exercise of constitutional power in the UK. As early as the fourteenth century,

**Table 2.1** The role and composition of forerunners of the Houses of Parliament

| Body | Role and composition |
| --- | --- |
| The *Curia Regis* (King's Court) | Formed in 1066 to replace pre-existing Anglo-Saxon *Witenagemot*, this council of 'tenants-in-chief' and senior clergymen advised the sovereign on prospective new laws. Although initially composed entirely of wealthy, landed individuals (or their representatives), the *Curia Regis* was the forerunner of the *Commune Concilium* (Common Council), as today's Houses of Parliament are collectively known. Set up on a semi-professional basis, it upheld a formal legislative framework. Arguably, the first meeting of a bona fide English parliament was convened by Simon de Montfort, sixth Earl of Leicester, during the reign of John's successor, Henry III. In 1265, in an act of defiance, he summoned a gathering of supporters without seeking the king's permission. By the end of Henry's reign, an embryonic parliament, comprising two houses, was meeting on regular basis. Edward II (1307–27), although derided for ignoring his barons' views, further formalized England's parliamentary arrangements by constructing the Star Chamber (or Starred Chamber) for the *Curia Regis*. |
| The *Magnum Concilium* (Great Council) | Although its existence was only formalized during the reign of Henry III (1216–72), this body had effectively begun under William I. A putative House of Lords, it was a gathering of landowners, barons, and church leaders who would meet the sovereign to discuss affairs of state (and their own interests) twice-yearly. Although technically still in existence, the Great Council has not been summoned since 1640. |
| The Privy Council | With the law courts and two other councils mentioned above, this is the fourth principal council of state. It was once a hugely influential body, comprising carefully chosen aristocrats who were trusted allies of reigning monarch and convened to provide them with sound, confidential advice. The Council still exists, in diminished form (although it numbers more than 500 members). Whereas once it helped the sovereign to exercise prerogative powers, its functions have largely been delegated to its most important committee, the **Cabinet** (see p. 95). Neither are its principal members today the landed gentry of old: it is now composed of current and ex-members of the Cabinet (i.e. senior ministers in government of the day), whose status as Privy Counsellors/Councillors is recognized by the title 'Right Honourable' with which they are addressed in Parliament. Leader of the Opposition and heads of other major parties are honorary members, with places also reserved for other senior public figures, including archbishops and judges—although only serving ministers take part in its actual decision-making. Barring expulsion for a serious offence, membership is for life. The Council has various responsibilities—principally agreeing Orders in Council with the monarch, advising on the use of the Privy Purse, and formally sanctioning the introduction of new public holidays. |

monarchs were increasingly forced to recognize that the earls and barons on whom they depended to maintain their authority must, for that reason, be consulted (and heeded) on major affairs of state. It was during this tumultuous century that kings came to accept, reluctantly, the need to gain consent from their landed supporters to levy taxes, and in the following century that a newly assertive Parliament of 'Commoners' secured the right to play an active part in converting royal petitions (or Bills, as they are known today) into statutes (Acts).

Then came the English Civil War of the seventeenth century, and with it the series of decisive breaks with tradition outlined in Chapter 1 ushered in a new order. But it was another 200 years or more (despite the lofty ambitions of the more revolutionary Parliamentarians—notably, the Levellers and the Diggers) before most people were granted the vote and, with it, a true stake in parliamentary democracy.

The above developments are discussed in detail in Chapter 4, which explores the British electoral system. But what exactly is this Parliament—this great organ of government and citizenship—in which UK citizens are expected to invest such faith? This chapter explores two key aspects of parliamentary democracy in Britain: the nature and composition of the various institutions of Parliament; and the range of roles, duties, and responsibilities that its members discharge on the country's behalf.

## Hansard

Before examining the workings of Parliament, it is worth pausing to mention how its practices are recorded. Since 1909 all debates, votes, and other proceedings have been transcribed for a sprawling record known as **Hansard**. Excepting the words of the serving prime minister, it is not verbatim—'*repetitions, redundancies, and obvious errors*' are deliberately omitted—but it is the nearest we have to a definitive account of Parliament's business.

Although Hansard has only been published by Parliament itself for about a hundred years, it has existed for longer. As early as 1771 a printer called Miller was hauled up before the Lord Mayor of London for producing illicit reports of parliamentary debates, while radical free speech campaigners John Wilkes and William Cobbett fought for the right to publish their own versions. The latter's *Parliamentary Debates* first appeared in 1802, courtesy of Thomas Curson  'TC' Hansard, the printer after whom the 'official' record is now named. Today Hansard is one of the most reliable sources of news stories for political journalists at both local and national level, providing full details not only of contemporaneously reported debates but also of written parliamentary questions and answers, early day motions, and petitions. Like live debates it carries qualified privilege, and can be accessed electronically (via www.publications.parliament.uk/pa/cm/cmhansrd.htm). A more critical overview of how individual MPs and peers vote in Parliament can be found at www.theyworkforyou.com.

## ▌ The House of Commons

The linchpin of modern constitutional government in the UK is the 'lower house': the House of Commons. It currently comprises 650 members of Parliament (MPs), each representing a seat—or *constituency* (electoral district)—averaging

65,000 inhabitants. Under coalition plans this number will be reduced to 600. Prior to 2010, there were 646 (see p. 116).

Unlike many other parliaments, including that of the European Union (EU), the Commons chamber is ranged along two sets of opposing benches, presided over by its chairperson, the *Speaker* (referred to by members as 'Mr Speaker' or 'Madam Speaker'). To the right of the Speaker's chair are the government benches—those occupied by the governing party and its allies—while to their left are the Opposition benches, home of 'Her Majesty's Loyal Opposition' (the Opposition)—generally the second biggest party after a general election. All other MPs not allied to the government of the day sit along this side.

The adversarial layout of the Commons chamber is a reflection of the 'two-party politics' that (barring occasional coalitions, like the present one) has tended to dominate the British parliamentary scene, for complex historical reasons, since its inception. Since the later medieval period, debate has been divided broadly along conservative versus radical/reformist lines with, at various times: Royalists ranged against Parliamentarians; landowning Whigs battling to preserve the status quo against progressive Tories during the Industrial Revolution; and latterly Liberal, then Labour, MPs championing the rights of the common man against the forces of a more establishment 'big C' Conservatism.

In modern times two-party politics has continued to prevail, largely due to the quirks of the UK's electoral system. As we will see in Chapter 4, the so-called 'first past the post' (FPTP) process sees only the candidates who win a *relative majority* of votes cast in their constituencies—that is, more than any of their rivals—elected to the Commons. This means that all votes cast in favour of anyone else are effectively 'wasted'. As a result, the electoral process favours parties that can muster sufficient concentrations of support in enough constituencies to win the number of seats needed to form a government. With the Conservatives traditionally representing the more affluent classes and Labour supplanting the Liberals in the early twentieth century as the party of ordinary working people (the recent realignment under Tony Blair notwithstanding), elections have generally ended up being a straight fight between these two parties. The FPTP system thus discriminates against minority parties and independent candidates.

While Commons debates are chaired by the Speaker, its business timetable is set by a Cabinet minister: the **Leader of the House**. The typical Commons year is outlined in Table 2.2, while its usual weekly sittings are set out in Table 2.3.

## The role of an MP in relation to constituents

As of April 2010, ordinary MPs received salaries of £65,738 a year, as well as generous personal allowances enabling them to employ their own personal secretaries or researchers. In return, they are expected to represent the concerns and interests of *all* of their constituents—regardless of individual voters' political affiliations.

**Table 2.2** The annual timetable of the House of Commons

| Date | Event |
| --- | --- |
| October/November | State opening of Parliament |
| December–January (for four weeks) | Christmas recess |
| February (one week) | Half-term recess |
| March/April (two weeks) | Easter recess |
| May (one week over Spring Bank Holiday) | Whit recess |
| July–September (two months) | Summer recess |
| September/October (three weeks) | Party conference season |
| October/November | **Prorogation** |

**Table 2.3** The weekly timetable of the House of Commons

| Day | Time of sitting |
| --- | --- |
| Monday | 2.30–10.30 p.m. |
| Tuesday | 2.30–10.30 p.m. |
| Wednesday | 11.30 a.m.–7.30 p.m. |
| Thursday | 10.30 a.m.–6.30 p.m. |
| Friday (13 days a year, for private members' business, including PMBs) | 9.30 a.m.–3 p.m. |

At any time the serving government has anything between 80 and 100 MPs in its ranks. All other MPs—save the 'shadow ministers' on the Opposition frontbench—are known as 'backbench MPs', or *backbenchers*.

The principal ways in which MPs discharge their constituency responsibilities include:

- holding weekly 'surgeries' in their constituencies;
- writing to the ministers responsible for relevant government departments to try to resolve grievances voiced by constituents;
- asking written or oral questions in the House of Commons at **Question Time**—both 'Prime Minister's Questions' on a Wednesday and other regular slots during which senior departmental ministers answer for their ministries;
- canvassing support among fellow MPs for 'early day motions' (EDMs)—formal parliamentary records expressing strong views on an issue;
- requesting leave from the Speaker for 'adjournment debates' or tabling urgent debates (with the Speaker's consent);
- introducing *private member's Bills (PMBs)*—a form of potential legislation that, if passed, would change the law of the land (see p. 65).

The three main forms of debate that may be tabled by backbenchers are explained in Table 2.4, but certain of their roles justify more detailed explanation.

**Table 2.4** Types of House of Commons debate that may be tabled by backbenchers

| Name | How it works | Example |
|---|---|---|
| Early day motions (EDMs) | Despite their title, these rarely result in actual 'motions' (votes) and seldom win sufficient signatures to warrant full debate in the House. This only usually happens when at least half the sitting MPs support the motion. Nevertheless, as they become part of the official record of the Commons immediately they are tabled, they have an official status over that accorded to more minor procedures. In practice, they often provide journalists with fodder for stories—meaning that, in this age of media-driven policy initiatives, they can, in time, influence governments. Perhaps the most important function of EDMs is to enable backbenchers to highlight issues of concern to them, gauging support among their colleagues for a more definite attempt to initiate change through a PMB (see p. 65). | The most significant EDM of recent times was that tabled by then Leader of the Opposition Margaret Thatcher in 1979, censuring Jim Callaghan's incumbent Labour government. Callaghan's administration had arguably been on its last legs since the collapse of the Lib-Lab Pact that he had negotiated with David Steel's Liberal Party the previous August and, in time, Mrs Thatcher's motion precipitated the vote of no confidence that brought it to an end. What followed for Labour, on 4 May 1979, was a landslide election defeat to the Tories. Others have included the hugely influential EDM signed by 412 of the 646 MPs days after the 2005 election, calling for a Climate Change Bill, which duly followed in 2006. Only three other EDMs have ever been signed by more than 400 MPs. |
| Adjournment debates | Half-hour debates on the motion that 'this House do now adjourn' held either on the floor of the Commons or in neighbouring Westminster Hall at the end of a day's business. It is an opportunity for a backbench MP to raise an issue of concern to his or her constituents—and, more importantly, to 'summon' a minister to respond to it. Although, as with EDMs, it is highly unusual for an adjournment debate to result in an actual vote, on rare occasions this has happened when the debate has raised a nationally significant issue over which there are strong differences of opinion between opposing sides. | Conservative Prime Minister Neville Chamberlain, signatory to the ill-fated Munich Agreement with Nazi Germany, was effectively brought down by a motion flowing from an adjournment debate: while the government won the vote—effectively a motion of confidence in his leadership in the wake of Adolf Hitler's breach of the agreement by invading Poland—it was by such a narrow margin that his credibility was left in tatters. He was swiftly replaced by Winston Churchill. |
| Urgent debates | Any MP may apply to the Speaker for an urgent debate—formerly an 'emergency debate'—'on a specific and important matter that should have urgent consideration' under **Standing Order** No. 24. In practice, far more MPs apply for these than are granted and the Speaker will only allow one or two per session. If granted, the debate will take place within 24 hours. | Recent urgent debates have included a three-hour session on the future of British troop deployments in Afghanistan, forced by then Shadow Defence Minister Bernard Jenkin on 20 March 2002. |

## Surgeries

Also known as 'clinics', these weekly drop-in sessions may be attended by any constituent who wishes to voice a concern. They are normally held on Fridays (when little parliamentary business is timetabled), or Saturdays in the case of MPs whose constituencies are distant from London. Although many MPs hold surgeries in the offices of their constituency party, they frequently take place in more informal surroundings—church halls, community centres, and even pubs.

## Question Time

This opportunity to quiz senior departmental ministers directly about their policy decisions and the day-to-day workings of their ministries is held for at least one hour a day whenever the Commons is sitting. On Mondays and Tuesdays it takes place between 2.30 p.m. and 3.30 p.m.; on Wednesdays, from 11.30 a.m. to 12.30 p.m.; on Thursdays, from 10.30 a.m. to 12.30 p.m. (the two-hour slot on this day is intended to make up for the fact that Parliament rarely sits on a Friday).

Each department takes its turn to answer questions from the floor of the House on a fortnightly rota. In addition to the departmental question times, questions can be put to the prime minister on Wednesday lunchtimes, between 12 noon and 12.30 p.m. Until Mr Blair's election in 1997, 'Prime Minister's Questions' (or PMQs) occupied a twice-weekly 15-minute slot: on Tuesdays and Thursdays, between 3 p.m. and 3.15 p.m. Mr Blair's decision to combine the two into a single session was widely criticized at the time as a high-handed presidential-style gesture calculated to limit opportunities for Parliament and his own party to scrutinize him publicly. Nonetheless, the advent of a bumper Wednesday PMQ slot—combined with the fact that, since 1989, it and other key Commons proceedings, such as the Budget Speech, have been televised live on BBC2—has become a knockabout media highlight of the weekly Commons timetable.

Questions posed at departmental question-time sessions tend to be for a verbal (oral) response. They are answered by ministers according to a rota called the 'Order of Oral Questions'. Prime Minister's Questions, in contrast, takes one of two forms:

- oral;
- written (officially 'questions for a written answer').

For obvious reasons (in that they are posed in front of television cameras), oral questions attract the most media attention—although more often for the 'Punch and Judy' nature of the proceedings, rather than the substance of what they contain. Because PMQs can be heavily oversubscribed, MPs keen to ask questions are advised to give the Speaker three days' advance notice of their intentions to ensure their names appear sufficiently early on the order paper for them to be called in the allotted time. Giving such notice in advance does *not*, however, mean that MPs must specify the *exact wording* of their questions at that stage—merely that they should let it be known they wish to ask one.

Prime Minister's Questions follows several curious conventions. The first question faced by the prime minister is always one asking him or her about the other engagements he or she has scheduled for that day. This will usually be immediately tailed by a 'follow-up' question tabled by whichever MP posed the initial procedural one. This is the *real* question and, while the prime minister may have prior notice of the subject to which it relates, he or she rarely knows exactly how it will be phrased. The prime minister's hope is that he or she will have been adequately briefed by civil servants on the issue concerned to be able to ad-lib a convincing answer (or at least sidestep it effectively). When, later in the session, prime ministers refer before taking a question to 'the reply I gave some moments ago', they are alluding to the fact that the MP about to ask them a question has used the same procedural nicety about their engagements to get his or her name on the order paper.

Despite being the most talked-about parliamentary activity, Question Time is often criticized by serious-minded observers for being superficial and insincere, and playing to the cameras. And it is not only ministers and their would-be replacements on the Opposition frontbench who are accused of this: the most derided questions are often those asked by jobbing backbenchers seen to be using the session either as an opportunity to curry favour with the media in their own constituencies (and by extension their electorates) by focusing on the minutiae of extraordinarily specific local issues or to massage ministers' egos in the hope of gaining promotion.

In general, MPs genuinely seeking to hold ministers to account for their actions and to influence decision-making on behalf of their constituents will pose *written questions* (which are not only written themselves, but intended for written answers). This enables them to be more forensic and to seek more detailed replies than are likely to be delivered during the theatrical point-scoring exercise that Question Time often resembles. An alternative is to table what, until recently, were known as 'private notice questions' (now 'urgent questions'). These are questions on issues that have suddenly come to light and do not require the MP to give the usual three days' notice.

Although ministers invariably try to put a positive gloss on their policies— and the luxury of being able to map out a considered written answer gives them ample scope to do so—they are under a constitutional obligation to reply to written questions thoroughly and accurately. From a journalistic point of view,  while snappy sound bites offered up in the heat of battle between harassed ministers and their counterparts on the Opposition benches may generate easy headlines, stories that emerge from skilfully worded written questions can be more newsworthy in the long run.

None of this is meant to downplay the importance of oral questions, or PMQs in particular. As a weekly barometer of how the political wind is swaying, there is nothing to rival it. While ordinary backbenchers may ask only one question, the Leader of the Opposition is allowed to pose six supplementary questions and that of the third largest party, normally the Liberal Democrats, is tradition-ally permitted two. At time of writing, however, the Liberal Democrat leader and Deputy Prime Minister, Nick Clegg, had forfeited his right to ask questions for the duration of the Lib-Con *coalition government*. Indeed, Mr Clegg was authorized to stand in for the Prime Minister, David Cameron, at times when he was away.

PMQs have long provided a lively, sometimes heated, exchange between the serving prime minister and the pretender who would dethrone him or her—and it has often been said to make or break party leaders. Despite a shaky start, Mr Blair became an adept operator at the Dispatch Box in his decade in power. Nonetheless, on handing over to Mr Brown in summer 2007, he admitted that, whatever his apparent bravado, he had always dreaded the weekly ordeal. For his part, there was criticism of Mr Brown's more stilted performances at PMQs (despite the experience he had gained handling tricky exchanges over the Budget during ten years as Chancellor of the Exchequer).

## The role of an MP in relation to Parliament and party

MPs' primary duty of care lies, constitutionally, with their constituents. In addition to this, elected members have a responsibility to Parliament and, through it, the British people as a whole to participate in debate, and to scruti-nize and hold accountable the executive (government and Cabinet). One of the chief ways in which they discharge this responsibility is through the commit-tee system—one of several 'checks and balances' built into the workings of the legislature to ensure the transparency and accountability of government.

In practice, however, the nature of Britain's party system means that these constitutional responsibilities can conflict with the pressure most MPs are under to act in accordance with the official policies of their parties. This sense of instilled discipline—increasingly enforced by a strict **whip** system—is known as 'toeing the party line'. The idiomatic expression refers to the clearly delineated lines drawn along the length of the Commons in front of each set of benches, behind which members sitting on either side are required to stand while debating. It relates to the somewhat arcane principle that opposing MPs should be made to stand sufficiently far apart to ensure that, if they were to draw their swords in the heat of debate, they would be able to hold their arms fully outstretched without their weapons clashing.

## Parliamentary scrutiny and the committee system

The majority of backbench MPs at any one time—and indeed peers, who have an equivalent, if smaller scale, system in the Lords—are members of at least one committee. Each is made up of between 11 and 14 members, and chaired by a sitting member. The proportion of committees chaired by an MP or peer drawn from one party or another customarily reflected the distribution of seats in the House. Between May 1997 and May 2010, therefore, Labour had proportionately more chairpersons than all of the other parties put together, reflecting its majority in the Commons.

Although committees have become more 'fluid' in the forms they have taken in recent years—a parliamentary committee against anti-Semitism was formed in 2005—they can generally be divided into four broad types:

- **select committees**;
- **public Bill committees**;
- ad hoc committees;
- joint committees.

## Select committees

The most frequently publicized type of committee is the select committee. These scrutinize the workings of individual government departments and Parliament itself, and as such are permanent (at least, until the department to which they relate is renamed or disbanded). At present, there are 19 select committees covering departmental issues and several others focusing on internal parliamentary matters—for example, catering and administration. Departmental committees include the Education Committee (until recently, the Children, Schools, and Families Committee)—which scrutinizes the recently 'reformed' Department for Education—and the Culture, Media and Sport Select Committee. There is also a Commons Liaison Committee, made up of the chairpersons of all other select committees, to which the prime minister submits him or herself for questioning on government policy twice a year. It was established by Mr Blair.

Select committees have the power to call MPs, senior civil servants, and other public officials as witnesses, and to publish reports on their findings. One of the most explosive hearings of the past few years occurred on 15 July 2003, when the late Dr David Kelly was grilled by members of the Foreign Affairs Select Committee in the wake of the controversy over a dossier compiled by the Blair  government to justify its case for war against Saddam Hussein's Iraq. Dr Kelly, who was found dead near his Gloucestershire home two days later, was subjected to intense questioning about whether he was the source of a story on Radio 4's *Today* programme by BBC defence correspondent Andrew Gilligan, which claimed that senior intelligence sources were concerned that ministers had 'sexed up' the dossier by exaggerating the likelihood that Saddam's forces could unleash weapons of mass destruction (WMDs) within 45 minutes of being ordered to do so.

Because they are permanent, the composition of select committees has become increasingly contentious in recent times, in light of their customary in-built bias towards the governing party of the day. During the Thatcher years and the first two Blair terms Parliament was often criticized for failing to do enough to hold serving ministers to account, and committees in particular often seemed neutered—not least because prime ministers had a habit of using their party whips to parachute favoured placemen and women into their chairmanships. It was against this backdrop (as well as the general loss of public trust in MPs sparked by the expenses controversy) that the Commons Parliamentary Reform Select Committee recommended in 2010 that all future select committee chairpersons should be formally elected by their fellow MPs. On entering office in May that year, the coalition implemented this recommendation, extending the scope of elections to cover all committee members. Henceforth, committee seats allotted to each party would be filled by MPs elected by their fellow party members.

## Public Bill committees

The other most influential type of committee is the 'public Bill committee' (formerly the 'standing committee'—the term 'standing' being an archaic reference to the fact that its members are not around long enough to warrant permanent seats). Its new name better reflects its function: to scrutinize, comment on, amend, and/or *refer back* to the Commons for further consideration Bills in the process of becoming Acts of Parliament.

As the work of public Bill committees can take some time, in recent years governments have increasingly tried to bypass them when rushing to pass legislation they deem urgent. Under these circumstances, if agreed by the Speaker, the Commons itself can take on the role of a public Bill committee, as a 'Committee of the Whole House'. The **committee stage** of Bills is explored in more detail below.

## Ad hoc committees

As their name suggests, ad hoc committees are also temporary in nature, but unlike public Bill committees are formed to focus on specific topical issues of wide public concern, rather than prospective legislation. Recently established ad hoc committees include the House of Lords Ad Hoc Committee on Intergovernmental Organizations, formed in December 2007 to examine how cross-border policy issues (such as the spread of communicable diseases) are being addressed through the UK's membership of intergovernmental bodies like the European Union.

## Joint committees

So-called because they are composed jointly of MPs and peers, joint committees include the Joint Committee on House of Lords Reform, formed in 2002 to consider a range of alternative options for the composition of the Upper House in the wake of the, as yet incomplete, reforms begun by Labour in 1999 (see pp. 61–4). Since 1894 there has been a joint committee devoted to assisting the swift passage of laws designed to rationalize the number of Acts on the statute book (the record of all parliamentary legislation in place at any one time). These 'consolidation Bills', normally introduced in the Lords rather than the Commons, seek to bring together a number of different Acts on the same or similar subjects in one all-encompassing Act.

## Party loyalty and the whip system

As discussed earlier, British MPs tend to be affiliated to political parties. There have been notable exceptions, like Martin Bell, the one-time BBC foreign correspondent who overturned disgraced former Conservative minister Neil Hamilton's huge majority in Tatton in 1997, standing as an independent candidate on an 'anti-sleaze' ticket. But, in most cases, the nature of Britain's electoral system tends to guarantee candidates backed by the full force of their party machines—and particularly those representing the three main ones—the best chance of election.

Party membership is a double-edged sword. On the one hand, being selected as an official candidate for a major party gives you access to a huge support network, including significant financial backing in the run-up to an election. Independents, in contrast, must largely use their own money to finance their campaigns or canvass for donations. But being a partisan MP comes at a price. Parties in Britain have traditionally painted themselves as 'broad churches' representing people united by common ideals, but who may hold a variety of shades of opinion on specific issues. In recent times, however, party leaders (particularly serving prime ministers) have been criticized for stifling dissent within their ranks by using the whip system to force their MPs to back the official line when voting.

There are three broad definitions of the term 'whip':

- whips;
- the party whip;
- three-line whips.

Whips are individuals (MPs or peers) charged with 'whipping into line' backbenchers when a debate or vote regarded as important by their leadership is pending. It is the job of whips, led by a chief whip, to persuade MPs whose views are known to differ from those of the party's leadership to 'toe the party line'—attending debates and voting with their party at the appropriate time.

Whips have frequently been accused of, at best, cajoling and, at worst, bullying MPs into doing their leaders' bidding. When John Major was struggling to pass the Maastricht Treaty into British law in May 1992 in the face of a backbench rebellion by Euro-sceptic Tories, ailing loyalists including one who had just had brain surgery—known as the 'stretcher vote'—were taxied to the

Commons to act as 'lobby fodder' for the government. Under Labour, whips would notoriously bombard MPs with pager alerts urging them to turn up and vote along party lines and stay 'on message' when making speeches and giving interviews.

Mr Blair's prolonged honeymoon with both the voters and his own MPs after his 1997 election victory ended with a bump in his second term, when he faced a succession of knife-edge Commons votes, despite retaining a large majority in the House. He squeezed through some of his more controversial reforms, such as foundation hospitals and university top-up fees, by wafer-thin margins. In his third term, he actually lost the vote to extend the length of time for which terrorist suspects may be questioned by police without charge from 14 to 90 days, in spite of rigorous arm-twisting by Labour Chief Whip and future Home Secretary Jacqui Smith.

In addition to being fixers, the whips also play a more 'constructive', less intimidating role. Crucially, they act as unofficial personnel officers for the party leadership, talent-spotting potential future ministers and frontbench spokespeople, and providing important lines of communication between leader and party.

The term 'party whip' effectively refers to an MP or peer's 'membership' of his or her parliamentary party. Like any such affiliation, this can be withdrawn if the member in question is felt to have broken the 'rules' attached to membership. Mr Major temporarily withdrew the whip from the 22 Maastricht rebels—including future party leader Iain Duncan Smith—as a punishment for their disloyalty. More recently, Labour backbencher George Galloway, MP for Glasgow Kelvin, had the whip removed in October 2003 following repeated public attacks on his leader, Mr Blair, over the invasion of Iraq. In 2005 he was re-elected to the Commons for a further term in a different constituency, Bethnal Green and Bow, this time as an MP for anti-war party Respect.

Votes judged by party leaders to be of the greatest importance are highlighted—and underlined three times—in a weekly circular sent to their MPs and peers, *The Whip*. These votes are known as 'three-line whips', and attendance and voting along party lines is regarded by party leaders as compulsory. There are two lower levels of voting:

- 'one-line whips' (or 'free votes') tend to be called on 'matters of conscience'—non-party-political issues, like foxhunting or euthanasia;
- with 'two-line whips', MPs are told they 'must attend' unless they have made legitimate arrangements to be absent under the *pairing* system.

Pairing is a traditional parliamentary convention that allows an MP sitting on one side of the House to miss a vote on which they would have voted one way at the same time as an MP with opposing views on the opposite side of the chamber. Although regarded as acceptable, leaders would obviously prefer all of their MPs to attend and vote along party lines, regardless of whether members on the other side are absent, to increase their chances of winning votes and of doing so decisively. In turn, certain 'tribal' members, such as former Labour MP Tony Benn, have refused on principle ever to participate in pairing.

Although technically still possible, pairing was last used in 1996. At that time, the Labour and Lib Dem Chief Whips—Donald Dewar and Archy Kirkwood, respectively—suspended the arrangement indefinitely in protest at an incident in which, encouraged by their 'pairing whip', Derek Conway, three Conservative MPs cheated by each pairing up with a member from both of Opposition parties—thereby cancelling out six, rather than three, votes.

Three-line whips have long been seen as the ultimate call to arms (and disciplinary device) for party leaders—so much so that the term has passed into the vernacular of many businesses and other organizations to denote events and activities attendance at which is compulsory. But, as with *collective responsibility* (see pp. 99–101), the Lib-Con coalition agreed early on to compromise established practice in areas of principled disagreement between the parties, in the interests of preserving their overall alliance. For example, the official coalition agreement indicated that, while a three-line whip would be used to force through the Referendum Bill paving the way for a public vote on electoral reform, Tories would be permitted to campaign against changing the voting system when the *referendum* came.

## MPs, conflicts of interest, abuses of privilege—and how to avoid them

In addition to being responsible to their constituents, Parliament, and their parties, recent years have seen MPs accused of compromising their integrity by affiliating themselves to 'outside interests' over and above those to which they have constitutional obligations. To promote greater openness about such outside interests—and to avoid charges of corruption or deceit about their motives—since 1974 they have been expected to declare any gifts or income received over and above their parliamentary salaries on a **register of members' interests**.

The idea that an MP might have a financial or non-pecuniary interest in an organization other than the Commons is hardly new. The MPs of the eighteenth and early nineteenth centuries were invariably industrialists, agriculturalists, and/or landlords first and foremost, and elected representatives second: their decision to stand in the first place was normally motivated as much by commercial self-interest as by concern to improve the lot of their fellow man Conversely, when the Labour Party was formed, one of its aims was to get working-class candidates elected to the Commons, to counter the long-standing dominance of the middle and upper classes. To enable people from poorer backgrounds to fight elections, the trades union movement (one of several bodies that united to form the party) offered to 'sponsor' them—a traditional source of funding that continued for more than a century, but was recently switched from MPs themselves to their constituencies. Despite repeatedly pledging to end direct union sponsorship, Mr Blair was himself sponsored by the now-defunct Transport and General Workers' Union (TGWU, later T&G) for much of his time as an MP. The Hull East constituency of his deputy, John Prescott, a former merchant seaman, was sponsored for many years by the Rail and Maritime Union (RMT) and its precursor, the Seaman's Union, until it withdrew its support in protest at Blairite industrial policies in June 2002.

While Labour—and some individual MPs—have long been accused of being in the unions' pockets, similar charges have been levelled at the Conservatives in relation to big business. When Kenneth Clarke, a former Tory Health Secretary and Chancellor, 'retired' (temporarily) to the back benches in 1997, after losing a leadership bid to the more youthful William Hague, he took on several company directorships, as well as the chairmanship of British American Tobacco. But the outside interests of some of his erstwhile frontbench colleagues were more controversial still. Jonathan Aitken, Minister for Defence Procurement in Mr Major's government, notoriously signed a 'gagging order' during the  'Iraqi Supergun' affair, preventing it being disclosed that a British arms company of which he was a non-executive director, BMARC, had sold weapons to Saddam's regime. It was controversies such as the latter and the 'cash for questions' scandal involving then Trade Minister Neil Hamilton that prompted Mr Major to order a wholesale tightening of the way in which MPs—and, in turn, peers and local councillors—declared their interests.

The 'cash for questions' saga erupted in October 1994 when Hamilton and a colleague, Tim Smith, were accused in *The Guardian* of receiving money in brown paper envelopes from Harrods owner Mohamed Al Fayed in exchange for asking parliamentary questions on his behalf—a breach of Commons rules. Both were forced to resign and, although Hamilton was granted immunity from  **parliamentary privilege** to sue both the paper and Al Fayed (see p. 9), he was unsuccessful.

Following the Hamilton debacle and a series of personal scandals involving other ministers, Mr Major established a new Committee on Standards in Public Life under distinguished judge Lord Nolan. After six months of deliberation, the Nolan Committee published *Seven Principles of Public Life* (see Table 2.5), to which it stated MPs and other senior public officials should in future adhere.

If 'cash for questions' marked a low point for Mr Major's government, the scale of its fallout was nothing compared to that from the MPs' expenses scandal that erupted under Gordon Brown. What began as a trickle of minor revelations about the questionable claims of a handful of MPs—exposed by Freedom of Information Act 2000 (FoI) requests from journalists Ben Leapman, Jon  Ungoed-Thomas, and Heather Brooke—had by May 2009 become a full-blown flood, with the release of unexpurgated details of the accounts of hundreds of MPs in a flurry of front-page scoops by the *Daily Telegraph*.

**Table 2.5** The 'Seven Principles of Public Life'

| Principle | Meaning |
| --- | --- |
| Selflessness | Duty to act solely in terms of public interest (i.e. not for financial gain for him or herself, his or her family or friends) |
| Integrity | Duty not to sustain any financial obligation to outside individuals or organizations that might seek to influence him or her in the performance of his or her duties |
| Objectivity | Principle that appointment to his or her position be based purely on merit |
| Accountability | Duty to be accountable for his or her actions to public and to submit him or herself to 'whatever scrutiny is appropriate' to his or her office |
| Openness | Duty to be open about his or her actions and decisions in office |
| Honesty | Duty to declare any private interests relating to his or her public duties and take steps to resolve any conflicts of interest |
| Leadership | Duty to promote all principles by leadership and example |

An early casualty of the furore was Conservative backbencher Derek Conway, who had the whip withdrawn by Mr Cameron after it emerged he had used his parliamentary allowance to pay his younger son, Freddie, £40,000 over three years and his eldest, Henry, a further £32,000 for purportedly working as his parliamentary researchers. The scandal centred less on the idea of their being employed by their father —it emerged at the time that nepotism was commonplace at Westminster—but over whether they actually carried out the duties, of which no records were kept. As well as being suspended from his party, Mr Conway was asked to repay £13,161 by the Committee. The three main parties swiftly ordered their MPs to make full declarations about any relatives whom they were employing, the nature of their engagement, and details of their remuneration.

The ensuing controversy led to further disclosures about the arcane allowances regime governing MPs. It transpired that many MPs—including then Speaker Michael Martin—were claiming allowances of up to £22,000 to help with mortgage repayments on their second homes (those in their constituencies), despite the fact that some had long since paid off the loans. Embarrassingly, Mr Martin was chairing a committee tasked with reviewing the expenses system at the time.

Scenting blood, the media was soon chasing every shred of information about the obscure rule system governing MPs' expenses. An early twist in the saga came when it emerged that MPs claiming £250 or less on expenses were not even required to submit receipts to the authority then in charge, the Commons Fees Office (formally titled the 'Operations Directorate of the House of Commons Department of Resources'). Although Mr Brown reacted swiftly, ordering a review of the system and slashing the minimum receipted claim to £25, this change only came into effect in June 2008—by which time the saga had moved on still further. In March that year, details were released under FoI requests of a so-called 'John Lewis list' of perks for which MPs were eligible in relation to their second homes. Members were able to claim (at taxpayers' expense) for furnishing the properties—including around £10,000 for a new kitchen, £300 for air-conditioning units, £35 per square metre for new carpets or wooden flooring, and £750 apiece for television sets.

From this point on, stories kept coming. Two months after details of the John Lewis list emerged, the High Court ruled that a request made some two years earlier under FoI for full disclosure of MPs' expenses should be granted. Under intense media pressure, the custodian of this information, Mr Martin, reluctantly agreed to publish a receipt-by-receipt breakdown—in so doing, revealing that Mr Brown had claimed £4,471 to modernize his kitchen in 2005, while his predecessor, Mr Blair, had been reimbursed £10,600 for a new kitchen at his former constituency home in Sedgefield. Only weeks after these disclosures, husband-and-wife Tory MPs Nicholas and Ann Winterton were found guilty by the Parliamentary Commissioner, John Lyon, of breaching rules introduced two years earlier to stop MPs claiming back rent on properties owned by family members. Having paid off the mortgage on their £700,000 London flat in the early 1990s, the couple had placed it in a family trust to avoid Inheritance Tax. But since 2002, they had occupied it again as tenants, paying the trust £21,600 a year out of a Commons entitlement, known as the 'additional costs allowance' (ACA), a subsidy of up to £24,000 a year to help MPs who needed to maintain second homes because of the distance between their constituencies and Parliament. The couple, who denied any intentional wrongdoing, were given a grace period up until September 2008, during which they were permitted to continue using their ACAs to pay rent while they made alternative arrangements.

Even worse was to come. In January 2009 Leader of the House Harriet Harman made a final vain attempt to prevent full disclosure of all MPs' expense accounts after nearly two years of stonewalling by members since the initial FoI requests by journalists. When the trio had passed their original enquiries to *Information Commissioner* Richard Thomas in June 2007, an immediate tussle had begun between him and the Commons. While he had ordered the disclosure of some of the requested information, the Commons authorities formally objected and MPs went on to vote to exempt their correspondences from his jurisdiction by approving the Freedom of Information (Amendment) Bill. A widely used excuse for doing so was that wholesale disclosure of MPs' personal information might compromise that of constituents with whom they had corresponded. In the event the Bill had been swiftly withdrawn when it became clear no peer could be found to 'sponsor' it (introduce it formally) in the House of Lords. So when, under intense media scrutiny, Ms Harman tried to revive the block to the wholesale release of expenses, it was only a matter of time before the Commons authorities buckled. Following the government's climb-down, it announced that full disclosure of all MPs' expense receipts going back to April 2004 would be published on 1 July that year.

Those impatient to know more did not have to wait that long, though. In May 2009, the *Daily Telegraph* published the first of a series of sensational instalments revealing just what MPs had been using their parliamentary allowances for—after a disc containing data on all 646 MPs was leaked to it by an ex-SAS officer, John Wick. For weeks, newspapers and radio and television bulletins were dominated by unravelling details of a variety of sometimes lavish, more usually trivial, and occasionally downright bizarre claims. In the event, but for the *Telegraph* investigation much of this, detail might never have come out: when the Commons finally got round to publishing MPs' receipts two months later, large chunks of information had been blacked out (or 'redacted'), supposedly to protect individuals' personal details.

Among the more outlandish claims exposed by the *Telegraph* were the purchase of a £1,645 'duck island' by Conservative MP Peter Viggers, the £2,115 former minister Douglas Hogg's reimbursement for the cost of cleaning his moat, and a rejected claim made by then Home Secretary Ms Smith (apparently unwittingly) for a £67 Virgin Media bill that included two pornographic pay-per-view films ordered by her husband. She eventually resigned, officially for family reasons, just ahead of the 2009 European elections, but after losing her seat in the 2010 Westminster poll conceded that one of her reasons for quitting had actually been the furore over her expenses.

Ms Smith's elevation to the status of 'poster girl' (as she would later describe herself) of the expenses scandal had stemmed in part from the earlier revelation that she had misused her ACA entitlement. For many, the suggestion that MPs could claim financial aid to furnish and make mortgage interest payments on their pieds-à-terres was dubious enough, but widespread public indignation intensified when it transpired Ms Smith had designated her sister's house in London as her 'first home'—leaving her able to claim £116,000 for her family home in Redditch. The phenomenon this exposed—the apparently widespread practice among MPs of switching the designations of their first and second homes, so as to maximize their ACA claims—became known as 'flipping'. Among those subsequently accused of profiting this way were then Communities Secretary Hazel Blears, Transport Secretary Geoff Hoon, and Michael Gove, who was appointed Education Secretary after the May 2010 election. Some members had added value to a property at taxpayers' expense before later selling it— avoiding Capital Gains Tax (see p. 187) to boot if they had designated it their first home—while others had refurbished one residence before flipping designations so that they could spend money on another.

Inevitably, the government had to act—and do so decisively. A handful of hurried tweaks to existing Commons rules (such as the earlier one governing receipts) was never going to be enough to satisfy a baying media. Wholesale reform was needed. In the end, Mr Brown's final response was threefold:

- to commission Sir Christopher Kelly, chairman of the Committee on Standards in Public Life, to examine the existing expenses regime and recommend reform;

- to establish a new **Independent Parliamentary Standards Authority (IPSA)** (see later in this chapter) to assume responsibility for policing the expenses system from the existing in-house Commons authorities, the Members' Estimate Committee, and the Fees Office;

- to ensure that questionable second-home expenses claimed since 2004 were repaid by MPs in full, by authorizing retired *Permanent Secretary* Sir Thomas Legg to conduct a backdated audit—invoicing anyone he judged in breach of existing rules.

Sir Christopher's report, published in October 2009, contained several recommendations, all of which Mr Brown immediately pledged to implement 'in full'. Among the most significant were:

- the scrapping of the ACA following an 'appropriate' transitional period;

- a ban on MPs employing members of their family, to be introduced within five years;

- an end, as of the next election, to the generous 'resettlement grants' to which retiring MPs had been entitled. These are currently worth up to a year's salary (around £65,000), depending on members' age and length of service—the first £30,000 being tax-free—but will be replaced with a mere eight weeks' pay;

- a handover of responsibility to IPSA for both determining MPs' expenses and also their salaries and pensions.

Not all MPs 'outed' for excessive or inappropriate claims took their punishments meekly. When in February 2010 Sir Thomas began issuing individual letters demanding repayment from 390 MPs (who had collectively overclaimed £1.3m), a number said they simply did not have enough money available, while others criticized what they saw as the injustice of applying a putative new set of rules to claims made in good faith under an old one. By the time his final report was published—exposing what he described as a 'culture of deference' at the Fees Office—70 MPs had formally appealed against his demands (at least nine winning their appeals). In the end, the most substantial repayments Sir Thomas requested included one for £42,458 from then Communities Minister Barbara Follett, and one for £24,878 by Dr Liam Fox, soon to be installed as Defence Secretary in Mr Cameron's Cabinet.

More unedifying still than the cries of unfairness over disputed claims for Kit-Kats and frangipani was the intervention by the Metropolitan Police in the case of three Labour MPs—former Fisheries Minister Elliot Morley, David Chaytor, and Jim Devine—and Conservative peer Lord Hanningfield. By February 2010, all had been referred to the Director of Public Prosecutions, Keir Starmer, and he subsequently charged them with false accounting. If it was possible for the accused to lower themselves in the estimation of the public any more, they had managed it. As each man appeared in court for the first time in April 2010, their solicitors confirmed their intention to invoke the constitutional protection of parliamentary privilege (see p. 8), arguing that allowing a court of law to try them would breach the principle of the *separation of powers* between judiciary and legislature. They cited the wording of Article Nine of the 1689 Bill of Rights, which reads:

> ❝ The freedom of speech and debates or proceedings in Parliament ought not to be impeached or questioned in any court or place out of Parliament. ❞

Their efforts to avoid a high-profile trial were short-lived, however: in June 2010 Mr Justice Saunders ruled that there was no 'logical, practical, or moral justification' for their immunity.

A fourth Labour MP, Eric Illsley, was charged with false accounting in May 2010, in relation to an allegedly dishonest claim for £20,000 in *Council Tax* and other bills, and in July that year, Tory peer Lord Taylor of Warwick was also charged, on six counts of false accounting. In January 2011 Mr Chaytor, by then a former MP, received an 18-month prison sentence. Mr Illsley became the first sitting MP to be convicted a week later.

## The Parliamentary Commissioner for Standards

To reinforce his determination to stamp out the perceived culture of 'sleaze' among certain members of his party, Mr Major had a formal code of conduct for MPs drawn up and appointed Sir Gordon Downey the first **Parliamentary Commissioner for Standards** in 1995. The new Commissioner's job was to oversee the register of interests, summoning and holding to account any member felt to have breached the code. He was later replaced by Elizabeth Filkin, but, controversially, in late 2001 her job was advertised while she was still in office. Many argued this was because she had been too robust in holding MPs and government to account. Her successor, Sir Philip Mawer, was replaced by Mr Lyon in summer 2008. To ensure that the Commissioner is correctly discharging his or her duties, a further layer of oversight exists, in the guise of the Committee on Standards and Privileges. Not to be confused with the Committee on Standards in Public Life, this is composed of sitting MPs, and has the same membership as the House of Commons Commission (see p. 70).

## Independent Parliamentary Standards Authority (IPSA)

In an effort to avoid future repeats of the expenses scandal, in his last year in power Mr Brown announced the formation of a new external body to take over responsibility for policing the expenses regime from the Commons authorities and MPs themselves. IPSA was charged not only with drawing up a new allowances system but also with setting and reviewing MPs' salaries and pensions. Although it began work on developing a firm 'scheme' of changes to the pre-existing expenses system in 2009, it was not until the end of March 2010 that this was published. While it was substantially the same as the recommendations made by Sir Christopher, finer details included the following.

- An end to MPs' ability to claim expenses in relation to second homes— to be replaced by an entitlement to help with the cost of rented accommodation. From summer 2010, a two-year transitional period was to be introduced for MPs then currently claiming mortgage interest expenses, enabling them to adapt to the changes.
- A widening of the definition of 'London area' hitherto used by MPs claiming accommodation expenses on the grounds that their constituencies were located too far from Westminster for them to commute. Members would no longer be eligible for help with overnight stays if any part of their constituency was within 20 miles of Westminster, or when a commute from any part of their constituency to Westminster was possible within 60 minutes by public transport at peak times.
- The limit on expenditure for any train journey would be the cost of a standard-class open ticket, as opposed to a first-class one.

The new scheme was introduced in full following the May 2010 election.

# ▌ The House of Lords

Before describing the means by which Parliament passes legislation, it is necessary to look at the nature and composition of the second chamber: the House of Lords. Since the passage of the House of Lords Act 1999, which Labour introduced to start the process of reforming or replacing this institution, it has been in a state of effective limbo—and currently remains a 'transitional' House.

## What is the point of the Lords?

Even among those who dispute the current make-up of the Lords, few believers in parliamentary democracy argue against the principle that the main lawmaking chamber in a bicameral legislature should be held to account by a second. The arguments that have raged in recent decades over whether the Lords should be reformed or abolished have been less about any real desire to scrap the Upper House altogether than a growing recognition that, in a modern democratic state, a second chamber composed primarily of political appointees and people entitled to sit there by birthright alone is fundamentally undemocratic. Few, however, dispute the need for some form of 'check and balance'.

As long ago as the early twentieth century, the Lords had begun to seem outmoded to many—its staunchly establishment outlook increasingly colliding with the reformist governments of Herbert Asquith and David Lloyd George. It was as Asquith's Chancellor that Lloyd George brought the matter of Lords reform to a head by introducing his seminal 'People's Budget' in 1909, which sought to raise taxes to fund social reform. The Budget was rejected by the disproportionately Conservative Lords, so after Asquith narrowly won a further election the following year he made it his mission to prevent the Lords ever again being able to reject legislation outright. The 1911 Parliament Act replaced its power of veto with a right merely to *delay* Bills—and for a maximum of two calendar years (or three parliamentary sessions). This delaying period was subsequently truncated, by the Parliament Act 1949, to two sessions over 13 months. Any attempt to delay further, in defiance of the Commons' will, has since seen governments 'invoke' the Parliament Acts. This happened recently when the Lords' repeated attempts to thwart Labour's ban on hunting with hounds were finally defeated.

Since Asquith's run-in with the Lords, and despite repeated promises to further curtail its powers and change its composition by Labour, nothing decisive has so far happened. Nothing, that is, apart from the House of Lords Act 1999, which finally sounded the starting pistol for reform of the chamber by abolishing all but a handful of the remaining hereditary peers at the time still sitting in the House. Its long-term aim, as yet unrealized, was to replace the hereditary principle with some form of membership entitlement based on individuals' contribution to society through public service or other major achievement.

The composition of the Lords prior to the 1999 Act was as follows.

1. *The* **Lords Spiritual**—26 peers comprising:

    (a) the Archbishops of Canterbury and York;
    (b) the Bishops of London, Durham, and Winchester;
    (c) the 21 next most senior Church of England diocesan bishops.

2. *The Lords Temporal*—1,263 peers comprising:

    (a) all 759 *hereditary peers* of England, Scotland, Great Britain, and the United Kingdom (but not including Northern Ireland);
    (b) *the Lords of Appeal in Ordinary (the Law Lords)*—27 peers 'created' by successive governments under the Appellate Jurisdiction Act 1876 to help the Lords to fulfil its role as the UK's final court of appeal;
    (c) the 477 other *life peers* who had been created in **honours lists** under the terms of the Life Peerages Act 1958.

Hereditary peers have long been permitted to disclaim their peerage rights to enable them to stand as MPs and this happened on several occasions in the second half of the twentieth century. Tony Benn inherited the hereditary title Viscount Stansgate while sitting in the Commons—thereby finding himself banned by law from retaining his seat. After several years of campaigning for the right to renounce his peerage and resume his seat as an MP, he persuaded Harold Macmillan's Conservative government to set up a joint committee to examine the issue and, ultimately, change the law through the Peerage Act 1963.

Others followed his lead. Quintin Hogg (Lord Hailsham) disclaimed his family seat to fight a by-election in, ironically, his father's old constituency of St Marylebone. He ultimately changed his mind, however, reverting to his inherited title to become a Tory *Lord Chancellor*. Most peculiarly, in 1963 Lord Home performed a double-flip by giving up an inherited title that had earlier forced him to resign a Commons seat to return to the Lower House as prime minister. His action—prompted by his election to replace Macmillan as Conservative leader—had the unique consequence of creating a two-week interval between his 'resignation' as a peer and re-election as an MP, during which Britain's prime minister was a member of neither the Commons nor the Lords.

## The House of Lords Act 1999

The House of Lords Act 1999 contained five key clauses designed to pave the way for an, at least partially, elected second chamber. After a series of run-ins between Mr Blair, his own backbenchers, the Tories, and the Lords itself, however, it was decided to move towards reform gradually by setting up a *transitional* chamber, which would remove the automatic membership rights of all but 92 hereditary peers. In the meantime, the thorny question of exactly what the final composition of a new Upper House should be was handed to a Royal Commission headed by former Tory minister Lord Wakeham.

Of the 92 hereditary peers allowed to remain in the House during the hazily defined transition period, 90 were elected—but by their fellow peers, not the public. The aim was to single out individuals with a history of making valuable contributions to Lords debates, rather than the many who rarely, if ever, attended proceedings in practice. As well as the 90 lords with **elected hereditary peerages**, however, a further two hereditary peers were permitted to remain as *ex officio* members, on the basis of their ceremonial significance to the chamber. These were the Earl Marshal, the Duke of Norfolk, and the Lord Great Chamberlain, the Marquess of Cholmondeley. In addition, ten new *life peerages* were controversially created to enable several hereditary peers *not* elected to remain. These included former Tory Leader of the House Lord Cranborne, ex-Foreign Secretary Lord Carrington, and the Earl of Longford. More contentious still was the decision to retain Lord Snowdon, Princess Margaret's ex-husband, who was widely felt to have demonstrated little interest in the chamber. The process by which the transitional House was set up was brokered as a compromise amendment to the Bill by Lord Weatherill, a former Commons Speaker.

After the internal election that followed the passing of the 'Weatherill Amendment', the composition of the Lords was as follows:

- 26 Lords Spiritual;
- 598 Lords Temporal, comprising 27 Law Lords, two non-elected hereditary peers, 90 elected hereditary peers, and 477 life peers.

Since then life peers have continued to be appointed at a prodigious rate and the balance of power between parties has fluctuated wildly, with Labour finally reaching the symbolic tipping point at which it had as many peers as the Tories and Lib Dems put together in 2009—12 years after regaining power. More recently, shortly after reaching their coalition agreement Mr Cameron and Mr Clegg revealed plans to create 170 new party-affiliated peers between them, in the short term, to ensure their Bills' uninterrupted passage through the Lords—a move condemned by Labour MP Chris Bryant, a former Deputy Leader of the Commons, as 'the single largest simultaneous act of political patronage probably since Charles II came to the throne in 1660'. Lords who have no declared party affiliation are known as *cross-benchers*. Appropriately enough, they sit on benches ranged in short rows across the width of the House, with the government benches to their left and the Opposition to their right.

## The Wakeham Commission, the 2001 White Paper, and moves towards further reform

The Wakeham Commission's remit was to address the following questions.

- What is to be the future role of the second chamber?
- How should it be composed (appointed or elected)?
- Is an entirely appointed second chamber the best option?
- Is an entirely elected second chamber the best option?

Its report, *A House for the Future*, published in January 2000, made several recommendations, subsequently crystallized in a 2001 House of Lords **White Paper** entitled *A Chamber Fit for the 21st Century*. This advocated a neutered version of the Wakeham proposals, including the removal of all remaining hereditary peers, the retention of existing life peers 'transitionally', and the eventual capping of Lords membership at about 600. The one concrete development that happened almost immediately was the establishment of an independent **House of Lords Appointments Commission** to ensure that, while the Lords remained in transition, life peerages would be awarded principally on merit, rather than as a result of political patronage. The main role of the Commission was to vet individuals nominated by the prime minister and other party leaders for any sign of rewards for favours—a power it memorably used to block three of Mr Blair's nominees in 2005 (see pp. 156–7). But it is also allowed to propose its own nominees, focusing on non-partisan individuals with 'a record of significant achievement' in their 'chosen way of life'. To date, 42 of these 'people's peers' have been appointed.

During his remaining years in office, Mr Blair slowly edged away from advocating a fully elected chamber to a partially elected and then fully appointed one—in defiance of an all-party motion as early as March 1999 demanding that it be entirely elected. Although he would cite in his defence well-rehearsed Conservative arguments—including the potential challenge an elected Lords might pose to the status of the Commons as Britain's primary legislature—the Tories branded his alternative idea an attempt to shore up his power base by appointing 'Tony's Cronies'. Memories were evoked of the 'Lavender List'—the notorious string of honours for trusted allies and confidantes that another Labour Prime Minister, Harold Wilson, had patronized on his retirement in 1975.

Leaving aside the problematic nature of steering any legislation designed to abolish the Lords through the Upper House itself, the 'settled' view of MPs now appears to favour a fully elected second chamber. Between 2006 and 2008, Jack Straw (first as Leader of the Commons, then Lord Chancellor) introduced two further White Papers. The former proposed a 50:50 split between elected and appointed peers, with a new £50,000 salary to encourage attendance, while the latter extended the elected component to between 80 and 100 per cent (on salaries of £55,000–60,000). This legislation would also have reduced the size of its membership to 400–450 maximum, with anyone found guilty of being 'lazy' or 'corrupt' being expelled (a rule that would surely have removed Lord Archer, the Tory peer jailed for perjury in 2000, and Dame Shirley Porter, surcharged by Westminster City Council for the 'homes for votes' scandal— see p. 411).

By the time Labour entered the 2010 election it had finally committed itself to a fully elected Lords as part of a wider packages of constitutional reforms, including a referendum on replacing Britain's first past the post (FPTP) electoral system with the **alternative vote (AV)** (see p. 131). With the Lib Dems advocating similar reforms, Mr Clegg persuaded Mr Cameron to include a commitment in their coalition agreement to push for a new 'Senate', to be wholly or largely elected using *proportional representation* (see pp. 130–1). At time of writing the two options had been referred to a committee, which was due to report back with a draft motion by December 2010.

The one significant further reform since 1999 to have affected the Lords was the creation in the Constitutional Reform Act 2005 of a new US-style *Supreme Court*—formally known as the *Supreme Court of the United Kingdom*. To further reinforce the principle of separation of powers in practice, then Lord Chancellor Mr Straw divested the House of Lords of its judicial function, transferred its status as highest court of justice and appeal in the UK to the Supreme Court, and installed 12 of the then 27 serving Law Lords as inaugural Justices of the Supreme Court. The Court began work on 1 October 2009. For the duration of their service as Justices, their ability to sit in the Lords was curtailed, although they would be entitled to return to the chamber on retirement (assuming that it still existed). Future appointees would not have seats in the Lords. Although the new Court is the ultimate bastion of English, Northern Irish, and Scottish law, and has taken over adjudication of devolutionary matters from the *Judicial Committee of the Privy Council*, Scotland retains its own supreme court in criminal matters: the *High Court of Justiciary*.

# ▌ Types of legislation

As Britain's legislature, the primary purpose of Parliament is to legislate. So how does it do this and what forms can legislation take?

British legislation is divided into two broad types: *primary* and *secondary*. Primary legislation is the umbrella term for all Bills passed by both Houses of Parliament and given the ***royal assent*** to become Acts. It is also known sometimes as 'enabling legislation', in that Acts must be passed to 'enable' the government and Parliament to issue the various rules, regulations, and instructions needed to implement changes in law on the ground.

## Primary legislation

The four main categories of primary Bill are as follows:

- public Bills;
- private Bills;
- hybrid Bills;
- private member's Bills.

### Public, private, and hybrid Bills

Public, private, and hybrid Bills all have one thing in common: they are all initiated at the behest of the government. But that is where their similarities end. Whereas public Bills change 'the law of the land', private Bills seek only to affect specific individuals or organizations—for example, companies or local authorities.

Briefly, the majority of new laws that gain media attention—and about which journalists normally find themselves reporting—are public Bills. The Academies Bill 2010, which controversially paved the way for *free schools*, and the numerous 'anti-terror' Bills of recent years all are, or were, public Bills affecting the entire population of England, if not Britain. Private Bills, in contrast, are usually introduced at the request of a specific individual or body, either to exempt them from a law otherwise affecting the whole country, or to grant them some other discrete privilege. The **Highways Agency**—the **executive agency** of the Department for Transport responsible for building and maintaining major

**trunk roads**, A-roads, and motorways—has often been granted private Bills to enable it to extend, or introduce, roads in new areas. Another recent example is the London Local Authorities Bill 2007, which invited complaints from the British Beer and Pub Association over the fact that it required pub landlords to submit any plans to extend or otherwise alter their licences to the authorities responsible for local litter policy—in addition to the eight other bodies they were already expected to inform.

Hybrid Bills are a mix of the other two. Like public Bills they affect the whole population, but they resemble private Bills in that they impinge on some people more than others. Examples of hybrid Bills include the one passed to sanction construction of the Channel Tunnel. As residents living along the length of the tunnel were affected by construction work significantly more than those who might occasionally use it, the government granted the enabling Bill hybrid status—giving those residents the right to be formally consulted on the legislation to a greater extent than the rest of the British public. The Bill enabling work to begin on the long-delayed Crossrail project in London, finally confirmed by ministers and then London Mayor Ken Livingstone in 2008, is another example of hybrid legislation.

## Private member's Bills

Private member's Bills (PMBs) warrant a separate category because, unlike all of the above types of legislation, they are introduced not by governments but backbench MPs. PMBs may be introduced in one of three ways listed in Table 2.6.

The primary purpose of **ten-minute rule** Bills is to enable MPs to raise issues that they deem important—rather than actually to get their measures onto the statute book. In practice, it is unlikely an MP will persuade his or her party, or the government, to allocate sufficient parliamentary time to take his or her Bill further (although there have been some celebrated cases in which this has occurred—see p. 66).

**Table 2.6** The three ways of introducing private member's Bills (PMBs)

| Method | Procedure |
| --- | --- |
| PMB Fridays | Early in each parliamentary session, MPs can take part in a 'ballot' for the opportunity to introduce their own Bill on one of 13 'PMB Fridays'. On these days PMBs take precedence over government and Opposition business. The first 20 names drawn in the ballot—effectively out of a 'hat'—may introduce their Bills. The six or seven at the top of the list are likely to have their proposals discussed in detail in the Commons. |
| The ten-minute rule | MPs may instead use the 'ten-minute rule' (officially, Standing Order No. 23), which applies on most Tuesdays and Wednesdays at the start of public business in the Commons. They may make a ten-minute speech outlining their proposals, provided that they have the support of at least ten other members. An opponent may make a ten-minute speech in reply. |
| Presentation Bills | MPs may introduce a presentation Bill (under Standing Order No. 57). This is a means of drawing limited attention to an issue of concern to the MP, because—unlike the other two methods—it does not allow him or her to make a speech outlining the Bill's details in the House. |

To qualify to introduce a ten-minute rule Bill, an MP must be 'the first member through the door' to the Public Bill Office on the Tuesday or Wednesday 15 working days prior to the date on which they wish to present it. They must also have the Bill proposed and seconded, and receive written backing from ten colleagues.

Many significant issues have been raised as a result of the introduction of PMBs. In 1997, after initial indications he would receive government backing, Labour backbencher Michael Foster introduced a PMB proposing a ban on hunting with dogs (a measure proposed in his party's manifesto). He later withdrew it when it became clear ministers were not going to accord it sufficient parliamentary time to see it through all of its stages in the face of mounting opposition from the Conservative Party and the Lords.

Perhaps the most celebrated PMB was former Liberal leader Mr Steel's Abortion Bill 1967, which legalized terminations of unwanted pregnancy for the first time in Britain, albeit only up to 24 weeks after conception. Touching on an issue of huge public concern at the time, it was allotted ample time for full debate and scrutiny, and duly passed.

## Secondary legislation

It has increasingly been the convention for primary legislation to cover only the fundamental *principles* underpinning a change in the law. In contrast, *secondary legislation*—or 'subordinate' or *delegated legislation*—refers to powers 'flowing from' Acts themselves, and rules, regulations, and guidelines drawn up to implement them. For primary legislation to be put into practice, ministers need the authority to introduce the measures it contains on the ground. This authority is exercised through 'delegated' legislative powers, the main types of which are listed in Table 2.7.

**Table 2.7** Main types of secondary legislation

| Name | Definition | Example |
|---|---|---|
| *Statutory instrument* | Rules, regulations, and guidelines issued by ministers to flesh out the detail of newly passed Acts or update that in existing ones. Although no further Act is required to implement the measures, they still require the formal agreement of Parliament. The 'parent' Act usually specifies whether affirmative or negative agreement is required (the former means a statutory instrument will not come into play unless Parliament formally approves a resolution, while the latter means it will automatically do so if, after 40 days, no motion has been passed objecting to it). | The complex instructions issued by the Department for Culture, Media, and Sport to enable local authorities and police to assume responsibility for issuing liquor and public entertainment licences under the Licensing Act 2003. These took so long to come into force that '24-hour drinking' was only introduced in pubs in November 2005—two years after the Act received royal assent. |

| Name | Definition | Example |
|------|-----------|---------|
| **By-law** | Localized laws passed on approval of the relevant government minister, the scope of which is enshrined in an existing Act. | City-centre street drinking bans introduced by local authorities in problem areas. |
| Order in Council | Submitted by ministers for approval by the sovereign at a meeting of the Privy Council. A draft is normally agreed by Parliament before being submitted by ministers. | Orders in Council were used to introduce much delegated anti-terror legislation relating to Northern Ireland in the 1960s and 1970s. |

# ▌ The passage of a Bill

Before it can be introduced into Parliament as a fully fledged Bill, the detail of prospective government legislation is publicly aired in two early draft forms: a **Green Paper** and a White Paper. The former is a sketchy consultation document outlining the *broad spirit* of a proposed Bill. It is open to significant redefinition depending on the response it elicits from the public and other interested parties. The latter is a more crystallized outline of a proposed law—again issued for consultation purposes—that normally prefigures a Bill to be introduced in the next session.

Bills can be introduced in either the Commons or the Lords, although they are normally instigated in the former. The process is as outlined in Table 2.8.

## Speeding up the legislative process

The legislative process can be very involved, and over the decades MPs of all parties have become increasingly adept at delaying the passage of Bills to which they object. Traditionally they have conspired to do so by making excessively long speeches designed to frustrate the government's attempts ever to get through the various stages through which a Bill must pass to become law. 'Filibustering' (as it is known) has at times been used sufficiently obstructively to delay indefinitely and, in some cases, 'kill off' prospective Acts. If a Bill were to be delayed by time-wasters long enough for a government to be voted out of office in an election, that might well spell its end, because the Opposition waiting to take over would be unlikely to resurrect it.

The term 'filibustering' was first coined in reference to pro-independence Irish MPs in the nineteenth century, who, in an effort to force the Westminster government to hand over 'home rule' for Ireland, would deliberately hold up Bills on other issues. Today, filibustering and other forms of time-wasting, repetition, and drawn-out debate can be countered in one of the four ways outlined in Table 2.9.

**Table 2.8** The passage of a Bill through Parliament

| Stage | Process |
| --- | --- |
| **First reading** | When Bills are first presented, the only thing that happens is that their titles are read out in the Commons. In practice, this can take several minutes, because the full titles of Bills tend to sum up the substance of their proposals and can be lengthy. |
| **Second reading** | The general principles of the Bill are read out, debated, and voted on for the first time. This normally happens in 'an afternoon' between 4 p.m. and 10 p.m. (barring a brief experiment, when late Leader of the House Robin Cook introduced a new 'family-friendly' parliamentary timetable more in keeping with the rest of the working population). The second reading can run over several days if the Bill has major implications. |
| Committee stage | A public Bill committee undertakes detailed consideration of the main clauses in the Bill. Sometimes this stage is carried out by the Commons itself, sitting as a Committee of the Whole House (this normally happens when a treaty is being ratified, or when a Bill needs to be passed urgently—e.g. recent anti-terror legislation). This also happens automatically following the annual Budget Speech, when aspects of the Finance Act flowing from it are fast-tracked. |
| **Report stage** | The committee's recommendations are referred to the Commons in a written report and further amendments can follow before the Bill proceeds to a *third reading*. This stage often involves late sittings. |
| Third reading | The Bill is reviewed and debated in its final intended form. At this stage all opportunities for the Commons to make amendments to it have passed (although the Lords can still do so). |

The Bill is now referred to the Lords (or 'another place' in parliamentary parlance). Here it follows much the same sequence of stages as those of the Commons, but this time its committee stage will usually be taken on the floor of the House.

| | |
| --- | --- |
| The House of Lords and the Lords' report to the Commons | Amendments made by the Lords must be agreed by the Commons before it can proceed to the Statute Book. Should there be significant differences of opinion between the two (e.g. over foxhunting legislation during Mr Blair's tenure), a joint committee will usually be set up to resolve them. Under the successive Parliament Acts, the Lords cannot delay a money Bill, and can only delay other Bills by up to 13 months, after which they are automatically given royal assent. |
| royal assent | The final seal of approval for a Bill, turning it into an Act, is notionally still given by the monarch, but the last time this formally happened was in 1854. It is conferred in Norman French, *La Reine le Veult*, and has not been refused since 1707, when Queen Anne declined to grant it for a Bill to settle the militia in Scotland. The sentence preceding every Act reads: '*Be it enacted by the Queen's Most Excellent Majesty, by and with the advice and consent of the Lords Spiritual and Temporal, and Commons, in this Parliament assembled, and by authority of the same, as follows...*' |

**Table 2.9** Devices used to speed up debate in the House of Commons

| Device | Definition |
| --- | --- |
| Allocation of time motion (the 'guillotine') | Used by the Leader of the House to restrict the amount of time that can be taken by specific stages of a Bill (i.e. to set a deadline). First used in 1887 to push through the Criminal Law Amendment (Ireland) Bill following a debate lasting 35 days (including all-night sittings), largely because of the obstructive actions of Irish MPs. Six years earlier, the Commons had sustained its single longest ever sitting: a debate over the Protection of Person and Property (Ireland) Bill 1881, lasting 41 hours and 31 minutes. The guillotine was used in June 1997 to force through the Referendums (Scotland and Wales) Bill, when opponents had tabled 250 amendments. |
| A motion of closure | Requires a petition of 100-plus MPs to be submitted to the Speaker calling for a vote to be swiftly taken. |
| The 'kangaroo' | The Speaker chooses to combine, in one hit for one vote, a number of virtually identical motions or amendments tabled by different MPs. |
| Programme orders | A relatively new device that replaces the guillotine in many cases, this allows the Leader of the House to set a fixed number of sittings for the passage of a Bill or a fixed date for its completion. Programme orders may be moved after the second reading stage. |

# ▌ Role of the Commons Speaker

The most important officer of the Commons, the Speaker is officially the chair of all its business. As such, he or she must preside over votes and debates, intervene to restore 'order' when members become rowdy, and choose which member should be next to speak when confronted by MPs waving their order papers in a bid to 'catch the Speaker's eye'. The Speaker is always drawn from the ranks of elected MPs, but on taking office he or she discards his or her previous party allegiance for the duration of his or her time in post.

The Speaker's main roles today are as follows:

- controlling debates, including deciding when those on specific subjects should end and be voted on, and suspending or adjourning sittings if they get out of hand. Debate over the Hutton Report into the death of Dr Kelly (see p. 48) was suspended after protesters invaded the public gallery in the Commons. Similar action was taken during two other protests in the House: in May 2004, when activists from Fathers4Justice, a pressure group campaigning for equal access rights to children for fathers separated from their partners, threw a missile containing purple powder from the guests' gallery at Mr Blair while he was addressing MPs, and again in September that year, when pro-hunt protestors led by Otis Ferry, son of singer Bryan Ferry, invaded the floor of the chamber;

- ordering MPs who have broken Commons rules to leave the chamber. Mr Galloway, was barred from the Commons for 18 days in July 2007 for failing to declare his links to the **United Nations (UN)** 'Oil for Food' programme—a charitable appeal allegedly partly funded by a supporter involved in the sale of oil under Saddam Hussein;
- certifying some Bills as 'money Bills' to give them swift approval;
- signing warrants to send members to jail for contempt of the House;
- chairing the House of Commons Commission—the main body that administers the procedures of the Commons;
- chairing the *Speaker's Committee on the **Electoral Commission**,* which recommends appointments to the board of the Commission (see p. 154).

Traditionally, the Speaker (the first of whom, Peter de Montfort, was appointed as Parlour of the Commons in 1258) is chosen by an election of MPs called by the 'Father of the House'—the backbench MP with the longest unbroken membership of the Commons. For nearly forty years it has also been customary for the two main political parties to alternate in providing Speakers. But when the post became vacant in October 2000 with the retirement of Betty (now Baroness) Boothroyd, backbenchers became so annoyed by the government's insistence that this tradition be upheld that they defied it by voting in another Labour MP, Mr Martin, instead of Mr Blair's preferred candidate, former Tory minister Sir George Young. After the 2005 election, however, then Father of the House, Labour's Tam Dalyell, faced the prospect of Mr Martin's re-election as Speaker being contested amid criticisms from the Tories about his alleged government bias.

Although Mr Martin survived several whispering campaigns in the ensuing parliament, his tenacity would ultimately deprive him of any opportunity to retire gracefully. A series of perceived errors of judgement began in November 2008, with his mishandling of the Damian Green affair (see p. 9). More damaging still was his response to the parliamentary expenses scandal. Mr Martin's personal expenses had been the subject of controversy for some time. In 2007, it emerged he had claimed £20,000 of taxpayers' money to pay

City law firm Carter Ruck to defend him against negative press stories. The following February it was revealed that his wife had claimed £4,000 in taxi fares while on a series of shopping trips to buy food and refreshment for receptions—and a month later that refurbishments to the couple's official residence, the Speaker's House, had cost £1.7m over seven years.

More damaging still was Mr Martin's response to the wave of revelations about MPs' expenses claims (see pp. 54–9). After appearing, to many, to do too little too late—by proposing only a prolonged sequence of meetings between party leaders and other internal Commons bodies to decide how best to reform the system, rather than any larger-scale changes—on 12 May 2009 he became the first Speaker in memory to face a motion of no confidence (tabled by Conservative backbencher Douglas Carswell). Within days, the Liberal Democrat leader Mr Clegg became the first party leader to demand his resignation, and Mr Martin had to defend his refusal to allow a debate on the confidence motion in the House—hesitantly citing obscure rules that, he said, prevented it unless either the government or Opposition formally made room in their timetables. Finally, on 19 May, a week after his initial motion, Mr Carswell tabled another—this time backed by 22 further MPs. Before matters proceeded to a formal vote, Mr Martin announced his resignation in the chamber, becoming the first Speaker since Sir John Trevor in 1695 to be forced out of office by a confidence 'vote'.

With Mr Martin's successor, the Commons reverted to its customary pendulum swing from Labour to Conservatives: in a hotly contested election that marked a break from the 'coronations' of past Speakers, John Bercow beat a host of other hopefuls, including fellow Tories Ann Widdecombe and Sir George Young, and former Labour Foreign Secretary Margaret Beckett. He was reconfirmed in office after the May 2010 election.

# ▌ The changing role of the Lord Chancellor

Officially the 'Lord High Chancellor of Great Britain', this ancient post—dating back at least as far as the 1066 Norman Conquest—has undergone significant (if not always smooth) changes over the past five years. The office of Lord Chancellor is the second most senior of the so-called 'Great Officers of State of the UK' (the highest ranking being the Lord High Steward—a post generally kept vacant, except during coronations, when it is filled temporarily). As explained in Chapter 1, the Lord Chancellor was, for centuries, a bastion of all three branches of the British constitution, being head of the judiciary, Speaker of the House of Lords (legislature), and, as Cabinet minister responsible for what until recently was known as the 'Lord Chancellor's Department', a member of the executive.

The Lord Chancellor still retains many of its ancient ceremonial roles. As 'Custodian of The Great Seal of the Realm', or 'The Great Seal of the United Kingdom', he or she has the ability to authorize the reigning sovereign's documents (most notably the royal assent) on his or her behalf—saving the monarch from having to sign each one personally. The Lord Chancellor also remains a minister.

Since 2003, however, the office has ceased to retain quite the authority it possessed previously—to the annoyance of the Lords, which sought initially to prevent Mr Blair from denuding its powers. In a notoriously botched Cabinet reshuffle, Mr Blair replaced outgoing Lord Chancellor Derry Irvine with Lord Falconer of Thoroton. In doing so, however, he sought to rename the post '*Secretary of State* for Constitutional Affairs'—effectively *abolishing* a constitutional role that had existed, more or less uninterrupted, since the Middle Ages.

In the end he was forced to step back from scrapping the post outright and, although he did abolish the Lord Chancellor's Department, Lord Falconer retained the dual titles of Constitutional Affairs Secretary and Lord Chancellor throughout his four years in office. Further changes, however, came about after the 2005 election, when the Constitutional Affairs Act 2005 handed responsibility for running the judiciary to the Lord Chief Justice, and created a new, elected post of *Lord Speaker* to assume the Lord Chancellor's role as chair of the Lords. The inaugural Lord Speaker, Baroness Hayman, was confirmed in office on 4 July 2006.

Jack Straw was named Lord Falconer's successor in Gordon Brown's first Cabinet and, although he retained responsibility for a department, it became the Ministry of Justice (MoJ). Mr Straw was also the first Lord Chancellor since Henry VIII's Cardinal Wolsey gave way to several laymen in the sixteenth century to be an MP—*not* a lord. Early signs under Mr Cameron's government were that this 'new tradition' would continue: Mr Straw's successor was another MP, Kenneth Clarke.

# ▌ The Opposition

The largest party other than the governing one (in terms of the number of seats that it has in the Commons) is known as 'Her Majesty's Loyal Opposition'. In recognition of its official status, the Leader of the Opposition, the Opposition Chief Whip, and the Opposition Deputy Chief Whip each receive allowances over and above their normal parliamentary ones to aid with their responsibilities.

The Opposition is charged with:

- holding the government to account by appointing a 'Shadow Cabinet' covering the main departmental briefs;
- contributing to the legislative process by proposing amendments;
- setting out its policies as an alternative government using designated 'Opposition Days', which are schemed into the parliamentary timetable to allow it, rather than the government, to dictate the flow of Commons business. In each parliamentary session, there are 20 Opposition Days in total (17 go to the largest Opposition party and three to the second largest).

# ▌ Devolution in practice—parliaments in the provinces

The first chapter laid out the overall constitutional framework governing the UK, while introducing the concept of devolution and how it was applied in the constituent countries of the UK outside England. This section explains how devolution has come to work in practice through the aegis of the new chambers created to implement it.

## The Scottish Parliament

Comprising 129 members of the *Scottish Parliament* (MSPs), the Scottish Parliament is, unlike Westminster's, a 'unicameral' legislature—meaning that it only has one House.

During the initial transition stage flowing from its establishment in 1998, some of the inaugural MSPs were permitted to remain as members of the House of Commons as well (a similar arrangement is currently under way in relation to Northern Ireland Assembly members, following the recent restoration of devolved government in that province). This swiftly changed, however, when they assumed their place as MSPs full-time and by-elections were held to find replacements for them in their previous Commons constituencies.

Long before Scottish devolution was established, concerns were raised about the so-called 'West Lothian Question' (see p. 32): the perceived inequity of allowing MSPs to sit and vote on English issues in the London Parliament while their Westminster equivalents would be barred from doing so in Scotland. Indeed, since devolution was introduced, the arrangement has proved incendiary: in November 2003, the votes of Scottish Labour backbenchers secured a knife-edge victory for the most controversial clauses of the government's Bill to introduce foundation hospitals in England (legislation with no bearing on their own constituencies). The Scottish Parliament—buoyed by the votes of Labour MSPs—had previously rejected the imposition of foundation hospitals in Scotland.

MSPs are elected using the additional member system (AMS) form of *proportional representation* (see Chapter 4), with 73 voted in via the UK's traditional first-past-the-post (FPTP) system and the remaining 56 from a regional list designed to give a fairer allocation of seats to each party at national level. Each elector is given two votes: one for his or her constituency, and the other for a political party the names of which appear on the list.

MSPs originally met in a temporary chamber at Edinburgh's Church of Scotland Assembly Hall on The Mound. This was belatedly replaced by a purpose-built parliament at Holyrood, at the foot of the Royal Mile, in 2004. One

MSP is elected to be 'Presiding Officer' (equivalent to the Commons Speaker), supported by two deputies. Parliament is elected for fixed terms lasting four years from the date of an election and each year is divided into a parliamentary session, which is further split into 'sitting days' and 'recess periods'. On sitting days, Parliament tries to finish its business at 5.30 p.m., except on Fridays, which tend to wrap up at 12.30 p.m.

MSPs can raise issues by:

- asking oral questions during parliamentary sittings;
- submitting written questions;
- giving notice of, or moving, a motion.

## Scottish parliamentary committees

Unlike at Westminster, much of the nitty-gritty work of the Scottish Parliament is performed by its 18 committees—a system intended to make it easier for individual members to hold the devolved government to account. Each committee comprises 5–15 MSPs and is chaired by a 'convener'. Meetings are held in public and can be convened anywhere in Scotland. This is meant to provide more direct access for ordinary people to the democratic process. A member of each committee is appointed as a 'reporter' and MSPs are allowed to participate in meetings of committees of which they are not members (although they cannot vote).

Committees are charged with examining the following:

- policy, administration, and financial arrangements of the *Scottish Government,* or *Scottish Executive* (see p. 110);
- proposed legislation in the Scottish and Westminster Parliaments;
- application of EU and international laws or conventions in Scotland.

## Role and responsibilities of the Scottish Parliament

The Scottish Parliament is responsible for *domestic is*sues specifically relevant to Scotland, but not foreign policy. The roles retained by the Commons include:

- foreign and defence policy;
- most economic policy;
- social security;
- medical ethics.

## The legislative process in Scotland

The four main types of Bill that can be introduced into the Scottish Parliament are:

- *executive*—introduced by a minister;
- *committee*—introduced by the convener (chair) of a committee;

- *member's*—introduced by individual MSPs, like private member's Bills at Westminster, with the support of 11 fellow members;
- *private*—introduced by private individuals or promoters.

When introduced in the Scottish Parliament, Bills must be accompanied by the documents listed in Table 2.10. To become law, they must pass through the four stages outlined in Table 2.11, in a streamlined version of the Westminster process.

## The National Assembly for Wales

Elected every four years, the Cardiff-based **National Assembly for Wales** has 60 members—40 elected for constituencies and 20 on the basis of four

**Table 2.10** The documents required to accompany different types of Scottish Bill

| Document | Definition |
| --- | --- |
| *All Bills* | |
| A written statement from the Presiding Officer | Confirming that the provisions of a prospective Bill come within the legislative remit of the Parliament, highlighting any provisions judged to be outside its authority |
| A financial memorandum | An estimate of the administrative, compliance, and other costs to be incurred by the Scottish Executive, local authorities, other bodies, and businesses and individuals in meeting the Bill's provisions |
| An Auditor General's report | Confirmation of the appropriateness of any charges to be incurred during legislative process by Scottish Consolidated Fund |
| *Executive Bills only* | |
| A written statement from a departmental minister | Confirming that the proposed Bill falls within the remit of the Scottish Parliament |
| Explanatory notes | A fair and thorough summary of the Bill's proposals |
| A policy memorandum | Setting out the Bill's objectives and any possible alternative proposals |

**Table 2.11** The passage of a Bill through the Scottish Parliament

| Stage | Process |
| --- | --- |
| Stage one | Examination of Bill's general principles, normally handled by *lead committee* (i.e. a committee specializing in the relevant subject area). |
| Stage two | More detailed, line-by-line examination of Bill, either by lead committee, another committee, or whole Parliament. Amendments can be made and debated at this stage. |
| Stage three | Final consideration of Bill by full Parliament. Amendments can be made and debated, and Parliament decides whether it should be passed. More than 25 per cent of all MSPs must vote on issue one way or another for it to pass. |
| Final stage | Parliament decides, finally, whether to approve Bill when it is referred back to a meeting of the full House. It is then automatically submitted by the Presiding Officer for royal assent (there is no House of Lords stage). |

for each of five larger regions. Assembly members (AMs) can be MPs at the same time, as in Northern Ireland, but it is proposed that joint membership will eventually cease, as progressively more power is devolved to the Welsh administration.

Each elector in Wales has two votes: one for a constituency member and the other for a name from the relevant regional list. The Secretary of State for Wales retains a degree of responsibility for the province and, unlike in Scotland, the Assembly does not yet have tax-varying powers. He or she is charged with ensuring that devolution works effectively, by chairing a joint ministerial committee between the UK and the devolved governments.

The Assembly's responsibilities include:

- determining budgetary priorities;
- funding, directing, and appointing managers of NHS bodies in Wales;
- administering EU structural funds aimed at Wales;
- determining the content of the *National Curriculum* in Wales.

A referendum on the potential transfer of new lawmaking powers to the Assembly, originally pencilled in by Labour for autumn 2010, was expected to be held by the end of March 2011.

## The legislative process in Wales

The legislative process in Wales resembles that of Scotland, in that it is overseen by a presiding officer and his or her deputy, elected by other members of the Assembly. Again, executive functions are wielded by a First Minister at the head of a devolved government. This was initially called the **Welsh Executive**, but is now referred to as the **Welsh Assembly Government**.

The Assembly meets in public in plenary sessions in Cardiff and business is directed by the presiding officer through a business secretary and business committee. Each session allows at least 15 minutes for oral questions of the First Minister and, each four weeks, similar sessions are held to allow Assembly Members (AMs) to question their departmental ministers. In addition, any member can propose a specific motion once a week, before the conclusion of a plenary session, and there are two forms of committee to consider matters in plenary session: 'subject committees' and 'regional committees', covering specific areas of the country.

Although it remains a poor relation of the Scottish Parliament in terms of the scope of its remit, the Assembly gained notable new legislative powers with the passage of the Government of Wales Act 2006. This introduced the *Measure of the National Assembly for Wales* (or *Assembly Measure*)—a form of second-tier primary legislation that allows ministers in the Welsh Assembly Government to enact statutory instruments in relation to particular areas of policy analogous to those introduced routinely by their Westminster counterparts. Assembly Measures may be proposed by any member of the Assembly, including a backbencher, and must be scrutinized by a committee, debated in plenary session, and approved in an Assembly vote before being adopted. Importantly, the 2006 Act also widened the ambit of the Assembly's powers to cover a wider range of policy areas, devolution of which had to first be approved through the passage of a form of Order in Council (see p. 67) known as a *Legislative Competence Order (LCO)*. These areas included:

- agriculture, fisheries, forestry and rural development;
- ancient monuments and historic buildings;
- culture;
- economic development;
- education and training;
- environment;
- fire and rescue services and promotion of fire safety;
- food;
- health services;
- highways and transport;
- housing;
- local government;
- public administration;
- social welfare;
- sport and recreation;
- tourism;
- town and country planning;
- water and flood defence;
- Welsh language.

## The Northern Ireland Assembly

Due to the ongoing fallout from 'The Troubles', the devolution process in Ireland has been long and complicated, and it was only in 2007 that devolved government at the Northern Ireland Assembly in Stormont finally came into effect, with the signing of a landmark power-sharing agreement between the two biggest parties—Dr Paisley's Democratic Unionist Party (DUP) and Gerry Adams's Sinn Féin—following fresh elections in the province. In April 2008, Dr Paisley (a stalwart of Northern Irish politics for more than four decades) retired as First Minister and DUP leader, to be replaced by East Belfast MP Peter Robinson (who subsequently lost his Westminster seat at the 2010 election, but continued as head of the Assembly). Deputy First Minister was Sinn Féin chief negotiator Martin McGuinness.

### Areas of responsibility retained over Northern Ireland by the UK

The Secretary of State for Northern Ireland remains responsible for:

- international relations;
- defence;
- taxation;

Several Whitehall agencies remain responsible for overseeing specific areas, including the Northern Ireland Prison Service, the Compensation Agency, and the Forensic Agency of Northern Ireland. Policing and justice powers were devolved in April 2010 (see p. 35). The former is overseen by a recently reconstituted Northern Ireland Policing Board, with members drawn from all of the main political parties.

### The legislative process in Northern Ireland

The Northern Ireland Assembly is home to 108 elected representatives, known as members of the Legislative Assembly (MLAs). The nature and titles of its senior politicians and officers and the nature of its legislative process are virtually identical to those in Wales.

## ☰ Topical feature idea

The MPs' expenses row was one of the biggest parliamentary scandals of modern times, and led to a huge shake-up in Commons rules. Many MPs who stood down at the May 2010 election did so at least partly under pressure from their parties and local voters over their involvement in the controversy. While many MPs accepted they were in the wrong and repaid some or all of the money they had claimed, others protested they had submitted claims in good faith. Still more said they did not have the money (particularly shorn of a parliamentary salary) to reimburse the public purse. How tarnished were MPs in your area by the expenses scandal? Were any of them asked to repay money, and if so, did they do so? Did any step down at the election? If so, how have they fared since, and what are they doing to rebuild their reputations?

## ✳ Current issues

■ **House of Lords reform:** the Lords' slow transformation from an 'Upper House' the members of which were chosen by birthright rather than political appointment or election into a more democratic second chamber began with the 1999 House of Lords Act. New Labour failed to finish the job, but as part of his coalition deal with Mr Cameron, Lib Dem leader Mr Clegg has secured a review of the Lords' composition, which was due to report preliminary findings before the end of 2010.

■ **Fewer MPs and more accountability:** the package of constitutional reforms unveiled by Mr Clegg in July 2010 included a commitment to reduce the number of constituencies from 650 to 600, with constituency population sizes also equalized to ensure a fairer allocation of votes at elections. The coalition is also proposing to allow disgruntled constituents collectively to 'recall' (or sack) their MPs between elections if they are found guilty of serious wrongdoing.

■ **The future layout of the House of Commons:** with the advent of Britain's first coalition government in 65 years after the 2010 election, and the prospect of a referendum on electoral reform (see p. 131), it is possible the old 'two-party' system is drawing to a close. Not only is the 'third party' now in government, but changing to a more proportional voting system is bound to increase the likelihood of Labour and the Tories having to rely on external support after future elections. If this happens, for how long will the adversarial layout of the Commons be fit for purpose?

## ? Review questions

1. Outline the role of backbench MPs. To whom do MPs owe primary responsibility—Parliament, party, or public?

2. What is meant by the terms 'party whip', the 'whip', and 'three-line whip'?

3. What are the arguments for and against an elected second chamber?

4. What is the role of private member's Bills and what do they actually achieve?

5. Has the creation of the Lords' Speaker and the removal of the condition that the Lord Chancellor must be a peer rendered the position redundant?

## → Further reading

Jones, B. (2004) *Dictionary of British Politics*, Manchester: Manchester University Press. **Thorough, accessible A–Z of terms and of recent developments on the British political scene.**

Jones, B., Kavanagh, D., Moran, M., and Norton, P. (2006) *Politics UK*, 6th edn, London: Longman. **Full-colour edition of established core text giving a comprehensive overview of the structure and workings of the British political system up to 2005.**

Norton, P. (2005) *Parliament in British Politics*, London: Palgrave Macmillan. **A thoughtful evaluation of the changing significance of the British Parliament in light of recent constitutional developments, such as devolution and the partial reform of the House of Lords.**

Rogers, R. and Walters, R. (2006) *How Parliament Works*, 6th edn, London: Longman. **Sixth edition of this indispensable layman's guide to the often complex, sometimes archaic workings of the British Parliament.**

##  Online Resource Centre

www.oxfordtextbooks.co.uk/orc/Morrison2e/

Visit the Online Resource Centre that accompanies this book for web links and regular updates.

# 3

# Prime minister, Cabinet, and government

Having examined the competing seats of constitutional power in Britain—the sovereign and Parliament—it is necessary to look in detail at the means by which, in practice, most of that power is exercised. This chapter focuses on the make-up and workings of the executive branch of the UK constitution—the government—and in particular the role of the inner circle of ministers known as the **Cabinet**, and the most senior of these: the prime minister.

## ▌ Origins of the role of prime minister

Compared to ancient posts like that of Lord Chancellor, the role of prime minister emerged surprisingly recently, and owes its origins to historical accident. When German-born George I succeeded to the British throne in 1714, he could speak little English. Traditionally the Cabinet had always been chaired by the monarch (albeit in an increasingly titular way since the passage of the Bill of Rights 25 years earlier), but with the newly crowned king literally incapable of understanding the language of UK government a practical need arose for a senior minister to perform this duty in his stead. Thus was born the idea of a post that became that of de facto head of government in Britain—or 'prime' minister.

But which government minister should assume this privileged position? After some debate, the honour fell to Sir Robert Walpole, holder of the extant post 'First Lord of the Treasury' (in effect, the Lord High Treasurer or official head of HM Treasury—the department responsible for raising taxes to finance government policy). His previous duties were generally assumed from this date by the Lord High Commissioners of the Treasury.

Despite assuming the day-to-day role of prime minister, however, Walpole retained his official Cabinet title, as did his successors for the best part of a century. In fact, although the term 'prime minister' was used informally within government from 1714 onwards and started appearing on government documents in the 1860s, under Benjamin Disraeli, it was only coined publicly during the term of Liberal premier Sir Henry Campbell-Bannerman (1905–08).

Given the disproportionate degree of power wielded by the prime minister, since the position arose it has been contentious constitutionally. Prior to its introduction, all ministers of the Crown were regarded as equals, with shared responsibility for governing the nation. The emergence of a Cabinet chairperson from within its own ranks made an immediate mockery of this idea, by implicitly elevating him or her to a level *more equal* than that of the others. This curious, somewhat contradictory, position spawned a Latin phrase that has been associated with prime ministers ever since: *primus inter pares*—or 'first among equals'. The notion is that prime ministers are 'equal' to their peers in the Cabinet—and, indeed, the House of Commons (the legislature)—in that, as elected members of Parliament (the last peer to have been prime minister was Lord Salisbury, who left office in 1902), they must be voted in to represent **constituencies** and can be removed by local people if they become unpopular. To this extent, they are ordinary MPs like any other. In contrast, they are 'first among' those notional 'equals' by dint of not only being senior ministers in the government, but also presiding over Cabinet meetings.

## The role of prime minister today

Today there are many established conventions surrounding the office of prime minister, almost all of which have grown up since the time of Walpole. The prime minister—or 'premier'—tends to be the leader whose party wins the most seats in the Commons at a general election. To this extent, although British voters are theoretically turning out to elect their local MP on polling day (not to mention the small matter of a national government for their country), the emphasis of elections is inherently 'presidential'. Everyone knows that if X party gets in, Y leader will become prime minister. Historically, the majority of premiers have hailed from either of the two biggest parliamentary parties at any one time. In the twentieth century, only five prime ministers were Labour, compared to 12 Conservatives. The Tories' dominance of the office until recently saw them regarded as the 'natural party of government'.

Although many of the prerogative powers exercised on behalf of the sovereign by government are discharged collectively by Cabinet (at least notionally), by custom the prime minister remains the only minister ever granted a private audience with the reigning monarch. Incoming prime ministers first meet the Queen in this capacity when they visit her at Buckingham Palace to be offered the post formally after their election. This behind-the-scenes ritual is known as the 'kissing of the hands'. Reportedly, Tony Blair actually did kiss the Queen's hands, although this has not generally been the practice for generations.

Despite widespread belief to the contrary, Mr Blair was not always so deferential in his handling of the Queen, however. Another long-standing tradition surrounding the relationship between the prime minister and the monarch is that they meet to discuss government business in person once a week. At the height of the Iraq War Mr Blair reportedly cancelled or cut short his weekly audiences more than once.

The prime minister's official London residence is at 10 Downing Street and he or she also has the use of a sprawling country estate at Chequers in the Chilterns. Like many conventions, of course, such rules are there to be bent when circumstances dictate: when Mr Blair came to power, he struck a deal with his Chancellor of the Exchequer, Gordon Brown, whose official residence was next door at Number 11, to swap domestic quarters. Mr Blair had a growing family of three children, while at the time Mr Brown was a childless bachelor.

By far the most important convention relating to the prime minister, however, is the fact that whoever holds the office has the authority to exercise, on behalf of the sovereign, the majority of the powers entrusted to him or her by the *royal prerogative.*

The principal prerogative powers discharged by the premier are to:

- appoint fellow ministers of the Crown;
- chair meetings of the Cabinet at least once a week;
- appoint members of **Cabinet committees**;
- keep the sovereign informed of government business on a weekly basis;
- declare war and peace;
- recommend the passage of government Bills to *royal assent*;
- recommend the **dissolution** of Parliament for a general election;
- recommend the *prorogation* of Parliament for the summer recess;
- draw up his or her party's manifesto at election time and write the **Queen's Speech**—the annual announcement of proposed government legislation;
- recommend for the sovereign's approval appointees to senior positions in the clergy, including the Church of England bishops and deans;
- recommend the appointment of senior judges;
- recommend appointees for senior positions in public corporations, including the posts of director-general and chairman of the British Broadcasting Corporation (BBC);
- recommend prospective recipients of honours and peerages in the Queen's Birthday *Honours List* and the New Year Honours List;
- answer for his or her government's policies and actions at Prime Minister's Questions (PMQs) every Wednesday lunchtime.

In addition to the above, the prime minister has an additional job title: Minister for the Civil Service. The 'department' he or she oversees in this capacity is the Cabinet Office (effectively the 'Ministry for the Civil Service') and his or her **permanent secretary** (the most senior civil servant) is the Cabinet Secretary.

## Towards 'elective dictatorship'—are prime ministers now too presidential?

The British prime minister may not be the country's head of state, but to many outside observers he or she may often appear to be. No monarch has had the temerity to challenge the passage of a government Bill since Queen Anne did so 300 years ago. And the notion that a king or queen would defy the will of the electorate to block the appointment of a premier to whose policies he or she opposed is the stuff of establishment conspiracy theories (although, for a time, more pessimistic Labour *backbenchers* are said to have envisaged such a scenario in the 1980s, when the party was lurching to the far left and appeared incapable of winning an election).

Perhaps unsurprisingly, therefore, power has been known to go to some prime ministers' heads. As long ago as 1976, Quintin Hogg—who as Lord Hailsham twice served as Conservative Lord Chancellor—used his Richard Dimbleby Lecture to criticize the 'elective dictatorship' of British governments. The thrust of his argument was that successive prime ministers had accrued substantial additional power over and above that vested in them constitutionally, and were increasingly using their parliamentary colleagues to steamroller policies through Parliament. Moreover, he argued, those same policies were often thought up (and effectively decided upon) behind closed doors—long before being debated in Parliament. At best this backstage policymaking would take place around the Cabinet table, among premiers and their ministerial colleagues; at worst it might be dreamt up more informally between the prime minister and a close-knit inner circle of trusted confidantes, not all of whom were even ministers. This mode of governing is often referred to as 'prime ministerial government'—or, more recently, 'sofa government'—as opposed to the collective decision-making embodied by traditional 'Cabinet government'.

Indeed, it was often said that the governments of the late 1960s and 1970s were prone to striking deals in 'smoke-filled rooms', with business leaders, trade union bosses, and other interest groups having a direct and unofficial input into policymaking. In the case of Labour governments, the phrase 'beer and sandwiches' was coined to refer to the cosy chats the likes of Harold Wilson and James Callaghan reportedly had with the leaders of unions that helped to bankroll the party prior to announcing new wage and industrial policies.

But these tactics—increasingly common to governments of both main parties—are far from the only examples of perceived presidential behaviour by modern prime ministers. Occasional slips of the tongue by premiers under pressure have spoken volumes about their apparent sense of superiority or infallibility. In 1989, Margaret Thatcher notoriously referred to herself using the 'royal we' when she spoke to the media outside Downing Street to express her delight at news that the wife of her son, Mark, had given birth. Her exact words were: 'We are a grandmother.'

Mr Blair—of all recent prime ministers beside Mrs Thatcher, the one most frequently described as presidential—was also prone to such lapses during his later years in office. In an interview on the ITV1 chat show *Parkinson* in March  2006, it was put to him by host Michael Parkinson that his job brought with it a huge amount of responsibility, in light of his status as commander-in-chief of the British Armed Forces. Mr Blair failed to challenge this assertion, despite the fact that, constitutionally, the office of commander-in-chief still resides with the Queen. In the same interview he intimated that God had guided his actions over Iraq (an echo of words used by President George Bush several years earlier).

So much for the sound bites, though: in what ways do our prime ministers act high-handedly? Broadly, the examples of such presidential actions can be broken down into four major categories:

- bypassing and/or downgrading the role of the Cabinet in devising policy;
- announcing policies to the media before informing Parliament/the Cabinet;
- ignoring popular opinion and protest;
- grandstanding on the international stage.

## Bypassing and/or downgrading the role of the Cabinet in devising policy

Prime ministers are charged with chairing meetings of the Cabinet. It is here that policies are traditionally first debated and fine-tuned, before being announced to the press and public. In recent decades, however, there has been a growing tendency for premiers to downgrade the role of Cabinet in policymaking—and, in some cases, to bypass it entirely, in favour of relying for their advice on a small posse of trusted friends and colleagues known as a 'kitchen Cabinet'.

'Kitchen Cabinets' have taken various forms, often closely reflecting the individual politics and personalities of individual prime ministers. One of the first manifestations of a UK kitchen Cabinet was Conservative Prime Minister Ted Heath's Central Policy Review Staff (CPRS), a group of advisers within the Cabinet Office (including some senior civil servants—see pp. 102–6) entrusted with streamlining the formulation of government policy across departments. The formation of the CPRS had been recommended by the Fulton Committee, set up by his predecessor, Labour Prime Minister Wilson, in 1966 to review the workings of the Civil Service. The Committee had also suggested there should be a separate 'policy unit' set up to coordinate long-term strategic planning in each ministry and, when Wilson was duly returned to power in 1974, he swiftly acted on this suggestion by forming the Downing Street Policy Unit (effectively his own kitchen Cabinet), chaired by Sir Bernard Donoghue.

Indeed, Mr Wilson (more than any earlier prime minister) had long had a reputation for valuing the views of personal friends over those of Cabinet colleagues when it came to devising policy. Among his closest confidantes were his private secretary, Marcia Williams, and his press secretary, Joe Haines. This fashion for consulting close allies—elected or otherwise—before presenting one's ideas to Cabinet, let alone Parliament, was also favoured by his successor-but-one, Mrs Thatcher, whose closest aides included her press secretary, Sir Bernard Ingham, and her private secretary, former businessman Charles Powell.

More recently, the plotting and ruminations of the kitchen Cabinet have become increasingly associated with the work of 'special advisers' and, in particular, the **spin doctors** employed by the Blair and (to a lesser extent) Brown administrations to put a positive gloss on government policy. This development will be discussed more fully later in this chapter, but it is worth reflecting on briefly here in relation to one particular casualty of the 'sofa government' favoured by Mr Blair: Cabinet decision-making. As with his weekly meetings with the Queen, when the Iraq War was in full swing Mr Blair reportedly downgraded formal Cabinet meetings to such an extent that deliberations that would traditionally take two or three hours were often reduced to  30 minutes or less. In addition, he is said to have left many detailed policy debates customarily held in full Cabinet to be discussed by Cabinet committees, appointing his most loyal colleagues to chair those hearings to reduce the likelihood that his own ideas would be disputed. It was for this and other tendencies that she saw as fundamentally undemocratic that former Cabinet minister Clare Short publicly dubbed Mr Blair a 'control freak' after resigning from the government over its handling of the post-invasion reconstruction of Iraq in 2003.

Recent prime ministers—in particular, Mrs Thatcher and Mr Blair—have also been accused of bypassing, or downgrading, the role of Parliament in the legislative process. The most common way in which this happens is through the use of the party *whip* system to coerce MPs and peers to attend votes and back the party line. Mr Blair was frequently accused of using his large Commons majority to 'steamroller' through Parliament policies unpopular with the public (not to mention his own backbenchers). Examples include the various anti-terror measures introduced following the attacks on the Twin Towers in New York and the 7 July 2005 bombings in London—many of which were rushed through in a matter of days, with *committee stages* taking place on the floor of the Commons. Other examples include the knife-edge votes on foundation hospitals, university top-up fees, and enabling police to detain terrorist suspects for up to 90 days without charge—which actually failed, in spite of the pressure put on backbench Labour MPs by party whips.

## Announcing policies to the media before Parliament/Cabinet

Briefing the media (or targeted sections of it sympathetic to government) on policy proposals ahead of formal announcements to Parliament and public has become a much criticized trend under recent administrations. Indeed, in some instances under Mr Blair this secondary form of bypassing the normal machinery of government has seen ministers close to the prime minister spoon-feeding policy details to favoured journalists before even the Cabinet (let alone the Commons) has had a chance to discuss them. Arrangements for the briefings invariably involved the spin doctors and/or special advisers with which Mr Blair surrounded himself—principally his official spokesman and long-time director of communications, Alastair Campbell, and/or Downing Street chief of staff Jonathan Powell. A fuller discussion of the roles of these two follows later this chapter.

So what forms do these 'off-the-record' briefings actually take and how often have they involved policy announcements yet to be debated in Cabinet? The most widely used form of policy briefing by ministers, special advisers, or government press officers acting on behalf of their superiors are explained in Table 3.1.

From a policy viewpoint, one of the most infamous examples of serious proposals being released to the press in advance of even full Cabinet discussion occurred in 2002, when then Health Secretary and close Blair ally Alan Milburn gave *The Times* a detailed explanation of his so-called 'Ten-Year Plan for the National Health Service' (NHS). Among the more controversial policy ideas he mooted (which has since come to fruition) was the introduction of foundation hospitals—a new type of **NHS trust** with far greater control over its own finances and management than had previously been the case (see pp. 174–5).

## Ignoring popular opinion and protest

During his first term, Mr Blair was notorious for consulting opinion pollsters and focus groups before taking radical policy decisions. His critics (including many within his own party) argued that this was, at best, a waste of the mandate he had achieved by winning such a large parliamentary majority in the 1997 election and, at worst, a betrayal of promises made in the Labour Party's manifesto.

In his second term Mr Blair developed a tendency to do precisely the opposite—becoming increasingly bold in his political judgements. The most notorious example of this headstrong approach was his pursuit of the case for war with Iraq, citing supposed evidence (which turned out to be deeply flawed, and remains unsubstantiated) that Saddam Hussein was stockpiling weapons of mass destruction (WMDs). Defying huge opposition in the country at

**Table 3.1** Types of media briefing used by ministers and special advisers

| Name | Definition |
|------|------------|
| Kite-flying | The government practice of releasing details of potential policy initiatives through media to gauge public's reaction before committing itself to them. Ideas mooted in this way have included extending the right to vote to 16-year-olds, banning teenagers from wearing 'hoodies' (hooded tops), and allowing the police to march those guilty of antisocial behaviour to cash points to pay on-the-spot fines. No such policies have yet been implemented. |
| Leak | Associated with the release of confidential and/or advance information of a controversial nature, often by someone 'in the know' who is unhappy about what is happening behind the scenes. A famous leak included that by civil servant Clive Ponting of details of the sinking of the Argentinian warship the *General Belgrano* during the Falklands War. More recently, there have been accusations of complicity by ministers in releasing potentially controversial information prematurely, in the hope that a gradual 'drip, drip' of information will lessen the impact of a later announcement. The Hutton Report into the circumstances leading to the apparent suicide of government scientist Dr David Kelly was leaked to *The Sun* the night before its publication—purportedly by a government source. |
| Rebuttal | The practice of issuing swift denials to criticisms, accusations, and announcements made by political foes (e.g. rebutting claims of wartime casualties by the enemy). Occasionally these pre-empt the claims they are meant to be 'rebutting', in an effort by the rebutter to neutralize their impact by 'getting in first'. |
| Trail | Similar to kite-flying, these are frequently offered to Sunday newspapers. Because they are published only once a week and there is generally less diary-based news (e.g. court hearings, parliamentary proceedings) around when they go to press than is the case for dailies, the Sundays rely more on exclusive stories. The more certain they are that they have an exclusive, the more likely they are to 'run it big'. Government press officers and special advisers are usually keen to offer such 'scoops' to Sundays with which they have good working relationships, because a large spread in a paper aimed at their target audience on a day of the week when more people read papers than at any other time will generate significant publicity. Government spin doctors and press officers release information in this way using a schedule known as 'the Grid'. This maps out, for their own reference, a putative timetable of when policy announcements, Cabinet and Commons debates, publication of reports, etc., are due, so press officers can release 'sneak preview' information strategically to ensure the maximum—or minimum—publicity. |

large—articulated by the biggest peacetime demonstration in Britain's history, when up to 500,000 protestors converged on Trafalgar Square just days before the war—he persuaded a reluctant Commons to vote for the invasion.

Mr Blair's new appetite for defying public opposition echoed the approach taken by Mrs Thatcher, particularly in her third term. The policy that most clearly demonstrated her stubbornness in the teeth of huge public opposition would ultimately—like the Iraq War, arguably, for Mr Blair—hasten her downfall. The introduction of the deeply unpopular Community Charge, or 'Poll Tax'—a replacement for the age-old rates system—provoked some of the largest-scale public protests in British history. Mrs Thatcher remained resolute, however, and it was only when her successor, John Major, came to power a year or so after the demonstrations that the tax was abandoned.

## Grandstanding on the international stage

As Britain's de facto head of state the prime minister has the biggest global profile of any UK politician. Nonetheless, some premiers take to the role of international statesperson more than others. In the nineteenth century, Liberal William Gladstone and Tory Benjamin Disraeli were two most accomplished and successful British premiers, but it was arguably the latter—famous, like Mrs Thatcher and Mr Blair after him, for his interventionist foreign policy—who really impressed on the international stage. Of twentieth-century prime ministers, Winston Churchill was widely regarded as the greatest statesman, principally because of the leadership he gave to Europe during the Second World War.

Examples of 'presidential-style' grandstanding on the global stage in recent times have included Mrs Thatcher's decisive handling of the Falklands War and high-profile 'love-ins'—frequently caught on camera at the White House—with US president Ronald Reagan. Her implacable opposition to communism and her determined negotiation of various British opt-outs from European Union (EU) legislation also helped to maintain her high international profile.

Mr Blair, meanwhile, waged at least four wars during his ten years in Downing Street. During his first term, he was a party to the launch of two military campaigns: the *North Atlantic Treaty Organization (NATO)* intervention over alleged 'ethnic cleansing' of Albanians by Slobodan Milošović's Serbs in Kosovo, and a decisive move to halt the civil war in the former British colony of Sierra Leone. In his second term he became forever wedded in the public eye to George Bush's US administration by pledging to 'stand shoulder to shoulder' with the country following the 11 September terrorist attacks, and backing the invasions of first Afghanistan, then Iraq.

Mr Blair's exhausting schedule of shuttle diplomacy in the run-up to the Iraq War—flying across Africa to persuade smaller *United Nations (UN)* member states to support Britain and the USA's calls for a 'second' UN resolution to justify military action—buoyed his profile still further. So, too, did his earlier missions to tackle poverty in Africa, forge peace in Northern Ireland, and promote a decisive 'two-state solution' to the long-running stand-off between Israel and Palestine in the Middle East. His involvement in brokering the latter saw him rewarded after stepping down as prime minister with a new diplomatic role as Middle East peace envoy for 'the Quartet'—a loose international consortium representing the EU, UN, USA, and Russia.

Finally, although the Queen is still responsible constitutionally for entertaining visiting heads of state on official visits (which she did for President Bush in 2004 and France's President Sarkozy in 2008), prime ministers also tend to get in on the action, often inviting world leaders to stay at Chequers after they have left her.

## Holding the prime minister to account

Given the degree of power accrued by the office of prime minister, what mechanisms exist to hold him or her to account? As we know, monarchs have long since lost their inclination (if not ability) to challenge premiers—Queen Anne's notable stand against a government Bill in 1707 being the last to date. Notwithstanding Queen Elizabeth II's predilection for wrong-footing Wilson and her reputedly frosty relationship with Mrs Thatcher, there has been little evidence in modern times of reigning monarchs displaying an appetite for confrontation. Nonetheless there remain significant means by which the actions of prime ministers can be influenced, if not directly controlled. These can be divided into four areas:

- public;
- press;
- Parliament;
- party.

### Public

The primary means of holding prime ministers to account goes back to that first principle—namely that they are ultimately MPs like any other and, as such, must stand for re- election in their constituencies come polling day. The parties they represent are similarly dependent on a public mandate for their Commons majorities: if enough of their MPs lose their constituencies' support at an election, other parties will emerge with more seats to replace them in government.

The resounding defeat of Mr Major's Conservative government in 1997 by 'New Labour' was perhaps the clearest example in recent times of an ailing administration being unceremoniously ejected by an electorate that had decided it wanted change. Not only did the Tories suffer a landslide defeat, but many senior MPs—including Defence Secretary Michael Portillo—lost their seats. Although Mr Major escaped this ignominy himself, it has been known for prime ministers in some countries to lose their own constituency seats, as well as their parliamentary majorities. Such a fate befell Australian premier John Howard, in the 2007 election, which booted him out of office after more than a decade in power.

Prime ministers are also accountable in other ways. It has long been the practice, for example, for by-elections, local, and European elections to be treated as 'protest votes' by electors disgruntled with serving governments, who will opt for candidates or parties other than the prime minister's to give him or her a 'bloody nose'. Others prefer to withhold their support from governing parties they might still back at general elections by abstaining altogether. There was significant anecdotal evidence that protest votes rose under New Labour, especially among traditional party voters disillusioned by the invasion of Iraq. The combined effect of protest votes and abstentions on the one side, and renewed determination to harness support on the other, can lead to situations like that witnessed in the 2007 and 2008 local elections, and the by-election in the previously solid Labour parliamentary seat of Crewe and Nantwich following the death of veteran backbencher Gwyneth Dunwoody, both of which were 'won' by David Cameron's then resurgent Conservatives.

Other forms of public pressure that can be put on prime ministers include demonstrations (such as the Stop the War Coalition marches over Iraq and the Countryside Alliance's over the hunting ban), industrial action by public sector employees—for example, the recent strikes by postal workers and local government employees—and the rejections of key policies in national *referenda*.  Although British governments rarely put individual questions to the public vote in this way—preferring to invoke the constitutional principle of **parliamentary sovereignty**, which leaves decisions to Parliament between elections—both Mr Blair and Mr Brown were accused of avoiding referenda on the EU's 2007 Lisbon Treaty for fear of losing it (see see p. 261).

## Press

If there is one thing guaranteed to send a prime minister scurrying in pursuit of populist policy ideas to regain public support it is a run of negative headlines in Britain's tabloid newspapers.

In recent years the national press—particularly the biggest-selling daily papers, *The Sun* and the *Daily Mail*—has been seen to wield disproportionately more influence than other media on the actions of successive governments. Mrs Thatcher's hat-trick of election wins in the late 1970s and 1980s were put down, in part, to the support of 'white van man' or 'Essex man'—terms used to denote a new breed of aspirational working-class voter weary of the 'class  warfare' espoused by old-school Labour politicians, and attracted by the doctrines of self-help and share and home ownership ushered in by Thatcherite ideology. Although formerly a red-blooded Labour paper (the *Daily Herald*), *The Sun* under Rupert Murdoch came to epitomize this new spirit of entrepreneurship, just as the high moral tone of the *Daily Mail* appealed to 'traditional' Conservatives.

Throughout the 1980s, *The Sun* remained one of the staunchest advocates of Thatcherism, using many memorable front-page headlines to bolster support for her resolute, patriotic brand of politics. Among its most controversial splashes was its celebration of the sinking of the Argentine warship *General Belgrano* with the headline 'Gotcha!' and the one with which it urged voters to support Mr Major rather than Labour leader Neil Kinnock in the

1992 election: '*If Neil Kinnock wins today would the last person to leave Britain please turn out the lights.*' After more than a decade of supporting the Conservatives, though, Britain's biggest-selling paper switched horses in the run-up to the 1997 election, backing Mr Blair (although it eventually returned to the Tories, declaring 'Labour's lost it' on the morning after Mr Brown's speech to the 2009 Labour Party Conference).

Although this was strenuously denied by both Mr Blair and Mr Brown, the liberalization of UK media ownership laws that enabled Mr Murdoch (despite his significant share of the national newspaper market) to buy a stake in ITV was rumoured to have come as a result of his behind-the-scenes lobbying. Mr Blair, in particular, is said to have frequently invited Mr Murdoch to private talks at Downing Street and Chequers, and visited him in Australia.

 While it has long been commonplace for newspapers to take a partisan stand, in Britain broadcasters are bound by a strict code of impartiality upheld by the *Office of Communications (Ofcom)* (see p. 217) and, in the case of the licence fee-funded BBC, the BBC Trust. There have been recent calls, however, from the likes of former *Sun* editor Kelvin Mackenzie for commercial broadcasters to be allowed to adopt a more political voice akin to that of the pro-Republican, Murdoch-owned Fox News Network in the USA.

## Parliament

Prime ministers are held to account by Parliament in various ways, the most demonstrable of which is Prime Minister's Questions (PMQs)—the weekly half-hour session in which he or she is quizzed about his or her actions (see p. 45).

Most MPs also sit on committees. Through participating in the work of *select committees*, they examine in detail the workings of individual government departments—and, indirectly, those of the Cabinet over which the prime minister presides. *Public Bill committees*, meanwhile, are there to scrutinize the wording of prospective legislation, the bulk of which will have originated in the in-trays of the prime minister and his or her most senior ministerial colleagues. Prime ministers also now subject themselves to twice-yearly scrutiny by the Commons Liaison Committee (see p. 48).

MPs can also use a variety of other parliamentary procedures outlined in the last chapter—including early day motions (EDMs), urgent debates, and adjournment debates—to influence and/or criticize prime ministers and their policies. Perhaps the single most powerful way in which MPs—and, to a lesser extent, peers—conspire to embarrass serving prime ministers is by voting down their policies in Parliament. Because most British governments tend to have a working majority in the Commons and can usually martial sufficient support from party loyalists, historically government legislation has rarely been comprehensively defeated. On occasion, however, prime ministers have found themselves so out of step with their parliamentary parties that (whatever their nominal majority) they have struggled to get their proposals passed.

Mrs Thatcher and Mr Blair generally managed to squeak through their more controversial legislation—barring the latter's attempt to allow anti-terror police to continue questioning suspects without charge for up to 90 days, which was defeated by one such backbench rebellion. But there have been times when the extent and frequency of indiscipline in a governing party's ranks has become so serious that it has had long-lasting, if not fatal, consequences for prime ministers and their governments.

## Party

When Parliament conspires to censure prime ministers, derail their legislative programmes, or otherwise undermine their authority, it usually succeeds in doing so only with the complicity of government backbenchers who have become so dismayed with their leadership's direction that they are prepared to vote against it en masse. During Mr Blair's second and third terms backbench rebellions became so frequent at times that Labour MPs were increasingly described as the 'unofficial Opposition' (particularly when the *real* Opposition, the Tories, were still under the stuttering leadership of William Hague, Iain Duncan Smith, and Michael Howard).

The most serious form this censure of serving prime ministers by their own backbenchers can take is through the aegis of a *motion of no confidence* (also known as a 'vote of no confidence', or a *censure motion*). This is when a device such as an EDM is put before the Commons—customarily by the Leader of the Opposition—inviting MPs to pass a motion (vote) expressing a loss of 'confidence' in the serving prime minister. If the prime minister loses the motion this normally means that even his or her own MPs have withdrawn their support, and an election must therefore be called.

The election that saw the end of Callaghan's Labour government in May 1979 was ultimately precipitated by a confidence vote tabled by Opposition leader Mrs Thatcher. Because Callaghan had been leading a minority government following the collapse of a fragile deal with the Liberal Party that stopped short of a formal coalition—the 'Lib-Lab Pact'—he had become increasingly reliant on the support of the Ulster Unionists and Scottish Nationalists in the Commons. When his government refused to implement a proposed Scotland Act to introduce **devolution** north of the border (a referendum had backed it, but only on a relatively low voter turnout—see p. 31), the nationalists tabled a confidence motion, which Mrs Thatcher swiftly emulated.

Prime ministers in desperate straits have even been known to call their own votes of confidence in an effort to instil discipline in their party ranks and force through unpopular legislation. In 1993 Mr Major tabled a high-risk 'back me or sack me' motion, to force the hand of the so-called 'Maastricht rebels' (Euro-sceptic Conservative backbenchers who had repeatedly voted against the Treaty on the European Union—popularly known as the 'Maastricht Treaty'—that his government was struggling to ratify). In the event, he won the vote—not least because most of the rebels represented marginal seats, and could easily have lost them to other candidates or parties in the event of an election.

Traditionally, confidence motions have only ever required a *simple majority* of MPs' votes—50 per cent of those cast, plus one—to bring down a government and force an election. So it was with alarm that some constitutional experts and politicians on both sides of the Commons initially greeted the Lib-Con coalition's proposals in May 2010 to introduce not only five-year fixed-term parliaments (see p. 131), but also a new rule preventing elections being called mid-term unless 55 per cent of MPs voted in favour of dissolution. Critics argued that the proposed '55 per cent rule' could be used to insure Mr Cameron against the possibility of his coalition partners pulling the plug on it prematurely by with-drawing from government (between them, the Lib Dems, Labour, and all of the minority parties together would only have been able to muster 53 per cent of Commons votes if the former were to switch loyalties).

But opponents complained that it would render redundant the confidence pro-cedure. Although a government could theoretically still be defeated by a simple no confidence vote, the backing of a further 5 per cent of MPs would be needed to force an election—potentially leaving a 'defeated' administration limping on indefinitely like a 'zombie'. In the coalition's defence, **Leader of the House** Sir George Young argued that its opponents were missing the point: rather than enabling prime ministers to prolong their tenures against Parliament's wishes,  the new rule would instead liberate the Commons by equipping it with a mecha-nism to demand a dissolution of the House off its own bat, without the need for a formal confidence vote. Nevertheless, when Mr Clegg confirmed the final shape of the proposals in a Commons statement two months later, he announced the 55 per cent rule was being dropped, and that elections would instead continue to be triggered by a no confidence vote alone. However, in performing his U-turn, he introduced a new lifeline for struggling minority governments—granting them a two-week breathing space after losing a confidence vote to try to form an alternative administration and avert an election. At the same time, he said the Commons would still be given the ability to prompt a dissolution without the need for a confidence vote, although only if two-thirds of MPs (as opposed  to the mooted 55 per cent) were to vote for it. The proposed new power echoed one previously adopted by the *Scottish Parliament*.

There are, of course, various other ways in which governing parties can hold their leaders to account—and even depose them. Once a week when Labour is in government leaders subject themselves to a lengthy meeting of the **Parliamen-tary Labour Party (PLP)**—essentially the body representing all elected Labour MPs. Although Mr Blair was given a famously easy ride for his first few years in power, in the aftermath of the Iraq debacle PLP meetings reportedly became increasingly strained, with the prime minister fielding harder questions and occasionally being heckled.

Conservative MPs have an even more ferocious means of grilling—and occasionally removing—their leaders. The **1922 Committee** is a body made up of all Tory MPs. Actually formed in 1923 (but taking its name from the 1922 election), this influential committee has an 18-strong executive committee charged with overseeing the election of new party leaders, and has, at times, acted to replace existing ones. As the 'voice' of the majority of Tory MPs, the 1922 Committee is seen to represent the collective 'mood' of the parliamentary party. If it passes a vote of no confidence in its leadership, therefore, it is normally only a matter of time before he or she will jump (assuming that he or she is not pushed first).

The 1922 Committee is examined in more detail in Chapter 5, but it is relevant here in relation to its involvement in the removal of a recent Tory premier: Mrs Thatcher. Her downfall was effectively instigated by her former Cabinet colleague, Michael Heseltine, when he challenged her for the party leadership in November 1990. Although she won the first round of voting in the election that followed, she did so by too small a margin to seal the contest outright. To do so, she had to secure the backing of an *absolute majority*—that is, more than half—of all Tory MPs and to achieve 15 per cent more votes than her nearest rival. She narrowly missed the target. Despite initially announcing her intention to continue fighting for her position through the second round, in the interim Mrs Thatcher was visited by a deputation of backbenchers who made it clear she had lost the backing of many of her MPs. After taking counsel from fellow ministers, she withdrew her candidacy—paving the way for Mr Major's election.

# Cabinet versus government—what is the difference?

Despite the clear moves towards a more presidential—or 'prime ministerial'—form of government, constitutionally speaking the role of the Cabinet remains of paramount importance in the exercise of elected power in Britain. So what exactly is the 'Cabinet', and how does it differ from and relate to the 'government'?

Essentially the Cabinet is a 'subset' of the government. While the latter is made up of *all* ministers appointed by the prime minister, the former is composed of only the most senior ones. Governments and Cabinets have been known to vary wildly in size from one administration to another, with some favouring a more compact, rationalized approach and others a more comprehensive one.

Historically, the average size of a Cabinet has been 20—although at times it has been, by turns, significantly larger and significantly smaller. For much of the Second World War, Winston Churchill ran a Cabinet numbering 68 ministers while in 1922 Andrew Bonar Law formed a peacetime Cabinet of only

16. In contrast, Labour prime ministers in particular have tended to appoint larger Cabinets—at least in part as a bulwark against what the party for many years saw as the intransigence of senior civil servants when presented with its policies in government. Wilson had one Cabinet comprising 24 members and Mr Blair raised the bar to 26. Mr Brown, meanwhile, appointed an enlarged 'hybrid' first Cabinet, effectively numbering 29. While only 22 of these were permanent members, an additional seven (including Olympics Minister Tessa Jowell and Attorney General Baroness Scotland) were permitted to attend its meetings on a de facto basis.

In his October 2008 reshuffle, he expanded the Cabinet even further, to 34 (including the 'occasional' members). Its numbers were boosted, in part, by his decision to create a new Department for Energy and Climate Change (DECC), and to reinstate two distinct offices for Defence and Scotland, in response to criticisms from military chiefs and the devolved *Scottish Government* respectively of his earlier decision to combine the two under one *Secretary of State*, Des Browne, who had decided to leave the government.

Cabinet ministers have, until recently, always been either MPs or peers. For some time the idea of even a peer—a lord or lady who has not stood for public office—being entrusted with a ministerial brief was viewed as highly contentious. Nevertheless, there have been many high-profile examples of such appointments, including Lord Young of Graffham (Trade and Industry Secretary under Mrs Thatcher, and recently appointed by Mr Cameron to lead a review of health and safety laws) and Lord Adonis (variously an Education Minister, and Transport Secretary in the Blair and Brown administrations). Today the appointment of peers to high government office (if not that of prime minister) scarcely raises an eyebrow.

Mr Brown took the prime minister's discretion to choose ministers from out-side the Commons to a new level, with his declaration on entering office that he wanted a 'government of all of the talents'. This assertion—an extension of the 'big tent' politics for which Mr Blair was so often criticized by Labour traditionalists—saw several individuals from outside his own party's ranks appointed to senior advisory positions in government. Perhaps most contro-versially, Baron Jones of Birmingham, former director-general of the Con-federation of British Industry (CBI), was appointed a minister at the then Department of Business, Enterprise, and Regulatory Reform (BERR)—despite making it clear he had no intention of joining the Labour Party. Sir Mark Mal-loch Brown, former UN deputy secretary-general and neither a peer nor an MP, was appointed Minister for Africa, Asia, and the UN. Mr Brown also dispensed with another Cabinet tradition: since 1963 its meetings had generally been held on Thursdays, but he switched them to Tuesdays.

Most Cabinet ministers have the title secretary of state, rather than **minister of state**, denoting their seniority. This normally means they head up a major government spending department, such as health, and often have several junior ministers—members of the government but not Cabinet—answerable to them. The choice of ministerial posts included in the Cabinet can vary greatly, depending on the political priorities of the day. For example, until Mr Blair's election win in 1997, overseas aid and development was treated as a relatively minor ministerial area and was the responsibility of a non-Cabinet minister in the Foreign Office. When Labour was re-elected, the post was promoted to become that of 'International Development Secretary'. Its first incumbent, Clare Short, gained her own dedicated department and was promoted to Cabinet.

In addition to the more obvious senior departmental posts, traditionally the Cabinet also contains one or two honorary ones awarded to loyal lieutenants of the prime minister whom he or she wants to keep close at hand, but for more general duties than overseeing a specific portfolio. One such post is that of 'Chancellor of the Duchy of Lancaster'—a sinecure deriving from an office once involved in the daily management of the sovereign's one significant surviving estate following the handover of the Crown Lands to the state (see p. 25). When veteran Labour MP Jack Cunningham was appointed to this post by Mr Blair in 1998, the media dubbed him variously 'Cabinet enforcer' and 'Cabinet fixer', because his brief was taking charge of coordinating the government's message in its dealings with press and public. Another such post is the recent addition of 'Minister without Portfolio', an office assumed after the 1997 election by Mr Blair's close ally Peter Mandelson (who made two subsequent returns to the Cabinet). In forming his coalition with the Liberal Democrats, meanwhile, Mr Cameron dispensed with convention by appointing the party's leader, Nick Clegg, Deputy Prime Minister without allocating him a departmental portfolio. On day one of their new collaborative administration the two party leaders also jointly took the stand at a press conference in the Downing Street garden, as if intending to share the top job. As of the end of May 2010, the coalition Cabinet was as listed in Table 3.2.

So much for the Cabinet: what of the government as a whole? Its size can also vary, but in modern times it has become customary for it to number anything up to a hundred ministers. The most junior ministerial post is that of **parliamentary under-secretary,** who ranks beneath both a minister and secretary of state. Also usually included in this overall tally are government whips and MPs given the role of **parliamentary private secretary (PPS)**. These are junior posts ascribed to ambitious MPs who aspire to become ministers. They serve as a point of contact or liaison in Parliament (or, as some would have it, 'spy') for serving ministers and are informally connected to those ministers' departments. The prime minister tends to have two PPSs at any one time.

## Ministerial salaries

In recognition of their higher levels of responsibility, ministers who are MPs receive substantially higher salaries than their backbench colleagues. The

**Table 3.2** Composition of the UK Cabinet (May 2010)

| Title | Name |
| --- | --- |
| Prime Minister/First Lord of the Treasury/Minister for the Civil Service | David Cameron |
| Deputy Prime Minister | Nick Clegg |
| Chancellor of the Exchequer | George Osborne |
| Secretary of State for Foreign and Commonwealth Affairs (Foreign Secretary) and First Secretary of State | William Hague |
| Secretary of State for Justice/Lord Chancellor | Kenneth Clarke |
| Secretary of State for the Home Department (Home Secretary) and Minister for Women and Equality | Theresa May |
| Secretary of State for Defence | Dr Liam Fox |
| Secretary of State for Health | Andrew Lansley |
| Secretary of State for Energy and Climate Change | Chris Huhne |
| Secretary of State for the Environment, Food and Rural Affairs | Caroline Spelman |
| Secretary of State for International Development | Andrew Mitchell |
| Secretary of State for Business, Innovation, and Skills | Vince Cable |
| Secretary of State for Work and Pensions | Iain Duncan Smith |
| Secretary of State for Transport | Philip Hammond |
| Secretary of State for Communities and Local Government | Eric Pickles |
| Chief Whip | Patrick McLoughlin |
| Secretary of State for Education | Michael Gove |
| Secretary of State for Culture, Olympics, Media, and Sport | Jeremy Hunt |
| Secretary of State for Northern Ireland | Owen Paterson |
| Secretary of State for Wales | Cheryl Gillan |
| Secretary of State for Scotland | Michael Moore |
| Leader of the House of Lords | Lord Strathclyde |
| Chief Secretary to the Treasury | Danny Alexander |
| Conservative Co-chairman and Minister without Portfolio | Baroness Warsi |
| *In addition, the following senior ministers are also allowed to attend Cabinet:* | |
| Minister for Universities, Science, and Skills | David Willetts |
| Attorney General | Dominic Grieve |
| Solicitor General | Edward Garnier |
| Cabinet Office Minister | Francis Maude |
| Minister of State for the Cabinet Office, with responsibility to the Prime Minister for policy | Oliver Letwin |
| Leader of the House of Commons | Sir George Young |

 NOTE: A regularly updated version of this table can be found on the Online Resource Centre that accompanies this book.

precise levels of ministerial salaries can vary significantly, depending on the degree of that additional responsibility and the overall complexity of their jobs. As of the 2008–09 tax year, then Prime Minister Mr Brown and his ministers chose to decline their automatic annual 1.5 per cent salary increases in a gesture of solidarity with public sector workers whose pay rises were being limited because of what he described as the 'economic uncertainty' of the time. This initially meant Mr Brown was paid £132,923 on top of his basic MP salary of £64,766 (a total income of £198,661—several thousand less than his entitlement), but soon after he left office in May 2010 it emerged that for the previous year he had quietly taken a further cut—bringing his salary nearer the level of ordinary senior ministers (£150,000). For the two years prior to Labour's electoral defeat, Cabinet ministers and the government Chief Whip had each been paid £145,492 in total. During his first week in power, Mr Cameron went still further, in an apparent goodwill gesture ahead of expected public spending cuts. By not merely continuing the ministerial pay freeze but cutting salaries of those around the top table by 5 per cent in absolute terms, he brought his own political earnings down to £142,500, those of Cabinet ministers to £134,565, and pay for ministers of state outside the Cabinet from £100,568 under Labour to £98,740.

Although peers are not paid as yet (see p. 62), those occupying positions in government do receive parliamentary remuneration. Cabinet ministers drawn from the House of Lords are paid £101,038 by the taxpayer, while ministers of state get £78,891. Until 2007 the highest-paid minister of all was not the prime minister but the Lord Chancellor, who was entitled to the princely sum of £232,900. But both the current incumbent, Kenneth Clarke, and his immediate predecessor, Jack Straw, are MPs, not peers, and have therefore drawn £145,492 and £134,565 respectively. .

Substantial salaries are also paid to the most senior members of the Opposition front bench, although at a lower level than those of their government counterparts. The Leader of the Opposition currently earns £139,355 a year.

## Collective responsibility versus ministerial responsibility

The actions of ministers, especially those in Cabinet, are governed by two constitutional conventions: **collective responsibility** and **individual ministerial responsibility**. While one of these relates to their role as part of a collective decision-making body, the other concerns their duty to manage the day-to-day running of their individual portfolio (department), 'taking the rap' if mistakes are made.

### Collective responsibility

Cabinet ministers are expected to endorse and support publicly the actions of the government of which they are a part, even if they do not agree with them privately. This doctrine—known as collective responsibility—rests on the assumption that individual ministers are broadly in favour of the policy programme adopted by their government, but may occasionally disagree with specific proposals. It has long been the custom, under these circumstances, for ministers to bite their tongues. On many notable occasions, however, individuals have found themselves increasingly out of step with the views of their Cabinet colleagues over time and have ultimately resigned—freeing themselves to speak out.

In 1986 then Defence Secretary Michael Heseltine quit the Cabinet over the controversy surrounding the proposed merger of Westland, Britain's last surviving helicopter manufacturer, with US company Sikorsky. He stormed out of a Cabinet meeting in full view of waiting television cameras, making it clear he had had enough of what he saw as Mrs Thatcher's dictatorial decision-making style. In 2003 the late Robin Cook, then Leader of the House, resigned from government in protest at Mr Blair's decision to invade Iraq. He was followed, some time after the invasion, by International Development Secretary Clare Short, who blamed the chaotic reconstruction of the country in the aftermath of Saddam Hussein's defeat for her decision. John Denham, reappointed to the Cabinet under Mr Brown, also resigned from a junior post over Iraq.

In a risky, but ultimately shrewd, tactical manoeuvre, in 1975 Labour Prime Minister Wilson took the, until now unique, step of temporarily suspending collective responsibility in relation to a debate over an issue he feared would otherwise create potentially fatal Cabinet divisions. Having called a national referendum on Britain's continued membership of the European Community (which he subsequently won), he allowed members of his Cabinet strongly opposed to the policy to campaign for a 'no' vote. Among the Euro-sceptics was left-winger Tony Benn, who argued that the 'Common Market', as it was widely known, would destroy British jobs by preventing the country from using protectionism—or customs duties—to inflate the price of imports of manufactured goods, in the interests of persuading people to 'buy British'. Asked about his similarly inclusive policy towards troublesome colleagues, US President Lyndon B. Johnson once remarked of FBI director J. Edgar Hoover:

> ❝ It's probably better to have him inside the tent pissing out than outside the tent pissing in. ❞

In the early days of the Lib-Con coalition, there were signs that Messrs Cameron and Clegg were looking to mimic Mr Wilson's tactic in relation to policies over which there remained clear divisions between their parties. In what some constitutional experts greeted as a major dilution of the binding nature of collective responsibility, to win the latter's support the Conservatives agreed to allow Lib Dem frontbenchers to 'continue to make the case for' alternative policies in areas such as the renewal of Britain's Trident nuclear programme. But, while the coalition agreement allowed for limited open Cabinet 'dissent' in specified areas, Lib Dem MPs (both front and backbench) found themselves bound by an undertaking not to vote *against* policy proposals with which they disagreed—only to abstain.

## Individual ministerial responsibility

The other major convention relating to the work of a Cabinet minister is that of individual ministerial responsibility. This is the doctrine that, should a serious error or scandal occur 'on the watch' of a departmental minister, he or she should do the honourable thing and resign. Lord Carrington, for example, stepped down as Foreign Secretary over the Argentine invasion of the Falkland Islands in 1982.

But he was something of an exception. In contrast to the position in relation to collective responsibility, recent history is littered with examples of significant departmental errors for which ministers have been reluctant to take the blame. The fiasco over Britain's sudden withdrawal from the European exchange rate mechanism (ERM) in 1992 would, on many other occasions, have seen the immediate departure of the Chancellor of the Exchequer—the minister in charge of the economy. In fact, then Chancellor Norman Lamont stayed on for several months before belatedly being sacked by Prime Minister Mr Major (see p. 279).

More recently, as Labour's Defence Secretary Geoff Hoon survived a series of explosive controversies surrounding everything from the non-discovery of Saddam's alleged WMDs to a scandal over the inadequate military equipment with which British soldiers were revealed to be fighting in both the conflicts in Iraq and Afghanistan. There have been noble exceptions. Estelle Morris quit  her job as Education Secretary in 2002 over a controversy surrounding the inaccurate marking of thousands of A-level exam papers, declaring she did not feel 'up to the job'. Ironically, many people—including some political opponents, teachers, and union leaders—felt she took her decision prematurely, and was not personally to blame. The controversy had erupted when it emerged that a disproportionate number of A-level students whose papers were marked by certain exam boards had received grades substantially lower than those they were predicted. Head teacher unions accused the boards of unfairly penalizing students because of pressure from Britain's then main examinations body, the Qualifications and Curriculum Authority (QCA), to limit the number of 'A' grades in the wake of past controversy over so-called 'grade inflation'. In the end, a mass re-marking took place and a number of students' grades were revised. Although Ms Morris arguably had nothing directly to do with the marking procedure and had acted promptly, she decided to 'fall on her sword'. In 2006, then Home Secretary Charles Clarke resigned voluntarily after a succession of controversies on his watch—including the revelation that more than a thousand foreign nationals convicted of criminal offences in the UK had been freed from prison without being considered for deportation.

In practice, ministers are often sacked by their prime minister before they have a chance to quit. The prime minister's ability to remove colleagues unceremoniously dates back to a convention initiated by William Pitt in the early nineteenth century. It almost always precipitates a 'Cabinet reshuffle', during which several other ministers will be moved from one job to another to fill gaps created by the removal of their errant colleague and his or her replacement.

## The Cabinet Office and Cabinet committees

The Cabinet Office is effectively the 'Civil Service of the Cabinet'—the administrative staff and machinery that organizes its meetings and keeps its business running on a day-to-day basis. It comprises a Cabinet Secretariat, responsible for organizing the **minutes** of Cabinet meetings, and the Office of Public Service, which oversees government business as a whole. It is headed by the Cabinet Secretary, or Head of the Home Civil Service.

In turn, the Secretariat is made up of six separate departmental secretariats:

- the Economic and Domestic Affairs Secretariat;
- the Defence and Overseas Affairs Secretariat;
- the European Secretariat;
- the Constitution Secretariat;
- the Central Secretariat;
- the Intelligence Support Secretariat.

In addition, Cabinet committees are increasingly formed to deal with the finer points of policymaking. They tend, in practice, to be chaired by ministers whose personal views are close to those of the prime minister. When Mr Blair was prime minister, a significant number were chaired by his loyal deputy, John Prescott. As with parliamentary committees, there are several types of Cabinet committee, as outlined in Table 3.3.

# ▶ The Civil Service

If ministers are the engine of government—brainstorming and formulating policies in Cabinet—civil servants are the stolid engineers on the factory floor, responsible for oiling the machinery of state that puts these ideas into practice. The 'Civil Service' is the collective term for the administrative structure that carries out the work of government departments and the numerous agencies and other bodies that implement policies on their behalf.

Dating back to the secretariats that first emerged, piecemeal, at the height of the British Empire in the eighteenth century, the Civil Service has become the

**Table 3.3** Types of Cabinet committee

| Name | Role and composition |
| --- | --- |
| Standing committees | These permanent committees focus on broad-ranging policy areas (e.g. transport or health), in an effort to encourage coordinated policymaking and avoid duplication. They tend to be composed of the most relevant senior departmental ministers—e.g. a health standing committee might involve the Health Secretary, Work and Pensions Secretary, and, say, the Education Secretary. |
| Ad hoc committees | Like parliamentary ad hoc committees, these are formed to look at temporary issues and disbanded when they are resolved. |
| Ministerial committees | Formed to consider the work of specific government departments. Despite their title, they are made up solely of civil servants. |

one true constant in the UK system of government. The fact that government continues to operate uninterrupted even after the governing party has changed at an election (and, indeed, while the country is without any MPs—although not without ministers—during election campaigns) is largely down to the continuity guaranteed by the professionals responsible for 'keeping things running'. Its continuity role has rarely been more starkly apparent than during the five days between the May 2010 election and the formation of the Lib-Con *coalition government*, when caretaker Prime Minister Mr Brown agreed to give both other main parties access to the Cabinet Secretary, Sir Gus O'Donnell, and other high-level mandarins as they worked on the terms of their prospective deal. He also revealed the existence of a working document he had asked Sir Gus to produce in the run-up to the election clarifying the constitutional position of sitting premiers and Opposition leaders in a **hung Parliament**.

The foundations of today's Civil Service were first laid down in the Northcote–Trevelyan Report 1854, which stipulated the following:

- all appointments should be made on *merit*;
- there should be *fair and open competition* for advertised posts.

Efforts were quickly made to establish a professional structure for the Civil Service and successive governments have made this progressively more rigorous. Senior civil servants—known in the profession as 'mandarins'—are recruited by independent Civil Service commissioners through the Civil Service Board. Some recruits rise to senior ranks very quickly, via the Fast Stream development programme, which admits around 300 graduates a year.

Altogether, Her Majesty's Civil Service comprises some 525,000 officials working across anything up to 60 departments of state and 100 associated bodies—*executive agencies* and **quangos** (see pp. 106–7)—based principally at

Whitehall and Millbank, a stone's throw from Parliament. Each department is headed by a permanent secretary. As with civil servants of lower ranks, they are employed because of their expertise in the particular areas overseen by their departments. They are not to be confused with secretaries of state, and indeed often have a far longer record of service to their departments than such individuals, given that they are permanent Crown employees and, as such, will remain in post irrespective of whether the government changes at an election. Although they come into close daily contact with ministers and often advise them on policy, as paid officials, permanent secretaries are expected to be politically neutral at all times.

## Political neutrality in practice

Although the doctrine of 'political neutrality' is held sacrosanct in the Civil Service, in recent times there have been controversies concerning civil servants who have acted in an apparently politically motivated way. The machinations of Sir Humphrey Appleby—the odious permanent secretary for the Ministry for Administrative Affairs in the classic 1980s BBC1 sitcom *Yes, Minister*—is said to have taken its inspiration from real-life shenanigans in certain Whitehall circles. But perhaps the most significant Civil Service scandal of modern times occurred in 1985, when Clive Ponting, a civil servant in the Ministry of Defence, was tried under the Official Secrets Act 1911 for passing classified details to an unauthorized person about the sinking during the Falklands War of the Argentine ship the *General Belgrano*—allegedly while it was both retreating and outside the 'exclusion zone' declared by the British government around the islands. Although Ponting, who has gone on to be a successful writer, was acquitted of breaching s. 2 of the Act, the case prompted then Cabinet Secretary Sir Robin Butler to issue the following 'Note'—by way of an addendum to the code of conduct earlier drafted for the Civil Service:

❝ The determination of policy is the responsibility of the minister . . . When, having been given all the relevant information and advice, the minister has taken the decision, it is the duty of civil servants loyally to carry out that decision . . . Civil servants are under an obligation to keep the confidences to which they become privy in the course of their official duties. ❞

In the aftermath of the Ponting affair and a series of smaller-scale 'leaks' by similarly ethically motivated officials, new stipulations were drawn up to clarify the *levels* of political neutrality expected of civil servants on different rungs of the professional ladder. While civil servants of all ranks were expected to remain politically impartial in their day-to-day behaviour in the workplace, it was decided the extent to which they had to be entirely neutral *outside* work would depend on their seniority (see table entitled 'Levels of political impartiality in the Civil Service', on the Online Resource Centre accompanying this book). Yet leaks have continued. The Home Office was embroiled in controversy after a series of leaks to then Opposition MP Damian Green led to the police searching his office (see p. 9) in November 2008, and months later a disc containing details of MPs' expenses claims was leaked to the *Daily Telegraph* (see pp. 55–7).

In running their departments on a day-to-day basis, civil servants are expected to abide by the 'three Es'—'economy, efficiency, and effectiveness'. This maxim has been underlined by two key milestones: the Efficiency Strategy published in 1979 by Sir Derek (now Lord) Rayner and the 1982 Financial Management Initiative, which sought to provide departmental managers with 'a clear view of objectives and performance' in the context of the responsibilities of their individual ministries.

## Civil Service accountability

Several recent government initiatives have attempted to give the Civil Service a better name by making it appear leaner and meaner. In 1991 Mr Major launched a 'Citizen's Charter' calling for a 'revolution in public services'. In theory, this gave the public recourse to complain about everything from lack of information to discourtesy in their dealings with government departments. In January 2002 Charter Mark services were extended to cover the conduct of purely *internal* departmental divisions that did not come into direct contact with the public. New Labour also coined the buzzwords 'joined-up government' to refer to its attempts to encourage individual departments to work closer together.

## Executive agencies

The work of the Civil Service is so all-consuming and involved that governments have often tried to rationalize departments, breaking them down into smaller, more manageable units. These units—effectively *subsets* of their parent departments—focus exclusively on the *delivery*, rather than *formulation*, of policy. Today they are generally known as 'executive agencies'.

Initially established in 1988 by Mrs Thatcher—who sought to move away from what she saw as an over-centralized, monolithic Civil Service structure—these smaller scale, breakaway departmental bodies were designed to resemble commercial companies, rather than traditional organs of government. As such, they were each given their own chief executive, who presided over a board of directors—at the time, a hugely radical departure from the more bureaucratic way the Civil Service had previously been run. Unlike commercial companies, executive agencies had no shareholders (and therefore no profit motive) and were staffed by civil servants seconded from their parent departments. But as time went on their managers were increasingly drafted in from industry, rather than graduating from the ranks of the Civil Service itself (the theory being that importing talent from the private sector would increase efficiency). This approach was ultimately to have a sweeping impact across the public sector that continues to be felt to this day, with everything from local NHS trusts to **further education** colleges adopting the chief executive and board model at their helm.

Initially there were only a handful of executive agencies, the first of which, the Vehicle Inspectorate—now the Vehicle and Operator Services Agency (VOSA)—was established in August 1988. Their number went on to mushroom, particularly under Labour, which ended up with 130 in total—90-plus reporting to government departments at Whitehall, with the remaining number answering to the three devolved administrations in Scotland, Wales, and Northern Ireland. While some smaller spending departments have only one or two agencies working under them, bigger ones like the Home Office and Department for Work and Pensions (DWP) allocate much of their day-to-day work to agencies. The single biggest agency, in terms of staffing and budget, is **Jobcentre Plus**, which employs 100,000 people and spends £4bn a year of taxpayers' money. With 36 agencies, the Ministry of Defence (MoD) has more than any other ministry.

One of the major criticisms of executive agencies is that they are used by ministers to absolve themselves from individual ministerial responsibility. By devolving power to 'breakaway' sections of their departments, ministers might disclaim personal liability for their mistakes. This arguably happened in November 2007 when Chancellor Alistair Darling refused to accept culpability for the loss of two unencrypted computer discs containing the names, addresses, birthdates, **National Insurance (NI)** numbers, and bank details of 25 million families by HM Revenue and Customs (HMRC), an executive agency of the Treasury (see p. 589). The Child Benefit-related data had been on its way to the National Audit Office (NAO) when it was mislaid. In the ensuing furore it was HMRC's chief executive, Paul Gray, who resigned—not Mr Darling.

## Quangos

Long before executive agencies existed, there were already a large number of taxpayer-funded organizations carrying out work delegated by government departments. But historically, these non-departmental public bodies (NDPBs) tended to be staffed not by seconded civil servants from specific departments of state, but by their own employees, which they recruited as discrete entities, notionally independent of government. Over time, an umbrella term has evolved for these bodies: 'quasi-autonomous non-governmental organizations', or 'quangos'.

Quangos are often confused with executive agencies and it is easy to see why. Like agencies, they have their own management boards—although these are headed by honorary chairpersons, rather than salaried chief executives. They also control significant budgets, largely funded by the taxpayer.

Perhaps unsurprisingly, therefore, quangos frequently come under fire from the media for their lack of accountability. Whereas agencies are at least answerable to ministers whose government can be ejected at an election if the electorate is unhappy with its actions, quangos have traditionally had a degree of autonomy that puts them beyond such direct 'control'. Yet, like agencies, they receive the bulk of their funding from taxpayers—through the aegis of related departments. Much of the budget for Arts Council England (ACE), for example, comes from the Department for Culture, Media, and Sport (DCMS).

Lack of accountability is one criticism levelled at quangos; another is nepotism. Because they, like executive agencies, are run by boards, the members of which have customarily been nominated (for which, read 'selected') by relevant ministers, how can we be certain that individuals are genuinely being chosen on merit, rather than because they are friends and/or political allies of the government? The recently disbanded BBC board of governors—charged with holding the Corporation to account for its public service broadcasting responsibilities—was a quango in all but name. Little surprise, then, that Mr Blair came in for criticism for choosing Gavyn Davies, a former Labour donor, as its chairman in 2000.

Sustained criticism of the 'quangocracy' has led to several recent moves to address the nepotism question. In 2000, the government introduced an Appointments Commission to appoint chairpersons and non-executive directors of NHS bodies, including hospitals, **primary care trusts**, and strategic health authorities (see Chapter 6). The body also has powers to vet appointees to other quangos at local, regional, and national levels. Its own appointments are regulated by an Office of the Commissioner for Public Appointments (OCPA).

In July 1996 a democratic audit identified 6,224 executive and advisory quangos, run by 66,000–73,500 people and responsible for spending £60.4bn. On coming to power, Mr Blair vowed to scrap 'unaccountable quangos' and Mr Brown spoke of a 'bonfire of the quangos'. But figures from the Cabinet Office published in August 2007 revealed that quangos had spent £167.5bn in the previous year.

## Taskforces

A new form of non-elected body created by New Labour, particularly during its first term, the number of taskforces in place by 2000 was already 44. They were generally set up to deal with short-term issues of public concern and were headed by senior public figures dubbed 'tsars' (effectively, hired troubleshooters). Examples include the Rough Sleepers' Unit, led by 'Homelessness Tsar' Louise Casey, which set out to tackle street homelessness, and a short-lived drugs taskforce run by 'Drugs Tsar' Keith Hellawell. Mr Cameron has continued the trend for 'tsars', allowing the term to be used to denote advisory roles he gave to former Labour MPs Alan Milburn and John Hutton (as 'Social Mobility Tsar' and 'Pensions Tsar' respectively) and current Labour MP Frank Field ('Poverty Tsar').

## Spin doctors and special advisers

The number of special advisers and, in particular, spin doctors—those largely concerned with the effective presentation of policy to the electorate through the media—has hugely multiplied in recent years. By the end of Mr Major's reign they had increased to 38, but under Mr Blair there were consistently as many as 74 at the highest level of government. At its peak the advisers' salary bill topped £3.6m, but their number has since declined.

Unlike civil servants, special advisers and spin doctors are *party*, rather than government, appointments. This was the case with most Downing Street big-hitters of the Blair years, including Alastair Campbell, the prime minister's official spokesman, and Jonathan Powell, his chief of staff. Sometimes, the edges are more blurred, however: Sir Bernard Ingham, Mrs Thatcher's bullish press secretary, started out as a civil servant, before switching to the Conservative Party's payroll while she was in government. When a party is in opposition, it picks up the pay bill for its advisers, but once in government they (like civil servants) are usually paid from public funds for the duration of a parliament.

In 2000, the Neill Committee on Standards in Public Life published a report entitled *Reinforcing Standards*, which recommended that Westminster, like Scotland and Wales, should place an upper limit of 100 on its tally of advisers. Yet their number continues to be high and their actions to be viewed as controversial.

Under Mr Blair some special advisers became bywords for cold-hearted calculation. Jo Moore, an adviser at the Department of Transport, Local Government, and the Regions (DTLR), was forced to resign in February 2002 following a series of controversies about her management style and, in particular, the publication of an explosive email she sent on 11 September the previous year—the date of the terrorist attacks on the Twin Towers—describing it as a 'very good day' to 'bury' bad news.

Mr Blair's reliance on advice from spin doctors and party appointees over senior civil servants frequently saw him accused of 'politicizing' the Civil Service by the back door. One of his first actions on taking office in 1997 was to pass an executive order allowing senior advisers like Mr Campbell and Mr Powell to issue orders to civil servants. Mr Brown revoked this, symbolically, within hours of replacing Mr Blair at Number 10, but cynics dismissed even this gesture as spin, in light of recent statistics indicating that the number of government special advisers, spin doctors, and press and marketing staff continued to climb during his time in power. A Whitehall audit found that 68 additional special advisers were employed by ministers during 2007, and all were still in post at the end of the year—six months after Mr Brown took over. The overall number of press office staff (many of them civil servants, but nonetheless employed to put a positive gloss on government policy) had risen to 3,250. Between 1997 and 2007 Labour increased the annual cost of 'government PR' (public relations) to £338m—with a £15m rise in 2007 alone.

In July 2001, following years of controversy about Labour's reliance on political advisors, a Code of Conduct for Special Advisers was published. It defined them as 'temporary civil servants' who did not necessarily have to be appointed 'on merit', but were nonetheless expected to comply with the Civil Service Code governing all other departmental civil servants, and could not use 'official resources', such as stationery, for party-political purposes. If they wished to campaign on behalf of their ministers during the lead-up to a general election, once it was called, they must stand down from their posts in recognition of their political affiliation. Mr Campbell did this in 2005.

## The Parliamentary Ombudsman

Despite its title, the **Parliamentary Commissioner for Administration** (part of a wider regulatory body known as the **Parliamentary and Health Service Ombudsman**) is charged with investigating public complaints not about Parliament itself, but about government departments and other public bodies, including quangos. The basis of an individual's complaint has to be that he or she has suffered an injustice due to maladministration arising from delay, faulty procedures, errors, unfairness, and/or bias. Complaints against judges, police officers, and local authorities are investigated by separate bodies and procedures.

The ombudsman is sometimes derided as 'a watchdog without teeth' because, even though it can recommend that a department or body found at fault should 'remedy' its mistakes, its findings of maladministration cannot be *enforced*.

Since devolution, there have been separate ombudsmen for Scotland and Wales.

# ▶ Devolved government—executive decision-making in the regions

Chapters 1 and 2 laid out, first, the manner in which devolution unfolded in Britain and, then, the forms of government subsequently settled on in each of the three countries outside England. There follows a brief overview of the manner in which *government* is constituted in those countries.

## The Scottish Government/Executive

Just as the legislative process prevailing in Scotland is distinct from that which applies in Wales and Northern Ireland, so too is its executive framework. Scotland now boasts its own Scottish Government. Until recently this was known as the Scottish Executive, but when the Scottish Nationalist Party (SNP) became the largest party in the Holyrood Parliament in May 2007 and its leader, Alex Salmond, replaced Labour's Jack McConnell as First Minister he renamed it. The Scottish Government is much more fully formed than either of its cousins in Cardiff or Stormont. Like the British government it has its own Cabinet. It meets on Tuesday mornings at Bute House in Edinburgh's Charlotte Square, the First Minister's official residence. The administration itself is based at St Andrew's House, along with its own secretariat, and has two subcommittees: a Cabinet subcommittee on legislation and a Scottish Executive emergency room Cabinet subcommittee.

## The Welsh Assembly Government/Welsh Executive

Like the Scottish Executive, the **Welsh Executive** recently changed its name to the **Welsh Assembly Government** to reflect the increasing autonomy granted to it since devolution. It, too, is led by a First Minister—Labour leader Carwyn Jones, who replaced his long-time predecessor, Rhodri Morgan, in December 2009. Since the 2007 Welsh Assembly election, Labour has been in coalition with the Welsh nationalist party, Plaid Cymru, under the banner 'One Wales'.

## The Northern Ireland Executive

The 'power-sharing executive' in Northern Ireland has been a coalition since its rocky inception more than five years ago—and only recently began to function properly, following the conclusion of a substantive peace agreement in spring 2007.

### ≣ Topical feature idea

The Civil Service is Britain's single biggest employer, with departmental head offices at Whitehall but staff based the length and breadth of the country—working everywhere from local tax officers to branches of Jobcentre Plus. Shortly after taking power, the Lib-Con coalition announced plans for an immediate job freeze across the Civil Service, as part of its move to make £6.2bn in public spending cuts in its first year to reduce the UK's Budget deficit. Actual job cuts soon followed, beginning with the loss of 240 posts in Coventry with the closure of Becta (formerly the British Educational Communications and Technology Agency), the government agency charged with promoting investment in ICT. How big an employer is the Civil Service in your area and how many job losses, if any, have there been in recent months? What does a typical day in the life for a civil servant working in your local Jobcentre Plus branch or tax office entail, how much are they paid, and what would happen if they were not there to do their job? How are staff at Jobcentre Plus coping with a recruitment freeze, pay freezes, and a high workload due to recent rises in overall UK unemployment?

## ✳ Current issues

- **The return of coalition government:** the 2010 election saw the formation of Britain's first formal coalition government since the Second World War. With a referendum on the introduction of a new electoral system scheduled for May 2011, it is possible that bipartisan or multi-partisan Cabinets might soon become the norm, rather than the exception, as in many mainland European countries.

- **The future of collective responsibility, the government whip system, and party discipline:** despite being in coalition, the Conservatives and Lib Dems have confirmed their intention to continue fighting council and European elections as distinct parties with distinct manifestoes, and Mr Cameron has allowed his MPs to actively campaign against electoral reform in the run-up to the pending May 2011 referendum on the *alternative vote*. Similarly, the Lib Dems are to be allowed to speak out against certain Tory policies, such as the renewal of Trident. It remains to be seen how strictly the two parties will enforce unity in parliamentary votes on their agreed policy priorities in relation to areas such as the economy, welfare, and defence.

- **Contraction of the Civil Service:** the coalition has announced an indefinite freeze on all Civil Service recruitment. Although portrayed as stasis, rather than a reduction in the number of civil servants, opposition MPs and independent commentators argue that it means job losses, as individuals who retire or move on will not be replaced. In June 2010 John Philpott, chief economic adviser for the Chartered Institute of Personnel and Development, warned up to 725,000 public sector jobs were likely to be lost as a result of the cuts—including at least 200,000 departmental civil servants.

## ? Review questions

1. Outline the role and powers of the prime minister. To what extent, in practice, does his or her position differ from that of a head of state?

2. To what extent can recent prime ministers be accused of being 'presidential'—and can they still claim to adhere to the maxim of 'first among equals'?

3. What is the distinction between 'collective' and 'individual ministerial' responsibility, and do Cabinet ministers always abide by either, or both?

4. What is the difference between the Cabinet and the government, and is there an optimum size and composition for either, or both?

5. To what extent can the use of 'kitchen Cabinets', special advisers, and spin doctors be said to have 'politicized' the Civil Service?

→ **Further reading**

Budge, I., Crewe, I., McKay, D., and Newton, K. (2007) *The New British Politics*, 4th edn, London: Longman. **Fourth edition of acclaimed critical introduction to British politics at dawn of twenty-first century, updated to cover Brown's administration.**

Burnham, J. and Pyper, R. (2008) *Britain's Modernised Civil Service*, London: Palgrave Macmillan. **Thorough examination of recent developments in Civil Service, incorporating analysis of the impact of changes introduced by the Thatcher, Major, Blair, and Brown governments.**

Campbell, A. (2007) *The Blair Years: Extracts from the Alastair Campbell Diaries*, London: Hutchinson. **Candid, if 'on message', personal diaries of Tony Blair's chief spin doctor, charting period from his employer's election as Labour leader in 1994 to his resignation as prime minister in 2007.**

Crossman, R. (1979) *The Crossman Diaries: Selections from the Diaries of a Cabinet Minister, 1964–1970*, London: Book Club Associates. **Widely regarded as among the most incisive and revealing political diaries written by a British minister, these highlights are edited by one of Britain's foremost contemporary political biographers.**

Hennessey, P. (2001) *The Prime Minister: The Job and Its Holders Since 1945*, London: Penguin. **Colourful run-down and evaluation of British premiers in post-war period, balancing serious academic discourse with story and anecdote.**

Jones, N. (2002) *The Control Freaks: How New Labour Gets Its Way*, London: Politico's Publishing. **Blow-by-blow unpicking of the 'New Labour' government's media strategy by a former BBC political correspondent.**

@ **Online Resource Centre**

www.oxfordtextbooks.co.uk/orc/Morrison2e/
Visit the Online Resource Centre that accompanies this book for web links and regular updates.

4

# The electoral system

Chapters 1–3 examined the constitutional framework governing the UK and the gradual shift from royal to **parliamentary sovereignty** that has taken place over the past four centuries. But the legitimacy of the UK legislature—and the executive, the members of which are drawn from it—today derives from more than mere historical precedent: it stems from the system of democratic elections that is the bedrock of modern British government.

## ▌ The origins of the British franchise

British social reformers were demanding the vote for their fellow citizens for centuries before it was granted. For the rank and file who comprised the New Model Army, the Levellers, and their offshoot, the Diggers, propelling Oliver Cromwell to power, the English Civil War was about far more than a tussle for constitutional supremacy between Parliament and Crown. To John Lilburne, radical leader of the Levellers, parliamentary sovereignty meant nothing if it was not exercised by ordinary people. For this to happen, he argued, all 'free-born Englishmen' must be given a direct say in how Parliament is run: in other words, a vote.

Lilburne's arguments would echo down the decades for some 200 years before being answered, even in part—through the writings of Thomas Paine, the marches of the nineteenth-century Chartists, the speeches of the Labour Party's firebrand first member MP, James Keir Hardie, and the campaigns of the suffragettes. But it was to be a further century or more before every adult (regardless of class or gender) was granted a say in the running of his or her country's affairs. The slow extension of the UK 'franchise'—the number and range of people entitled to vote in parliamentary elections—is charted in the timeline in Table 4.1.

**Table 4.1** Acts of Parliament that extended the UK franchise

| Year | Act | Effect |
|---|---|---|
| 1432 | Electors of Knights of the Shire Act | Voting rights restricted to men living in county areas. All men owning freehold property or land worth 40 shillings in a county could vote in that county. |
| 1832 | Representation of the People Act ('Great Reform Act') | Huge extension of franchise—by 50–80 per cent, with one in five men (653,000) now allowed to vote—but women excluded. In counties, vote given to all owners of land worth £10 or more in 'copyhold' (a medieval form of title deed), all owners of land worth £10 on long-term lease (60 years or more), and holders of land on medium-term lease (20–60 years) worth £50. In boroughs, all men with property worth £10 gained vote, except in 'freeman boroughs', where rights went only to those with 'freedom of the borough'. |
| 1867 | Representation of the People Act ('Second Reform Act') | All male urban householders given vote, along with all male lodgers paying £10 or more a year for unfurnished rooms. Electorate nearly doubled, with extra 1.5 million men added. |
| 1884 | Representation of the People Act | Electorate increased to 5.5 million through extension of voting rights given to boroughs in 1867 to countryside. All men owning or renting property worth £10 now had vote. |
| 1918 | Representation of the People Act | Franchise extended to all men over 21 and women over 30. Voting still subject to minimum property qualifications, but less strict than previously. Electorate tripled from 7.7 million to 21.4 million. |
| 1928 | Representation of the People Act | Universal suffrage extended to all adults over 21. |
| 1969 | Representation of the People Act | Voting age lowered to 18 universally. |

While the primary significance of the above acts was to extend the voting entitlement to more people, the most radical went further. To ensure that parliamentary democracy operates in as fair and equitable a way as possible, it has been necessary for governments periodically to introduce additional structural and procedural reforms.

The 'Great Reform Act 1832' owes its place in history less to a wholesale extension of the franchise and more to its abolition of so-called 'rotten boroughs'—by that point an anachronistic and shameful hangover from medieval times. The term 'rotten borough' was used to refer to areas of the country in which *constituency* boundaries ought to have been altered to reflect dwindling population numbers, but had not. In other words, there existed (prior to the Act) boroughs in which MPs were dependent for their election on a fraction of the number of adults whose votes had to be sought by their parliamentary colleagues.

In some cases the number of local electors was so minimal that it was, quite literally, possible for a parliamentary candidate to win a seat by bribing voters. In 1831, the year before the Act was passed, the constituency of Old Sarum in Wiltshire had just three houses and 11 registered voters. Gatton in Surrey had 23 houses, but only seven voters. As a result rotten boroughs had become a byword for corruption, with some constituencies effectively being bought and sold, and others passed from father to son like inheritances. Before being awarded a peerage (and eventually becoming prime minister) Arthur Wellesley, the Duke of Wellington, once served as MP for the rotten borough of Trim, County Meath. Rotten boroughs were memorably satirized in the BBC1 sitcom *Blackadder the Third*, in which a dog won the fictitious seat of 'Dunny-on-the-Wold'.

Another significant reform—but one that took a lot longer coming—was the abolition of 'plural voting'. This was the tradition that allowed individuals who owned properties in two or more areas—or those attending university in one area when their family home was in another—to have a multiple say in the outcome of an election, by voting in each constituency. This practice (not to be confused with that, still common today, which allows individuals in these positions to choose in which constituency they would like to vote) was ended by the Representation of the People Act 1948.

## The British franchise today—who can vote?

Elections to the House of Commons are known as 'general elections'. They have traditionally taken place up to five years to the day after the previous Parliament was assembled following a poll and, for convoluted historical reasons, tend to be held on Thursdays.

However, the ability of sitting UK prime ministers (unlike governments in practically any other developed democracy) to call elections at times that suit them—often quitting while they are ahead in the polls, rather than seeing through policies that might be for the good of the country, if not their own approval ratings—has long been contentious. So in its maiden *Queen's Speech* in May 2010, the Lib-Con *coalition government* confirmed legislative plans to introduce fixed-term parliaments—commencing with an election on Thursday 7 May 2015—as part of a wider-ranging package of constitutional reform. The decision to plump straight for five-year (rather than the more usual four-year) terms provoked some early criticism. Similarly contentious was the coalition's (arguably unconstitutional) decision in September 2010 to drop the customary autumn Queen's Speech that year and in 2011, thereby extending the length of its first full parliamentary session until spring 2012—the longest interval between state openings for 150 years. The excuse given at the time by the coalition's *Leader of the House*, Sir George Young, was that a generous time slot was needed to allow MPs and peers to fully scrutinize the then new government's packed legislative agenda.

As its name implies, at a general election all sitting MPs formally resign to contest their seats on polling day. This means elections are held simultaneously in all 650 Commons constituencies, and a new Parliament is normally summoned by the sovereign as soon as all votes are counted and seats allocated. After the May 2010 election, the distribution of seats in the Commons was as outlined in Table 4.2—leaving Britain facing its first *hung Parliament* since February 1974 (see pp. 120–1). Under these circumstances it typically takes several days for the shape of a new government to be finalized, and true to form the Lib-Con coalition deal was only signed on Tuesday 11 May—five days after polls closed.

Whereas in local and European elections the franchise has gradually been extended to include European Union (EU) citizens resident in Britain at the time of a poll, voting is more restricted in general elections. Currently it is open to citizens of Britain, the Irish Republic, and the Commonwealth normally resident in the UK, subject to the following criteria:

- the citizen's name must be on the **electoral register** for the constituency in which he or she lives;
- he or she must be over the age of 18 at the time of the election—although he or she may enter his or her name on the electoral register when aged 17.

Despite these broad qualification criteria, the following individuals are barred from voting:

- peers entitled to sit in the Lords;
- foreign nationals (including citizens of other EU states);
- patients detained under mental health legislation in relation to criminal activities;
- convicted people detained in prison (but not those awaiting trial on remand);
- people convicted during the preceding five years of 'corrupt' or 'illegal election practices'.

The rules governing eligibility to vote in general elections also have the following quirks:

- members of the Armed Forces and Crown servants of British embassies, the Diplomatic Service, and the British Council employed overseas (and their partners and other family members) may vote in the constituencies 'where they would normally live';
- UK citizens living abroad ('ex-pats') but resident in Britain and registered as electors *within the previous 15 years*, can make annual declarations allowing their names to be included in the register for constituencies

**Table 4.2** The distribution of seats in the House of Commons following the May 2010 election

| Party | Seats | Gains | Losses | Net gain/loss | Votes (%) | Votes | Change in % of vote |
|---|---|---|---|---|---|---|---|
| Conservative | 307 | 101 | 3 | +97 | 36.1 | 10,706,647 | +3.8% |
| Labour | 258 | 3 | 94 | -91 | 29.0 | 8,604,358 | -6.2% |
| Liberal Democrat | 57 | 8 | 13 | -5 | 23.0 | 6,827,938 | +1.0% |
| UK Independence Party | 0 | 0 | 0 | 0 | 3.1 | 917,832 | +0.9% |
| Scottish National Party | 6 | 0 | 0 | 0 | 1.7 | 491,386 | +0.1% |
| Green | 1 | 1 | 0 | +1 | 1.0 | 285,616 | -0.1% |
| Democratic Unionist | 8 | 0 | 1 | -1 | 0.6 | 168,216 | -0.3% |
| British National Party | 0 | 0 | 0 | 0 | 1.9 | 563,743 | +1.2% |
| Plaid Cymru | 3 | 1 | 0 | +1 | 0.6 | 165,394 | -0.1% |
| Sinn Féin | 5 | 0 | 0 | 0 | 0.6 | 171,942 | -0.1% |
| Ulster Conservatives and Unionists—New Force | 0 | 0 | 1 | -1 | 0.3 | 102,361 | -0.1% |
| Social Democratic and Labour Party | 3 | 0 | 0 | 0 | 0.4 | 110,970 | -0.1% |
| Independent Community and Health Concern | 0 | 0 | 1 | -1 | 0.1 | 16,150 | +0.0% |
| Respect-Unity Coalition | 0 | 0 | 1 | -1 | 0.1 | 33,251 | -0.1N/A |
| Scottish Socialist Party | 0 | 0 | 0 | 0 | 0.0 | 3,157 | -0.1% |
| Alliance | 1 | 1 | 0 | +1 | 0.1 | 42,762 | +0.0% |
| English Democrats | 0 | 0 | 0 | 0 | 0.2 | 64,826 | +0.2% |
| Trade Unionist and Socialist Coalition | 0 | 0 | 0 | 0 | 0.0 | 12,275 | N/A |
| Christian Party | 0 | 0 | 0 | 0 | 0.1 | 18,623 | N/A |
| Others | 1 | 1 | 1 | 0 | 1.1 | 319,891 | +0.0% |

NOTE: A regularly updated version of this table can be found on the Online Resource Centre that accompanies this book.

'*where they were living before they went abroad*'. They can vote by proxy—appointing a friend or relative to vote on their behalf—at any Westminster, *Scottish Parliament*, Welsh Assembly, and **European Parliament** (but not local) election;

- holidaymakers are allowed 'absent votes' in national elections under the Representation of the People Act 1985—provided that the electoral registration officer is '*satisfied that the applicant's circumstances on the date of the poll will be or are likely to be such that he cannot reasonably be expected to vote in person*';

- although there is nothing stopping reigning monarchs and their immediate heirs from voting in theory, were they to do so in practice, this would be seen as unconstitutional.

Registers of electors are compiled by local electoral registration officers and completion of electoral registration forms is compulsory—although, unlike in countries such as Australia, voting is *not*. Many people technically broke the law when local taxpayers were charged the Community Charge ('Poll Tax')—a head tax payable by each individual, rather than household (see pp. 357–8)—by deliberately not filling in forms to avoid being billed.

The Representation of the People Act 2000 has changed the way in which registration takes place in the following respects.

- Prior to the Act, electors were registered to vote wherever they were living on 10 October each year. Although an annual canvass is still conducted—on 15 October—a rolling registration system now exists, enabling electors to register themselves at a new address at the beginning of any month.

- Draft registers used to be open for inspection until 16 December. This date has now been brought forward to 1 December. The register cannot (except as the result of a formal appeal) be altered once the final date for registration has passed.

The Labour government also liberalized some pre-existing voting disqualifications, while remaining strict about others. Until recently, many people detained under mental health legislation in a hospital or other institution (as opposed to being there voluntarily) were barred from voting, on the grounds that they were not of 'sound mind'. This is no longer the case (unless they have been convicted of a crime). Homeless people were also enfranchised formally for the first time with the passage of the 2000 Act. People with no permanent address may now vote subject to a 'declaration of local connection'. Following repeated appeals by convicted prisoners against their prohibition from voting under the European Convention on Human Rights (see pp. 11–12), the coalition has agreed to amend the law to allow some categories of prisoner to vote.

Although its stance was more liberal than those of previous governments in some respects, Labour tightened up certain qualifications. The Representation of the People Act 1989 made it easier for ex-pats to vote in UK general elections, by allowing them to do so up to 20 years after emigrating. At the time this was viewed by critics of the then Conservative government as a manoeuvre designed to boost its vote (the assumption being that many people who had retired abroad were likely to be wealthy and inclined to vote Tory). After the 2001 election, Labour reduced this entitlement period to 15 years.

# ▶ General elections and candidacy— who can stand?

As of June 2007 any citizen of the UK, the Irish Republic, or a Commonwealth country resident in Britain and over the age of 18 on the day he or she is nominated (the age qualification was previously 21) may stand for election—provided that he or she is not disqualified from sitting in the Commons. Such disqualification might arise because he or she is:

- a peer retained in the House of Lords;
- an undischarged bankrupt subject to a bankruptcy restriction order under the Enterprise Act 2002 in England and Wales. These are made by the Insolvency Service—an **executive agency** of the Department of Business, Enterprise and Regulatory Reform (BERR)—if a bankrupt individual is found to have acted dishonestly, or in an otherwise 'blameworthy' way. In Northern Ireland, anyone adjudged bankrupt is barred from standing, while in Scotland, anyone whose estate has been sequestered is banned;
- a patient detained for criminal activities under mental health legislation;
- someone sentenced to, and currently serving, more than one year's imprisonment;
- a person found personally guilty of *corrupt* election practices during the preceding ten years (if in the same constituency) or in the last five years (if in a different one);
- someone found personally guilty of *illegal* election practices in the last seven years (if in his or her constituency) or five years (if elsewhere);
- a holder of the offices listed in the House of Commons Disqualification Act 1975:
  - **politically restricted posts** within the Civil Service—that is, senior civil servants in close day-to-day contact with government ministers or elected councillors;

- members of the regular Armed Forces or the Ulster Defence Regiment;
- serving police officers;
- holders of judicial office;
- members of specified commissions—for example, the **Commission for Equality and Human Rights (CEHR)**, the **Independent Police Complaints Commission (IPCC)**, and the Lands Tribunal.

Some disqualifications are more liberal than others. While convicted prisoners have long been denied the vote in general elections, they may stand as candidates—provided that they are serving 12 months or less for their crimes. This 'loophole' was once even more open-minded: Provisional Irish Republican Army (IRA) member Bobby Sands was imprisoned for 14 years for possessing firearms in 1977, yet managed to get himself elected as MP for Fermanagh and South Tyrone in April 1981, after standing on a so-called 'Anti-H Block/Armagh Political Prisoner' ticket. He was on hunger strike at the time, however, and died a few weeks later. After his death Margaret Thatcher's government hastily passed the Representation of the People Act 1981, which introduced the current 'maximum 12-month sentence' qualification for serving prisoners with parliamentary ambitions. The swiftness with which it did so stopped any of Sands's fellow hunger strikers standing for election in his stead.

## How the British electoral system works

The system used to elect MPs in British general elections is colloquially known as 'first past the post' (FPTP) (its technical name is *plurality voting*). Essentially this means that, in each of the 650 constituencies, the candidate with the highest number of votes cast—a simple majority—is automatically elected as its MP. Similarly, the political party that gains the most seats in the House of Commons once all constituency votes are counted nationwide will normally form the government. Historically, one party has tended to win an *overall majority*—more seats than all of the other parties and independent MPs put together (or a majority 'over all'). In rarer circumstances, one party emerges with only a handful more seats than its nearest rival—allowing it to form only a *minority* administration (as Labour did temporarily in February 1974), or to forge a coalition with another party or parties. This type of result is known as a 'hung Parliament'.

Britain's most recent hung Parliament followed the May 2010 election, when no single party won an overall majority, but the Conservatives secured 307 Commons seats, Labour 258, and the Lib Dems 57. With Lib Dem leader Nick Clegg holding the balance of power—despite a disappointing election-night result, which saw his party make a net loss of five seats—he was invited into swift negotiations with David Cameron's Tories. After five days of furtive dealmaking, which at one point saw Mr Clegg holding parallel talks with Labour, the

Lib Dems formally agreed to join a Conservative-led government—marking the start of the UK's first formal coalition since the end of the Second World War. Unlike the fragile 'Lib-Lab Pact', which had seen David Steel's then Liberal Party keep James Callaghan's Labour government in power for 15 months between 1977 and 1978, the 2010 arrangement—dubbed 'a new politics' by Mr Clegg—saw Lib Dem frontbenchers enter the *Cabinet* in senior positions, with their leader appointed deputy prime minister.

The British electoral system has long been controversial, because of the frequent imbalance between the number of votes cast for a particular party and the share of seats into which they translate. As only the first-placed candidate in a given constituency is elected, all other votes cast (often numbering tens of thousands) are effectively 'wasted'. For many years, it has been only the Conservatives and Labour who have stood a realistic chance of forming a government in their own right, because in order to win sufficient seats to do so parties have had to rely on *concentrations* of support. Traditional heartlands—for the Tories, the affluent south-east; for Labour, the post-industrial north and Scotland—have tended to swing the pendulum from one to the other.

General elections have also produced governments with numbers of seats vastly outstripping their share of the vote. Recent examples include the 1997 election, which saw not one Conservative MP elected in Scotland—despite the fact that a number of Scots still voted for the party. The 2005 poll saw Labour win well over half of the available seats, despite only gaining 35 per cent of the vote (equivalent to 21 per cent of registered voters, given the low turnout on the day). And the in-built Labour bias under FPTP was underlined still further when in 2010 the Tories won 36 per cent of the vote, compared to Labour's 29 and the Lib Dems' 23, but were 19 seats short of the winning post. Detailed analysis of the 2005 election results had found that the average Labour MP needed only 26,858 votes to be re-elected at that time, with Tories requiring 44,241 and Lib Dems 98,484. Hardly surprising that, in a move interpreted as an attempt to rectify this imbalance (as well as cutting the cost of Parliament to taxpayers), Mr Cameron's Lib-Con coalition plans to reduce the number of MPs to 600 and make constituency populations more equal. An example of the wild disparities in the sizes of UK electorates at the time of his election was the fact that the Isle of Wight (a Tory stronghold) boasted 110,000 voters, while a populace of 22,000 was sufficient to return an SNP MP in the Western Isles.

Some election results have been notoriously unfair. In February 1974, incumbent Prime Minister Ted Heath's Tories won 200,000 more votes than Labour, but secured four fewer seats. Heath's attempts to secure a deal to keep himself in power with then Liberal leader Jeremy Thorpe failed within days—due largely the Conservatives' unwillingness to give ground on electoral reform. Within days Wilson took office, consolidating his victory in October that year by securing a small working majority of three and a million more votes than the Tories, but this did little to defuse the initial sense of injustice. It has not always been this way around: in 1951, Labour Prime Minister Clement Attlee was beaten by Winston Churchill's Tories, who won seven more seats despite polling more than a million fewer votes.

## Tactical voting

In recent elections it has become increasingly common for people in certain constituencies to vote *strategically*—backing candidates other than those they would most like to see elected, in the hope of preventing the election of those they like least. This method of casting votes—rejecting one's 'sincere preference' in favour of a compromise candidate who is more likely to win—is known as **tactical voting**.

An oft-cited example of this is when a voter who strongly identifies with Labour, but lives in a constituency in which the sitting MP is Conservative, votes Lib Dem instead. If at the previous election, the Labour candidate were to come third, behind not only the Tories but also the Lib Dems, on this basis a vote for Labour would be 'wasted'. So, as the Lib Dems are better placed to beat the Tories, it is worth the Labour supporter voting tactically, backing his or her 'least worst option' over the one he or she most favours.

Examples of MPs elected by tactical voting in recent years abound. Lib Dem Mark Oaten's decisive 1997 victory in the Winchester by-election prompted by an electoral petition from Tory Gerry Malone, described later in this chapter, is believed to have been due largely to a wholesale tactical switch by Labour supporters to the Lib Dems. Indeed, by 1997 the Conservatives had become so unpopular, after 18 years in power, that widespread tactical voting was used to boot them out—whatever the cost—across the UK. In 2001 protest singer Billy Bragg organized a national campaign designed to prevent the Tories winning seats by getting fellow opponents of the party to 'trade' their tactical votes with electors living elsewhere in Britain. A Lib Dem voter living in a Labour/Tory marginal constituency, for example, might 'vote by remote' for his or her preferred party in a distant Lib Dem/Tory marginal—trading his or her own constituency vote with a Labour supporter whose home was in that area.

# The election process

The sequence of events leading to a general election is as outlined in Table 4.3.

Each candidate must put down a £500 **election deposit**, which will be returned provided that he or she receives at least 5 per cent of the votes cast in the relevant constituency. The deposit was introduced in 1918 as a means of discouraging 'frivolous' candidates—and, cynics suggest, boosting the Treasury's coffers (it made £800,000 from forfeited deposits in 2001).

**Table 4.3** The general election process

| Event | Condition |
|---|---|
| Election date announced | Elections must be called *at least 17 working days* before polling day |
| Nominations for candidates—until recently prospective parliamentary candidates (PPCs)—entered | Nomination process closes at 12 p.m. on 19th day before election (excluding Sundays and Bank Holidays) |
| Checking that nomination meets basic conditions for eligibility and registration | Each candidate must have his or her nomination proposed and seconded by two 'subscribing' electors, and signed by eight other 'assenting' electors—all registered in the constituency. Nominations include brief description of candidate (up to six words including name and political affiliation) identifying them on ballot paper. Candidates do not have to be backed by parties (i.e. can be 'independent'). Each candidate allowed to post one 'election communication' to registered voters |
| Disqualification of invalid nominations | **Returning officers** may reject nomination papers deemed 'out of order' on day of voting |

# Voting procedure on the day—role of the returning officer

Local administration of voting in general elections follows a tightly regulated procedure. After polling closes it culminates in an election-night 'count' at a chosen venue—normally a large local authority building somewhere near the constituency's geographical centre—which is overseen by a returning officer. In practice, the role of returning officer has tended to be discharged by a senior officer in the local authority containing, coterminous with, or neighbouring the constituency—often its *chief executive*—but in theory it is the responsibility of the council's chairperson or **mayor**. This position was confirmed by then Justice Secretary Jack Straw in 2007, with the exception of 'county constituencies' (rural ones), in which the role now falls to 'acting returning officers', in the shape of the electoral registration officers employed by specified nearby district councils. Electoral procedure on the day is outlined in Table 4.4.

Should results be especially close and it be felt that disallowed ballot papers might have produced a different result if included, dissatisfied candidates can apply to the High Court for an 'election petition' against the returning officer. This happened in 1997, when Mr Malone lost his Winchester seat by just two votes to Mr Oaten (see p. 122)—the closest result since 1945. Mr Malone's petition succeeded, but when the election was rerun in November the same year he lost by a 21,566-vote landslide (suggesting there is more than a little truth to the adage that nobody likes a bad loser!). The by-election result is almost certain to have been nearer the electorate's original wishes than the knife-edge outcome of the general election poll, given that on the earlier occasion many voters had been confused by the candidacy of Richard Huggett, who listed himself on the

**Table 4.4** The electoral process on the day of voting

| Event | Conditions |
|---|---|
| Polling stations open at 7 a.m. and close at 10 p.m. | Registered electors who have not chosen to vote by post, email, or proxy may cast them at stations based at schools, community centres, and, increasingly, pubs and supermarkets. |
| Absent votes may be cast in advance | Those who cannot reasonably be expected to vote in person (e.g. are on holiday) can apply for 'absent votes', while the physically incapacitated or those unable to vote because of the nature of their work or the fact that they have moved to a new constituency since the electoral roll was last compiled can apply for 'indefinite absent votes'. Anyone entitled to an absent vote can either vote by post or have someone else do so in person at a polling station on his or her behalf (a 'proxy vote'); postal ballot papers *cannot*, however, be sent to addresses outside the UK. Assuming electors follow the normal process, ballot papers are issued to them at the polling station by election staff (with official marks impressed on the papers at this stage). |
| Secrecy of ballot preserved—no interference with ballot boxes | Ballot boxes are sealed at the close of poll, before being taken to the counting place to be counted. |
| Official count starts after close of poll—only valid papers counted | The count is supervised by the returning officer—observed by the candidates, their agents, the media, and a small number of 'scrutineers'. Any 'spoilt' ballot papers—e.g. those defaced or with a cross placed beside the name of more than one candidate—are disallowed. |
| Recount if result is too close to call | If the winner's victory is marginal, the candidates can demand a recount (and, on occasion, more than one—until the returning officer decides the result is clear). In the event of a dead heat, the returning officer is required by law to settle victory by intervening more directly. He or she will normally do so by either by tossing a coin, or by asking the neck-and-neck candidates to write their names on slips of paper and drawing the winner out of a hat. |

official ballot paper as 'Liberal Democrat Top Choice for Parliament' (forcing Mr Oaten to have the words 'Liberal Democrat Leader Paddy Ashdown' written alongside his name). Mr Huggett stood again in the ensuing by-election—this time under the label 'Literal Democrat'—but the adverse publicity generated by his first campaign blunted his vote. The use of such deliberately confusing labels was subsequently banned by the Registration of Political Parties Act 1998, which established the **Electoral Commission**.

Disputes over close-run contests are far from the only thing that can cause headaches on election night. Occasionally, more serious administrative problems occur. Besides being the first election for 36 years to produce a hung Parliament, the May 2010 poll was notable for widespread controversy over the number of electors unable to cast their votes because of localized organizational hiccups. As early results were announced on the evening of 6 May, live reports about registered voters being denied the right to vote began flooding in from areas as disparate as Hackney, Liverpool, and Newcastle-upon-Tyne.

Some voters had spent hours queuing only to be locked out of polling stations at the last minute when the clocks struck 10 p.m. In Sheffield Hallam (Mr Clegg's constituency), the returning officer blamed a last-minute influx of students without polling cards for delays that resulted in a number of people being denied votes. A swift investigation by the Electoral Commission (see pp. 154–5) found that, in all, 1,200 voters were barred from voting, and for a variety of reasons. The Commission's initial recommendation was for a wholesale modernization of the voting process—which to date has relied largely on paper records, rather than computerized ones—to avert similar problems in future.

## Limits on election spending

Election spending is closely controlled by the Electoral Commission to stop any one candidate or party having a significant advantage over his or her/its competitors. Each candidate must appoint an election agent with an office in the constituency. The maximum sum candidates may spend campaigning in their seats is fixed by law. At time of writing, it was just under £7,150, plus 5p per voter in urban constituencies and 7p in rural ones. At a national level, however, parties may also spend £30,000 fielding each candidate.

In addition, so-called 'recognized third parties' may separately spend money campaigning in support of, or against, a candidate—up to £500 apiece. They are, however, permitted to spend considerably more in support of a party as a whole. **UNISON** is registered as a 'recognized third party' supporter of Labour. It is allowed to spend up to £793,000 on the party's behalf at a general election, or £30,000 in elections to devolved assemblies. Other organizations or individuals wishing to campaign on behalf of a political party as a whole (rather than an individual candidate)—but 'unregistered'—are legally limited to spending £10,000 in England, or £5,000 in the other UK countries.

In **referenda**, meanwhile, 'permitted participants'—those registered to campaign for a 'yes' or 'no' vote—may spend up to £500,000 on a UK-wide poll, but only £10,000 may be spent by anyone *not* so permitted. The Commission may 'designate' specific permitted participants to campaign for a 'yes' or 'no' vote to ensure order. Such bodies may claim up to £600,000 to finance their campaigns and spend up to £5m.

# ▌ Before the event—how constituency boundaries are decided

There are currently 650 Commons constituencies in England, Wales, Scotland, and Northern Ireland. Until recently, however, there were 659 and from time to time the number rises or falls in line with population changes. Variations in population not only have an impact on the number of constituencies, however; they also influence the size and shape of individual constituencies in areas especially affected by those changes. In some cases, constituencies with falling populations might cease to exist or be merged with neighbouring ones, while large localized increases in population can lead to the introduction of additional seats or existing ones being split up.

Parliamentary electoral boundaries are reviewed on an 8–12-year cycle, to ensure that they keep pace with demographic fluctuations in the UK. The task of conducting these reviews until recently fell to four independent 'boundary commissions'—the **Boundary Commission for England**, and those for Scotland, Wales, and Northern Ireland.

Boundary changes are often controversial. The act of abolishing constituencies, creating new ones, subdividing them, and/or merging two or more can often have a significant impact on the ability of particular political parties to win seats at subsequent elections. Although the commissions are required to operate on a strictly non-partisan basis, successive governments have been accused of trying to influence their decisions, to ensure that any proposed changes are favourable to their own parties at election time. The most recent boundary review, completed under Labour, was, however, widely interpreted as a boost to the Tories, particularly given the eventual outcome of the May 2010 election. Completed by the English and Welsh Commissions in April 2007, with new boundaries for Assembly member (AM) constituencies in place for the National Assembly of Wales elections in May that year, it proved controversial in some parts of the north and in Labour heartlands, because all four new constituencies were in the south. As of the next boundary review (to be carried out between 2014 and 2018) responsibility for redrawing constituencies has been transferred to the Electoral Commission: a *quango* established by the Political Parties, Elections, and Referendums Act 2000 to provide comprehensive oversight of the election process in Britain. It is likely to be significantly more comprehensive than previous ones, in light of the Lib-Con coalition's decision to cut the number of constituencies (and MPs) by 50 and better equalize the size of their electorates (see p. 121).

The Commission's other responsibilities include:

- registering political parties (and preventing their names being used by others);
- ensuring that people understand and follow the rules on party and election finance;
- setting standards for running elections and reporting on how well this is done;
- ensuring that people understand they should register to vote, and know how to do so;

- making sure that candidates fund their election campaigns in a legal and transparent way.

In addition to overseeing election-related funding, the Commission is also responsible for policing party finance as a whole, by vetting how parties raise money and declare their donations (see pp. 154–5).

# How parties select their candidates

Just as different political parties have their own membership policies, so too do they have their own preferences about how to select the candidates they wish to field at general elections. The workings of Britain's main political parties, and the internal structures and procedures that distinguish one from the other, are the subject of Chapter 5, but it is worth looking here at significant trends and developments in candidate selection procedures.

## The Conservative Party

Historically, the Conservatives have favoured a centrally controlled selection procedure, which sees a list of 'approved candidates' compiled by **Conservative Campaign Headquarters**. This initially involves staff from the party's candidates' department sifting through CVs and letters from applicants, and inviting a selection of them to attend a 'candidates' weekend', at which they face aptitude tests to ascertain their suitability. A central list is then drawn up and distributed to local Conservative constituency associations, who advertise vacancies for prospective candidates in their areas as and when they arise (sitting MPs wishing to run again are normally automatically reselected, as in the other main parties). After a series of public meetings, at which three to five competing applicants have the chance to prove their mettle in debates with rivals, a vote on which individual should be adopted to fight the seat will be held among local party members.

While this process remains in place, Mr Cameron's tenure as party leader has already seen several significant moves towards even greater centralization. Perhaps the most controversial illustration of this was the drawing up of the so-called 'A list' of aspiring Tory MPs prior to the 2010 election, with included several minor celebrities, including 'chick lit' author Louise Bagshawe and and Zac Goldsmith, editor of the *Ecologist* magazine and son of late Tory defector Sir James Goldsmith, whose Referendum Party stood against Europhile Tory  MPs in the 1997 election. Both were subsequently elected. Another, equally contentious, development has been the introduction of 'open primaries' modelled on the US voting system. This unprecedented move gives everyone on the electoral register in a constituency a chance to vote on which prospective candidate should stand for the Conservative Party at the next election—irrespective of whether they are Tory members, or even supporters.

## The Labour Party

Labour's selection process has traditionally been more democratic than the Conservatives'. In recent years, however, it has become increasingly centralized and, given moves by the Tories to encourage greater public involvement in their internal party procedures, Labour can no longer so easily claim to be more transparent.

Up to 31 January 2001, constituency Labour parties (equivalent to the Tories' constituency associations) and affiliated organizations, such as trades unions, could each nominate up to two candidates from a list approved by local party leadership. The general council of the Constituency Labour Party (CLP) then drew up a shortlist, which was circulated to local party members who could vote by either postal ballot or at a 'hustings'—a public meeting involving a debate between the rival candidates, as described above.

On the pretext of speeding up this time-consuming process, Mr Blair introduced a streamlined version of it after 31 January 2001. To reduce the time taken up with initial vetting procedures, future lists of candidates would be centrally approved by the party's ruling National Executive Committee (NEC). Constituency Labour Parties needing a new candidate would be presented with this list and asked to vote for one of the approved names. Critics of Mr Blair saw this as a clear attempt to weed out left-wing candidates and impose a more Blairite agenda on the party's grass roots.

An earlier example of the centralizing tendency among recent Labour leaders was the party's adoption of all-women shortlists for parliamentary candidates in 1993. The positive discrimination policy was brought in to increase the number of women MPs to reflect better the gender balance in the British population (51 per cent of which is female). In 1996 Labour's stand was judged unlawful, in a case brought under the Sex Discrimination Act 1975, but once in power Labour introduced the Sex Discrimination (Election Candidates) Act 2002, which guaranteed the legality of all-women shortlists until 2015. More recently, in the run-up to the May 2010 election, Mr Cameron became a convert to all-women shortlists. Nonetheless, the policy still has its critics—most notably some groups representing ethnic minorities, who argue that white women may get selected in some areas known for their racial diversity at the expense of strong potential candidates from minority communities.

## The Liberal Democrat Party

Although they often claim to be more democratic than their bigger Westminster rivals, the Liberal Democrats use a similarly centralized selection system. A list of approved names is drawn up centrally. Constituencies looking for new candidates must first advertise this fact in the *Liberal Democrat News*, the party's main publication, and individuals whose names are on that list may apply for vacancies. A selection committee will then interview them and a shortlist will be put before the local party membership.

# Quirks of the electoral system

Parliamentary candidates may stand, and even be elected, in more than one constituency. If returned in both, however, they must immediately decide which constituency they would like to represent and 'stand down' from the other. The seat forgone will pass to the second-choice candidate in that constituency. This follows rules set out in Erskine May (see p. 16) and laid down in House of Commons procedures.

Candidates may withdraw their nominations for election—provided that they do so in writing (with one witness attesting) by noon on the 16th day before polling day. This throws up the intriguing possibility that an individual might one day be elected to serve as an MP, despite having decided against standing at the last minute.

Since 1935 elections have generally been held on Thursdays. The precise historical reasons for this are obscure, but the day is thought to have been arrived at through a process of elimination. As the traditional Christian day of worship, Sundays are out, and weekends, as a whole, are seen to present too many leisure options to ensure voters will discipline themselves to vote. Mondays have the highest employee absence record of any working day—making it difficult to be sure of a solid turnout—while Tuesdays and Wednesdays are the main working days (providing few opportunities for people to escape the workplace to vote). As the traditional market day in many towns and cities, Thursday has traditionally been favoured. In addition, holding elections before a weekend is seen to have advantages if there is a change of government, as it allows the new administration to use Saturday and Sunday to prepare itself to start work in earnest the following week.

The British electoral system produces a clear divide between 'marginal constituencies' (or 'marginals') and 'safe seats'. In marginals—the key battlegrounds on election day—incumbent MPs have small majorities (in some cases, having won only a handful more votes than their nearest rivals at the previous election), so their seat is considered vulnerable and a key target for competing candidates. Candidates concentrate their energies on attracting the support of 'swing voters': individuals with no firm historical loyalty to one party or another. Safe seats, in contrast, are those in which sitting MPs have large majorities that (barring a huge upset) they are unlikely to lose. These tend to be located in party-political heartlands—for example, the north for Labour and the Home Counties for the Tories. Such seats would require huge 'swings' (switches of support from one candidate or party to another) if they were to change hands.

Other than local and European elections, one of the biggest litmus tests of British public opinion has traditionally been the by-election—a vote in a single constituency to replace a sitting MP who has either retired, been deselected, or died between general elections. Towards the end of Mrs Thatcher's time in the late 1980s and under Mr Major in the early 1990s, by-elections frequently produced bruising results for the Tories, reflecting their growing unpopularity in the country at large. By 2008 it was Labour's turn to suffer in by-elections and, over a three-month period before the summer recess, the party sustained a series of humiliating defeats, including two in previously safe seats: the Crewe and Nantwich constituency of veteran *backbencher* Gwyneth Dunwoody, whose 7,000–strong majority was overturned by the Conservatives, in their first by-election victory over Labour for thirty years, and Glasgow East, a dyed-in-the-wool Labour seat on Mr Brown's doorstep, where the Scottish Nationalists achieved a 22.5 per cent swing to snatch the seat (although Labour regained it at the 2010 election). The most peculiar by-election of modern times, however, was held the same summer in Haltemprice and Howden, the constituency of former Tory Home Affairs spokesman David Davis. In an unprecedented move, Mr Davis resigned his safe seat to contest a symbolic contest over his opposition to the government's then recently passed Bill to give police powers to detain terrorist suspects for up to 42 days (see p. 246). Neither Labour nor the Lib Dems contested the seat—each arguing his move was a vanity exercise—but he was faced by a record 26 minority candidates. Of these, 23 lost their deposits and Mr Davis was duly re-elected with 72 per cent of the vote.

# ▶ Proportional representation (PR) and other voting systems

Such are the inequities of the British electoral system that pro-democracy campaigners have long argued for its replacement by one the outcome of which more accurately reflects the distribution of votes between rival candidates or parties. Pressure groups like the Electoral Reform Society and Charter 88 (recently incorporated into Unlock Democracy) advocate *proportional representation (PR)*—an umbrella term referring to a variety of alternative models they judge to be fairer. Such a switch has, for many years, been official policy for the Lib Dems, who have long suffered more than any other party under the FPTP system, due to the wide dispersal of their vote across the country.

It has long been observed that, given Labour and Tories' vested interest in keeping the old system in place, the Lib Dems would need to get into power to be able to introduce it—but that without it this is unlikely to ever happen. However, the eventual outcome of the May 2010 election—which saw Mr Clegg and several of his Lib Dem colleagues take their seats at Mr Cameron's Cabinet table—meant that, at time of writing, Britain was closer to the prospect of electoral reform than at any point in its recent history. As one of the principal bargaining chips used to secure the Lib Dems' support, Mr Cameron agreed to hold a referendum on whether to adopt the *alternative vote (AV)* system used in Australia (a proposal to which Labour also committed itself in its manifesto). Briefly, AV requires electors in each constituency to mark candidates in order of preference. If one wins an immediate absolute majority, he or she is elected; if not, the name of the lowest-placed candidate is struck off the ballot paper and his or her second preferences distributed among the remaining contenders. This process continues until one candidate finally has a majority. The referendum was scheduled to be held on 5 May 2011.

Although the adoption of AV would stop significantly short of the Lib Dems' desired option, the single transferable vote (STV) (see Table 4.5, where it is explained alongside other PR systems), the proposed referendum marks the belated revival of a review of the electoral system that originally began in December 1997. Unsure that it would win a working majority in the May 1997 election, Labour committed itself to re-examining FPTP, and duly did so with the appointment of an Independent Commission on the Voting System under the chairmanship of the late Lord Jenkins of Hillhead, a Lib Dem peer and former Labour Chancellor. He reported in 1998, advocating either a hybrid system modelled on that to be used in Scotland and Wales (see below and p. 82) or a new system called 'alternative vote plus' (AV+).

Alternative vote + would have involved a reduction in the number of constituencies, but with the number of MPs remaining the same as at present. Between 80 and 85 per cent of MPs would have continued to be elected on a constituency basis, with the rest voted in via a 'top-up process'. This would work 'correctively'—on the basis of electors' second votes— to better reflect the electorate's overall preferences. Although Lord Jenkins never lived to see his advice acted upon, it is worth noting that in the aftermath of the May 2010 election a number of senior Labour politicians, including outgoing Home Secretary Alan Johnson and Welsh Secretary Peter Hain, indicated their enthusiasm for a more radical form of PR than AV, perhaps modelled on AV+.

Key arguments used by advocates and opponents of the introduction of PR in the UK are outlined in Table 4.6.

# ▌ Elections under devolution

The devolved parliaments in Scotland, Wales, and Northern Ireland are elected on a set timetable every four years—an electoral cycle bearing more resemblance to those of local authorities than the Commons. But this is not the only difference from Westminster: more significantly, the voting systems used to elect members of the Scottish Parliament (MSPs), Assembly members (AMs),

**Table 4.5** Different types of proportional representation (PR) and how they work

| Name | How it works | Where used |
|---|---|---|
| The single transferable vote (STV) | System favoured by the Liberal Democrats. STV states have multi-member constituencies—making it more likely that voters will end up with at least one local representative from a party they support. Electors mark each candidate in order of preference and, once one has achieved a predetermined quota (e.g. one-fifth of all votes cast if there are five seats available), he or she is elected. The second choices listed on all 'surplus' papers naming that candidate as 'first choice' will be treated as first choices and distributed accordingly among the remaining candidates. The means by which some ballot papers are designated 'surplus' varies: in some countries 'surplus' papers are selected randomly from all those with initial winning candidate as first choice, while elsewhere papers are accorded primacy on 'first come, first served' basis (those submitted later become 'surplus'). The process of reallocating second choices, third choices, etc., as 'first choices' continues until the required number of candidates are elected. | The Irish Dáil; Scottish local authorities; the Northern Ireland Assembly; local and European elections in Northern Ireland |
| Party list systems | Seats allocated to parties in direct proportion to number of votes they receive. Candidates chosen by voters from lists supplied by their parties—meaning they can theoretically opt for someone with a local connection to area, even if the 'constituency link' preserved by UK elections is more remote. In an *open*-list system, they can vote for both a party and an individual: parties supply lists of candidates; electors choose the ones they want; the party then allocates the seats it wins to named candidates, according to those expressed preferences. In *closed*-list systems, parties have already decided which candidates they wish to take seats in parliament, if they win enough votes. Britain, like all other EU member states already uses the party list system as its means of electing **members of the European Parliament (MEPs)**. In the 2004 European Parliament elections, UK Independence Party used a closed-list system to cherry-pick candidates it wanted to represent it as MEPs—ensuring that former BBC talk show presenter and ex-Labour MP Robert Kilroy-Silk was elected. | European elections in most member states; regional and national parliamentary elections in European states, including Sweden and the Netherlands; Israel's Knesset |

| Name | How it works | Where used |
|------|-------------|-----------|
| Alternative vote (AV) | Similar to STV, except only one MP elected per constituency—meaning the extent to which election's outcome please most voters is more limited. AV is, however, widely seen as producing more accurate reflections of voters' preferences than FPTP. If, after votes are counted, one candidate has a simple majority—more than half the votes cast—he or she is immediately elected. Otherwise the candidate with least 'first choice' votes is struck out and 'second choices' on all papers putting them top are redistributed among others as if first choices. This process continues until one candidate has more than half votes cast. | Australia's House of Representatives |
| The supplementary vote (SV) | Modified version of AV. If no candidate initially obtains absolute majority—support of more than half of eligible voters—all but the top two are eliminated and their 'second choices' are reallocated to produce a winner. | English mayoral elections, including that for London mayor |
| The additional member system (AMS) | A hybrid of different systems, this sees some candidates elected in single-member constituencies (normally using FPTP) and second—'additional'—votes used to top up from regional lists, introducing a measure of 'proportionality' between votes and parties. As with party list system, lists can be either open or closed. | Elections for the Scottish Parliament, Welsh Assembly, and London Assembly; parliaments in Germany, Italy, Mexico, New Zealand, and Venezuela |

Table 4.6 Pros and cons of PR

| For | Against |
|-----|---------|
| Governments elected under FPTP are often parties that win a majority of seats despite only securing a minority of votes cast. | PR produces more coalition governments. These can be less decisive and coordinated in policymaking. Extremist parties (e.g. the National Front in France) can sometimes hold balance of power because their support is vital to enable mainstream ones to form governments. |
| Many votes wasted because numerous electors are denied representation by MPs of same or a similar persuasion. PR produces overall results that are fairer reflections of distribution of votes cast. | PR means voters are less able to hold a particular government responsible for its actions by decisively voting it out. |
| Changes in government between left and right can bring abrupt changes of policy and direction—leading to a lack of long-term continuity. | Some PR systems break the constituency link between individual voters and MPs—a cornerstone of Britain's democracy. |
| FPTP denies voice in Parliament to minority parties that have significant support in the country but no elected MPs. | PR can lead to frequent elections and big policy compromises, because many coalitions are unstable. Sometimes leadership and firmer action are needed. |

and members of the Legislative Assembly in Northern Ireland (MLAs) use elements of PR.

In Northern Ireland, the single transferable vote (STV) is now used, in line with the system used in Southern Ireland since 1919. Both Scotland and Wales have adopted the 'additional member' system (see p. 133 ).

# ▶ The future of voting

Since 2001, electoral turnout has been consistently lower than at any other time since the Second World War, although it rose by nearly 4 per cent in 2010—from 61.3 to 65.1 per cent—in the midst of a period of political and economic upheaval following the *recession* and the MPs' expenses scandal. This has prompted an ongoing debate about the perceived disengagement of voters—whether due to the increasingly indistinguishable nature of many Labour and Conservative policies, or the perception that politicians say one thing in their manifestos and do another once elected.

Although there remains a wide spectrum of different views on the merits and pitfalls of FPTP, there is a growing cross-party consensus that more needs to be done to encourage people to vote. One approach to this quandary—in recognition of the increasingly hectic lifestyles led by many British adults—is to make voting *easier*. The Representation of the People Act 2000 authorized various pilot schemes to see which worked best, including:

- electronic voting—via email, text messaging, the Internet;
- global postal voting;
- voting spread over a number of days;
- voting on Saturdays;
- taking polling stations to the voter—for example, to supermarkets, GP surgeries, etc.

Although Labour was a big advocate of postal voting, presiding over a 60 per cent rise in the take-up of this method in some areas in 2010, there have been huge controversies over its vulnerability to fraud. In multi-occupancy households, one resident could theoretically vote multiple times by completing and sending off his or her housemates' forms. Indeed, elections for Birmingham City Council in 2004 exposed systematic corruption after a number of Labour Party workers were implicated in fraudulently submitting forms in support of it.

## ⊞ Topical feature idea

The Lib-Con coalition government is due to hold a referendum on the alternative vote (AV) on 5 May 2011. If adopted, the new system would probably lead to a fairer distribution of Commons seats between parties at future general elections. The coalition also proposes reducing the number of MPs by around 10 per cent to cut the costs of Parliament to the public purse, while equalizing the size of constituencies. How would either or both of these proposed changes affect the likely outcome of elections in your area? Would the number of local MPs rise or fall, and which parties would be likely to be the biggest winners and losers?

## ✳ Current issues

- **Electoral reform:** in the horse-trading between Mr Clegg and Mr Cameron's Conservatives that led to the formation of the Lib-Con coalition, the Tories eventually made the 'final offer' of a referendum on the alternative vote (AV)—a system used in Australia that Labour had already pledged to explore in its manifesto. It remains to be seen how actively Tory MPs will be permitted to campaign for a 'no' vote in the referendum, due to be held in May 2011, and whether the Lib Dem grass roots will continue to support its leadership remaining in the coalition if AV is rejected.

- **Fixed-term parliaments:** the Lib-Con coalition is introducing fixed-term parliaments in the mould of France, the USA, and other countries—ending the age-old constitutional convention allowing sitting prime ministers to 'quit while they're ahead' by dissolving Parliament mid-term. Elections will be held every five years, rather than four (as in the USA), and to bring down a sitting government in between would require either a no confidence vote or a motion with the backing of two-thirds of MPs.

- **Open primaries:** the Conservatives have become the first UK political party to experiment with the idea of US-style *open primary* selection process for its parliamentary hopefuls (that is, allowing electors living in a given constituency, regardless of their past political affiliations, to vote on which prospective Tory candidates they would like to stand for election to the Commons). Will others follow?

## ? Review questions

1. What are the arguments for lowering the voting age in the UK to 16?
2. Given the imbalance between votes cast and seats won under the first-past-the-post (FPTP) system, what are the arguments for and against proportional representation (PR)? Give an explanation of two or more different types of PR.

3.  What are the qualifications for electors and candidates in UK parliamentary elections, and how can people be barred from standing for the Commons?

4.  How are constituency boundaries determined, how many constituencies are there at present, and what role does the Electoral Commission play at general elections?

5.  How is the government trying to increase turnout at general elections and can you think of any additional or alternative ways of improving voter engagement?

## → Further reading

Crewe, I. (ed.) (1998) *Why Labour Won the General Election of 1997*, London: Frank Cass. **Illuminating critique of techniques of media management and triangulation used by 'New Labour' to improve its standing with middle classes.**

Denver, D. (2006) *Elections and Voters in Britain*, 2nd edn, London: Palgrave Macmillan. **Second edition of authoritative text focusing on UK voting patterns. Includes data from British Electoral Study (BES) surveys.**

Gallagher, M. and Mitchell, P. (2008) *The Politics of Electoral Systems*, Oxford: Oxford University Press. **Comprehensive examination of different electoral systems used in 22 countries, including Britain, incorporating comparative data and examples.**

Johnston, R. and Pattie, C. (2006) *Putting Voters in Their Place: Geography and Elections in Great Britain*, Oxford: Oxford University Press. **Thoughtful examination of geographical differences in voting and turnout patterns in local, national, and European elections. Examines issues including the emergence of safe seats, and the role of marginal wards and constituencies in winning polls.**

##  Online Resource Centre

www.oxfordtextbooks.co.uk/orc/Morrison2e/
Visit the Online Resource Centre that accompanies this book for web links and regular updates.

# 5

# Political parties, party funding, and lobbying

The 'party system' has long been one of the cornerstones of Britain's brand of representative democracy. It derives from a series of nineteenth and early twentieth-century works of political science, most notably *American Commonwealth* (1885) by English scholar James Bryce and later writings—also focusing on the emergence of what was seen as a model democratic system in the USA—by Charles Merriam and William Nisbet Chambers. The notion of groups of like-minded individuals banding together to form 'parties' that would campaign collectively to win power might have been relatively new across the Atlantic, but in the UK the party was already a long-established institution, as was the country's own peculiar version of party politics—the 'two-party system'.

Britain's 'first past the post' (FPTP) electoral system has always favoured candidates representing the two or three main parties. Given the fact that British general elections produce a 'winner takes all' outcome at **constituency** level—with a single representative returned from each one—it has tended to be those candidates most closely identified with the (frequently polarized) concerns of each area who have been elected (historically, social reformers in the industrial north and conservatives in the wealthier south). The formation of a coherent nationwide government is only possible if a number of elected representatives agree to share power and ascribe particular responsibilities to individuals from among their number. For both these reasons, the emergence of a party system in Britain was logical, pragmatic, and arguably inevitable.

From the point at which Parliament wrested sovereignty from the monarch in 1689, up to the emergence of the Liberal Party nearly 200 years later, the two-party system revolved around two political groupings: the Whigs and the Tories. While the former are often crudely identified with the progressive tendencies later embodied by the nineteenth-century Liberals of William Gladstone and the latter with the modern-day Conservative Party (the term

'Tory' is still often used as shorthand for 'Conservative'), in truth the distinction between the two was more nebulous. Both were associated, to a greater or lesser degree, with the moneyed classes and aristocracy. What differences there were initially rested largely on Christian denominational grounds, with the Whigs identifying more with the non-Anglican believers ('dissenters' such as the evolving Presbyterian Church in Scotland) and the Tories with the Church of England 'establishment'.

By the late eighteenth century, however, clearer party lines had emerged, with the ascendancy of Charles James Fox and William Pitt the Younger as Whig leader and Tory prime minister respectively. Within a few short decades, the Whigs would be advocating the abolition of slavery, the introduction of overseas free trade, and wider voting rights.

Although the purpose of this book is to give journalists a clear understanding of the present-day political framework governing the UK, no explanation of the British party system would be complete without a brief summary of how today's main parties came about.

# The Conservative Party—a potted history

For much of the period from the 1950s to the 1990s, the Conservative and Unionist Party, to use its full title, was viewed as the 'natural party of government'. Of the 21 prime ministers who served in the twentieth century, 13 were Conservative, compared to three Liberals and five from Labour. The Tories were in power for 55 years, the Liberals for 17, Labour for 28.

Although William Pitt the Younger is widely regarded as the first 'Conservative' prime minister, he was really the last of a long line of political leaders whose affiliation was rooted in that looser, more general Tory persuasion spawned in the seventeenth century. It was only after his death, in 1812, that a cohesive Tory Party organization began to emerge, initially under Lord Liverpool (who, as prime minister for 15 years, remains the longest-serving premier to date). Not until a decade later, however, was the term 'Conservative' tentatively coined by his short-lived successor, George Canning.

The title 'Conservative Party' was officially adopted in 1834 by Sir Robert Peel, now widely credited as its true founder, who formalized it in a paper viewed as the blueprint for its later constitution, *The Tamworth Manifesto*. Ironically, he later all but destroyed the party, splitting it down the middle over his decision to repeal the 'corn laws'—tariffs protecting the profits of British agriculturalists, by artificially inflating the prices of imported foreign crops— to allay the suffering caused by the Irish potato famine of 1845–46. After being deposed as party leader, Peel formed his own faction in Parliament—the

'Peelites'—and was briefly courted by a coalition of Whigs and Radicals (later to form the Liberal Party) in 1849.

The late nineteenth century was notable for the emergence of two progressive political giants in the Conservative Party: Benjamin Disraeli, who served twice as prime minister between 1868 and 1880, and his successor, Lord Salisbury. Despite his imperialistic approach to foreign policy, Disraeli marked a break with tradition in the Tory ranks, extending the right to vote and embodying a more paternalistic attitude towards the poor. He even introduced a right to peaceful picketing in industrial disputes.

Disraeli's brand of moderate conservatism foreshadowed the 'One Nation Toryism' that would characterize post-war twentieth-century premiers such as Harold Macmillan and Sir Alec Douglas-Home. Only with the emergence of Thatcherism—and its adherents' derogatory labelling of their ilk as 'Wets'—did the party's pendulum swing decisively back to the right, adopting a more solidly free market approach to its handling of the economy and social welfare than ever before.

The last Conservative prime minister of the twentieth century was John Major, who served from 1990 to 1997. Today the party is still associated with certain core Tory values—privatization, low taxes, tough anti-crime measures, and a free market approach to the economy—but its latest leader, David Cameron, has also modernized its approach to issues traditionally associated with Labour, the Lib Dems, and even the Green Party. While in opposition he launched several policy reviews focusing on everything from renewable energy to the widening gap between rich and poor. The author of the latter report, former leader Iain Duncan Smith, coined the term 'broken society' to describe Labour's legacy after a decade in power, and Mr Cameron's 2010 election campaign centred around his pledge to promote a 'Big Society'. Yet if this  was intended as a rhetorical rebuff to Margaret Thatcher's oft-cited remark that there was 'no such thing as society', it was also founded, in part, on a repackaging of Thatcherite values like self-help, individual responsibility, and small government.

# ▶ The Labour Party—a potted history

Despite having long since supplanted the Liberal Party (today the Liberal Democrats) as the second of Britain's two main political parties, Labour is little more than a hundred years old. For much of the nineteenth century the Liberals were the 'progressive' party—advocating what would later become core Labour values, such as social reform, wider democracy, and a foreign policy founded on internationalism rather than imperialism. Only when the vote was finally extended to men on more modest incomes—ironically, a policy ushered in by both Disraeli's Tories and Gladstone's Liberals—did rumbling calls for a voice in Parliament for the working classes, to counter that of the middle and upper echelons who had so far dominated, become a clamour.

Unlike the Conservative Party, which emerged 'organically' from the ranks of the propertied classes over a period of decades, Labour was formed through the coordinated amalgamation of several organizations founded to safeguard the interests of ordinary working people, and united by a shared belief in democratic socialism. The first of these were the trades unions, which had evolved out of the aftermath of the Industrial Revolution to provide protection and representation for employees in the workplace. Having failed to persuade the Liberals to sponsor sufficient numbers of working-class candidates to stand in general elections in the later nineteenth century, the unions turned their attentions towards establishing their own party.

Around the turn of the century, several like-minded organizations began talking seriously about forming a new party: notably two early think tanks, the Fabian Society and the Marxist Social Democratic Federation, and a body of aspiring parliamentary candidates and their supporters calling itself the Independent Labour Party (ILP). In 1900, at a special conference convened by the Trade Union Congress (TUC) in Farringdon, London, they formed between them the Labour Representation Committee (LRC). With future Labour Prime Minister James Ramsay Macdonald as secretary, the LRC began sponsoring candidates to fight the coming election. In the event the so-called 'khaki election', which returned the Tories under Arthur Balfour that October following his perceived success in the Boer War, delivered the first two Labour MPs: Richard Bell for Derby and James Keir Hardie for Merthyr Tydfil, who was to become its first leader.

Although hardly meteoric, the party's progress in Parliament was steady from hereon in. The 1906 election ushered in 17 years of reforming Liberal government, but a combination of infighting and growing Labour momentum during its later years ensured that this marked the party's last term as a majority administration. Labour had gained 27 additional seats in 1906—thanks in part to a secret pact between Macdonald and Liberal Chief Whip Herbert Gladstone designed to stop Labour and Liberal candidates cancelling out each other's votes by contesting the same seats—but by 1910 it was up to 42. In 1924, aided by the Liberals' divisions, it won 191—enough to form its first government under Macdonald.

By now Labour was the second party. It secured its first decisive election victory in the wake of the Second World War, in 1945—a landslide win for Clement Attlee and a radical team of ministers who introduced the National Health Service (NHS) and free state education, and consolidated earlier moves towards establishing a welfare state to provide benefits for the unemployed, the low-paid, and the elderly. Three further periods of government followed:

under Harold Wilson (1966–70); Wilson and James Callaghan (1975–79); and Tony Blair and Gordon Brown (1997–2010).

# ▌ The Liberal Democrat Party—a potted history

Although technically the youngest of the three main parties, the Liberal Democrats—or 'Lib Dems'—are essentially the successors to the Liberal Party. The Liberals were a dominant force in British politics until a combination of the erosion of their grass-roots support by Labour and internal divisions caused by the bitter rivalry between the last Liberal Prime Minister, David Lloyd George, and his predecessor, Herbert Asquith, led to their sharp decline in the late 1920s.

Between the 1920s and 1980s the Liberals cemented their status as Britain's 'third party', with modest parliamentary gains that were never again sufficient to propel them to power in their own right, but at times gave them a toehold in government. In 1977, buffeted by rising **inflation** and wildcat union strikes, Callaghan kept himself in Number 10 by negotiating a Lib-Lab Pact with Liberal leader David Steel. The Liberals held the balance of power for a year, but the alliance soon broke up, and Labour were brought down on a Tory-instigated confidence vote in March 1979 (see p. 44).

In 1981, as Labour swung to the left following its election defeat, four of its senior moderates—former Chancellor Roy Jenkins, Foreign Secretary David Owen, Science Minister Shirley Williams, and Transport Secretary Bill Rodgers—quit to form the Social Democratic Party (SDP). By 1983 the so-called 'Gang of Four' had recruited enough supporters to form a credible new party, joining Steel's Liberals to form the SDP-Liberal Alliance. Such was the state of the UK economy in the early 1980s that the Tories began flatlining in opinion polls—with the Alliance initially reaping the benefit, due to infighting within Labour. At one point in 1982, it reached a poll rating of 50 per cent, with the Tories and Labour virtually neck and neck on around half that. But for the Falklands War, it is possible the next election would have produced a *hung Parliament*, with the Alliance the biggest 'party'. In the event, buoyed by victory in the South Atlantic, Mrs Thatcher increased her majority and the Alliance went on to perform modestly in both the 1983 and 1987 polls, before disbanding.

In 1988, more than two-thirds of existing Liberal and SDP members—and all of their serving MPs—regrouped to form a new party: the Liberal Democrats. Initially led jointly, like the Alliance, by Steel and Robert Maclennan (Mr Owen's successor as SDP leader), it soon elected Paddy Ashdown to replace them. He was succeeded by Charles Kennedy, Sir Menzies 'Ming' Campbell, and Nick Clegg.

# ▶ The structure and constitution of the modern Conservative Party

Many aspects of the internal organization of the Conservative Party remain the same today as a hundred years ago. It has, however, introduced significant changes since the 1990s, most notably democratizing its leadership elections.

As with any organization, the lifeblood of the party is its grass-roots membership. It is ordinary members who swell the party's coffers by paying annual subscriptions and raising funds; it is they who troop out, unpaid, on cold winter evenings to canvass in the run-up to elections—and who can usually be relied on to vote loyally come polling day. In return, it is incumbent on the party's leadership to give something back to members—policies they can support and a sense of involvement. This can come through everything, from participating in fund-raising events to attending the annual party conference. Like those of Labour and the Lib Dems, this is held at the end of the summer recess, traditionally in a large coastal town such as Brighton, Bournemouth, or Blackpool.

Notwithstanding Labour's close ties with the unions, traditionally the Conservatives have had the largest individual subscribing membership of any British party. Although recent years have seen a noticeable decline in party membership across the board, the Tories remain the biggest at grass-roots level, with around 250,000 members as of September 2010. Members are customarily connected to the national party through local constituency associations, which began springing up around the UK in the wake of the Reform Act 1832. Unlike in the Labour Party, in which membership activities have always been directed from the centre, these associations initially sprouted independently. They could, however, wield considerable clout: in affluent areas, associations would recruit candidates and finance their campaigns.

Despite being gradually incorporated into the overall party structure, constituency associations retained a large degree of notional independence until 1998, when then newly elected leader William Hague formalized their party status in an effort to discipline what he perceived as errant elements (some of whom he controversially labelled 'out of touch' and 'racist'), and kick-start a grass-roots Tory revival. To this end he introduced the party's first codified constitutional document, *Fresh Future*. This imposed new conditions on associations, but gave them significant new rights. Their position in the modern Tory Party's internal hierarchy—beneath its constitutional college and *Conservative Campaign Headquarters* (formerly 'Conservative Central Office')— is explained in Table 5.1, while the way in which the various components of the party's central organization fit together is shown in Table 5.2.

Although the Tories traditionally perform poorly in elections in Scotland and Wales—they secured only one Scottish MP in May 2010—unlike Labour they still contest some seats in Northern Ireland. This is a hangover from the party's

**Table 5.1** The internal structure of the modern Conservative Party

| Level | Party in the country | Party in Parliament |
|---|---|---|
| Top table | **Chairman of the Conservative Party** (head of Conservative Campaign Headquarters) and Conservative Party Board | Party leader |
| Middle tier | Constitutional college, incorporating National Conservative Convention (made up of MPs, **members of the European Parliament (MEPs)**, and other senior activists) | 1922 Backbench Committee |
| Grass roots | Constituency associations | Individual **backbenchers** |

**Table 5.2** Main components of central Conservative Party organization

| Body | Role and composition |
|---|---|
| Conservative Party Board | Ultimate decision-making body, comprising 18 members, including chairman of Conservative Party and deputy chairman. Tories' equivalent of National Executive Committee (NEC) of the Labour Party. |
| Conservative Campaign Headquarters | Main fund-raising, campaigning, and recruitment body, which coordinates its electioneering and marketing. Headed by Party Chairman. |
| Constitutional college | Body comprising representatives from all levels of party, including constituency associations and rank-and-file members, with say in questions of reform and long-term policy strategy. Incorporates National Conservative Convention—made up of MPs, MEPs, and senior party activists. |
| Constituency associations | Grass-roots member organizations, originally only loosely affiliated to the party, but now formally incorporated. Now permitted to play significant role in selecting prospective candidates for Parliament, *European Parliament*, and elections for devolved assemblies. |

strong historical ties to the province, as evidenced by its official 'Conservative and Unionist Party' title. In July 2008, Mr Cameron and the leader of the Ulster Unionists, Sir Reg Empey, published a joint letter in the *Daily Telegraph* pledging to revive their parties' historic electoral alliance, dating back to the 1880s, which had been severed some thirty years earlier due to infighting.

## How the Conservatives choose their leader

From the mid-1960s until 1998, Conservative leaders were always elected by their parliamentary colleagues—with no formal input from rank-and-file party members. Today only the first stage of this process is handled exclusively by MPs and peers. Once two frontrunners have emerged this way, their names are put forward to ordinary members around the country—on a 'one member, one vote' basis—and the final say rests with them.

While the introduction of this huge extension of party democracy signalled that then new, young Tory leader Hague (he was aged 36 at the time) was serious about modernizing his party, it was not long before his fellow MPs were ruing the day they voted for it. When Hague was defeated at the 2001 election he swiftly resigned, to be replaced by the little-known Mr Duncan Smith. Although widely perceived by both his colleagues in Parliament and political commentators as uncharismatic, he beat his more dynamic challengers, Kenneth Clarke and Michael Portillo, because of his solid support among grass-roots Tories. An ex-Army officer, devoted family man, and Euro-sceptic, he chimed far more than his rivals with typical Tory members—the average age of whom, despite Hague's reforms, was 64. In contrast, Clarke's Europhile views and Portillo's admission of a previous homosexual relationship did little to endear them.

Duncan Smith's later removal in a vote of no confidence instigated by a group of Tory MPs paved the way for a new leader before the following election, in former Home Secretary Michael Howard. Recognizing the need to ensure that the party elected leaders more in touch with the wider public in future, after losing the May 2005 election he tried to reverse Hague's reforms in his remaining months in office. That September Howard's proposals were defeated, however, after failing to win the required two-thirds majority among Tory MPs and activists in the party's 1,141-strong constitutional college.

## The 1922 Committee

Also known as the '1922 Backbench Committee', the **1922 Committee** comprises all Conservative MPs apart from the leader, and can therefore number in the hundreds. It has often been referred to as 'influential'—an understatement, given that it represents all elected Tory members and is therefore able to articulate the 'mood' of the parliamentary party like no other organization. Traditionally, leaders have ignored its views at their peril.

Far from being a 'talking shop', the Committee retains huge constitutional clout in the party. It is headed by an 18-member executive committee, the chairperson of which is often referred to as the party's 'shop steward', charged as he or she is with organizing elections for its leadership (even under the new rules). He or she also oversees votes of confidence. Such a vote can be triggered by a letter to the chairperson signed by 15 per cent of Tory MPs. The last time this happened was in 2003, when Mr Duncan Smith was deposed. The Committee also instigated the final twist of the knife that unseated Mrs Thatcher following Michael Heseltine's 1990 leadership challenge (see p. 95).

The Committee meets every week when Parliament is in session and is governed by curious conventions. For the first 88 years of its existence, frontbenchers were only permitted to attend its meetings when the party was in Opposition. Even then, the leader was barred—so his or her Shadow Cabinet colleagues would act as his or her intermediaries. When in government, neither leader nor **Cabinet** colleagues used to be able to attend, but barely a week after forming his May 2010 *coalition government* Mr Cameron surprised the committee by demanding an immediate vote on whether frontbenchers should be both admitted and granted full voting rights. Arguing that the Conservatives needed to be 'one party' in Parliament, he successfully orchestrated a secret ballot, and his rule change was passed by 168 votes to 118. He was later forced into a partial U-turn, agreeing to drop his call for frontbenchers to be allowed a vote in the committee. His initial move had provoked fierce reactions from stalwart backbenchers such as Euro-sceptic Bill Cash, who described it as 'a great tragedy' and warned that, when seen in conjunction with other constitutional changes Mr Cameron was proposing at the time (including the '55 per cent rule'—see p. 94), it smacked less of the 'new politics' about which he and Mr Clegg had evangelized than of an 'old politics' of shoring up their positions.

Although the 1922 Committee is by far the largest and most powerful sub-group of the Conservative Party, MPs and peers may choose to join several smaller such 'clubs', depending on where their views fall on the wide political spectrum embraced by the party. These associations of like-minded left or right-wingers—or members united over a particular issue, such as Europe—have traditionally been known as 'ginger groups', although in recent times many have morphed into semi-professional think tanks. Among the most active today are the Bow Group, which describes itself as Britain's 'oldest centre-right think tank', and the Thatcherite group Conservative Way Forward. In addition, the Conservative Party has a long tradition of support from upmarket gentlemen's clubs such as the Carlton Club.

# ◗ The structure and constitution of the modern Labour Party

Unlike the Conservative Party, which emerged in 'top-down' fashion from one of the two principal parliamentary factions that evolved in the late seventeenth and early eighteenth centuries, the Labour Party emerged in a 'bottom-up' way—as a membership-led movement formed through a coalition of establishment outsiders campaigning for greater parliamentary representation for the working classes. Its creation was also more *deliberate*, with several distinct groupings coalescing to establish it formally in 1900. As such, it has had a codified constitution since its inception.

In addition to its de facto union members, the Labour Party today is made up of some 177,000 subscribing individuals. For a brief period under Tony Blair its membership reached an all-time peak—at 400,000 overtaking that of the Conservative Party, many of whose older subscribers were, quite literally, dying off—but this later fell due to growing disenchantment with his leadership. Although it has had traditional strongholds in Scotland, Wales, and northern England, Labour does not organize in Northern Ireland. In that province its closest equivalent is the centre-left Social Democratic and Labour Party (SDLP).

The main constituent elements of the Labour Party today are as outlined in Table 5.3. Of its main leadership bodies, the most significant is the **National Executive Committee of the Labour Party (NEC)**. Its role in relation to two other organizations, the National Policy Forum (NPF) and the Labour Party Conference, is explained in Table 5.4.

## Clause 4 and the birth of 'New Labour'

The most significant internal victory for Mr Blair's leadership came not in his frequent run-ins with his own backbenchers after being elected prime minister but in his first year as leader, with the party still in opposition. At its 1995 Easter conference, bolstered by his rabble-rousing deputy, John Prescott (whose similarly tub-thumping speech had helped John Smith, his predecessor, to win the 'one member, one vote' debate—see Table 5.3), Mr Blair successfully passed a motion to reword one of the most sensitive and symbolic sentences in the Labour Party's constitution.

'Clause 4' had been written in the context of a pre-war British society in which ownership of the country's assets and wealth was concentrated in the hands of very few individuals, and the absence of any state provision meant 'public services' like free health care and education were largely reliant on charity. As a result, its wording bore the imprint of the Marxist ideology on which the party's original values were based—focusing on the need to take into public ownership the 'means of production' (industry and agriculture) and give workers a greater share in their fruits. The clause, penned by Marxist intellectual Sidney Webb in 1917 and formally adopted by the party a year later, vowed:

❛❛ To secure for the workers by hand or by brain the full fruits of their industry and the most equitable distribution thereof that may be possible upon the basis of the common ownership of the means of production, distribution and exchange, and the best obtainable system of popular administration and control of each industry or service. ❜❜

Basing his version on a pamphlet he had written for the Fabian Society, Mr Blair reworded it:

❛❛ The Labour Party is a democratic socialist party. It believes that by the strength of our common endeavour we achieve more than we achieve alone, so as to create for each of us the means to realise our true potential and for all of us a community in which power, wealth and opportunity are in the hands of the many, not the few, where the rights we enjoy reflect the duties we owe, and where we live together, freely, in a spirit of solidarity, tolerance and respect. ❜❜

**Table 5.3** Member organizations of the Labour Party

| Organization | Role and functions |
| --- | --- |
| Constituency Labour Parties (CLPs) | Equivalent to the Conservatives' constituency associations, these are the voice of ordinary party members and activists. Their influence has diminished in recent years, as party leadership has exerted greater control over their activities—in particular, the selection of parliamentary candidates. CLPs still technically have the final say over who represents their constituencies, but they must choose from a centrally vetted list of applicants. In addition, the party's central National Executive Committee (NEC) may overrule decisions of their selection panels, parachuting in favoured candidates over the heads of those chosen locally. |
| | CLPs are normally run by two committees: a general management committee (GC), and an executive committee (EC). The former are made up of delegates from branch Labour parties (smaller-scale ones in individual towns), local socialist societies, Co-operative Party branches, and unions. In addition, each CLP has several elected officers, including a chair, two vice-chairs, a secretary, a treasurer, a women's officer, a youth and student officer, and, increasingly, a black and ethnic minority officer. Each CLP elects representatives to national policymaking bodies, including the Labour Party Conference, and nominates candidates for election to its other two ruling bodies: the National Policy Forum and the NEC. |
| Affiliated trades unions | Certain trades unions are formally affiliated to the party—many 'sponsoring' individual constituencies. These include **UNISON**—representing local authority and healthcare workers—and Unite (formed in 2006 from the amalgamation of technical union Amicus and the Transport and General Workers' Union (T&G)). Among those that have disaffiliated in recent years, in protest at Labour's policies in government, are the Rail and Maritime Union (RMT) and the Fire Brigades Union. If an employee is a member of an affiliated union, he or she automatically becomes a de facto Labour member, although he or she may opt out of the party. |
| | Affiliated unions wield considerable influence on party decision-making, selecting 12 of the 32 members of the NEC and electing half of the delegates to the party conference. In voting at the conference, however, their wings have been clipped in recent years. Until the early 1990s, despite significant reforms introduced in the 1980s under Neil Kinnock, unions still wielded a 'block vote' at party conferences—allowing them to deliver votes for or against particular policy proposals en masse on behalf of their memberships, regardless of individual members' views. This led to numerous run-ins between a leadership intent on pursuing more modest social and economic goals through its policies, in an effort to appear more 'voter-friendly' in future elections, and unions determined to stick to a more socialist agenda. In 1993, Kinnock's successor, John Smith, abolished the block vote, in favour of 'one member, one vote'. |
| Socialist societies | An umbrella term referring to various smaller associations instrumental in the party's foundation. Like unions, they pay an affiliation fee to the party and may elect one delegate between them to sit on its ruling NEC. The most famous socialist society is the Fabian Society, the early members of which included George Bernard Shaw, H. G. Wells, and Emmeline Pankhurst, one of the founders of the British suffragette movement. Other societies include the Christian Socialist Movement and the Society of Labour Lawyers. |
| The Co-operative Party | A small socialist party formed in 1881 through the establishment of a joint parliamentary committee to act as a watchdog on activities at Westminster from the viewpoint of under-represented working people, this has a long-standing arrangement with Labour not to contest the same seats separately at elections. Instead, it often fields joint candidates with Labour under the banner 'Labour and Co-operative Party'. |

**Table 5.4** Main constitutional bodies of the Labour Party

| Body | Role and composition | Notes |
|---|---|---|
| National Executive Committee of the Labour Party (NEC) | Often described as its 'ruling' body, the National Executive Committee of the Labour Party (NEC) is meant to represent all wings at a national policymaking level, taking delegates from all affiliated groupings (see Table 5.2). It has traditionally acted as a counterweight to the party leadership, although its influence declined under Mr Blair, who formed the National Policy Forum. As of September 2010, the NEC had 31 members—not counting its two *ex officio* ones: the party leader and deputy leader. These included former *EastEnders* actor and MEP Michael Cashman, and stalwart backbencher Dennis Skinner. The NEC also enforces party discipline. In 2003, it considered the case of George Galloway, former Labour MP for Glasgow Kelvin, who was accused of bringing the party into disrepute in a series of speeches criticizing Mr Blair's actions in Iraq. Labour's constitutional committee (made up largely of NEC members) expelled him in what Galloway described as 'a kangaroo court'. | Mr Blair's neutering of the NEC was partly a response to the frequent run-ins his predecessors had in the 1980s and early 1990s over proposed policy changes, such as the party's abandonment of its commitment to scrap Britain's nuclear weapons after the 1987 election, and with the repeated election to its membership of vocal critics of the leadership, such as veteran left-wingers Tony Benn and Ken Livingstone. |
| National Policy Forum (NPF) | Set up by Mr Blair in 1997, under his 'Partnership in Power' initiative, this draws 184 members, from all levels of the party. It meets over two or three weekends a year to examine in detail proposal documents generated by six policy commissions, the members of which include representatives of the leadership, NEC, and NPF. Its recommendations are passed to the Labour Party Conference for ratification. | Introduced officially as a means of widening party democracy in Labour's ranks, but often perceived as the leadership's instrument for quelling dissent. |
| Labour Party Conference | Unlike the Conservative and Lib Dem conferences, the Labour Conference has traditionally been viewed as less of an event and more as the party's supreme decision-making body. Presiding over the Conference is one of the Labour Party's most senior officers: its general secretary. | Theoretically, the Conference still has the final say on major policy and constitutional changes. In practice, since 1997 the party's leadership has made clear its willingness to overrule Conference decisions. Mr Blair also reduced the weight of the vote by affiliated organizations at conference from 80 to 50 per cent (four-fifths of which are still wielded by union members). |

The rewriting of Clause 4 was a defining moment in the creation of the 'New Labour' brand—a project initiated years earlier under Neil Kinnock, who had softened the party's image by replacing its Soviet-style, Red Flag-inspired logo (and conference anthem) with the now familiar red rose motif. Under Mr Blair, this process was accelerated, as the party embraced more mainstream policies, the language and aspirations of business, and an affinity with media management—or 'spin'—designed to improve its public image after years in the political wilderness (see pp. 208–9). Soon terms such as 'third way', 'big tent politics', and 'triangulation' had entered the political vernacular to explain the tactics used by Mr Blair and his apparatchiks to neutralize their opponents, by bringing together people from a variety of shades of 'liberal' opinion in a new coalition against what he would describe in a later conference speech as 'the forces of conservatism'.

## How Labour chooses its leader

Labour's leadership election procedure has trodden a long, slow road towards democratization over recent decades—beginning the process well in advance of more recent Tory moves to involve ordinary party members. From 1922 to 1981 leaders were elected solely by the party's MPs. Annual contests were held at the party conference, but in practice leaders were normally re-elected unopposed, so these were mere formalities.

In 1981, although it was to be some years before wholesale reform of the party's constitution, Labour established an electoral college: in future, only 30 per cent of votes in leadership elections would be cast by Labour MPs, with another 30 per cent going to Constituency Labour Parties (CLPs) and 40 per cent to the unions. Further reform followed in 1993, when the union block vote was scrapped and the weighting equalized to give each grouping a one-third share of the vote. There remain some inequities, however: individuals who are members of two or more affiliated organizations— for example, a union and a CLP—may vote more than once. Other anomalies abound: although Labour balked at introducing *proportional representation (PR)* for parliamentary elections while in office (see pp. 130–1), it uses the single transferable vote (STV) for its leadership elections.

## The Parliamentary Labour Party (PLP)

Like the Conservative Party, Labour has a body that represents the views of rank-and-file MPs—known as the *Parliamentary Labour Party (PLP)*. It, too, meets in a room in the Palace of Westminster on a weekly basis and it, too, has a chairperson elected from among its number annually, normally at the start of the parliamentary session.

Between 1921 and 1970 the chair of the PLP was the party leader. But since 1970, the two posts have been permanently split and the PLP has become (like the 1922 Committee) largely a means for backbenchers to hold their leaders to account. Unlike the 1922 Committee, however, leaders have always been able to attend the PLP, even when in government. In his last months in office, Mr Blair endured hostile receptions from the PLP on several occasions (although he received a standing ovation at the meeting following his resignation). Like the 1922 Committee, the PLP can instigate a vote of no confidence in its leadership, but in practice Labour has refrained from dumping unpopular leaders, who have generally jumped before being pushed despite murmurings of rebellion.

As well as the PLP, Labour has within it a number of ginger groups and is associated with various think tanks. One of the most historic, the left-leaning Tribune Group, was revived in 2005 by backbencher Clive Efford as a direct challenge to the leadership's perceived move to the right. More Blairite examples have included the Institute of Public Policy Research (IPPR), although this publicly distanced itself from Labour in 2009.

# ▌ The structure and constitution of the Liberal Democrat Party

As the 'youngest' of Britain's major political parties, the Liberal Democrat Party also has the newest constitution. Unlike either Labour or Conservatives, the party has a *federal* organization, comprising separate but conjoined parties for England, Scotland, and Wales. It currently has 64,000 paying members, and like Labour encompasses several affiliated groupings, known as 'specified associated organizations' (SAOs). These each represent particular sections of the membership, such as women, ethnic minorities, lesbian, gay, bisexual, and transgender (LGBT) members, trades unionists, and youths and students.

Like Labour and the Tories, the Lib Dems have a parliamentary party to act as a voice for ordinary MPs: in fact, they have three, in recognition of their federal structure. The party also organizes in Northern Ireland, but, rather than contesting elections under its own banner, has a semi-official arrangement to support the Alliance Party of Northern Ireland.

## How Liberal Democrats choose their leader

Of the three main Westminster political parties, the Lib Dems have the most obviously democratic process for electing their leaders. Once a leadership election is called, every paid-up member of the party—from Commons frontbenchers down to local activists—has an equal say in the outcome. The various means by which an election may be triggered, however, range from grassroots-led (receipt by the party's president of a requisition from at least 75 per cent of local parties) to decidedly 'top-down' (a vote of no confidence passed by a majority of Lib Dem MPs).

In recent years the Lib Dems have been more than willing to depose leaders with whom they become dissatisfied. Despite leading his troops to their biggest tally of Commons seats to date under the Lib Dem banner in 2005 (62), Mr Kennedy was persuaded to resign in January 2007 following his public admission of a drink problem. The weeks beforehand had seen several of his parliamentary colleagues call for his resignation, and a poll of his MPs for BBC2's *Newsnight* suggested that only 17 were willing to give him their unqualified backing. Less than two years later, Kennedy's successor, Campbell, also quit, after senior colleagues, including his deputy, Vince Cable, made it clear to journalists there were concerns among the party hierarchy about his lacklustre performance in the media and during Prime Minister's Questions.

## The Lib Dem Ideology—left, right, or in-between?

The question of where the Lib Dems fall on the left–right political spectrum has long been debatable. Traditionally, like the Liberals before them, they have been seen as centrists—pro-welfare state on the one hand, but in favour of the free market (subject to effective regulation) on the other. It is this that has arguably been their great electoral asset—enabling them to appeal to Labour voters in Tory-held marginals and Conservatives in Labour ones. In recent years, however, the Lib Dems have often appeared more conventionally left-wing in their policy ideas than Labour—thanks in part to Labour's rhetorical embrace of many Thatcherite economic reforms, the encroachment of market forces into public services, and its increasingly interventionist foreign policy. For many years, the Lib Dems advocated a 50 per cent higher rate of Income Tax (something Labour abandoned for some time until its introduction in April 2010 of a new 'top rate' pegged at that level for people earning £150,000 a year or more). The Lib Dems still support a local income tax to replace the *Council Tax*, arguing it would take more account of individuals' ability to pay.

Under Nick Clegg and his recent predecessors, the party has reasserted many centre-left tendencies, but there have also been signs of the return of a more free market approach—including a commitment (first floated by Mr Campbell) to reduce the Income Tax burden on middle-income families. In 2004, Mr Clegg, along with several fellow leading lights, including Mr Cable, co-authored the *Orange Book*, a collection of essays advocating more free market policies, greater private sector involvement in public services, and a return to a more Gladstonian, nineteenth-century vision of Liberalism. The resurgence of this 'laissez-faire' philosophy appeared to be confirmed when, after the May 2010 election returned no majority government for a single party, Mr Clegg allied himself with Mr Cameron's Conservatives rather than join a 'coalition of the defeated' with Mr Brown. It was not long before many left-leaning Lib Dem supporters and activists began openly voicing concern about the long-term implications for the party's independence.

Barely a week after the formal coalition agreement was signed, ex-leader Mr Kennedy—one of a long line of Liberal leaders who had nurtured the idea of an eventual 'realignment of the centre-left', perhaps bringing the Lib Dems and Labour together— became the firsts 'big shot' to out himself as having opposed it (he had abstained when the parliamentary party voted to endorse it). In an  article for *The Guardian* on 15 May, he expressed alarm at Mr Cameron's use of the term 'Liberal Conservative' to describe the new government in his first Downing Street press conference, and warned of the danger that the Tories might try to absorb the Lib Dems in time. This had happened to sections of the party on two previous occasions—first, when Joseph Chamberlain split it over home rule for Ireland in 1886 (ending up a Liberal Unionist), and second, when a decision by Lloyd George to continue in coalition government with the Conservatives after the end of the First World War sparked a prolonged period of factional infighting resulting in the formation of various splinter groups and the Liberals' ultimate relegation to 'third-party' status.

As well as possessing the tools to remove their leader, the Lib Dem rank and file have access to an unusual constitutional mechanism enabling them to prevent their leadership from steering them in political directions with which they are uncomfortable. The 'triple lock' was originally agreed by the party's conference in 1998 amid growing concern among some of its members about the increasingly close relations between then Lib Dem leader Ashdown and the Labour government. It is designed to come into effect whenever the Lib Dem leadership makes a 'substantial proposal that could affect the party's independence of political action'—for example, announcing its intention to join a coalition government. To secure such a deal leaders are required to first win the support of at least three-quarters of members of both the parliamentary party and the Lib Dems' Federal Executive (an elected committee of 35 senior activists, MPs, and party officials). If no such backing can be obtained, a special conference must be convened to decide the matter, mirroring the composition and voting rights of a standard annual gathering of the party. The triple lock was invoked for the first time on 12 May 2010, to approve the Lib Dems' entry into the coalition.

# ▌ The deselection process

Once a parliamentary candidate has been selected by his or her constituency party or association and elected to Parliament, he or she will usually serve until voted out at another election, or until he or she retires. Under certain circumstances, however, it is possible for a candidate to be 'deselected'—or sacked—by either his or her local party or that party's leadership. The process by which this can happen varies from party to party, but, in general terms, follows much the same pattern.

The most recent formal deselection was that of Jane Moffat, Labour MP for East Lothian, who was removed by her local party in March 2010 for allegedly failing to work hard enough for her constituents. In exceptional circumstances, MPs can be 'sacked' in other ways: former Immigration Minister Phil Woolas was barred from standing again for Labour after a specially convened election court stripped him of his Oldham East and Saddleworth seat for lying about his Lib Dem rival during the 2010 election campaign.

Notable examples of MPs who have avoided deselection included several Conservatives who defected to other parties in the last years of Mr Major's government. Emma Nicholson, MP for Torridge and West Devon, switched to the Lib Dems in 1995, but continued serving her constituency (despite quitting her local Tory Party) until the 1997 election. Fellow Tories Alan Howarth and Shaun Woodward both jumped ship to Labour, but retained their seats after the election and went on to serve as ministers.

Between general elections, deselection of MPs normally leads to a by-election—an election in his or her constituency alone—giving his or her local party a chance to field a replacement candidate and retain the seat, and its opponents an opportunity to win.

# ▌ Party funding now and in future

One endlessly debated issue surrounding the party system is that of funding. Because political parties are intrinsic to British parliamentary democracy, there has long been a vocal lobby calling for them to be financed, at least in part, by the state. At present, only Opposition parties receive any state subsidies in Britain—a privilege designed to counteract the advantage governing parties have because of the resources that can be marshalled by their sitting MPs. Introducing wholesale state funding of parties would signal a major change. But the idea of using taxpayers' money to fund the activities of political organizations the beliefs of which many of them are unlikely to share could be deeply problematic. Given the scale of Britain's current Budget deficit, without significantly increasing the tax burden, where would 'the state' find the extra cash needed to fund parties? And, if state funding were to become an entitlement for registered political parties, would it only be the larger and/or more mainstream ones that benefited—or could taxpayers expect some of their money to go to minority extremist parties like the British National Party (BNP)?

For these and other reasons, successive governments have sidestepped the question of state funding. But in the absence of such grants, how do parties fund their campaigns? Because membership subscriptions provide only a modest, if regular, source of revenue, parties have come to rely increasingly on bequests, loans, and donations from wealthy supporters. Naturally, this has given rise to charges of inequity—if one party attracts higher donations than another, it can mount a bigger campaign—and suspicions that rich donors are using their money to buy levels of influence denied to ordinary supporters.

The 1990s witnessed various controversies over party finance. During the Major years, there was growing unease about the Conservatives' use of anonymous multimillionaire donors and money originating in offshore tax havens—particularly the so-called 'Ashcroft millions' funnelled away by the party's ex-patriot treasurer, Lord Ashcroft. Labour promised to deal with these issues by limiting the ability of 'non-domiciles'—individuals living and/or working in Britain but registered for tax purposes in another country (see p. 200)—to finance parties, and making the source of their donations transparent. But within months of its election Mr Blair was embroiled in his own controversy  when Formula One boss Sir Bernie Ecclestone was identified as the source of a £1m donation to his campaign. The fact that Formula One had just been granted a temporary exemption from an impending ban on tobacco sponsorship fuelled suspicions he had used his money to buy influence.

To wrest back the moral high ground, the party subsequently returned the donation and began reforming the rules governing party funding in two ways: by introducing a statutory register of all significant donations, and by creating new criminal offences relating to false and late declarations. But 11 years after he thought he had laid it to rest, the Ecclestone affair returned to haunt Mr Blair in October 2008, when then Commons *Speaker* Michael Martin announced he would be investigating claims the former prime minister had deliberately  misled Parliament at the time of the original controversy. Newly released papers suggested that, contrary to Mr Blair's protestations that he was a 'pretty straight kind of guy', within hours of holding a meeting with Ecclestone he had begun frantically looking for ways of exempting Formula One from the sponsorship ban. Because Mr Blair had ceased to be an MP more than a year earlier, however, it was far from clear what sanctions, if any, would be able to be imposed even if he were to be found 'guilty'.

Under the Political Parties, Elections, and Referendums Act 2000, registration of donations now rests with the *Electoral Commission*, which, in addition to overseeing election procedures, has the responsibilities laid out in Table 5.5.

Thirteen years after the 1997 election, the Ashcroft saga resurfaced in the run-up to the May 2010 poll. This time Mr Brown's former *spin doctor*, Charlie Whelan (by now political director of the Unite union), mounted an aggressive  counter-attack in the marginal constituencies the peer was said to be targeting. Lord Ashcroft, whom it emerged was still a non-dom despite having given undertakings to then Tory leader Mr Hague a decade earlier that he intended to take up UK residency (and tax liability), was accused of pumping millions into target seats prior to the official launch of the campaign (thereby avoiding

**Table 5.5** The role of the Electoral Commission in relation to donations and loans

| Role | Process |
|---|---|
| Registers donations and loans | Established a statutory register of donations, requiring all political parties and affiliated organizations to declare donations, loans, or benefits in kind of more than £1,000 made to constituencies or local party offices in a single year, and donations or loans of £5,000-plus paid to central offices. Parties must detail them in quarterly reports. |
| Defines 'permissible donors' | Clamps down on anonymous donors. Anyone donating more than £200 to a party is named on register and such donations are only accepted from 'permissible donors'—individuals on the UK **electoral register** or organizations registered in the EU and carrying out business in the UK. 'Donations in kind' (e.g. office space, printing of campaign literature) are treated as donations. |
| Limits spending | Monitors compliance with spending controls during election campaigns (see Chapter 4). |
| Refers abuses to Crown Prosecution Service (CPS) | There are now three levels of offence relating to false or late declarations:<br>1. failure to submit a return in time—a civil offence by the party and a criminal offence by the treasurer;<br>2. submitting a return that fails to comply with the Act—a criminal offence by the treasurer;<br>3. making false declarations on a return—a criminal offence by the treasurer. |

breaking election rules) in an effort to 'buy' votes. Two months after the election, with a Conservative once more in Downing Street, Lord Ashcroft finally relinquished his non-dom status—agreeing to pay UK tax in return for keeping his seat in the Lords.

By way of a postscript, figures published by the Electoral Commission in August 2010 found overall donations made to Britain's political parties in the run-up to that year's election had been £6m higher than before the 2005 poll—reaching a record level of £26.3m. For the first time since 1997, the Conservatives trumped Labour into second place, raising some £12m to its £11m, although the two biggest single donations went to the latter (including £1m from a long-time supporter, steel magnate Lakshmi Mittal).

# ▶ 'Lobbygate', 'cash for honours', and Labour's deputy leadership row

Mr Blair's government was frequently embroiled in controversies concerning alleged lack of financial transparency on the one hand, and underhand links with business on the other. By the time Mr Brown succeeded him in Downing Street, the tension between the government's pledge to be 'whiter than white' financially while still raising enough money to keep the Labour Party machine afloat had reached breaking point. Successive scandals about undeclared—or, at best, underdeclared—donations and loans had forced ministers into embarrassing admissions. The political initiative was consequently handed to Mr Cameron, who demanded a cap of £50,000 on all individual payments—including its main lifeline, union donations. Whatever his political instincts, Mr Brown was hardly in a position to comply, arguing instead that union contributions should be viewed as comprising a number of smaller individual donations. With 'Middle England' deserting the party in favour of a resurgent Conservatives, disclosure of Labour's annual accounts in July 2008 revealed the full extent of the party's mounting debt—£24m was owed to various creditors, including a number of individual donors whose money was due back that year.

## 'Lobbygate'

Political lobbying is nothing new. The Conservatives have never been coy about their links to business, while Labour MPs in certain constituencies have been sponsored by unions for decades. But the emergence of specialist lobbying companies purposely set up to help individuals and interest groups to gain access to ministers, in the hope of influencing government policy, was a phenomenon not widely witnessed until the 1990s.

The involvement of one such company, Ian Greer Associates, as an alleged intermediary in the 'cash for questions' affair (see pp. 9 and 53) was for many the first they had heard of such practices. Labour promised to eradicate such activities, but within a year of regaining power senior ministers—including Mr Blair's right-hand man, Peter Mandelson—were being linked to lobbying firms boasting of their ability to buy access to ministers. One such firm was Lawson Lucas Mendelsohn, run by former Labour campaign strategy adviser Neal Lawson, business intermediary Jon Mendelsohn, and Ben Lucas, one of  Mr Blair's political briefers. Another, GPC Market Access, employed one of Mandelson's ex-special advisers, Derek Draper, who is alleged to have bragged to clients he could buy them tea with Geoffrey Robinson, Labour's then Paymaster General, or dinner with Mr Blair.

## 'Cash for honours'

If 'Lobbygate' and the Ecclestone affair were early shots across the bows for Labour, then the various 'cash for honours' rows that followed provided the smoking gun that proved for many the party was as guilty of succumbing to the advances of big business as the Conservatives.

Of these by far the most damaging was the so-called 'loans for peerages'  scandal exposed by *The Independent on Sunday* in October 2005. The controversy erupted in earnest the following March, when the then recently formed

*House of Lords Appointments Commission* rejected several nominees Mr Blair had forwarded for *life peerages*. It quickly emerged that each of the men concerned had recently loaned the Labour Party substantial sums of money on an anonymous basis. A loophole in the 2000 Act meant that, although all *donations* of £200-plus had to be properly declared, the same rule did not apply to loans— provided that they were taken out on normal commercial terms.

With the party in huge debt in the run-up to the 2005 election, Mr Blair and his advisers appeared to have deliberately sidestepped a law they themselves had introduced under the premise of wanting to make party funding more transparent, by courting loans rather than actual donations. Although the revelation that the party had gone 'cap in hand' to anonymous lenders was embarrassing enough for the government, there was no suggestion the letter of election law had been breached (even if its spirit might have been). What led to the subsequent criminal investigation—and the spectacle of Mr Blair becoming the first serving prime minister to be questioned by police, albeit as a witness—was the allegation, levelled by Scottish Nationalist MP Angus McNeil, that attempts had been made by some of his aides to 'sell' honours (an offence under the Sale of Peerages Act 1925).

In the ensuing months the spotlight came to focus on Lord Levy, Labour's chief fundraiser (who was alleged to have asked one of the lenders, Dr Chai Patel, director of the Priory healthcare group, to change a gift he planned to offer the party into an unsecured loan for £1.5m, to sidestep the new donation rules. As the controversy escalated, Lord Levy—known as 'Lord Cashpoint' in some Labour circles—briefly faced the prospect of being charged with conspiracy to pervert the cause of justice, while Downing Street adviser Ruth Turner was subjected to a dawn raid by the Metropolitan Police amid rumours she faced similar charges.

No charges were ultimately brought, but the year-long investigation, which ended weeks before Mr Blair left Downing Street, cast a shadow over his final year in office. To regain the political initiative at the height of the controversy, Mr Blair launched a cross-party review of political funding, chaired by Sir Hayden Phillips, chairman of the National Theatre and a senior partner with corporate financiers Hanson Westhouse. But in October 2007, the talks were suspended amid scenes of dissent between Labour and the Tories. This did not stop Sir Hayden making his own recommendations public. They included a proposal to cap individual donations after a transitional period at a maximum of £50,000.

## The Labour Deputy leadership donations

If Mr Brown had hoped to close the lid on allegations of financial sleaze on entering Downing Street, his dream was swiftly dashed. Within months of joining his Cabinet, several colleagues were immersed in a new funding controversy, this time surrounding donations made to their individual campaigns in the party's deputy leadership election.

In November 2007 it emerged that David Abrahams, a property magnate and one-time Labour parliamentary candidate, had bypassed the new law on donations by using a third-party intermediary to pay £5,000 into Harriet Harman's winning campaign. The money had been passed to Harman's team by a friend of Abraham, Janet Kidd. Apparently accepting the gift at face value, Harman wrote to Mrs Kidd to thank her.

She denied any wrongdoing, stressing she had registered the donation with the Electoral Commission (albeit under Mrs Kidd's name), but there was surprise at her apparent ignorance of the party's own rules on donations, let alone the wider law. Both Hilary Benn, a fellow deputy leadership candidate, and Mr Brown had turned down offers of donations by Mrs Kidd—the latter because she was 'not known' to his team. It was the New Year before the deputy leadership affair claimed its first scalp, though, after it emerged that Peter Hain, then Work and Pensions Secretary and Welsh Secretary, had failed to declare 17 donations to his deputy leadership bid, together worth £103,000, until four months after the contest ended. He blamed his ministerial workload for the poor organization of his campaign, but when his case was referred to the Met, he accepted he had 'no choice' but to resign.

Problems with Labour donations soon surfaced north of the border, too. In July 2008, Wendy Alexander, Leader of the Scottish Labour Party, resigned over an undeclared £950 donation to her 1997 campaign to succeed Jack McConnell.

## ☰ Topical feature idea

The May 2010 general election delivered no overall majority for any individual party, and produced 19 MPs representing interests other than those of Labour, the Conservatives, or the Liberal Democrats. The Green Party secured its first MP, Caroline Lucas for Brighton Pavilion, after fielding candidates across the UK, and while neither the United Kingdom Independence Party (UKIP) nor the British National Party (BNP) won any seats, they put up 560 and 326 candidates respectively. In many constituencies they secured votes in the hundreds or low thousands—indicating a groundswell of support for their views. Did any minority party candidates win seats in your area? What level of support do minority parties have in your area, and how might this translate into seats in future local, national, and European elections? Would local minority candidates do better under an alternative electoral reform?

## ✳ Current issues

- **The future of 'two-party politics':** the advent of the coalition government has put electoral reform firmly on the agenda. With both Labour and the Tories polling progressively smaller shares of the popular vote compared to the other parties, a fairer allocation of Commons seats between competing parties under a more proportional system is likely in future.

■ **Party funding:** controversies over political loans and donations have led to renewed calls for the introduction of state funding for parties, as practised in other countries.

■ **'Deselection' by the public:** new rules are due to be introduced to enable constituents to sack their own MPs between Parliaments if they are found guilty of serious wrongdoing, such as fiddling their expenses.

## ? Review questions

1. Which is the oldest UK political party—Conservative, Labour, or Liberal Democrat?

2. To what extent has Labour stayed true to its democratic socialist roots, and are traditional labels such as 'left-wing', 'right-wing', and 'centrist' still relevant today?

3. Outline the similarities and differences between the role of the 1922 Committee in the Conservative Party and the Parliamentary Labour Party.

4. What is the difference between a political donation and loan in UK law?

5. What are the arguments for and against state funding of political parties in Britain?

## → Further reading

Marr, A. (2008) *A History of Modern Britain*, London: Pan Books. **Critically acclaimed tie-in to 2007 BBC2 documentary series of same name, chronicling British social and political history from post-war period to present day.**

Roy, D. (2005) *Liberals: A History of the Liberal and Liberal Democratic Parties*, London: Hambledon Continuum. **Overview of the complex history of the Liberal Party and its successors, tracing the origins of liberalism in the eighteenth and nineteenth centuries, the party's decline in the early twentieth century, and its resurgence in the 1970s and 1980s.**

Seldon, A. and Snowdon, P. (2004) *The Conservative Party*, Stroud: The History Press. **Colourful history of Conservative Party from late eighteenth century to present day, including analysis of party's recent troubles over Europe.**

Thorpe, A. (2001) *A History of the British Labour Party*, 2nd edn, London: Palgrave Macmillan. **Second edition of this comprehensive history of the Labour Party, chronicling evolution of its policies and institutions from late nineteenth-century origins up to 2001 election.**

## @ Online Resource Centre

www.oxfordtextbooks.co.uk/orc/Morrison2e/

Visit the Online Resource Centre that accompanies this book for web links and regular updates.

# 6

# The National Health Service (NHS)

If there is one British institution beside Parliament capable of dictating the country's news agenda it is the National Health Service (NHS). For many journalists, however, the newsworthiness of the NHS is matched only by its complexity.

Founded in 1948, three years into Clement Attlee's reforming post-war Labour government, the NHS was designed to be exactly what it said on the tin: a *national* health service providing high-quality medical treatment, 'free at the point of need', on a uniform basis wherever one lived in the UK. But the story of subsequent decades—in particular the past thirty years—has been of the gradual fragmentation of this idealized model of social health care. What was once a single, monolithic health service, run directly by central government, was transformed in the 1980s and 1990s into an umbrella organization encompassing a series of connected, but increasingly autonomous, units. Much like individual companies in the commercial marketplace, most of these units were given their own boards of directors and delegated budgets, and allowed to 'commission services from' and 'sell services to' one another. And with the introduction of the concept of 'patient choice'—allowing those in need of operations and other treatments to shop around between hospitals like customers—they even began to compete.

With the advent of the Conservative-led *coalition government*, market reforms initiated by Margaret Thatcher and consolidated by first John Major, then New Labour, looked set to be taken to a new level in England, through the wholesale dismantling of parts of the NHS—with general practitioners (GPs) given direct charge of purchasing care for their patients and many hospitals allowed to opt out of the health service altogether to become fully fledged not-for-profit companies. This chapter charts how the NHS in its current (and likely future) form came about and tries to explain how its many strands link together.

# ▌ The origins of the NHS

Although not formally established until the National Health Service Act 1946, the NHS emerged from mounting concern over a period of decades about the ever starker inequalities in personal well-being between the richest and poorest Britons. It had its roots in two key developments. These were the 'Beveridge Report' (of which more in a moment) and the introduction by Liberal Chancellor David Lloyd George, as far back as 1911, of a *National Insurance (NI)* scheme, which, in exchange for docking 4d a week from their wages, insured low-paid workers against sickness and unemployment.

When this modest measure was introduced the concept of an NHS offering a comprehensive range of treatments was still some way off. It was not until Labour ministers were invited into Winston Churchill's wartime national government in 1940 that the idea of a system of universal, needs-based health care was born. Arthur Greenwood, then Minister without Portfolio, commissioned Liberal economist William Beveridge to head up an interdepartmental committee on social insurance and allied services in 1941. Its report, published a year later, was to form the blueprint for not only the NHS, but also the all-encompassing 'welfare state' of which it became part—leading to Attlee's famous pledge, on entering Downing Street, to harness the spirit of collectivism born out of the war effort to look after the poor, sick, and vulnerable 'from the cradle to the grave' during peacetime.

The Health Minister entrusted with launching the embryonic NHS was Aneurin 'Nye' Bevan, whose vision was inspired by his memories of witnessing the suffering of steelworkers and miners in his native Tredegar, south-east Wales, as a younger man, and the work voluntary societies and charity-funded cottage hospitals had done, in the absence of government funding, to care for such people. He reputedly modelled the NHS on the Tredegar Medical Aid Society, a community-run healthcare collective set up in 1874.

With no pre-existing national template for the NHS, Bevan initially had a fight on his hands persuading family doctors and consultants—most of whom had previously been able to dictate their own working conditions and pay—to sign up to his project. In the end he did so by offering them generous contracts that, by his own admission, 'stuffed their mouths with gold'. When he triumphantly unveiled the new NHS at its inaugural outlet, Park Hospital in Manchester, on 5 July 1948, Bevan declared:

❛ We now have the moral leadership of the world. ❜

Although Bevan's vision of a health service for all was largely fulfilled, it was not long before the economics of providing universal health care on such a massive scale began to chip away at some of its guiding principles—notably that of universal free access to treatment, regardless of ability to pay. In May 1951, buffeted by global economic turbulence and its dependence on US loans to continue financing its social welfare programme, the Labour government reluctantly introduced the first NHS charges: £1 for spectacles prescribed by an optician and a half-cost price for dentures. A year later a flat rate £1 fee for visiting the dentist was introduced, along with a 5p generic prescription charge. In what was to be a mortal blow for Attlee, Bevan—the architect of his greatest achievement—resigned from the government even before the first of these charges had taken effect. Among those who joined him was a young Harold Wilson, a future prime minister.

## How the NHS is funded

Although the proportion of Britain's *gross domestic product (GDP)* ploughed into the NHS each year has varied wildly between governments—with Labour traditionally investing more, even if not always wisely—the general break-down of sources from which this investment derives has remained broadly the same as in the early 1950s. Around 80 per cent comes from general taxation (Income Tax, VAT, duties on tobacco and alcohol). The remaining 20 per cent stems from:

- the NHS element of National Insurance contributions;
- charges to patients for drugs (prescriptions) and treatment;
- income from land sales and income-generation schemes;
- funds raised from voluntary sources—for example, local hospital appeals.

Given the direction in which the coalition is currently pushing health policy, this balance is likely to shift in future years, with substantially more coming from income-generation.

# ▶ End of the post-war consensus and the birth of the internal market

For forty years or more the NHS retained largely the same structure: it was funded centrally through taxation, with ministers and civil servants filtering the money down to hospitals, surgeries, and ambulance services. Of the tens of thousands of nurses, doctors, and paramedics (not to mention catering and cleaning staff) working in the health service at any one time, most were effec-tively on the government's—and, by extension, taxpayers'—payroll.

This is no longer the case. A series of institutional reforms since the late 1980s have transformed the NHS into a different organization entirely. Nowadays, the bulk of family doctors, or 'general practitioners' (GPs), are self-employed; many specialists work as freelance locums, moving from hospital to hospital, and public to private sector, as demand arises; and junior doctors, nurses, and care workers are increasingly employed through agencies, rather than as full-time members of staff. Catering, cleaning, and security workers are routinely supplied by outside contractors, rather than being employed in-house, and even treatment itself is increasingly contracted out to external and/or commercial providers.

So, how and why did this apparent sea change in the day-to-day running of the NHS come about, and who is responsible for running the modern-day health service?

It is impossible to understand the shape of the NHS today without first examining the emergence of the 'internal market'. As long ago as 1973, the National Health Service Reorganization Act spearheaded by then Conservative Health and Social Security Secretary Keith Joseph (in time, one of the architects of 'Thatcherism') aimed to shake up the NHS by introducing a more efficient management structure, with 'generalist' managers joining existing clinical experts on hospital boards, and incentives to generate revenue by letting out unused wards for the use of private patients. These themes were revisited a decade later when, alarmed at the escalating cost of NHS treatment and wage bills, another Tory Health Secretary, Norman Fowler, commissioned then deputy chairman and managing director of Sainsbury's Sir Roy Griffiths to chair an inquiry into making the health service more efficient. His remit was to recommend an alternative management structure, and find ways of cutting running costs by using resources more economically.

The resulting Griffiths Report proposed a wholesale restructuring of the NHS, putting the onus on two key recommendations:

- introduction of *general managers* to run the existing district health authorities (DHAs)—essentially the administrative presence on the ground in each area of the then Department of Health and Social Security (DHSS), and responsible for directing funding to local hospitals and surgeries. These would oversee the efficient use of NHS budgets at local level, replacing the 'management by consensus' philosophy (under which medical practitioners had effectively been their own managers) used since previous, smaller-scale, reforms had occurred in 1974. Griffiths felt this approach had provided little more than crisis management;

- greater focus on *community-based* health care—with GPs, dentists, and other primary care providers given control of their own budgets, along with the freedom to commission services on behalf of their patients without needing to go through the government, or even their local health authorities. The aim was to make the allocation of finite

NHS funds more efficient by replacing the 'one-size-fits-all' approach to funding GP surgeries of old with a more targeted allocation of resources tailored to the particular needs of the individual patients on their books.

Amid criticisms from Labour that they were primarily motivated by saving money (and accusations that they were privatizing the health service by stealth), the Tories initially took only tentative steps towards implementing the report's findings. But a series of *White Papers* flowing from the inquiry in ensuing years eventually paved the way for an internal market that was, if anything, more far-reaching.

The Act that finally established this internal market (in so doing, defining this term for the first time) flowed from a further review of the NHS announced by Prime Minister Margaret Thatcher in 1988. At about the same time, she decided to split the mammoth DHSS in two, in recognition of its burgeoning workload: creating the Department of Social Security (DSS) to run the benefits system and a separate Department of Health (DH).

The National Health Service and Community Care Act 1990 implemented two of the previous White Papers: *Caring for People* and *Working for Patients*. It ushered in a phased reorganization with the following key features:

- hospitals, mental health units, ambulance services, and other NHS bodies directly involved in patient care became *NHS trusts*—with their own management boards, incorporating both practitioners (consultants and other senior clinical staff) and general managers charged with improving their efficiency;
- GPs were offered the opportunity to become 'fundholders'—'opting out' of district health authority control to take charge of their own budgetary decisions;
- GP fundholding practices, DHAs, and family health service authorities (FHSAs) were redefined as 'purchasers' of NHS care on behalf of their patients. While GPs would now focus on *primary care*—providing 'first-port-of-call' treatments such as diagnoses, vaccinations, and purchasing X-rays, tests, and small operations on behalf of their surgery patients—FHSAs would buy in other community-based services, with DHAs purchasing acute hospital services such as accident and emergency (A&E) facilities;
- NHS trusts were defined as 'providers' of services.

In theory the new internal market would operate as illustrated in Figure 6.1.

In practice, its implementation was far from smooth. For a start, as independent contractors GPs had to *want* to be integrated into it in the first place.

**Figure 6.1** How the Conservatives' NHS internal market was structured

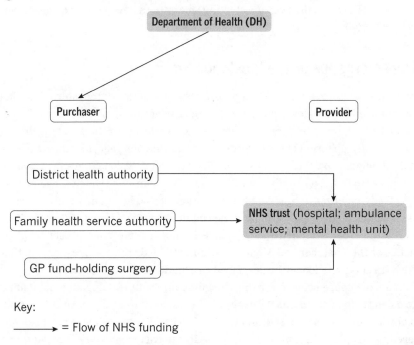

Key:

⟶ = Flow of NHS funding

While some relished the opportunity to control their own budgets and direct spending towards areas they felt were in need of cash, others were alarmed at the increased workload and, potentially, making the wrong decisions about how to spend their money—only to face tricky dilemmas should unforeseen needs arise during a financial year. Only family practices with more than 5,000 patients in England and Northern Ireland (4,000 in Wales and Scotland) were allowed to apply for fundholder status. By the time Labour came to power in 1997, some 3,500 practices had signed up, involving 15,000 GPs—fewer than half the estimated 40,000 practising across the UK. By mid-1996 there were more than 520 trusts in place, but mergers had reduced this tally to 450 by 1999.

The internal market was also criticized for placing too much emphasis on management and recruiting high-salaried senior staff, armed with clipboards and flow charts, at the expense of frontline workers like nurses. Managers were increasingly headhunted from the private sector—a reflection of the Conservatives' belief that those with business expertise were likely to be better at running the organization than medical practitioners whose skills lay primarily in patient care. This trend has continued to this day, with chief executives of most NHS trust boards earning six-figure salaries. In 2005, a survey by Incomes Data Services identified Derek Smith, chief executive of Hammersmith Hospitals, as the first NHS manager to top the £200,000 mark. It also found chief executive salaries across the board had risen 70 per cent in the previous decade. At the time, the average starting salary for a newly qualified nurse was around £17,000.

## The emergence of the 'postcode lottery'

There was widespread agreement before the introduction of the internal market that the original 'top-down' NHS model needed adapting to the changing needs of a society on the cusp of a new century—not least because of the widening disparities between different areas in terms of average income, age, healthcare needs, and other demographic factors. Nonetheless, the decision to grant increased autonomy to DHAs and individual GPs was to have one unintended consequence: the steady emergence of significant variations in the level and nature of treatment available to people with the same conditions living in different areas. This increasing trend—dubbed the 'postcode lottery' or 'postcode prescribing' by critics of the Thatcher and Major governments—led many to question whether the NHS could any longer be described as a 'national' health service.

A famous cause célèbre for those arguing against the delegation of funding decisions to local level was the case of beta interferon—an expensive drug that, according to some experts, dramatically decreases the number of relapses suffered by people with multiple sclerosis. In the early 1990s, it emerged that a number of DHAs were refusing to fund beta interferon on the NHS—arguing that the £10,000 a year per patient needed to buy in the drug would be better spent on other treatments, such as physiotherapy. Its supporters argued that prescribing the medicine early could save the NHS money in the long run, by delaying the need for residential and/or palliative care.

Another commonly cited example of the postcode lottery is the differential availability of fertility treatment for childless couples and, in particular, *in vitro* fertilization (IVF)—the process by which egg cells are fertilized by a man's sperm outside a woman's womb before being transferred back to stimulate pregnancy. Despite Labour's early attempt to end the postcode lottery by establishing national service frameworks (NSFs) to harmonize provision of essential health services across the country (see p. 170), wide disparities remain. In November 2005 it emerged that Ipswich Hospital NHS Trust and a number of Suffolk *primary care trusts (PCTs)*—the bodies that currently run the healthcare commissioning process—were rationing hip and knee replacement operations by refusing to offer them to patients judged obese, other than in exceptional circumstances. Dr Brian Keeble, director of public health for Ipswich PCT, justified the decision by telling the press it was for patients' own good, because overweight people 'do worse after operations' and hip replacements might fail.

But critics of the move—since emulated by several other trusts—condemned it as discrimination against patients whose conditions were judged to be self-inflicted. Their concerns were compounded when, just days later, a leaked paper from the *National Institute for Health and Clinical Excellence (NICE)*—the agency that vets potential new treatments and recommends to the government whether they should be funded on the NHS—indicated that plans were afoot to ration treatment for heavy smokers and drinkers.

The postcode lottery is now such a political 'hot potato' that ministers have increasingly found themselves drawn into disputes over individual cases of patients denied treatment by their local PCTs. So potentially damaging had the issue become by June 2008 that then Health Secretary Alan Johnson pledged to end it once and for all—by banning PCTs from denying patients costly treatments approved by NICE for NHS use. Despite this, inequities remain, and there are fears that the introduction of wholesale GP commissioning heralded by coalition Health Secretary Andrew Lansley could see widening disparities emerge in primary health provision from area to area.

## NHS waiting lists and the origins of Blair's health reforms

Perhaps more controversial still, in light of escalating criticisms of the Thatcher and Major governments' emphasis on spending NHS money more efficiently rather than pouring more in, was the waiting-list crisis that emerged in the early 1990s. By the time Labour was elected in May 1997, 1.3 million people were listed as awaiting operations or other inpatient treatments, with 'guaranteed maximum waits' from initial GP referral to actual treatment of 18 months. In the final months of Mr Major's government the tabloids were filled with stories about elderly and vulnerable patients falling seriously ill or even dying while awaiting surgery. Equally alarming were the numerous stories printed about the lengthy queues people were enduring in A&E units—and the often overcrowded and undignified conditions they were forced to accept.

Such was the public outcry that one of Tony Blair's central election pledges in the campaign leading to his 1997 landslide was to cut waiting lists by 100,000 by releasing £100m from so-called 'NHS red tape'. Despite a sluggish start, by November 2004 official figures indicated waiting lists had hit a 17-year low: although 857,000 people were still listed, this was down 300,000 in 1997. Perhaps more importantly for the individuals concerned, waiting *times* were found to have fallen, with only 19 patients having waited longer than a year for treatment and 122 for more than nine months. Health Minister John Hutton declared  at the time that, by the end of 2008, no patient should be waiting longer than 18 weeks—and this target remained official government policy until Labour left office in 2010. However, within weeks of becoming Health Secretary Mr Lansley signalled an end to target culture (a long-standing bête noire of the Conservatives) by scrapping the 18-week hospital appointment 'guarantee' in England, together with the condition stipulating that all NHS patients should be given a GP appointment within 48 hours of requesting one.

# New Labour's restructuring of the NHS

The success of Mr Blair's blizzard of NHS reforms was mixed. Significant achievements in some areas—bolstered by unprecedented public investment—were marred by apparently inconsistent, even contradictory, policymaking in others.

When Labour returned to power after 18 years in opposition it inherited a health service widely seen as being in crisis. After an initial period of caution, during which the new government stuck to public spending limits imposed by the Tories before leaving office, then Chancellor of the Exchequer Gordon Brown announced a huge increase in NHS funding—taking it above and beyond the average annual investment of other European countries in public health care. In 1997 the proportion of Britain's GDP spent annually on the NHS was 6.7 per cent, but in his 2002 Budget Mr Brown used his first tax rise (a 1 per cent National Insurance increase) to raise it to 7.4 per cent a year. By 2007–08 it was due to have risen to 9.4 per cent—more than a percentage point higher than the European average. By 2010, NHS spending was equivalent to 9.7 per cent of GDP, but even before the coalition took power and announced its multibillion-pound savings programme the influential King's Fund charity was predicting that by 2016–17 it would fall back to 7.9 per cent as a result of public spending cuts—wiping out all real terms increases since 2000.

Mr Blair quickly decided that pouring more money into the NHS was not enough. To ensure that this investment was spent wisely, like Mrs Thatcher before him he set about restructuring the health service. Having promised to dismantle the 'wasteful' internal market while in opposition (and initially doing so under his first Health Secretary, Frank Dobson), he began to introduce a new form of localized management and budgetary control seen by many as his own version of the Tory model.

New Labour's version of the internal market originated in the Health Act 1999 and the White Paper preceding it, *The New NHS: Modern and Dependable*. Its main emphasis was on the primacy of community-based health care—steering patients wherever possible away from hospital, and giving GPs and other primary care providers the money and autonomy needed to offer a wider range of treatments through their practices.

On the face of it, the resulting reforms were initially modest. In place of fundholding, which had effectively fostered an element of 'competition' between GP surgeries, Mr Blair introduced greater cooperation between practices, by establishing *primary care groups (PCGs)*. These collaborative bodies brought together GPs, community nurses, and other related practitioners in a given geographical area to promote closer liaison and, ultimately, a more coordinated use of NHS resources. The idea was that, as PCGs grew in confidence and evolved, they would have increasing levels of responsibility delegated to them. In the end, like fundholding GP practices, they also assumed control of their own budgets, establishing NHS trust-style boards to take their financial decisions for them.

By 2002 the bones of a new NHS structure were established, which over time came to take the following form.

- PCGs were replaced by primary care trusts (PCTs), local administrative organizations covering populations of 100,000 or more. Like fundholding GP practices, these bought in clinical services from NHS trusts on behalf of their patients—except that, rather than calling this 'purchasing', Labour used the term 'commissioning'. PCTs took control of 80 per cent of the overall NHS budget, and with it virtually all local commissioning. But it was only a matter of time before health policy would return full circle, with the coalition's pledge to abolish PCTs and hand commissioning powers direct to GPs (see p. 176).

- After initially being replaced by 96 health authorities (HAs), DHAs later gave way to much more arm's-length administrative bodies, *strategic health authorities (SHAs)*, of which there were initially 28—a number reduced to ten in July 2006. As the population covered by each authority increased, its level of direct involvement in patient care dwindled. At time of writing, SHAs were due to be abolished, but in the meantime they remained responsible for monitoring local health care to ensure fair access to services like GP surgeries and dentists, and for publishing three-yearly health improvement plans (HIPs) identifying local health concerns (such as rates of heart disease or diabetes) and promoting healthier lifestyles and disease prevention.

- NHS trusts continued to be classed as service 'providers', but with the prospect of gaining greater autonomy over their budgets if they performed well in NHS 'league tables'. Ultimately, many were granted the 'self-governing' status of **foundation trusts**—a form of autonomy to be granted to all NHS hospitals by the Lib-Con coalition (see p. 176).

- County councils and unitary authorities established **local involvement networks (LINks)** to act as the voice of service users. Run directly by local taxpayers, LINks could demand specific changes to health and social care in their areas. They replaced a prior Labour invention, patients' forums, which had been staffed by volunteers from local communities, and the earlier 'community health councils' (CHCs), run by paid officers for the previous 25 years. LINks (due to be replaced by Mr Lansley with a new national *HealthWatch quango*—see p. 176) had to be formally consulted on major structural changes in their areas and allowed to view related documentation.

Labour's revamped internal market therefore works as outlined in Figure 6.2.

Since the initial Labour restructure, the NHS has been rationalized more than once. On 1 October 2006 the number of PCTs was halved, from 303 to 151.

**Figure 6.2** Labour's version of the internal market

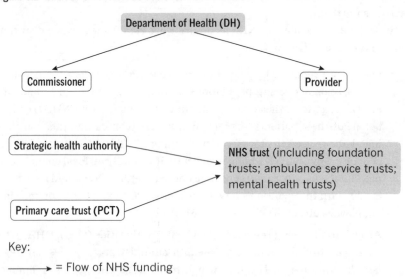

The mergers enabling this to happen were intended to produce efficiency savings by preventing duplication between trusts in neighbouring areas with broadly similar needs. As a result, by the time the coalition announced it was scrapping PCTs many were covering populations of up to 600,000. There are now fewer hospital trusts, too (partly as a result of closures and mergers). At time of writing, there were 168 acute trusts and 73 mental health trusts covering 1,600 hospitals and specialist care centres.

In addition to its structural reforms, Labour strengthened the hand of the DH and the *Secretary of State* for Health, giving them the power to set nationwide targets and standards of care in priority areas to which all SHAs, PCTs, and NHS trusts must adhere. These 'national service frameworks' (NSFs), established in 1998, were described as 'long-term strategies' designed to provide consistency of care across the UK, reducing the postcode lottery. In effect they amounted to a set of 'rules', similar to the *National Curriculum* used to enforce uniformity of teaching in core subjects in schools. By the time Labour left office, there were NSFs covering ten conditions, as outlined in Table 6.1. The scope of NSFs was next due to be reviewed on 31 January 2012.

The use of NSFs to impose uniformity of health care for priority conditions was strengthened in the early years of the Labour government by the introduction of 'health action zones' (HAZs) in deprived areas. These were used to address 'health inequalities' between rich and poor districts by targeting additional resources at communities with high rates of unemployment, poverty, and poor housing, to ensure that public health—and quality of health care—in those areas kept pace with that in more affluent ones.

A further attempt to tackle the postcode lottery came with the formation of NICE in 1999. This *executive agency* of the DH is charged with approving

**Table 6.1** NHS national service frameworks (NSFs) (to 31 January 2012)

| Condition/Service area | Target/Aim |
|---|---|
| Blood pressure | To work with the Blood Pressure Association (BPA) to raise awareness about the risks of hypertension (high blood pressure) through initiatives like National Blood Pressure Testing Week |
| Cancer | To improve preventative measures, like vaccination and screening, for cervical, breast, and bowel cancer, as part of the DH's wider Cancer Reform Strategy |
| Children | Covers specific aims for improving treatment for children with disabilities, and implementation of 'Every Child Matters' agenda through children's services departments (see p. 511) |
| Chronic obstructive pulmonary disease (COPD) | Improving drug therapy for a wide range of respiratory illnesses, like bronchitis and emphysema |
| Coronary heart disease | Specific target of 40 per cent cut in the death rate for people under 75 from heart disease and strokes by 2010 |
| Diabetes | Ten-year programme of improvements to all aspects of diabetes treatment, running until 2013 |
| Long-term conditions | Five outcomes to improve treatment and quality of life for people with long-term conditions, by reducing dependency and improving choice—including introduction of direct payments (see p. 512) |
| Mental health | Specific focus on disproportionate number of black and minority ethnic (BME) people with diagnosed mental health issues—one in five, compared to one in ten of general UK population |
| Renal | Raising quality of care available to people with kidney conditions, especially in the last days or weeks of their lives |
| Strokes | Target to reduce the under-75 death rate from this condition—the third biggest killer in the UK—by 40 per cent by 2010 |
| Vascular | Commitment to cut the number of deaths from this disease, which causes 39 per cent of all mortality in Britain each year and disproportionately affects people from deprived backgrounds and specific ethnic groups, such as South Asians |

NOTE: A regularly updated version of this table can be found on the Online Resource Centre that accompanies this book.

drugs and treatments for use by the NHS, promoting improved public health, and ensuring that consistent, high-quality healthcare provision is available across the country, by:

- offering guidance on the prevention of illness to NHS workers, local authorities, and wider public and voluntary sectors;

- advising government on whether new and existing clinical treatments, medicines, and procedures should be made (or remain) available on NHS;

- giving advice to ministers and public on the most appropriate treatment for individuals with specific ailments and diseases.

NICE's decisions have often been controversial. Campaigners representing sufferers from specific conditions frequently accuse it of penny-pinching by failing to endorse new drugs, or recommending the abandonment of others (in a preliminary ruling in 2001, it ruled beta interferon should no longer be available on the NHS). On many occasions, however, its interventions have taken a more positive approach to countering postcode prescribing. In June 2006 NICE issued draft guidance to PCTs recommending the use of the then recently licensed drug Herceptin® for early-stage breast cancer. Its decision followed the case of Barbara Clark, a 49-year-old nurse who persuaded Somerset Coast PCT to pay for the £20,000-a-year drug by threatening it with litigation in the *European Court of Human Rights (ECtHR)*.

The DH's other key roles under New Labour included:

- setting the *direction* of health policy—by outlining an overall health service strategy, formulating policies, passing legislation, setting regulations, allocating resources, determining the overall NHS operating framework, and fostering local area agreements between partner organizations to implement DH policy on the ground;

- supporting the *delivery* of NHS services—by monitoring and evaluating the performance of health service bodies and professionals, increasing capacity, improving the NHS skills base, and ensuring value for money for service users;

- promoting health and well-being among the population—by working with public, private, and voluntary sectors to encourage healthier lifestyle choices, and liaising with international bodies like the European Union (EU), WHO, and the Organization for Economic Co-operation and Development (OECD);

- accounting to Parliament and the public for the performance of the NHS—by answering parliamentary questions, responding to correspondences from the public, and communicating through speeches and public events.

## From Labour's 'Ten-Year NHS Plan' to the coalition's 'social enterprise' revolution

Health professionals who hoped for respite after the second wholesale NHS reorganization in a decade were to be disappointed. Even before the new Blairite version of the internal market had fully taken shape, his ministers were signalling plans for more fundamental change—taking the Thatcher reforms to their logical next stage by freely introducing market terminology such as 'choice' and 'competition' into the health service lexicon, and redefining patients and service users as 'consumers'.

The blueprint for this transformation first appeared in the 'Ten-Year NHS Plan' unveiled in 2000. Pledging to 'give the people of Britain a health service fit for the twenty-first century', it signalled the formation of a 'Modernization

Board', chaired by the Health Secretary, to judge if change was happening fast enough, with NHS 'taskforces' 'driving' that change 'at the coalface'. But it was not until the flesh was put on the bones with a series of stage-managed ministerial announcements that the full scale of the overhaul became apparent. At carefully timed intervals between early 2001 and 2003, its architect, Mr Dobson's archly 'New Labour' successor Alan Milburn, outlined the plans listed in Table 6.2.

Not everyone welcomed this reinvention of the NHS. For some long-serving Labour *backbenchers* and party loyalists, the idea of *any* private sector involvement in the NHS—direct or indirect—was heresy.

**Table 6.2** Key reforms flowing from the 'Ten-Year NHS Plan'

| Reform | Detail |
| --- | --- |
| Pragmatic approach to cutting waiting times | To speed up cuts in waiting times, a 'concordat' was negotiated with private healthcare providers like BUPA. Anyone who had spent six months on a waiting list could have his or her operation in private hospital—or elsewhere in the EU. Special terms were negotiated with private providers allowing the NHS to buy up their spare capacity at reduced rates comparable to the cost of standard NHS treatment. |
| 'Patient choice' extended to surgery | People waiting for operations were given the option of having surgery fast-tracked by travelling elsewhere in UK—or even abroad—to hospitals with shorter waiting times. League tables began offering detailed information on waiting times of individual trusts to help patients to choose between hospitals in informed way. Star ratings were awarded for everything from hospital cleanliness to the standard of its food. |
| More and better hospitals | Huge hospital-building programme began, fast-tracked with help of up-front investment from private sector. These were financed through **public–private partnerships (PPPs)**— Labour's version of the Tories' **private finance initiative (PFI)** (see p. 222). In addition to offering commercial companies a profit from lucrative leaseback arrangements, ministers offered them stakes in the day-to-day running of some NHS hospitals. |
| More independence for hospitals | Successful hospital trusts were given greater autonomy, as foundation hospitals (now foundation trusts). They were allowed to manage own budgets and set own pay scales for key staff above national wage agreements negotiated with unions. |
| Division between general and specialist hospitals | Increased emphasis on hospital 'specialization', with trusts renowned for treating specific conditions like cancer becoming specialist hubs and highest performing ones given 'super hospital' status. Lower-performing hospitals and those in less populated areas later merged or closed, while still others lost costly, underused departments—including maternity and A&E units. |
| High-street NHS treatment | Network of NHS 'treatment centres' opened on high streets. These focus on routine diagnostic procedures, like blood and allergy tests, to relieve pressure on overstretched GP surgeries and hospitals. By 2005, at least 25 had opened and plans were announced to open them in branches of chain stores like Boots. |

Facing accusations that allowing NHS patients to be treated in private clinics and hospitals, and using private money to pay for new hospitals, was tantamount to privatizing it 'by the back door', the government argued that it was no such thing. Mr Blair retorted that it was the ends, not the means, that mattered—and that if using a spare BUPA ward meant that frail pensioners would have to wait 18 months less for hip replacements than previously, neither they nor their families were likely to be fussed about outdated ideological objections. Yet the media was quick to highlight the incongruous spectacle of the first NHS patients being flown overseas for surgery—and criticize the principle that anyone should be expected to travel hundreds of miles for operations that, by rights, ought to be available equally soon locally.

Among the vocal critics of this shake-up was Mr Dobson, who accused his party's leadership of being 'elitist' and 'following a Tory consensus'. He argued that, by naming and shaming 'failing' hospitals in league tables and allowing 'successful' ones (foundation trusts) to offer inflated salaries for the most qualified and experienced staff, Labour risked creating a 'two-tier health service'. Higher performing trusts would inevitably become yet more successful, gaining even greater freedoms in the process, while those stuck at the bottom of the ladder would continue spiralling downhill, devoid of the reputation, resources, and autonomy needed to improve their performance.

&#x275D;&#x275D; Others argued 'patient choice' was a sham. Given the option of having an operation at a poor-performing hospital in one area or a better one elsewhere, no patient would choose the former, so the 'choice' was illusory. And like the most popular schools, the best-performing hospitals ultimately had finite capacity—meaning they might quickly become oversubscribed and incapable of coping with demand. The waiting time/list spiral would then start all over again... &#x275E;&#x275E;

As if taunting his critics, Mr Milburn went further in an interview with *The Times* in January 2002, when he dispensed with constitutional etiquette by unveiling policy to the media before consulting either **Cabinet** or Parliament (see p. 87), and described the NHS as 'Britain's last great nationalized industry', suggesting it represented a model unsuitable for the twenty-first century.

But for Labour opponents of the changes, the final insult came at the hands of some of their fellow backbenchers, on a glacial November evening in 2003. With the help of a handful of Scottish MPs—many of whom personally opposed to the imposition of foundation hospitals in their own country, where members of the **Scottish Parliament** (MSPs) had rejected them—Mr Blair scored his lowest Commons victory to date, squeezing the Health and Social Care Bill through with a majority of 17.

New Labour's version of the internal market had an even bumpier ride outside England. With Scotland having rejected foundation hospitals at the outset, the overall structure of the NHS north of the border still bears a strong resemblance to the way it looked nationwide before Mrs Thatcher. Meanwhile, in Wales, a year after Labour was forced into an uneasy coalition with Plaid Cymru in the Welsh government, the country began systematically abandoning the internal market in time to mark the 60th birthday of the health service—returning to an old-style model that saw funding channelled directly from the health department down to trusts and *health boards, the* Welsh equivalent of SHAs .

Nonetheless, by the time of the May 2010 election a broad consensus existed between the three main parties over a desire to move towards granting all NHS trusts foundation status—giving staff and local residents increasingly hands-on involvement in their running. Today's foundation trusts, overseen by an *Independent Regulator of NHS Foundation Trusts* (known as *Monitor*), have been likened by some to mutuals or cooperatives. Staff and members of the public can become 'members', earning the right to elect members to the trust's board, or even to stand for it themselves. Once on a board, they have a direct say in the appointment (and dismissal) of the trust's chairpersons and non-executive directors, and a veto over their choices of chief executive.

Other recent reforms have only added to the concerns of critics of 'backdoor privatization'. Within days of Parliament reconvening after the 2008 Summer Recess, a commercial drugs company revealed that it had signed contracts with 30 hospital trusts to provide private 'top-up' treatment not available on the NHS to cancer patients in their own homes. At the time ministers' official position was that any patient who paid privately for costly drugs not available on the NHS would lose their entitlement to treatment on the health service. But in November that year, on the advice of 'Cancer Tsar for England' Mike Richards, Mr Johnson overturned the top-up ban—provided that any additional treatments were administered at a 'different time and in a different place' from the NHS care.

If Mr Blair's repeated restructuring of the NHS was controversial, the biggest earthquake was to come. Despite earlier declaring a 'moratorium' on any further 'top-down' reform, coalition Health Secretary Mr Lansley signalled a change of mind by using the May 2010 *Queen's Speech* to announce a 'slimming down' of the DH, and the formation of a single *NHS Board* to replace the ten remaining STAs by 2012. Around the same time, he published a contentious report by management consultants McKinsey (commissioned but suppressed by Labour), indicating support for its recommendation that £20bn be cut from the NHS budget by 2014 through a 10 per cent staff reduction. Similar figures emerged in the wake of Chancellor George Osborne's October 2010 **Comprehensive Spending Review (CSR)**, with administrative savings demanded as a quid pro quo for the Treasury's commitment to maintain real-term increases in NHS spending in the face of massive cuts to other government departments. The promised above-*inflation* rises of 4 per cent over as many years (1 per cent a year) were, however, greeted with mute applause by some commentators, who pointed out that this represented the smallest growth in health spending since the early 1980s. Respected business-to-business magazine *Health Service Journal* calculated that the true rise amounted to barely 0.6 per cent once £1bn previously set aside for capital projects but redirected towards running costs was removed from the equation.

The biggest shocks to the NHS system were, though, to be announced not by Mr Osborne but by the Health Secretary himself. In July 2010, Mr Lansley unveiled a reform package widely depicted as the biggest structural shake-up in NHS history. In a throwback to the abortive fundholding policies of the Major years, he announced the abolition of PCTs and the handover of their commissioning role to GPs. Unlike fund-holding practices (which had managed their finances individually) the new breed of GP commissioners would be able to form local consortia to purchase services collaboratively. But this time GPs would be forced to participate, rather than be allowed to decide for themselves whether to 'opt in' or not (as was the case with fundholders)—a curious element of compulsion amid a raft of other proposals predicated on the freedom of choice principle. More controversial still, potentially, was Mr Lansley's pledge to create 'the largest social enterprise sector in the world' by encouraging foundation trusts to break out of the NHS entirely—becoming not-for-profit, mutual-style companies with the ability to generate their own revenue by charging paying customers for private treatment as well as providing traditional health care free at the point of delivery. The flipside of these freedoms is that, like commercial firms, hospitals that mismanaged their finances could go bankrupt.

Facing immediate criticisms from unions and opposition MPs that he was preparing to hand £80bn of NHS funds over to private contractors—with no PCTs or SHAs left to police them—Mr Lansley said GPs' decisions would be scrutinized by a new HealthWatch regulator with local offshoots based on the extant LINks bodies, and a beefed-up version of the **health service scrutiny committees** established by Labour (see p. 180). To oversee the buying in of specialist services, meanwhile, there would be a new quango, the NHS Commissioning Board, which (along with the DH) would act as a hub of the new-look healthcare market.

So seismic was the proposed overhaul that in August 2010 healthcare union *UNISON* (concerned about its members' job security) launched legal action against the DH, in protest at the speed and scale of the reforms. It argued that the public consultation process ministers had instigated around the proposals was a 'sham', as within 24 hours of Mr Lansley's unveiling his White Paper, NHS chief executive Sir David Nicholson had written to all English trusts urging them to start implementing the changes 'immediately'—despite the fact that they had yet to be approved. On a different tack, respected health charity the King's Fund warned that, while GPs were best placed to judge the needs of patients, many had little inclination (or ability) to become their own accountants—raising the prospect that, over time, they might end up paying for the costly expertise of multinational private health providers like United

Healthcare and McKinsey, or effectively reinventing the PCT model by hiring their own managers, administrators, and finance directors. In the months since, GPs themselves have raised similar concerns. The British Medical Association (BMA), the professional body representing doctors, has warned that giving GPs direct control of their own budgets (with all of the tough decisions this will inevitably entail) risks fostering distrust between them and their patients—with the latter likely to interpret decisions not to prescribe them costly treatment as being motivated as much by a desire to 'balance the books' as genuine medical opinion.

## Other recent controversies in the NHS

If Mr Lansley were minded to insure his new brand of hospitals against the vicissitudes of the free market, as they begin the process of becoming independent businesses, he might do well to consider the cautionary tale of the huge deficits accumulated by some trusts under Labour In 2006, then Health Secretary Patricia Hewitt responded to the deficit crisis by giving debt-ridden trusts permission to borrow money from 'better performing' trusts with financial surpluses. The coalition government might also reflect on the difficulties Labour encountered negotiating with GPs. In 2004 it emerged that Mr Blair's government had 'botched' a new contract for family doctors by offering them bonuses for providing certain services—for example, flu vaccinations for asthmatics and the elderly—over and above their general practice, and in so doing inflating their salaries to as much as £100,000. Rumbling controversy over this perceived injustice at a time when many practices offered little or no out-of-hours service led eventually to a new agreement between the government and the BMA, which saw GPs reluctantly agree to renegotiate their collective contract, and offer limited weekend and evening appointments. Mr Lansley has vowed to go further, forcing local GPs to take back formal control of all out-of-hours provision from the private companies that delivered it under Labour. He has also promised to ensure that any foreign doctors providing out-of-hours care have 'the relevant language skills to ensure they are safe'—in reference to  a succession of scandals relating to allegedly poor levels of care administered by some overseas practitioners under the previous system. In the most high-profile case, retired engineer David Gray died after being given ten times the correct dose of diamorphine by German locum Dr Daniel Urbani.

One Labour reform opposed by many GPs for which the coalition appears to have little enthusiasm is the creation of an England-wide network of Continental-style 'polyclinics' (one-stop shops for NHS treatment, where patients can drop in to see doctors, district nurses, and specialist practitioners under one roof). Launching the policy in 2008, then Health Minister Lord Darzi argued these 'super-surgeries', which would open from 8 a.m. to 8 p.m. seven days a week, could only benefit the public. But the BMA, marshalling a

1.2 million-strong petition, claimed they would undermine existing GP services by poaching their patients and depriving them of funds. They added that involving private firms in running the clinics amounted to backdoor privatization of NHS primary care—making patients subservient to shareholders. By the time Labour left office, there were only seven polyclinics in place— all in London—and Mr Lansley swiftly put a further rollout on hold.

Other recent controversies have revolved around a familiar bugbear of critics of NHS market reforms: the fines and bonuses culture. In 2008, Lord Darzi published the recommendations of a year-long review into the next ten years of NHS funding, unveiling plans to award hospitals multimillion-pound bonuses for demonstrating top-quality clinical performance. Assessments of their success would be based both on hard data—covering everything from waiting-times to individual surgeons' 'death rates'—and patients' own views about the quality of treatment they received. Also proposed was a new 'NHS constitution' outlining what patients had a right to expect from the health service, including dignity, privacy, and confidentiality (an echo of the 'Patients' Charter' introduced by Mr Major and updated in Mr Blair's first term). In addition, 15 million people with long-term health conditions, including asthma and diabetes, would be given new personalized care plans, with 5,000 participating in a pilot giving them greater control over their treatment through 'personal health budgets'— a reform already in place in relation to domiciliary care provided by council social services departments for the elderly and mentally ill, and broadly supported by the other parties.

➜     see also local government, pp. 531–2.

Before leaving office, Labour also undertook to introduce free prescriptions for patients with long-term conditions, but this pledge was abandoned by the coalition in its October 2010 *CSR*—along with plans for one-on-one care for cancer patients.

The coalition has also reawakened the spectre of financial rewards and penalties for hospitals. While Mr Lansley offered trusts greater autonomy, he also warned that those that readmitted patients within 30 days of discharging them for a related complaint would be forced to carry out any additional treatment without having its costs covered by ministers. Defending the move, he cited statistics showing hospitals had become over zealous in discharging patients to alleviate 'bed-blocking': between 1998–99 and 2007–08, emergency readmissions in England rose from 359,719 to 546,354. According to warnings from charities and professionals, however, hospitals were likely to need more free beds than ever to cope with the impact of cuts to social care budgets flowing from the CSR, because of expected reductions in the number of residential and nursing home places.

➜     see also local government, pp. 532–4.

Deficit reduction was also the motivation for Lib Dem and Tory manifesto promises to cut wasteful spending on consultants, managers, and IT projects—while protecting 'frontline services'. Once in office, however, the Lib-Con coalition quickly reneged on a related pledge: its undertaking to scrap the Summary Care Record (SCR) database, commissioned by Labour to store all electronic patient records on one system so they can be accessed by NHS professionals working anywhere in England. The database—from which patients must 'opt out' if they want their details kept private—began rolling out in April 2010, and in an early U-turn the new government decided to retain it.

Meanwhile, Mr Lansley found himself provoking further controversy in August 2010, when, amid intense media speculation, he appeared to confirm plans to abolish *NHS Direct*—the telephone service introduced more than a decade earlier to offer the public round-the-clock health advice to prevent unnecessary out-of-hours GP appointments and overcrowding at hospital accident and emergency units. It was rumoured that the service would be replaced by a new 1-1-1 helpline, already piloted in the North East, which ministers and NHS Direct's own chief executive argued would be more efficient and easier to access.

Critics immediately accused the government of penny-pinching by replacing NHS Direct, which cost £123m a year to run and boasted 3,000 staff, 40 per cent of them trained nurses—with an alternative Mr Dobson described as little more than a 'call centre'. Hardly surprising, perhaps, that in an apparent U-turn (although one denied by ministers) Mr Lansley subsequently announced NHS Direct would be continuing after all.

# ▌Complaining about NHS treatment

Anyone dissatisfied with his or her NHS care may make a formal complaint, initially at local level, and his or her case may be referred to one of four ombudsmen—one each for England, Scotland, Wales, and Northern Ireland. In England, complaints about the NHS are handled by the *Parliamentary and Health Service Ombudsman*, in Wales by the *Public Services Ombudsman for Wales*, in Scotland by the *Scottish Public Services Ombudsman*, and in Northern Ireland by the *Northern Ireland Ombudsman*.

Each ombudsman produces an annual report for consideration by its national assembly or parliament, and handles complaints in relation to:

- failure in service standards from an NHS body;
- failure to provide a service to which a person is entitled;
- maladministration by an NHS body;
- failure in the exercise of clinical judgement by hospitals or GPs.

Complaints are handled according to the sequence outlined in the table entitled
'The complaints process to the Health Service Commissioner (Health Service
 Ombudsman)', to be found on the Online Resource Centre that accompanies
this book.

In addition, there exists an independent watchdog charged with promoting ongoing improvements in the health service and reviewing complaints
by service users unhappy with the local resolution of their cases. Individuals
must, however, have gone through the full NHS complaints procedure before
their cases can be referred to this quango. Since April 2008, health and social
care providers in England have been monitored by the **Care Quality Commission (CQC)**. Formed from the merger of the Healthcare Commission and Commission for Social Care Inspection (CSCI), it is authorized to issue trusts with
fines, fixed penalties, and enforcement notices for breaking the terms of their
registrations. It can even withdraw NHS licences from acute hospitals that persistently fail cleanliness inspections. In Scotland the CQC's role is assumed by
the *Scottish Commission for the Regulation of Care (SCRC)* (Care Commission
for short), in Wales by *Healthcare Inspectorate Wales (HIW)*, and in Northern
Ireland by the *Regulation and Quality Improvement Authority (RQIA)*.

> → see also local government—Chapter 18

The performance of NHS services at local level is also now regulated by
health service scrutiny committees set up by county councils and unitary
authorities. These comprise around 15 members, including a chairperson and
vice-chairperson. Membership is drawn not only from the county or unitary
authority, but also local district or *borough councils* and relevant voluntary
organizations, including Age Concern, the National Society for the Prevention of Cruelty to Children (NSPCC), and the National Association for Mental
Health (Mind). Finally, the NHS is also held accountable in England and Wales
by the *Audit Commission*, which scrutinizes the accounts of individual trusts,
PCTs, and STAs (although it is due for abolition by 2012). Its Scottish equivalent
is Audit Scotland, while the Northern Ireland Audit Office (NIAO) performs
this role in that province.

> → see also local government, pp. 408–9

# ▌ NHS changes under devolution

The act of handing day-to-day NHS management to the devolved executives in
Scotland, Wales, and Northern Ireland was always likely to create disparities in
the way in which the health service was administered in different parts of the UK.

Aside from major structural contrasts—for example, the continued absence of foundation trusts in Scotland—the past few years have seen the emergence of clear 'inequalities' between the nations, arising from political decisions taken by individual legislatures. In April 2007 the *National Assembly for Wales* became the first devolved chamber to scrap prescription charges, having previously reduced them from the £6 an item levied elsewhere in Britain to £3. The Northern Ireland Assembly followed suit in April 2010, and the Scottish Parliament was due to do likewise in 2011. Perhaps understandably, there have been increasingly vocal calls for the same to happen in England.

Marginally less controversial have been the decisions by all three devolved administrations to abandon parking charges at NHS hospitals—a move former Labour Health Minister Ben Bradshaw refused to adopt in England, arguing that many trusts needed the revenue generated to subsidize patient care.

## ☰ Topical feature idea

The article in Figure 6.3 is taken from the *Manchester Evening News* of 23 June 2010. It concerns an announcement by Health Secretary Andrew Lansley that two maternity units earmarked for closure since 2006 might now be saved. His intervention came as part of a nationwide review of Labour's controversial moves to rationalize the NHS by closing or merging some hospitals and centralizing core services like accident and emergency in major ones in towns and cities. The proposed closure of the two units made national headlines when announced because Salford MP Hazel Blears joined a protest march despite being a minister in Mr Blair's government. How would you follow up this story to develop it into a background feature for the paper? Who would you approach for interviews, and what questions would you ask them?

**Figure 6.3** Article from the *Manchester Evening News*, 23 June 2010

# Decision to Shut Maternity Units to be Reviewed

Amanda Crook

*Manchester Evening News*

21 June 2010

Web link: http://menmedia.co.uk/manchester eveningnews/news/health/s/1262823_deci sion_to_shut_maternity_units_to_be_reviewed

The controversial closure of maternity units in Salford and Rochdale is to be reviewed, the M.E.N. can reveal.

Bury's maternity services won a reprieve last week from health secretary Andrew Lansley—and now government officials say they will also look again at units in Rochdale and Salford.

The news means a £100m shake up of maternity care across Greater Manchester is now in chaos.

Fairfield General in Bury was due to stop providing overnight care next summer with mums and babies transferring to new, multi-million pound units at Bolton Hospital and North Manchester General.

Rochdale and Salford were due to close in 2012. Overnight maternity services have already closed at Trafford General.

Mr Lansley has promised results of the review would be ready 'in weeks'.

Greater Manchester health chiefs agreed to centralise all maternity and children's care from 12 units into eight almost two years ago after a decade of planning and consultation.

The shake-up of baby services, called 'Making it Better', was finalised in 2007.

It caused huge controversy, with local Labour MPs including Hazel Blears and Ian Stewart defying the government to join protests aimed at saving local units.

NHS bosses said the shake-up would stop expert care being spread too thinly and provide the best possible facilities.

Fairfield's future was at the heart of the tightly-contested election fight in Bury North—narrowly won by Tory David Nuttall, who pledged to save it.

Now Labour MPs Hazel Blears, in Salford, and Simon Danczuk, in Rochdale, are to have an urgent meeting with Andrew Lansley.

Ms Blears said: 'It's absolutely clear here that Salford people want these services and we are negotiating for a midwife-led service, which will mean babies can continue to be born in Salford.'

Mr Danczuk said: 'I've always taken the view that maternity services should be retained at Rochdale Infirmary. My son was born there just eight weeks ago, and there's no doubt they provide an excellent service.'

## ✱ Current issues

- **Return of GP commissioning and creation of independent hospitals:** the Conservative-led coalition has announced the most radical set of changes since the health service's inception. PCTs and SHAs will be scrapped and commissioning handed directly to up to 500 consortiums of GPs, with foundation trusts encouraged to opt out of the NHS altogether to become 'dynamic' social enterprises.

- **Future of NHS prescription charges:** prior to the May 2010 election, Labour pledged to abolish prescription charges for those with long-term conditions in England. As of 2011 no one living in Scotland, Wales, or Northern Ireland has to pay for prescribed medicines. Plans to cut charges in England have been put on hold by the coalition, sparking criticisms of an emerging national postcode lottery.

- **Scaling back of NHS targets, or just changing their emphasis?** The Lib-Con coalition has vowed to reduce the use of top-down NHS targets, placing greater emphasis on assessing 'quality' of care, rather than simply the quantity and speed of procedures performed. However, early on in the Parliament, Health Secretary Mr Lansley announced several new sets of data to be published regularly to inform patients. The first to be introduced, in June 2010, were weekly updates on rates of infection at individual hospitals by meticillin-resistant *Staphylococcus aureus* (MRSA) and *Clostridium difficile* (C. diff.). These are now published on a single national website (http://data.gov.uk).

## ? Review questions

1. What were the founding NHS principles? To what extent were they ever achieved?

2. Labour pledged to scrap the Conservatives' internal market when it returned to power, but many argue that it actually consolidated the Tory model. Who is right and why?

3. Can the NHS still be described as a 'national' health service? If not, why not?

4. Given the variable needs and demands of different areas of the UK, what are the arguments for and against pursuing the NHS ideal?

5. Outline what is meant by the concept of 'patient choice'. What measures have been introduced so far to put this idea into practice—and how successful have they been?

# → Further reading

Ham, C. (2004) *Health Policy in Britain: The Politics and Organisation of The National Health Service*, 5th edn, London: Palgrave Macmillan. **Fifth edition of leading text on history of NHS, including updates on the Blair reforms and developments in Scotland, Wales, and Northern Ireland.**

Klein, R. (2006) *The New Politics of the NHS: From Creation to Reinvention*, Abingdon: Radcliffe Publishing. **Comprehensive overview of the evolution of the health service.**

Pollock, A. M. (2006) *NHS plc: The Privatisation of Our Health Care*, London: Verso Books. **Thoughtful critique of growing involvement of the private sector in running the NHS by a professor of health policy and health services research at University College London.**

Pollock, A. M. and Talbot-Smith, A. (2006) *The New NHS: A Guide to Its Funding, Organisation and Accountability*, London: Routledge. **Indispensable guide to the changing internal structure and practices of the NHS since the introduction of the first internal market, including the growth of patient choice.**

#  Online Resource Centre

www.oxfordtextbooks.co.uk/orc/Morrison2e/

Visit the Online Resource Centre that accompanies this book for web links and regular updates.

# 7

# The Treasury, industry, and the utilities

During the 1992 US presidential election race, James Carville, campaign strategist for then aspiring Democratic nominee Bill Clinton, coined a phrase that would go down in political (and journalistic) folklore. Commenting on the issue he judged most crucial in persuading the US electorate to back a candidate he said simply, 'the economy, stupid'. So it is, arguably, in Britain. Although political historians have observed that UK voters do not always switch horses at times of economic crisis (the deep **recession** of the early 1990s saw John Major return the Conservatives to power, albeit with a drastically reduced majority), perceived economic competence has proved the making of certain prime ministers (Margaret Thatcher, Tony Blair) and incompetence the downfall of others (Ted Heath, James Callaghan).

This chapter explores the work of the two principal government departments charged with overseeing the British economy: HM Treasury and the Department for Business, Innovation, and Skills (BIS). It also examines the remit and composition of the main non-departmental bodies charged with managing specific areas of economic performance, such as the **Bank of England's Monetary Policy Committee (MPC),** the **Office of Fair Trading (OFT),** and the recently established **Office for Budget Responsibility (OBR).**

# ▌ The role of the Treasury and Chancellor of the Exchequer

In recent years it has become customary for prime ministers to appoint deputy prime ministers to stand in for them when they are absent on foreign business or on holiday. If there can be said to be a 'true' deputy prime minister, however, it is the Chancellor of the Exchequer. Charged with controlling the government's purse strings, the Chancellor is indisputably the most powerful minister in the **Cabinet** beside the premier. The workings of government would grind to a halt if it were not for taxes and loans, and it is the Chancellor's job to raise this money. Even the name of the department he or she heads—the Treasury—testifies to his or her authority: not for nothing is the prime ministers's official title 'First Lord of the Treasury'.

The Chancellor has the following key responsibilities:

- overseeing the government's public spending commitments by managing fiscal policy—raising or lowering taxes and/or duties, and investing them in public services (schools, hospitals, prisons);
- managing the national debt—the level of borrowing needed to top up taxation revenues in order to finance the government's spending programme;
- promoting economic growth in the UK economy and encouraging British exports;
- controlling domestic *inflation* (rises in the cost of living) and unemployment.

In recognition of the huge degree of responsibility that comes with the post, he or she is assisted by one of the largest ministerial teams of any Whitehall department. Unlike most other ministries, the Treasury boasts at least three secretaries of state in addition to the Chancellor: the Chief Secretary to the Treasury, the Financial Secretary to the Treasury, and the Economic Secretary to the Treasury.

## Fiscal policy and taxation

One of the principal means by which British governments have traditionally attempted to control the economy is through 'tax and spend' tactics—more formally known as 'fiscal policy'. Based on the writings of Liberal economist John Maynard Keynes, fiscal policy involves the raising or lowering of taxation to influence consumer behaviour—and to improve the health of the government's finances. A 'Keynesian' approach might see the Chancellor raise Income Tax rates, for example, in so doing cutting individuals' take-home pay and, by extension, spending power. In theory this should have the knock-on effect of reducing demand for goods and services, thereby curbing inflation. At the same time, raising taxes increases government revenue for public spending on schools, hospitals, etc., reducing the need for the Chancellor to *borrow* money (in so doing increasing the 'national debt').

Until the 1980s there was a broad post-war consensus in favour of managing the economy via fiscal policy (although, on balance, it tended to be favoured more by Labour than Conservative governments). Labour's enthusiasm arose largely out of its traditional emphasis on taxation as an instrument for redistributing income from higher to lower earners through benefits (see Chapter 8). From the advent of the National Health Service (NHS) onwards, Labour also gained a reputation as the 'high tax party' on account of its ideological commitment to strong investment in state health care and education (all of which required high tax revenues). Prior to the Thatcher years the party also favoured the public ownership of many industries and these, too, required huge injections of money to maintain them. The Conservatives, in contrast, have traditionally been the party of tax cuts and breaks (particularly for business)—favouring a 'supply-side' approach to running the economy that leaves more money in individuals' pockets in the hope of boosting growth through private, rather than public, expenditure. The theory is that keeping taxes as low as possible for everyone, including the rich, ultimately has a beneficial 'trickle-down' effect on the wider economy and, by extension, lower-income households.

There are two broad forms of taxation: *direct taxes* and *indirect taxes*. Direct taxes are 'up-front'—those explicitly taken from individuals or businesses as deductions from their basic earnings. The main types are outlined in Table 7.1.

The fact that direct taxation is charged at different rates, according to an individual's or company's income, means it is often referred to as 'progressive taxation'. By taking into account people's ability to pay, it is seen as fairer than a flat rate charge—such as a water bill or a television licence—which costs the same to everyone, regardless of their earnings.

Indirect taxes do the opposite and, as a result, are often described as 'regressive'. Unlike income or corporation taxes, they are built into the prices of goods and services consumers buy (including basic utilities like gas and electricity). Because these 'pay as you spend' charges—often described as 'hidden' or 'stealth taxes'—are levied at across-the-board rates, they take no account of individuals' ability to pay. The most familiar—VAT, tobacco/alcohol duties, and fuel duty—are set out in Table 7.2.

Table 7.1 Types of direct taxation in the UK—and how they work

| Tax | How administered | Rates (2011–12) | Notes |
| --- | --- | --- | --- |
| Income | Paid by working people through either Pay As You Earn (PAYE) contributions deducted from their gross salaries by employers, or as retrospective payments to HM Revenue and Customs (HMRC) by the self-employed | Personal allowance—£7,475 Standard rate—20% (20p in £) Higher rate—40% (40p in £) Additional rate— 50% (50p in £) for those earning £150,000 or more | As of the 2010–11 tax year (4 April–3 April), the Income Tax 'personal allowance' (the amount a person can earn before paying tax) was due to rise by £1,000 to £7,475, taking 900,000 of the lowest earners out of Income Tax. The level at which the 40% higher rate of Income Tax kicks in was also lowered by £1,500, to £42,375. |

| Tax | How administered | Rates (2011–12) | Notes |
|---|---|---|---|
| Corporation | Paid by companies on their profits—an 'income tax for companies' | Small companies' rate—20% (20p in £ from April 2011—down from 22% or 22p in £) Main rate—27% (27p in £) from April 2011 (down from 28% or 28p in £), and due to fall to 26% (26p in £) in 2012–13, 25% (25p in £) in 2013–14, and £24 (24p in £) in 2014–15 | The standard rate (known as the 'main rate') was reduced in 2008–09, from 30% to 28%. It was due to fall by 1% every year for four years beginning in April 2011. The main rate applies to any company whose profits in a given tax year are £1.5m or more. The small companies' rate rose in 2009 from 19% to 22% (compensated for by a 100% relief for small businesses on any capital investment up to £50,000, and a 175% tax credit to encourage research and development). The small companies' rate was due to fall to 20% in April 2011. |
| Capital gains (CGT) | Paid by the owners of financial assets, property, and other items, such as expensive jewellery or sports cars, sold by them for personal gain | Entrepreneurs' rate—10% (10p in £) on first £5m made during lifetime General rate—18% (18p in £) Higher rate taxpayers' rate—28% (28p in £) | There has been prolonged controversy about capital gains in the British media, in light of the mammoth profits made by 'private equity firms'—groups of wealthy speculators who club together to buy underperforming companies, improve their fortunes, and sell them for profit. Amid mounting criticism of the sector (some directors were reputed to be paying less tax than their cleaners), Labour introduced an 18% flat rate for CGT for anyone whose gain exceeded £1m (albeit with a 10% 'entrepreneurs' rate' for gains of less than £1m). Before George Osborne's first Budget there was speculation that CGT might rise to 40 or even 50%, but it was finally raised to just 28%—and only for higher rate Income Tax payers. At the same time the entrepreneurs' rate was extended to apply to the first £5m of an individual's lifetime gains. |
| Inheritance (IHT) | A 'death duty' paid on the value of estates (including financial assets, property, and other valuable items) handed down from | 40% (40p in £) for legacies of over £600,000 | Until recently it was charged at 40% on all estates worth over £300,000, but mounting controversy over this low threshold (average house prices were near that level by 2007) prompted |

| Tax | How administered | Rates (2011–12) | Notes |
|---|---|---|---|
| | the deceased to friends or family members by the executors of their wills | | Mr Darling to double it for married couples and those in civil partnerships seeking to bequeath their estates to their children. He was widely criticized, however, for 'stealing' a Conservative policy, and the Tories entered the May 2010 election pledging to raise the threshold to £1m (although this change has yet to materialize). |

 NOTE: A regularly updated version of this table can be found on the Online Resource Centre that accompanies this book.

**Table 7.2** Types of indirect taxation in the UK—and how they work

| Name | How administered | Rates (2011–12) | Notes |
|---|---|---|---|
| Value added tax (VAT) | A 'hidden tax' embedded in the retail prices of items that consumers buy in supermarkets, high-street stores, and online | 20% (20p in the £) | For essential items like domestic fuel and power there is a reduced rate of 5%, while certain items are exempt— including food, children's clothes, books, newspapers and magazines, and some equipment for the disabled. At the height of the recession, Labour cut the rate for 13 months from 17.5% (17.5p in the £) to 15% (15 in the £). In its first Budget, the **coalition government** raised it as of January 2011 to 20% (20p in the £). |
| Tobacco products duty and alcohol excise duties | Embedded in the retail price of items that are subject to excise duty | 24% (24p in £) on packet of 20 cigarettes, plus £119.03 per 1,000 cigarettes £23.80 per litre of spirits and wine exceeding 22% ABV £288.20 per hectolitre of made-wine and sparkling wine of 8.5–15% alcohol by volume (ABV) | Always controversial among smokers and drinkers, these are higher in Britain than elsewhere in the EU. Duties on alcohol products range widely from one to another. Petrol duties have also been a source of unrest recently, in light of the increasing underlying |

| Name | How administered | Rates (2011–12) | Notes |
|------|------------------|-----------------|-------|
| | | 17.32% (17.32p in £) per hectolitre of beer | price of car fuel caused by the ongoing global peak oil crisis. Mr Osborne froze tobacco and most alcohol duties in his June 2010 Budget, and announced no further rise in fuel duty, but motorists were still set to be hit by the ensuing increase in VAT. |
| Fuel tax escalator | Additional tax added to VAT on motor fuel | 59% (59p in £) per litre for unleaded petrol, diesel, biodiesel, and bio-ethanol | In 2000 Mr Brown angered farmers and long-distance hauliers by raising fuel duty—known as the 'fuel tax escalator'—at a time of already rising petrol prices. His action led to the first large-scale protest of the Blair era, as convoys of angry fuel protestors clogged the M1 and M6. Aware of the political sensitivity of fuel duty, Mr Darling delayed planned rises more than once. In his last Budget, in March 2010, he announced he was phasing in a proposed 'all in one go' rise or nearly 3p a litre in three stages—in April 2010, October 2010, and December 2011. |

NOTE: A regularly updated version of this table can be found on the Online Resource Centre that accompanies this book.

As these two tables illustrate, the British tax system has long been characterized by its complexity. For this reason, coalition Chancellor George Osborne established a new *Office for Tax Simplification* in July 2010 to rationalize the 11,000-page Exchequer fiscal code he had inherited, and end what he described as the 'spaghetti bowl' of UK tax law. Meanwhile, in an effort to crack down on tax evasion and avoidance—which together are estimated to cost the British economy some £14bn a year—Mr Osborne's Lib Dem deputy, Chief Secretary to the Treasury Danny Alexander, announced at his party's 2010 conference that he would be placing the accounts of everyone earning £150,000 or more under greater scrutiny in an effort to recoup at least half of these lost fiscal receipts.

Major public spending announcements have historically been reserved for *the Budget* (see pp. 199–201), but in 1997 Mr Brown introduced a new innovation designed to set out publicly his spending plans for three years at a time. The idea was partly motivated by a desire to create the appearance of greater financial transparency. It was also intended to encourage individual spending departments dependent on Treasury handouts to plan in a more long-term way, rather than from year to year as previously. Spending reviews have generally been held on a three-yearly basis since then, with less frequent (but more far-reaching) *Comprehensive Spending Reviews (CSRs)* occurring so far on just three occasions (in 1998, 2007, and 2010). Labour delayed its final CSR until after the May 2010 election, and it eventually fell to the Lib-Con coalition to deliver it in October that year (see p. 192).

## Managing national debt

*National debt*—sometimes referred to as 'public', 'government', or increasingly 'sovereign debt' (see p. 281)—is the term describing the total of all credit owed at any one time by every level of government (or government-owned institution) in a given state. Other than raising taxes, the principal way in which governments finance public spending is through borrowing. On a month-by-month basis, Chancellors run a **public sector net cash requirement (PSNCR)**. Formerly the 'public sector borrowing requirement' (PSBR), this is effectively the difference between the total the government intends to spend on public services in a given year and the amount available to it through taxation. To avoid unpopular tax rises or spending cuts, governments have historically favoured loans as a means of financing costly public expenditure. Usually, these are raised by selling bonds (known as 'gilt-edged securities', or 'gilts') to the public. By borrowing from investors to maintain or increase spending, governments often run up short-term 'debts', much like individuals using their bank overdrafts or credit cards. An overspend of this kind within a given financial year is known as the *annual deficit*.

Since a more 'monetarist' approach to running the economy was adopted in the 1980s (see p. 196), successive governments have made a virtue of trying to 'balance the books' within overall *economic cycles* (periods, usually of a few years, during which economies 'naturally' fluctuate between bouts of expansion and contraction) by reining in taxation and controlling spending. But the impact of the 2008 global financial crisis and ensuing recession (see p. 197) changed this. In 2009–10, the last tax year before the May 2010 election, government borrowing reached a peacetime record of £163.4bn—*excluding* the cost of aid to the banking sector.

The principal debate in Britain since the most recent recession has centred on the state of the country's 'structural', rather than 'cyclical', deficit. The latter phenomenon—a familiar concept in most market economies—is the periodic budgetary overspend most governments incur during periods of short-term economic turbulence (such as recessions). The former, in contrast, is more deep-rooted. It results from what the *Financial Times* newspaper describes as a 'fundamental imbalance in a government's receipts and expenditure, as opposed to one-off or short-term factors'. In other words, a structural deficit tends to emerge after a prolonged period during which a government has consistently spent more money than it was able to raise through taxes or selling off state assets—forcing it to borrow more (often at high commercial interest rates) as a consequence.

When the Lib-Con coalition took office in May 2010 and examined the previous government's balance sheets in detail, its ministers claimed the 'black hole' in Britain's public finances—and the true extent of its structural deficit—was even worse than previously feared. In his last Budget Labour Chancellor Alistair Darling said this overspend (estimated at around £77bn of Britain's overall £167bn deficit) had peaked at 8.4 per cent of GDP during 2009–10, and would fall to 2.5 per cent by 2014–15 on the back of a phased programme of £73bn in spending cuts and tax rises. He repeated an earlier Labour pledge to halve the country's overall deficit within four years.

But neither Mr Darling's figures nor the speed of his response to Britain's debt crisis impressed the Conservatives. Delivering his own 'emergency' Budget barely two months later, Mr Osborne unveiled a swingeing package of austerity measures—principally a squeeze on welfare benefits (see p. 233) and annual spending cuts of £40bn by 2015, *in addition to* the billions earmarked by Labour. In so doing, he put government spending departments other than those that had previously had frontline funding ring-fenced on notice that their budgets would fall by up to a quarter (later asking ministers to 'model' even deeper cuts of 40 per cent to identify any further slack). Mr Osborne and his supporters in the right-leaning press, notably the *Daily Telegraph* and the *Spectator*, argued this was much-needed 'medicine'—although the precise nature of the cuts would not be known until the October 2010 CSR (to be informed, controversially, by recommendations from Sir Philip Green, billionaire owner of the Arcadia retail group, which includes the British Home Stores and Top Shop high-street chains).

By 2015–16, Mr Osborne predicted the structural *current* deficit—the part of the structural deficit used to fund public sector running costs like wages and maintenance, rather than capital investment—would have turned into a modest surplus, allowing him to start addressing Britain's overall national debt. Based on his Budget, the Office for Budget Responsibility predicted this debt would peak at £70.3bn in 2013–14—compared to the £74.9bn anticipated for 2014–15 under Labour's plans. However, Mr Osborne's contention (and that of his Lib Dem allies) that his Budget had been 'fair'—by, for example, raising the personal Income Tax allowance to £7,475, thus taking 900,000 low-paid workers out of tax altogether—was questioned in August 2010, when the independent

Institute of Fiscal Studies (IFS) think tank published an in-depth analysis of its likely impact on different income groups over the period up to and including 2014. Branding the Budget 'clearly regressive', it claimed the poorest 10 per cent of households stood to lose 5 per cent of their income as a result of its measures, while non-pensioner households without children in the richest tenth would sacrifice less than 1 per cent. The IFS analysis—reflected in a similar assessment four months later when Mr Osborne slashed welfare further in his October CSR—prompted an unusual intervention by the director general of the Equality and Human Rights Commission, Neil Kingham, who publicly reminded ministers of their obligation under the Equality Act 2010 (passed months before Labour left office) to 'have due regard' before announcing Budget measures to ensuring that their impact does not fall disproportionately on 'vulnerable groups' such as the disabled and other minorities. He warned that the Commission might need to take 'enforcement action' if the Treasury was unable to prove it had properly assessed the likely long-term fallout of the Budget against 'equality impact assessments', and said he would be issuing further guidance in the autumn.

The CSR itself went on to slash some £81bn from public expenditure—the biggest cut by a British government since at least the 1970s—and the Treasury's own predictions estimated that nearly 500,000 jobs would be lost in the public sector as a result.

During acute economic crisis, it has sometimes been necessary for governments to approach global financial institutions. In the mid-1970s then Labour Prime Minister James Callaghan borrowed money from the International Monetary Fund (IMF)—a crisis bank Britain had helped to found in the wake of the Second World War (see pp. 309–10)—to stabilize the UK economy as it was buffeted by stagflation (simultaneous rises in inflation and unemployment). The IMF only agreed on condition that the government made substantial public spending cuts to save money. Documents released by the National Archive in December 2006 under the '30-Year Rule'—a convention stipulating that all but the most sensitive government papers should be made public 30 years after being written (a gift for journalists!)—revealed that the country nearly had to scrap its nuclear deterrent simply to balance the books.

More recently, it emerged that the huge injections of extra funding into the NHS and state education system under New Labour were financed largely by borrowing—meaning that, even before it was forced into the position of considering a multibillion-pound bailout for the banks, the government was accumulating a mounting structural deficit (see pp. 190–1). According to figures released in 2008, having initially dropped sharply after the party returned to power in 1997, national debt more than doubled between 2001–02 and 2007–08, leaping from £315.5bn to £650bn. It rose by £100bn in one stroke when the government bailed out the Northern Rock bank to save its customers' deposits and restore confidence in the financial sector following the bank's near-collapse in 2007. Northern Rock—which had overstretched itself by making high-risk home loans to customers without the guaranteed means of repaying them—initially made an emergency plea for support to the Bank of England (reflecting trends in the US 'sub-prime market'—see p. 207). It was eventually nationalized by the government, as a 'temporary measure', after months of talks to find a private buyer failed.

By this time, however, the bill for propping up the beleaguered bank had topped £100bn (more than the total annual spend on the NHS), and the cost of repaying Britain's national debt was costing taxpayers £31bn a year in interest—marginally less than the country's defence budget. In a symbolic move, in July 2008 Mr Darling revealed that he was reviewing Mr Brown's fiscal 'Golden Rule': the principle, adhered to for more than a decade, that the government should only borrow for public *investment*, rather than *current spending*. In a swift move designed to signify ministers had learned lessons from the Northern Rock debacle, in September 2008 Mr Darling wasted little time nationalizing the assets of another bank, the Bradford and Bingley, to avert its collapse. While some critics immediately accused him and Mr Brown of again using taxpayers' money to secure irresponsible loans made by a reckless bank at the height of the credit boom, they were widely praised for some innovations, including the creation of a new Financial Services Compensation Scheme (FSCS). Triggered by the since reconfigured Financial Services Authority (FSA), this effectively forced the banking sector as a whole to absorb Bradford and Bingley's losses, while still guaranteeing protection to those with savings in the bank of initially up to £35,000.

Towards the end of its 13 years in power, Labour reverted even more overtly to a Keynesian approach to buoying up the economy. As the recession bit, Mr Brown and Mr Darling committed themselves to a 'fiscal stimulus' designed to limit job losses by boosting growth through strategic tax cuts (including a short-term cut in VAT—see Table 7.2) and increased public investment. The idea was that, by bringing forward capital projects originally earmarked for future years, the sharp decline in activity in the by then free-falling housing and small business sectors could be offset by the state keeping people in employment directly. Figures published by the ONS in July 2010 suggested it may indeed have been the fiscal stimulus that hauled the British economy out of recession: the statistics showed that Britain's 'peak to trough' decline in output was equivalent to 6.4 per cent of GDP (rather than the previously estimated 6.2 per cent), and the 0.3 per cent growth rate for the first quarter of 2010 was achieved largely through extra government spending. Mr Darling also claimed credit for second-quarter growth figures of 1.1 per cent, published that July and revised upwards to 1.2 per cent a month later—Britain's strongest economic performance for four years.

At the height of the downturn, Labour also launched a number of discrete aid initiatives to help those hit hardest by the downturn. These included a

Homeowner Mortgage Support Scheme, to give short-term financial aid to those with mortgages of up to £400,000 and savings of £16,000 or less who had lost their job but expected to return to work soon. Its aim was to avoid a repeat of the 1980s and 1990s recessions, during which home repossessions had soared. By 2010 there were indications its impact had been positive: according to the Council of Mortgage Lenders, while 46,000 homes were repossessed in 2009, this was only 61 per cent of the 75,500 seized by banks and building societies in 1991.

To stimulate a recovery in property and small business, meanwhile, the government began using its stake in the part-nationalized banks to nudge them into lending more money (at affordable rates) to consumers and struggling companies. An Asset Protection Scheme was also introduced to insure the major British banks against potential losses caused by previous 'toxic debts' (see p. 207). At the same time, in a move unseen for decades, the Bank of England opted to use its own device to encourage more lending—pumping liquidity into the system by increasing the supply of sterling, in a process known as *quantitative easing*.

## The Office for Budget Responsibility

In a symbolic move intended to take responsibility for making medium to longer-term economic forecasts out of the hands of politically motivated Chancellors, Mr Osborne introduced the Office for Budget Responsibility shortly after entering Number 11 Downing Street. While the OBR gave a broad thumbs-up to the cutbacks and tax changes Mr Osborne introduced to tackle Britain's deficit in his maiden Budget, one of its earliest pronouncements was remarkably positive about the economic competence of his predecessor.

Although it revised down Mr Darling's predicted growth rates of 3 per cent or more from 2011 onwards (instead predicting fluctuations between 2.6 and 2.8 per cent), it revealed that surprisingly buoyant tax receipts in the early part of 2010—boosted by the introduction of a new 50p top Income Tax rate—meant government borrowing over the following five years was likely to be £22bn less than he had warned. Perhaps more directly embarrassing for the coalition was the OBR's prediction in June 2010 that by 2015 around 1.2 million fewer people would be employed across the public and private sectors (although ministers emphasized other figures suggesting that this could be offset by the creation of new jobs).

At the same time as he formed the OBR, Mr Osborne appointed former *Observer* editor, executive vice-chair of the Work Foundation, and Labour sympathizer Will Hutton as 'Fair Pay Tsar' to look into future salary settlements for senior public sector managers, the unrelated former Business Secretary John Hutton to advise on the future of public sector pensions, and Labour **backbencher** Frank Field to brainstorm new ideas for tackling poverty.

# Controlling inflation and unemployment

Inflation and employment have a 'seesaw' relationship. Historically, when inflation is rising, unemployment tends to be low, and vice versa. Only usually at a major crisis point—such as the Depression, or the late 1970s oil crash—do both rise noticeably at the same time. This is known as *stagflation*.

The reasons for this trade-off relate to basic economics. When the prices of goods and services rise, this tends to mean one of two things: either demand for them is high (that is, shops and manufacturers can get away with charging more, because people are willing and able to pay), or the cost of producing them is rising. If production costs are rising, this will often be down to mounting wage bills—in other words, the fact that more workers have been taken on to produce and deliver those goods or services and/or their salaries have risen.

Conversely, at times when demand for goods is falling, the first casualties tend to be at least some of the workers employed to produce them. Employers lay off staff to reduce their running costs and enable them to continue in business on a more manageable scale, cutting prices to attract more custom if necessary. If such redundancies become more widespread in the economy, overall unemployment will rise. And, of course, at times of high unemployment, people have less money to spend on goods and services—so prices will have to fall further if consumer demand is to be sustained.

Therefore, rising unemployment tends to lead to falling inflation. A knock-on effect of this is a reduction in economic growth—the expansion of the economy through rising demand for goods and services, and increased private sector investment, job creation, and exports. Theoretically, growth can be a virtuous circle: more jobs should mean more people with money to buy things, more companies manufacturing goods, and higher employment. In practice, the promotion of free trade has meant that many of the products that British people are now buying are cheap imports from the Far East and elsewhere—which means they no longer necessarily lead to industrial expansion and job creation in Britain.

Given the tensile nature of this relationship between inflation and unemployment—referred to by economists as the 'inflation–unemployment seesaw'—governments find it difficult to keep a grip on both for any length of time. When New Labour was elected in 1997, Mr Brown pledged to end 'boom-and-bust' by doing just this—words that would return to haunt him in years to come. But despite the fact that Britain proceeded to enjoy a decade of sustained growth, in the second quarter of 2008, the country's economy officially slipped into recession for the first time since the early 1990s—only emerging 19 months later.

## The Bank of England's role in monetary policy

If fiscal policy was the favoured approach to keeping the British economy afloat in the 1950s and 1960s, *monetary policy* has been the vogue since the 1980s. Widely credited as the 'invention' of free market US economist Milton

Friedman (a hero of Mrs Thatcher's), the contrasting approach to economic management favoured by monetarism involves **interest rates**—the cost of borrowing money—being used to direct consumer behaviour and control inflation. The theory is that if rates rise, people will be more likely to *save* (banks and building societies should theoretically be offering them a profitable return for their investment) and less likely to borrow and spend (credit cards and loans cost more).

In Britain, inflation is calculated monthly. The government uses two tools to measure it: the **retail price index (RPI)** and the **consumer price index (CPI)**. Both track movements in the prices of notional 'baskets' of 650-odd items bought regularly by 'typical' households—including food, clothes, and tobacco. The difference between the two is that the CPI—the measure preferred by governments and the *European Central Bank* (see p. 280)—*excludes* housing costs such as *Council Tax* and mortgage rates, while 'core CPI' (also often quoted) omits day-to-day expenses, such as food and energy bills. Both place more emphasis on goods people buy only occasionally—for example, DVD players and other electronic products. Given that routine purchases like food and utilities are the costs that most burden households, critics view the CPI as highly misleading. Nonetheless, the use of these statistics enabled Labour to maintain low rates of both 'headline' (CPI) and 'underlying' inflation (CPI adjusted to exclude volatile items, like tax rises) on the whole throughout its tenure, even when the RPI figures cited by the Opposition and some economists began to rise.

Until 1997 responsibility for reviewing interest rates each month rested with the Chancellor. Within days of taking on that job, however, Mr Brown made the Bank of England independent—and handed it the task of controlling inflation on his behalf. Decisions about interest rates have since rested with the Monetary Policy Committee (MPC), composed of nine members, including the bank's chief economist, and chaired by its governor. The government sets an inflationary target—currently 2 per cent—and if this is missed (according to CPI figures) the governor is expected to write to the  Chancellor explaining, and setting out the action the MPC intends to take to lower it. In April 2007 Mervyn King became the first incumbent to have to do this, when headline inflation hit 3.1 per cent. It has been almost a monthly ritual ever since.

## The quest for full employment

Successive Chancellors, particularly Labour ones, have dreamt of the holy grail of 'full employment'—an ideal state in which everyone capable of work can find a job suited to their abilities and aspirations. In practice, this goal has remained elusive.

At certain times, unemployment in Britain has reached levels that have been politically damaging for the government of the day. In the early 1980s Mrs

Thatcher's mass closure of coal pits, steelworks, and shipyards in northern England, Wales, and Scotland, combined with her crackdown on trades union power (see p. 213), saw the national jobless total rise to between 3 million and 4 million. While Labour largely maintained a much lower official unemployment rate than this—using a combination of 'carrot' and 'stick' policies, such as tax credits and its 'New Deal' to entice people off benefits and back to work—nationwide unemployment still hovered around 1.5 million-plus even before the recession pushed it up to nearer 2.5 million. Moreover, there has been huge criticism of the increasing 'casualization' now widespread in the British working environment—with many new jobs created since the early 1990s taking the form of part-time and/or short-term contracts devoid of the entitlements (for example, pensions, holiday pay) available to full-time, permanent staff.

## Promoting economic growth and UK exports

If one word strikes terror into the hearts of prime ministers and Chancellors it is 'recession'—the term used to denote two successive economic quarters in which the economy 'shrinks'. Such periods of negative growth generally lead to less money being borrowed and spent by consumers, lower sales and profits for businesses, the scaling back of production, and redundancies. Britain has lived through three recent recessions: in the early 1980s, the early 1990s, and again between April 2008 and December 2009, when the country's economic output slumped by a total of 6 per cent.

Little wonder governments have become so obsessed with achieving growth. Two engines are traditionally used to achieve it: rising employment and prosperity among a country's citizens, leading to increasing domestic demand, and the development of overseas export markets for products manufactured at home. In theory, each of these should lead to wealth creation.

This chapter has already examined the inflation–unemployment quandary and how British governments have tried to boost the economy by juggling these 'twin evils'. But how do they go about promoting the UK's exports abroad—and measuring their success or failure in doing so? Taking the latter question first, there are two measures:

- the **balance of trade**—the difference in value between the total of all goods and services bought by British residents from overseas (imports) and that of all British-made goods and services sold abroad (exports) in a given year. This includes both 'visible' products (physical goods, like food, clothes, and television sets) and 'invisible' ones (virtual goods, such as information technology and financial services);

- the **balance of payments**—the difference in value between the total of *all* payments of every kind flowing between the UK and other countries, including imports and exports, but also financial transfers and debt payments to foreigners. The balance of trade is therefore a 'subset' of the balance of payments.

If, in a given financial year, Britain is found to be buying more foreign imports than it is selling exports overseas, its current account will be in *deficit*. In contrast, if the UK sells more abroad than it buys in it is in *surplus*.

Recent decades—particularly since the advent of Britain's membership of the European Union (EU) (see Chapter 9)—have seen the UK importing disproportionate quantities of cheap foreign clothing, toys, electrical items, and motor vehicles. The slow decline of indigenous industries like shipbuilding and coalmining, meanwhile, has seen the emphasis of the country's economic output switch to services such as telecommunications, information technology (IT), and finance. As a result, while the UK has historically had a significant balance of trade deficit in terms of visible items, its service sector has often generated a surplus. According to the Office of National Statistics (ONS), the UK's overall trade deficit in goods and services was £3.26bn in April 2010—at the end of the first quarter of positive growth since the end of the recession. When broken down into the two categories, it showed a £4bn surplus in the service sector, compared to a £7.3bn deficit in goods.

In view of the high importance attached to the balance of trade, successive Chancellors have tried to incentivize people to 'buy British', both at home and abroad. Prior to its entry into the then European Economic Community (EEC) in 1975, Britain had a history of doing this through 'protectionism'. It would levy customs duties (tariffs) on companies seeking to import foreign goods into the UK—a tactic designed to inflate their prices artificially and encourage consumers to seek out home-grown alternatives (saving jobs as a consequence).

An alternative approach is to try to influence international exchange rates for the British currency, the pound sterling. Both Labour and Tory Chancellors have, in the past, 'devalued' the pound—for example, by issuing more banknotes to increase the overall money supply in the economy. The idea was that, by reducing sterling's value, they would cut the price of British goods abroad—making them more attractive to foreign buyers and boosting exports.

But the relative value of the pound is affected by other factors, too—including the 'demand' for sterling in world money markets. Fear of *undermining* the value of the pound was at the heart of Tory Chancellor Norman Lamont's decision to pull Britain out of the European exchange rate mechanism (ERM)—which was designed to harmonize the exchange rates of all EU member states (see pp. 278–9).

In addition to the balance of trade and balance of payments, there are two other 'litmus tests' of the state of economic growth in the economy:

- **gross domestic product (GDP)**—the market value of all goods and services produced within Britain's borders in a given year, irrespective of which country derives income from them (sometimes referred to as 'national output');
- **gross national product (GNP)**—the market value of all goods and services produced by British-owned companies, labour, and property in a given year, irrespective of where those assets are based (sometimes referred to as 'national income').

It has become customary for governments to cite favourable GDP as evidence of the strong performance of their economies. In reality, however, while a high GDP should reduce unemployment (a foreign-owned company on UK soil is as likely to generate jobs as a British one) contributing to increased spending and investment in the local economy where a factory or call-centre is based, this is only part of the picture. Most income generated by foreign-owned companies flows back to the countries in which they are based, limiting the longer-term benefits to the British economy brought by businesses that choose to locate here. Conversely, GNP may often give a truer indication of levels of wealth generation for the UK economy: the numerous British-based telecoms firms that have recently outsourced their call centres to the Far East, where labour costs are cheap, may do little to help Britain's employment figures, but most of the income they generate comes back to the Treasury.

# ▌The Budget process

The highlight of the Treasury's calendar is the annual Budget Speech and accompanying Finance Act. This used to take place in autumn, but is now held in spring. However, Mr Brown introduced an annual Pre-Budget Report (or 'Pre-Budget Statement'), which has since been delivered each autumn. Initially, this was intended simply to set the scene for prospective tax and spending plans to be announced in the Budget, acting as a 'health check' on the performance of the British economy over the preceding 12 months. More recently, it has become almost as much of a media event as the Budget itself—with Chancellors making increasingly firm policy announcements, and using it as an opportunity to test public opinion on changes they are considering.

In his inaugural Pre-Budget Report, Mr Darling signalled several headline-grabbing changes—including his intention to introduce a flat rate tax of 18 per cent on all capital gains over £1m. After several months of sustained lobbying on behalf of small businesses, led by the Confederation of British Industry (CBI), he performed a U-turn, announcing that upcoming 'entrepreneurs' would qualify for an 8 per cent reduction. Fearing further reprisals from within the business community, he also backtracked on plans to tighten up tax regulations relating to wealthy UK-based 'non-domiciles' (see p. 154). Mr Darling had been expected to force them to disclose details of offshore financial holdings, but instead limited his actions to introducing a promised £30,000 a year 'wealth tax'. Beyond this, they would continue to pay only tax related to their UK-based earnings in Britain.

The Budget itself, generally held in early March, has two elements:

- the Budget Speech;
- the Finance Act.

## The Budget Speech

The Budget Speech is designed to:

- forecast short to medium-term movements in the economy (one–three years), and review how it has performed in the preceding 12 months;
- announce rises and/or cuts in direct and indirect taxation, and public spending, and the prioritization of particular areas over others (for example, health, education, defence);
- announce new taxes, tax breaks, and/or benefits to finance investment and/or help low-income groups (for example, tax credits, cold weather payments for the elderly);
- give the Chancellor a platform for political grandstanding—allowing him or her to boast about the country's economic performance.

The speech—which occasionally runs for more than an hour—is immediately followed by a similarly lengthy retort from the Shadow Chancellor or Leader of the Opposition and a debate on the floor of the Commons. More than 150 years after the event, William Gladstone holds the dubious honour of having delivered the longest ever continuous Budget Speech. His 1853 address lasted four hours and 45 minutes.

## The Finance Act

For measures announced in the Budget to take effect, the Commons must legislate to implement them. Unlike most laws, however, the Bill needed to deliver the proposals is given swift passage and substantially passed on the same day as the Speech. Dubbed the Finance Bill, it is designated a 'money Bill' by the *Speaker*—enabling it to bypass the usual stages Bills must negotiate before receiving *royal assent* (see p. 68). The initial 'stages' are effectively gone through in one fell swoop, with the Speech itself treated as the *first reading*. The Commons must pass individual resolutions to approve each specific tax or duty change within ten sitting days, but, under the Collection of Taxes Act 1968, minor changes can be agreed immediately—enabling the business of government to continue in the interim. A *second reading* must be heard within 30 days, but the *committee stage* may be split, with more important resolutions heard by a committee of the whole house and remaining ones considered by a standing committee of 30–40 MPs. Following this, the *third reading* will be steamrollered through, usually on the second day of the *report stage*.

Since the confrontation between the Commons and House of Lords over Lloyd George's 1909 'People's Budget', there has been no Lords stage to the Finance Bill. Nonetheless, even today there is scope for Budgets to fall at a late hurdle. The row over Labour's abolition of the 10p starting rate of Income Tax so raised the hackles of backbench rebels led by former Welfare Minister Mr Field that, before announcing a compensation package for low earners penalized by the change, it looked as if Mr Darling's first Budget (in 2008) might be defeated—forcing his resignation. In the event, he staved off this prospect by issuing an 'emergency Budget' designed to compensate the losers—some of whom stood  to be left £230 a year worse off. This raised the Income Tax threshold—by £600, lifting 600,000 people out of tax. The move was backdated to 1 April—meaning everyone paying the new 20 per cent basic tax rate, but not earning enough to pay 40 per cent, gained a staggered 'rebate', through their pay packets, of £120. In that year's Pre-Budget Report, this 'bonus' was made permanent—and raised to £145 from 2009–10.

## Public spending outside England—the Barnett Formula

To ensure that Scotland, Wales, and Northern Ireland benefit fairly from central government tax revenues, public spending is allocated on a per capita basis across Britain using a system called the 'Barnett Formula'. In theory, the formula—devised in the late 1970s by then Labour Chief Secretary to the Treasury Joel Barnett—ensures that the amount given to each country corresponds to its population size (and, by definition, the extent to which its inhabitants have contributed to taxes).

In practice the formula has proved highly controversial—successive recalculations have benefited Scotland, in particular, relatively more than the rest of Britain. Resentment between it and the other countries has escalated since *devolution* was introduced in 1998, because not only has Holyrood continued to do disproportionately well out of taxes, but the *Scottish Parliament* has also used its freedom to spend its share of the money as it chooses to subsidize its public sector in ways unseen elsewhere. Barnett has, among other things, enabled Scotland to reject university top-up fees and phase out NHS prescription charges—two highly controversial levies that remain in England (if not Wales and Northern Ireland). In his June 2010 Budget, Mr Osborne confirmed plans to review the Barnett Formula .

# ▌ The government's role in promoting British industry and commerce

For the past thirty years, British governments have taken an increasingly laissez-faire approach to running the economy as a whole. The mass privatization programme of the 1980s saw a swathe of industries sold into private ownership, from motor manufacturer British Leyland to British Airways, British Steel, all major utilities (gas, electricity, water), and ultimately the railways. In the decades since, the mantra has been one of 'consumer choice', with successive governments promoting competition between rival private-sector providers over any state monopoly. In theory, this allows people to shop around for the best deals on virtually any product—with market forces (supply and demand) ensuring that they are high quality and competitively priced.

In practice, however, the government continues to play an interventionist role in promoting British industry and protecting it from the worst ravages of **globalization**—the process by which national economies are becoming increasingly interdependent. Recent decisions by ministers to shore up failing banks and try to broker a rescue package for the Rover car company—the last surviving British-owned motor manufacturer until its collapse in 2005—demonstrate this. Moreover, the free market ideal of a private sector that, left alone, will 'regulate itself' efficiently and fairly has proved elusive—forcing the state to introduce greater regulation.

## The Department for Business, Innovation, and Skills (BIS)

The department responsible for promoting British industry and commerce and overseeing regulation of the free market within the UK is the Department for Business, Innovation, and Skills (BIS). Between summer 2007 and May 2010 it was known as the Department of Business, Enterprise, and Regulatory Reform (BERR), and before that as, variously, the Department of Trade and Industry (DTI), the Department of Trade, and the Board of Trade.

The Department's website describes it as 'the *voice for business across government*'. It has the following responsibilities:

- creating conditions for business success and raising productivity in the UK economy;
- championing the interests of employees and employers;
- promoting consumer interests;
- encouraging sustainable business development.

Although formal regulation of the business environment is delegated to a series of non-departmental bodies, when BERR replaced the DTI under Labour, its

*Secretary of State* began to play a more hands-on role than previously. In January 2009, then Business Secretary Lord Mandelson tried to jump-start Britain's ailing car industry by pledging £2.3bn in loan guarantees—including £1.3bn from the European Investment Bank—for motor manufacturers prepared to invest in 'high technology' and green alternatives to conventional engines. BERR was proactive in enforcing regulatory judgments, too. In 2008, Mr Mandelson's predecessor, John Hutton, publicly ordered BSkyB, the satellite broadcaster part-owned by Rupert Murdoch's multinational media company News Corp, to sell more than half its shares in rival company ITV. He was endorsing a ruling by the **Competition Commission** (see p. 205) that the shareholding represented '*a substantial lessening of competition*' in the television market.

As well as overseeing the regulatory framework, it is the Secretary of State's job to liaise regularly with the main bodies representing employees and employers: the Trades Union Congress (TUC) (see p. 212) and the CBI respectively.

# The regulatory authorities

While it is BIS's responsibility to draft the laws governing fair competition, consumer protection, and sustainable business, until recently these have been administered on the ground by two principal regulatory authorities: the Office of Fair Trading (OFT) and the Competition Commission. A week before the coalition's October 2010 CSR it emerged that the two authorities were set to be merged. However, with formal consultation on the merger only due to begin in January 2011, it was unclear how soon this would happen, and at time of writing the two institutions remained in place, retaining their distinctive roles.

## The Office of Fair Trading (OFT)

Established in 1973, this *quango* has been charged with ensuring that the 'rules' of fair play—genuine choice and competition—are applied in practice. Its founding remit was to protect both consumers and companies, ensuring that small businesses in particular were protected from anti-competitive practices by larger, more established rivals. Until 2003 the OFT was headed by a Director General of Fair Trading, but it is has since been run by a board and chairperson.

According to its most recent statement of aims, the OFT's duties are to:

- encourage businesses to comply with competition and consumer law, and improve their trading practices through self-regulation;
- act decisively to stop hardcore or flagrant offenders;
- study markets and recommend action where required;
- empower consumers to make informed choices and get the best value from markets, and help them to resolve problems with suppliers through Consumer Direct—a regionally based, government-funded advice service established in 2000.

It has been for the OFT to launch investigations into allegations of 'restrictive practices'. These have taken various forms, but most commonly a small or medium-sized business has complained that its attempt to break into an established market (such as telecoms) was being frustrated by larger-scale, more-established companies offering discounts on their wares that it could not hope to match as it struggled with initial overheads. To some extent, being initially 'out-competed' by the big boys is inevitable as one tries to set oneself up in a new marketplace, but history is littered with examples of competition being deliberately stifled by established players using underhand means. The most notorious examples occur when rival companies collude to peg their prices at the same level and/or undercut potential new competitors by offering 'loss leaders' (cheap deals at below-cost price) to lure customers. These unofficial alliances—'cartels'—can effectively stop new competitors getting established, by using economies of scale achieved through years of trading in the sector to sell certain items at unrealistically low prices.

Companies have also been accused of unfair trading in relation to the prices they pay their suppliers. In recent years there has been concern about the below-cost prices allegedly offered by supermarket chains like Tesco and Asda to producers in developing countries for everything from bananas to coffee, while British farmers have complained of being offered unsustainably low prices for meat and dairy products. The appalling press generated by such controversies has prompted retailers to embrace 'fair trade' goods and invest millions in corporate social responsibility programmes.

Of course it is not only other businesses that are hurt by restrictive practices: price-fixing can work upwards, as well as downwards, and at times consumers get the worst deal. In December 2007 Asda and Sainsbury's were among several companies to admit having conspired to fix the price of milk, following an OFT investigation. The supermarkets charged inflated prices for the product—despite offering farmers minimal payment —and as a result British consumers were left £270m out of pocket.

In 1997, a separate regulator was set up to oversee the financial services sector—banks, building societies, and insurance companies—assuming responsibilities previously held by the Bank of England. But the effectiveness of this body, the *Financial Services Authority (FSA)*, was called into question following its failure to act on the banking sector's increasingly cavalier mortgage lending policies prior to the collapse of Northern Rock and the subsequent 'credit crunch' (see pp. 192–3).

For this reason, shortly after entering the Treasury Mr Osborne announced plans to downsize the FSA, dividing its responsibilities between three authorities as follows:

- a new *Consumer Protection and Markets Authority* to police the overall conduct of every financial company authorized to provide services to the public;

- a *Prudential Regulatory Authority* created as a subsidiary of the Bank of England to prevent financial companies ranging from banks and building societies to insurers and brokers taking imprudent risks with their investors' money;

- a *Financial Policy Committee*, again within the Bank of England, charged with identifying potential financial and macroeconomic risks to the stability of the UK economy and where possible taking pre-emptive action to avert them.

## The Competition Commission

Formerly the 'Monopolies and Mergers Commission', the Competition Commission has been less concerned with the day-to-day market practices preoccupying the OFT than with movements in company ownership that may affect future competition. Although most markets are now 'deregulated'—open to full free market competition—in practice there has been huge consolidation in many of them over the past decade, with more profitable companies taking over or merging with smaller ones. As a result, markets that once offered dozens of alternatives from which consumers could choose are increasingly dominated by a handful of providers—and sometimes only one or two.

Nowhere is this lack of genuine competition more obvious than on supermarket shelves. While most stores offer myriad varieties of essentially the same products, superficially different brands are often made by the same company. Other than supermarkets' own-brand options, household cleaning products tend to be manufactured by Unilever or Procter and Gamble; many chocolate bars lining confectionary counters will somewhere bear the small print of Nestlé or Cadbury.

It has been the Commission's job to ensure that, wherever possible, choice has been genuine. One way of doing this has been to prevent mergers and takeovers that would otherwise restrict it—avoiding 'monopolies', which occur when one company has more than a 25 per cent market share in a particular product. High-profile recent rulings by the Commission have included its decision to approve supermarket chain Morrisons' takeover of rival Safeway in 2003—provided that it first agreed to sell 53 stores in areas where local competition might suffer as a result of the acquisition. In February 2008 the Commission issued a report focusing on whether the proliferation of out-of-town supermarkets was contributing to the decline of town centres and local grocery stores. It angered critics by finding no conclusive evidence to support this assertion—although it did argue a new 'competition test' should be applied by local authorities when deciding whether to grant *planning permission* for superstores. It cited the example of the 'Tesco town' of Bicester in Oxfordshire, which is ringed by five branches of the chain. The report also disappointed campaigners by failing to compel major supermarkets to dispose of 'land banks'—areas of prime development land they have acquired to prevent rivals building there.

→
see also
local
govern-
ment,
pp. 476
and 478

## Types of company

There are three main types of corporate structure in the UK:

- limited liability companies (ltds);
- private limited companies;
- *public limited companies (plcs)*.

The principal differences between the three are explained in Table 7.3.

# The role of the Stock Exchange

Shares in plcs are traded on global stock markets, one of the biggest being the London Stock Exchange (LSE). Established in 1760, when 150 brokers expelled from the Royal Exchange for rowdiness formed a spontaneous share-trading club at Jonathan's Coffee House, it registered as a private limited company in 1986, and finally as a plc in 2000. Like all plcs, the LSE is susceptible to potential takeover bids. In 2004, it became the first stock market to be targeted by a prospective purchaser when it faced an £822m hostile bid from little-known Swedish company the OM Group, a technology manufacturer that runs the Swedish Stock Exchange. Four years later, its shareholders rejected a £1.35bn offer by its German rival, Deutsche Börse.

Table 7.3 Types of company in the UK

| Type of company | Definition |
| --- | --- |
| Limited liability companies (ltds) | One up from a sole trader, this is a common form of company in the small and medium-sized enterprise (SME) (small business) arena. Introduced to provide some security for individuals who would otherwise have to shoulder all the burden of risk associated with running their own businesses, it provides them with a statutory guarantee not enjoyed by larger commercial companies. Limited companies—which can include theatres, charities, and voluntary trusts—instead only allocate 'liability' (risk) to their investors to the value of a nominal sum (usually £1). This will be agreed with them when they initially sign the company's 'original memorandum' and 'articles of association'. |
| Private limited companies | Again usually small or medium-sized, these are not permitted to issue shares to the public via the stock market. The liability of individual investors for any shortfalls or debts incurred by such companies is limited to the nominal value of shares with which they were initially issued. |
| Public limited companies (plcs) | These have at least two shareholders and may offer shares to the public. Their owners will 'float' them and they will be listed on the LSE. They must have issued shares to the value of £50,000 before being allowed to trade. Larger plcs are often referred to as 'blue chip' companies, and include household names such as BP and Marks and Spencer. |

Today the LSE has regional bases in Belfast, Birmingham, Glasgow, Leeds, and Manchester. Some 2,600 UK and overseas companies are listed on it at any one time, and shares are traded electronically via a computerized system called 'CREST'. Minute-by-minute movements in share prices of listed companies are tracked by a series of nine indices collectively known as the 'Financial Times Stock Exchange' ('FTSE', or 'FOOTSIE'). The most famous of these is the **FT100 Share Index**, which lists the 100 highest-valued companies at any one time in order of value, and monitors the movements in share prices of these firms. The FT All-Share Index, meanwhile, lists all of the 2,500-plus companies on the stock market, again in order, and monitors daily movements.

All manner of factors can impact on company share prices. Mergers and takeovers—or the mere prospect of them—can send prices soaring or crashing, according to the market's assessment of how favourable such outcomes are for its commercial fortunes. Shares in iconic high-street companies like Marks and Spencer (M&S), meanwhile, are notoriously prone to fluctuations depending on the state of their profits—particularly at Christmas.

Often, companies' share prices suffer because of factors beyond their control. Amid growing suspicions among share traders that the 1980s stock market bubble was about to burst, 'Black Monday' on 1 October 1987 saw the biggest one-day crash in history. By the end of the month, the value of LSE shares alone had plummeted by 26.4 per cent.

As well as the LSE, London also now boasts an Alternative Investment Market (AIM), launched in 1995, on which shares in smaller developing companies, ethical traders, and/or those whose value has fallen so low that they have decided to 'delist' from FTSE are traded. Sometimes, the trend goes in reverse: when The Body Shop™ was acquired by French cosmetics giant L'Oréal in 2006, it moved from AIM to FTSE.

## The 2008 global banking crisis

After years of unsustainable growth in the mortgage and banking sectors and the credit market as a whole, autumn 2008 witnessed the onset of the biggest global financial meltdown since the Wall Street Crash of 1929 and the ensuing Great Depression. Eighteen months after the term 'sub-prime' had first seeped into the mainstream media—in relation to the crisis of insecurity sparked by defaults on 'toxic' mortgage loans made by US banks to people without the means to repay them—major financial institutions from Europe to the Far East were brought to their knees by the knock-on effects of these and similar practices elsewhere. In the end the position of household-name banks, from Merrill Lynch to Barclays, became so perilous that governments in Britain, the USA, and mainland Europe were forced into doing what the long-standing 'neoliberal' consensus would previously have deemed unthinkable: pouring vast sums of money into the sector to shore up savings and pensions and keep the system going. But even this was not enough in itself, and before long Mr Brown's government was leading the way by going a stage further—taking controlling stakes in several major high-street banks. After decades of runaway privatization and deregulation, the term 'nationalization' (see pp. 215–6) re-entered the political lexicon.

The escalating financial crisis came to a head in late September 2008 when, within a week, investment bank Lehman Brothers filed for bankruptcy, Merrill Lynch was taken over by the Bank of America, and the US Federal Reserve Bank (the country's equivalent of the Bank of England) announced an $85bn rescue package and effective nationalization of America's biggest insurance firm, AIG. Within a fortnight an even bigger collapse occurred, when Washington Mutual—the largest US mortgage lender—was shut down by regulators and sold to JP Morgan Chase. To prevent other financial giants facing a similar fate, the White House administration was left battling to force a $700bn rescue package for the country's entire banking sector through a Congress furious at the conduct of reckless bankers.

In Britain, even more dramatic state interventions were to come. Barely a week after Lloyds TSB stepped in to announce a buyout of Halifax Bank of Scotland (HBOS), one of Britain's biggest mortgage lenders, the government nationalized the bulk of Bradford and Bingley's assets, while selling off its branches and savings operation to Spanish bank Santander. The Treasury then moved to guarantee all savings deposits in UK banks of up to £50,000, to prevent a 'run on the banks'—the mass withdrawal of savings by panicked investors worried about losing their money if a bank were to collapse. Meanwhile, the FSA announced a temporary ban on 'short-selling'—a shady form of stock market speculation that entails gambling on a company's share price falling, and which had been blamed in some quarters for undermining confidence in the banking system. Short-selling involves seasoned speculators 'borrowing' shares the value of which they expect to fall from a third party, selling them on, and then buying them back after their value has plummeted, before returning them to their original owner for a profit. It has since been unilaterally banned in Germany, and the EU is considering outlawing it across the union. Then, on 8 October, amid feverish rumours and jittery fluctuations on the stock market, Mr Brown and Mr Darling announced details of a £500bn bailout for the UK's banking sector, which would see up to eight high-street banks and building societies part-nationalized in a last-ditch attempt to persuade financial institutions to resume lending to each other, and—more importantly for the 'real economy'—

small businesses and the public. While only Lloyds TSB, HBOS, and the Royal Bank of Scotland (shares in which had plummeted) initially accepted the government's offer—other major banks like Barclays opting to raise capital on the open market—the price paid by these institutions for their cut of the 'final' £37bn Treasury share offer was significant. First, the FSA ordered the government to acquire not only 'preference shares' (which give shareholders priority in the payment of dividends, but no voting rights), but also 'ordinary' ones—thereby giving ministers a direct say in running the companies. Second, it emerged the government would be appointing its own directors to the banks' boards, and that no bonuses would be paid to senior staff for at least the first year. This latter measure went some way towards allaying mounting public outrage at the scale of the 'bonus culture' that had exploded during the boom years, with directors often taking home multimillion-pound perks—irrespective of how well their company was performing. The government replaced several leading bankers at the helm of the semi-nationalized institutions, including the chief executive of RBS, Sir Fred Goodwin—known as 'Fred the Shred' because of his notoriously ruthless cost-cutting in a previous job at the Clydesdale Bank. The Royal Bank of Scotland was 60 per cent nationalized, while the state took a 41 per cent stake in Lloyds TSB, and HBOS.

In the same tumultous week Mr Brown entered into a public row with Iceland, after several of the country's leading banks collapsed like dominoes, and it emerged dozens of British local authorities, charities, universities, and other bodies had substantial sums invested in them. When Iceland's prime minister Geir Haarde announced he was guaranteeing the safety of all Icelanders' deposits, but not those of Britons, Mr Brown used anti-terror legislation to freeze the £7bn in assets held in the UK by Landsbanki, the country's national bank, to recoup some of the costs.

→ see also local government, pp. 368–9

After months of criticism of his leadership at home, and amid flat-lining opinion poll ratings, Mr Brown was widely praised for his statesmanlike handling of the financial crisis in the international media. His model of state intervention was swiftly emulated by the USA and a number of mainland European countries. At a press conference in London with foreign journalists, he was asked by one if he considered himself a superhero like 1920s comic book space explorer Flash Gordon. With trademark seriousness, he replied: 'Just "Gordon", I can assure you.'

The aftermath of the banking crisis, and its ongoing impact on Britain's public finances (see pp. 190–4), saw opposition politicians and media commentators pour scorn on City traders and demand firm action from the government to ensure that there would be no repeat of the reckless practices that had led to the near-collapse of so many institutions. Among the most vocal critics was Lib Dem Treasury spokesman Vince Cable, who ridiculed what he saw as Mr Darling's ineffectual response—a call for international action to impose strict new trading conditions on the banking sector, and a one-off 50 per cent tax on bonuses of £25,000-plus that was only levied in April 2010 (18 months after the crisis began). Once in office, though, the Lib-Con coalition wavered in its professed determination to make the sector pay for its past errors: Mr Osborne has so far imposed only a modest levy on the banks, based on their overall balance sheets rather than individuals' bonuses. The tax, starting at 0.04 per cent of profits in April 2011 and rising to 0.07 per cent in 2012, is expected to raise little more than £2.5bn a year. However, the *European Parliament* recently announced an

EU-wide cap on bankers' bonuses (see p. 270), which in time might pave the way for the kind of global agreement that has continued to be favoured by Labour.

The Lib Dems' pre-election proposal to 'break up' bigger banks into retail and investment arms to stop ordinary customers ever again being exposed to the perils of high-stakes risk-taking is currently the subject of an independent review. More concrete, perhaps, is the coalition's pledge to proceed with plans for a Green Investment Bank announced in Mr Darling's last Budget. When originally announced, the bank—to be backed by £2bn in combined public and private sector cash—was envisaged as an engine for future investment in green energy projects and high-speed rail links. In October 2010 Mr Osboma confirmed plans to press ahead with it, but its precise composition and remit was the subject of a select committee inquiry at time of writing.

# ▶ The government's role in industrial relations

In the 1960s and 1970s, when many industries were still state-owned, battles between the government and trades unions over wages policy, working conditions, and their ability to take industrial action when relations broke down were frequently in the news. After years of struggle between the unions and employers, and growing infighting within the Labour movement, tensions exploded in 1978–79 during the 'Winter of Discontent'—a prolonged period of wildcat action across the public services during which, at one point, the dead infamously went unburied when even funerary workers joined the mêlée.

Hand in hand with its mass privatization programme, Mrs Thatcher's government introduced swingeing clampdowns on the rights of workers to take industrial action. Legal barriers were introduced to block strikes, while the new generation of private sector employers with which unions were now confronted no longer had even to 'recognize' their existence—let alone formally negotiate with them over job cuts or changes in working practices. Mrs Thatcher also ended:

- the 'closed shop'—a rule forcing employees in certain trades or industries to join a specific trade union;
- 'secondary picketing'—the ability of workers in trades *related* to others in dispute with their employers to take 'sympathy action'.

Although both the above remain illegal, when Labour returned to power in 1997 certain workers' rights were restored. Many of these—the right to sick pay and paid leave, and a maximum number of weekly working hours—were guaranteed under the European Social Chapter, signed by Mr Blair in 1998 (see p. 283). The new government introduced a *national minimum wage (NMW)*. It also moved to extend some rights previously the preserve of full-time permanent employees to those on part-time and temporary contracts. Despite these early moves, it took nearly 13 years before a more thorough-going equalization of the rights of temporary and agency workers and those employed on full-time contracts was introduced, in the Agency Workers Regulations, which were finally adopted by the British government despite opposition from the Conservatives and some business leaders, shortly before the May 2010 election. Derived from the EU's Agency Workers Directive, and due to come into force in October 2011, these should give temporary and agency employees the same rights as permanent staff after 12 weeks' continuous employment.

## The role of unions

As discussed in Chapter 4, the unions initially emerged in the eighteenth and nineteenth centuries. They were formed to provide representation for the large groups of workers recruited by the owners of Britain's emerging manufacturing industries. In time, dismayed by the lack of attention paid to their cause by politicians of their day, they began seeking their own stake in power and, to that end, joined with other bodies to form the Labour Party—to which many of them remain formally affiliated to this day (see pp. 140–1).

Although many workers' rights are today enshrined in British and/or European Union law, unions have historically adhered to a self-help approach to representing their members' interests known as 'voluntarism'—a tradition that shies away from seeking legal intervention in workplace disputes in favour of a form of group negotiation known as free collective bargaining. In material terms, unions' principal aims are to:

- negotiate and protect a fair wage for given trades and professions;
- negotiate fair working conditions—working hours, holiday entitlement, sick pay, compensation in the event of work-related injuries or illnesses;
- provide their members with training, educational and social opportunities, and a 'fighting fund' for living costs in the event of prolonged industrial disputes.

In addition, unions traditionally offer legal and financial support in the event of disputes between employees and employers. Unions have historically achieved many favourable settlements for aggrieved workers unfairly dismissed from their jobs, or bullied at work by colleagues or bosses. Sometimes this is done on an out-of-court basis, but on other occasions unions represent employees at employment tribunals.

Over the past thirty years, the number of unions has declined by a third, with many pooling their resources to strengthen their voice at the negotiating table. The most recent amalgamation was that of the Transport and General Workers' Union (TGWU) and Amicus, Britain's biggest technical union, which together became Unite in 2007. The senior officer of a trade union is usually called the 'general secretary'. Like the Labour Party, it will also usually have an elected national executive committee that debates changes of policy and practice, and beneath that regional and district organizations. There will also be branch organizations, often based in individual workplaces, and houses or shop stewards' committees, which act as focal points for negotiations between employees and employers.

The 'big three' British unions as of 2011 are as set out in the table entitled 'Britain's "big three' trade unions", to be found on the Online Resource Centre accompanying this book.

Most unions are affiliated to a single representative body, the Trades Union Congress (TUC), which holds an annual conference like those organized by the main political parties to rally opinion from members and ratify changes in policy. The serving Labour Party leader is traditionally invited to give its keynote speech.

The TUC dates back to 1868 and its membership currently consists of 58 unions, representing 6.5 million people (equivalent to 80 per cent of union members). It has eight regional councils in England and a single one for Wales. Scotland has its own equivalent body: the Scottish Trades Union Congress (STUC).

## Union recognition—and what it is worth

For unions to be able to negotiate with employers about working practices, pay, and conditions, they first need to be *recognized* by employers. After years of having their rights diluted, unions were given a new impetus to recruit in the Employment Relations Act 1999, which introduced a statutory process through which they could demand recognition on meeting specific criteria.

If claims for recognition cannot be satisfied bilaterally between a union and the relevant employers, it has the right to apply for help from a Central Arbitration Committee (CAC), which assigns a three-person panel to each case. There are two main ways in which a union may achieve recognition through the CAC—regardless of whether this is desired by the employers with which it is in dispute:

- *without* a ballot—a union is entitled in law to *automatic* recognition if *more than 50 per cent* of its 'bargaining unit' (that is, all employees entitled to join it) have done so;

- *with* a ballot—if *at least 40 per cent* of the bargaining unit vote in favour of recognition in a ballot and this number constitutes a majority of those who vote. A worker in a bargaining unit does not need to have joined a union to vote in strike ballots.

Ironically, one of the most notorious industries for union recognition is journalism. There have been many cases in which the managers of larger regional newspapers and some nationals (including Express Newspapers and Independent Newspapers) have fought to prevent it. Prior to the 1999 Act, some regional newspaper groups tried to argue that, to achieve recognition, the unions representing their journalists would need to obtain the support of 40 per cent of their *overall workforces*—including advertising and sales staff, etc.—rather than simply the writers and sub-editors who constituted the bargaining unit.

From the mid-1980s to late 1990s unions were restricted from taking strike action in the sense that any withdrawal of their labour over a dispute constituted a breach of contract. Theoretically this entitled bosses either to sack striking workers or to sue them for damages and loss of business. However, the 1999 Act entitles 'recognized' unions to be consulted formally over changes in working conditions for employees they represent—for example, the movement of a British-based call centre to the Far East or a proposed merger with another company. It also gives unions immunity from prosecution for industrial action provided that:

- action is '*wholly or mainly in contemplation or furtherance of a trade dispute between workers and their employer*' (that is, not secondary picketing);
- the union goes through the correct ballot procedures beforehand. This involves a secret postal ballot, followed by a letter giving the employer seven days' notice of the intended action and details of the ballot result.

Some restrictions remain, however. In addition to being barred from secondary action, unions must keep picket lines to negotiated levels to avoid intimidating colleagues who opt not to take part. This latter clause was inserted to avoid the kinds of harassment to which 'strike-breaking' coalminers and other workers were allegedly subjected in the 1980s by picketers.

Interestingly, while secondary action is illegal, the definition of this term has been tested in recent years. In 2005 British Airways baggage handlers walked out in a two-day 'wildcat strike' in sympathy with employees of Gate Gourmet, a company that supplied BA's airline meals. The workers had been ordered to sign new contracts cutting their wages and benefits following the sudden sacking of 670 colleagues. Because Gate Gourmet had previously been owned by BA and was being subcontracted by BA management to produce meals for its passengers, it was a moot point whether the smaller company's workers were still 'employed' by the airline. If so, was this action 'secondary'?

## Avoiding strikes—role of the Arbitration, Conciliation, and Advisory Service (ACAS)

When negotiations break down, one or other party (or sometimes the government) may seek impartial help in reaching a settlement from the *Advisory, Conciliation, and Arbitration Service (ACAS)*.

This quango's role is to:

- *advise* warring parties on how to avoid industrial action;
- *conciliate* in disputes when invited to do so and try to encourage the parties to reach agreement peacefully;
- *arbitrate* to restart negotiations in disputes that result in industrial action;
- mediate over grievances between individual employees and their employers—notably in relation to prospective employment tribunal cases (relating to unfair dismissal, gender, age, or racial discrimination, etc.).

ACAS has been involved in numerous recent disputes. In July 2007 its chair was called in by ministers to report on the issues arising from a strike by Royal Mail workers over the imposition of new modernization plans and a below-inflation 2.5 per cent pay deal. In May 2005, it was approached by the National Union of Journalists (NUJ) to mediate between it and British Broadcasting Corporation (BBC) director general Mark Thompson over his plans to slash 4,000 jobs.

## Workplace and safety

Health and safety in the workplace is regulated by the Health and Safety at Work Act 1974, which covers the operation of work-based equipment, and a number of subsequent regulations, including the Control of Substances Hazardous to Health (COSHH) Regulations 1999, relating to exposure to virtually all potentially dangerous substances.

Since April 2008 the job of both developing policy guidelines on workplace health and safety and enforcing these rules through inspections fell to the *Health and Safety Executive (HSE)*.

The HSE's day-to-day work is carried out by its Field Operations Directorate (which incorporates separate factory, agriculture, and quarries inspectorates), and regional officers of the Employment Medical Advisory Service. Its powers are set out in the table entitled 'The responsibilities of the Health and Safety Executive (HSE)', to be found on the Online Resource Centre accompanying this book.

In addition, some health and safety legislation (covering shops, offices, warehouses, restaurants, etc.) is enforced by local authority environmental health departments. In its drive to reduce 'red tape'—particularly that afflicting small businesses—the Lib-Con coalition is to review existing health and safety legislation, and the future of the HSE.

# ▶ The utilities

A 'utility' is an organization—whether publicly or privately owned—that is responsible for maintaining and delivering reliable and affordable supplies of a commodity essential to the lives of a country's citizens. The main utilities are those charged with providing 'natural monopolies'—the basic services needed to sustain a society, like water and energy (gas and electricity). Traditionally the railways, postal services, and telecommunications have also been grouped under the utilities umbrella.

In recognition of the vital nature of water and power—and the conviction that everyone should have guaranteed, equitable access to them—the post-war Labour government nationalized all utilities in 1948. Until then, like schools and hospitals, they had been owned by an ad hoc medley of local corporations and charities, with the result that service standards varied wildly from place to place.

For forty years the utilities remained in the public sector. While individuals still had to pay their own rail fares and electricity bills (according to how much of any service they individually used), the industries were hugely subsidized through general taxation. Despite the fact that there was no outside competition from other suppliers to drive down prices, subsidies generally enabled utilities to keep charges at reasonable levels.

## Privatization of the utilities

In the 1980s the ethos governing the way in which state-owned utilities were perceived began to change, as free market economics infiltrated public services for the first time. Mrs Thatcher's government began a wholesale privatization of the utilities, arguing the monolithic state-owned industries were inefficient, over-bureaucratic, and offered the public too little 'choice'. Arguments for and against privatization are set out in Table 7.4.

The first utility to be privatized was British Telecom—a then state telecommunications provider that was once owned and run by the General Post Office. The British Gas Board followed two years later, with electricity changing hands in 1990, and the railways in 1993. Each privatization is explored in more detail below.

**Table 7.4** Arguments for and against utility privatization

| For | Against |
|---|---|
| Privatization makes utilities more efficient by introducing competition from rival suppliers, and enabling them to woo managers with commercial experience. | Introducing the profit motive—and private companies' reliance on shareholders to raise finance for investment—raised suspicions that their main priority was to boost revenue, rather than using cost and/or efficiency savings to lower prices and improve services. |
| It enables them to respond to consumers' wishes by reacting to supply and demand with a wider choice of services—rather than assuming 'the state knows best'. | Periods of intense competition between rival gas and electricity suppliers, combined with ineffective regulation, led to consolidation under fewer, large companies. The public monopolies of old could eventually be replaced by private monopolies and whereas unpopular governments can be removed at elections, the boards of private companies are not publicly accountable. |
| Privatization removes the old 'statist' philosophy imposed on publicly owned utilities, allowing them to cut waste and contract out ancillary services—cleaning, catering, and maintenance—to smaller specialist companies . Doing so saves money on overheads, which can be ploughed into improving the product. | Some privatized utilities—particularly private monopolies like the water companies—have been accused of passing costs on to consumers rather than bearing them internally, to placate shareholders. The major infrastructural investment in the water industry required by recent EU Directives led to disproportionately high increases in water bills, while share dividends continued rising. |
| It raises revenue for future government spending, while saving the state money by cutting the cost of maintaining huge resources. | Privatization divests the country of significant assets built up through investment of taxpayers' money over long periods and gives commercial companies 'something for nothing'. Former Tory Prime Minister Harold Macmillan described it as 'selling off the family silver'. |

Privatization was to be only the first step in Mrs Thatcher's mission to 'liberalize' Britain's utilities. Unusually for someone revered and reviled for her radical handling of the economy, she initially moved tentatively—allowing minimal competition in the privatized utilities to ensure that the transition from public to private sectors had time to bed down before being opened to the ravages of the free market. But by the early 1990s, the gas, electricity, and telecommunications industries had been totally 'deregulated'—allowing a variety of different companies to compete for business in each sector for the first time. On the railways, travellers were soon being referred to as 'customers' rather than 'passengers'.

The onward march of deregulation continues to this day, even in the few sectors still dominated by major public sector providers. In January 2006 the Royal Mail was opened up to free market competition for the first time in 350 years, as industry regulator the **Postal Services Commission (Postcomm)** gave the go-ahead for any licensed business to deliver letters.

Although British governments today favour a 'light-touch' approach to regulation—preferring to let the free market determine prices and services—they continue to set certain minimum standards for each sector. For example, BT (the successor to British Telecom) is still required by the terms of its licence to maintain public telephone boxes to ensure that there is provision for people without mobile phones. In addition, each industry is overseen by at least one regulator with a statutory duty to ensure that customers receive value for money and appropriate access to essential services. Overall responsibilities of regulators include:

- laying down limits on price increases;
- monitoring service quality;
- ensuring that true competition is maintained.

Over the years, however, there has been considerable criticism of these regulators—often derided as 'watchdogs without teeth', in light of their perceived reluctance to interfere in the way in which the utilities they oversee are managed. In April 2008 in the absence of regulator action, the chair of an all-party committee on fuel poverty, Labour backbencher John Battle, tabled a Commons motion publicly demanding that ministers force the gas and electricity regulator, the **Office of Gas and Electricity Markets (Ofgem)**, to stop energy companies charging higher unit rates to poor households reliant on prepayment meters than better-off customers paying by direct debit.

## Communications

British Telecom was privatized in 1984. Initially only limited competition was allowed, with a single alternative provider, Mercury Communications Ltd (a digital phone then owned by the Cable and Wireless Group), entering the market.

After a well-received trial, this 'duopoly' ended in 1991. Some 150 licensed telecommunications companies, including 125 cable operators and 19 regional and national public telecoms operators, soon sprang up, although the market has since radically rationalized through mergers and takeovers. Today consumers can also choose from a range of mobile phone companies, the largest of which include Orange, O2, Vodafone, and T-Mobile, not to mention numerous Internet service providers, including BT Broadband, Virgin, and Tiscali.

Confusingly, most telephone landlines are still provided by engineers from BT, but customers are billed by the suppliers they pay to deliver services to them through those lines. A similar division between the companies that own the physical infrastructure and those who provide services via it exists in most utilities.

In recognition of the growing convergence of telecommunications and broadcast media, since 2003 telecoms regulation has been the responsibility of the **Office of Communications (Ofcom)**, a 'super-regulator' that also oversees television, radio, and digital media services providers. As a media regulator, Ofcom is solely concerned with broadcast and digital/online platforms. Oversight of the print media is the responsibility of the **Press Complaints**

**Commission (PCC)**: unlike Ofcom, a self-regulatory (as opposed to statutory) body with a governing board comprised of industry professionals, the responsibility of which it is to ensure newspapers and magazines comply with an editors' code of practice covering everything from respect for the privacy of the bereaved to the protection of confidential sources.

Previously, telecoms was policed by the now-defunct Office of Telecommunications (Oftel), while the broadcast industry was overseen by several disparate regulators, including the Independent Television Commission (ITC) and the Radiocommunications Agency. The BBC occupied an unusual position in that it has a discrete overseer to monitor its editorial independence, the BBC Trust, with taste and decency issues falling within Ofcom's remit.

In recent years, the postal industry has been regulated by the Postal Services Commission (Postcomm), but in the run-up to the October 2010 CSR Cabinet Secretary Francis Maude unveiled plans to merge it with Ofcom. In addition, the consumer-run body, *Consumer Focus*, which channels complaints from the public to government in relation to most of the utilities, was to be scrapped, with its role franchised to the charity Citizens Advice as part of the government's 'Big Society' rollout. Consumer Focus had lasted barely two years, after being formed in October 2008 from the merger of a prior watchdog, **Postwatch**, Energywatch, and the Welsh, Scottish, and National Consumer Councils.

Until its merger, Postcomm was due to retain the following responsibilities:

- protecting a universal postal service;
- licensing postal operators;
- introducing competition into mail services;
- regulating Royal Mail;
- advising the government on the Post Office network.

With nine out of ten letters still delivered by Royal Mail, a former monopoly, it is unsurprising that Postcomm is usually in the news pronouncing on that organization's performance. In May 2008 it issued a report warning that, unless Royal Mail were part-privatized, allowing it to raise investment on the open market, it might have to axe Saturday postal deliveries to save money. In the year to March 2010, the company made a pre-tax loss of £262m, which it blamed on growing competition from private providers and consumer resistance to the rising price of first-class mail during the recession.

Given its continued dominancy of postal services, Royal Mail can also uniquely be fined by Postcomm for failing to meet government targets (a threat used in 2002 to chivvy up Consignia—as it was then known—after it failed to speed up business mail delivery).

At time of writing, Mr Cable had recently confirmed coalition plans to privatize Royal Mail fully—a step further than Labour had ever dared tread, even under his predecessor, Lord Mandelson, who shelved proposals for a part sell-off in the dying months of Mr Brown's government. Under Mr Cable's scheme, 10 per cent of

Royal Mail shares would be sold to its own employees, with the remainder floated on the open market. It was also expected that the Post Office—the end of the 'postal chain' responsible for running post offices, rather than delivering mail—would be 'mutualized'. This would entail turning it into a cooperative-style company, run (in 'Big Society' fashion) by its own staff and, to a lesser extent, the public.

## Energy

In 1986 gas—then the preserve of the British Gas Board—was privatized. Although the newly rechristened 'British Gas' was initially a private monopoly, the industry soon became the first utility to be fully deregulated. At first the emerging new generation of gas companies (like electricity suppliers later) were regionally based—households and businesses in south-east England, for example, were given a choice of only one alternative to British Gas, the headquarters of which was located in the region. Today it is possible for most people to buy their gas from suppliers based anywhere in Britain, or even abroad, and many companies including British Gas supply 'dual fuel' (both gas and electricity).

As with telecoms, there is a division between supply companies that bill customers and the single firm that owns the infrastructure used to 'transport' fuel to them. Both the network of pipes for gas and the cables and pylons used to transmit electricity are owned by National Grid plc, a monopoly. Suppliers pay the company for using the network.

When electricity was privatized in 1990 it was originally split into three generating companies and 12 suppliers. An example of a regional supply company was the South East Electricity Board (Seeboard), subsequently bought by French-owned company Électricité de France (EDF Energy) in 2002. Since then the electricity supply chain has evolved into the three-stage process outlined in the table entitled 'The energy industry supply chain', to be found on the Online Resource Centre accompanying this book.

While England and Wales are governed by this system, Scottish Power plc and Scottish Hydro-Electric generate, transmit, and distribute all electricity in Scotland.

The gas and electricity utilities used to have separate regulators, but are now overseen by the Office of Gas and Electricity Markets (Ofgem) and the Director General of Gas and Electricity Markets. Following a number of controversies over double-digit rises in energy bills (blamed by companies on the rising price of crude oil—despite the fact most have continued to report substantial profits), a succession of consumer watchdogs have also emerged. The first of these, *Energywatch*, was absorbed by Consumer Focus in 2008.

## Water and sewerage

The most controversial utility privatization was that of the water industry, which was sold off in 1989. Given the essential nature of clean, safe water supplies, many critics of privatization (and some supporters) saw the idea of opening it up to free market competition as a step too far.

There were also practical objections. Given the peculiar difficulties of 'subdividing' the industry's infrastructure—to take an extreme, splitting stretches of a reservoir between different companies—it quickly became clear that conventional competition would be almost impossible. As a result, to this day water is supplied to British consumers by companies that are local monopolies—making a mockery, critics argue, of the premise of privatization.

Initially, ten water and sewerage companies were formed. Each was given responsibility for supplying water, storing, and recycling it, and treating and disposing of sewerage. Confusingly for consumers (and journalists), the industry today is regulated by not one, but three bodies, the roles of which are outlined in Table 7.5.

Industrial and commercial water users are metered nowadays, and households may be charged on the basis of their Council Tax band or opt to be metered, depending on where they live. Consumers with a record of unpaid bills are often forced to install meters to avoid them slipping into future arrears. As in the energy industry, there has been periodic controversy about meters, with campaigners arguing they leave poor people vulnerable: if they do not have change available at a given time, their water supply is effectively cut off. Moreover, companies have been criticized for charging higher rates per unit to customers with meters than to those who pay by conventional bill. These and other concerns prompted the emergence of another watchdog: the **Consumer Council for Water**.

In Scotland, water effectively remains a nationalized utility. Three regional water authorities, covering the north, east, and west of the country, were merged in April 2002 to form a single state-owned company: Scottish Water. Scottish Water is overseen by the Water Industry Commission for Scotland (WICS) and its accounts are audited by Audit Scotland.

## Railways

Privatization of the railways took a different route from that of other utilities and today, albeit by default, the industry remains a *public–private partnership (PPP)*

**Table 7.5** Regulation of the water industry

| Regulator | Remit |
| --- | --- |
| **The Water Services Regulatory Authority** (Ofwat—formerly the *Office of Water Regulation*) | Regulates the industry's structure and financial transparency (examining annual accounts, and vetting proposed mergers/takeovers) |
| The Drinking Water Inspectorate | Regulates the quality of water supplies to consumers |
| The **Environment Agency** | Monitors pollution and regulates the water quality in inland, estuary, and coastal waters. It also has responsibility for flood protection |

(see p. 222). In 1993, following years of negotiation with the private sector to sell franchises covering marginal and unprofitable lines, British Rail was finally privatized. It was initially fragmented under 100-plus private operators—companies that bought up engines, carriages, and other rolling stock to manage individual routes on renewable franchises. Meanwhile, as in the energy industry, ownership of the rail network (the tracks, signals, and stations) was transferred from the government to Railtrack, a private monopoly. Following a spate of controversies and rail disasters—including the 1999 Paddington train crash, in which 31 people died—ministers wound down Railtrack in 2002, replacing it with a not-for-dividend company: **Network Rail**. The infrastructure was therefore effectively taken back into a form of qualified public ownership.

Network Rail charges the remaining 25 operators for using its infrastructure, although in practice many operating companies run their local stations as subcontractors. Franchises are awarded by the government on the basis of a guaranteed 'minimum level of service' specific to each route and companies are invited to tender for renewable terms of anything between seven and twenty years. The company that wins a franchise will usually be that willing to run the service with the lowest government subsidy—giving rise to concerns about underinvestment and price rises. Current examples of franchisees include Southern (which runs the main London to Brighton line and manages stations for Network Rail along that route), and Virgin (operator of the west coast mainline).

In some areas two or more companies operate services in competition with each other, but elsewhere there are local monopolies. In practice, any competition that does exist is limited because it is physically impossible for two companies to run directly competing services (no two trains can use the same track between the same stations at the same time).

Huge increases in the number of people commuting to work in Britain in recent years have put growing pressure on the rail network and fare prices have repeatedly risen well above inflation, even at times when service quality has deteriorated. Overcrowded carriages, broken-down engines, late arrivals, and cancellations—at a time when annual government subsidies to the rail network remained significantly higher than those before privatization—have made the railways an enduring ministerial headache.

Regulation of the rail industry is currently split between two authorities. The Office of Rail Regulation ensures that prices are fair and there is equitable access to tracks for operators. Meanwhile, the Department of Transport (DoT) itself recently took responsibility for awarding and reviewing franchises and fining operators for repeated lateness, cancellations, and other aspects of poor performance back in house. Beforehand, this role fell to the Strategic Rail Authority (SRA).

As with the other utilities there is also a watchdog to represent consumers: **Passenger Focus.**

# Private finance initiative (PFI) and public–private partnerships (PPP)

As with major public sector building projects, the huge infrastructural invest-ments required by utilities are often funded through the *private finance initiative (PFI)*—the system introduced by Mr Major's Conservative govern-ment in 1992, initially to finance new prisons at a time of acute overcrowding and repeated breakouts (see p. 254). The classic PFI model sees a private com-pany financing the bulk of the initial capital investment (buildings and equip-ment), often along with some ancillary staff to man the facility, and effectively 'owning' it for years or decades afterwards. The public sector gradually 'buys it back', a long-term leaseback arrangement akin to a mortgage.

Although initially sceptical, Labour wholeheartedly embraced the PFI concept as it moved to fund an extensive programme of new schools and hospitals, rechris-tening such projects 'public–private partnerships' (PPPs). Today, virtually all new public sector capital outlays are financed this way—and so, too, are some related to the utilities. The proposed new generation of nuclear power stations approved in 2008 is likely to be largely, if not wholly, financed by the private sector.

One big advantage to governments of using private finance to fund capital projects is that initial outlays do not appear on the Treasury's balance sheet—meaning they do not technically 'count' as public expenditure. In contrast to the huge start-up costs of some projects, the face value of contracts awarded to pri-vate businesses as an incentive to carry out building work is relatively low. Critics argue, however, that PPPs have notable disadvantages—as outlined in Table 7.6.

**Table 7.6** Criticisms of the private finance initiative (PFI) and public–private partnerships (PPPs)

| Criticism | Explanation |
| --- | --- |
| Can only generally be financed through borrowing | Because governments' borrowing is better secured than the private sector's, interest rates faced by private companies investing in PPP projects will be higher than those offered to states. |
| Companies put sharehold-ers before the public (or 'customers') | Private companies have legal responsibility to earn profits for their shareholders—making it likely that, whatever the short-term savings to the government, final costs to the taxpayer will, over time, be greater than if the state had wholly financed the project itself. |
| PFI/PPP agreements are like credit card debt or 'hire pur-chase' agreements—money bor-rowed on the 'never never' | PFI/PPP creates confusion over who actually 'owns' the project. Some regard it as akin to hire purchase (HP) agreements entered into by governments in the 1960s. |
| Who is responsible if something goes wrong—the private investor or the taxpayer? | The closure of Railtrack by ministers increased pres-sure on the state to provide guarantees underpinning the private sector's investment in prospective PPP projects, so as not to deter them. |

## 📃 Topical feature idea

The news story in Figure 7.1 appeared in *The Guardian* on 22 June 2010. It concerned
the announcement by coalition Chancellor George Osborne of a two-year pay freeze
for all public sector workers earning more than £21,000 a year—including nurses,
schoolteachers, and social workers—and the furious reaction from trades unions who
accused him of 'declaring war' on the sector. The coalition had earlier announced a
recruitment freeze across the Civil Service. How would you follow up this story for your
local newspaper and its online operation?

**Figure 7.1** Article from *The Guardian*, 22 June 2010

# Budget 2020: George Osborne 'Declaring War on Public Sector'

Anna Bawden

*The Guardian*

22 June 2010

Web link: http://www.guardian.co.uk/uk/2010/
jun/22/budget-public-sector-cuts-pay

The government was today accused of waging war on public services as the Chancellor,
George Osborne, announced a two-year public
sector pay freeze and a crackdown on public
sector pensions.

The pay freeze, which applies to all public
sector workers earning £21,000 or more, will
save £3.3bn a year by April 2015. To mitigate
accusations of unfairness, Osborne promised
an extra £250 for the 1.7 million public sector
staff earning less than £21,000.

Osborne also promised to ensure that senior
salaries are more closely linked to those of the
lowest earners.

Will Hutton, executive vice-chair of the
Work Foundation, has been asked to draw up
plans for fairer pay so that those at the top of
public organisations are paid no more than 20
times the salaries of those at the bottom.

The chancellor confirmed measures to
reduce the cost of public sector pensions
would be in place by next year. 'We need to do
something about the spiralling costs of public
sector pensions,' he said, citing figures from
the Office for Budget Responsibility showing
that the funding shortfall between contributions and pensions paid out will have reached
£10bn by April 2016.

An independent commission, chaired by
former Labour minister John Hutton, will
conduct a review of public service schemes.
An interim report will be published in September and final recommendations in time for
next year's budget.

Osborne said: 'Many millions of people in the
private sector have in the last couple of years
seen their pay frozen, their hours reduced,
and their pension benefits restricted.

'They have accepted this because they knew
that the alternative in many cases was further
job losses.

'The public sector was insulated from these
pressures but now faces a similar trade-off.
I know there are many dedicated public sector workers who work very hard and did not
cause this recession—but they must share the
burden as we pay to clean it up.'

He added: 'The truth is that the country was
living beyond its means when the recession
came. And if we don't tackle pay and pensions,
more jobs will be lost. That is why the government is asking the public sector to accept a
two-year pay freeze.'

Dave Prentis, general secretary of Unison,
said that the budget was the most draconian
in decades.

'This budget signals that the battle for
Britain's public services has begun with the
government declaring war,' he said. 'Public
sector workers will be shocked and angry that
they are the innocent victims of job cuts and
pay freezes.

'Freezing public sector pay when inflation is
running at 5.1% and VAT is going up will mean
a real cut in living standards for millions of
ordinary workers and their families already
struggling to pay rising bills.'

John Philpott, chief economic adviser at
the Chartered Institute of Personnel and

Development, said curbing public sector pay would not improve the public finances a great deal.

'In the short term, while a pay freeze will stop the public deficit getting any worse, it will do little to help the deficit get any better,' he said.

'The CIPD says the budget measures will lead to 725,000 job losses in the public sector by 2015. With average redundancy payouts in the region of £17,000-£18,000, the potential cost to the public purse could be extremely high,' Philpott said.

He also warned of the damaging effect on attracting and keeping staff.

'The government needs to be wary of the dangers of a prolonged squeeze on public sector pay. Keeping the lid on pay for year after year would cut costs at the expense of severe public sector recruitment and retention difficulties,' he said. 'This would harm the quality of public service provision as public sector employers would have to make do with lower quality staff, while history suggests that periods of tight pay restraint are subsequently followed by periods of significant public sector pay inflation when earnings are raised to competitive rates.'

The pay freeze will not affect public sector workers equally. For council workers, the announcement is particularly galling as a pay freeze this year means that local authority employees will now not receive a pay rise for three years.

In contrast, teachers will not be affected until 2011.

Michael Gove, the education secretary, confirmed that teachers' three-year pay deal would be honoured in full and that they would still receive a pay rise due in September, the last instalment of that three-year deal.

© Guardian News & Media Ltd 2010

## ✳ Current issues

- **The Office for Budget Responsibility:** Chancellor George Osborne has established a new Office for Budget Responsibility to produce independent assessments of the UK's public finances for each Budget and Pre-Budget Report, forecast the country's likely future economic performance, and challenge the government on tax and spending decisions it deems unwise.

- **Tax rises and spending cuts:** in Mr Osborne's first Budget, he pledged public spending cuts of up to £31.9bn a year by 2014–15, to bring down Britain's Budget deficit. Significant rises in taxes—notably a 2.5 per cent hike in VAT—were also announced in Mr Osborne's emergency budget on 22 June 2010, and two weeks earlier Prime Minister David Cameron warned that the British 'way of life' would be disrupted for years.

- **Regulation of the banking sector:** the Bank of England regained authority for overall bank regulation following the May 2010 election, but the Financial Services Authority was scheduled for closure, and despite their pre-election pledges to introduce unilateral taxes to curb the City's 'bonus culture', the Tories and Lib Dems settled on a modest £2bn-a-year balance-sheet tax.

## ? Review questions

1. What role does the Budget play in fiscal and monetary policymaking in Britain?

2. What was the thinking behind Gordon Brown's decision to make the Bank of England independent and to give it responsibility for setting interest rates?

3. Outline the present-day rights of trades unions and the process by which individual unions gain legal recognition. Who has the most power: employers or employees?

4. How effective has regulation of the privatized utilities proved in the UK?

5. What are the arguments for and against the privatization and deregulation of the utilities?

## → Further reading

Edwards, P. (2003) *Industrial Relations: Theory and Practice in Britain*, 2nd edn, London: Wiley-Blackwell. **Second edition of acclaimed text focusing on recent developments in worker–employer relations in Britain, and the growing casualization/flexibility of labour markets.**

Grimsey, D. and Lewis, M. (2007) *Public Private Partnerships: The Worldwide Revolution in Infrastructure Provision and Project Finance*, London: Edward Elgar. **Illuminating overview of the growing role of private capital in major public sector infrastructural investment and costs this brings to the public purse. Includes comparative examples of PPP-style projects from several states outside Britain.**

Michie, R. C. (2001) *The London Stock Exchange: A History*, Oxford: Oxford University Press. **Acclaimed history of Britain's biggest money market—one of the largest in the world—incorporating up-to-date explanations of the Stock Exchange and how FTSE works.**

Monbiot, G. (2001) *Captive State: The Corporate Takeover of Britain*, London: Pan Books. **Critically acclaimed exposé by leading campaigning journalist of the creeping growth in influence of commercial companies in British public affairs.**

Swann, D. (1988) *Retreat of the State: Deregulation and Privatisation in the United Kingdom and the United States of America*, London: Prentice-Hall. **Accomplished exploration of the privatization revolution on both sides of the Atlantic, and the introduction of competition into formerly state-owned public services.**

Wrigley, C. (2002) *British Trade Unions Since 1933*, Cambridge: Cambridge University Press. **Textbook giving a comprehensive overview of the evolution of industrial relations policy in Britain since the 1940s.**

## Online Resource Centre

www.oxfordtextbooks.co.uk/orc/Morrison2e/

Visit the Online Resource Centre that accompanies this book for web links and regular updates.

# 8

# Social welfare and home affairs

Chapter 1 explored the rights and responsibilities of British *subjects* in the rather abstract context of the country's constitution. This chapter focuses on the rights and responsibilities of UK *residents* in relation to the more tangible areas of social welfare, criminal justice, and that most contested and politically sensitive of terms: 'citizenship'.

Alongside the National Health Service (NHS) and education, the twin briefs of 'social affairs' and 'home affairs' occupy more newspaper column inches, current affairs airtime, and web pages than almost any other areas of British life (save, perhaps, those heavyweight topics of sport and celebrity). From government crackdowns on 'welfare scroungers' to controversies about immigration, prison breakouts, or gun crime, barely a week passes without at least one major story generating screaming headlines.

The story of British citizenship in the modern age is one of 'carrot' and 'stick': carrot, in terms of the rights, entitlements, and benefits to which UK citizens who 'play by the rules' are eligible; stick, in terms of prosecution, punishment, and, ultimately, imprisonment for those who 'break the rules' by failing to meet the responsibilities expected of them.

## Basis of the 'welfare state'

Before exploring the ways in which social welfare is applied in Britain today, it is worth considering its underlying premise and the extent to which this has ever been fulfilled.

The primary purpose of the 'welfare state' initiated by the Liberal government of Herbert Asquith and David Lloyd George, and solidified by the post-war reforms of Clement Attlee's Labour administration, was to provide a safety net for members of society who fell on hard times, whether temporarily (through losing a job or falling sick and being unable to work) or more indefinitely (because of the diagnosis of a serious injury or long-term illness). Other than in exceptional situations, life 'on the social', 'on the sick' or, in the case of unemployment, 'on the dole' was never envisaged as a permanent state of affairs for anyone. Rather, it was meant to prevent those who, through no fault of their own, found themselves unable to work, earning low wages, or in other economically impoverished circumstances. The concept of 'deserving' and 'undeserving' poor was arguably enshrined in the minds of Britain's governing classes well before the Thatcher revolution.

According to eminent historian Asa Briggs, the term 'welfare state' was first coined by William Temple, Archbishop of Canterbury, during the Second World War. It is widely recognized, however, that the practical foundations of a prototype welfare state were laid during Lloyd George's time as, first Chancellor of the Exchequer, then prime minister. His 1909 'People's Budget' (see p. 60) introduced both old-age pensions and *National Insurance (NI)*—the progressive tax that remains the bedrock of the benefits system to this day. From the outset, the welfare state was to be a safety net based on both *need* and *entitlement*: the needy would be looked after, but their eligibility for this support derived from the presumption that when they were able to work and pay their way, they would do so. Even today, a British citizen's ability to claim higher-rate benefits to help them through periods of sickness and/or unemployment is contingent on their having made sufficient NI contributions and paid enough tax during periods of work.

Nonetheless, while a certain amount of 'responsibility' has always been expected of benefit claimants and those receiving other forms of welfare support, in return for their 'rights' to such help, there has been a marked hardening of attitude under recent governments. The early 1980s saw a huge increase in unemployment as entire industries were effectively dismantled through Margaret Thatcher's radical market reforms. Few could argue at the time that the hundreds of thousands of workers made redundant had themselves to blame for their predicament. Yet it was not long before Mrs Thatcher's ministers were invoking the image of the jobless layabout. Shortly after the Handsworth and Brixton Riots of 1981, her Employment Secretary, Norman Tebbit, was asked by a journalist if he felt rising unemployment had anything to do with these outbreaks of civil unrest. He replied:

❝ I grew up in the 1930s with an unemployed father. He did not riot. He got on his bike and looked for work, and he went on looking until he found it. ❞

Mr Tebbit's reply has gone down in British political folklore. In many ways it was to set the tone for future policy by not only the Conservatives, but also New Labour. When Tony Blair was elected in 1997 his Chancellor, Gordon Brown, initiated an ambitious plan to reduce unemployment under the 'Welfare to Work' banner. His 'New Deal for the Unemployed' (based on a model adopted in some

US states) aimed to provide a wider choice of work-related opportunities for the long-term unemployed, rewarding those who undertook specified training programmes and/or voluntary work with an initial £10 top-up to their weekly benefits. In return for these entitlements, however, it would demand ever more stringent demonstrations of their efforts to find work, organizing regular interviews with 'supervisors' in the then Employment Service to monitor their rate of applications and help them with job searches. This built on tough measures introduced under John Major's government, when high-profile crackdowns were introduced to target 'welfare scroungers'—particularly those who accepted cash-in-hand work on top of their benefits but failed to declare it.

# ▌ Social welfare services today

The social security bill represents the single largest area of government expenditure in Britain. Defined broadly as welfare provision allocated to guarantee *a basic standard of living for those in financial need*, it accounts for more than 30 per cent of Britain's overall public spending budget and 21 per cent of its *gross domestic product (GDP)*.

Over the years, social welfare services have been administered by a succession of, often overlapping and sometimes conflicting, government departments and agencies. The landscape today is no less patchwork, as illustrated in Table 8.1.

Because the first half of this chapter is primarily focused on the social security system—specifically the benefits and tax incentives introduced by governments to promote welfare and employment—it concentrates on the work of the two biggest players: the Department for Work and Pensions (DWP) and HM Treasury.

# ▌ Department for Work and Pensions (DWP)

The DWP has overall responsibility for the Welfare to Work programme. When Labour returned to power in 1997, its immediate concern was to tackle the growing problem of intergenerational unemployment—the increasing numbers of long-term unemployed (those who had been without work for six months or more and, in many cases, a number of years), as well as the growing number of 18–25-year-olds with little or no employment record (many hailing from the same families as long-term claimants). The New Deal policies that followed were criticized as much for their narrow focus on these two target groups, to

**Table 8.1** A breakdown of the main government departments involved in social welfare

| Department | Role |
| --- | --- |
| Department for Work and Pensions (DWP) | Formerly Department for Social Security (DSS), this ministry oversees welfare benefits and job creation. Led by **Secretary of State** for Work and Pensions. |
| Department for Education | Replaced Department for Children, Schools, and Families when David Cameron became prime minister. Has hand in welfare services in promoting affordable early-years childcare through tax credits and nursery vouchers, and policing child welfare. Headed by Secretary of State for Education. |
| Department of Health (DH) | Under Labour, this department played a greater role in promoting child welfare, and there were attempts to involve both DH and DCSF (and its precursors) more directly in addressing inequalities in distribution of high-quality health and education services. This was done through such early New Labour initiatives as health and education action zones, and subsequently through greater involvement of NHS 'service users' in influencing the direction of health policy through, first patients' forums and **local involvement networks (LINks)**, and now HealthWatch. |
| Department of Communities and Local Government (DCLG) | Responsible for various areas linked to welfare, including providing low-cost affordable housing for key workers (nurses, teachers) and social housing for those on low incomes. |
| HM Treasury | Under Labour, Chancellors played more hands-on role in providing welfare services. The New Deal programmes, cold-weather payments for pensioners, the tax credit system, and the now-defunct Child Trust Fund all derived from Treasury initiatives. Much of Treasury's welfare-related work has been carried out on its behalf by HM Revenue and Customs (HMRC)—the huge tax-gathering agency formed through the amalgamation of the Inland Revenue and Customs and Excise. |

→

see also local govern-ment, p. 485

the exclusion of others like under 16-year-olds and older unemployed people, as for the stiff conditions they imposed on those they were designed to help.

Following the 2001 and 2005 Labour victories, the New Deal was gradually extended to cater for various other target groups, including over-25s, over-50s, lone parents, people with disabilities, and even musicians—who were offered various forms of support in pursuing music careers, including government-funded open learning modules.

The vast and complex benefits system over which the DWP presides is administered in practice by a range of **executive agencies**, the roles of which are outlined in Table 8.2.

## Types of benefit and their relationship to NI

There are two categories of UK welfare benefit. Whether a particular payment falls into one or the other depends on the extent to which NI contributions have been made, as follows.

**Table 8.2** A breakdown of the executive agencies involved in social security

| Agency | Role |
|---|---|
| *Jobcentre Plus* | As the 'plus' in its title indicates, this has a wider remit than providing employment-related welfare—although that accounts for much of its work. A replacement for the Benefits Agency (BA), it administers most state benefits, ranging from Child Benefit, maternity benefits, and widows' pensions to *Income Support*, Incapacity Benefit, Disability Living Allowance (DLA), and *Jobseeker's Allowance (JSA)* (today's principal unemployment benefit). Local authority housing departments administer *Housing Benefit*/Local Housing Allowance (see p. 485) on its behalf. |
| Child Support Agency (CSA) | Assesses and collects maintenance payments for children from parents under terms of arrangements made in the family courts. |
| Pension Service | Agency that helps people to navigate the complex web of alternative pension options and related benefits and tax credits. |

- **Contributory benefits** are those that are available to people subject to their prior payment of sufficient NI contributions. These include contributions-based Jobseeker's Allowance (the higher rate of JSA) and *Incapacity Benefit*.

- **Non-contributory benefits** bear no relationship to an individual's prior NI contributions. Most are 'needs-based' payments available to anyone whose income falls below a certain level and/or who meets certain other criteria (e.g. disability in relation to DLA). These include Income Support and the basic level of JSA. Some, however, are 'universal': for example, Child Benefit, which is paid to all mothers with dependent children under the age of 16 (or under 20, and in specified forms of education or training), irrespective of their personal financial circumstances.

There are five 'classes' of NI contribution. The one affecting most people is Class 1—paid by both employers and employees in proportion to their levels of earnings. One oft-cited advantage of working for someone else (as opposed to being self-employed) is that for every pound invested into the NI 'pot' entitling a person to future benefit, should they need it, a further pound at least is paid in by his or her employer. By contrast, self-employed people have sole responsibility for making their NI contributions. They are also subject to two types: Class 2 (paid weekly or monthly at a flat rate by those earning above a minimum threshold) and Class 4 (a profit-based rate for higher earners).

In addition, there are two further classes of NI: Class 1A, paid by employers operating company car and fuel schemes for their employees for private use, and Class 3, which is paid voluntarily by those with money to do so to safeguard future eligibility to benefits. By way of a long service award, those who continue working after pensionable age—presently 65 for men and 60 for women, although the Lib-Con *coalition government* proposes to raise the retirement age to 66 for both genders by as early as 2016—no longer have to pay NI. However, their employers continue doing so on their behalf.

## Jobseeker's Allowance (JSA)

JSA is paid to adults working fewer than 16 hours a week and 'available for and actively seeking' full-time work. There are two levels of benefit: contributions-based (for those who have paid sufficient NI contributions in the past) and lower-rate income-based (for those who satisfy a financial means test, regardless of prior NI contributions). People with savings of £16,000 or more are unlikely to be eligible for JSA, whatever their circumstances, while those with between £6,000 and £16,000 will receive reduced payments.

As with other forms of unemployment benefit that preceded it, JSA has been the subject of periodic criticism from all sides over the nature of the criteria used to award or refuse it, not to mention the level of the benefit itself. For decades British governments have agonized over the benefits-related 'poverty trap'—put crudely, the fear that giving too much money to the unemployed will act as a disincentive for them to work. In taking up a job, an unemployed person instantly loses any entitlement to unemployment benefit and, even if he or she continues to qualify for certain other payments—for example, Housing Benefit—he or she will instantly be paying Income Tax and NI contributions out of his or her wages. For some, such as single parents, the option of taking up a low-paid, temporary and/or part-time job rather than remaining on JSA often seems impractical: the cost of childcare they would otherwise not need, combined with immediate loss of benefits, can make the prospect of remaining unemployed (however unpalatable) a preferable option. It has long been acknowledged that at the point at which unemployed people move into work, they are subject to extremely high 'marginal tax rates'—losing up to 95p for every pound earned initially, as benefits cease, working tax credits wait to kick in, and emergency tax is deducted from their first pay packets.

Few would dispute that benefit levels need to remain lower than pay rates to encourage people to return to work when they find a suitable job. But for some campaigners, including trades unions and social policy think tanks like the Joseph Rowntree Foundation, the poverty trap arises less out of overinflated benefits than the fact that wages for many jobs are too low. As of the 2010–11 tax year, maximum weekly rates of JSA stood at £51.85 for 18–25-year-olds and £65.45 for over-25s—hardly the stuff of which millionaires are made!

Labour tried to address the issue of low wages by introducing Britain's first national minimum wage in 1997 (see p. 211), backed by a free-phone hotline to help people to report employers who tried to sidestep the legislation. Yet many workers—particularly those in low-skilled jobs like security and care work—continue to receive poverty wages that take little account of the cost of living where they are based. Employment agencies in towns and cities across the south-east—where costs are only marginally lower than those in London—still routinely offer £6–7 per hr for basic catering and office-based 'temping' work.

Concern about the poverty trap led Labour to roll out a newer form of payment for people on low incomes directed to them through their pay packets, rather than the traditional giro cheque-based benefits system: tax credits. These are discussed further in the section below on HM Revenue and Customs (HMRC). Such measures have, however, been tempered by continuing threats to make life harder for the minority of people that successive governments have insinuated are 'refusing' to work, despite being capable of doing so. In February 2008 Labour launched a major 'rethinking' of welfare, in contracting out Jobcentre Plus-style job search advice and support services to the private sector—with companies paid for successfully finding work for claimants and keeping them in those jobs for six months or more. Fees are currently paid according to a sliding scale, with placements for the long-term unemployed netting companies the biggest bonuses. Claimants who do not turn up for interviews or appointments with their personal supervisors have money docked from their benefits, with similar penalties faced by unemployed drug addicts who fail to attend rehab programmes.

The Lib-Con coalition government has taken an even tougher stance. The Work and Pensions Secretary, Iain Duncan Smith, who in opposition had headed the party's Centre for Social Justice, announced in May 2010 his intention to simplify the benefits system (the complexities of which he admitted he himself did not understand!), replacing existing job schemes with a single work programme that would make receipt of benefits even more conditional on individuals' willingness to take up employment. Among the mooted sanctions was a 'three strikes and you're out' policy for those who repeatedly refused offers of work. First-time 'offenders' would lose their benefits for three months, second-timers for six months, and third-timers for up to three years.

The manifesto had also suggested that unemployed claimants might be expected to work for benefits in future, in the manner of the US Workfare scheme. At the same time, though, ministers signalled a willingness to address the poverty trap they argued was locking some claimants into welfare dependency— allowing unemployed people to retain more benefits in the short term as they moved into work, and raising the bar for payment for the private companies, charities, and other providers contracted to find them jobs, by requiring them to place people in posts lasting at least a year.

The commercial sector stood to profit considerably, however, from an initiative announced by Mr Cameron in August 2010 to crack down on welfare fraud. Defying criticisms from civil liberties groups and some Opposition MPs, and provoking a call for an 'urgent meeting' from the *Information Commissioner* (see Chapter 20), he confirmed private credit rating firms would be used to snoop on the financial affairs of benefit claimants in an effort to identify those whose spending habits suggested they were guilty of fraud. The companies—likened to 'bounty hunters'—would be paid on results, receiving taxpayer-funded fees for every fraudulent claim they exposed. Although Mr Cameron highlighted an annual cost to the public purse of £5.2bn, official DWP and HMRC figures suggested the bulk of this was attributable to overpayment and paperwork errors by officials and only £1bn was down to wilful fraud.

Aside from toughening eligibility conditions for claimants and cracking down on fraudsters, in his June 2010 Budget Chancellor George Osborne also trained his sights on costly benefits as part of his deficit reduction package. As well as freezing Child Benefit for three years and reducing eligibility for child tax credits to families with household incomes of £40,000 or more, he announced that customary annual rises in the value of other benefits enabling them to keep pace with *inflation* would in future be pegged to the *consumer price index (CPI)* rather than the traditionally higher *retail price index (RPI)* (see p. 196)—a move designed to save the state £6bn a year. He also capped Housing Benefit at £280 a week for a one-bedroom flat and £400 a week for a four-bedroom house, aiming to save another £2bn a year.

Barely a fortnight after Mr Osborne announced his benefits squeeze, Mr Duncan Smith signalled a return to a decidedly pre-Beveridge approach to welfare. In response to warnings from Christian charity the Trussell Trust that many claimants had been left 'on the edge' after being refused crisis loans or while awaiting reassessment of their entitlements, he commissioned a review into whether Jobcentre Plus staff should be allowed to distribute food vouchers to those in the greatest need. If approved, the vouchers would be exchangeable at 'food banks' operated by the charity for up to six days' worth of groceries at a time.

## Income Support

Income Support is a flexible non-contributory benefit available to people aged 16–60 on low incomes, not in full-time paid employment, and who satisfy various other criteria (for example, being single parents, full-time carers, or registered blind). As of summer 2010–11, there were two rates for single people:

- £51.85 for single 16–24-year-olds;
- £65.45 for single people aged 25 or over.

As with other benefits, payments to couples take account of their ability to cut costs by shopping and cooking together, and to pay joint utility bills. These combined payments are relatively lower as a consequence. The standard rate for all couples in which both partners were aged 18 or over was £102.75. Eligible single parents were entitled to £51.85 if aged 16 or 17, and £65.45 if 18 or over, but since 2008 incremental changes have been introduced to encourage mothers and fathers to take up jobs once their children reach a certain age by withdrawing Income Support at that point. Lone parents with children over the age first of 12, then of 10, had their entitlements stopped in November 2008 and October 2009 respectively, while from October 2010 eligibility was withdrawn for anyone whose child was due to turn 7 within the following year.

As with JSA, there are restrictions on individuals' ability to claim Income Support if they have savings of £6,000-plus.

## Incapacity Benefit (IB), Employment and Support Allowance (ESA), and Disability Living Allowance (DLA)

Just as there are different levels and types of JSA, so, too, there is more than one form of benefit for the sick and/or disabled. Although it is in the process of being reformed, Incapacity Benefit (IB) has long been the contributions-based benefit paid to people judged incapable of working, who are under state pension age, and meet one or more of the following criteria:

- have received Statutory Sick Pay through their employer that has ended, despite the fact they remain incapable of working;
- are self-employed or unemployed;
- have been receiving Statutory Maternity Pay (SMP), but have not gone back to work because they are incapable.

There were three rates of weekly Incapacity Benefit for people of working age as of 2010–11:

- short-term (lower)—£68.95;
- short-term (higher)—£81.60;
- long-term (which kicks in after someone has been claiming for 53 weeks)—£91.40.

Pensioners are eligible for short-term rates only, at £87.75 and £91.40 respectively.

Due to its relatively generous size and the sheer number of claimants (2.6 million as of 2008, at an annual cost of £12bn), IB has become a huge political issue. Labour announced a root-and-branch reform of the rules governing it in 2005, vowing to reduce the number of recipients by 1 million. The resulting Welfare Reform Act 2007 introduced these changes, but only in relation to new claimants initially. As of October 2008, they were entitled to a new Employment and Support Allowance, paid at one of two rates: a higher one for people with serious long-term conditions who remain unable to work, but a lower one for those considered capable of returning to work who fail to do so. As of 2010–11, single people under 25 received £51.85 and those over that age £65.45 (in line with JSA rates) for the first 13 weeks of a claim, while a decision was made on their ability to work on the basis of a new work capability assessment. Those subsequently placed in a 'work-related activity group', because they are felt to have the potential to return to employment, then receive £91.40 a week, while those judged to have limited capability to work get £96.85. Regular employment interviews have since been arranged for the latter, while 'work capability assessments' were introduced to put the accent on claimants' abilities, rather than their disabilities. Those judged capable of work, but who failed to take it up, have faced benefit cuts.

Since taking office, Mr Cameron's government has signalled an intention to move further and faster towards reducing Britain's disability benefits bill. In May 2010, Mr Duncan Smith confirmed plans to reassess all existing IB claimants (including those in receipt of the payments for many years), and transfer those who remained eligible onto ESA, but as many as possible onto the (far cheaper) JSA, with a view to their moving into the job market. However, in the week of his announcement, a report by Citizens Advice Scotland labelled the ESA system 'unfit for purpose' after finding that up to two-thirds of claimants were being declared fit for work on the basis of their medicals (20 per cent more than the previous government had anticipated), resulting in 8,000 appeal cases per month. Of these, two-fifths led to decisions being reversed, at significant cost to the taxpayer. A BBC investigation found that many GPs involved in conducting the medical tests used to establish eligibility had strong reservations about their efficacy, particularly in relation to people with mental health problems and other less 'visible' conditions.

The second principal sickness-related payment, Disability Living Allowance, is a non-contributory benefit based purely on assessments of mental or physical need (regardless of income, savings, or ability to work). People under 65 have traditionally been able to claim DLA if physically or mentally disabled. Because it covers both of these aspects, DLA comprises both a *care component* and a *mobility component*. It has been possible for some individuals to qualify for both. But George Osborne signalled the start of a radical overhaul of DLA in his Budget, announcing that from 2013 all new claimants would have to undergo a medical assessment. In October he removed the entitlement for disabled people living in residential homes to receive the mobility component. As of 2010–11, the higher rate of care component was £71.40, the middle rate £47.80, and lower rate £18.95. The mobility component has only a higher and a lower rate (£49.85 and £18.95, respectively).

# ▌ HM Revenue and Customs (HMRC)

HMRC plays an integral role in the welfare system in two respects: it raises taxes to pay for benefits, and makes discrete payments to families, pensioners, and others on limited incomes through tax credits—a system designed to encourage low earners to stay in employment by rewarding them with modest 'rebates' through their pay packets, in place of the old-style handouts designed to compensate them for being out of work. As the tax credit system has evolved, it has expanded to provide 'minimum income guarantees' (MIGs) for other vulnerable groups, including pensioners. The main types are outlined in Table 8.3.

**Table 8.3** A breakdown of the main tax credits available from HMRC

| Name of credit | Purpose and scope |
| --- | --- |
| Working Tax Credit (WTC) | Replacement for both Working Families Tax Credit (WFTC) and Disabled Person's Tax Credit (DPTC), this is paid through low earners' pay packets, in addition to their wages. Means-tested, it is a way of topping up earnings of employed or self-employed people on low or middle incomes. A single WTC is paid to each eligible household, normally monthly, comprising several elements: basic (one per individual, couple, or family); extra 30-hour (if at least one household member works for 30 hours or more a week); disability (if one or more adults have, or a child, has one); child (an extra top-up for each dependant); childcare (up to 70 per cent of eligible approved costs). Three types of household are eligible:<br>1. those with dependent children and at least one partner working 16 hours or more a week;<br>2. households without dependent children in which at least one partner is aged 25 or over and works at least 30 hours a week;<br>3. those in which one or more adults has a disability but works at least 16 hours per week. |
| Child Tax Credit (CTC) | Formerly Children's Tax Credit, this means-tested payment is designed to encourage new parents to return to work. Credits are awarded on a sliding scale to families whose household incomes are £58,175 or less (£66,350 if they have a child under the age of one), and who have savings of £8,000 or less. The Lib-Con government is expected to remove eligibility for some families, with those earning £50,000 or more potentially losing their entitlements entirely. |
| Pension Credit | In recognition of the fact that many elderly people did not earn sufficient income while still working to save for their retirements, Labour introduced this additional tax credit to help poorer pensioners—raising the level of personal savings they could have without losing their eligibility to £10,000 from November 2009. As of 2010–11, all over-60-year-olds were guaranteed minimum weekly incomes of £132.60 for single people or £202.40 for couples. This system is administered by the government's Pensions Service (see Table 8.2). |

The other principal welfare innovation administered until recently by HMRC was the Child Trust Fund (CTF). All British babies born between September 2002 and 2011 were entitled to one-off payments by the government of between £250 and £500 (depending on parental income). While parents could decide where to invest the money on behalf of their offspring, only their children were entitled to withdraw it—and only then on their 18th birthdays. In the meantime, parents were encouraged to top up their children's CTF accounts, to a maximum of up to £1,200 a year, either in one-off payments or instalments of as little as £10 a time. Estimates varied widely as to how much a fund might be worth by 2020, but according to the Nationwide Building Society's annual *Children's Savings Report*, published in 2006, if the initial £250 were invested in a share-based option, it could top £40,000 over 18 years (assuming a £1,200 annual top-up and annual growth of 7 per cent). It estimated that putting £43 a month away ought to cover the cost of a deposit on a first home (estimated at £15,200 on the basis of current trends). However, during the 2008–09 global *recession*, the value of shares in many blue-chip companies, let alone smaller-scale funds, plummeted.

When the CTF was launched, its stated aim was to foster a culture of saving among young people—particularly those from poorer backgrounds with less parental financial support upon which to rely. To this end, under Labour the Treasury later announced that further one-off payments would be made into funds when children reached their 7th birthdays, with talk of further injections at age 11. However, the Lib-Con coalition has vowed to scrap the fund in 2011 as part of its wider plan to tackle the UK's budget deficit—a move its advocates condemned as considerably less progressive than the parties' pre-election pledge to take it away only from better-off families.

## Other forms of welfare support

In addition to the needs-based benefits outlined above, a number of other sources of support are available on a 'universal' basis.

Child Benefit is paid to mothers for each child under the age of 20 and still in full-time education or training. It has long been controversial, given that high-income families arguably have little need for it, but receive the same amount per child as low-earning ones. The same principle applies to certain forms of welfare targeted at the elderly, notably free bus passes for use on local bus services anywhere in England and Wales (for which everyone qualifies from their 60th birthdays) and the one-off annual *winter fuel payments*, which currently amount to £250 for individuals living alone who were born on or before 5 July 1950 or £400 for those aged 80 or over on or before 26 September 2010. As with other benefits, couples qualify for reduced sums (£125 and £275 respectively).

Statutory maternity and paternity pay are paid via employers to parents of recently born children. Mothers are now entitled to up to nine months' paid maternity leave, albeit pegged at 90 per cent of their usual income for the first six weeks and whichever is the lower of £124.88 a week or 90 per cent of their normal earnings for the next 33 weeks. Labour had pledged to increase paid maternity leave to 12 months, but having delayed introducing the extension in 2009 was voted out at the 2010 election. Fathers are currently only eligible for two weeks' paid paternity leave, at either 90 per cent of their normal earnings or the £124.88 rate (whichever is lower)—although an eligible father whose child is due on or after 3 April 2011 will be able to use up to six months of the mother's maternity leave entitlement if she earns more than him and/or decides to return to work sooner.

Other state entitlements include Statutory Sick Pay, which is available for up to 28 weeks to those in full-time employment unable to work through ill health (although the requirement for employees to provide their employers with 'sick notes' was changed to a new emphasis on 'fit notes' as of April 2010), and widows' pensions, which are lump sums paid to women whose husbands were below retirement age when they died. Payments begin from the date at which they would have qualified for pensions had they lived.

The sheer scope of their coverage means universal benefits cost the Treasury a huge amount each year. Hardly surprising, then, that at a time of major public spending cuts the debate about universalism versus means-testing has been reignited. Supporters of means-testing (including some formerly staunch opponents on the left) argue that, by paying Child Benefit and winter fuel allowance to people irrespective of their financial need, the welfare state is needlessly subsidizing the wealthy when it should be focusing on the poor. Advocates of universalism, meanwhile, broadly fall into two camps. Pragmatists argue that means-testing would be too complex (and, for that reason, costly), given the need to repeatedly reassess households should their annual incomes fluctuate for any reason—for example, if the main 'bread-winner' were to lose his or her job, take a lower-paid alternative, or become self-employed. They point to problems encountered by families who have lost their entitlement to child tax credits—and in some cases been asked to repay substantial sums—as warnings against such a process. Others, including many on the left, cite more ideological objections: means-testing, they argue, can stigmatize the poor, while universalism gives everyone (including, admittedly, those who do not strictly need benefits) a 'stake' in the welfare state, which (as with the NHS) helps to preserve popular support among taxpayers for costly social welfare programmes on which others rely.

One type of welfare support that is targeted at those on low incomes (whether employed or unemployed) is the one-off payment. This can take several forms, but the most common are crisis loans (lump sums to help out in the event of emergencies or disasters, like floods or fires in the home), and the Social Fund, which offers either 'regulated' (compulsory) help to those who meet the criteria (for example, one-off payments to help with funeral costs) or 'discretionary' awards, such as short-term budgeting loans to help people through rocky patches while waiting for their next pay packets or benefit cheques.

## Future of the state pension

Although there has been much debate in recent years about the size of the basic state pension—and its decreasing value in relation to living costs and average earnings—Britons retain an automatic entitlement to a retirement pension funded out of general taxation.

At present British men retire at the age of 65, while women can draw their pensions from 60, but this is in the process of changing. Equalization of the retirement age for men and women is due to be phased in over ten years from 2010. Women born before April 1950 will still retire at 60, but those born between 1950 and 1955 will instead do so at 65. As a reflection of the demographic changes currently facing the country—a rapidly ageing population, with pensioners living longer and relatively few people of working age available to support them—Labour recently planned to raise the age at which UK citizens become eligible for state pensions to 66 in 2024, 67 in 2034, and 68 in 2044. At time of writing, the Lib-Con coalition was reviewing the date at which the retirement age should rise to 66, although this was unlikely to be before 2016 for men and 2020 for women. A further rise, to age 70 or beyond, is likely in coming years.

The introduction of the basic state retirement pension was one of the founding initiatives of the welfare state in 1948. The basic provision—funded through NI contributions—was supplemented in 1978 with the introduction of the now contentious State Earnings-Related Pension Scheme (SERPS), championed by bastions of 'Old Labour', principally the late Baroness Castle, who, as then Health and Social Security Secretary, was its main architect. SERPS was seen by many as guaranteeing a civilized degree of comfort to people in their retirement because of the principle that underpinned it—namely, that the value of state pensions should keep pace with the average wage.

By the late 1970s, the majority of working people were required by their employers to contribute to a second, occupational, pension, normally through their wage packets. Nowadays, however, the framework of pension provision in the UK is patchwork, with many workers having neither the security of employment nor level of income needed to pay into a pension scheme over and above their state one.

Mrs Thatcher's government actively encouraged employees to opt out of SERPS and use their money to invest instead in potentially more lucrative (if riskier) private or personal pensions. In recent years, the vulnerability of some personal pension schemes has been exposed by several major controversies—most notably the mis-selling scandals that hit Royal and Sun Alliance and Standard Life, and the fraudulent misuse of the Mirror Group pension fund by late newspaper tycoon Robert Maxwell.

Since the mid-1990s, the pensions issue has become increasingly pressing. There is a growing awareness of the fact that, as the population is living longer, radical steps are needed to ensure that everyone can retire on a liveable income. As the proportion of the population of working age diminishes, the pressure for people to save for their own retirement is increasing: no longer is there a guarantee that there will be enough money in the public purse to pay for them when they reach pensionable age.

The Welfare Reform and Pensions Act 1999 paved the way for potentially radical pension reform. But ministers' attempts to move from this to a definitive

**Table 8.4** The three types of government-backed pension

| Type of pension | How it works |
| --- | --- |
| State retirement pension | A contributory benefit, the 'real value' of which has plummeted in recent years, as living costs have risen. It is currently linked to inflation, rather than average earnings (as under SERPS). Those who do not pay enough NI contributions during their working lives qualify for Income Support on retirement. |
| Stakeholder pension | Introduced to help those without occupational pensions (e.g. the self-employed) but earning enough to save something for retirement. They are distinct from most personal pension schemes operated by banks and building societies in being cheaper and more flexible (people can move them from job to job). The government pays monthly contributions in place of the employers who do so for those with occupational pensions. |
| State second pension | Introduced to replace SERPS in April 2002, this is aimed at providing a minimum income guarantee (MIG) for people who do not have the money to save much for their old age through NI credits. In practice, the main beneficiaries are carers and disabled people with sporadic work records. |

and coherent framework for state-funded pensions stuttered for years afterwards, and only after several high-profile reviews of the policy by independent commissions and numerous changes of Pensions Secretary was a conclusion of sorts reached. There are currently three types of government-backed pension, as outlined in Table 8.4.

Following a report by Lord Turner's Pensions Commission, in May 2006 then Work and Pensions Secretary John Hutton proposed a radical shake-up of state pensions, including the following changes:

- co-opting all workers into a new national pension savings scheme from 2012. Individuals would be able to opt out, but those who did not would pay 3 per cent of their salaries into a top-up pension pot, with another 3 per cent contributed by their employers and 1 per cent by the government through tax relief;

- in an echo of SERPS, the state pension to be relinked to average earnings, rather than living costs, from as early as 2012 (a move subsequently brought forward to April 2011 by the coalition);

- entitlement to the state pension to be reduced to 30 years' worth of NI contributions.

The Lib-Con coalition is to reintroduce the earnings link from April 2011 (a policy to which Labour also committed itself before the May 2010 election), It is also pledging to increase pensions annually by the higher of prices, earnings, or 2.5 per cent. But its wider, perhaps more painful, reforms are currently under review by Lord Hutton, who, in recognition of his unfinished business, was recently appointed 'Pensions Tsar'.

## Reviews and appeals under the benefits system

If claimants are dissatisfied with a decision on their eligibility for benefit, or a move to withdraw it, they may appeal against the decision. Before lodging an appeal, however, the claimant must first go through a lengthy process, requiring him or her to file a formal complaint with a so-called 'local decision-maker'. Should he or she be dissatisfied with the outcome, the complainant may apply for a 'review' by the decision-maker.

Finally, the claimant has recourse to one last stab at 'justice': an appeal, handled by a branch of the *Tribunals Service* known as Social Security and Child Support (SSCS) (formerly the ***Appeals Service***). Incorporated into the Tribunals Service in 2006, this agency handles appeals about claims for all kinds of benefit—from DLA to SMP.

Once the SSCS has reached its decision, appeals can only ever be taken further *on a point of law*. In such circumstances, they are dealt with by either a Social Security Commissioner or a Child Support Commissioner (independent ombudsmen).

## The changing face of home affairs

One of the biggest offices of state, the Home Department (to use its official title), was split in two in spring 2007 by Mr Blair's final Home Secretary, John Reid. He had declared the unwieldy Home Office 'not fit for purpose' on succeeding his predecessor, Charles Clarke, in 2006. Mr Clarke had endured a succession of public embarrassments over the department's handling of anti-terrorism and asylum policy, and presided over a ticking time bomb in a prison service creaking under the weight of too many inmates.

Mr Reid stepped down when Gordon Brown replaced Mr Blair as prime minister, but not before instigating one of the biggest shake-ups in this sprawling department's 225-year history. For some years, there had been an artificial 'Chinese Wall' between the responsibilities of the Home Office and those of the Lord Chancellor's Department (renamed the 'Department for Constitutional Affairs' by Mr Blair in 2005) in relation to crime and disorder. With the emergence of a raft of new internal security issues in relation to the growing threat of Islamist terrorism, Mr Reid judged that the department needed to cede some of its criminal justice powers to enable it to focus more effectively on the various other policy areas in its ambit.

When Mr Brown arrived in Downing Street he replaced the Department for Constitutional Affairs with a new 'Ministry of Justice' (MoJ), headed by Lord

Falconer's replacement as Lord Chancellor, Jack Straw. Mr Straw became the first Lord Chancellor in more than 300 years to be a member of Parliament, rather than a peer. As a reflection of this, he was given the additional title 'Secretary of State for Justice'. This better described his powers, in light of the fact that his post had lost several of the Lord Chancellor's traditional trappings—notably his chairmanship of debate in the House of Lords, which went to the then newly appointed **Lord Speaker** (see p. 72). The division of responsibilities between the dual departments for internal affairs resulting from these reforms are now as outlined in Table 8.5.

To aid the Home Office in its new responsibilities for counter-terrorism policy, it was given a new 'subdepartment': the Office for Security and Counter-Terrorism. A 'National Security Board' (NSB)—a weekly forum chaired by the Home Secretary—was also formed to discuss security threats when they occurred, as well as a National Criminal Justice Board (NCJB) tasked with promoting 'joined-up government' between the two departments responsible for different aspects of criminal justice policy (chaired jointly by the Home Secretary, the Justice Secretary, and the Attorney General).

# The new-look Home Office

In a break with generations of male dominance at the top table in the **Cabinet**, Mr Brown appointed Jacqui Smith as Britain's first female Home Secretary in July 2007. Mr Cameron later followed this example, appointing Theresa May to the post in his inaugural Cabinet.

### Policing and crime prevention

The role of Her Majesty's Constabulary is explored in depth in Chapter 11. In examining the work of the Home Office, however, it is important to outline the extent to which police forces in England and Wales remain under the department's overall authority.

The Home Office funds the police, and is responsible for recruitment, training, and pay. Responsibility for organizing policing on the ground, like so many areas of public policy, has long since been delegated from central to local government. In theory, it is down to individual local **police authorities** *to* appoint, hold to account, and occasionally dismiss the **chief constables** *res*ponsible for

**Table 8.5** A breakdown of the responsibilities of the Home Office and the Ministry for Justice (MoJ)

| Home Office | Ministry of Justice (MoJ) |
| --- | --- |
| Policing and crime prevention | The court system and sentencing policy |
| Security and counter-terrorism | Prisons |
| Asylum, immigration, and citizenship | Probation and prevention of reoffending |

running police forces in their areas. In practice, even today the Home Secretary must endorse these appointments and, if there is a perception of declining confidence in either the chief constable or the authority he or she may intervene to remove either or both against their wishes. In June 2001, then Home Secretary David Blunkett publicly urged Sussex Police Authority to consider sacking local chief constable Paul Whitehouse over his handling of an inquiry into the fatal shooting by a police marksman of an unarmed alleged drug dealer, James Ashley, in St Leonards three-and-a-half years earlier. Mr Whitehouse, who had recently promoted two of the officers involved in the incident, subsequently resigned. On entering office in May 2010, Ms May signalled her intention to press ahead with a Tory manifesto pledge to replace police authorities with directly elected police commissioners.

→
see also
local
govern-
ment,
p. 337

The traditional responsibility of the Home Secretary for overseeing policing in London, through the Metropolitan Police Commissioner, was formally handed to a newly created police authority answerable to the **Greater London Authority (GLA)** in 2000. The GLA passed a vote of no confidence in Sir Ian Blair, then Met Commissioner, in November 2007, following the Old Bailey's decision to convict his force for breaching health and safety legislation when anti-terror officers mistakenly shot dead Jean Charles De Menezes, an innocent Brazilian man, at Stockwell Tube station in July 2005. Despite widespread calls for Sir Ian's dismissal, Ms Smith and then London Mayor Ken Livingstone publicly defended him. Critics of the shooting were ultimately vindicated when an inquest jury returned an open verdict into his death in December 2008—pointedly disbelieving testimony by police officers who insisted they had shouted a warning to him before opening fire—and it was only a matter of time before Sir Ian was forced out. In October 2008, five months after Conservative Boris Johnson unseated Mr Livingstone, the new *mayor* publicly called for a change of leadership at the Met—leaving the Commissioner little option but to resign. Mr Johnson's immediate criticisms of Sir Ian appeared to have been sparked by accusations of unfair treatment for black and Asian officers in the force. Two of Sir Ian's harshest critics, Assistant Commissioner Tarique Ghaffur, Britain's most senior Muslim officer, and Ali Dizaei, had only recently been suspended, with the former placed on 'garden leave' in response to his public conduct on filing a £1.2m racial discrimination claim against the Met. Mr Johnson immediately launched a new inquiry into allegations of racism in the Met—underlining his insinuation that the former Commissioner had presided over a force that remained 'institutionally racist', despite its protestations to the contrary. (The term had been coined a decade earlier by Sir William Macpherson's report into the murder of black teenager Stephen Lawrence. Police botched their investigation into the racially motivated crime, scuppering an initial trial, and Lawrence's killers have yet to be brought to justice.)

The timing of Mr Johnson's intervention coincided with the launch of an advertising campaign by the Met's Black Police Association to deter people from the black and Asian communities from joining the force. The Met aside, Labour's reign was marked by periodic run-ins with the police as a whole—usually over issues relating to pay and recruitment. In December 2007, the Metropolitan Police Federation declared itself 'at war' with the government over its decision to stagger a 2.5 per cent pay rise, awarding increases only when it was satisfied that productivity targets were being met in relation to crime detection and prevention. There was also frequent controversy over crime rates under Labour. In the decade from 1997 to 2007, police funding rose by 77 per cent in real terms (£4.8bn), yet statistics were far from conclusive about the extent to which crime had fallen. According to British Crime Survey figures published in January 2008, the risk of becoming a crime victim in Britain was at a 27-year low, with a year-on-year fall in reported crime of 9 per cent. But figures obtained from the police themselves showed drug offences had soared by nearly a quarter in the previous 12 months. The number of firearms-related arrests had risen by 4 per cent.

Like hospitals, schools, and care homes, police forces must submit themselves to independent inspection. The body responsible, Her Majesty's Inspectorate of Constabulary (HMIC), is actually the oldest organization of its kind—dating back more than 150 years, to the County and Borough Police Act 1856. Its remit covers England, Wales, and Northern Ireland (there is a separate inspectorate for Scotland), and it is headed by a Chief Inspector of Constabulary. Like the Chief Inspector for Schools (see p. 449), this official is semi-independent from government—and, as such, has been known to speak out critically over aspects of policy. In July 2010, then incumbent Sir Denis O'Connor published a joint report with the *Audit Commission* and Wales Audit Office warning that projected police budget cuts of 25 per cent would adversely affect frontline policing. He said that, while 12 per cent could be saved through a 'total redesign' of the way forces operated, further cuts would hit beat numbers unless they were 'prioritized over everything else'.

## Security and counter-terrorism

When 52 commuters were killed in coordinated suicide bombings in central London on 7 July 2005, the British government decided at once that security policy must be at the heart of its future political agenda. Ever since the attacks on New York's World Trade Center on 11 September 2001, and the UK's subsequent support for US-led military action in Afghanistan and Iraq, the country had been periodically threatened with its own atrocity—both covertly, through tip-offs gathered by its intelligence services, and overtly, by the increasingly bellicose online proclamations of Osama bin Laden, his chief 'lieutenant' Ayman Al Zawahiri, and Abu Musab al-Zarqawi, late leader of 'Al-Qaeda in Iraq'.

Because of these threats—real and perceived—Mr Blair's government had already passed a succession of 'anti-terror' laws long before the 7 July bombings. In fact, so proactive had it been that critics of his policies (not to mention the Iraq invasion itself) argued that, far from preventing further attacks, they might actually provoke them.

Of all anti-terror policies introduced in Britain in the wake of the 11 September attacks, the most controversial and far-reaching were those relating to the detention of terrorist suspects. At the heart of the controversy was ministers' cavalier willingness—in the eyes of critics—to dispense with more than 800 years of due legal process by detaining people for prolonged periods without charge. Civil liberties campaigners saw moves like the internment in Belmarsh Prison of individuals suspected of (but not immediately tried for) terror offences as a breach of the sacrosanct constitutional principle of habeas corpus—the right to a fair trial before one's peers—first introduced under Magna Carta. Signed by King John in 1215 (see p. 6), this mammoth document stipulated:

> ❝ No free man shall be seized or imprisoned . . . except by the lawful judgement of his equals or by the law of the land. ❞

The policy of detaining 'terror suspects' summarily (before trial) at Belmarsh began in late 2001, shortly after the 11 September attacks. It was not long before the government—which had opted out of the article of the Human Rights Act 1998 barring it from taking such action—faced significant challenges to its authority. As early as July 2002, the Special Immigration Appeals Commission (SIAC)—a Home Office *quango*—ruled in response to an application by four detainees that the Anti-Terrorism, Crime, and Security Act 2001, under which they had been imprisoned, unjustifiably discriminated against foreign nationals. Although this ruling was later overturned by the Court of Appeal, worse was to come for the Labour government. Most significantly, in December 2004 the Law Lords ruled eight to one that continued detention of the 12 individuals still in custody was incompatible with human rights legislation.

Despite an initial show of defiance, then Home Secretary Mr Clarke was forced to release the suspects early in 2005, replacing indefinite detention with 'control orders'—sweeping powers to confine suspects in the community through the use of electronic tagging, curfews, and even house arrest. But these soon ran into trouble, too. Because an order could be introduced for between six and 12 months at the Home Secretary's behest, with little or no  opposition, the policy again upset civil liberties campaigners. Neither was it an unqualified success at a practical level: in May 2007, it emerged that three men allegedly plotting to kill British troops abroad, Lamine Adam, 26, his brother Ibrahim, 20, and Cerie Bullivant, 24, had absconded while under control orders. This prompted a call from the independent reviewer of terrorism laws, Lib Dem peer Lord Carlile, for the system to be tightened up. The most recent controversy concerning terror suspects relates to the period of time for which police are permitted to detain them for questioning without charge. In November 2005, Mr Blair suffered his first House of Commons defeat in eight years as prime minister by staking his authority on a vote to increase the period from an existing limit of 14 days to 90 days. Mr Blair—who said senior police officers had told him the case for extending their detention powers to nearly three months was 'compelling'—had to accept a compromise of 28 days.

His successor, Mr Brown, later tried to raise this to 42 days by offering rebellious *backbenchers* a series of compromises and forcing the measure through the Commons on a three-line *whip*. But he and Ms Smith were finally forced to shelve the plans after being defeated in the Lords by a majority of 191 votes. Among those who voted against the measure were Mr Blair's former Attorney General, Lord Goldsmith, and Lord Falconer, the ex-Lord Chancellor and one of his closest friends. Erstwhile MI5 heads Dame Eliza Manningham-Buller and Dame Stella Rimington also opposed it. Ms Smith insisted the following day that the government would revisit the proposal in the form of emergency legislation at a later date, should Britain face a further terrorist attack, but this opportunity was never to arise.

Having fought the May 2010 election, at least partly, on a pro-civil liberties platform, the Tories and Lib Dems launched a wholesale review of anti-terrorism policies on entering government. Among the measures earmarked for reform or abolition were control orders, police stop-and-search powers, and the 28-day detention period for terrorist suspects.

## Asylum, immigration, and citizenship

Before terrorism shifted the goalposts in 2001, perhaps the single biggest home affairs issue of the New Labour years was the dual question of asylum and immigration. The term 'asylum seeker' entered the media lexicon around the time war broke out in the Balkans in the early 1990s. Tabloids and broadsheets alike were quick to focus on this new 'threat' to Britain's borders, and by 2002 the red-tops were filled with scare stories about impending invasions of 'illegal immigrants' lured by the UK's 'soft-touch' benefits system. Their agitated prose was fuelled by the initially laissez-faire attitude of the French government to a burgeoning refugee camp at Sangatte, near Calais, from which 1,600 asylum seekers from around the world were apparently planning to sneak into southern England.

More recently, **enlargement** of the European Union (EU), first to 25 then 27 countries, has led to a significant influx of economic migrants from other parts of Europe—and, in particular, from former Eastern Bloc countries like Poland—in pursuit of paid work. This, too, has been controversial, with national newspapers such as the *Daily Mail* and the *Daily Express* pandering to the concerns of local communities in some areas of the country that foreign workers were 'stealing' jobs from long-standing residents and putting pressure on already overstretched public services, such as social housing, schools, and health care. There have also been numerous headlines blaming immigrants for rises in certain types of crime. In fact, according to two reports published in

April 2008, immigrants have actually had little or no negative impact on either demand for public services or crime. The first, published by the Association of Chief Police Officers (ACPO), found that offending rates in the Polish, Romanian, and Bulgarian communities (the focus of the study, due to the influx of economic migrants from those countries following their accession to the EU) were proportionate to that within the British population as a whole. The second, a joint study by the *Commission for Equality and Human Rights (CEHR)* and the Local Government Association (LGA), found little evidence that migrants were queue-jumping to obtain social housing before local people: in fact, 60 per cent of those who had moved to Britain in the previous five years were in private rented accommodation.

But not every survey paints a rosy picture of immigration: in December 2007, analysis of employment data by the Statistics Commission found that 80 per cent of all new jobs created in Britain since 1997 had gone to foreign-born workers (1.4 million out of 1.7 million). Around the same time, Ms Smith admitted as many as 11,000 non-EU nationals licensed to work in the security industry might be illegal immigrants. One had been involved in repairing Mr Blair's car; another was found to be working as a cleaner in the Commons in February 2008. And a report by the Lords Economic Affairs Committee, published in April 2008, concluded that immigrants had had 'little or no impact' on the UK's economic well-being. The Committee recommended a formal 'cap' on immigration numbers. An annual cap on migrants from outside the European Union was promised in the Conservatives' 2010 election manifesto, and on 19 July that year Ms May introduced a temporary cap on entry into the UK by non-EU citizens (of 24,100 between then and April 2011) to avoid a rush of people trying to migrate before the permanent limit had come into force. The Lib-Con government also announced plans early on for a new dedicated Border Police Force.

Despite widespread perceptions, asylum seekers, illegal immigrants, and economic migrants often have a far from cushy time when they arrive in Britain. In 1999, papers across southern England were filled with reports about the appalling housing conditions some families were enduring while their asylum applications were processed and as they waited to be 'dispersed' around the country. Meanwhile, an emerging black market in cheap foreign labour (employed on rates well below the minimum wage) fostered by unscrupulous people traffickers has led to high-profile tragedies. In February 2004, 21 Chinese refugees were drowned in Morecambe Bay, Lancashire, while illegally working as cockle-pickers.

Sensationalism aside, Britain's population is rising fast: according to the Office for National Statistics (ONS), it soared by 8 per cent between 1971 and 2008, and had reached 62 million by early 2010. By 2029, it is expected to top 70 million at current rates of growth. In September 2007, the ONS predicted the number of immigrants arriving in Britain would continue rising by up to 190,000 a year—three times higher than previous estimates—while three months later it reported that the birth rate among foreign-born women living in the UK had overtaken that of British-born mothers. These and other demographic trends have made immigration and asylum perhaps one of the most problematic and divisive issues facing government.

The decision by aspiring immigrants and economic migrants to relocate to the UK can also have a negative knock-on effect on their countries of origin. The migration of large numbers of skilled Polish workers, such as plumbers and electricians, to the UK following the country's admission into the EU produced as many negative newspaper headlines in Poland as it did in Britain. In some media, whole towns were depicted as being 'drained' of their most highly trained artisans by Britain and other west European countries. Meanwhile, the backlash among some sections of the electorate over the perceived impact of inward migration and immigration on the availability of job opportunities for native Britons led to the UK imposing restrictions on migration from the two newest member states, Bulgaria and Romania (both of which joined in January 2007), and to Mr Brown's controversial pledge to work towards a guarantee of a 'British job for every British worker'.

But what do terms like 'asylum seeker' and 'illegal immigrant' actually *mean*—and what is the difference? Put simply, the term 'asylum seeker' is generally used as a synonym for 'refugee', which the 1951 **United Nations (UN)** Convention Relating to the Status of Refugees described as follows:

❝ A person who owing to a well-founded fear of being persecuted for reasons of race, religion, nationality, membership of a particular social group, or political opinion, is outside the country of their nationality, and is unable to or, owing to such fear, is unwilling to avail him/herself of the protection of that country. ❞

The term 'asylum' is also distinct from 'immigration', in that it is often used to describe a *temporary* state of affairs—an individual fleeing tyranny in his or her home country is not necessarily seeking to remain permanently in the land to which he or she has fled.

Immigration, in contrast, is used to describe the process of becoming a 'naturalized' citizen of a different country. The term 'illegal immigrant' is frequently used pejoratively by right-wing politicians and newspapers. It refers to individuals who illegally cross borders to enter a country without following the official asylum procedure. Before the Sangatte camp was closed, there were several instances of refugees illicitly entering Britain through the Channel Tunnel.

Asylum policy is overseen by the UK Border Agency (previously the Border and Immigration Agency), a Home Office executive agency. The question of whether to grant asylum does not arise in the case of Irish Republic or Commonwealth citizens who had the right of abode in Britain before January 1983, nor other EU citizens. It applies only marginally to nationals of the European Economic Area (EEA), a region of *potential* EU countries, which encompasses the Union itself, plus neighbouring states such as Iceland, Liechtenstein, and Norway. Residents of these countries are already allowed (subject to certain limitations) to work in the UK and, if they can support themselves, live here too. But nationals of most countries outside these areas, including many African and Asian nations, require a visa before entering Britain. Some also require 'entry clearance'.

In an effort to reassure UK taxpayers that the country is no 'free for all' for foreign immigrants, the Home Office has introduced tough new measures designed to make it harder for foreigners to claim asylum the table entitled 'Recent rule changes covering asylum and immigration policy', on the Online Resource Centre accompanying this book. In addition, successful applicants  for British citizenship must now sign up to a number of 'responsibilities' in order to be able to claim the 'rights' that go with it. These are outlined in Table 8.6.

## The great 'Big Brother' debate

If one issue during New Labour's era raised the hackles of civil liberties campaigners more even than detention without trial it was the perceived 'Big Brother' approach ministers took towards crime detection and prevention. This tactic was symbolized for many by two signature Blairite policies (both since abandoned by the Lib-Con coalition): national identity cards and the national DNA database.

Between 2009 and 2010, British citizens applying for or renewing adult passports were offered a choice between being issued with ID cards containing both their specific personal details (name, age, address, etc.) and biometric data (fingerprints, facial characteristics, irises), or new-style 'biometric passports' containing more limited information. The aim of the 'biographical footprint' held on ID cards was to enable certain accredited organizations to use it—with the cardholders' permission—to confirm their identities. Foreign nationals living and working in the UK began being issued with biometric ID cards in 2008. Although having a card was not initially compulsory, the Labour government sought to make it so eventually.

Opponents of ID cards broadly fell into two camps: pragmatists and idealists. Pragmatists, like former Conservative Shadow Home Secretary David Davis, argued that questions over the reliability of the technology used to produce the cards, combined with the fact that owning one was not initially intended to be  compulsory, threatened to make the scheme an ineffective waste of taxpayers' money. Idealists, such as campaign group Liberty and many other MPs, saw the cards as a dangerous next step on the road to turning Britain into a paranoid surveillance society. They also highlighted inconsistencies in the arguments ministers used to justify the measure: when first mooted, in the aftermath of 11 September, it appeared they were primarily intended as a weapon in the 'war on terror', but towards the end of Mr Blair's premiership he said the government's

**Table 8.6** New 'rights and responsibilities' measures for 'successful' immigration applicants

| Device | How it works |
|---|---|
| Vouchers | To avoid accusations they were prepared to give asylum seekers cash handouts, Ministers introduced vouchers to be exchanged for food and toiletries by refugees applying for asylum. The scheme was scrapped by Mr Blunkett in 2002 following a riot at the Yarl's Wood detention-centre, but reintroduced in 2006, following controversy about the cash payments that replaced it. 'Failed' asylum seekers who cannot be deported to their home countries because of human rights concerns also qualify for the vouchers, worth £35 a week, in addition to a bed. Alternatively, they can claim three meals a day and no financial support. |
| Citizenship ceremonies | Intended to steady community relations between British residents and new foreign immigrants moving into their areas, these were introduced in 2004. On 26 February that year, in the presence of the Prince of Wales, 19 people—including three children—swore allegiance to the Queen, sang the national anthem, and vowed to respect the rights and freedoms of British citizens. Citizenship ceremonies have since been held repeatedly across the UK. New immigrants receive an 'immigration handbook', and are expected to attend classes in the English language, UK institutions, and the law, to familiarize themselves with Britain's cultural heritage. |
| Points system | Introduced for *economic migrants* in early 2008, this five-tier system limits the ability of unskilled workers from non-EU countries to work in Britain, while welcoming skilled migrants as 'key contributors' to the UK economy. Points for 'highly skilled migrants' are awarded on the basis of age, qualifications, and previous salary. Around 75 points are needed to guarantee entry. |
| Probationary citizenship | Non-EU economic migrants applying to settle in Britain permanently must now serve a probation period before gaining full citizenship. Under the previous system, migrants could apply for a British passport after five years of living and working in the country. The new system requires them to serve a one–three-year probationary period of 'earned citizenship' following their initial five-year stay. The prospect of someone gaining full citizenship increases if he or she takes part in voluntary work, but reduces if he or she commits a crime. In the meantime, benefit and social housing entitlement is limited. |

main intention was to protect people against the growing threat of identity fraud.

Concerns about ID cards were compounded by publicity surrounding the expansion of the national DNA database—a sprawling electronic record of genetic samples taken from crime scenes and individuals held in police custody. Originally established in 1995, by the end of 2009 it contained 5.9 million samples from 5.1 million people (equivalent to nearly one in ten of the population). By comparison, the US database contains samples from a mere 0.5 per cent of its citizens. Since 2004 anyone penalized for an arrestable offence—even those given a simple police caution—have had their samples added to the database. In December 2006, then Home Secretary Mr Reid admitted more than a million of those whose details were on the database had not even been cautioned! One reason for the apparent anomaly was the fact that police had failed to remove the details of individuals arrested and charged with criminal offences, but subsequently acquitted.

To ensure that the database is not misused, it is regulated by a board comprising members of the Home Office, ACPO, the Association of Police Authorities (APA), and the Human Genetics Commission (HGC).

A series of high-profile convictions of serial murderers and sex attackers in early 2008 led to calls from some senior police officers for the government to extend the scope of the database to include the whole British population. But in its May 2010 *Queen's Speech* the Lib-Con coalition announced plans to restrict the future use and growth of the database by passing a Freedom (Great Repeal) Bill that would also regulate closed-circuit television (CCTV) cameras, ease existing limitations on peaceful protest, and reduce the state's ability to monitor individuals' email and Internet records (another crime prevention measure introduced under Mr Brown). As with ID cards, defenders of the database—including those who believe it should be made universal— argued the innocent had nothing to fear from it. But its opponents said such views were counter-intuitive and that inclusion of non-offenders on a police record contradicted the basic tenet of British justice that individuals are 'innocent until proven guilty'. Not all critics have been Opposition MPs, disgruntled backbenchers, or people with other obvious agendas. In August 2004, the government's own Information Commissioner, Richard Thomas, warned in an interview with *The Times* that the country might unwittingly 'sleepwalk into a surveillance society'.

Three years later one of Britain's most senior judges, Lord Justice Sedley, described the database as 'indefensible' and suggested it be extended to cover the whole population—if only to address what he perceived as its intrinsic discrimination against people from ethnic minorities.

## Safeguarding human rights for British citizens

Despite Labour's predilection for vigilance, the passage of the 1998 Human Rights Act (see p. 11) marked the beginning of a sustained championing of equality of opportunity and basic freedoms for British citizens in other ways, which led to everything from the equalization of the age of consent for gay and heterosexual sex to the introduction of civil partnerships for homosexual couples.

To spearhead the government's drive to guarantee British citizens equal opportunities—regardless of age, gender, race, or disability—it established three new quangos on entering office in 1997:

- the Equal Opportunities Commission (EOC);
- the Commission for Racial Equality (CRE);
- the Disability Rights Commission (DRC).

Ten years later, these bodies were merged into a single Commission for Equality and Human Rights (CEHR), also known as the 'Equality and Human Rights Commission'. The Commission's remit was extended to cover sexual orientation and religious beliefs, in addition to the areas dealt with by the three former quangos.

In addition to investigating individual complaints about discrimination, the Commission:

- enforces the law in relation to equal opportunities and rights;
- influences the development of the law and government policy;
- promotes good practice;
- fosters better relations between communities.

# ▌ Ministry of Justice (MoJ)

The British criminal justice system has two core elements—the court system and the treatment of offenders—both of which are now the responsibility of the Justice Secretary.

## The court system and civil law

The day-to-day business of running the British courts is performed by an MoJ executive agency, Her Majesty's Courts Service. The Justice Secretary is personally responsible for promoting more general reforms of the civil law and the legal aid system.

The government's principal legal advisers are the Attorney General and Solicitor-General, both of whom are members of either the Lords or the Commons. In Scotland their roles are performed by the Advocate General for Scotland (who has assumed the roles previously held by the Lord Advocate and the Solicitor General for Scotland).

Subordinate to the Attorney General are the Director of Public Prosecutions (DPP), who runs the Crown Prosecution Service (CPS)— the state-owned legal service that brings prosecutions on behalf of the Crown—and the DPP for Northern Ireland, along with the Director of the Serious Fraud Office. At present there remains an as yet unresolved debate about the future role of the Attorney General stemming from controversy about the perceived over-politicization of the 750-year-old post under Mr Blair's government. Lord Goldsmith was seen to be torn between party loyalty and legal protocol in advising ministers on the legitimacy of invading Iraq, as well as the later decision (subsequently overturned by the Serious Fraud Office) not to press charges against BAE Systems over its controversial overseas business dealings.

# Criminal law

The Justice Secretary has overall responsibility for criminal law and introducing Bills needed to change it. In this respect, his or her work is delegated to the following two principal agencies:

- the *National Probation Service (NPS)*—which oversees the supervision of individuals serving community-based sentences for criminal offences, or periods in prison during which they are permitted to live in the community. Each year the NPS supervises 175,000 offenders (90 per cent male), a quarter of whom are 16–20-year-olds. There are 42 county-based probation services in England and Wales spread across ten regions. Their boundaries correspond with those of local police forces. Since 2001, the NPS has come under a new National Probation Directorate in the Home Office and been supervised by an independent HM Inspectorate of Probation;
- the **National Offender Management Service (NOMS)**—the body that runs all 135 prisons in England and Wales (in Scotland, this role is retained by the Prisons Service, which did so before). Formed in April 2008, NOMS oversees *all* prisons—whether publicly or privately funded and/or owned—and its chief executive office has been left with ultimate responsibility for administrative mistakes arising from its conduct. The Prisons Service still exists—but only as one 'unit' of NOMS, with responsibility for publicly funded jails.

## Recent and future developments in the prison system

NOMS employs the 50,000-plus wardens, officers, and governors who administer prisons on the ground. Since the Criminal Justice Act 1991, management of many prisons has been contracted out to the private sector—as has transportation of defendants held in custody to and from court. The first four newly built prisons handed over to private managers were the Wolds (Humberside), Blakenhurst (Worcestershire), Doncaster, and Buckley Hall (Rochdale).

In addition, all new jails built since the early 1990s have been funded through the *private finance initiative (PFI)* or *public–private partnerships (PPPs*—see p. 222). The first four privately financed jails, opened in 1998–99, were on Merseyside, and in Nottinghamshire, South Wales, and Kilmarnock.

Complaints about the prison and probation services are handled by a single authority: the independent Prisons and Probation Ombudsman for England and Wales (PPO). HM Prison Inspectorates—one for each of England, Scotland, and Wales—are charged with visiting prisons every three years to report on conditions and treatment. Individual prisons and young offenders' institutions also have 'boards of visitors'—groups of local people appointed by the Home Secretary to relay complaints from prisoners in the same way as *HealthWatch* groups operate in the NHS (see p. 176).

Since the early 1990s prisons have seldom been out of the news. Typically, stories about them tend to be negative, focusing on overcrowding, riots, and periodic breakouts. To provide spare capacity, successive governments have done everything from adapting military camps to act as temporary prisons to commissioning a 'prison ship', *HMP Weare*, moored off Portland, Dorset. During his time as a tough-talking Home Secretary in Mr Major's government, Michael Howard vowed to cut the number of community sentences and send more people to jail, particularly violent offenders. But his famous cry of 'Prison works!' set him on a collision course with then Director-General of the Prisons Service, Derek Lewis, who warned of dangerous overcrowding. In January 1995, the simmering prisons crisis came to a head during a succession of riots and breakouts, first at Everthorpe Jail, Humberside, then Parkhurst. A damning report into the state of the system saw Mr Howard sack Mr Lewis in October that year—but not without facing tough questioning from Jeremy Paxman in a now legendary interview for BBC2's *Newsnight*, during which he was asked 12 times if he had 'threatened to overrule' Mr Lewis.

Overcrowding has remained a serious concern for recent governments. In May 2007 the prison population reached 80,500—within a whisker of its maximum capacity. At the time, a further 300 prisoners were being held in police and court cells. Lord Falconer, then Lord Chancellor, issued an appeal to the courts to limit their use of prison sentences for people convicted of minor offences and it emerged the government was considering the early release of 3,000 inmates to free up cells for more serious offenders. To add to ministers' blushes, Lord Phillips, the Lord Chief Justice, declared in a public statement that the country's jails were 'full' and that the rate of prison sentencing would soon 'outstrip the capacity of the prisons'. By the time Labour left office in May 2010 the prison population had climbed to a record high of 85,201—nearly twice the level under the previous Tory government.

In June 2010 the *Scottish Parliament* unilaterally reduced prisoner numbers north of the border, through a new Criminal Justice and Licensing Bill introducing a presumption against sentences of three months or less alongside a commitment to tougher community sentences. The Bill also raised the age of criminal responsibility in Scotland from 8 to 12—two years higher than in England and Wales, where a decision had earlier been taken by Mr Brown's government to keep it at 10.

Other recent controversies have focused on the plight of staff themselves, and in particular, the poor pay and conditions of many prison officers. In August 2007, 20,000 members of the Prison Officers' Association (POA) threatened a 24-hour wildcat strike in protest at overcrowding and a below-inflation pay rise of 1.9 per cent.

## Rehabilitation of offenders

Convicted offenders receive sentences that are either *custodial*—detention in a prison or young offenders' institution—or *non-custodial* (for example, conditional discharge, community service, probation, fines, or compensation order). The latter are supervised in England and Wales by the NPS; in Scotland, by local authority social workers.

Other than in the exceptional cases in which royal pardons are issued on the advice of the Justice Secretary (see p. 21), prisoners are only generally granted early release from jail in recognition of 'good behaviour' in custody. This system is known as **parole**. Although the application process is relatively simple, parole itself is complex, in that prisoners' eligibility to apply for it depends on various factors—most notably, the nature and severity of their offences. Those eligible for parole may apply in the first instance six months before their earliest possible release date (normally specified at the time they were sentenced). A file on the prisoner will be compiled and three members of the Parole Board—the body that advises the government on applications—will meet to decide whether to grant the prisoner's wishes.

A swift decision may be taken for more minor offenders to allow them parole 'on licence'—under which they may be released early subject to the condition that they do not reoffend. If they do so within the remaining period of their original sentence they may end up serving the remainder of that term in jail after all, in addition to any further period relating to their latest conviction. A full Parole Board hearing tends to be called only for the most serious offenders.

Due, in part, to concerns about prison overcrowding, in practice parole has become all but automatic for most offenders. In 1991, however, Mr Howard toughened up the procedure. The conditions he introduced to guide future decisions included that:

- prisoners other than the most serious offenders (rapists and murderers) serving *four years or more* should be released on Parole Board recommendation after serving half their sentence, and normally automatically after serving two-thirds;

- final decisions on the early release of prisoners serving *more than four but less than seven years* should be taken by the Parole Board;

- prisoners sentenced to life imprisonment for certain kinds of murder— those of police officers, terrorism, and child killings—would tend automatically to serve at least 20 years. Early release of such 'mandatory life prisoners' could only be authorized by the Home Secretary in consultation with the Parole Board and judiciary;

- those sentenced to life for offences other than murder would normally be released by the Home Secretary after a period set by the judge at their trial. The Board would still have power, though, to order continued confinement beyond this period if necessary to protect the public. Such sentences—known as 'indeterminate sentences for public protection' (IPP)—have caused headaches for recent governments. In February 2008 three Court of Appeal judges and the Lord Chief Justice ruled the board

→
see also
local
govern-
ment,
p. 519

was not sufficiently independent of ministers to approve IPPs at their request, and that then Justice Secretary Mr Straw had acted 'unlawfully' in his prior treatment of such prisoners. Among the high-profile prisoners repeatedly refused release on grounds of public safety, as well the peculiar seriousness of their crimes, were late Moors murderer Myra Hindley, and serial killer Rose West. Peter Sutcliffe, the 'Yorkshire Ripper', who was told by a High Court judge in July 2010 he would never be released. Others, including Tracey Connolly, mother of child domestic abuse victim Peter Connolly ('Baby P'), are serving indefinite sentences.

In addition to the 1991 Act, the Crime (Sentences) Act 1997 further toughened the sentencing regime by putting greater emphasis on the idea of prisoners *earning* parole—restyling them 'early release days' and introducing the idea that they could be gained and lost.

It also introduced:

- automatic life sentences for those convicted twice of serious sexual or violent crimes;
- mandatory minimum prison sentences for drug dealers and serial burglars.

In opposition the Conservatives consistently called for increased funding for additional prison places. On re-entering government, however, coalition Justice Secretary Kenneth Clarke performed an apparent volte-face, announcing a 'rehabilitation revolution' intended to cut the jail population. Pledging to 'shut the revolving door of crime and reoffending', he unveiled a new scheme analogous to that introduced by Mr Brown to find work for the long-term unemployed, under which private firms and voluntary organizations would be paid by results for turning repeat offenders (particularly those previously jailed for petty crimes) into 'law-abiding citizens'. Until 2006 Scottish parole policy was more lenient than those elsewhere in the UK—with prisoners serving between four and ten years released on the Parole Board's say-so after serving half their sentences, and only those serving more than ten years needing the Home Secretary's consent, but under the Custodial Sentences and Weapons Act 2007 (passed by the Scottish Parliament) conditions for early release were toughened. Automatic early release without conditions for prisoners serving less than four years was replaced with a new licensing system. Anyone released early who breaches his or her licence terms is now returned to jail. In addition, sentencing judges who consider a defendant to be of particular risk to the public can stipulate that such individuals wait longer than the usual halfway mark before qualifying for parole. The Parole Board also has powers to increase this custodial period at a later date, should the circumstances arise. The Management of Offenders (Scotland) Act 2005, meanwhile, ended unconditional early release for sex offenders sentenced to between six months and four years, subjecting them to a new licence-and-supervision system.

In Northern Ireland special circumstances apply in terrorism cases, in recognition of the unique nature of The Troubles. Until 1995, terrorists sentenced to five years or more were usually paroled only after serving two-thirds of their terms, but this has since been brought in line with the rest of the UK—that is, eligibility after serving half a sentence. Terrorists convicted of another offence before the end of their original sentences must complete these before their next starts. In response to the positive progress of the Northern Ireland peace process at the time, a one-off arrangement was made allowing inmates of the Maze Prison out on licence for Christmas 1999 and New Year 2000.

## ☰ Topical feature idea

Despite its controversy, the national DNA database has been praised by many senior police officers for providing crucial leads in the pursuit of dangerous criminals who might never have been caught or convicted were it not for the genetic information it contained. Under Labour, the Home Office argued that some 45,000 matches were identified each year between DNA samples on the database and those retrieved from crime scenes. Have any convictions occurred in your area through the use of such DNA evidence? If so, what do the victims of those crimes, their relatives, and/or local police officers feel about the Lib-Con coalition government's plans to reduce the future scope and use of the database?

## ✳ Current issues

- **Welfare reform:** the Lib-Con coalition government is committed to reducing Britain's welfare bill as part of its programme to cut the country's Budget deficit, and the perceived 'dependency culture'. According to the Office of National Statistics, 8.2 per cent of British adults of working age are currently 'economically inactive' (neither employed or self-employed, nor officially unemployed), although critics argue many of these are students or those in early retirement. As of autumn 2010, some 2.7 million were on Incapacity Benefit or Employment and Support Allowance.

- **The Freedom (Great Repeal) Bill:** Deputy Prime Minister Nick Clegg has pledged to usher in 'the most significant programme of empowerment by a British government since the great enfranchisement of the nineteenth century' by introducing constitutional reform and rolling back several New Labour policies criticized for infringing civil rights—including ID cards, biometric passports, and the retention of genetic profiles of innocent people on the national DNA database.

- **Reform of the role of Attorney General:** the last Labour Attorney General, Baroness Scotland, published a draft Bill designed to reform her office to remove potential conflicts of interest identified during the tenure of her predecessor, Lord Goldsmith, but these were criticized for failing to go far enough, and have yet to be implemented. Reform of the role, which originated in the mid-thirteenth century, has yet to be addressed by the coalition partners.

## ? Review questions

1. What is the difference between a 'contributory' and a 'non-contributory' benefit?

2. Outline the history, aims, and responsibilities of the Home Office. To what extent have these changed and been extended since its inception?

3. To what extent has the welfare state remained true to its founding principle to look after British citizens—regardless of their means—from the cradle to the grave?

4. Outline the recent developments in UK pensions policy, explaining the main types of state-funded pension and some of the alternatives.

5. Which government department—the Home Office or the Ministry of Justice—has the greater jurisdiction over criminal justice matters in the UK? Outline the specific responsibilities in relation to crime, policing, and the courts of each department.

## → Further reading

Bartholomew, J. (2006) *The Welfare State We're In*, London: Politico's Publishing. **Critique of welfare state, using examples of its failings in state education and pensions system to argue Britain would have been better off without it.**

Glendinning, C. and Kemp, P. (2006) *Cash and Care: Policy Challenges in the Welfare State*, Bristol: Policy Press. **Overview of recent trends in social security policy, including evaluations of the impact of tax credits and Welfare to Work, and the changing socio-economic profile of benefit recipients.**

Hansen, R. S. (2001) *Citizenship and Immigration in Post-war Britain: The Institutional Origins of a Multicultural Nation*, Oxford: Oxford University Press. **Accomplished evaluation of the socio-economic and cultural impact of immigration since 1945.**

Lowe, R. (2004) *Welfare State in Britain Since 1945*, 3rd edn, London: Palgrave Macmillan. **Third edition of standard work on the evolution of the welfare state, incorporating analysis of recent trends in welfare provision, such as tax credits and Welfare to Work.**

Reiner, R. (2000) *The Politics of the Police*, 3rd edn, Oxford: Oxford University Press. **Fully revised third edition of standard text on the origins, history, and present-day make-up of British police. Includes detailed analysis of current issues, including those arising from the Macpherson Report into the Stephen Lawrence case.**

Sanders, A. (2006) *Criminal Justice*, London: LexisNexis UK. **Critical analysis of the British criminal justice system, focusing on all aspects of crime and punishment including habeas corpus, the penal system, and sentencing procedures.**

## 🌐 Online Resource Centre

www.oxfordtextbooks.co.uk/orc/Morrison2e/
Visit the Online Resource Centre that accompanies this book for web links and regular updates.

# 9

# The European Union (EU)

The European Union (EU) is a subject that divides British politicians, the public, and, for that matter, the media into two equally vociferous camps. On the one side are 'Europhiles'—those who see closer economic and political integration as a logical, common-sense, and desirable state of affairs that can only enhance mutual understanding and, ultimately, prosperity. Ranged opposite them are the 'Euro-sceptics'. While some are merely critical of its current composition (seeing it as overly bureaucratic, undemocratic, and lacking accountability), others still view the very idea of the union as an anathema, arguing that it threatens individual nations' rights to sovereignty and self-determination.

As befits such a contentious issue, Europe generates extensive (if not always well-informed) coverage in the British press. Although EU press officers are forever complaining about how difficult it is to interest editors and reporters in writing meaningful news stories about its work, the number of column inches devoted to supposed diktats from 'Brussels' (to cite the commonly used shorthand) has steadily increased since the dramatic parliamentary scenes of the early 1990s surrounding the passage of the 'Maastricht Treaty' (see pp. 269 and 279). The furores have often verged on the farcical. In 1998, *Daily Mail* readers were greeted by near-hysterical headlines in response to the **European Commission**'s attempt to force British chocolate manufacturers such as Cadbury to redefine their products as 'vegelate', reflecting the high percentage of vegetable fats they contained in comparison to cocoa butter.  More recently, in 2005 *The Sun* launched a 'Save our Jugs' campaign in protest at a supposed attempt by 'EU killjoys' to force busty barmaids to cover up  their cleavages. The actual proposal (dropped in light of the opposition) was a draft 'Optical Radiation Directive' designed to protect workers from builders to park-keepers from excessive exposure to the sun. It made no mention of barmaids' breasts.

So what *does* EU membership mean for Britain and how did it come about?

# ▌ Britain's twisty path to EU membership

The European 'Common Market' (as it was widely known in Britain until the 1970s) began its slow emergence in the post-war period, as the continent struggled to rebuild itself after six years of bruising conflict. But although it shared many of the same economic interests as its neighbours, for a long time Britain's attitude towards them was lukewarm at best. Buffered by the existence of its Commonwealth of dependent nations on the one hand and its emerging 'special relationship' with the USA on the other, it was reluctant to be too tied to the activities of its Continental cousins.

By 1961, however, the positive economic impact membership of the European Economic Community (EEC) appeared to be having for its member states encouraged the UK, under then Conservative Prime Minister Harold Macmillan, to apply for membership alongside Denmark, Ireland, and Norway. But its application was blocked by France's then President Charles de Gaulle twice (in 1963 and 1967), because he argued Britain was not sufficiently 'European' to join.

In the ensuing disagreement with fellow member states, De Gaulle precipitated one of the biggest constitutional upheavals in the history of the embryonic EU by refusing to send representatives from France to meetings of any of the three Communities from 1965–66 (an affair known as the 'empty chairs crisis'). His action led, in 1966, to the passing of the Luxembourg Compromise—an informal understanding that agreements between member governments must in future be made *unanimously*, rather than by *majority vote*, as had been the case before.

Following the resignation of de Gaulle in 1969, negotiations began in earnest for Britain's accession to the new Community and the country was taken into it by Edward Heath's government in 1973. Ireland and Denmark joined at the same time.

Yet any hope that the country's accession would finally end years of squabbling between Britain and its European neighbours—not to mention the internecine fighting over the European Community (EC) within the UK's main political parties—were short-lived. By the time of the next general election in 1974, divisions were so marked within Harold Wilson's Labour Party and (according to opinion polls) in the country at large that Labour pledged to hold a *referendum* on the issue if returned to power. This it did, on 5 June 1975, but only after Mr Wilson had waived the decades-old convention of *collective responsibility* (see pp. 99–101) to allow members of his *Cabinet* who opposed his pro-European stance to campaign actively for 'no' votes. These included then Industry Secretary Tony Benn and Employment Secretary Michael Foot, who blamed rising unemployment figures on the UK's membership of the EC. They argued free trade between Britain and its Continental neighbours was allowing cheap imports to flood high-street shops, undermining the profits of British-based manufacturers and leading to job cuts.

Despite the best efforts of the 'no' lobby, Wilson got his way decisively enough to lay to rest the EC membership debate for the time being (although not, it transpired, forever). Two months after weathering a humiliating defeat on the issue by members of his own party at a one-day Labour conference, his 'yes' campaign clinched more than 67 per cent of the vote in the referendum on a 64 per cent turnout.

Mr Wilson's triumph was pyrrhic: Britain's troubled admission into the EU marked the beginning of what has continued to be, at best, a love–hate relationship with the union. At various points during its membership, the country has refused to toe the line—negotiating 'opt-outs' from clauses to treaties that bind most, if not all, of its peers (John Major's refusal to sign the Social Chapter of the 'Maastricht Treaty' being a famous example) and struggling to win parliamentary approval for various others. In 1992, Mr Major's government was almost brought down by its own **backbenchers** over Maastricht—an episode explored in depth later in this chapter—while more recently Tony Blair and Gordon Brown both resisted the clamour for a referendum on the 'Lisbon Treaty', a similarly controversial agreement that many Euro-sceptics (and some Europhiles, such as former Tory Chancellor, now Justice Secretary, Kenneth Clarke) argued was essentially the same document as the ill-fated 'EU Constitution' (see p. 283). Although in coalition with the predominantly Europhile Liberal Democrats (whose leader, Nick Clegg, is both a former MEP and 'Eurocrat'), David Cameron's Conservatives remain a largely Euro-sceptic party. Prior to gaining power they formed a breakaway right-wing political grouping in the **European Parliament**. Since doing so, they have refused to cede any further powers to the EU without a referendum—and at time of writing were calling for a cap to the Union's budget spending to reduce the UK's contributions in line with the austerity measures that ministers were introducing domestically.

Aside from Sweden and Denmark, the UK is the only EU state to have held out against joining the *euro*, while its refusal to sign the **Schengen Agreement** (see Table 9.1, below) is the reason why Britons are still expected to show their national passports when crossing internal EU borders—including returning to their home country—while citizens of fellow member states are not.

# ▶ Evolution of the EU

So how did today's EU come about? What happened to transform it from a loose confederation of states cooperating over trade in core post-war raw materials (principally steel and coal) into a sprawling supranational alliance exercising a degree of control—often contentiously—over everything from employment rights to economic migration?

Its growth and transformation can best be charted with reference to the succession of key treaties and summits that paved the way for it to become the hugely influential entity it is now. Providing a detailed explanation of every agreement signed during the six decades since the concept of a 'European Union' was first committed to paper would require a chapter in itself. Instead, the most significant developments in the evolution of the EU are outlined in Table 9.1.

**Table 9.1** Chronology of the evolution of the European Union (EU)

| Agreement | Year | Main provisions |
|---|---|---|
| The Treaty of Paris | 1951 | Established earliest forerunner of EU: the European Coal and Steel Community (ECSC). Membership initially limited to France, Germany, Italy, Luxembourg, Belgium, and the Netherlands. The Treaty initiated joint production of the two materials most central to the war effort (coal and steel) and a fledgling European assembly, which met for the first time in Strasbourg in September 1952. |
| The Treaties of Rome | 1957 | Often erroneously referred to in the singular, these twin treaties spawned two organizations ultimately to coalesce into the modern EU: the European Economic Community (EEC) and the European Atomic Energy Community (EURATOM). Their aim was to foster trading links between member nations by ending tariffs imposed by one nation on imports from another and removing other distortions in operation of the market, as well as:<br><br>1. introducing the *Common Agricultural Policy (CAP)*—a means of encouraging free trade in agricultural products within the EEC, while guaranteeing farmers' incomes in relation to competition from third-party countries through subsidies, as consolidated in 1962 by the formation of the European Agricultural Guidance and Guarantee Fund (EAGGF);<br>2. creating a 'common market' for the free movement of goods, services, and capital between member states (in practice, only free trade in goods followed until the Single European Act 1986). |
| Merger of the three European Unions | 1965 | In 1967 the ECSC, EURATOM, and EEC were merged into a single European Community (EC). This consolidated alliance was framed around four core institutions: the European Commission (the EC's 'Civil Service'); the European Assembly (later renamed European Parliament); the **European Court of Justice**; and the future Council of Ministers. |
| Launch of the European Monetary System (EMS) | 1979 | Designed to relax, if not abolish, exchange rates between member states, this eventually led to the launch of the euro (see pp. 278–80). |
| *Enlargement* | 1981 | Greece admitted into EC. |

| Agreement | Year | Main provisions |
|---|---|---|
| The Single European Act and further enlargement | 1986 | First full-scale revision of original 1957 European Treaties, encapsulating in one document the structure of the new-look EC and paving way for following extensions of community:<br>1. greater economic integration;<br>2. strengthened supranational institutions;<br>3. practical moves towards a single European currency and linked exchange rates in the form of economic and monetary union (EMU).<br>In the same year, Spain and Portugal entered the EC. |
| The Treaty on the European Union ('Maastricht Treaty') | 1992 | Formally renamed the EC the European Union (EU) adding new areas of responsibility. Although signed in February 1992, it had to be formally ratified by each member state and its passage was far from smooth in Britain (see pp. 266 and 279). It:<br>1. introduced a new EU-wide commitment to move towards full EMU in three stages—ultimate ends being either a single currency or a 'common' one (native currencies retained, but in parallel with an EU one);<br>2. established a single European Union from existing communities;<br>3. set up framework for potential common foreign and security policy;<br>4. increased cooperation on domestic issues, particularly criminal justice;<br>5. defined principle of '*subsidiarity*'—system defining EU institutions as 'subsidiary to' those of individual member states, and safeguarding their ability to run their own internal affairs without consulting EU unless they cannot achieve their objectives unilaterally;<br>6. introduced concept of 'EU citizenship'. |
| The Corfu Treaty | 1994 | Allowed Austria, Finland, and Sweden to join EU in January 1995, and paved way for Norway to be admitted (it subsequently declined to join). |
| The Amsterdam Treaty | 1997 | Arose out of 1996 inter-governmental conference convened by heads of EU states. It extended the rights of EU citizens in relation to:<br>1. consumer protection;<br>2. the fight against crime and drugs;<br>3. environmental protection.<br>The Treaty also introduced a Charter on Fundamental Workers' Rights.<br>The Summit had attempted to persuade member states to agree EU-wide immigration and asylum policy, but Britain, Ireland, and Denmark opted out of plans, leaving the rest to form the Schengen Group, which the UK declined to join at the 2000 Nice Summit. Its name referred to a deal—signed in two stages, in 1985 and 1990—which abolished border controls between participating nations. |

| Agreement | Year | Main provisions |
|---|---|---|
| The Helsinki Summit | 1999 | This removed existing system under which notional target dates had been set for the accession of specific countries to EU membership. From now on, any country meeting qualifying conditions would be eligible for swift entry. Entry talks quickly began with Slovakia, Malta, Lithuania, Bulgaria, Latvia, and Romania. Turkey also entered talks soon after, despite having previously been rejected in 1997. |
| Agenda 2000, *For a Stronger and Wider Europe* | 2000 | This European Commission discussion document set out a blueprint for onward development of the Community in twenty-first century. Many of its provisions were intended to prevent future disagreements between member states like those provoked by discussion of EMU, the proposed common defence policy, and CAP. It also signalled an attempt to set firm rules for acceptance of new countries. Among its stipulations were:<br><br>1. any country now wishing to join EU must meet economic and political criteria for membership and adopt the *acquis communitaire*—the laws and policies of EU—before being accepted (as Cyprus had just been admitted, the new regulations kicked in with accession negotiations for the ten additional states that entered in 2004);<br>2. to redefine the CAP and 'structural funds' used to ensure equitable socio-economic infrastructure across Europe;<br>3. to express then Commission's view on proposed accession to the EU of countries in central and eastern Europe;<br>4. to propose new budgetary framework for EU, with initial proposals for Community-wide budget 'not exceeding 1.27 per cent of EU's GNP'. |
| The Nice Treaty | 2000 | 'Proclaimed' EU Charter of Fundamental Rights (a conflation of principles outlined in the preceding European Convention on Human Rights, devised in 1950 by the **Council of Europe**—see pp. 306–7). The Charter's 53 'Articles' were not legally binding at the time, but expressed shared set of aims, including:<br><br>1. equality between men and women;<br>2. fair and just working conditions;<br>3. workers' rights to collective bargaining and industrial action;<br>4. public rights to access EU documents;<br>5. right of elderly to life of 'dignity'.<br><br>The Nice Summit also aired many concerns that have since coloured political discussion about the EU—including the implications of accepting 12 prospective additional members who have since joined.<br>Consensus emerged that the EU's main governing institutions would have to be changed over time for following reasons:<br><br>1. arrival of 12 potential new member countries would mean they needed votes at the negotiating table in the Council of Ministers, their own EU commissioners, seats in the European Parliament, and judges;<br>2. reunification of Germany, following fall of Berlin Wall in 1990;<br>3. impact of EU enlargement on asylum, immigration, and economic migration. |

| Agreement | Year | Main provisions |
|---|---|---|
| The Goteburg Summit | 2001 | Focused on the perceived conflict between EU membership and the Irish Constitution, particularly in relation to the province's neutrality. At around same time, Ireland narrowly voted 'no' in referendum on EU membership. Another controversy stemmed from realization of larger member states that enlargement might result in reductions in monetary benefits they received from EU. |
| *White Paper* on *EU Governance* | 2001 | Produced in response to mounting distrust of unelected EU policymaking institutions, this sought to pave the way for more democratically accountable EU by: <br><br> 1. involving individual states, especially smaller ones, more openly in decisions; <br> 2. introducing 'better policies and regulations'; <br> 3. moving towards a system of 'global governance'; <br> 4. 'refocusing' the EU's core institutions. <br><br> These ideas were underpinned by a clearer list of principles that the EU pledged to embody in future: <br><br> 1. openness—encouraging its institutions to work together more; <br> 2. participation—encouraging all members to take an active part in decision-making; <br> 3. accountability—giving clearer definitions of the roles of EU institutions; <br> 4. effectiveness—ensuring policies are appropriate to the current socio-economic climate, and are promptly implemented once decided upon; <br> 5. coherence—making sure that policies can be easily understood; <br> 6. proportionality; <br> 7. subsidiarity—ensuring 'action' by the EU in relation to member states is only taken when strictly necessary. |
| Enlargement of the Union | 2004 | Czech Republic, Estonia, Hungary, Latvia, Lithuania, Poland, Slovakia, Slovenia, Malta, and Greek Cyprus joined the EU. |
| Enlargement of the Union | 2007 | Romania and Bulgaria joined. |
| The European Union Reform Treaty ('Treaty of Lisbon') | 2007 | Almost as contentious as 'Maastricht', this followed hot on heels of the short-lived 'EU Constitution'—which was abandoned after being rejected in French and Dutch referenda. 'Lisbon Treaty' also rejected—by Ireland—but eventually came into force in December 2009. Its main provisions were to: <br><br> 1. make the Charter of Fundamental Rights legally binding; <br> 2. extend the role of the directly elected European Parliament; <br> 3. introduce a permanent *president of European Council* in place of current 'rotating presidency'; <br> 4. give the EU as a whole the legal status of a single entity capable of signing international treaties with other institutions or bodies. |

Of all of the treaties listed, the British government found it particularly difficult to ratify 'Maastricht' (see below), but it was not alone in encountering hurdles. In June 1992, the people of Denmark—who were given a direct say in a national referendum—rejected it. The Danish government finally squeaked it through 11 months later, after being forced to negotiate 'opt-outs' from two of its key provisions: economic and monetary union (EMU) and the move towards a common European defence policy.

# From 'three pillars' to one EU

One of the key sticking points of the Maastricht Treaty for individual member states was its underlying emphasis on fostering a 'supranational' approach to major policy areas over and above the EU's traditional drive towards Europe-wide free trade. Where several countries—notably Britain, Sweden, and Denmark—were keen to limit the EU's influence to the economic sphere (ideally preferring an 'intergovernmental' approach to even that based on bilateral negotiated agreements between independent member states), the likes of France and Germany were keen to roll out the Union's responsibilities to encompass everything from criminal justice and drugs policy to defence and security. In so doing, they also appeared willing to surrender varying degrees of national sovereignty—giving EU institutions the power to determine policies governing these areas with limited input from national parliaments.

The process of negotiating the Maastricht settlement led to the emergence of three broad areas of policy to be overseen subject to the principle of subsidiarity (see p. 283), by the European Parliament (EP), the European Commission (EC), the *Council of the European Union (Council of Ministers)*, and the European Court of Justice (ECJ). These areas known as the 'pillars' of the EU—corresponded with the three strands of its mission from that point on: the European Communities pillar (covering economic, social, and environmental policies); the Common Foreign and Security Policy (CFSP) pillar; and the Police and Judicial Cooperation in Criminal Matters (PJCC) pillar. With the advent of the Lisbon Treaty (see p. 284), the pillars were abolished—to be replaced by a single, consolidated structure for the EU.

# The main EU institutions

Journalistically, the best EU stories invariably arise out of conflict and confrontation. Notwithstanding ongoing wrangles over the Union's future direction and scope, many contentious issues emerge from the day-to-day deliberations of the EU's four principal governing institutions:

- the European Commission;
- the European Parliament (EP);
- the *Council of the European Union (Council of Ministers)*;
- the European Court of Justice (ECJ).

Each institution is chaired by its own president, whose method of election or appointment varies from one to the other. In addition, there is one further body that asserts a significant influence on the direction of EU policy (although, unlike the above, it wields no formal executive or legislative powers). This is the *European Council*—more commonly referred to as the 'European Summit', to avoid confusion with the Council of Ministers. Composed of the heads of state or government of all 27 member states of the EU, it meets up to four times a year, usually in the Justus Lipsius Building in Brussels, which is primarily the headquarters of the Council of Ministers.

Since the Lisbon Treaty finally came into force on 1 December 2009, the European Council has for the first time been chaired by a full-time 'permanent' president selected by members of the Council. The inaugural president, whose initial term is due to expire on 31 May 2012, is former Belgian Prime Minister  Herman Van Rompuy. Previously, chairmanship of the Council rotated between member states, with individual heads of government taking it in turns to hold it for periods of six months at a time, in tandem with their parallel presidency of the Council of Ministers (see pp. 272–5). While the European Council has no legislative power (unlike its near-namesake), a member state may complain to it formally about a decision taken in the Council of Ministers with which it disagrees under a procedure known as the 'emergency brake'. The Council may then choose to settle the matter by holding its own vote—giving it what some observers see as the ultimate veto over disputed EU policy.

## The European Commission

Formed in 1951 and based in Brussels, this is the Civil Service and executive (government) of the EU rolled into one. It employs 25,000 staff working at various levels across more than thirty 'departments and services' or 'Directorates-General'.

Each Directorate-General is headed by one of 27 commissioners—one from each member state, appointed for a five-year period. Meetings are chaired by one of their number, elected president by the European Parliament (on the recommendation of the European Council/Summit). The president chairs meetings of the Commission in the same way as a prime minister sitting in Cabinet. Although the Council of Ministers (composed of representatives from each member state's government) takes the final decisions on major political developments and structural changes within the EU (subject to 'emergency break' intervention by the European Council in exceptional cases), the Commission is the primary institution responsible for *initiating* policy. It does this in much the same way as national policy is originated through Cabinet government, with the commissioners sitting around a table devising and debating ideas for prospective legislation.

What makes this process more controversial in relation to the Commission than the workings of the British Cabinet is that none of the commissioners are elected: all are 'proposed' (nominated) by the governments of their native countries. The fact they are chosen by democratically elected politicians arguably gives them some degree of legitimacy, but they are not directly answerable to the European citizens whose lives their proposals affect. This perceived lack of accountability was famously described in a 1980s pamphlet as a 'democratic deficit' by the British Liberal Democrat MEP Bill Newton Dunn.

The Commission issues its policy proposals in three broad guises: *regulations*, *decisions*, and *directives*. Both 'regulations' and 'directives' must be scrutinized by the European Parliament and Council of Ministers before they can be enacted, but this is where the similarity between them ends. The former are EU-wide laws similar to British primary legislation that, once passed in Council, will automatically apply in all member states. The latter, in contrast, are broader 'end results' that must be achieved in each state, but it is left up to individual members to decide for themselves how to do this by, if necessary, introducing new or adapting existing national legislation. 'Decisions' are binding laws (akin to private Bills in the UK—see pp. 64–5) used to impose conditions or confer rights on an individual or authority in a particular state—for example, forcing a government department or *quango* to issue new guidelines to local authorities on kerbside recycling.

Not that policies devised by the Commission are automatically a done deal: elected *members of the European Parliament (MEPs)* have ample opportunity to scrutinize them and the authority to reject them, and ultimate say-so for new regulations rests with the Council of Ministers. Moreover, although it has far greater political clout than the British Civil Service—the job of which is merely to implement government policy 'on the ground' once Parliament has approved it (see pp. 267–9)—the Commission also fulfils this basic administrative function. The EP may also dismiss the Commission in exceptional circumstances (although, curiously, it is prevented from removing individual commissioners and must instead sack all of them). This scenario has arisen more than once in recent years. In March 1999 the Commission under then President Jacques Santer resigned en masse following the publication of a damning report into its alleged nepotism. Although it stopped short of suggesting that any commissioner was directly involved in corrupt practices, the 144-page report, by five independent 'wise persons', singled out former French Prime Minister

Edith Cresson for her 'dysfunctional' organization and favouritism in staff appointments.

Although not elected to their EU posts, most commissioners are experienced politicians and/or public figures who have previously served in senior positions in their home countries. Until the EU's membership expanded from 15 to 25 states in the 2004 enlargement, the countries with the biggest populations—Britain, Germany, France, and Italy—had two each, with smaller states having just one. Among those who served in this capacity were former Labour leader Neil Kinnock, who was Commissioner for Transport, and ex-Conservative Home Secretary Sir Leon Brittan, onetime Commissioner for External Trade Relations. Former Northern Ireland Secretary Lord Mandelson became Britain's first single Commissioner in 2004 (overseeing trade), but after being recalled to the British Cabinet in Gordon Brown's second reshuffle in October 2008 he was replaced by Baroness Ashton of Upholland. Following implementation of the Lisbon Treaty in December 2009, the Commission was dissolved and reconstituted, and Lady Ashton was elevated to the newly created role of **High Representative for Foreign Affairs and Security Policy** (and one of seven vice-presidential positions). Her swift promotion was interpreted by some in the media as a consolation prize for Britain in the wake of the EU's 'snub' to former Prime Minister Mr Blair's designs on the first 'EU presidency'. Having been formally approved by the EP, the new Commission took office in 2010.

Enduring controversy over the composition, powers, and privileges of the Commission has led to repeated attempts to reform it. For many years, its mammoth expenses bill was cited as one of the main causes of concern for EU taxpayers, and terms such as 'Brussels bureaucrats' and 'gravy train' were frequent bedfellows in the British tabloids. This issue was somewhat addressed in the 1999 report and subsequent reforms—some instigated by Lord Kinnock, who, in his role as Commission vice-president, tried to clean up its act by establishing an internal audit service and ethics committee. But concerns about the perceived power it wields—and the apparent dominance of certain countries in its decision-making—led to several further reforms being proposed in the 'Lisbon Treaty'. These were to have included a reduction in the number of commissioners, with only two-thirds of member states being represented at any one time from 2014, with seats distributed fairly on a rotating basis. However, Ireland's initial rejection of Lisbon in its 2008 referendum prompted the European Council to take the executive decision to retain the existing 'one member, one commissioner' system for the time being, by way of a peace offering to it and other smaller nations. The Council's ability to do this was itself formalized by Lisbon, which gives it the right to unilaterally alter the number of commissioners at any time, subject to unanimous approval by its members.

The composition of the current Commission is outlined in the table entitled 'The current composition of the European Commission', which can be found on the Online Resource Centre that accompanies this book.

## The European Parliament (EP)

Although the EP has the appearance of a legislature, until recently it had considerably less influence on EU lawmaking than either the Commission or Council of Ministers. Traditionally it has tended to be consulted on decisions, rather than taking them itself, in the manner of a giant House of Commons committee rather than a legislative assembly per se. For this reason, it was for many years caricatured as a supine talking shop. However, Maastricht gave it the ability to *reject* legislation it dislikes, according it 'joint' legislative status with the Council in certain areas under a process known as *co-decision*. Briefly, this works as follows: the Commission will pass a proposal for a new regulation or directive to the EP, which then expresses its opinion at a 'first reading'. If the Council approves of this opinion, the 'law' is passed, but if not it will deliver its own verdict to the EP, together with an explanation of its thinking. The EP then enters a '*second reading*' stage at which it can either approve the Council's changes (in which case the law is passed), amend them, or reject the law outright. All the while, the Commission will also be giving its opinion on suggested amendments, and if it rejects any of them, the Council must vote to approve the amended law unanimously, rather than by a majority. If, on the other hand, a stalemate exists between EP and Council and it lasts more than three months, the presidents of the two institutions may convene a *conciliation committee* made up of equal numbers of MEPs and Council members to broker a compromise.

→
see also
local
govern-
ment,
p. 371

This equal-weighted, if drawn-out, approach to lawmaking—renamed the 'ordinary legislative procedure' under Lisbon—used to exist in relation to only a few areas, such as health, culture, science, sport, and some aspects of asylum policy. But Lisbon extended it to most others, including agriculture, transport, and decisions over how to allocate European structural funds. The EP also has powers to legislate in relation to the smooth operation of the 'eurozone' (see pp. 280–1) and, crucially, to veto the EU budget. And (subject to agreement with the Council) it may also take action over other aspects of economic policy: in July 2010 the EP passed legislation capping bankers' bonuses. As of January 2011, cash bonuses were due to be subject to an initial cap of 30 per cent of the total (or 20 per cent for 'particularly large' bonuses), with between 40–60 per cent deferred. In a move designed to deter excessive risk-taking by bankers, the rules also stipulated that at least 50 per cent of the total bonus should be paid as 'contingent capital'—meaning it would be the first money to be called upon in the case of future debt or liquidity problems.

Despite its title, when originally christened in 1958 the EP's representatives were not elected at all, but appointed, one by each member country. Since 1979 the EP has been a fully elected institution. By the time of its first election, the number of representatives—today known as MEPs—had increased from 142 to 410.

The EP's current membership numbers 754, although it will fall back to 751 in 2014. Elections are held every five years and prior to 1999 were conducted on a 'first past the post' (FPTP) system analogous to that used in UK general elections (see p. 120). The European Parliament Act 1999 changed this by introducing *proportional representation (PR)*, generally based on the party list system. Parties are awarded a number of seats proportional to their share of the vote.

The UK is currently divided into 12 European electoral regions (including Northern Ireland, which uses its own version of PR). Each region returns between three and ten MEPs, depending on its population size. There are 72 British MEPs altogether: 59 elected in England, six in Scotland, four in Wales, and three in Northern Ireland.

Like the Commission, the EP has its own president (elected by absolute majority in a secret ballot of members for renewable terms of two-and-a-half years), and its principal base is in Brussels, where it sits for three weeks of every month. For the other week, its members travel to Strasbourg in neighbouring France, convening in an identical chamber.

As at the British Parliament, members of the EP sit in political groupings reflecting their ideological affiliations, rather than regional or national delegations. The minimum number of MEPs needed to form a group is:

- 29 if they all hail from a single member state;
- 23 if they come from two member states;
- 14 if they come from four or more member states.

There are currently seven political groupings in the EP, although at time of writing 27 MEPs remain 'non-attached' (independent). The groupings sit at designated points around the hemispherical parliamentary chamber, according to their notional position on the left–right political spectrum. Communist MEPs will sit to the far left of the central seat occupied by the EP president, while fascists and extreme right parties such as France's National Front will occupy the seats on the far right.

The current political groupings are:

- European People's Party (EPP) (265 members as at August 2010);
- Progressive Alliance of Socialists and Democrats (S&D) (184);
- Group of the Alliance of Liberals and Democrats for Europe (ALDE) (85);
- The Greens-European Free Alliance (Greens-EFA) (55);
- European Conservatives and Reformists (ECR) (54);
- European United Left-Nordic Green Left (EUL/NGL) (35);
- Europe of Freedom and Democracy (EFD) (31).

While Britain's Labour Party remains part of the socialist grouping (despite its recent drift to the centre-ground), after much internal debate the Conservatives finally made good on a long-standing promise to pull out of the centre-right EPP after the June 2009 European elections. Mr Cameron, who had made this pledge a central plank of his 2005 campaign for the party's leadership, announced the formation of the ECR—a Eurosceptic alliance including several parties the views of which have invited disdain in the liberal media. Of these, Poland's Law and Justice Party, which draws much of its support from ultra-conservative Catholics, has been accused of homophobia, while Latvia's Fatherland and Freedom Party counts among its members a number of former recruits to Hitler's Waffen SS. The Tories' decision to quit the EPP has been the subject of several barbs from centre-right European leaders such as French President Nicolas Sarkozy and German Chancellor Angela Merkel, and it looks set to remain a point of contention in coming months and years as the EU moves to consolidate reforms introduced by the Lisbon Treaty and to fortify the euro against the threat of sovereign debt crises (see p. 281)

Administration of the EP's functions is overseen by yet another layer of EU bureaucracy: a 'bureau' run by the president, 14 vice-presidents, and five 'quaestors' (civil servants responsible for accounting matters directly affecting the MEPs themselves). All of these officials are elected, like the president, for two-and-a-half years at a time.

## The Council of Ministers of the European Union

The *Council of Ministers of the European Union* is the single most powerful EU institution. Comprising departmental ministers from each of the 27 member states, its precise composition varies according to the issue being debated on a given day. If, for example, the Council is debating health policy, a health minister from each member state will attend, while discussions about crime, policing, and security issues will involve interior ministers (in Britain's case, the Home Secretary or another Home Office minister).

The Council has ten 'configurations', reflecting the broad policy areas under its jurisdiction:

- General Affairs;
- Foreign Affairs;
- Economic and Financial Affairs;
- Justice and Home Affairs;
- Employment, Social Policy, Health, and Consumer Affairs;
- Competitiveness;
- Transport, Telecommunications, and Energy;
- Agriculture and Fisheries;
- Environment;
- Education, Youth, and Culture.

Although policy ideas are often proactively proposed by the Commission, all but the most minor must be formally approved by the Council to make them 'law'. To this end, it is supported by a related institution, the Committee of Permanent Representatives (COREPER), made up of civil servants seconded from each member state or each state's EU ambassador (itself backed by a further 150 committees and working groups).

All meetings of the Council are chaired by a senior politician (normally the president or prime minister) from the country currently holding the rotating EU presidency. The UK last held the presidency in 2005. In view of the need for continuity emphasized by this rota, the Council has its own dedicated civil service in the shape of the General Secretariat of the Council.

## Qualified majority voting (QMV)

The voting system used in the Council is complex and, as such, warrants its own section, given its importance in determining the direction of EU policy.

The unanimous approval of member states is normally required to pass major decisions with implications for the future of the EU—such as whether to admit additional countries into the Union. The annual confirmation of the EU's budget also traditionally requires unanimity. Since Maastricht, however, an increasing number of (often significant) decisions have been agreed through a process known as **qualified majority voting (QMV)**. As its name suggests, the premise of QMV is for agreement on a policy to be reached without the need for every member state to approve it—that is, on a majority basis. This majority system is 'qualified', however, in two respects:

- member states are not accorded an equal say in the Council—rather, the number of votes allocated to each state is weighted to reflect the size of its population, giving some countries greater clout than others;

- a simple majority system (like that which determines whether Acts are passed in the UK Parliament) would require only one more 'yes' vote than the total number of 'no' votes—but under the Nice system (still in force at time of writing) approval by QMV requires the backing of 74 per cent of weighted votes in the Council, representing 62 per cent of the EU's population and either 50 per cent (if voting on a proposal put forward by the Commission) or 67 per cent of member states.

Of these bigger countries, France, Britain, Germany, and Italy presently have the most votes, with 29 apiece. The smallest populated country, Malta, has just three. The overall breakdown of vote allocations under QMV is spelt out in Table 9.2.

Perhaps unsurprisingly, QMV has its critics. Some smaller EU member states argue that at times they have policies imposed on them—regardless of their views—by more heavily populated ones. Euro-sceptics, meanwhile,

**Table 9.2** Allocation of voting power under qualified majority voting (QMV)

| Country | Population | Number of votes |
| --- | --- | --- |
| Germany | 82m | 29 |
| France | 63m | 29 |
| UK | 60m | 29 |
| Italy | 59m | 29 |
| Spain | 44m | 27 |
| Poland | 38m | 27 |
| Romania | 22m | 14 |
| Netherlands | 16m | 13 |
| Greece | 11m | 12 |
| Portugal | 11m | 12 |
| Belgium | 11m | 12 |
| Czech Republic | 10m | 12 |
| Hungary | 10m | 12 |
| Sweden | 9.0m | 10 |
| Austria | 8.3m | 10 |
| Bulgaria | 7.7m | 10 |
| Denmark | 5.4m | 7 |
| Slovakia | 5.4m | 7 |
| Finland | 5.3m | 7 |
| Ireland | 4.2m | 7 |
| Lithuania | 3.4m | 7 |
| Latvia | 2.3m | 4 |
| Slovenia | 2.0m | 4 |
| Estonia | 1.3m | 4 |
| Cyprus | 0.77m | 4 |
| Luxembourg | 0.46m | 4 |
| Malta | 0.40m | 3 |
| EU | 493m | 345 |

see the absence of a 'one member, one vote' system in the Council as evidence that individual countries are increasingly being subsumed within an embryonic 'European super-state', rather than treated as a confederation of independent—and equal—countries.

Given the inequitable allocation of votes between member states, the fact that some decisions need only obtain a simple majority to be passed can prove especially controversial. In the past, it has been possible for a handful of the most populated countries to muster sufficient votes to approve a policy by rallying support from a bare 50 per cent of the member states.

It is for these reasons—as well as the need to give fair representation to newer members—that the 'Lisbon Treaty' will usher in significant moderations to the existing voting system from 1 November 2014, balancing out the population weightings that favour larger states with a new 'one country, one vote' element designed to placate smaller countries. Future votes by QMV will be determined as follows:

- *either* at least 55 per cent of member states (if vote is on a Commission proposal) *or* 72 per cent of all member states will need to back a proposal for it to become EU law—these state percentages must represent at least 65 per cent of the EU population;
- a minimum of four countries will be needed to block any decision (preventing two or three larger states 'ganging up' to do so), and at least 15 backers to bring it into force.

An alternative reform proposed by Poland, known as the 'Penrose Method' (or 'square-root system'), would have dropped the requirement for there to be a majority of states in favour of a proposal entirely, replacing it with the need for a 61.4 per cent share of all of the votes cast (however that total was achieved).

## The European Court of Justice (ECJ)

Established in 1952, the European Court of Justice (ECJ)—officially the 'Court of Justice of the European Communities'—is the EU's supreme legal institution. Unlike other bodies it is based in Luxembourg City, but like them it has its own president (appointed by their fellow judges on a renewable three-year term).

Again like the other key EU institutions, the Court comprises 27 members—that is, one judge per member state. For practical reasons, however, a maximum of 13 judges will usually hear a case at any one time, sitting as a so-called 'Grand Chamber'. The judges are assisted by eight 'advocates-general'—lawyers tasked with presenting to the judges impartial 'opinions' on cases assigned to them. Judgments are made in a collegiate way and must be unanimous.

Judges are nominated by the member states from which they hail on renewable six-year terms. Five of the advocates general are nominated by the biggest EU member states—Britain, France, Germany, Italy, and Spain—with the other three rotating in alphabetical order between the remaining 22. During negotiations over Lisbon, Poland repeatedly argued that, because its population is only marginally smaller than Spain's (and its representation under QMV the same), it should have an automatic right to nominate an advocate-general, too. This has yet to materialize.

The Court may be required to pass judgment in a variety of circumstances—for example, if there is evidence a member state has not implemented a treaty or directive, or a complainant alleges that a governmental institution, non-government organization (NGO), or commercial business has in some other way broken EU law.

Areas of EU law covered include:

- free trade and the movement of goods and services in the EU single market;
- employment law and the European Social Chapter (see p. 283);
- competition law (cartels, monopolies, mergers and acquisitions);
- public sector regulation.

In practice, it is unusual for a case involving an individual or small group of individuals to go before the ECJ itself. And even when a case *is* heard by the Court, this will often be by three or five judges, rather than 13. Only in exceptional cases (such as when an EU commissioner is alleged to have seriously failed to fulfil his or her obligations) will it ever sit as a 'full court', and even then only a quorum of 15 judges—rather than the full complement of 27—are needed.

In lesser cases, hearings will be convened by a junior body established in 1988 to deal with the growing number of routine complaints being generated as the EU extended its influence: the General Court (until Lisbon, the 'Court of First Instance'). Like its more illustrious counterpart, this Court also boasts 27 judges, one from each member state, and a president appointed by them for renewable three-year terms. Unlike the ECJ, however, it has no advocates-general, so a judge from among its own number is sometimes nominated to fulfil this role. A 'judge-rapporteur' will also be appointed to oversee proceedings and to draft a provisional judgment—to be deliberated on by the judges—after hearing representations from complainant and respondent.

The General Court's responsibilities encompass the following policy areas:

- agriculture;
- state aid;
- competition;
- commercial policy;
- regional policy;
- social policy;
- institutional law;
- trade mark law;
- transport.

It has the authority to impose a variety of penalties, as outlined in the table entitled 'Forms of ruling that can be made by the European Court of Justice (ECJ)',  which can be found on the Online Resource Centre.

Judgments by the General Court are subject to a right to appeal to the ECJ. In addition to the General Court, meanwhile, two further courts exist to deal with more specific cases: the Civil Service Tribunal, which handles complaints about maladministration by EU employees, and the Court of Auditors (responsible for overseeing its accounts).

For individual member states, the extent to which European law can be said to take precedence over national legislatures, judiciaries, and (where relevant) constitutions is a subject of intense interest and ongoing debate. In recent years, however, a series of landmark Court judgments have pointed towards a growing sense that the EU holds supreme. In 1999 Mr Blair's government faced a compensation bill of up to £100m after the ECJ ruled that Margaret Thatcher had broken European law by passing a 1988 Act of Parliament intended to ban Spanish trawler-men from using British-registered boats to fish in UK waters—a practice known as 'quota-hopping'. The final judgment in this case, known as *Factortame* (after the name of one of the 100-plus Spanish fishing companies that brought the original action), only came after a decade of legal ping-pong between London and Luxembourg.

Several 'test case' rulings have focused on the scope of EU employment law—and in particular the extent to which private sector companies and other non-government organizations can be bound by it. In the case of *M. H. Marshall v. Southampton and South-West Hampshire Area Health Authority* (1986), a Ms Marshall sued her employer after being dismissed from her job on reaching the then state retirement for women (60). She argued this contravened EC Directive 76/207 (focusing on non-discrimination), because men were not expected to retire until the age of 65 and the Directive created rights that could be enforced 'horizontally' between individuals. The ECJ ruled against this interpretation—stipulating that directives generally only applied 'vertically' (that is, through the aegis of the specific individuals or organizations at whom they were directed). However, there was a silver lining for Ms Marshall: as the health authority employing her was 'an organ of the state' (meaning it was bound by the Directive on a vertical basis), she still won her case. Some ECJ judgments have proved so momentous that new legal concepts have been named after them: in a 1991 case, a group of Italian workers who lost their jobs when their employer became insolvent successfully sued the country's government for failing to implement EC Directive 80/987, which would have guaranteed them compensation. The ECJ's ruling in favour of the workers established the principle that member states are liable for compliance with EU law by all bodies based on their soil, including private companies. This has been christened the '*Frankovich* Principle' (after the surname of one of the victors).

But not all ECJ judgments have gone the way of claimants, and some outcomes suggest a rather less clear-cut balance of power between UK courts and the EU. In *Van Duyn v. the Home Office* (1974), the ECJ found in favour of Britain after a Dutch national, Yvonne Van Duyn, sued under the Treaty of Rome for being denied entry to the country because she was a practising Scientologist. The Court ruled that member states could bar individuals on the basis of their 'personal conduct' if this conflicted with their national 'public policy' objectives, and the UK's public policy was to prevent the spread of Scientology. More significantly, in 1993 the German judicial system successfully asserted its supremacy over the EU in internal constitutional matters. In a case known as *Brunner v. the European Union Treaty*, the German Constitutional Court ruled that it was for it alone to determine whether European laws, and the powers conferred on individual Union institutions, were compatible with Germany's constitution. And, in a warning similar to Mr Cameron's recent refusal to cede any further powers to the EU without consulting the British public first, it ruled that the country would not be bound by any interpretation of the Treaty that extended the Union's overall remit (or 'kompetenz'), or any laws subsequently adopted by the EU that increased its existing powers—unless German law decided that such laws should apply.

# ▌ Evolution of the euro

The concept of moving towards some form of single European currency has been quietly fermenting for decades. But what started out as the seed of an idea in the minds of European commissioners in the late 1960s took some thirty years to reach fruition. The following section focuses on the more decisive stages in the development of the euro project.

## The exchange rate mechanism (ERM) debacle and 'Black Wednesday'

In an effort to control *inflation*, encourage trade, and stabilize exchange rates between individual EU member states' currencies—in doing so kickstarting the process of introducing a single European currency—in 1979 the EU introduced the exchange rate mechanism (ERM). The ERM was based on the idea of fixing narrower margins between which member states' currencies would  be permitted to fluctuate in value in relation to those of other members— effectively 'pegging' one country's exchange rate to another's. Prior to its introduction, bilateral exchange rates between EU states were based on the European currency unit (ecu)—a 'virtual' European currency traded in stock markets—the value of which was equivalent to a weighted average of those of the individual EU members' currencies. As a condition of EU membership, states were required to contain fluctuations in the value of their currencies within a 2.25 per cent margin either side of their bilateral exchange rates (excepting Italy, which was allowed a variance of up to 6 per cent).

The Maastricht Treaty envisaged the European monetary system (EMS) moving towards full monetary union in three stages, as set out in the table entitled 'The three stages of Economic and Monetary Union (EMU)', which can be found on the Online Resource Centre.

Britain was characteristically slow to sign up. It finally did so in 1990, when John Major was Chancellor, but pulled out dramatically on 16 September 1992 after a panic-stricken day of stock market speculation and *interest rate* hikes by his successor, Norman Lamont.

'Black Wednesday'—as this day came to be known—arose out of the unsustainable position in which the British currency (the pound sterling) had found itself during the months after the country signed up to the ERM. Throughout much of the 1980s Margaret Thatcher's Chancellor Nigel Lawson had 'shadowed' the German Deutschmark when deciding whether to raise or lower *interest rates* to maintain sterling's value. By September 2002 this had had the effect of valuing sterling unsustainably high compared to the US dollar. Because many British exports were valued in dollars—not sterling—the UK was potentially losing significant income from overseas markets by allowing the gap between the dollar and pound to widen. But with Britain pegged to the ECU in the ERM, there was limited room for the Chancellor to devalue sterling in the way he otherwise might have done to remedy this.

The approaching crisis reached its tipping point when US speculators, including billionaire George Soros, began frenziedly borrowing pounds and selling them for Deutschmarks in mid-September, in the belief that sterling was about to be devalued and they could therefore profit by repaying their loans at deflated prices. This prompted Mr Lamont to raise interest rates from 10 to 12 per cent on 16 September (with the promise of a further increase, to 15 per cent, later the same day), in an effort to stop sterling's value falling too far by tempting speculators to buy pounds. But, apparently disbelieving him, speculators continued selling pounds, in anticipation of a slump in its value.

With sterling's value plummeting as a result, at 7 p.m. Mr Lamont pulled Britain out of the ERM—freezing interest rates for the time being at 12 per cent, rather than raising them to the promised 15 per cent. During the course of one day, he had spent £27bn of Britain's gold reserves propping up the pound. By the time the Conservatives lost to Labour five years later, official Treasury estimates calculated that the ultimate cost to the taxpayer of 'Black Wednesday' was £3.4bn. The Tories' previous reputation for economic competence was dealt a body blow by the events of that day from which it took years to recover.

# Launch of the euro and growth of the eurozone

The euro has existed in a 'non-physical' form—that is, in the guise of travellers' cheques, electronic transfers, etc.—since 1 January 1999, but it officially came into being on 1 January 2002, when the **European Central Bank (ECB)** in Frankfurt began issuing notes and coins in the 12 EU member states that had signed up to join. At the time there were only 15 EU states, and membership of the euro has since been extended to include two of the additional 12 countries admitted through enlargement: Malta and Slovenia. Of the 'original' 15 EU members, Britain, Sweden, and Denmark are the only three so far to have resisted joining. Both the Swedish and Danish populations have rejected the single currency in national referenda (the latter twice), and the former has since circumvented any pressure from 'eurozone' states to make a fresh attempt to join them by failing to adhere to the 'convergence criteria' that countries are expected to meet before being accepted into the euro.

The main convergence criteria, designed to promote price stability across the participating states, require applicants to achieve the following:

- an inflation rate no more than 1.5 per cent higher than that of the three lowest-inflation member states of the EU;
- a ratio of no more than 3 per cent between their annual government deficit and *gross domestic product (GDP)* at the end of the preceding tax year;
- a ratio of gross government debt to GDP no greater than 60 per cent at the end of the preceding tax year (it is sometimes acceptable to approach this target);
- membership of the successor to the original ERM—ERM II—for at least two consecutive years without at any point simultaneously devaluing their currencies;
- a nominal long-term interest rate no more than 2 per cent higher than that of the three lowest-inflation EU member states.

At time of writing, the 16 countries in the eurozone were (in alphabetical order): Austria, Belgium, Cyprus, Finland, France, Germany, Greece, Ireland, Italy, Luxembourg, Malta, the Netherlands, Portugal, Slovakia, Slovenia, and Spain. In addition, Denmark has recently made tentative steps towards joining the euro by becoming a member of ERM II in preparation and there is talk of a further referendum.

For its part, Britain remains a refusenik. Mr Major's government negotiated an 'opt-out protocol' before belatedly signing the Maastricht Treaty, removing any obligation on its part to move from stage two to stage three of EMU. On entering office, Mr Blair (widely seen as a Europhile, compared to the more cautious Mr Brown) promised to hold a referendum before committing the UK to the single currency. He repeated this pledge at various points during his ten years in power and is thought always to have been broadly supportive of the idea of one day joining. But in 1997 Mr Brown announced that, before surrendering the strength of sterling to the untested vagaries of the euro, he would need to be convinced Britain had met 'five economic tests'. These 'tests'—actually questions to determine whether the UK economy would benefit from entry—are outlined in the table entitled 'Gordon Brown's "five economic tests" for Britain's entry into the euro', to be found on the Online Resource Centre  accompanying this book.

Critics argued that these questions—which effectively kept Britain out of the euro for the duration of the New Labour government—were at best susceptible to obfuscation and at worst unanswerable. In reality, many claimed, they were introduced to enable Mr Brown to place continual delays in the way of a referendum—arguing at any point in time that one or more had yet to be satisfactorily answered.

## Doubts over the euro's future

Because several EU member states have yet to join the single currency, the Union is often described as a 'two-speed' Europe. Some observers argue that a time will come when Britain and all other member states outside the euro will be forced to join it, if only to retain their influence at the negotiating table over other issues affecting the Union. Former French President Jacques Chirac and German Chancellor Gerhard Schroeder each made several speeches when in office emphasizing the need for Britain to commit more fully to the EU by entering the euro.

However, recent events in the 'eurozone' have encouraged long-time euro doubters, not least Mr Cameron's Conservatives, to dig in their heels about any future prospect of Britain joining. In May 2010, the euro was plunged into the biggest crisis in its history after first Greece, then a succession of other European Union member states using the single currency, became the subject of intense concern over the extent of their 'sovereign debt': that is, the individual budget deficits they had built up in the wake of the global financial meltdown.

Trouble began in Greece, where a package of austerity measures unveiled by the government provoked a wave of wildcat public sector strikes and violent demonstrations. Financial analysts Standard & Poor's swiftly reduced the status of the country's government bonds to 'junk' (the UK's, by contrast, were still at 'AAA'—the highest possible level—in spite of its own deficit). In an effort to contain Greece's downturn—preventing it from having a knock-on effect to the euro and, by extension, the economies of other EU states—on 2 May the 'eurozone' countries teamed up with the International Monetary Fund (IMF) to offer the country an unprecedented €110bn (£93bn) loan bailout, on condition it imposed harsh domestic spending cuts. Within a week, though, a further massive cash injection was required to stabilize the euro as a whole. This saw Europe's finance ministers collectively approve a loans package worth £624bn aimed at ensuring financial stability across Europe by shoring up the 16 states by that point struggling to service their debts. In one of his last actions as Labour Chancellor, Alistair Darling signed off the deal—committing the UK to providing between £9.6bn and £13bn to support a new £95bn 'stabilization mechanism' designed to stop individual countries' economies collapsing.

In the ensuing weeks, governments in a succession of other eurozone states, including Spain, Portugal, and Italy, began implementing similarly tough austerity measures. But as international money markets indicated a new wariness towards the previously unassailable euro, the crisis came closer to home, as Ireland was forced to accept a joint £85bn (£71bn) bailout by the IMF and the eurozone countries.

# ▌ Towards an EU 'super-state'?

Of all of the issues to divide the main British political parties in recent years, none has been more damaging than what many see as the gradual shift from an EU based on mutual cooperation between sovereign nations towards a 'federal' union more akin to that of the USA. By the late 1980s, the perception that many mainland European countries (in particular France and Germany) wanted to create a 'European super-state' provoked staunch resistance from Mrs Thatcher and her more Euro-sceptic ministers to almost any prospect of further UK involvement. Perhaps most symbolically, during a Commons debate on the charismatic European Commission President Jacques Delores' plans to accelerate further EU integration, she declared 'no, no, no' to his vision.

Although as Leader of the Opposition Mrs Thatcher had supported the 'yes' campaign for Britain to remain in the then EEC, a decade into her premiership she saw things quite differently. By then, the pace of integration had stepped up a gear, and the likes of Mr Delores and German Chancellor Helmut Kohl were championing ever-closer ties between member states, with the contents of the Maastricht Treaty a particular bone of contention. High-profile resignations by pro-European Cabinet colleagues, such as Chancellor Nigel Lawson and Foreign Secretary Sir Geoffrey Howe, did little to dent her resolve. It was the Tories' growing internal rift over Europe as much as the Poll Tax riots that led to her being challenged for the party's leadership in 1989 by a 'stalking

horse' candidate, the obscure backbencher Sir Anthony Meyer, and her ultimate downfall in her ill-fated defence against the 1990 challenge by Michael
Heseltine (see p. 95).

Despite producing a more mild-mannered replacement, the ensuing leadership election failed to heal the party's wounds. Mr Major did much to placate
his Euro-sceptic colleagues in his first months in Downing Street. In particular,
he negotiated British opt-outs to various clauses in the Maastricht Treaty—
notably the Social Chapter (the section, later signed by Mr Blair's government, which enshrined new rights for EU workers, including the Working Time
Directive barring employers from forcing staff to work more than 48 hours a
week, and recognition of their right to trades union membership and collective
bargaining).

But such fillips to the right could only delay an inevitable confrontation over
Maastricht (which effectively *had* to be signed if Britain were to remain in the
EU). By May 1992, having secured a narrow fourth successive Tory victory in
an election earlier that month with a majority of just 18 MPs, Mr Major found
himself held to ransom by a hardcore of Euro-sceptic backbenchers, known
collectively as the 'Maastricht rebels' (see pp. 50–1). Only by temporarily with-
drawing the *whip* from these MPs, building a fractious alliance with the Ulster
Unionists and Democratic Unionists, and threatening his party with a further
election, which it would almost certainly have lost, did Mr Major manage to
force through the European Communities (Amendment) Bill on a wafer-thin
majority. Among those actively rebelling from the backbenches were bullish former Employment Secretary Lord Tebbit and a certain Mrs Thatcher.
In addition to the usual suspects, such as stalwart right-wingers Bill Cash and
Teddy Taylor, the rebels included no fewer than three future ministers in Mr
Cameron's government: David Willetts, Dr Liam Fox, and Iain Duncan Smith.

As the Tories' Euro-sceptic resolve has hardened, old divisions have also
resurfaced in the Labour Party. The publication in 2004 of a draft 'EU Constitution'—or Constitutional Treaty—ostensibly did little more than draw together
in a single (if mammoth) document various earlier agreements, such as the
1986 Act and Maastricht. But those already wary of earlier shifts towards a
more centralized EU power structure saw in it a clear attempt to consolidate
the Union, leading to greater *federalism*—a reduction in status of the sovereign
governments of member states akin to the limited *devolution* accorded to individual states in the USA.

Ironically, the Treaty emphasized the concept of subsidiarity—the antithesis
of federalism, which defines member states as being paramount and the EU as
only a 'last port of call' should individual countries' self-determination falter. It
also, for the first time, set out the practical steps to be taken by states wishing
to withdraw from the EU altogether. Nonetheless, under mounting pressure
from the Tories and his own backbenchers, Mr Blair promised a referendum on
the constitution if he were to win a third term in the 2005 election.

It was his handling of the issue from his 2005 victory onwards—not to mention that of his successor, Mr Brown—that was to cause the greatest disquiet among not only Tory but also Labour MPs. Having taken cover from the collapse of the constitution proposals following their rejection by both France and the Netherlands in national referenda, both Mr Blair and Mr Brown refused to follow through on their earlier pledge with the advent of the Lisbon Treaty. This was despite the fact that, even according to many of its supporters, in content if not name it was substantially the same document.

After months of pressure from his own backbenchers and a Commons debate lasting 12 days, Mr Brown formally settled the issue in February 2008 with a slim victory in support of ratifying Lisbon on a three-line whip (to the fury of Euro-sceptic papers like the *Daily Mail*, the front-page headline of which

described the outcome as *'The Day They Betrayed British Democracy'*). Some 29 Labour MPs defied the party whip by backing a referendum and it was only Mr Clegg's decision to whip Lib Dem MPs into abstaining (rather than opposing the government) that carried the day for the prime minister. In doing so, Mr Clegg angered some in his own ranks: three frontbenchers resigned and 15 voted for a referendum, despite his using a three-line whip to discipline them. Oddly, the Lib Dems had spent much of the previous week in Parliament demanding a referendum on Europe—but on Britain's ongoing membership of the EU, rather than the constitutional issue in particular.

While Lisbon ultimately had a smoother passage than the abortive constitution, Britain was not the only country to have trouble ratifying it. On 13 June 2008, the only EU nation granted a referendum on it, the Irish, rejected it by 53.4 to 46.6 per cent (paving the way for a failed last-ditch attempt by Tory peers to delay its passage through the Lords). Facing the threat of isolation or,

worse, expulsion from the EU, Ireland finally approved Lisbon in October 2009. But it was not until December that year—18 months after the country's first referendum and two years after it had been signed in principle by EU leaders— that the Treaty finally came into force.

Today substantial questions (and divisions) remain as to the future direction of travel of the EU, and Britain's continuing place in it. With a Euro-sceptic Tory-led government returned to power in May 2010, the next few years may well prove decisive one way or the other.

# ▌ Other issues facing the EU

Although the twin issues of the euro and further EU integration undoubtedly remain the biggest sticking points for both Euro-sceptics and Europhiles, several other thorny issues continue to surround Britain's membership of the EU. Some of the more potentially explosive issues are explained in Table 9.3.

**Table 9.3** Major issues facing Britain's membership of the EU

| Issue | Explanation |
|-------|-------------|
| Common Agricultural Policy (CAP) and the British rebate | For more than fifty years, the CAP has taken a bigger annual chunk out of the EU's budget than any other area—equivalent to 44 per cent of spending each year. Mrs Thatcher negotiated a generous annual rebate for Britain from the CAP and other EU subsidies in the late 1980s, in recognition of the fact that Britain received less from them than other states, like France, that rely more on agriculture. But in December 2005, Mr Blair reluctantly accepted a £1bn a year cut in Britain's £3.6bn rebate following a row with then French President Mr Chirac that had threatened to paralyse negotiations over the EU's budget. His opponents argued that increased subsidies from richer western European countries were needed to assist then new member states—particularly former Soviet countries. |
| Common Fisheries Policy (CFP) | This long-standing policy is designed to protect fish and seafood stocks in European seas by using a 'quota' system for fishing rights, supposedly fairly allocated among relevant member states. In the mid-1990s, there were frequent confrontations between Britain and Spain over accusations of 'quota-hopping'—the alleged practice by Spanish trawlers fishing in British waters of registering boats under a third county's flag of convenience to enable them to exceed their country's quota. Many UK trawler-men were forced to scrap their boats and change jobs because of the strict quotas introduced in the waters they fished. |
| Common defence policy | The concept of greater cooperation over defence was formally introduced in the Maastricht Treaty. In Britain, Euro-sceptics saw this as another step too far in terms of loss of sovereignty, but then Defence Secretary Michael Portillo (a Euro-sceptic) vowed in a patriotic speech at the Conservative Party Conference that Britain would never surrender the right to maintain its independent Armed Forces. His headline-grabbing tirade ended with him quoting the SAS motto: 'Who dares, wins.' It remains unclear to what extent the EU will ever try to develop its own 'European army', but talk of an EU 'Rapid Reaction Force' designed to intervene swiftly in the event of a member state being threatened or invaded remains on the table (see p. 306). |
| Economic migration | Expansion of the EU to encompass former Eastern Bloc countries has seen an increase in economic migration from poorer to richer countries, fostered by the free movement of labour (as well as goods, services, and capital) enshrined in various treaties. This has put a strain on community relations and public services in some areas—creating tensions between migrants and indigenous peoples. In 2007 Britain became the first member state to introduce new restrictions on migrant workers from the two newest EU entrants, Bulgaria and Romania. |

## ☰ Topical feature idea

The press release in Figure 9.1 was issued on 29 April 2009, at the start of a lengthy process of consultation over proposals for a new EU-wide regulatory framework to police the actions of managers of 'alternative investment funds', who had been held partly to blame for the systemic instability in the financial sector exposed by the 2008 banking crisis. These include managers of *hedge funds*—operators of varied portfolios of speculative financial investments, principally *derivatives* ('virtual', rather than actual, purchases of assets that take the form of contracts between traders based on anticipated future movements in the value of those assets). At time of writing the European Parliament was expected to adopt the draft directive shortly, but it remains current because even with the Council of Ministers' approval the policy will need to be formally passed by the parliaments of individual member states. If you were working on the business section of a national or major regional newspaper, how would you follow up this press release to make it most relevant to your readers?

**Figure 9.1** Press release issued on 29 April 2009

# Financial services: Commission proposes EU framework for managers of alternative investment funds

The European Commission has proposed a Directive on Alternative Investment Fund Managers (AIFM). The proposed Directive is an *'important part of the European Commission's response to the financial crisis, as set out in the Communication on Driving European Recovery. It aims to create a comprehensive and effective regulatory and supervisory framework for AIFM in the European Union. AIFM, which include the managers of hedge funds and private equity funds, managed around €2 trillion in assets at the end of 2008. This is the first attempt in any jurisdiction to create a comprehensive framework for the direct regulation and supervision in the alternative fund industry. The proposal now passes to the European Parliament and Council for consideration.*

Internal Market and Services Commissioner Charlie McCreevy said:

'Alternative investment fund managers have become important participants in the European financial system and their activities have had a significant impact on the markets and companies in which they invest. There is now a global consensus—as expressed by the G20 leaders —over the need for closer regulatory engagement with this sector. In particular, it is essential that regulators have the information and tools necessary to conduct effective macro-prudential oversight. The crisis has also underscored the importance of robust risk and liquidity management systems and the need for reliable investor information as the basis for effective due diligence. I look forward to working with the European Parliament and Council to secure the adoption of this important piece of legislation.'

The proposed Directive will require all AIFM within scope to be authorised and to be subject to harmonised regulatory standards on an ongoing basis. It will also enhance the transparency of the activities of AIFM and the funds they manage towards investors and public authorities. This will enable Member States to improve the macro-prudential oversight of the sector and to take coordinated action as necessary to ensure the proper functioning of financial markets. The proposal will help to overcome gaps and inconsistencies in existing regulatory frameworks at national level and will provide a secure basis for the development of the internal market.

The proposed AIFM Directive will:

- Adopt an 'all encompassing' approach so as to ensure that no significant AIFM escapes effective regulation and oversight, while recognising the legitimate differences in existing business models and providing exemptions for smaller managers for whom the requirements would be disproportionate. Therefore, the Directive will only apply to those AIFM managing a portfolio of more than 100 million euros. A higher threshold of 500 million applies to AIFM not using leverage (and having a five year lock-in period for their investors) as they are not regarded as posing systemic risks. A threshold of €100 million implies that roughly 30% of hedge fund managers, managing almost 90% of assets of EU domiciled hedge funds, would be covered by the Directive.

- Regulate all major sources of risks in the alternative investment value chain by ensuring that AIFM are authorised and subject to ongoing regulation and that key service providers, including depositaries and administrators, are subject to robust regulatory standards.

- Enhance the transparency of AIFM and the funds they manage towards supervisors, investors and other key stakeholders.

- Ensure that all regulated entities are subject to appropriate governance standards and have robust systems in place for the management of risks, liquidity and conflicts of interest.

- Permit AIFM to market funds to professional investors throughout the EU subject to compliance with demanding regulatory standards.

- Grant access to the European market to third country funds after a transitional period of three years. This should allow the EU to check whether the necessary guarantees are in place in the countries where the funds are domiciled (equivalence of regulatory and supervisory standards, exchange of information on tax matters).

**More information is available at:**

http://ec.europa.eu/internal_market/investment/alternative_investments_en.htm

© European Union, 1995–2010

## ✳ Current issues

- **The sovereign debt crisis in the 'eurozone':** in spring 2010, several EU member states were forced to introduce swingeing austerity measures because of rising concern on the international money markets about their ability to service their national debts. Greece was loaned €110bn by the International Monetary Fund, and had its credit rating downgraded by Standard & Poor's to 'junk bond' status, as its government announced massive public spending cutbacks in the face of angry street protests and death threats. Spain, Portugal, and several other countries in the eurozone followed suit. EU finance ministers (including Britain's then Chancellor, Alistair Darling) agreed a comprehensive rescue package worth nearly $1tn—prompting some British commentators and Eurosceptics to respond with relief to the fact the UK remains outside the euro.

- **Turkey's accession to the EU:** negotiations over Turkey's accession to the EU began seriously in 2004, but the country's questionable human rights record and historical tensions with other member states, including Germany, have so far conspired to slow progress. In June 2010 US Defence Secretary Robert Gates criticized the EU for pushing the majority Muslim country towards eastern countries politically by snubbing its advances, after it voted against a **United Nations (UN)** Security Council resolution proposing new sanctions against Iran over its suspected nuclear weapons programme.

- **Britain's defence of its EU 'opt-outs':** following the Conservatives' decision to leave the centre-right European People's Party grouping in the European Parliament and form a new alliance, the party has remained solidly Euro-sceptic in government. While the need to join the Lib Dems in coalition has deterred the party from pursuing its pre-election pledge to repatriate control over social and employment law (including the Working Time Directive), the Tories have vowed not to cede any further powers to the EU without a referendum, and are resisting pressure from other member states for Britain to renegotiate its annual budget rebate.

## ? Review questions

1. Outline the roles, structures, and composition of the main European Union institutions. Which is the most powerful and why?

2. How does qualified majority voting (QMV) work, where and how often is it used, and can it be described as fair and democratic? If not, why not?

3. What were the main stages leading up to full economic and monetary union (EMU)? What are the arguments for and against Britain joining the euro?

4. Is the EU a federal super-state in the making, or one that has stayed true to its stated aim of preserving subsidiarity? To what extent, if any, is national sovereignty threatened by recent developments in European integration?

5. List some of the main issues affecting the future of the EU, explaining why they are significant to the UK's membership of the Union.

## → Further reading

Bomberg, E. and Stubb, A. (eds) (2008) *The European Union: How Does it Work?* Oxford: Oxford University Press. **Concise introductory text focusing on demystifying key EU institutions and their sometimes arcane governing procedures.**

Daniels, P. and Ritchie, E. (1996) *EU: Britain and the European Union*, London: Palgrave Macmillan. **Analysis of the relationship of Britain and its main governmental institutions with the EU.**

Jones, A. (2007) *Britain and the European Union*, Edinburgh: Edinburgh University Press. **Invaluable introduction to the EU, its history, and its institutions, with particular emphasis placed on the changing relationship between the EU and UK.**

McCormick, J. (2008) *Understanding the European Union: A Concise Introduction*, London: Palgrave Macmillan. **Leading introductory text to the history, institutions, and treaties of EU. Latest edition includes a comprehensive assessment of the Lisbon Treaty and the impact of EU enlargement.**

## Online Resource Centre

**www.oxfordtextbooks.co.uk/orc/Morrison2e/**

Visit the Online Resource Centre that accompanies this book for web links and regular updates.

# 10

# International relations

We live in an era in which terms like *globalization*, 'development', and 'fair trade' are part of most people's everyday cultural vocabulary. More than at any time in its history, Britain's fortunes are tied to those of its neighbours in Europe. But its involvement in international affairs stretches well beyond the European Union. Until recently, the country was involved in at least two ongoing conflicts, in Afghanistan and Iraq. UK-based multinationals like Shell and BP retain oil and mineral interests across Africa, Latin America, and the Middle East. And then there are those last vestiges of the once sprawling British Empire, in the guise of Northern Ireland, the 53-nation Commonwealth, and a handful of island protectorates, including Gibraltar, the Falklands, and Diego Garcia.

At the same time as Britain is flexing its military and economic muscle, it has become one of the biggest players in the fight to eradicate global poverty, contributing nearly £7bn a year in overseas aid to developing countries in Africa, Asia, and South America, and leading the way at recent **G8** and *G20* summits for binding multilateral agreements on debt relief. The country has also played a significant—if so far limited—role in brokering international agreements on issues ranging from climate change to human rights abuse.

Any attempt by a textbook of this nature to examine the UK's role in global politics and economy must necessarily be selective. The purpose of this chapter is to outline the work of the principal government departments and agencies involved in international relations, and the most significant institutions and issues with which they are engaged.

## ▶ The Foreign and Commonwealth Office (FCO)

The Foreign and Commonwealth Office (FCO)—commonly known as the 'Foreign Office'—is the government department overseeing Britain's overall foreign policy. It was formed in 1968 from the merger of the existing Foreign Office (dating from 1782) and the then separate Commonwealth Office. At its head are several ministers, the most senior being the Foreign and Commonwealth Secretary, or 'Foreign Secretary'.

The FCO's main roles are to:

- maintain diplomatic and/or consular relations with 188 different countries;
- maintain diplomatic missions with a further nine countries;
- act as the UK's main broker in the drawing up of international treaties, common defence policies, and economic sanctions;
- use its overseas embassies to act as local focal points for diplomatic relations between Britain and the countries concerned;
- help to promote the UK as a trading partner with countries through its embassies.

When Labour regained power in 1997 its newly installed Foreign Secretary, the late Robin Cook, vowed to pursue an 'ethical foreign policy', which would put diplomacy and human rights campaigning ahead of narrow national interests and warfare. But in 2001 he was replaced by Jack Straw, who had earned a reputation as a tough-talking Home Secretary in the government's first term. Within months, the FCO was dealing with the fallout from the 11 September terrorist attacks on New York. In 2006, under then Foreign Secretary Margaret Beckett (the first woman to hold the post), the FCO announced ten new 'strategic priorities' for the next five to ten years (as outlined in Table 10.1).

Unlike most government departments, the FCO has only one *executive agency:* Wilton Park International Conference Centre organizes summits on international social problems attended by academics, business people, and other relevant professionals. Although staffed by FCO civil servants, Wilton Park prides itself on its academic independence. This is assured by the fact that its members are selected by an advisory council—not ministers. Nonetheless, because the council is appointed by the Foreign Secretary it is a moot point as to whether its independence is largely notional.

There are also several independent think tanks with close links to the FCO, the most famous being the Royal Institute of International Affairs, founded in 1920 and based at Chatham House, St James's Square, London (commonly known simply as 'Chatham House'). It is from Chatham House that the oft-cited 'Chatham House Rule'—beloved of (and cursed by) editors in equal measure—originates. This is a 'gentleman's agreement' allowing journalists access to candid discussions and debates held by private or public organizations in return for their agreement to respect the anonymity of participants. Reporters are normally permitted to use some or all information gained from such meetings,

Table 10.1 Ten-year strategic objectives of the Foreign and Commonwealth Office (FCO)

| | Objective |
|---|---|
| 1. | Making world safer from terrorism and weapons of mass destruction (WMDs). |
| 2. | Reducing harm to Britain from international crime, including drug trafficking, people smuggling, and money laundering. |
| 3. | Preventing and resolving conflict through strong international system. |
| 4. | Building effective and globally competitive EU in 'secure neighbourhood'. |
| 5. | Supporting UK economy and business through open and expanding global economy, science and innovation, and secure energy supplies. |
| 6. | Achieving climate security by promoting faster transition to sustainable, low-carbon global economy. |
| 7. | Promoting sustainable development and poverty reduction, underpinned by human rights, democracy, good governance, and protection of the environment. |
| 8. | Managing migration and combating illegal immigration. |
| 9. | Delivering high-quality support for UK nationals abroad—in 'normal times' and crises. |
| 10. | Ensuring the security and good governance of the UK's overseas territories. |

but on the strict condition that they do not attribute it to named individuals. The precise wording of the 'Chatham House Rule' is as follows:

> ❝ When a meeting, or part thereof, is held under the Chatham House Rule, participants are free to use the information received, but neither the identity nor the affiliation of the speaker(s), nor that of any other participant, may be revealed. ❞

The civilized, if rather quaint, rule reflects the overall culture of the FCO, which is often criticized for its antediluvian procedures and maintaining a cosy 'old boy' approach to business more redolent of a Graham Greene novel than the harsh realities of twenty-first-century *Weltpolitik*. In August 2005 Andrew Mackinlay, a Labour member of the Commons Foreign Affairs *Select Committee*, leaked details of a report by management consultancy Collinson Grant, which suggested it was hugely overmanned and needed reform to address the following weaknesses:

- a 'slowness to act';
- a lack of delegation within its management structure;
- poor accountability;
- overmanning—with at least 1,200 jobs, £48m a year capable of being saved.

Of the recent controversies involving the Foreign Office, none has been more damaging than the debacle over Iraq. There is insufficient space here to go into detail about the circumstances leading to the US-led invasion of the country over Saddam Hussein's alleged stockpiling of weapons of mass destruction (WMDs), or the subsequent failure to locate any such arms. It is fair to say, however, that the spectre of this ongoing conflict—not to mention the threat of terrorism, as brought home to Britain in the multiple bombings of 7 July 2005—is reflected in the wording of the FCO's new statement of 'priorities'.

Many other recent issues faced by the FCO—and played out in the media—have also stemmed in large part from Britain's involvement in the 'War on Terror' (although this expression was pointedly dropped by the UK government, if not the USA, after Tony Blair left Downing Street). These have included Britain's belated intervention to secure the release of UK-based terrorist suspects held in the US Guantanamo Bay detention camp on Cuba, from which  the first four finally returned to their families in 2007—five years after being captured by the US military in Afghanistan. During Gordon Brown's premiership, meanwhile, a row broke out over Foreign Secretary David Miliband's admission—contrary to previous assurances by ministers—that a British territory had been used for so-called 'extraordinary rendition' by the USA. This is the process by which suspected terrorists are flown to a third-party country to be interrogated by agents working on behalf of the Central Intelligence Agency (CIA). The process has been criticized as 'torture by proxy' by human rights organizations, which argue that, by allowing prisoners to be questioned in countries known for their strong-arm tactics, the USA is giving tacit approval to interrogation practices banned in its own country. In a speech to the Commons in February 2008, Mr Miliband revealed he had been told by then US Secretary of State Condoleezza Rice only after the event that US planes, each carrying a single suspect, had stopped on the British island of Diego Garcia in the Indian Ocean. One had been en route to Guantanamo Bay; the other to Morocco.

In July 2010 David Cameron launched an inquiry into allegations that British operatives had colluded in torture, to be led by Intelligence Services Commissioner Sir Peter Gibson—promising compensation to victims if the allegations were proven. His choice of appointment proved immediately contentious  among human rights campaigners, including the charity Reprieve, who argued his impartiality was 'fatally compromised' by his other job—and by the fact he had personally fronted an earlier (internal) inquiry into similar issues.

Earlier in the month, there had been other indications of the possible future direction of British foreign policy under the coalition. Foreign Secretary William Hague had signalled a new, more 'clear, focused, and effective' approach to international diplomacy—emphasizing the need for Britain to be proactive in Europe, and build strong relations with emerging economic superpowers like China, Brazil, and India. In a swipe at Labour's legacy, he argued the UK had come to be seen by some as a state that only engaged with them in the event of disaster or when it needed their support for crucial votes (an oblique reference to the elusive 'second resolution' Mr Blair had sought to legitimize the invasion of Iraq). He added he hoped British troops would be able to leave Afghanistan by 2014.

## The Diplomatic Service

A 'sub-department' of the FCO, this is staffed by seconded administrators and is responsible for manning the embassies and consulates through which Britain discharges its diplomatic relations with their host countries. It employs some 20,000 officials and is headed not by a government minister, but a career civil servant. Despite the fact he or she is a salaried official, rather than an elected MP, this civil servant has a title similar to a certain type of minister: 'Permanent Under-Secretary of State at the FCO'.

Personnel employed by the service at all levels enjoy 'diplomatic immunity'—freedom from prosecution under the laws of the countries in which they are based. They may, however, be expelled for committing an offence, and may well be tried back in Britain.

# ▌ The Ministry of Defence (MoD)

What with the continuing military operations in Iraq and Afghanistan, controversies over the treatment of service personnel at home and abroad, and periodic outbursts about both these and other issues by retired senior officers, the Ministry of Defence (MoD) has grabbed more recent headlines than virtually any other government department. When Mr Blair was elected in 1997 he made a now infamous speech declaring himself part of the 'first generation' able to  *'contemplate that we may live our entire lives without going to war or sending our children to war'*. Yet, by the time he stepped down ten years later, he had taken Britain into no fewer than four conflicts: to prevent ethnic cleansing by Serbia's Slobodan Milošević in Kosovo (1999), to intervene in the civil war in Sierra Leone (2000), to support the US-led invasion of Afghanistan (2001), and to 'liberate' Saddam Hussein's Iraq and root out his supposed WMDs (2003). In addition, UK planes were heavily involved in the sustained bombing of Iraq by Bill Clinton's US administration in 1998.

Mr Blair's last Defence Secretary and Mr Brown's first, Des Browne, became the subject of unwitting controversy after being given two ministerial briefs (he remained Scottish Secretary after his appointment). In November 2007  a sustained attack was mounted by five retired chiefs of staff (heads of the Armed Forces) over his dual role and other cutbacks in the defence budget at a time when British troops were stretched to the limit in the Middle East. Former Royal Navy chief Admiral Lord Boyce accused the government of leaving 'blood on the floor' of the MoD by failing to resource the department adequately. Mr Brown went some way towards addressing this concern with his second reshuffle, in October 2008, when he replaced Mr Browne with former Business Secretary John Hutton—in so doing, stripping him of the role overseeing Scotland.

Formed in 1964 from the amalgamation of four other departments of state—the War Office, Admiralty, Air Ministry, and Ministry of Aviation—the MoD is, ironically, most often in the news in times of conflict. Once diplomacy has broken down and Britain has declared war on another nation, the FCO tends to fade out of the picture, to give way to the department charged with coordinating the military. Although its original aim was (as its name suggests) to provide a first line of 'defence' for Britain against foreign aggressors, in practice it is more likely to see action at times when the UK is doing the attacking.

The principal roles of the MoD in its present form are as outlined in Table 10.2.

In recent years the MoD's *raison d'être* has changed in light of global developments, principally the end of the Cold War and rise of the terrorist threat. The current operation in Afghanistan notwithstanding, so-called 'conventional warfare'—involving ground troops, tanks, helicopters, planes, and ships—is becoming less common. For a time during the 1980s—before the collapse of the Berlin Wall and the break-up of the Soviet Union—the consensus was that future wars would generally be fought 'by remote', with computerized missile systems replacing traditional armaments. While nuclear strikes have yet to occur, today's field weapons are increasingly sophisticated and the number of soldiers required to fight conflicts continues to diminish as their equipment becomes capable of doing more of the work for them. In response to the new challenges and opportunities presented by modern warfare, the Labour government published two major reviews of defence expenditure.

**Table 10.2** Principal roles of the Ministry of Defence (MoD)

| | Role |
|---|---|
| 1. | Deterring threats and, if necessary, defending freedom and territorial integrity of UK and dependent territories (e.g. the Falkland Islands). |
| 2. | Contributing to promotion of UK's wider security interests, including protection of freedom, democratic institutions, and free trade. |
| 3. | Promoting peace and helping to maximize Britain's international influence. |
| 4. | Acting as international headquarters for British Armed Forces—wherever they are in the world. |
| 5. | Financing and maintaining permanent army, navy, and air force, and weaponry, uniforms, and other military equipment. |
| 6 | Financing and maintaining accommodation for UK Armed Forces at home and overseas (barracks), and land and facilities for training and equipment. |

The 1998 Strategic Defence Review and the 2003 **White Paper** *Delivering Security in a Changing World* both envisaged the following approach for the armed forces:

- the ability to support three simultaneous small to medium-scale operations, with at least one as an enduring peacekeeping mission—for example, Kosovo or Afghanistan. These forces must be capable of representing the UK as lead nation in any coalition operations;
- the ability, at longer notice, to deploy forces in a large-scale operation while running a concurrent small-scale operation.

Unlike the FCO, the MoD contains numerous executive agencies responsible for specific operations. These include a British Forces Post Office (in charge of all postal communications for the military), Defence Estates (responsible for maintaining MoD barracks and land), and such agencies as the Defence Storage and Distribution Agency and the Defence Aviation Repair Agency.

The Chief of the Defence Staff—effectively the *permanent secretary* of the Armed Forces as a whole—is supported by a Vice-Chief of the Defence Staff and the following heads of three individual Armed Forces:

- First Sea Lord/Chief of the Naval Staff;
- Chief of the General Staff;
- Chief of the Air Staff.

Aside from the ongoing criticisms of levels of defence expenditure—the MoD's annual budget is said to be less than the £100bn spent by the Treasury on 'rescuing' Northern Rock from collapse (see pp. 192–3)—the ministry has weathered numerous other storms in recent years. At the height of the Iraq War then Defence Secretary Geoff Hoon was accused of failing to provide adequate equipment for British troops. Mr Hoon, like Mr Blair, had also been repeatedly

criticized for his apparent eagerness to invade Iraq on the basis of questionable intelligence about Saddam's WMD threat—and his unwillingness to apologize for the ensuing loss of life when it later emerged that no such weapons existed. Years after the event, during his January 2010 appearance before the Iraq Inquiry convened by Mr Brown to identify lessons from the ill-starred conflict, Mr Hoon sought to blame this 'scandal' on his former boss, claiming that, during his time as Chancellor, he had forced 'difficult cuts' on the MoD. Appearing before the inquiry himself two months later, Mr Brown insisted defence spending had risen continually during his time in the Treasury, but he later apologized for what he insisted was an inadvertent inaccuracy—conceding that during four years it had fallen in real terms.

The MoD has also been castigated in the press for failing to maintain barracks and domestic quarters for personnel to a civilized standard, and for selling off large amounts of military accommodation to private landlords—only to end up renting it back from them. In March 2008 it emerged that British taxpayers were paying a private housing company £29m a year to rent 8,200 marital homes that were lying empty in lieu of any Forces families to move into them. In October 2010 coalition Defence Secretary Liam Fox published a strategic defence and security review of upcoming MoD procurement projects, which he had earlier described as 'wholly unaffordable'. In August 2010 he signalled his intention to start out by addressing a £37bn 'unfunded liability' bequeathed by Labour. One commitment saved from the chop was the plan to renew Britain's independent Trident nuclear deterrent—despite the fact the Lib Dems opposed this in opposition—but equally eyebrow-raising was the coalition's decision to press ahead with two new aircraft carriers despite not having any planes for them to carry for up to ten years.

# ▌ The Department for International Development (DfID)

Until the 1997 election the fields of humanitarian aid and investment in developing countries were the responsibility of a minister in the Foreign Office, the Minister for Overseas Development. When Mr Blair was elected, however, this post was incorporated into the *Cabinet*. Its first incumbent was Clare Short, a passionate advocate of overseas aid and sustainable development, who resigned from the Cabinet over her reservations about the post-war reconstruction of Iraq. When the coalition took power, the Department for International Development (DfID) was one of very few to have a proportion of its budget (which relating specifically to overseas aid) ring-fenced in the teeth of impending public spending cuts.

Today, DfID works directly with 150 developing countries—principally in Africa, parts of Asia, Latin America, and the Far East. Its annual budget is more than £4bn and it has two headquarters: in London and East Kilbride, near Glasgow.

The Department for International Development initially stipulated a time frame within which it hoped to achieve key goals designed to tackle child poverty and improve the welfare of children and women worldwide. In its 1997 White Paper, *Eliminating World Poverty: A Challenge for the 21st Century*, it outlined the key objectives for Britain's overseas aid policy listed in the table entitled 'Key objectives of the Department for International Development', to be found on the Online Resource Centre accompanying this book.

More recently these were revised—and made decidedly more modest and less time-specific—in the form of so-called 'Millennium Goals', as listed in Table 10.3.

**Table 10.3** DfID 'Millennium Goals'

| | Goal |
|---|---|
| 1. | Halving number of people living in extreme poverty and hunger. |
| 2. | Ensuring all children receive primary education. |
| 3. | Promoting sexual equality and giving women a stronger voice. |
| 4. | Reducing child death rates. |
| 5. | Improving the health of mothers. |
| 6. | Combating HIV/AIDS, malaria, and other diseases. |
| 7. | Ensuring the environment is protected. |
| 8. | Building global partnership for those working in development. |

# ▶ Britain's role in the United Nations (UN)

In addition to the EU, Britain is a member of several major international organizations with differing, if sometimes overlapping, remits. Of these perhaps the most significant is the *United Nations (UN)*—a global body set up after the Second World War with the stated aim of promoting peace, preventing future conflicts, and achieving international cooperation on economic, social, cultural, and humanitarian issues. From the outset the UN has been committed to solving disputes between nations by peaceful means, wherever possible, and when it sends troops into a country this tends to be in a *peacekeeping* capacity—to police borders, protect aid routes, etc.—rather than to engage in active hostilities against any party.

Formally established in October 1945, the UN set out to avoid the perceived errors of its precursor, the League of Nations. The League—born in the wake of the First World War—had imposed crippling reparations on Germany, in so doing contributing to the dire economic woes that were to foster Nazism. While the UN was pointedly to exclude Germany from the top table in its main governing institutions (a state of affairs that largely remains the case to this day), it was determined not to make the mistake of isolating the country entirely, let alone financially penalizing it, as it struggled to rebuild its shattered infrastructure (and reputation) following Hitler's defeat.

Initially founded by 51 states, today the UN embraces 192 participating nations. The most senior UN official is its Secretary-General (at time of writing Ban Ki-Moon). In theory UN membership is open to every recognized state in the world, but in practice individual countries have been periodically excluded—or have chosen to exclude themselves—in disputes over the legitimacy of their governance (or, occasionally, that of the UN itself).

The UN is based in New York—a fact that has periodically led some member states (particularly those with a history of disagreeing with the USA) to argue that the US government wields a disproportionate influence on its decisions. In

October 2006, deputy leader of Somalia's Islamic Courts Hassan Turki, one of several parties wrestling for control of the war-ravaged country, declared he did not recognize the UN—dismissing it as an 'American interest group'.

## The UN Security Council

The term 'United Nations' was coined during the Second World War itself, when Winston Churchill and US president Franklin D. Roosevelt used it in speeches to refer to the Allies: the countries opposing Hitler. But it was only born in earnest after the UN Conference on International Organization convened in April 1945, and a formal UN Charter was drafted and signed by the majority of its founding states on 24 October. Giving substance to Churchill's famous remark that '*history is written by the victors*', of these 51 nations the five who had played arguably the most significant role in defeating Hitler were awarded permanent seats on a newly formed UN Security Council—the body charged with allocating peacekeeping forces around the world, ratifying economic sanctions, and in extreme cases authorizing military action.

According to the UN Charter, its role is to:

- investigate any situation threatening international peace;
- recommend procedures for peaceful resolution of a dispute;
- call on other member nations to completely or partially interrupt economic relations as well as sea, air, postal, and radio communications, or to sever diplomatic relations;
- enforce its decisions militarily, or by any means necessary.

The five permanent members of the UN Security Council are: the USA, Britain, France, the Republic of China (later to be renamed the People's Republic of China), and the Soviet Union (now the Russian Federation). They are joined at any one time by a further ten members, elected by the UN's 'parliament', the General Assembly, for two-year terms. These are chosen from among the remaining 187 UN countries on a rotational basis. For the two-year period commencing 1 January 2010, the temporary members of the UN Security Council were as outlined in the table entitled 'The temporary membership of the UN Security Council (2010–11)', which can be found on the Online Resource Centre that accompanies this book.

As a mark of its seniority, each permanent member has the right to veto votes on prospective UN actions. It was this fact that presented the biggest stumbling block to Britain and the USA's campaign to win support for the invasion of Iraq. Both the French president, Jacques Chirac, and his Russian counterpart, Vladimir Putin, made it clear they had no intention of supporting any such further resolution authorizing military strikes without conclusive proof that Saddam was stockpiling WMDs. Their immovability blocked the passage of the 'second resolution' the USA and UK sought, forcing them to abandon pursuing it and go it alone.

In recent years there has been some discussion about the possibility of increasing the number of permanent members on the Security Council. Representations have been made not only by Germany (now a key player on the international stage), but also Japan, Brazil, and India. In 2004 then Secretary-General Kofi Anan proposed doubling the number of permanent members to include each of these states, as well as one from Africa and/or one from the Arab League (a regional organization of Arab nations in the Middle East and North Africa, with members including Egypt, Iraq, Saudi Arabia, and Libya). A two-thirds 'yes' vote by the UN General Assembly would be needed to approve this.

## The UN General Assembly

The primary purpose of the other UN's second governing body is to approve its annual budget and appoint non-permanent representatives to the Security Council. It also receives reports from the UN's various other subsidiary bodies, and wields considerable influence over policy areas including international aid and climate change.

Unlike the Security Council the Assembly gives each UN member state an equal say at meetings. It convenes for regular annual sessions, lasting from September to December, but can be assembled for emergency meetings at other times. Meetings are chaired either by the serving Secretary-General or by a president, elected by Assembly members on a yearly basis. Votes are passed if a two-thirds majority of those present is achieved.

Like Britain's Parliament at Westminster, the Assembly has various committees charged with overseeing specific policy areas, in addition to seven commissions, six boards, five panels, and numerous working groups. Of the 30 committees, the most influential are numbered one to six and focus on the following issues:

1. Disarmament and International Security (DISEC);
2. Economic and Finance (ECOFIN);
3. Social, Humanitarian and Cultural (SOCHUM);
4. Special Political and Decolonization (SPECPOL);
5. Administrative and Budgetary;
6. Legal.

## Other UN bodies and agencies

Like every major organization, national or international, the UN requires administrators. The UN Secretariat employs 8,900 staff, the majority of whom are based at the UN headquarters in New York. Others are stationed in its regional headquarters in Addis Ababa, Bangkok, Beirut, Geneva, Nairobi, Santiago, and Vienna. The Secretariat's responsibilities are divided, like those of the British Civil Service and *European Commission*, into separate departments overseeing discrete policy areas:

- Division for the Advancement of Women (DAW);
- Department of Disarmament Affairs (DDA);
- Department of Economic and Social Affairs (DESA);
- Department of Political Affairs (DPA);
- Department of Peacekeeping Operations (DPKO);
- Office for the Coordination of Humanitarian Affairs (OCHA);
- Office of the High Commissioner for Human Rights (OHCHR);
- United Nations High Commissioner for Refugees (UNHCR);
- United Nations Development Fund for Women (UNIFEM).

Other significant agencies of the UN and their responsibilities are outlined in Table 10.4.

**Table 10.4** Subordinate bodies of the UN

| Body | Role and remit |
|------|----------------|
| The International Court of Justice (ICJ) | Comprising 15 judges elected for nine years at a time, this sits in the Peace Palace in The Hague, the Netherlands. It hears cases referred to it by member states and adjudicates between warring parties. Several countries—including the USA, France, Germany, and China—have refused to be bound by its rulings. Its most famous cases have included the protracted trial of late Serbian dictator Slobodan Milošević on 66 charges of genocide and 'crimes against humanity', and the recently opened hearings into similar charges against Bosnian Serb leader Radovan Karadžić. (Membership of the Court for the nine years beginning March 2007 can be found in the table entitled 'The membership of the International Court of Justice (ICJ)', to be found on the Online Resource Centre.) |
| The United Nations Economic and Social Council (ESOCOC) | Promotes cooperation between UN states on economic and social policy—all 54 members are elected by the General Assembly for three-year terms. It has a president, elected for a one-year term from among smaller and 'middle-ranking' states represented on the ESOCOC. Historically it meets once a year for four weeks, in July, but since 1998 has also convened in April to liaise with finance ministers heading the key committees of the World Bank and International Monetary Fund (IMF). The ESOCOC consults with 2,000 non-government organizations (NGOs) and oversees numerous agencies, including UNESCO, UNICEF, WHO, UNDP, ILO, and UNHCR. |

| Body | Role and remit |
| --- | --- |
| The United Nations Educational, Scientific and Cultural Organization (UNESCO) | Formed to promote cultural understanding through education, science, and the arts. With 193 member states and six associate members, it has more notional participants than the UN itself, a base in Paris, and 30 other offices. |
| The United Nations Children's Fund (UNICEF) | Formerly the 'United Nations International Children's Emergency Fund', this provides urgent food and health care to children whose countries have been devastated by natural or manmade disasters. It is a voluntary agency, reliant for income on governments and private donations. |
| The World Health Organization (WHO) | Established on first World Health Day, 7 April 1948, this body coordinates international efforts to monitor outbreaks of deadly diseases like malaria, cholera, typhoid, and AIDS, sponsoring vaccination programmes and medical research. Among its famous pronouncements is its 'Breast is Best' advice to mothers in developing countries, to encourage the use of breast milk to rear infants, rather than formula, which relies on clean water supplies to make it safe. UN-affiliated NGOs like UK-based Baby Milk Action have repeatedly come into conflict with the multinational Nestlé over its alleged promotion of powdered milk. |
| The United Nations Development Programme (UNDP) | An executive board within the Assembly, but funded by voluntary donations, this is the world's largest source of aid for investment in industrial and agricultural development. |
| The International Labour Organization (ILO) | Based in Geneva, Switzerland, this body aims to promote opportunities for both men and women to 'obtain decent and productive work, in conditions of freedom, equity, security, and human dignity'. Its focus has been increasingly on the unequal plight of women in developing countries. It meets three times a year—in March, June, and November—and holds an International Labour Conference in Geneva each June. The ILO boasts a governing body comprising representatives from 28 governments, 14 workers' groups, and 14 employers' groups. Ten seats are held permanently by the USA, UK, Brazil, China, France, Germany, India, Italy, Japan, and the Russian Federation; the remaining ones are elected by member states on a three-year basis. |
| The Office of the United Nations High Commissioner for Refugees (UNHCR)/The United Nations Refugee Agency | Established in 1950, this coordinates international efforts to protect refugees and relieve situations that might lead to indigenous peoples fleeing their countries. It employs 6,300 staff in 110 countries. |

The present composition of the International Court of Justice is explained in the table entitled 'The membership of the International Court of Justice (ICJ) (July 2010)', which can be found on the Online Resource Centre.

# ▌ Life after the Cold War—Britain's ongoing role in NATO

Founded in 1949, the *North Atlantic Treaty Organization (NATO)* is (unlike the UN) a *military* alliance established against the backdrop of the emerging Cold War between East and West, and the ensuring nuclear arms race, to protect the security of Western powers. NATO comprises 26 member states—principally the USA, Canada, and a collection of western European countries, although in the wake of the collapse of the Soviet Union it has also embraced several former Eastern Bloc nations.

NATO's origins lay in an earlier agreement, the 1948 Treaty of Brussels, which founded the Western European Union, a smaller-scale forerunner composed entirely (as its name suggests) of western European countries. In fact its only signatories were Britain, France, and the Benelux countries: Belgium, the Netherlands, and Luxembourg. As the Western Union began deliberating, its members concluded that, for any military counterweight to the Soviet Union to be effective, it would need to embrace the USA. Hence the decision was taken to open its doors to the USA, and on 4 April 1949 the North Atlantic Treaty was signed in Washington DC. Along with the USA and Canada, Portugal, Italy, Norway, Denmark, and Iceland were admitted at the same time. Greece and Turkey joined in 1952. Perhaps unsurprisingly, given the nature of the then current global political climate, West Germany had to wait longer, but it finally signed up on 9 May 1955. East Germany was effectively absorbed in 1990, following the reunification of Germany a year earlier.

Given the rapid expansion of NATO and its hostility to Stalin's growing empire in the East, it was only a matter of time before the Soviet Union retaliated by establishing an equivalent organization. On 14 May 1955, it signed the Warsaw Treaty of Friendship, Cooperation, and Mutual Assistance—better known as the 'Warsaw Pact'. This came to encompass all Soviet countries, except Yugoslavia. But, in belated recognition of the redundancy of the Warsaw Pact following the collapse of Communism in the East, on 12 March 1999 the following former members joined NATO: Hungary, Poland, and the Czech Republic. Bulgaria, Estonia, Latvia, Lithuania, Romania, and Slovakia followed suit in March 2004.

NATO remains based in Brussels, but as with the UN this has not stopped some countries accusing it of being in the USA's pocket. In 1958 French President Charles de Gaulle provoked its first constitutional crisis by proposing a new tripartite NATO 'directorate', headed jointly by the USA, Britain, and France. Writing to US President Dwight D. Eisenhower and then British Prime Minister Harold Macmillan, he accused them of undermining NATO's collective decision-making process through their cosy 'special arrangement'.

# The North Atlantic Treaty

The foundation stone of NATO was the North Atlantic Treaty. Perhaps its most defining (and oft-cited) clause is Art. V, which sets down the principle of 'collective defence'. Its precise wording is as follows:

> " The Parties of NATO agreed that an armed attack against one or more of them in Europe or North America shall be considered an attack against them all. Consequently they agree that, if such an armed attack occurs, each of them, in exercise of the right of individual or collective self-defence will assist the Party or Parties being attacked, individually and in concert with the other Parties, such action as it deems necessary, including the use of armed force, to restore and maintain the security of the North Atlantic area. "

The most recent invocation of Art. V came in the aftermath of the 11 September attacks on New York, when the USA argued that the terrorist strikes on the World Trade Center effectively amounted to a military attack on the country and therefore required a joint response from NATO members. There was some dispute about whether the usual rules applied, given that precise nationalities of all the terrorists were not immediately known, making any decision to target a specific country in retaliation problematic. Having asserted an Al-Qaeda link, the USA argued that the Taliban in Afghanistan was principally answerable, since its then leader, Mullah Omar, was believed to be harbouring leaders of the Al-Qaeda movement, including Osama bin Laden.

In the event, action in defence of the USA was authorized on 4 October 2001 (despite rowdy scenes in some NATO meetings) and the alliance participated in two subsequent operations: Operation Eagle Assist and Operation Active Endeavour. The former was a series of precautionary sorties over US skies performed by planes from 13 NATO states. The latter was to become an ongoing naval operation in the Mediterranean Sea designed to intercept the passage of WMDs. Since Operation Active Endeavour commenced, it has involved 12 NATO members and five partner countries (Russia, Egypt, Tunisia, Morocco, and Ukraine). At time of writing more than 100,000 ships had been monitored and 155 suspect vessels boarded.

Previous attempts to invoke Art. V have also failed. In 1982, Margaret Thatcher's government attempted to persuade NATO to do so in response to  the Argentine invasion of the Falklands, but because those islands are located thousands of miles from the UK (in the South Atlantic), the invasion was not deemed to be an attack on Britain.

# The North Atlantic Council (NAC)

NATO's principal governing body, the North Atlantic Council (NAC), meets twice a week: on Tuesdays, for informal lunch meetings, and on Wednesdays, for formal decision-making sessions. Its composition varies: on some occasions, so-called 'permanent representatives' (PermReps)—salaried career diplomats from each state—will do so, but when major issues are due to be debated, member states usually send their foreign or defence ministers.

The most senior official in NATO, as in the UN, is its civilian Secretary-General, currently former Danish Prime Minister Anders Fogh Rasmussen, whose job it is to chair meetings of the NAC and to act as the alliance's public figurehead.

The Secretary-General is supported by a Deputy Secretary-General.

## The Military Committee

NATO's status as an alliance focusing on security and defence-related issues means that some of its operational decisions require direct input from military personnel. To facilitate this, the Organization has its own Military Committee, which (unlike the NAC) comprises members of the armed forces rather than civil servants. Each member state sends to its meetings a military representative (normally a chief of staff). The Committee has its own permanent chairman.

The Committee also has several subsets: an Allied Command Europe, Allied Command Atlantic, Allied Command Channel, and Regional Planning Group (for North America), each under its own 'supreme commander'.

## The NATO Parliamentary Assembly

Not actually part of NATO's official structure—but created in 1955 to complement and liaise with it—the NATO Parliamentary Assembly is a fairly informal annual convention of parliamentarians/legislators (MPs) from each member state that meets to discuss common policy issues.

## The future of NATO

There has been much debate in the media about whether NATO remains 'relevant' in a post-Cold War world. Leaving aside the recent diplomatic contretemps between Russia and the USA over the latter's decision to expand its new Missile Defence Shield to cover former Soviet states such as Poland and the Czech Republic, and the stand-off between Mr Putin and Britain (of which more later), few observers argue that we are about to be plunged back into a new East–West arms race. Nevertheless, the Western world can hardly be described as safe from outside attack, given the events of 11 September 2001 and 7 July 2005 (not to mention the 2004 Madrid bombing). While terrorist attacks of this kind may be harder to defend—let alone retaliate against—than conventional invasions or missile strikes, recent secretary-generals have argued the alliance has a clear role to play in devising strategies to counter them. Its ongoing presence in Afghanistan symbolizes this resolve.

Then there are the flashpoints of more conventional conflict that still erupt periodically on European soil. In the 1990s NATO did a good job of redefining itself as a proactive third-party fighting force in the Balkans—first during the Bosnian War, then the Serbian assaults on Albania and Kosovo. Recent events in Serbia, including the unilateral declaration of independence by Kosovo and rumblings of discontent in Belgrade, have led some to question whether the alliance's work in the region is yet concluded.

These developments aside, NATO faces an emerging challenge from the European Union. As the threat of terrorist attacks on European soil grows, EU leaders have placed the development of their embryonic 'Rapid Reaction Force' squarely on the agenda for the next few years (see p. 285). The 'Force', as it stands, is little more than notional: the term refers to the EU's ability to mobilize up to 60,000 troops, 400 combat aircraft, and 200 ships drawn from member states at short notice to defend its borders, and there is no talk yet of formally establishing a collective 'European army'. Nonetheless, in the eyes of some Western governments the threat to NATO's hegemony remains.

# ▌ The Council of Europe

Founded in 1949, the *Council of Europe* pre-dates by two years the European Union (with which it and its institutions are often confused). As such, it has the distinction of being the longest-running organization dedicated to promoting European integration and cooperation. Recognized under international law, it has 47 member states (20 more than the EU to date).

Its prime purpose is to foster the adoption of common legal standards and human rights among its members. To this end its most famous institution is the *European Court of Human Rights (ECtHR)* in Strasbourg, and by far its most celebrated achievement the European Convention on Human Rights (ECHR), which the Court upholds (see pp. 11–12).

Moves to establish some form of European political and social confederation, of which the Council of Europe became the first expression, arose out of the anti-Nazi alliance forged in the Second World War. In a famous speech at the University of Zurich in 1946, Winston Churchill (at the time Britain's Leader of the Opposition, following his defeat by Labour in the 1945 election) called for the formation of a 'United States of Europe', with France and Germany at its head. Although he pointedly stopped short of suggesting Britain should be a part of this alliance—instead saying it should join with the USA in embracing it—his coining of the term is conveniently forgotten by many of his fans on the right of today's Conservative Party. In due course, the Council of Europe was established by the Treaty of London, on 5 May 1949, and a 'Statute' outlining its statement of principles was signed by the following ten countries: Belgium, Denmark, France, Ireland, Italy, Luxembourg, the Netherlands, Norway, Sweden, and the UK.

Article 1 of this Statute declared:

" The aim of the Council of Europe is to achieve a greater unity between its members for the purpose of safeguarding and realising the ideals and principles which are their common heritage and facilitating their economic and social progress. "

Its overall list of aims and objectives are as set out in the table entitled 'The aims and objectives of the Council of Europe', which can be found on the Online Resource Centre.

## Governing institutions of the Council of Europe

The main decision-making bodies within the Council are the Parliamentary Assembly (PACE)—comprising parliamentarians (MPs) from each of the 47 member states—and the Committee of Ministers, made up notionally of foreign ministers from each participating country (but, in fact, by permanent representatives, as on NATO's General Assembly). As with NATO and the UN, its most senior official is styled Secretary-General. He or she is elected for five-year terms by PACE, and heads up the Council of Europe Secretariat (its civil service).

The Council also has a number of *quango*-style structures, known as 'partial agreements', to which member states may send representatives. It also set up a Congress of the Council of Europe in 1994, to draw together representatives from local and regional government in the Council's member states.

# ▌ International trade and economy

Promoting peace is one key area of international cooperation in the modern world; the other is fostering free trade and financial investment between nations. Over and above the EU, the UN, and the Council of Europe, several key bodies were founded in the second half of the twentieth century to achieve these and related goals.

## From G8 to G20

The G8—or Group of Eight—is not a formal body like many of the others in this list, but rather a forum comprising the world's biggest industrialized nations and military superpowers. Its membership is as follows: Canada, France,

Germany, Italy, Japan, the Russian Federation, the UK, and the USA. The most recent country to join was Russia and, even today, the group sometimes convenes in its absence. On such occasions it reverts temporarily to the title 'Group of Seven' (G7).

The G8 has its origins in the seismic economic turmoil created in Europe by the 1973 oil crisis involving the USA, Japan, Britain, and other western European countries on the one hand, and the Arab members of the Organization of the Petroleum Exporting Countries (OPEC), plus two of their allies, Egypt and Syria, on the other. At the time, these countries were refusing to ship oil to the West in protest over its support for Israel in the Yom Kippur War. In response, the USA convened the 'Library Group'—an informal meeting of financial experts from the USA, Britain, France, Japan, and West Germany—and in 1975 then French President Valéry Giscard d'Estaing called a summit in Rambouillet that led to the formation of a Group of Six (G6), comprising the future members of the G8 minus Canada and, obviously, Russia. Canada joined the following year.

Since then the G6 and its successors have held annual meetings at different locations within participating countries, under a rotating presidency. Although the group has no economic or constitutional powers per se, it is one of the most influential talking shops in global politics. At the G8 Summit in Gleneagles in July 2005, Mr Blair used his chairmanship to secure a £29bn boost to international aid and cancel the debt of the 18 poorest African nations. Despite criticisms from some campaigners, Sir Bob Geldof and Bono described the date of the agreement as 'a great day'.

More recently, Russia's ongoing membership of the G8 was briefly called into question in light of the initially belligerent foreign policy of President Dmitry Medvedev. When the country invaded Georgia in August 2008—ostensibly to protect the neighbouring territory of South Ossetia in the Caucuses from Georgian aggression—it invited widespread condemnation. There were calls from some quarters for its G8 membership to be suspended.

Since the 2008–09 global financial crisis, the G8 has been eclipsed in influence (and media coverage) by the G20, which announced in September 2009 its intention to formally supplant the G8 as the world's main economic council of wealthy nations. This expression of confidence came five months after its most significant and heavily publicized meeting to date: a conference hosted by Mr Brown in London at which, in the teeth of mass marches by everyone from climate change protestors to the Stop the War Coalition, it reached what appeared to be firm agreement on the following measures to stabilize the global economy:

- the formation of an international *Financial Stability Board*—a beefed-up version of the *Financial Stability Forum* (an advisory body launched in 1999 to promote stable global markets). Its mission is to forecast potential future economic problems, conducting 'early warning exercises' and periodic reviews. Its 'supervisory college' monitors the performance of the world's leading financial services companies;

- more general reform of the global banking system, bringing hedge funds and private equity firms under global regulation for first time;
- publication of a list of 'tax havens' (states allowing foreign investors to bypass tax obligations in their native countries). Sanctions would be introduced against states that do not comply with 'anti-secrecy' regulations;
- the creation of international colleges of supervisors for national regulatory bodies (like the then Financial Services Authority—see p. 204), to ensure that all signatory countries implement their new regulatory regimes in the same way;
- a pledge to do 'whatever is necessary' to promote growth in individual countries, which sanctioned the British and US governments' use of 'fiscal stimulus' (see p. 193);
- an injection of $1tn (£685tn) into the global economy through a $500bn (£343bn) rise in IMF funding (largely provided by emerging economies less severely hit so far by the credit crunch, including China and Saudi Arabia), and an increase in money for developing countries through the IMF's 'special drawing rights' to $250bn (£171bn) and $250bn (£171bn);
- reform of the IMF, World Bank, and other institutions, allowing countries like China and developing nations to wield influence at their top tables;
- renewed commitment to the 'Millennium Development Goals' for eradicating child poverty, and an extra $50bn (£34.3bn) for the world's poorest countries.

Although the summit (and Mr Brown's chairmanship) was widely hailed a success, there has been criticism since of the slow pace of implementation of its promised reforms. In theory, though, the G20 remains committed to them.

## The International Monetary Fund (IMF)

Like many other supranational organizations, the International Monetary Fund (IMF) was formed in response to the Second World War. It was founded in July 1944, when the representatives of 45 governments met at Bretton Woods, New Hampshire, and its remit from the outset was intrinsically economic: to restore and maintain stability in the world's financial sector and prevent widespread **recessions** through mechanisms including exchange rate agreements and short-term monetary aid packages. Indeed, one of its key roles in the ensuing decades was to provide loans to countries experiencing temporary financial blips. This money is borrowed from a pool contributed to on a rolling basis by member states.

The IMF today counts 185 countries among its members. All UN states, apart from North Korea, Cuba, Andorra, Monaco, Liechtenstein, Nauru, and Tuvalu, are included. Its headquarters are in Washington DC—a fact that has led to repeated accusations by some that it is effectively a puppet of the USA (a similar charge is often levelled against the World Bank).

As with most banks, including the **Bank of England**, the IMF has its own board of governors. While every member state has a presence on the board and may vote on resolutions, as with the EU Council of Ministers some countries wield more power than others. The extent of an individual state's say on the board is governed by its 'quota' of the votes available. This relates as much to the amount of money it has contributed to the IMF in the past as to its population size. Each state also has a corresponding right in relation to how much it is permitted to borrow, should it need to, from the bank's pool of finance— entitlements known as 'special drawing rights' (SDRs).

Both Britain and the USA do relatively well out of the IMF. Britain wields nearly 5 per cent of the available votes, while the USA commands 17 per cent. In terms of borrowing ability, the USA has access to 37,149 million SDRs and Britain 10,739—compared to just 2,396 for Sweden. It is perhaps just as well: in 1976, Prime Minister James Callaghan had to ask the Fund for an emergency loan to enable his government to plug a huge hole in its public finances (see p. 192).

The IMF has seen its fair share of controversy. Perhaps giving succour to criticisms that the USA and certain European countries wield a disproportionate influence on its decisions, the governing board has in the past approved significant loans to dictatorships friendly to the West. Pinochet's Chile and Musharaf's Pakistan are two of the states helped out by the Fund, despite being boycotted by other organizations and non-government organizations (NGOs) because of their alleged human rights abuses. The Fund has also been heavily criticized for imposing strict 'conditionalities' on developing countries that approach it for assistance. The most frequently cited conditionality is a 'structural adjustment programme' that essentially obliges the country seeking aid to privatize state-owned utilities and other industries as a prerequisite for its loan. Similarly contentious is the IMF's habit of charging high interest to countries judged at risk of defaulting and recalling loans at short notice—practices that helped precipitate severe financial crises in Argentina and Bolivia in the 1990s.

## The World Bank

Also based in Washington DC, the World Bank was formally established on 27 December 1945. Its remit has evolved over the decades and now revolves, principally, around the so-called 'Millennium Development Goals' designed to eliminate child poverty and promote sustainable development in poorer countries. The Bank comprises five constituent parts, the most powerful being:

- the *International Bank for Reconstruction and Development (IBRD)*— originally formed to fund the rebuilding of countries devastated by the

Second World War, but now primarily devoted to providing loans through secure bonds to developing countries to relieve poverty and build infrastructure. The bonds it issues are rated 'AAA' (indicating they are as secure as possible). This is guaranteed by the fact they are backed by member states' share capital;

- the *International Development Association (IDA)*—provides long-term, interest-free loans to the world's 81 poorest countries for help with education, health care, sanitation, clean water, and environmental protection. Since its inception, it has made loans totalling nearly £80bn (on average, £4bn–14bn a year).

The World Bank, like the IMF, has encountered increasing hostility from some development charities, not to mention certain countries, on account of the stringent conditionalities it requires before agreeing to assist struggling states. Some see the criteria it expects them to meet before recognizing them as a stable business environment as an attempt to impose an imperialistic, Western capitalist model on nations the indigenous institutions and sociocultural makeup of which do not sit easily with it. The 'five key factors' stipulated by the Bank as necessary for promoting economic growth are listed in the table entitled 'The five key objectives of the World Bank', to be found on the Online Resource Centre that accompanies this book.

In terms of the USA's influence on the Bank, a high-profile row occurred in March 2005 when then President Bush nominated his erstwhile Deputy Defence Secretary, ardent 'neo-Conservative' Paul Wolfowitz, to its presidency. Mr Wolfowitz was criticized during his short-lived tenure (including by his own colleagues) for trying to skew the Bank's policies on issues such as family planning and climate change towards a right-wing agenda. But by far the most significant controversy arose when it emerged he had abused his position to award a disproportionate pay rise and promotion to Shaha Riza, a former bank employee with whom he had had an affair. Mr Wolfowitz resigned in June 2007 after admitting his actions to the board of governors—although he maintained he had 'acted ethically and in good faith'.

## The World Trade Organization (WTO)

Established on 1 January 1995, the World Trade Organization (WTO) replaced the General Agreement on Tariffs and Trade (GATT) originally set up after the Second World War to foster free trade and industrial harmony between member states. It is based in Geneva.

Although it theoretically promotes fair trade between nations, the USA has often been accused of ignoring or bypassing its rulings: the UK/EU tried to protect the Caribbean states by supporting the price of their banana exports recently, but the USA complained about this. In the end the WTO backed the USA.

More recently, the USA itself has tried to impose tariffs on its imports of foreign steel, inflating their market price relative to domestically produced steel. Other UN nations have complained that this amounts to protectionism—a claim the WTO is investigating.

The WTO is governed by:

- a Ministerial Conference, comprising finance ministers from all of the member states, which meets every two years;
- a General Council, which takes day-to-day decisions and runs its administration;
- a director-general appointed by the Council.

Originally, the *agenda* for WTO meetings revolved around the so-called 'Uruguay Round'—a set of concerns agreed by member states on its formation—but this has since been replaced by the 'Doha Development Agenda', which has focused on liberalizing trade between developed and developing countries, with the aim of removing all remaining customs barriers. Kick-started in 2001, discussions reached a rocky phase in July 2008, with the USA and EU refusing to give ground on free trade terms that some negotiators, including then EU Trade Commissioner Peter Mandelson, argued were vital to protect developing countries' interests as they prepared to open their markets up to global competition.

# The Organisation for Economic Co-operation and Development (OECD)

Based in Paris and formerly called the 'Organisation for European Economic Co-operation' (OEEC), the Organisation for Economic Co-operation and Development (OECD) is made up of 29 industrialized member countries. It was formed in 1948, initially to help implement the Marshall Plan for the reconstruction of war-ravaged Europe, but changed its name in 1961 when the decision was taken to admit non-European members.

The OECD's primary aims are to promote global free trade, together with representative democracy, and to this end (along with the G8 and World Economic Forum) its focus is the encroachment of globalization—the term denoting the increasingly interdependent nature of the global economy.

As with most supranational organizations, the OECD is run by a ruling council, and has a Secretary-General and its own secretariat (civil service), which is divided into the following 15 directorates:

- Centre for Entrepreneurship, SMEs (small to medium-sized enterprises) and Local Development;
- Centre for Tax Policy and Administration;
- Development Co-operation Directorate;

- Directorate for Education;
- Directorate for Employment, Labour, and Social Affairs;
- Directorate for Financial and Enterprise Affairs;
- Directorate for Science, Technology, and Industry;
- Economics Department;
- Environment Directorate;
- Public Governance and Territorial Development Directorate;
- Statistics Directorate;
- Trade and Agriculture Directorate;
- General Secretariat;
- Executive Directorate;
- Public Affairs and Communication Directorate.

## The World Economic Forum (WEF)

The World Economic Forum (WEF) is a not-for-profit foundation based in Geneva, the aim of which is to improve the distribution of economic opportunity throughout the world by fostering interaction between governments, businesses, academic institutions, and the arts. Its members meet each year at the Davos Symposium in Switzerland. Two hundred government leaders, 800 chief executives, and 300 assorted experts, scientists, artists, and media representatives take part in its summits.

# ▌ End of empire—the Commonwealth and the British Council

The British Empire may have long since collapsed, but two more benign aspects of its legacy continue, in the institutional guises of the Commonwealth and the British Council.

## The Commonwealth of Nations (the Commonwealth)

The Commonwealth today is comprised of 53 countries—most (but not all) former British colonies. It takes its name from a remark by Lord Rosebery, then Foreign Secretary (and future prime minister), who, on visiting Adelaide in 1884, described what remained of the UK's then crumbling empire as 'the Commonwealth of nations'. The current membership of the Commonwealth is as outlined below in Table 10.5.

Table 10.5  Current membership of the Commonwealth

| Country | Year joined | Population |
|---|---|---|
| Antigua and Barbuda | 1981 | 81,000 |
| Australia | 1931 | 21,134,563 |
| Bahamas | 1973 | 319,000 |
| Bangladesh | 1972 | 139,215,000 |
| Barbados | 1966 | 269,000 |
| Belize | 1981 | 264,000 |
| Botswana | 1966 | 1,769,000 |
| Brunei | 1984 | 366,000 |
| Cameroon | 1995 | 16,038,000 |
| Canada | 1931 | 33,039,367 |
| Cyprus | 1961 | 826,000 |
| Dominica | 1978 | 79,000 |
| Fiji | 1970 1997 | 841,000 |
| Gambia | 1965 | 1,478,000 |
| Ghana | 1957 | 21,664,000 |
| Grenada | 1974 | 102,000 |
| Guyana | 1966 | 750,000 |
| India | 1949 | 1,087,124,000 |
| Jamaica | 1962 | 2,639,000 |
| Kenya | 1963 | 33,467,000 |
| Kiribati | 1979 | 97,000 |
| Lesotho | 1966 | 1,798,000 |
| Malawi | 1964 | 12,608,000 |
| Malaysia | 1957 | 27,356,000 |
| Maldives | 1982 | 321,000 |
| Malta | 1964 | 400,000 |
| Mauritius | 1968 | 1,233,000 |
| Mozambique | 1995 | 19,424,000 |
| Namibia | 1990 | 2,009,000 |
| Nauru | 1968 | 13,000 |
| New Zealand | 1931 | 4,109,000 |
| Nigeria | 1960 1999 | 128,709,000 |
| Pakistan | 1949 1989 2004 | 161,488,000 |
| Papua New Guinea | 1975 | 5,772,000 |
| Saint Kitts and Nevis | 1983 | 42,000 |
| Saint Lucia | 1979 | 159,000 |

| Country | Year joined | Population |
|---|---|---|
| Saint Vincent and the Grenadines | 1979 | 118,000 |
| Samoa | 1970 | 184,000 |
| Seychelles | 1976 | 80,000 |
| Sierra Leone | 1961 | 5,336,000 |
| Singapore | 1965 | 4,680,600 |
| Solomon Islands | 1978 | 466,000 |
| South Africa | 1931 1994 | 47,208,000 |
| Sri Lanka | 1948 | 20,570,000 |
| Swaziland | 1968 | 1,034,000 |
| Tanzania | 1961 | 37,627,000 |
| Tonga | 1970 | 102,000 |
| Trinidad and Tobago | 1962 | 1,301,000 |
| Tuvalu | 1978 | 10,000 |
| Uganda | 1962 | 25,827,000 |
| United Kingdom | 1931 | 60,609,155 |
| Vanuatu | 1980 | 207,000 |
| Zambia | 1964 | 11,479,000 |
| **Total** | | **1,921,974,000** |

The Commonwealth's main purpose is to foster cross-cultural understanding and collaboration between some of the world's developed economies and the large number of developing nations that are also members. The broad policy areas over which it seeks to reach consensual agreement are:

- democracy;
- economics;
- education;
- gender;
- governance;
- human rights;
- law;
- treatment of small states;
- sport;
- sustainability;
- youth.

In addition, in 1971 the Commonwealth formally committed itself to upholding the following list of core values, by signing the Singapore Declaration, which was further cemented in 1991 with the drafting of the Harare Declaration:

- world peace and support for United Nations;
- individual liberty and egalitarianism;
- opposition to racism;
- opposition to colonialism;
- eradication of poverty, ignorance, disease, and economic inequality;
- free trade;
- institutional cooperation;
- multilateralism;
- rejection of international coercion.

While the Queen remains head of the Commonwealth, she is now head of state of only 16 of its member states (known as the 'Commonwealth realms'): Antigua and Barbuda; Australia; the Bahamas; Barbados; Belize; Canada; Grenada; Jamaica; New Zealand; Papua New Guinea; Saint Kitts and Nevis; Saint Lucia; Saint Vincent and the Grenadines; the Solomon Islands; Tuvalu; and the UK itself. Australia narrowly voted to retain her as head of state in a *referendum* in 1999.

There have been significant ructions in the Commonwealth in recent times. South Africa rejoined in 1994 after a 33-year absence following the election as president of Nelson Mandela. In contrast, Pakistan was temporarily expelled in 1999, following the military coup of then President Musharaf. Zimbabwe, meanwhile, withdrew voluntarily after previously being suspended in light of President Robert Mugabe's dubious human rights record.

Like most other supranational organizations, the Commonwealth has its own governing and administrative institutions, as listed in the table entitled 'Commonwealth institutions and their functions', to be found on the Online Resource Centre that accompanies this book.

## The British Council

The British Council is a registered charity that receives core grant aid from the FCO, but earns half of its total income from teaching English, running British exams, and managing training and development contracts. It is the UK's main agency for maintaining cordial, mutually beneficial cultural relations with other nations and, to aid it in this role, it has some 254 offices and teaching centres in 110-plus countries.

Among the technological, scientific, and artistic initiatives sponsored by the British Council is the UK's entry to the Venice Biennale, which showcases the work of a leading contemporary visual artist every two years. In recent years Britain has been represented by such 'Brit Art' luminaries as Chris Ofili,

Gilbert and George, and Tracey Emin. The British Council supports student exchange programmes between the UK and numerous other nations through its Central Bureau for Educational Visits and Exchanges.

Although generally perceived as a benign organization, the British Council has encountered notable diplomatic difficulties in recent times. Since 1994 it has operated in Russia under an interim intergovernmental agreement focusing on the fields of education, science, and culture. But the cordial relations between the charity and the Russian authorities were abruptly cooled when, in May 2007, the British government demanded the extradition by Russia of Andrei Lugovi. Mr Lugovi had been identified as the prime suspect in the murder of Alexander Litvinenko, a former lieutenant-colonel in the Russian Federal Security Service who was poisoned with the radioactive chemical polonium-210 while staying in London in November 2006.

Having already closed all of its branches in Russia, other than in Moscow, St Petersburg, and Ekaterinburg, the British Council was ordered to shut up shop everywhere except the capital in December 2007. Justifying its actions, the Russian Foreign Ministry alleged the Council was 'operating illegally' and had 'violated tax regulations, among other laws'.

## ☰ Topical feature idea

The number of British troop deaths in Afghanistan topped 300 in June 2010—with more than 100 killed in 2009 alone. News of the grim watershed came amid growing rumblings of unease among military 'top brass' and backbench MPs about the prospect for any clear-cut military 'victory', and calls from Afghan President Hamid Karzai for formal peace talks to be opened with the Taliban. How many British troops with links to your area have been killed or injured in Afghanistan? What do they, their friends and families, and local politicians feel about Britain's continued military presence in the country?

## ✳ Current issues

- **Funding of Ministry of Defence:** with Britain still involved in overseas conflicts and the death toll among troops continuing to mount, all three main parties entered the May 2010 election promising to ring-fence defence spending from budget cuts. However, several commentators have questioned the wisdom of protecting any single ministry from cuts, and some, such as *The Guardian* columnist Simon Jenkins, have called for its budget to be axed entirely—arguing it is unnecessary in a post-Cold War age.

- **Prioritizing overseas aid spending:** the Department for International Development is also having much of its budget ring-fenced, but in June 2010 International Development Secretary Andrew Mitchell warned the World Bank, United Nations, and 28 other bodies through which £3bn a year of UK aid funding is channelled that to continue qualifying for it they needed to provide proof of value for money.

■ **Future of global financial regulation under G20:** at the height of the 2008–09 global financial crisis, the G20 leaders agreed in principle to establish several new international regulatory institutions and move towards tougher rules about bank lending. However, recent summits have seen finance ministers from the world's 20 biggest economies shy away from introducing any new cross-border taxes, and firm reforms of global banking regulation remain to be implemented.

## ? Review questions

1. What are the main government departments responsible for overseeing Britain's participation in international affairs? Which is most significant?

2. Outline the founding principles of the UN, and the specific roles and responsibilities of its main institutions. How true would it be to say that the UN is in the pocket of the USA?

3. Outline the founding principles of NATO, and the roles and responsibilities of its main institutions. How has NATO adapted in the post-Cold War era?

4. What are the main supranational bodies responsible for overseeing the global economy and promoting free trade? Which are most influential?

5. What are the modern-day roles of the Commonwealth and the British Council?

## → Further reading

Brown, C. and Ainley, K. (2005) *Understanding International Relations*, London: Palgrave Macmillan. **Useful introduction to international relations and diplomacy.**

Evans. G. and Newnham, R. (1998) *The Penguin Dictionary of International Relations*, London: Penguin. **Indispensable A–Z of international relations jargon, covering terms ranging from 'ambassador' to 'weapons of mass destruction.'**

Jackson, R. and Sorensen, G. (2003) *An Introduction to International Relations: Theories and Approaches*, Oxford: Oxford University Press. **Succinct introduction to the main political theories surrounding international relations.**

Young, J. and Kent, J. (2003) *International Relations Since 1945: A Global History*, Oxford: Oxford University Press. **Concise single-volume analysis of international relations during and since the Cold War, including an overview of topics ranging from conflict in the Middle East to the evolution of the European Union.**

## @ Online Resource Centre

www.oxfordtextbooks.co.uk/orc/Morrison2e/
Visit the Online Resource Centre that accompanies this book for web links and regular updates.

# 11

# Origins and structure of local government

The history of government in Britain can be rationalized into two phases: the gradual unification of the UK beneath first a single monarch and then a centralized Parliament, and the more recent trend towards handing back much of the sovereign power accrued by the centre to regional and local administrations.

When the process of nation-building first began in the UK, competing kings vied with each other to extend their realms to encompass first England, then Wales, Scotland, and, in due course, Ireland. Ironically, by the time these countries were formally consolidated into a single UK, in the 1707 Acts of Union (see p. 10), the monarchy's power was already waning and it was not long either before Parliament would begin ceding a significant amount of self-rule to 'the provinces'.

That said, the evolution of local government in Britain has been as much a bottom-up as a top-down process. Medieval monarchs had a vested interest in appointing locally based courts and creating titled landowners to maintain loyalty and public order among their subjects. Conversely, pressure for jurisdiction over issues as diverse as public health, road maintenance, and refuse collection to be handed to locally based individuals, guilds, and, in due course, elected councils came from the artisans and merchants whose trade and enterprise fostered the emergence of the first towns. Their motive was self-interest: without adequate sanitation, water supplies, and housing, they would have no peasants to till the land or textile workers to spin their yarn; devoid of well-kept highways, they would have no trade routes through which to export their wares to ports and markets; without local law courts to assert their ownership rights, guarding them against theft and robbery, they would have no protection for their property or wealth. Over time, these early moves towards local government were to become increasingly sophisticated and multifaceted. Today there are 433 UK local authorities—353 in England, 22 in Wales, and 32 in Scotland. At time of writing, Northern Ireland's tally was expected to be cut from 26 to 11, but it was unclear whether this would take place in 2011, as originally planned, or be delayed until 2015.

What follows is the story of how Britain's highly developed local government framework came about.

## The first 'British' local authorities

Long before the emergence of anything that could be described as a 'council'—the term by which we refer to local authorities today—it suited those in power at the top of British society to maintain a rudimentary 'local government'. Even the absolutist monarchs of the early medieval period promoted this—if only to maintain a stable administration of land ownership, to collect taxes to fund wars and public building works (and food surpluses and tributes to sustain their luxury lifestyles), and to prevent anarchy at grass-roots level by upholding the ***rule of law*** (see p. 6). To this end the Saxon kings set up 'shire courts' across the countryside—local bodies with executive, legislative, and judicial powers rolled into one—and their Norman successors established a feudal system based on this, with vassals (peasants) kept in check by lords of the manor who, in time, became the squires of the seventeenth, eighteenth, and nineteenth centuries. By the twelfth century, demographic changes had led to the emergence of the first true towns, as the population began to cluster around the newly flourishing markets and ports. With urbanization taking root, the individuals and groups whose activities provided the bedrock of their local economies—artisans, merchants, and guilds—began to see the virtue of establishing a strengthened form of local autonomy to protect their rights to land, property, and free-flowing trade routes. Their pleas were rewarded with the granting of the first 'letters patent' and 'Royal Charters'—special privileges, approved on the advice of the ***Privy Council***, conferring the status of an 'incorporated body' (a self-governing entity) on first cities, then 'municipal boroughs' (smaller towns recognized as having legitimate claims to run their own affairs on a commercial and legal basis). These areas were run by nominally elected 'municipal corporations'.

Both cities and boroughs continue to exist to this day, albeit largely in name, as their powers have been brought in line with those of other forms of local council. In rural areas, however, the shire courts were more short-lived. Struggling to maintain the same degree of order over local subjects as their urban equivalents—notably in the aftermath of the Black Death, which killed up to 60 per cent of the British population in the 1340s—they were eventually replaced by a new, solidified local regime: the Justices of the Peace (JPs). Unlike the shire courts, JPs' authority arose out of Acts of Parliament rather than common law and, over time, they were assisted in their work by their local 'parishes'. These bodies—comprising representatives of the local community elected by their propertied peers—were a form of embryonic local government structure based initially around ecclesiastical parish boundaries, but they ultimately evolved into the civil parish council structure that remains in place, in diluted form, today. This is further discussed later in this chapter.

## The emergence of the modern idea of local authorities

It was in the early nineteenth century, at the height of the Industrial Revolution, that a combination of commercial, political, and simple logistical pressures combined to foster the emergence of the first true local authorities.

By the close of the eighteenth century, there were some 800 boroughs, most governed by a local major (*mayor*) and council. Unlike today's elected mayors and councillors who theoretically can hail from any background, class, or occupation, these were elected exclusively from among the wealthiest local merchants, industrialists, and landowners. The electorate (to the extent there was one) was limited to other equally moneyed individuals and a handful of marginally less affluent tradesmen. Such public services as were performed—street lighting and road maintenance, for example—tended to be done largely to make conditions better for commerce.

No new charters were granted in the eighteenth century, so major emerging industrial towns and cities like Manchester and Birmingham had to make do with more limited autonomy, in the form of 'improvement commissioners' approved by Parliament. In rural areas, meanwhile, the by-then-established JP/parish combination continued to hold sway. JPs and parish councils met four times a year in so-called 'quarter sessions', which tended to take place in public houses. They collected 'rates'—a form of local taxation based on the 'rateable' (or rental) value of land and property, which continued in one form or another until the late twentieth century—from local households to pay for the following core officials:

- parish constables;
- surveyors of the highways;
- overseers of the poor.

The origins of today's local government system lie in the key Acts listed in Table 11.1.

By 1894 the following five types of local authority—which have continued in more or less the same form for the best part of eighty years—were established outside London:

- county councils;
- county **borough councils**;
- municipal borough councils;
- urban district councils;
- rural district councils.

**Table 11.1** A chronology of the main Acts instrumental in the emergence of local government

| Act | Effect |
| --- | --- |
| Great Reform Act 1832 | Extended the right to vote in parliamentary elections to all 'ten-pound households' (those with property worth £10 or more). Abolished the majority of the 'rotten boroughs' (see p. 114). |
| Municipal Corporations Act 1835 | Abolished the pre-existing government structure in urban areas, reforming constitutions of existing municipal boroughs to standardize their election methods and modus operandi. Extended the right to vote in municipal elections to *all* local ratepayers—regardless of the value of their properties—to prevent the corporations that ran them becoming self-perpetuating oligarchies. Some 178 boroughs were reformed this way, with a further 62 towns incorporated under the Act, after petitioning the Crown for borough status. |
| Public Health Acts 1848, 1872, and 1875 | First of these reforms prompted by the sweeping cholera epidemics of the 1840s. Under it, central government began allocating more money to local areas for building houses and improving sanitation (domestic hygiene and sewage disposal) to combat the spread of disease. Two new forms of local authority emerged, responsible for promoting sanitation in towns and country areas respectively: *urban sanitary districts* and *rural sanitary districts*. They were administered in towns by boroughs, new local boards of health, and improvement commissioners, and in rural areas by voluntary Poor Law unions (charities often run with Church involvement). |
| Local Government Act 1888 | Set up a more formal system of county councils to assume roles previously undertaken by Justices of the Peace (JPs) in quarter sessions. County (rural) areas with populations of more than 50,000 given county borough status, meaning they could continue running their own affairs, retaining the privileges granted to the extant municipal boroughs. Other rural areas renamed county councils. Some towns with smaller populations, such as Worthing in West Sussex, granted municipal borough status, giving them the same powers of self-government as larger towns. |
| Local Government Act 1894 | Renamed the sanitary districts in towns and country areas not yet granted borough status by the Crown urban and rural district councils (forerunners of today's district councils). |

# ▌ The rolling reorganization of local government

Since the 1970s there have been four significant reorganizations of local government:

- the 1974 introduction of the *two-tier structure* in England and Wales;
- the 1986 abolition of metropolitan counties in major urban areas;
- the 1990s phased introduction of unitary authorities;
- the gradual introduction of *directly elected mayors* in major towns and cities.

The following section examines each of these developments in more detail.

Because the evolution of local government in both London and Scotland followed different trajectories from the rest of the UK, they will be looked at separately.

## The 1974 reorganization

Perhaps the largest-scale restructure of the local authority framework in England and Wales (excluding London), the '1974 reorganization' has its origins in the conclusions of a Royal Commission on Local Government set up in 1965 by Richard Crossman, then Minister for Housing in Harold Wilson's Labour government.

When it reported in 1969 the Commission (chaired by Lord Redcliffe-Maude) recommended the 1,000 existing local authorities should be replaced by a rationalized system of 61 'local authority areas', of which 58 would be 'all-purpose authorities'. These would effectively be unitary authorities (see pp. 326–8), taking responsibility for all areas of local service provision—from sanitary issues and waste collection to education and transport—while conurbations (major urban centres where two or more towns and cities had merged to form single built-up areas), like Manchester and Birmingham, would have their own two-tier *metropolitan* authorities, in recognition of their larger populations and community needs.

Labour lost the 1970 general election and the Commission's recommendations were deemed too revolutionary by Ted Heath's incoming Conservative administration. In the event it was not until John Major's tenure as prime minister in the 1990s that unitary authorities finally began appearing.

Despite his reluctance to adopt many of the Redcliffe-Maude proposals, Heath's government recognized the need for reform. It instituted this in the guise of the Local Government Act 1972, which took effect in 1974 and introduced:

- a two-tier structure of county councils and district councils, which remained more or less intact until the mid-1990s and still exists in some areas today. Many of the new districts applied for Royal Charters subsequently, entitling them to call themselves 'borough councils' or **city councils** (like the boroughs and cities of old). This move led to the amalgamation of some district and county councils, reducing the overall number of local authorities to 39 counties and 296 districts in England, with an 8:37 split in Wales;

- an alternative two-tier 'metropolitan county' local authority structure in six pilot areas, covering these conurbations—the West Midlands, Merseyside, Greater Manchester, West Yorkshire, South Yorkshire, and Tyne and Wear. A breakdown of the towns and cities encompassed by each is contained in the table entitled 'The composition of metropolitan county/borough areas', to be found on the Online Resource Centre accompanying this book. This saw each conurbation split for administrative purposes into several 'metropolitan borough councils', each taking charge of financing and running most day-to-day local services—for example, rubbish collection, housing, and environmental health. The conurbations would each be overseen by a single 'metropolitan county council', in charge of services affecting the area as a whole, such as strategic town and country planning, main roads linking neighbouring towns, public transport, emergency services, and civil protection.

The new two-tier structure saw the end of long-standing counties like Cumberland, Westmorland, and the three different parts of Lincolnshire, and the introduction of new ones like Avon, Cleveland, Cumbria, Humberside, Clwyd, Dyfed, and Gwent. Some of these were never wholly accepted by local people and have subsequently vanished (Avon was merged with neighbouring Somerset as part of the post-1992 unitary authority settlement). The reorganization also saw certain cities stripped of their pre-existent 'municipal borough' status. These included Nottingham, Bristol, Leicester, and Norwich—although by way of compensation they were allowed to retain their city status, not to mention 'lord mayors' (senior officials who perform ceremonial duties and in other towns are called simply 'mayors').

Under the rationalized two-tier structure, district councils, borough councils (districts with a historic Royal Charter status), and the new metropolitan borough councils were equivalent to each other, and as such were each given the same responsibilities—largely providing the most localized, 'door-to-door', services such as rubbish collection. Likewise, county councils and metropolitan county councils became responsible for providing countywide services, with social care and education being the biggest spending areas. A full breakdown of the responsibilities of the current types of local authority is outlined in Table 11.2. A list of the central government departments at Whitehall responsible for overseeing each local authority service area is given in Table 11.3.

Northern Ireland's local government reorganization took a different form and happened at a different pace. In 1973 26 district councils emerged, but many functions were transferred from local to central government at Westminster. The number of councils in the province was due to be reduced to 11 in 2011 following a recent wide-ranging review of public administration (RPA).

## The 1986 reorganization

The Tory Party's 1983 election manifesto described the six metropolitan county councils it inherited on regaining power in 1979—alongside the then Greater London Council (GLC), under the leadership of Ken Livingstone—as a 'wasteful and unnecessary tier of government'. It promised to abolish them and return their functions to the second-tier metropolitan borough councils (or, as they were redesignated in law, 'metropolitan district councils') that still existed 'beneath' them.

**Table 11.2** A breakdown of council services offered by different types of local authority

| District councils, borough councils, metropolitan borough councils, and unitary authorities | County councils and unitary authorities |
|---|---|
| Environmental health (sanitation, drainage, pollution, food hygiene) | Education (schools and *further education*) |
| Development control (**planning permission**) | Social services (care for elderly, mentally ill, and vulnerable children) |
| Housing and the homeless | Highways (road-building and maintenance, and on-street parking) |
| Refuse collection (now incorporating recycled waste) | Refuse disposal (landfill sites) |
| Car parks | Emergency planning |
| *Council Tax* and *uniform business rate (UBR)* collection | Cultural and leisure services (libraries, museums, sports centres) |
| Local strategic planning | County-wide strategic planning |
| Licensing | Passenger transport (buses, trams) |

**Table 11.3** Links between local authority service areas and Whitehall departments

| Service area | Department responsible |
|---|---|
| Antisocial behaviour | Home Office; Department for Communities and Local Government (DCLG) |
| Car parks | Department for Transport (DfT) |
| Children's services (schools, child protection) | Department for Education; Department of Health (DH); DCLG |
| Council Tax and *uniform business rates (UBR)* collection | DCLG; HM Treasury |
| Cultural and leisure services | Department of Culture, Media, and Sport (DCMS) |
| Education (further education) | Department for Business, Innovation, and Skills (BIS) |
| Emergency planning | Department for the Environment, Food, and Rural Affairs (Defra) |
| Environmental health (sanitation, drainage, pollution, food hygiene, waste management) | Defra; Home Office; Ministry of Defence (MoD) |
| Highways (road-building and maintenance) | DfT |
| Housing and the homeless | DCLG |
| Licensing | DCMS |
| Passenger transport (buses, trams) | DfT |
| Police | Home Office |
| Social services (care for the elderly, mentally ill, and vulnerable children) | DH |
| Town and country planning | Defra |

To this end it passed the Local Government Act 1985, which, as well as establishing metropolitan boroughs, set up new *police authorities*. Tyne and Wear was unusual, in that its police provision fell under the Northumbria Police Authority. Metropolitan areas also gained their own fire and civil defence authorities and passenger transport authorities, and some acquired joint boards responsible for handling their waste disposal services. This happened in Merseyside and Greater Manchester (except Wigan), although in the West Midlands, for example, joint arrangements between neighbouring boroughs were established on an ad hoc and purely voluntary basis. In other areas, in contrast, the commissioning and/or running of public transport services and waste disposal services continued to fall under the auspices of county councils.

Other than the introduction of these new, service-specific types of local authority, in all other respects the effect of the 1986 changes was to replace the pre-existing metropolitan two-tier structure with what were effectively the first unitary authorities—all-purpose councils responsible for fulfilling the roles split in other areas between districts/boroughs and counties. Opponents of the move saw in it a clear attempt by the Conservatives to diminish the authority of metropolitan councils by reducing them to lower-level, more localized administrations on the one hand and hiving off responsibilities formerly overseen by the scrapped metropolitan counties to new bodies with clearly defined and limited scope on the other. Mr Livingstone and other left-wing council leaders, including Sheffield City Council and South Yorkshire County Council's David Blunkett (a future Labour Home Secretary), saw the diluted powers as an assault on their socialist policies by a right-wing government fearful of major populated areas becoming 'states within states'. Referring to this notion explicitly at one point in the late 1980s, Sir Cyril Irvine Patnick, Tory MP for Sheffield Hallam, famously described Mr Blunkett's domain as 'the People's Republic of South Yorkshire'.

## The 1990s introduction of unitary authorities

The most significant restructuring of local authorities since the 1974 reorganization began in 1992, with the start of a process of phased change designed to rationalize local government across much of England and Wales. The aim of introducing a **unitary structure** was to improve the efficiency and transparency of local administration by reducing service duplication, slashing bureaucracy, and establishing a simplified, uniform council structure across the country. Unitary authorities, which to date number 55 in England, 32 in Scotland, and 22 in Wales, are defined in law as being '*any authority which is the sole principal council for its local government area*'.

Despite the bold claims made in favour of the new unitary system, critics argue it has only added to the confusion, by ushering in a patchwork landscape of local government, with unitary authorities in many areas sitting directly alongside councils that have retained the existing two-tier structure. Counties in which both unitary and two-tier authorities coexist are described as having a **hybrid structure**. Examples include Lincolnshire, where Lincoln City Council (a unitary authority) sits beside Lincolnshire County Council and borough/ district councils in nearby towns such as Grantham and Gainsborough. In East Sussex, Brighton and Hove Council is a unitary authority, while down the road Lewes District Council and Eastbourne Borough Council retain the classic borough/district responsibilities, with East Sussex County Council providing 'county-wide' services. The chronology of the phased introduction of unitary authorities followed is outlined in Table 11.4.

**Table 11.4** Chronology of the phased introduction of unitary authorities

| Year | Phase |
| --- | --- |
| 1992 | Local Government Act replaced English Boundary Commission with new Local Government Commission for England under chairmanship of Sir John Banham and answerable to government. In Wales, process was overseen instead by Welsh Secretary, leading to some discord, as existing system there swiftly replaced by framework of 37 new district councils and 22 unitary authorities. |
| 1994 (December) | First of several periodic reviews of local authorities coinciding with an initial tranche of conversions to unitary status. 'Big Bang' approach à la 1974 avoided in favour of gradual reorganization. Subsequent reviews due every 16 months. The phased approach took some surprising turns—when detailed guidelines were formulated, it emerged the government was not going to stipulate that each unitary authority area should cover a minimum or maximum population size. This marked major departure from previous reviews, although in practice only one council emerged to govern an area of fewer than 100,000 inhabitants: Rutland, with a population of only 33,700. Tensions soon emerged between rural areas and urban areas, with former accusing ministers of elevating the latter in importance by granting them unitary status. Rival publicity campaigns launched by the Association of District Councils (ADC) and the Association of County Councils (ACC). |
| 1995 (1 April) | Following detailed area-by-area reviews, four maiden unitary authorities emerged: the Isle of Wight and one for each of Avon, Cleveland, and Humberside (the so-called 'unpopular' or 'unofficial' counties created in 1974). |
|  | In the following counties, the Commission initially recommended no change: Cornwall; Cumbria; Hertfordshire; Lincolnshire; Northumberland; Oxfordshire; Suffolk; Surrey; Warwickshire; West Sussex. |
| 1995 (July) | New Commission chairman Sir David Cooksey replaced Sir John Banham, following his resignation. This led to 21 district councils being reviewed with a view potentially to becoming unitary authorities. Sir David's inquiry focused on preserving the 'stability, viability, and identity' of these areas. |
| 1995 (September) | New-look Commission produced its first set of recommendations: the creation of ten new unitaries, eight from existing districts and two, in the 'Thames Gateway', from the merger of two districts each. |
| 2009 (1 April) | Counties of Cornwall and Northumberland became unitary authorities after all, alongside fellow newcomers Wiltshire, Shropshire, and County Durham, as a total of 44 district/borough and county councils made way for just nine unitaries. Two of the abolished authorities, Congleton Borough Council, Cheshire, and Shrewsbury and Atcham Borough Council, Shropshire, had previously mounted unsuccessful legal challenges to the reforms. |

In addition to hybrid counties, the unitary authority system has produced other quirks. A growing number of unitary authorities encompass entire counties—notably the Isle of Wight, Rutland, County Durham, and Cornwall. The Isles of Scilly, meanwhile, have a unique form of council that, although not officially designated as such, is a *sui generis* ('in a class of their own') form of unitary authority.

# ▌ City councils and the meaning of city status

Between Henry VIII's reign and the end of the nineteenth century cities were generally synonymous with ecclesiastical seats of power and, more specifically, the presence of Church of England cathedrals and diocesan bishops. But even in the Tudor period this was not always the case: in practice city status could be conferred by the sovereign through letters patent (a legal instrument issued by a monarch), the granting of a town's Royal Charter, or even, over time, accepted custom and practice.

In the nineteenth century the Church of England actively sought to increase the number of its urban dioceses, creating more cities in the process. These included Ripon, Liverpool, St Albans, and Britain's most south-western city, Truro. But not all towns designated as cities had prior royal borough status: Ely, for example, was a humble urban district when recognized as a city. In addition, by the close of the nineteenth century cities had begun to spring up in places that did not have cathedrals—for example, Birmingham, which successfully petitioned Queen Victoria in 1889 on the basis of its large population and history of effective local government under its charismatic Liberal mayor, Joseph Chamberlain. It was around this time that Scotland gained its first cities by letters patent and Royal Charter—prior to 1889, major medieval towns such as Edinburgh and Perth were often referred to by the term 'civitas' and, although the word 'city' had been coined for them by the eighteenth century, their status remained unofficial.

Today, city status is no longer dependent on the presence of a cathedral, or any significant ecclesiastical influence. Neither are cities always major population centres: with a mere 2,000 inhabitants, Britain's smallest city, St David's in Pembrokeshire, has a population significantly smaller than most towns.

For most of the twentieth century it was the Home Secretary's job to advise the monarch on which towns should be made into cities. This happened to Lancaster in 1937, Swansea in 1969 (marking the investiture of the Prince of Wales), and Sunderland in 1992 (to mark the 40th anniversary of the Queen's accession to the throne). More recently, however, the rules have been bent somewhat. In December 2000 three new cities were created, in the form of Brighton and Hove, Wolverhampton, and Inverness, as part of a 'Millennium City' competition launched by the Labour government. The Queen created a further five in 2002 to mark her Golden Jubilee—Stirling, Preston, Newport, Lisburn and Newry—bringing the overall number of cities in the UK today to 66.

Just as the criteria used to determine whether a town qualifies for city status are nebulous, so, too, is the degree to which becoming a city has any tangible effect. A city council—the moniker adopted by local authorities with an official city designation—is not a type of council or administration in itself; rather, the term is really no more than an honorary title. In terms of their functions, city councils are actually other, standard types of local authority in all but name. Some operate as unitary authorities (Brighton and Hove, York, and Stoke-on-Trent); others are metropolitan boroughs or districts (Birmingham, Wolverhampton). Most, however, remain district or borough councils in a two-tier structure.

Confusingly, seven English cities—Chichester, Ely, Hereford, Lichfield, Ripon, Truro, and Wells—are actually no more than civil parishes, in terms of their administrative status. This means that they technically fall within the remit of parish councils—the lowest tier of local government (see the next section). Even more confusingly, while the term 'city council' is used to denote the parish council in some of these places (Chichester and Hereford), in others (Truro and Ely) this is the title used by the principal service-providing local authority. In addition to these unconventional examples, in two English cities (Bath and Salisbury) city status is the preserve of so-called 'charter trustees'—an arcane form of local administration intended to be a temporary stopgap for towns the borough status of which has been removed by the Crown prior to the formation of a parish council. Meanwhile, in two Welsh cities (Bangor and St David's) city status is possessed by local community councils (the equivalent of parish councils in Wales and Scotland).

A full rundown of designated cities, together with details of the type of local authority to which the designation applies in each place, is listed in the table entitled 'Local authorities with city status and the types of council in each case', to be found on the Online Resource Centre accompanying this book.

# Parish councils, town councils, and community councils

The lowest tier of local government is represented by elected parish councils in England and community councils in Wales and Scotland. Civil parish councils—not to be confused with the pre-existing *ecclesiastical* parishes established by the Church—were set up under the Local Government Act 1894 to oversee social welfare and basic civic duties in villages and small towns and act as the collective 'voices' of their local communities. Historically, some parish and community councils in larger villagers and small towns have called themselves town councils. Those that do so tend to have their own town mayors—not to be confused with the more official (if also largely ceremonial) mayors of borough and city councils, or the directly elected mayors now found in some towns and cities (see pp. 396–8). Councillors take turns to spend a year as mayor, on rotation, with a formal 'mayor-making ceremony' often held in the town hall to mark the handover from one to another. The role of mayor is largely ceremonial (opening church fetes, switching on Christmas lights), although he or she also tends to chair full council meetings during his or her year in office.

Under the 1972 Act all parishes with more than 150 inhabitants were compelled to have their own parish council—a stipulation that has significantly increased their number. Those with smaller populations are only required to hold **parish meetings**—regular gatherings open to all local registered electors. Unlike the meetings that might be held in towns and villages with formal parish councils, those convened in lesser populated parishes have statutory powers to act as de facto parish councils. In such circumstances a clerk and chairman are elected to preside over business.

Today, many of the limited day-to-day powers once exercised by parish, community, and town councils are wielded by higher-level local authorities: county and district/borough councils or unitary authorities. But parish councils are still allocated budgets by those authorities—dubbed 'parish precepts'—which, unlike revenue raised by higher level councils, cannot be capped by central government (see pp. 363–4). Therefore, in areas in which parish councils are more proactive, parish precepts can be high: Thurston Parish Council in Suffolk, for example, put its share of the Council Tax up by 214 per cent in 2008–09. In most areas, however, the precept is usually only sufficient to finance its rent of the town council buildings in which it holds its monthly meetings, and minor local improvements such as replacement street lights, park benches, or new goalposts for the village football pitch.

Parish councils do, however, play a significant advisory role. For example, they have a statutory right to be consulted formally by, and represented on, public inquiries into major planning applications affecting their localities. In fact, often the first time a reporter—and, by extension, his or her news organization—will hear of a potentially controversial planning proposal or other council-related issue will be by attending a meeting at which it is thrashed out by his or her local parish council. And far from being mere talking shops, in truth there has been something of a resurgence in the importance of parish councils in recent years. Labour experimented with new models of service delivery, involving partnerships between neighbouring authorities and delegation of certain responsibilities to voluntary and lower level statutory bodies, including parish councils.

The two most influential partnership initiatives are as follows:

- local area management (LAM);
- **quality parish councils**.

## Local area management (LAM)

LAM refers to the promotion of 'joined-up' service delivery and shared 'best practice' between neighbouring local authorities, including parish, community, and town councils. Some parish, town, and community councils have joined forces with their local district/borough, county, or unitary authorities in recent years to form 'local strategic partnerships' (LSPs) or 'local area partnerships' (LAPs). These are semi-formal alliances designed to streamline services within individual local authority boundaries by drawing together public, private, and voluntary sector organizations to pool their resources, reduce their collective costs, and improve efficiency. LSPs are set up under the terms of local area agreements (LAAs), approved by the Department for Communities and Local Government (DCLG). At time of writing, LSPs, LAPs and other forms of collaboration between local authorities looked to be more necessary than ever, in light of the two-year Council Tax freeze (see p. 364) and multibillion-pound public spending cuts announced in George Osborne's June 2010 Budget. Their emphasis on collaboration between public, private, and voluntary ('third') sector partners also appeared well suited to the vision of bottom-up, community-run local services envisaged by David Cameron's 'Big Society'.

## Quality parish councils

Introduced by Labour in 2003, quality parish councils are parish, community, and town councils that have been granted 'quality' status in recognition of their efficiency in overseeing the limited local services they have up to now provided. Their 'reward' has been additional responsibilities (matched by variable rises in budget) commensurate with their efforts to:

- be representative of, and actively engage with, all parts of its community, providing vision, identity and a sense of belonging;
- be effectively and properly managed;
- articulate the needs and wishes of its community;
- uphold high standards of conduct;
- be committed to work in partnership with principal local authorities and other public service agencies;
- deliver, in proportion to its size and skills, deliver services on behalf of principal local authorities when this represents the best deal for the local community;

- work closely with voluntary groups in its community;
- provide leadership to the community through its work on parish plans;
- act with their partners as an information point for local services.

In practice, quality parish councils have, as a bare minimum, played a greater role than previously in organizing community-based activities, such as youth activities, childcare, home support, and transport for the elderly and disabled. More proactive ones have gone further, by taking over responsibility for delivering on the ground many of the services funded by their principal local authority, or authorities, such as libraries or buses. They are also expected to draw up and publish a parish plan, outlining medium and long-term proposals for their areas.

# ▌ The evolution of local government in London

London's autonomy has always been exercised in a distinct way from the rest of Britain, although at times its local government structure has resembled that of the major English conurbations described earlier in this chapter. Today, London operates under a unique two-tier system, with responsibilities for service provision split between the *Greater London Authority (GLA)*, headed by the capital's elected mayor, and 33 second-tier councils (a system akin to the pre-1986 metropolitan county/borough structure abolished by Mrs Thatcher's government).

Of these 33 councils, 32 are London boroughs, elected in similar fashion to the metropolitan boroughs that still operate in the other conurbations, but the last is a unique entity run by an unreformed medieval-style City old boys' network. The City of London Corporation—officially, the 'Mayor and Commonalty and Citizens of the City of London'—is Britain's oldest surviving local authority. It covers the 'Square Mile' containing the capital's central commercial district and, although democratically accountable like other local authorities, has long attracted criticism for the anachronistic nature of its electoral processes and its peculiar customs.

The City of London was the only corporation to escape the axe when the Municipal Corporations Act 1835 abolished all others and it continues to be presided over by a non-partisan administration of a kind that prevailed more widely before the emergence of formal political parties (see Chapter 5). At its head is the Lord Mayor of London, his attendant aldermen, and a Court of Common Council, beneath which are a range of committees responsible for specific areas of local policy. Again uniquely, the City of London Corporation was allowed to retain a system of *non-residential voting* (often referred to as the 'business vote') following its abolition elsewhere in 1969. This concession was, in part, in recognition of its tiny resident population (some 9,000 at the time of the 2001 census). (A fuller explanation of the voting system used here and elsewhere in London is given in Chapter 14.)

Vocal critics of the corporation—which many see as a self-perpetuating, privileged cabal—include Labour *backbencher* John McDonnell (an unsuccessful candidate for the party's leadership following first Tony Blair's, then Gordon Brown's, resignations). In the debate over the City of London (Ward Elections) Act 2002, which significantly increased the size of the business franchise in the capital, he said of it:

❝ The corporation is a group of hangers-on, who create what is known as the best dining club in the City . . . a rotten borough. ❞

A timeline of the evolution of local government in London is presented in Table 11.5.

## Modern-day local government structure in London

As with *devolution* for Scotland, Wales, and Northern Ireland, Labour advocated the re-establishment of a single overarching local authority for London long before winning the 1997 election. The 1986 abolition of the Greater London Council (GLC), under its then leader Ken Livingstone, had been seen by some in the party as an act of war by the Conservative government. Others had viewed it as an error of judgement that needed redressing for more pragmatic reasons should their party regain power.

In its 1997 manifesto Labour pledged to introduce a new form of 'elected city government', topped by an EU-style elected mayor. A year after it regained power, the promised vote was held, and 72 per cent of London's electorate voted in favour of the proposed GLA. A year later the Greater London Authority Act 1999 formally paved the way for the establishment of the new authority and, with more than a hint of déjà vu, Mr Livingstone was duly elected London mayor in March 2000.

Mr Livingstone's return to power in the capital was hardly smooth. As had happened (with variable success) in Wales and Scotland, the Labour leadership attempted to parachute in a cherry-picked candidate, in defiance of his support among the party rank and file. But its official choice, former Health Secretary Frank Dobson, was no match for the former GLC leader, who resigned his parliamentary seat and the Labour *whip* to fight for the mayoralty as an independent. In the event, he returned to the party fold prior to his 2004 re-election, by which time Mr Blair had reluctantly endorsed him as Labour's prospective candidate.

Although the GLA has become a model for certain other towns and cities that have since adopted elected mayors (see Chapter 13), initially its method of conducting business was unique among British local authorities. In a manner akin to the way in which the US President shares power with that country's parliament (Congress), the London mayor is elected separately to the 25-strong London

**Table 11.5** Timeline of the evolution of local government in London

| From | Legislation | System |
|------|-------------|--------|
| 1835 | Municipal Corporations Act 1835 | The small, ancient, self-governing City of London remains unreformed by legislation covering the other major city corporations and does not expand into the growing metropolitan area surrounding it. The area now known as Greater London is administered by parishes and hundreds in the counties of Middlesex, Essex, Kent, Surrey, and Hertfordshire, with very little coordination between them. Special areas, such as the Liberty of Westminster, are exempt from county administration. In other areas, ad hoc single-purpose boards are set up. |
| 1855 | Metropolis Management Act 1855 | Metropolitan Board of Works created to provide the infrastructure needed in the area now known as Inner London. Its members are nominated by the vestries and boards. |
| 1889 | Local Government Act 1888 | County of London created from the area of responsibility of the Metropolitan Board of Works. A London County Council shares power with the boards and vestries. The City of London is outside its scope. Croydon and West Ham (and, later, East Ham) become county boroughs outside the County of London, but also outside the control of the newly formed Surrey and Essex county councils. |
| 1894 | Local Government Act 1894 | Rest of England, including area around 'County of London' and county boroughs (but not within it), divided into urban districts and rural districts. In Greater London area, they are consolidated over next seventy years into municipal boroughs and urban districts with no rural districts remaining. Many districts later become populous enough to apply for county boroughs status, but are rejected. Royal Commission on the Amalgamation of the City and County of London attempts, but fails, to facilitate the merger of the City and County of London. |
| 1900 | London Government Act 1899 | Metropolitan boroughs created within County of London, their functions shared with the London County Council. The existing vestries, boards, and liberties in the area are abolished. |
| 1965 | London Government Act 1963 | Enlarged Greater London replaces County of London, the county boroughs, and all local government districts within 12-mile radius. The mostly strategic Greater London Council shares power with 32 London boroughs and the City of London. |
| 1986 | Local Government Act 1985 | Greater London Council abolished and London boroughs work as unitary authorities with strategic functions organized by joint boards and **quangos**. Residual Inner London Education Authority remains for inner area, but is abolished during national reform of education. |
| 2000 | Greater London Authority Act 1999 | Regional Greater London Authority, consisting of Mayor of London and London Assembly, assumes strategic function, sharing power with London boroughs and City of London. |

Assembly with which he shares power over the GLA. As with the US president, it is the mayor's job to propose policy and set out a prospective annual budget to cover the cost of the services he or she proposes to provide in the coming financial year. The Assembly must then approve or amend these proposals, in the manner of Congress, and its committees and subcommittees (like their congressional equivalents) may scrutinize the mayor's actions in office and the performance of services provided by the GLA. The parallels between the London mayoral and US parliamentary systems have gone further in recent years, in light of changes to the political composition of both. Just as President George W. Bush (a Republican) was forced to share power in his last two years in the White House with a Democrat-dominated Congress, Mr Livingstone had to work with Conservatives following the 2004 elections (nine members to Labour's seven). With the election of Conservative Boris Johnson as his successor, alongside a largely unchanged allocation of seats on the Assembly, the capital reverted to a period of Tory hegemony in May 2008.

The GLA is the top tier of local government in London, with individual boroughs continuing to provide day-to-day services for Londoners. The division between GLA and borough roles is explained in Table 11.6; of the major roles fulfilled by the GLA, the majority are overseen by the agencies listed in Table 11.7.

**Table 11.6** Breakdown of local authority responsibilities in London

| Greater London Authority (GLA) | London boroughs |
| --- | --- |
| Transport | Schools and further education (FE) |
| Policing | Social services |
| Fire and rescue | Waste collection |
| Congestion charging | Highways repair and maintenance |
| Environmental policy | Libraries and local leisure and cultural services (museums, theatres) |
| Strategic development and planning | Development control |

**Table 11.7** Main agencies of the Greater London Authority (GLA)

| Agency | Responsibilities |
| --- | --- |
| Transport for London (TfL) | Manages most aspects of London's transport system, including public transport (London Underground, Docklands Light Railway, London Buses), main roads, and traffic management (incorporating the congestion charge zone) |
| Metropolitan Police Authority (MPA) | Oversees Metropolitan Police Service |
| London Fire and Emergency Planning Authority (LFEPA) | Administers London Fire Brigade and coordinates emergency planning |
| London Development Agency (LDA) | Responsible for strategic development planning across London, focusing on rejuvenation of deprived areas |

# ▌ Local government in Scotland

As with several other aspects of public affairs—notably its legal and education systems, the latter of which is explored in Chapter 15—Scotland has a different local government framework from the rest of Britain.

Until the 1974 reorganization, the country effectively had a single-tier form of local administration. The Local Government (Scotland) Act 1929 had replaced the pre-existing parish councils with a nationwide network of district councils with significantly increased autonomy and budgets. This structure—refined by the Local Government (Scotland) Act 1947—distinguished between smaller and larger 'burghs', which were a form of local unit derived from medieval administrative boundaries. The latter—burghs with populations greater than 20,000—were handed more power.

All this changed with the passage of the Local Government (Scotland) Act 1973, which ushered in a two-tier system along the lines of that implemented in England and Wales. The district councils remained—albeit with slightly refined borders and some variation in their levels of responsibility—but the first tier authorities introduced were named 'regional councils', as opposed to county councils. Three notable exceptions—the Western Isles, Shetland, and Orkney—were, however, effectively given unitary status even at this early stage, in recognition of their perceived homogeneity.

When Mr Major's government began its phased reorganization of local authorities in the early 1990s, Scotland was again treated as an exception. In a 'Big Bang' approach that ministers avoided elsewhere, unitary authorities were introduced across the country in one fell swoop. While rationalizing a patchwork system, this 'one-size-fits-all' strategy caused controversy in some areas—not least because of the wildly varying population sizes covered by individual councils. The unitary authority for Inverclyde (an area with relatively few inhabitants) followed the same boundaries as the extant district council, while that of Clackmannanshire embraced the whole of that county, and that of Highland a sprawling 30,650 km swathe of north-west Scotland, encompassing chunks of the former counties of Inverness-shire, Ross and Cromarty, Caithness and Nairnshire, as well as the whole of Sutherland.

Today, there are 32 'council areas' covered by unitary authorities in place across the country.

# ▌ Emergency services at the local level

While ambulance services are today part of the National Health Service (NHS) (see Chapter 6), with trust status akin to that accorded to hospitals, the other core emergency services are overseen by discrete forms of authority, as explained in the following section.

## Origins of the British police force

Until the early nineteenth century Britain had no countrywide police force. Instead local law and order fell to town magistrates to maintain, and before then, ad hoc arrangements had existed. Perhaps unsurprisingly, London was the first UK city to adopt its own police force. In 1749 the author Henry Fielding and his brother, Sir John, set up a group of semi-professional law enforcers known as 'The Bow Street Runners'. Operating out of Henry's house at 4 Bow Street, these early police officers wore civilian clothes and did not patrol the streets routinely like their modern-day equivalents. Rather, they acted to intercept criminals and bring them before the courts on the authority of local magistrates, who had become increasingly frustrated at their inability to prevent offenders absconding and enforce punishment without the help of an arresting force.

Shortly afterwards, an embryonic Thames Police was formed, partly based on the model established by the Fielding brothers. It was not until some eighty years later, however, when Sir Robert Peel was Home Secretary, that the first true constabulary was formed in the guise of the Metropolitan Police, based at Scotland Yard. Established in 1829 and variously dubbed the 'Bobbies' and the 'Peelers' after their founder, the 'Met' were funded by a local tax—'the police rate'—which citizens were obliged to pay in addition to the 'poor rate' (used to fund limited handouts for the poorest members of society and to finance workhouses). In due course similar innovations followed in the emerging borough council areas and the introduction of a new breed of county magistrates.

Today, the UK Police Service, although notionally a nationwide organization, is actually divided into 43 local forces in England and Wales, and a further eight in Scotland. Northern Ireland has its own dedicated police force, dubbed the Police Service of Northern Ireland, which replaced the erstwhile Royal Ulster Constabulary (RUC) in November 2001. Most forces in England, Scotland, and Wales have historically respected county boundaries, although there have long been some exceptions: a single force, Sussex Police, covers the two counties of East and West Sussex, while the south-westernmost force is Devon and Cornwall Police. In 2006, then Home Secretary Charles Clarke proposed merging a number of forces (among them the five existing East Midlands forces, which would be turned into a single 'super-force'), bringing down the total number in England and Wales to just 24, in an effort to streamline the Service and better equip the country to fight terrorism. His plans—heavily criticized by both the Police Federation (the union representing police officers) and the Association of Chief Police Officers (ACPO)—were shelved by his successor, John Reid, later that year, although a *White Paper* published in December 2009 signalled the then Labour administration's determination to cut £500m from the police budget by 2014 by, among other things, encouraging them to collaborate in areas such as forensics and procurement (recruitment, commissioning, and investment). More recently, individual police forces in certain regions have voluntarily entered into negotiations about possible mergers. At time of writing, talks were ongoing between the Durham and Northumbria forces.

### The role and powers of local police authorities

Other than in London, where the Metropolitan Police Authority was handed executive control over the Met by ministers in the Greater London Authority Act 1999, UK police forces all come under the overarching control of the Home Secretary (or, in Scotland, the Deputy First Minister). Until 1995 forces were regulated by police committees that were answerable to their local county councils or unitary authorities, but the advent of the Police and Magistrates' Court Act 1994 saw these replaced by a new second tier: the police authority. The change, consolidated by the Police Act 1996, has reduced the involvement of councillors from relevant local authorities in favour of a mixed membership intended to represent local residents and the business community better.

Police committees were made up entirely of officials—usually two-thirds councillors and one-third magistrates. The typical composition of a modern police authority is outlined in Table 11.8.

Police authorities raise their revenue by levying precepts (annual budget requests) on their local **billing authorities**, which are then included explicitly in local Council Tax bills (see Chapter 12).

Their responsibilities are to:

- maintain an effective and efficient force for their areas—and if they fail, the Home Secretary and/or Home Office Inspectorate have powers to 'act in default';

- publish an annual policing performance plan, in consultation with the *chief constable;*

**Table 11.8** Typical composition of a local policy authority

| Members | How chosen |
|---|---|
| *Nine* councillors | Appointed from councils covered by police authority area, including county and metropolitan borough councils, and unitary authorities. Where there is more than one relevant local authority, appointments made by special joint selection committee on which each one is represented. |
| *Three* magistrates | Chosen by selection panel answerable to a local advisory committee. |
| *Five* independent members | Co-opted from among local electors and business community by councillor and magistrate members, following complex selection process. Shortlists must be approved by Home Secretary. |

- publish their own local policing objectives, which must be consistent with the spirit of national objectives and ministerial priorities laid down by the Home Secretary;
- appoint the local chief constable and his or her assistant chief constables, one of whom will be designated by the chief as his or her deputy;
- hold open public meetings along the lines of those held by local authorities, at which their members are expected to answer questions on their activities;
- oversee the management of their land and buildings by the chief constable.

Northern Ireland's Police Service is overseen by an independent Police Board.

At time of writing, coalition Home Secretary Theresa May had recently confirmed her intention to implement Conservative manifesto plans to further reform the governance of police forces by replacing existing authorities with US-style directly elected police commissioners. There were signs, however, of mounting opposition among senior officers, including Sir Hugh Orde, president of the Association of Chief Police Officers, who warned against 'politicizing' the police.

## The role of chief constables

Chief constables have always had statutory responsibilities separate from those of their governing committee or authority. It is their role to deliver the policies agreed by their police authority on the ground. This entails appointing all officers in their force below the rank of assistant chief constable, producing an annual report on their performance in the preceding 12 months (covering specific categories of offence, along with other areas highlighted as being of local concern, like violent crime), and disciplining officers for misconduct.

In operational terms it is the job of the chief constable and his or her assistants to manage the force's budget, hire and fire other officers, and ensure that personnel are suitably allocated to maintain adequate patrols across the force area. But over the past twenty years, as both population levels and the range of responsibilities faced by the police have increased out of proportion with rises in the number of officers, successive governments have tried to remove some of the burden of more mundane patrol duties from the professionals by bolstering them with semi-trained back-up officers recruited from the local community. These include part-time volunteers known as 'special constables' or 'specials' and semi-trained policemen and women introduced by the Blair government called **police community support officers (PCSOs)**.

At time of writing, some 16,000 PCSOs were employed across England and Wales. In November 2007 they were given enhanced powers—partly in response to complaints by senior police officers that their trained staff were overstretched due to increased paperwork generated by legislation designed to make the stop-and-search and arrest procedures more transparent. Although they are entitled to paid overtime, a minimum of 21 days' annual leave, and various other benefits, PCSOs earn significantly less than fully trained officers. Starting salaries for professional police constables (PCs), the lowest rank, are around £22,000; in contrast, a PCSO will initially earn about £16,000. This fact—combined with evidence that police recruitment has been failing to keep pace with government targets in recent years—has led to many critical newspaper headlines about perceived underfunding of the police service.

In addition to PCSOs, Labour introduced another layer of partially trained, community-based officials, in the guise of **neighbourhood wardens**. A type of glorified Neighbourhood Watch coordinator, these uniformed individuals were an initiative of the DCLG's Neighbourhood Renewal Unit. They are meant to patrol, and be otherwise readily available in, areas with large numbers of elderly and/or vulnerable residents—particularly those notorious for property crime, graffiti, and antisocial behaviour. They currently have limited powers of intervention (reflected in their modest £15,000–20,000 salaries), but there has been talk of extending these to give them a semi-official 'assistant constable' status. Since 2005 both PCSOs and wardens have worked alongside fully qualified police officers on the one hand and groups of volunteers on the other, in a new breed of de facto police force called a **neighbourhood policing team** (also known as 'safer neighbourhood teams' and 'safer, stronger community teams'). Some 3,600 have been set up across England and Wales.

PCSOs have considerable clout. They are authorized to issue summary fixed-penalty notices on members of the public for offences ranging from littering and cycling on footpaths to failing to keep their dogs under control. Under the authority vested in them by Labour's 'Respect' agenda, they may also require names and addresses from people they apprehend for antisocial behaviour—for example, fighting or swearing in the street. These details may subsequently be used by police or local authorities to apply to magistrates' courts for permission to impose **antisocial behaviour orders (ASBOs)** on individuals. Given their proto-legal status, more detail on ASBOs—the subject of huge controversy on their initial introduction in Labour's second term—can be found in *McNae's Essential Law for Journalists*. They are civil penalties in the first instance, but individuals who breach their conditions—for example, by failing to respect a curfew or remain resident at a specified address—may be prosecuted for criminal offences. The Crime and Disorder Act 1998, which introduced ASBOs, defines antisocial behaviour as conduct that has:

" caused or was likely to cause alarm, harassment or distress to one or more persons not of the same household as him or herself and where an ASBO is seen as necessary to protect relevant persons from further anti-social acts by the defendant. "

The ASBO concept was recently extended to tackle lower-level problematic behaviour, through **acceptable behaviour contracts (ABCs)**. These are agreements that young people identified as having previously acted in an anti-social way may be asked to sign, with input from their parents or guardians, pledging to change their ways and/or take specified action to make amends.

In addition to being able to impose orders and contracts on named individuals, both neighbourhood wardens and PCSOs have the power (like ordinary police officers) to apply to councils for **dispersal orders** to cover locations judged to be antisocial behaviour 'black spots'. Groups of two or more people alleged to be causing 'harassment, alarm, or distress' may be forcibly broken up and/or moved on from a location under the terms of such orders. Failure to comply can lead to fines of up to £2,500. As with ASBOs, breaching the terms of a dispersal order may lead to prosecution.

Police can also obtain and enforce **designated public places orders (DPPOs)**— a variation on the dispersal order concept designed to clear specific streets, squares, or alleyways of drink-related antisocial behaviour. Anyone caught drinking in such locations who refuses to surrender his or her alcohol is liable for a £50 fixed penalty or for arrest and a fine of up to £500.

Despite the widespread ridicule with which news of some ASBOs was greeted in the media (a man was banned from his own home after being given one for playing his music too loudly, while several have been imposed on grumpy pensioners for relatively minor 'offences' such as cursing at their neighbours), they have proved hugely popular among law enforcement agencies and many local communities blighted by unruly behaviour in the past. According to Ministry of Justice figures, 14,972 ASBOs were issued in total between their introduction in April 1999 and December 2007. Unsurprisingly, Greater London (with 1,808) came out top, but hot on its heels were Greater Manchester (1,642), West Midlands (1,168), and West Yorkshire (1,122). Labour used the popularity of the orders as a springboard to expand the scope of its antisocial behaviour crackdown by increasing the range of 'offences' for which summary penalties could be issued by the police and local authorities, and giving parish and community councils powers to impose them.

At time of writing, however, Home Secretary Theresa May had just ordered a review into antisocial behaviour measures, signalling that ASBOs might soon be abolished.

## The police complaints process

Allegations of misconduct initially follow the same process as other complaints about the local police force. This process is as outlined in Figure 11.1.

All cases involving deaths in police custody or at the hands of officers in the community—for example, the shooting of a drug dealer—are automatically passed to the **Independent Police Complaints Commission (IPCC)**. Even when matters are handled locally by the chief constable or the police authority, the IPCC may intervene if dissatisfied with the choice of investigating officer. Alternatively, it will approve his or her appointment by issuing an 'appropriate statement'.

**Figure 11.1** A flow chart outlining the police complaints process

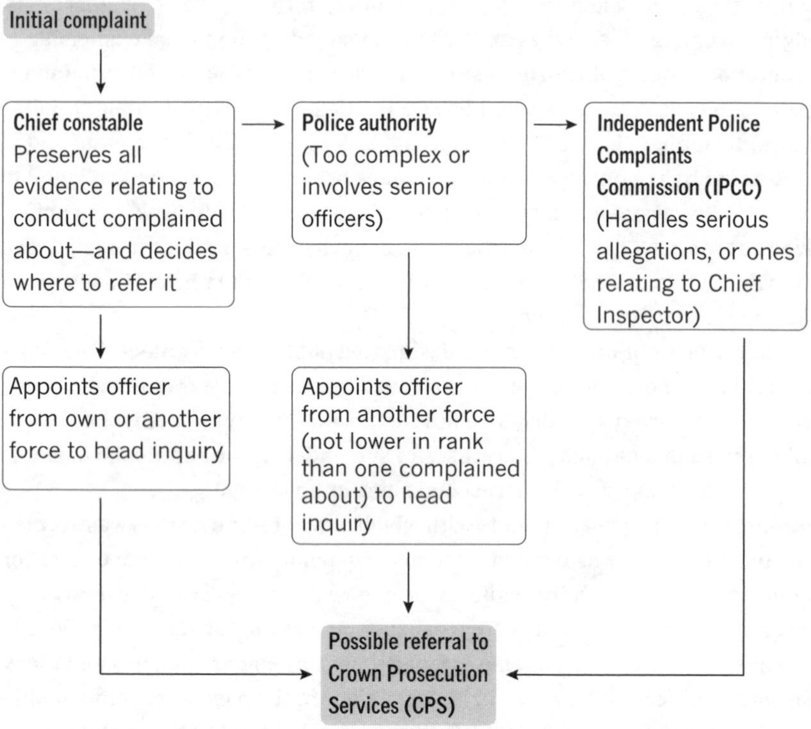

```
Initial complaint
      │
      ▼
┌─────────────────┐      ┌─────────────────┐      ┌─────────────────┐
│ Chief constable │ ───▶ │ Police authority│ ───▶ │ Independent     │
│ Preserves all   │      │ (Too complex or │      │ Police          │
│ evidence relating│     │ involves senior │      │ Complaints      │
│ to conduct      │      │ officers)       │      │ Commission (IPCC)│
│ complained      │      │                 │      │ (Handles serious│
│ about—and decides│     │                 │      │ allegations, or ones│
│ where to refer it│     │                 │      │ relating to Chief│
└─────────────────┘      └─────────────────┘      │ Inspector)      │
      │                          │                └─────────────────┘
      ▼                          ▼                         │
┌─────────────────┐      ┌─────────────────┐               │
│ Appoints officer│      │ Appoints officer│               │
│ from own or     │      │ from another    │               │
│ another force to│      │ force (not lower│               │
│ head inquiry    │      │ in rank than one│               │
│                 │      │ complained about)│              │
│                 │      │ to head inquiry │               │
└─────────────────┘      └─────────────────┘               │
      │                          │                          │
      │                          ▼                          │
      │                 ┌─────────────────┐                 │
      └──────────────▶  │ Possible referral│ ◀──────────────┘
                        │ to Crown        │
                        │ Prosecution     │
                        │ Services (CPS)  │
                        └─────────────────┘
```

Taking disciplinary action is a matter for the police authority in relation to the most senior officers, or the chief constable in relation to all others. The authority has to follow a formal disciplinary procedure and can impose disciplinary sanctions on senior officers (including chief constables). If a chief constable indicates he or she is *unwilling* to take action where the IPCC has become involved, the Commission can *direct* him or her to do so. Disciplinary charges imposed on officers are heard by chief constables (unless it is they, or an assistant chief constable, who are accused) and punishment can include cautions, demotions, or in certain cases dismissal. There is a right of appeal from the chief constable's decision—and this must go to a police disciplinary appeals tribunal. In the last resort, members of the public left unhappy by the way in which a complaint has been dealt with may apply to the courts for a private summons to prosecute the officers concerned (as was attempted unsuccessfully by the family of Mr De Menezes, prior to their successful private prosecution of the Met for breaching health and safety legislation).

In recent years there has been some controversy over the stringent 'standard of proof' required before disciplinary charges may be brought. This is illustrated by the stark contrast between the wording of the 'civil' standard—that which applies in most employment-related situations—and the 'police' standard. The former is worded thus:

❝ Is it more likely than not, on the balance of probabilities, that the police officer committed the disciplinary offence? ❞

The latter reads:

❝ Did the police officer commit the disciplinary offence, beyond all reasonable doubt? ❞

### Future of the police

In light of the increased organizational autonomy given to hospitals and schools in recent years, senior police chiefs have been calling for more delegated powers. In June 2008 Ken Jones, president of ACPO, announced he had submitted a proposal for some forces to be granted *foundation* status (see p. 169) to the Home Office. With the coalition minded to introduce elected police commissioners, however, it appears unlikely that these proposals will reach fruition.

Mr Jones, who qualified his statement by saying major policy areas such as counter-terrorism should be kept within the centralized remit of Whitehall, revealed that four forces were already piloting a 'common-sense' approach to policing, using their own discretion about whether to arrest certain kinds of minor offender. Others, including the Durham force, were keen to experiment with formal foundation status.

## Fire and rescue authorities

In contrast to the police (which, although divided into local forces, all fall under the umbrella of one national police service), technically speaking fire and rescue services—or 'fire brigades' as they once were—are entirely locally based. In common with the police, they are managed by a separate authority, but unlike it they do not have their own discrete body. Instead, in two-tier areas, the 'fire and rescue authorities' are usually county councils, but for fire services based in unitary areas, 'combined' fire authorities are established. In metropolitan areas, fire services are overseen by separate fire and civil defence authorities (as in London). Table 11.9 is a timeline outlining the history of Britain's fire services.

An important distinction between fire services that fall under county councils and combined fire authorities (and fire and civil defence authorities) is that the former are supervised by county council committees and have their budgets managed by them, while the latter two determine their own budgets like police authorities. They are, however, answerable to the *Secretary of State* for Communities and Local Government.

**Table 11.9** Timeline for the emergence of the UK fire services

| Year | Event |
|------|-------|
| Before 1938 | Volunteer fire brigades set up on ad hoc basis by local parish and town councils and fire insurance companies (the latter only fought fires in houses belonging to their policyholders, however—indicated by a 'fire mark' plaque fixed to the exterior of a home). |
| 1938 | Fire Brigades Act makes it compulsory for county borough councils, non-county borough councils, and urban district councils to provide fire brigades. |
| 1939–45 | All fire brigades combined for duration of Second World War in one National Fire Service. |
| 1947 | Fire Services Act returns all fire brigades to local authority control, this time under the auspices of county councils (designated 'fire authorities'). |
| 1963 | London Government Act updates the above by creating the GLC in London. |
| 1972 | Metropolitan county councils are designated as fire authorities in the relevant areas by the Local Government Act. |
| 1985 | Local Government Act abolishes the GLC and the metropolitan counties, and creates seven new 'fire and civil defence authorities'. In the six metropolitan areas, these were composed of councillors nominated by each new metropolitan borough council, and numbers were based on the size of each authority and the political balance of the councils. In London, one councillor was nominated from each of the 32 boroughs, plus one from the City of London. |
| 1992 | Rolling reorganization of local government ushers in new combined fire service authorities in unitary areas. |
| 2000 | Formation of the Greater London Authority sees the pre-existing fire and civil defence authority replaced by a new London Fire and Emergency Planning Authority (LFEPA). |
| 2004 | Fire and Rescue Services Act harmonizes fire service provision across England, introducing a new Fire and Rescue National Framework (including services for which they may charge) from July that year, and devolved responsibility for fire services to Wales (this had already happened in Scotland and Northern Ireland). Reserve powers introduced enabling the government, if necessary, to set up new independent bodies to oversee negotiations over firefighters' pay and conditions. |

It is the Communities Secretary's role to check each year the establishment schemes in place in each fire service area—that is, the level and precise nature of provision it makes available to local people. In law, all fire services must:

- equip and train a firefighting force;
- make arrangements for dealing with calls for help;
- gather information about local 'risk' buildings—for example, high-rises, timber-framed structures, or ones housing large numbers of elderly or disabled people;
- give advice on fire protection to the business community, local schools, etc.;

- make sure that any local water companies maintain an adequate supply of water at a pressure suitable for firefighting;
- draw up mutually beneficial 'reinforcement schemes'—that is, pool their resources—with neighbouring fire services to help them to deal with major fires.

Fire services are also called on to deal with other emergencies in addition to blazes. These so-called 'special services' are divided into two broad categories: humanitarian (for example, serious road accidents and floods) and non-humanitarian (less urgent calls, such as a request to help a resident gain access to their home after leaving their keys inside). Whereas firefighters would once willingly answer calls to scale trees in pursuit of errant cats, it has become increasingly commonplace for today's fire services to charge for such 'non-essential' operations.

Under the Fire Precautions Act 1971, various types of premises are now barred from operating without an official fire service seal of approval in the form of a fire certificate. These are issued, after an inspection, by the fire authorities. The types of premises affected include:

- offices;
- sports grounds;
- hotels;
- theatres.

Other Acts passed to increase fire safety include:

- the Public Health Act 1936—which stipulated that fire escapes must be provided in buildings such as hotels and theatres;
- the Fire Safety and Safety of Places of Sport Act 1987—which introduced tough new seating standards in the aftermath of the 1985 Bradford City Football Club tragedy (including a cut in attendance limits at UK football grounds).

# Emergency planning and civil defence

The aspect of 'emergency services' provision in which local authorities have historically been most directly involved is the broader category of contingency planning and civil defence. The notion of 'civil defence' in particular—namely, the idea that councils might be expected to help to protect citizens against enemy attack or other forms of security emergency—arose in the aftermath of the Second World War. As a policy, it was initiated by the post-war Labour government, but has remained largely a notional responsibility for the most part in 'peacetime'—perhaps its most tangible application being the plans for a hypothetical nuclear attack expected to be updated by local authorities at various junctures during the Cold War. Notable exceptions included the strategies employed to safeguard's London population from terrorist bombs during The Troubles and the measures that had to be implemented following the Real IRA's attack on a Manchester shopping centre in 1996. In this age of increased security threats, however, it is not hard to imagine a time when renewed importance may be attached to civil defence departments.

As recently as 2004, a new Civil Contingencies Act effectively replaced the entire body of existing emergency planning legislation on the statute book. The most significant aspect of the shake-up, ordered by then Secretary of State for Transport, Local Government, and the Regions John Prescott, was the new requirement placed on so-called 'responder' organizations in each local area to appoint a full-time **emergency planning officer** (sometimes known as a 'civil contingencies officer', 'civil protection officer', or 'resilience officer') to coordinate the measures that would be implemented in the event of a civil emergency. As well as security threats, such civil emergencies might include any number of natural or manmade disasters: for example, floods, major fires, landslides, or nuclear accidents. Responder organizations are divided under the Act into 'Category 1' and 'Category 2'. The list of bodies in each category is outlined in the table entitled '"Responder" bodies that are required to appoint emer-

gency planning officers', which can be found on the Online Resource Centre that accompanies this book.

The history of local government's involvement with civil defence began with the passage of the Civil Defence Act 1948, under which the Home Secretary was empowered to direct local authorities to take 'appropriate measures' to ensure that the civil defence requirements for their populations were met. These were further defined by the Civil Defence (Planning) Regulations 1974, which gave county councils the power to *make plans to deal with hostile attacks* and, in certain circumstances, to prepare for war, in consultation with boroughs/districts. It was only in the 1990s, in the wake of the end of the Cold War, that the term 'emergency' was explicitly redefined to cover peacetime disasters such as floods. Finally, in 2001, responsibility for civil defence shifted from the Home Secretary to a new Cabinet Office Coordination Unit.

A further type of agency involved in preparing for civil emergencies is the recently formed 'regional resilience board'. Sometimes referred to as 'regional control and resilience boards', these are joint bodies drawing together representatives from local police forces, fire service authorities, and council civil defence departments to oversee overall emergency planning for entire regions. The 2004 Act also required responder organizations to set up collaboratively more localized versions of the regional boards—'local resilience forums' (LRFs)—based in each police area. All are expected to produce a community risk register that is specific to their areas, outlining particular localities, buildings, businesses, or residential areas that are seen to be particularly vulnerable. They are overseen at national level by a new *executive agency* within the Cabinet Office: the Civil Contingencies Secretariat.

The government's much-vaunted new 'resilience' strategy for the country was prompted, in large part, by the 11 September 2001 terrorist attacks and the 2004 Madrid bombings (not to mention persistent fears of an avian flu pandemic, which have been periodically publicized by the media since 2003). But this new state of preparedness failed to prevent the 7 July 2005 attacks on London. And more embarrassing still for ministers was the organizational chaos and buck-passing between local authorities, the *Environment Agency*, and central government that greeted the widespread winter floods that devastated parts of Britain in 2007 and 2009.

At the top of the chain of command for emergency planning is an ad hoc government committee, codenamed 'Cobra' and headed by the prime minister, which meets in a Cabinet Office briefing room whenever necessary. (Despite its James Bond-style title, the acronym actually stands for something rather mundane: 'Cabinet Office Briefing Room A'.) Among the emergencies for which Cobra most recently convened were the 2007 foot-and-mouth outbreaks and  the terrorist attack on Glasgow Airport—all of which occurred within weeks of Gordon Brown's becoming prime minister. When the premier is unavailable, his or her place is taken by the Home Secretary. This happened at the time of the 7 July bombings, because then Prime Minister Tony Blair was at a *G8* summit in Gleneagles when the news broke.

# ▌ Local government associations

The Local Government Association (LGA) was established in 1997 to give a collective voice in Whitehall policymaking to all 388 English local authorities. A self-styled 'voluntary lobbying organization' (as opposed to a trades union or association), it is based close to Parliament, at Smith Square, in the former Transport House: the historic headquarters of the Labour Party. In addition to representing district/borough councils, county councils, metropolitan borough councils, and unitary authorities, the LGA also speaks on behalf of subscribing police authorities, fire authorities, **national park** authorities, and passenger transport authorities. Local authorities in Wales are represented by a Welsh Local Government Association (WLGA), which is a subset of the LGA.

In 2007–08, the LGA published the strategic objectives summarized in the table entitled 'Local Government Association (LGA) strategic objectives', to be found on the Online Resource Centre that accompanies this book.

In addition to the central LGA, there are 13 regional **local government associations**, the remits of which broadly follow the boundaries of the government's English regions.

## ≣ Topical feature idea

At a time of wide-scale government spending cuts, and an impending Council Tax freeze, media attention is focusing increasingly on the quality of services provided by local authorities and perceived disparities—or postcode lotteries—between one area and another. Two aspects of service delivery likely to face greater scrutiny are the perceived overlap and duplication between upper and lower-tier councils in two-tier areas, and the wide variations in the range and nature of services provided by the same types of council in different areas. How is local government organized in the catchment of your news organization? What types of local authority are present, where do the responsibilities of one end and the other's begin, and how might finite resources be better harnessed to improve services, making them more accountable, in these tough economic times?

## ✳ Current issues

- **The future of unitary authorities**: one of the coalition's first actions in relation to local government was to abandon already advanced plans for unitary authorities to be introduced in Norwich and Exeter. Nearly two decades after John Major introduced the gradualist unitary programme, a question mark remains over its future.

- **Elected police commissioners to replace police authorities**: to make police forces more accountable to those they serve, Home Secretary Theresa May plans to replace police authorities with US-style directly elected local police commissioners. However, the proposal has been condemned by many senior police officers, including Sir Hugh Orde, head of the Association of Chief Police Officers, who argues that they could lead to police forces being accused of kowtowing to 'political influence'.

- **Poor transparency of some council provision**: an ongoing concern for some local government observers (not to mention councillors) has been the proliferation of local strategic partnerships and other collaborations between neighbouring councils and/or external bodies over service delivery. Critics warn that 'outsourcing' increasingly significant chunks of council business to quango-style bodies overseen by unelected boards is undermining the accountability of service providers to the public.

## ? Review questions

1. When did the first local authorities emerge, and what was their initial role and purpose?
2. What were the main reforms instigated in the 1974 reorganization of local government?

3. Outline the current local government framework in England and Wales. What are 'two-tier areas', 'unitary authorities', and 'hybrid structures'?

4. In two-tier areas, what is the division of responsibilities between district/borough and county councils?

5. How is the UK police force structured, and how and by whom can local chief constables be held to account?

## → Further reading

Atkinson, H. and Wilks-Heeg, S. (2000) *Local Government from Thatcher to Blair*, Cambridge: Polity Press. **Comprehensive account of the succession of local government reforms passed by the Thatcher, Major, Blair, and Brown administrations.**

Stallion, M. and Wall, D. S. (2000) *The British Police: Police Forces and Chief Officers 1829–2000*, London: M. R. Stallion. **Exhaustive handbook to the UK police service from its inception to the new millennium, including profiles of every force past and present and introductory essays.**

Stevens, A. (2006) *Politico's Guide to Local Government*, 2nd edn, London: Politico's Publishing. **Fully updated second edition of the comprehensive guide to every aspect of local government, including the interplay between local and central administrations.**

Stewart, J. (2003) *Modernising British Local Government: An Assessment of Labour's Reform Programme*, London: Palgrave Macmillan. **Meditative examination of the impact of the Local Government Act 2000, focusing on the tension between the idea of increasing localism and complaints of diminishing council accountability.**

Wilson, D. and Game, C. (2006) *Local Government in the United Kingdom*, London: Palgrave Macmillan. **Revised fourth edition of the standard text on contemporary local government in Britain. This covers all of the major recent developments, including the introduction of unitary authorities and elected mayors.**

Wilson, D., Ashton, J., and Sharpe, D. (2001) *What Everyone in Britain Should Know about the Police*, London: Blackstone Press. **Fully revised second edition of the informative core text charting developments in the UK police service from its origins in the early nineteenth century up to the present day, with a focus on recent changes from the idea of the traditional 'Bobby on the beat' to today's target-led—and frequently armed—officers.**

## ⓐ Online Resource Centre

www.oxfordtextbooks.co.uk/orc/Morrison2e/
Visit the Online Resource Centre that accompanies this book for web links and regular updates.

# 12

# Financing local government

Some of the most newsworthy and politically contentious local government stories arise from the way in which it is financed—and how the funding it raises is spent. Above-*inflation* rises in councillor allowances, cutbacks in funding for local schools, all-expenses-paid 'fact-finding' junkets for members and officers, and the question of how much taxpayers and businesses are being charged for their local services are among the bread-and-butter issues that typically make local headlines.

## ▌ Revenue versus capital finance

Local authorities need money for two types of spending: to build infrastructure (offices, roads, traffic crossings, schools, and housing), and to operate and maintain these facilities on a day-to-day basis. The cost of building things is known as **capital expenditure**. Cash spent staffing, lighting, heating, and repairing them is called **revenue expenditure**.

## ▌ Revenue expenditure and how it is financed

Revenue spending is financed through the council's *income*: the grants it receives from central government, the taxes it raises and/or has allocated to it locally, and any up-front fees or penalties it charges for local services (for example, parking permits and library fines). Each of these income streams is examined in detail below, starting with the source of funds that underpins all others—the government grant system.

# The reformed government grant system

The overwhelming majority (75 per cent as of 2010–11) of local authority revenue finance derives from government grants. Of this, until relatively recently the bulk came in the form of the **revenue support grant (RSG)**—or **general block grant**—which individual local authorities were left to spend at their discretion, focusing on particular local funding needs. After Labour's return to power in 1997, the process by which central government grants were allocated to local authorities became steadily more baffling. At the same time the importance of the RSG progressively diminished as more and more government money became 'ring-fenced' and directed to specified areas of spending—notably schools. This process—known as 'passporting'—has seen over time a steady decline in the size of the RSG, to the extent that by 2010–11 it represented only around 4 per cent of local authorities' annual revenue budgets in England. By far the biggest portion—65 per cent—was allotted to councils in the form of discrete, increasingly sizeable chunks, many of which had to be spent in prescribed ways dictated by central government. Local authorities' own reserves and annual grants given to the police between them made up a further 5 per cent. Perhaps surprisingly, given the controversy it generates in the media, the *Council Tax* has for some time accounted for a mere quarter of revenue income. Figure 12.1 gives a full breakdown of the sources of local government revenue funding in England in 2010–11. Figure 12.2 summarizes the overall percentages of English local authority revenue spending in each service area.

While the way in which the overall revenue finance 'cake' is divided to prioritize particular service areas tends to be fairly uniform across the UK, *devolution* has seen widening disparities open up between central government's approach to funding local authorities in Britain's constituent countries. In 2010–11, 34 per cent of the Welsh local government budget was earmarked for education, 19 per cent for social services, and 9 per cent for policing—on a par with spending allocations in England. However, while the percentages of income Welsh authorities derived from Council Tax, redistributed UBR, and police grant (plus floor funding) were comparable to those received by English ones (at 23, 16, and 4 per cent respectively), the remaining 57 per cent was made up not of passported grants but of an old-style RSG, allowing individual councils to allocate money at their discretion.

These are the facts and figures—but how exactly are the various grants defined and allocated in practice? It is probably easiest to explain the patchwork government grant system by splitting the payments into two broad categories: *formula* and *non-formula grants*.

**Figure 12.1** A breakdown of regular local authority revenue income in England for 2010–11

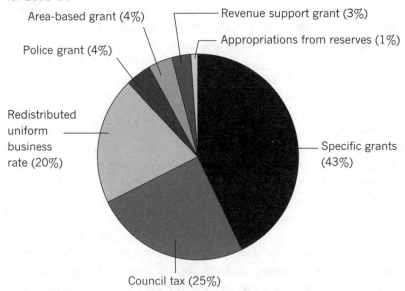

Source: Department of Communities and Local Government (DCLG)

**Figure 12.2** A breakdown of overall revenue spending patterns for English local authorities in 2010–11

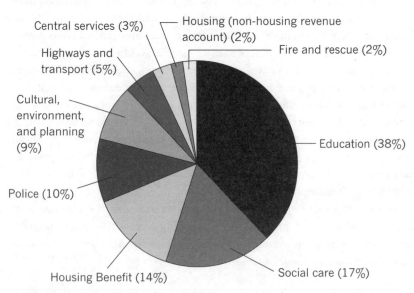

Source: Department of Communities and Local Government (DCLG)

## Formula grants

Central government makes a calculation—traditionally each year—of how much money it thinks individual local authorities need to provide services for their communities up to the required national standards. With effect from 2008–09, ministers began to calculate their allocations on a three-year basis, with the aim of helping local authorities to improve their long-term planning. The grants that ministers allocate on the basis of these calculations are known collectively as 'formula grants' and comprise the following three types:

- the revenue support grant (RSG);
- *uniform business rates (UBR)*—also known as **national non-domestic rates (NNDR)**;
- the principal formula police grant (PFPG).

UBR—a tax levied on businesses based in an area, but redistributed by central government elsewhere according to need—is explored in detail later in this chapter. Both the RSG and the PFPG have, since the 2006–07 tax year, been worked out on the basis of a two new calculations: the *relative needs formula (RNF)* and the *relative resource amount (RRA)*.

The RNF, as its title suggests, is a formula based on detailed information about the population size, social structure, and other characteristics of a local authority area. By taking into account precise local factors, such as the number of pensioners and school-aged children living in an area and its relative economic prosperity, the government aims to allocate funds that fairly and accurately reflect the needs of that area, and the cost of servicing those needs to its local authorities. Within the RNF, separate formulae are used to decide how much should be allocated to individual local authorities to cover the likely expenses associated with each of the 'major service areas': education, social services, police, fire, highways maintenance, environmental, protective and cultural services (EPCS), and capital financing. The RNF plays the same role in the current system as the now defunct formula spending share (FSS)—an earlier attempt at making the system more responsive to specific demographic factors (also introduced by Labour). Prior to the FSS, grants were calculated on the basis of standard spending assessments (SSAs), which were notorious for using a simple 'per head' approach (relating to population size and previous years' spending).

The RRA, in contrast to the RNF, is a *negative* figure. It is based on the logical assumption that an area with a large number of Council Tax-paying households—particularly those in higher tax bands, indicative of a relatively affluent population—needs less financial help from central government than a poorer area. The RRA is essentially subtracted from the previously calculated RNF to give a figure more accurately reflecting what an individual area should be allocated in government formula grants. The resulting grant is shared between local authorities in that area in proportion to the level of responsibility that each has—with 'upper-tier' county councils and unitary authorities gaining more than 'lower-tier' district or **borough councils**, and police and fire authorities.

Over and above the core chunk of formula grants allocated in this way, a small percentage has remained in the overall 'formula pot' to be distributed between local authority areas on a purely per head basis. This has been the same for all local authorities delivering the same services—that is, all district/borough councils receive identical per capita amounts. This is known as 'central allocation'. In addition, Labour introduced a procedure known as 'floor-damping' to ensure that every local authority—no matter how poorly it fared from a grant settlement compared to others—received at least a *minimum* year-on-year increase in its formula grant. Four different 'floor levels' were set (one for each of the aforementioned types of authority). To cite a current example, for the year 2010–11, education and social services authorities (the upper-tier counties and unitaries) were guaranteed a 1.5 per cent increase in grant, whatever their perceived 'relative needs' and 'relative resource amounts'. Early indications from the coalition were that the days of floor-damping might be numbered. Announcing a plan to trim £1.166bn from his department's budget as part of the government's deficit reduction programme, Communities Secretary Eric Pickles pledged to protect the then £29bn general block grant for the time being, but said some local authorities might face cuts to their overall revenue grants of up to 2 per cent.

The total value of formula grants allocated by the British government to England for 2010–11 was £29bn.

## Non-formula grants

Alongside formula grants, Labour introduced various other types of central government handout for local authorities—a growing number of which have, over the years, been 'passported' (or targeted) for specific purposes. The main categories of *non-formula* grants inherited by the coalition were:

- **specific grants;**
- area-based grants (ABGs).

Despite their name, not all specific grants have had to be spent by councils in equally strictly defined areas. In fact, specific grants have been further subdivided into: **ring-fenced grants** and **unfenced grants** (sometimes also called *targeted grants*). Ring-fenced grants—as their name suggests—are tied to spending in a particular area. One of the most famous is the **Dedicated Schools Grant (DSG)**, which councils may not spend on anything other than staffing and maintaining schools, or providing related services such as special needs teaching. As well as having to be spent on schools generally, the DSG is sometimes prescribed further still, with ministers stipulating that it goes towards particular running costs, such as buying more textbooks or improving extracurricular activities (to take a recent illustration, the ministerial priority for 2006–07 and 2007–08 was personalized learning). But such passporting can prove a source of conflict between central and local government. In 2005 there was a high-profile contretemps between several local authorities and then Education Secretary Alan Johnson after it emerged they had spent part of their schools grant on improving less generously funded local services.

Mr Johnson was also in charge when another ring-fenced school grant was introduced, in the shape of the extra £627m payment that it pledged, in two stages, to roll out healthier school meals between 2005 and 2011. The initiative followed the high-profile 'Feed Me Better' media campaign fronted by television chef Jamie Oliver.

The other form of specific grant—the unfenced grant—has been allocated to councils to spend however they see fit, within certain parameters determined by ministers. Confusingly, this has made it superficially resemble the RSG. Unlike the RSG, however, unfenced grants have not been calculated on the basis of a formula related to local demographic and socio-economic factors; rather, they are residual pots of money to be spent on services judged equally worthy of central government funding across the country. An example of an unfenced specific grant is the Housing and Planning Delivery Grant (HPDG), which, although councils have only been able to spend it on services related to housing and/or planning, has been used in a number of different ways by individual local authorities.

The government's stated aims for specific grants are to:

- help local authorities to achieve a specific purpose—for example, reducing Council Tax or bringing in uniform standards of domestic upkeep or disabled access provision;
- help poorer areas in which the Council Tax base—the number households eligible to pay it—is too low to meet the cost of local needs;
- cut the cost of services that are either spread unevenly across the country—for example, the maintenance of flood barriers—or of benefit to the nation as a whole (for example, roads);
- fund services for which ministers have laid down statutory requirements—for example, the Mental Illness Specific Grant (MISG), introduced under the Community Care Act 1990 to provide community-based support for people with mental health problems.

The final type of revenue grant—the area-based grant (ABG)—is a relatively new addition to local authorities' financial armouries. Introduced in 2008–09, it was designed to encourage them to work with 'partners'—other organizations, such as charities, local businesses, and even neighbouring authorities—to improve local services across the shared localities in which they operate. The idea is that, by forming partnerships, authorities will achieve efficiency savings and avoid duplicating or overlapping with other service providers.

The total value of specific and area-based grants combined for 2010–11 was £47bn. A summary of the main types of central government-directed revenue grant is given in Table 12.1.

Some critics of passporting see it as a means by which governments can get away with massaging public spending figures. In February 1999 a £50m additional grant for schools was very publicly allocated by ministers as an 'increase' in the value of the revenue support grant. In reality, however, this money was provided by taking it away from other local government services—a sleight of hand derided by Sir Jeremy Beecham, then chairman of the Local Government Association (LGA), who accused ministers of 'holding local authorities to ransom' by a 'smoke and mirrors trick'.

Government efforts to constrain local authorities' ability to spend revenue income where they please have not stopped with ring-fencing and area-based grants. It was once commonplace for councils that found themselves with unexpected shortfalls in one spending department during a financial year to transfer money from the budget of others that were in surplus, in a process known as **virement**. But in recent years repeated extensions of the passporting regime have rendered all but the most modest shuffling of books impossible. At time of writing, Chancellor George Osborne had just used his October 2010 *Comprehensive Spending Review (CSR)* to announce the end of wide-scale passporting—with all 'ring-fencing' of revenue grants, aside from simplified payments aimed at schools and a new public health grant, due to end from the 2011–12 financial year. Although the precise extent of the reforms remained unclear, the Treasury's official CSR document revealed that the number of separate core grants would be reduced from 90 to ten, and £4bn of revenue grant cash would be 'rolled' back into councils' formula grant pots—putting decisions about how and where to spend money squarely back at the feet of individual authorities. The Chancellor heralded the change as a triumph for localism, but some commentators, including BBC political editor Nick Robinson, remarked that it was a shrewd political manoeuvre by ministers designed to deflect the blame for painful cuts to local services onto councils. Writing on his BBC blog, he evoked the following 'old Whitehall saying':

❝ Governments with money centralize and claim the credit, those without decentralize and spread the blame. ❞

Mr Pickles pledged to restore councils' say in how to their own income should be spent by transferring progressively larger portions of money previously allocated through specific grants to the overall RSG pot. He began by using a novel form of central government-directed virement—reducing the level of ring-fencing of both revenue and capital non-schools allocations from 10.7 per cent of councils' budgets (£4.5bn) to 7.7 per cent (£3.2bn) during 2010–11.

**Table 12.1** Different types of government revenue grant (2010–11)

| Formula grants | Non-formula grants |
| --- | --- |
| Revenue support grant (RSG) | Specific ring-fenced grant |
| Uniform business rates (UBR) | Specific unfenced grant |
| Principal formula police grant (PFPG) | Area-based grant (ABG) |
| Floor-damping grant | |

# Local taxation and evolution of the Council Tax

The idea of local taxation dates back to a time when medieval churches charged 'tithes' to parishioners renting land from them and lords of the manor used bailiffs to extract land taxes from peasant farmers. But as early as 1601 it began to become a more systematic affair, with the emergence of 'rates'—a property tax based on the **rateable value** of an individual's home, which was to remain in place (with some modifications) for four centuries.

The rates were a tax levied on domestic properties, rather than the individual citizens who occupied them. The broad assumption was that the bigger a property and the higher its rateable—or rental—value, the better off its occupants were likely to be. But over time, the rating system (to use its full title) produced peculiar anomalies that led to growing calls for reform. Prior to its eventual abolition by Margaret Thatcher's Conservative government in 1990 (1989 in Scotland), the most oft-cited illustration of its unfairness was that of the elderly pensioner living alone, on a fixed income, in a house for which he or she had spent his or her lifetime paying—next door to several sharing professionals whose combined incomes were far greater. Because rates were property-based, both 'households' might be charged exactly the same, meaning each professional would be paying significantly less than the pensioner.

Although there was widespread agreement that rates needed reforming, their immediate successor was short-lived. Ushered in by the Local Government Finance Act 1988, the Community Charge—dubbed the 'Poll Tax' by its opponents—sought to address the grievances of ratepayers 'punished' for living alone by shifting the onus away from property and onto people. In future individual residents would be billed for their use of local services—forcing everyone to pay their way. But, while it may have seemed fairer in theory, in practice this new 'head tax' soon became even more unpopular than the rates. While various rebates and exemptions were introduced to take account of the inability of certain groups (for example, the unemployed) to afford it, working people living in the same area ended up paying identical amounts—regardless of any differences in their incomes. A multimillionaire tycoon might be charged exactly the same as his or her cleaner. In addition, some low-income groups previously excluded from local taxation altogether were suddenly included for the first time. Full-time students, for example, became liable (albeit with a 75 per cent discount).

Such was the furore that greeted the introduction of the Community Charge that it has been widely viewed as the tipping point in the loss of confidence in Mrs Thatcher among Conservative MPs that ultimately led to her resignation part-way through a leadership contest in 1990 (see p. 95). The tax also proved extremely costly to administer, due in part to the fact that many of its opponents seemed prepared to forgo their right to vote, by dropping off the electoral roll, rather than allowing themselves to be tracked down by the *billing authorities*. Others openly refused to pay, leading to costly litigation by councils (much of which never bore fruit). In the end, the government was forced to increase its grants considerably temporarily to allow for a gross reduction in Community Charge bills of £140 a person, funded by a 2.5 per cent increase in VAT. In 1990–91, the Poll Tax paid for 44 per cent of local expenditure, but this was halved to 22 per cent following the cut (compared to 25 per cent for today's Council Tax).

Following the biggest peacetime protests ever seen in Britain (at least prior to the 2003 'Stop the War' marches), Mrs Thatcher's successor, John Major, abandoned the charge—replacing it with the Council Tax. This 'hybrid' tax reinstated the property link, but unlike rates related it to market or *capital* values, rather than rateable ones. To placate critics of the rates, it also retained an element of 'individual' liability introduced by the Community Charge. Each household was billed on the assumption it comprised two adults (meaning bills did not increase for three or more). But to avoid returning to a time when households occupying identical properties paid exactly the same—regardless of how many working adults lived in each—a range of reductions and exemptions for single people and low-income groups were introduced to make the system fairer, as outlined in Table 12.2.

Table 12.2 Council Tax exemptions and reductions

| Exemption/reduction | How it works |
| --- | --- |
| Single person discount | 25 per cent off a full Council Tax bill |
| 'Reductions for Disabilities' scheme | Lowers bills of homes in Bands B–H if they have been adapted to meet needs of disabled people. Exists to ensure house is not unfairly overvalued because of expensive modifications |
| Exemptions | Applies to severely mentally impaired, carers, and full-time students, and certain categories of dwelling, such as student halls of residence |
| Unoccupied dwelling discount | Discount of up to 50 per cent—although councils now have discretion to charge more in 'ghost towns' |
| Council Tax Benefit | Writes off Council Tax bills for unemployed and certain other people on low incomes and other benefits |
| 'Transitional relief' | Provided during transition from Community Charge to Council Tax for those whose local tax bills suddenly leapt as a result |

Although designed to deal with many of the anomalies and inequities preserved by previous local tax regimes, the Council Tax benefits and exemptions system inevitably ushered in its own. Full-time students might have been exempt from Council Tax in theory, but in practice those renting from private landlords invariably found themselves having to pay it on the homeowner's behalf—or seeing their rent artificially inflated to cover the cost. Students sharing houses with one or more adults in employment also lost their exemptions by default, because the household automatically became liable for the tax.

Perhaps most controversial has been the 50 per cent reduction traditionally available to households with two or more properties whose additional homes are generally unoccupied. In Wales and south-west England, in particular, the 'ghost towns' created in picturesque areas favoured by wealthy city-dwellers as holiday home locations have been exacerbated by the relative cheapness of keeping such properties empty for large parts of the year, in light of the Council Tax discounts they receive. In certain areas blighted by this trend, councils have been given limited discretion by government to charge more than the standard 50 per cent, to deter property owners from leaving them unoccupied. A recent statutory instrument—the Council Tax (Prescribed Classes of Dwellings) (England) Regulations 2003—gave individual billing authorities the power to determine classes of discount in their areas for the first time, in recognition of the 'ghost town' issue (not to mention the risk of such properties being broken into). Unoccupied but furnished properties—those most likely to be used as second homes—became liable for reduced discounts of 10 per cent, while some long-term empty homes faced losing their reduction altogether. In April 2008, Newcastle City Council used this new power to scrap its 50 per cent reduction for unfurnished and uninhabitable homes—charging them the full Council Tax for the first time.

Council Tax remains highly controversial to this day, however, and is seen by many as far from progressive. Newspapers have frequently featured stories about the financial problems it has caused for pensioners and others on modest fixed incomes who do not fall into a category making them eligible for a reduction. Some have even been fined or jailed for 'refusing' to pay. In September 2005 Sylvia Hardy, a 73-year-old retired social worker from Exeter, was sent to prison for refusing to pay £53.71 in Council Tax arrears on time. She told Exeter magistrates' court defiantly that she was following the example of other individuals in history who had fought to change 'unjust laws'.

Such is the ongoing concern about the unfair impact of Council Tax on low-income households that for many years in opposition the Liberal Democrats argued for replacing it with a 'local income tax'—a system, based on the calculations used to determine national Income Tax bands, that should more closely match a household's Council Tax bill with its ability to pay. In Scotland, where the *Scottish Parliament* has the power to make changes to local taxation, the Scottish Nationalists have long been planning to introduce a local Income Tax.

Table 12.3 outlines arguments for and against a property-based (rather than people-based) local tax system.

## Council Tax banding

But enough about those who do not pay the Council Tax: how does the system work for the overwhelming majority who do?

Council Tax bills in England, Scotland, and Wales are based on a *banding* system that divides domestic properties into one of eight bands (nine in Wales)—A–H (A–I), respectively—according to their notional capital values. In Wales, these bandings were most recently revised in 2005, to take account of changes in property prices in the 14 years that had elapsed since the original ones were set on 1 April 1991. Controversially, however, neither England nor Scotland has had its bandings changed since they were originally set—meaning they remain exactly the same as on 1 April 1993 (by which time even the original valuations were out of date). Despite pledging in its 2005 election manifesto to revise the bands across the UK if re-elected, Labour dropped the policy on returning to power. Cynics saw its reluctance to tackle the issue anywhere but in Wales as an example of political

**Table 12.3** Arguments for and against property-based and people-based local taxes

| Property-based tax | People-based tax |
| --- | --- |
| Cheap to administer and collect and provides predictable source of income | Boosts local finances, because number of bills sent out hugely increases to reflect fact that all adults—rather than households—are being charged |
| Difficult for people to avoid paying rates because property, unlike people, is immobile | Some argue it is fairer in principle, because burden of paying for local services is spread across all adults—including those who might otherwise be 'invisible' to taxes based on property values. 'Head tax' does not need to be 'one size fits all': a local income tax would reflect individuals' ability to pay |
| Simple, clearly understood system | Fosters greater local authority accountability, because all adults charged and can voice views on use of their money at local elections |
| Fair in theory, in that people occupying larger dwellings likely to be better off | Because individuals have to fill in forms accepting liability for taxes such as the Community Charge, there is a huge disincentive for them to register. When introduced in Britain, many councils ended up collecting barely half what they were owed—and those unable or unwilling to pay lost voting rights by dropping off the electoral roll |
| Property taxes can be disincentive to home improvement, because major refurbishment or extension is likely to hike bills | Straight head taxes like Community Charge also mean low-income groups such as students, pensioners, and working people on modest wages are charged same as vastly richer ones—unless explicit exemptions and reductions are introduced |

back-pedalling motivated by a fear that it would lose future votes in marginal *constituencies* where people whose house prices had significantly increased in the previous decade might find themselves moving into higher bands. In fact, according to research by the LGA, the number of households likely to lose out in a revaluation is the same as the number that would benefit (around 4 million).

Whatever the merits of the argument for retaining existing bandings, it is undeniable that the property values to which they relate are anachronistic today, in light of the substantial rises in house prices seen across most of the UK since the early 1990s. In England, he highest Council Tax band (H) currently applies to all homes valued at more than £320,000 in 1991, while in Scotland the top rate starts at just over £212,000. As stated previously, only in Wales has there been any rebanding since 1993: as of 1 April 2005, a new top band (I) has applied there for properties worth more than £424,000. Homes built since the dates on which the bandings were set are given nominal values based on what they would have been worth had they existed on 1 April 1991 (1 April 2003 in Wales). The lowest Council Tax band (A) is set for homes worth £40,000 or less in England, £44,000 in Wales, and £27,000 or less in Scotland, while the 'average band' (D) applies to those worth between £68,000 and £88,000 in England, £91,000 and £123,000 in Wales, and £45,000 and 58,000 in Scotland.

The introduction of a revised banding system in Wales has led to complaints that the country is no longer on an equal footing with the rest of Britain. Moreover, despite the fact that the price ranges covered by each of the bands in Wales were all adjusted upwards to reflect the general surge in property values since 1993, the revaluation was not simply a question of mapping properties in the old Band A over into the new one. Instead, it produced clear winners and losers. Because house prices in some areas had risen significantly further than in others—with some previously cheaper homes overtaking in value those that were once more expensive—many households found themselves moving into a higher band than before. Most went up at least one band, while some jumped two or more. Only 8 per cent of homes moved down.

At present, around 25 per cent of homes fall in the lowest band in England and Scotland as a whole, although in north-east England this proportion rises to 60 per cent. The current Council Tax bandings in England, Scotland, and Wales are outlined in Table 12.4.

### How individual bills are calculated—and who collects the money

As explained above, domestic properties are charged Council Tax in line with the bands into which they are placed based on their capital values in April 1991 (2003 in Wales). But who actually puts them in these bands and determines the nominal 1991/2003 value of a home built in the years since the bands were originally set?

Responsibility for valuing homes rests with the Valuation Office Agency (VOA), an *executive agency* of HM Revenue and Customs (and, ultimately, the Treasury), but it is for individual billing authorities to maintain lists of

**Table 12.4** Current Council Tax bands and values in England, Scotland, and Wales

| Band | England | Scotland | Wales |
|---|---|---|---|
| A | Up to £40,000 | Up to £27,000 | Up to £44,000 |
| B | £40,001–£52,000 | £27,001–£35,000 | £44,001–£65,000 |
| C | £52,001–£68,000 | £35,001–£45,000 | £65,001–£91,000 |
| D | £68,001–£88,000 | £45,001–£58,000 | £91,001–£123,000 |
| E | £88,001–£120,000 | £58,001–£80,000 | £123,001–£162,000 |
| F | £120,001–£160,000 | £80,001–£106,000 | £162,001–£223,000 |
| G | £160,001–£320,000 | £106,001–£212,000 | £223,001–£324,000 |
| H | £320,001 and above | £212,001 and above | £324,001–£424,000 |
| I | N/a | N/a | £424,001 and above |

valuations. Based in 85 regional offices, the VAO's day-to-day work is undertaken by a team of *listing officers*, who compile and update lists of the properties grouped in each band in their area. Overall responsibility for running each district office falls on the local *valuation officer* (also sometimes known as the **district valuer**). It is his or her job to hear any formal appeals initiated by households unhappy with their property valuations.

Although the Council Tax banding system has never been reset in England and Scotland since the government's original mass valuation, homes originally placed in one band can still be moved into a different one under certain circumstances. A property might go up or down for any of the reasons outlined in Table 12.5.

Over the years considerable vitriol has been aimed at the VOA, not least by those whose homes are in higher bands. When they were initially set in 1991 it became an urban myth that the agents employed by the VOA to help valuation officers in the mammoth task of valuing millions of homes for Council Tax purposes for the first time did so simply by driving past houses and awarding them a notional market value purely based on their location and outer appearance. These were jokingly dubbed 'second-gear valuations'.

Local authorities that charge Council Tax to help to finance their services fall into two broad categories, depending on their degree of involvement in actually collecting the money:

- *billing authorities* (or *collection authorities*)—councils that actually send out bills to households, and collect the proceeds to be distributed between themselves and other authorities in their area. In two-tier areas, the billing authority is the district or borough council, while in unitary areas, it is the unitary authority;
- **precepting authorities**—all types of authority entitled to issue a 'precept' (instruction or order) to their local billing authority asking for a share of Council Tax proceeds. In two-tier areas this applies to the billing authority

**Table 12.5** Ways in which properties can change Council Tax bands between revaluations

| Band change | How it happens |
| --- | --- |
| Neighbourhood changes or alterations to buildings | Property falls in value because part of it has been demolished, or the state of its locality has changed significantly (e.g. a sewerage works has been built) |
| Non-domestic use of property | Householder has started—or stopped—using his or her home for business purposes |
| Rise in value due to material change to property | Home can increase in value because of an extension or other major alteration—although an increase in band will not occur unless or until property is sold |
| Home adaptations | Changes made to a home to adapt it for a person with a disability (e.g. disabled ramps, stair lifts, etc.) |
| Incorrect original valuation | Mistake made with original valuation. To determine this, the new occupants of the property must appeal to listing officer within six months of moving in |

itself, the county council (in its role as both top-tier council and local fire authority), and the local *police authority*, while in unitary areas there are still three precepting authorities: the unitary, police, and fire authorities. Every annual Council Tax bill received by a paying household should include a breakdown of the shares allocated to each precepting authority over the financial year. The largest portion goes to the top-tier council (unitary or county). Parish councils also issue precepts for the modest local services they provide, so precepting authorities are grouped into 'major' (county/district/unitary) and 'minor' (parish).

When Council Tax bills for each band for the coming tax year have been determined by local precepting authorities, they will express their precepts publicly in terms of an 'average rate' of Council Tax and the 'average rise' in the value of this rate faced by local taxpayers in comparison to the previous year. As indicated earlier, the 'average rate' is that which applies to a Band D property. It is determined by the following formula:

Total amount the authority intends to spend – Total non-Council Tax revenue

Council Tax base (number of eligible households)

## How central government 'controls' Council Tax bills

Ministers have powers to prevent local authorities charging excessive Council Tax by introducing formal ceilings to stop bills rising above specified levels. This process—known as **capping**—was introduced by the Tories in the Rates Act 1984, and used with increased frequency during the 1980s and 1990s to restrict bill increases by supposed high-spending councils (often Labour ones in poorer areas, which argued that they faced above-average costs in housing, education, and social care). New Labour was generally reluctant to cap authorities, although it retained reserve powers allowing it to do so under certain circumstances and did so increasingly towards the end of its 13-year term. In 2008–09 ministers threatened to cap Portsmouth City Council and seven police authorities—Bedfordshire, Cheshire, Leicestershire, Lincolnshire, Norfolk, Surrey, and Warwickshire—after each announced Council Tax rises above the 5 per cent ceiling it had urged them to respect. David Williams, Portsmouth's *chief executive*, argued the cost of rebilling taxpayers in his area would be £90,000, while only £40,000 would be refunded to 'overcharged' households—causing a deficit of £50,000. Ultimately, only Lincolnshire—which increased its precept by 78.9 per cent—was actually capped, although the other authorities faced limits on precept increases in future.

Such examples aside, Labour's approach to holding down Council Tax bills largely remained that of using its reserve powers to target specific authorities, rather than favouring the across-the-board capping occasionally used by the Conservatives. In November 2007 David Cameron revealed the Tories were considering readopting a version of this 'universal' approach. Under his proposals a so-called 'trigger threshold' would be introduced to limit bill rises. This would essentially be a government-dictated level above which authorities would not be allowed to raise Council Tax without first obtaining the permission of local people in a *referendum*. Critics argued that requiring the public to approve rises in Council Tax bills was tantamount to asking turkeys to vote for Christmas—making it capping by another name. In his June 2010 Budget, coalition Chancellor George Osborne aimed to offset the impact of a series of tax rises slightly by freezing Council Tax rates across England for two years. His action prompted an urgent call from the LGA for the projected £625m loss of revenue to councils that would result from the freeze to be made up by central government, prior to a wholesale review of local authority funding designed to improve fairness.

A further way in which governments have sought to keep Council Tax at reasonable levels is by banning authorities from issuing supplementary precepts—last-minute increases to the sums they request from their local billing authorities because of previously unforeseen changes to their budgetary predictions for the coming year. This was outlawed under the Local Government Finance Act 1982.

## The 'gearing' effect

Notwithstanding central government's ability to 'cap' bills, Council Tax is the one device available to local authorities to generate significant income over and above their annual grants to finance costly expenditure. Therefore, any decision by the government to *reduce* its contribution to a local authority (either by cutting or freezing grants) has tended to push authorities into increasing bills significantly to make up for resulting shortfalls. Similarly, if a council suddenly faces unforeseen revenue demands, but its contribution from government is already set, it will again turn to the Council Tax. The disproportionate rise in bills that can result in such circumstances is known as the 'gearing' effect.

To cite a theoretical example, if a council raises a total revenue income for the coming year of £100m—approximately £25m from the Council Tax—but ends up needing £101m to meet its final spending demands, it will need to raise Council Tax by significantly more than the 1 per cent shortfall to achieve this. In fact, its average Council Tax bills would have to rise by 4 per cent:

$$\text{Projected Council Tax increase} = \frac{£1m}{£25m} = 4 \text{ per cent}$$

# Uniform business rates (UBR)

In addition to their responsibilities for valuing domestic properties, listing officers and valuation officers are also charged with administering the 'equivalent' tax for occupiers of local business premises. While this may sound straightforward enough, uniform business rates (UBR)—otherwise known as 'national non-domestic rates' (NNDR)—have proved almost as controversial as the Council Tax. Introduced alongside the Community Charge in 1990, UBR's initial tax bands were based on a revaluation instigated at the time (aligned to rateable values in 1991), but they have since been revalued every five years. The most recent revaluation took place in 2010, based on rateable values at 1 April 2008.

### How UBR works and why it is unpopular

Like both the long-standing domestic rates system and the previous local business tax before it, UBR is based not on a property's capital value but its *rateable* one. Local listing officers keep a rating list covering all business premises in their area. When first introduced in 1990, UBR caused uproar among many occupants of commercial and industrial land and buildings because of the huge increases in the values of those premises that had occurred since 1973, when the previous business tax—the 'general rate'—had been set.

UBR works as follows. Business premises are valued by the local listing officer (in Scotland, 'assessors'), based on how much they could have been let for at the relevant date. The amount they are actually charged in UBR annually will then depend on a centrally determined calculation made by the Communities Secretary, known as the 'national multiplier' ('poundage' in Scotland). The multiplier is the number of pence in each pound of the value ascribed to a given business premises that its owner is liable to pay for that year. It is set at two levels: a 'standard' rate for middle-range and bigger companies, and a 'small business' rate for those that meet the necessary criteria to be defined as such by the Department for Business, Innovation, and Skills (BIS) and Treasury. Whichever category it falls into, the multiplier is normally held below the level of inflation for business properties with 'average' values.

UBR is therefore determined by the following formula:

$$\text{Rateable value of property} \times \text{National multiplier}$$

To cite a hypothetical example, a business, the premises of which have a rateable value of £50,000, would be expected to pay £25,000 in a year when the multiplier was set at 50p.

As of April 2008, empty business premises became liable for UBR for the first time—although, as with all bills, companies may challenge their ratings through a formal appeals process.

Separate multipliers are currently set for England and Wales. Scotland, in contrast, retains a different system of business rates, which is largely the same as that which first came into existence there in 1854. Although the 1988 Act amended the existing Scottish system as it did elsewhere in the UK, it remains distinct to this day. Until recently, when the **Scottish Government** began to 'pool' the revenue culled from business rates and redistribute it from the centre, one of its primary differences to the English and Welsh UBR was the fact that it was still a 'local tax'—that is, one both collected and spent in each area.

And this is the single most contentious aspect of UBR. As with Council Tax, UBR bills are sent out to businesses by local billing authorities and revenue generated is initially collected by them—but that is where the similarities end. Having been raised locally, UBR revenue is gathered up by central government, which redistributes it to councils according to a population-based formula, taking into account variations in local socio-economic factors in a similar way to the RSG. In effect, this means certain areas of the UK are 'subsidizing' others: the City of London sees millions of pounds raised through its UBR contribution siphoned off to poorer areas. Towards the end of 2010 Mr Pickles announced plans to 'repatriate' UBR for local communities—allowing councils to spend the money raised on their areas locally. An exact timetable had not been set at time of writing, however.

Another controversial aspect of the UBR is the emphasis it places on charging businesses according to the rateable values of the physical premises they occupy, rather than profit levels. A company operating a large factory on an out-of-town industrial estate, for example, will be charged significantly more than a neighbouring business based in a single office—irrespective of which earns the most money. Changes in the British economy over the past two decades have seen many businesses that offer IT services or legal and financial advice (the 'service sector') generate huge profits—despite the fact they often run their affairs from modest premises, with small overheads. In contrast, the decline of the manufacturing sector has seen the turnovers of old-style industries producing large consumer goods from expensive plants, using equally costly machinery, plummet.

These examples aside, like the Council Tax, UBR does offer reductions and exemptions for certain kinds of business property. In addition to those left unoccupied for large parts of the year, the exemptions include the following:

- agricultural land and buildings;
- place of public worship—for example, churches and mosques;
- property used by the disabled;
- fish farms;
- sewers;
- public parks;
- road crossings over watercourses—that is, traffic bridges;
- properties built in specified 'enterprise zones'—designations intended to rejuvenate deprived areas;
- property occupied by visiting armed forces.

## Other sources of local authority revenue income

In addition to the Council Tax and grants, local authorities derive income from:

- council house rents;
- leisure service use—for example, swimming pools, sports centres, library fines, etc.;
- the collection of trade refuse;
- car parking tickets, fines, etc.;
- income from private contractors;
- the *European Social Fund (ESF)*, which provides grants to companies, voluntary groups, and communities in deprived areas to improve training and employment prospects.

## The annual budget timetable at local level

As with most other organizations, the financial year for local authorities runs from 1 April to 31 March. While capital expenditure (to be dealt with next) has traditionally been planned on three–five-year cycles, only recently has the government sought to move revenue expenditure onto the same footing by introducing three-year grant settlements for authorities.

The process by which local spending is decided and provided for is outlined in Table 12.6.

Stories about local authorities being forced to make redundancies and/or slash budgets for essential services because of real-term reductions in government grants have long been a staple of British newspapers. But in October 2008, as the full impact of the global banking crisis unfolded, it emerged that at least 100 councils were facing a highly unusual threat to their solvency. The LGA revealed that up to £1bn of taxpayers' money had been collectively

**Table 12.6** The local authority budget-setting timetable

| Time | Stage |
| --- | --- |
| April | Council holds provisional meeting early in financial year to draw up overall 'budget strategy' for next one. |
| Late April/early May | Follow-up meeting held to decide levels of Council Tax needed to help to finance expenditure for coming year. |
| Late May/early June | Full council meeting follows earlier meetings of main financial committee. Until recently, this was normally known as the **policy and resources committee**; in new-style local authorities, its role falls to **cabinets** (see p. 391). Council leader or elected **mayor** in charge of the council must obtain formal endorsement of their cabinet for major budgetary decisions. |
| July–September | Once overall budget strategy determined, broad revenue estimates for following years must be ironed out. |
| October–December | Government will normally announce following year's formula grant allocations around this time, forcing authorities to make significant adjustments to budgeting for coming financial year. This is usually the last stage at which it is possible for individual departments to increase requests for revenue funding from authority's 'pot' for coming year. To do so, they must submit a **supplementary estimate**, outlining reasons for their increased outgoings. |
| January–February | Council is usually able to confirm and publish final draft estimates for revenue spending. |
| February | Full council has its say formally at special meeting, deciding definitively on levels of spending and Council Tax for next financial year (budgets normally approved in broad terms, but often with modifications). |

invested by councils and police authorities in collapsed Icelandic banks—notably the high-interest online institution Icesave. One authority alone, Kent County Council, had invested £50m, while *Transport for London (TfL)* had deposited £40m and the Metropolitan Police £30m. The news led to a media backlash against individual councils, which were criticized for putting so much faith— and, more particularly, local taxpayers' money—in commercial institutions offering unrealistically generous rates. While a few had been remarkably canny (Brighton and Hove Council decided not to trust the banks' promises), others were named and shamed. For example, Winchester City Council had invested £1m in Heritable, a subsidiary of Iceland's national bank Landsbanki, barely a fortnight before its parent company's collapse—apparently ignoring early warning signs that the country's institutions were on the brink.

With the blame game still in full swing, and many councils lobbying the British and Icelandic governments for help in recouping their losses, in March 2009 the *Audit Commission* published a report in which it criticized seven local authorities for 'negligently' ignoring official warnings by continuing to invest in Icelandic banks even after their credit ratings had been downgraded below acceptable levels. It found that £32.8m had been deposited between the reclassification of the Landsbanki and Glitnir banks as 'adequate' on 30 September 2008 and their collapse barely a week later, on 7 October. Among the biggest investors were the South Yorkshire Pensions Authority, which deposited £10m in one go on 2 October, and Kent County Council, which paid in £8.3m in two chunks on October 1 and 2.

# ▶ The local authority capital budget

Spending on infrastructural improvements—land, roads, buildings, and major items of equipment—is known as 'capital expenditure'. The main sources of local government capital finance are as outlined in Table 12.7.

## Capital borrowing

Although capital projects are funded in discrete ways significantly different from those used to finance revenue spending, they do incur a financial cost to local payers of the Council Tax. One regular outgoing local authorities are compelled by central government to factor into their annual revenue budgets is a 'minimum revenue provision' to cover the systematic repayment of any outstanding debt. This is usually equivalent to 2 per cent of housing debt and 4 per cent of that incurred for other capital purposes in a given year. In addition to paying back the debit itself, it must also make provision for any interest

**Table 12.7** Main sources of capital finance available to local authorities

| Source | How it works |
|---|---|
| Supported borrowing | 'Prudential borrowing' introduced in the Local Government Act 2003 to replace pre-existing system of 'credit approvals'—limits agreed by government—which had been in place since 1990, when brought in to switch emphasis away from controlling council *spending* to limiting *borrowing*. Today, borrowing determined in two ways, as follows. |
| | 1. Each council allowed to borrow up to 'affordable' figure in line with Prudential Code endorsed by Chartered Institute of Public Finance and Accountancy. Up to 2004 authorities were allocated annual basic credit approvals (BCAs)—aggregate figures decided by government departments in relation to areas of activity they covered (e.g. education), against which they issued annual capital guidelines (ACGs) relevant to these areas. This system was criticized for penalizing councils that did not spend their entire allocation each year. Councils could also apply for supplementary credit approvals, which were sometimes agreed late in day for specific projects (e.g. allocation of revenues from one-off 'windfall tax' on profits of privatized utilities that funded the 1997 New Deal for Schools programme).<br>2. Low-interest loans for specific projects from central government, through the **Public Works Loan Board (PWLB),** a body that operates within the UK Debt Management Office, a Treasury executive agency. |
| Prudential borrowing | Councils borrow money and repay it from their own resources without government support. They calculate how much they can afford to borrow according to a code drawn up by CIPFA. |
| Capital receipts | Money raised through local authority's sale of capital assets such as land or buildings, these are divided into two parts:<br>1. the *usable* part;<br>2. the *reserve* part. |
| | Council must set latter aside for use in specified ways, including paying back existing debts. Former can be used to supplement BCAs to invest in new buildings, land, etc. **Secretary of State** determines percentage of usable capital receipts at any given time. In 1998 the agreed percentage was 50 per cent—except, controversially, for receipts from the sale of council houses, only 25 per cent of which could be used for capital spending. The 2003 Act revoked stipulation that a proportion of housing receipts must be set aside by councils for debt reduction, introducing a centralized 'pooling' arrangement under which 75 per cent of capital receipts from council home sales under 'Right to Buy' scheme (see pp. 494–7), and 50 per cent of other housing-related receipts, are redistributed from authorities with less of a housing shortage to those in greater need. |

| Source | How it works |
|--------|--------------|
| Capital grants | In addition to RSGs, local authorities sometimes allocated grants to help finance specific projects. These can come from government departments, public bodies distributing National Lottery money, or hybrid arrangements that combine elements of borrowing with grants (e.g. Transport Supplementary Grant, Single Regeneration Budget, etc.). |
| European Union grants and loans | Money from EU pots including: *European Regional Development Fund* (for specific infrastructure projects and industrial development, usually in deprived areas); European Social Fund (for training and employment initiatives aimed at young people); and structural funds covering various 'objectives' (among them Objective 5b, which helped to fund socio-economic spending in deprived areas such as North Devon). |
| Private sector investment | Often takes form of 'in kind' offer—such as that of development land—and/or funding for capital works like road access or traffic management from private company, in exchange for the ability to recoup investment at later date by running profit-based business related to land in question (so-called *planning gain*— see pp. 472–3). The favourite means of encouraging private capital investment today is through PFI or PPP arrangements for building new schools, care homes, etc. (see also p. 222). These see private companies footing much of initial construction cost, enabling projects to go ahead quicker than if they were relying solely on public funds. In return, companies are paid back—with interest—over period of years, in arrangements similar to mortgages. This means that final costs to taxpayers will be significantly higher than if projects were funded up front by councils. Recent examples of PFI-funded projects include Brighton and Hove's award-winning solar-powered £14m Jubilee Library. |
| Local lotteries | Local authorities permitted to run own lotteries under conditions outlined in National Lottery Act 1993. |
| Local strategic partnerships | In January 2001 government launched a new £36m Community Empowerment Fund designed to encourage community and voluntary organizations to cooperate in LSPs to tackle social deprivation. It aimed to give £300,000-plus to each of the designated LSP areas through government offices for regions. |

on its long-term capital borrowing—the so-called 'revenue implications of the capital programme'. These repayments of capital interest from the revenue account are known as the **debt charge**.

Despite the fact it incurs interest and can take years to pay off, borrowing money to finance capital investment is often seen as politically desirable by both central and local government. The rationale is that, by taking out loans, authorities are 'spreading the costs' of their spending over a number of years—meaning it is not only local taxpayers living in the area at the time a decision is taken to invest in a project who shoulder the costs, but also anyone moving into the area during its lifetime. In addition, borrowing avoids authorities having to fund expensive projects entirely up-front, enabling them to fast-track the construction of schools, libraries, and other amenities that they would otherwise take decades to afford.

Similar arguments have been made by recent governments in favour of local authorities forming cofunding alliances with the private sector—*public–private partnerships (PPPs)* or ***private finance initiatives (PFIs)***—to pay for capital projects that would otherwise take years to finance through public funds alone (see p. 222).

# ▌ The future of local government finance

In the Local Government Act 2000, which introduced sweeping changes to the governance of local authorities, Mr Blair outlined a view of their financial future free of significant shake-ups (the subsequently shelved nationwide review of Council Tax bands notwithstanding). Under pressure to address the continuing anomalies and anachronisms prevalent in the existing funding framework for councils, however, the government appointed Sir Michael Lyons to lead a full-blown inquiry into local government finance. In March 2007 he issued wide-ranging recommendations for short-term, medium-term, and long-term reform, but these have yet to be implemented. They are outlined in the table entitled 'Sir Michael Lyons' recommendations for the reform of local government finance', to be found on the Online Resource Centre accompanying this book.

## Financial transparency at local level

For journalists, some of the best (and most accessible) stories can be found in the publicly available accounts of local authorities. Under s. 15 of the Audit Commission Act 1998, press and public have the right to both inspect and copy these accounts, and all books, deeds, contracts, bills, vouchers, and receipts relating to them. On completing their audited accounts for the previous tax year (usually by a date in June), all authorities are expected to make them formally available for public inspection for 20 working days, advertising this fact in advance. Those inspecting their authority's accounts may address questions about them to the *district auditor*, although the questions must relate to the period inspected and not be about council policy. Those unhappy with items listed in the accounts may lodge a formal grievance with the auditor, in the form of a written 'notice of objection'.

Several notable court judgments have flowed from the 1998 Act—the majority upholding the public's right to disclosure. In December 2009, the case of *Veolia ES Nottinghamshire Ltd v. Nottinghamshire County Council* saw the High Court uphold the council's decision to open the files on confidential documents relating to its signing of a waste management contract with Veolia. Citing a line in the Act compelling authorities to disclose 'all the financial movements or items of account of the council's funds', it confirmed the Act contained no exemption for commercially confidential information (unlike the law governing access to council meetings—see pp. 412–16).

However, while the Act has certainly made it easier for Council Tax-payers to inspect their local authorities' balance sheets, the media's attempts to assert similar rights have not always gone unchallenged. In 2004 ITV West (previously HTV West) narrowly won a High Court judgment forcing Bristol City Council to recognize its status as a 'person interested'— allowing it access to information relating to payments made to a former council officer sacked in 1998 for gross misconduct. Justice Elias ruled in the company's favour on a technicality, saying that it was only in its status as a local 'non-domestic rate taxpayer' that it qualified.

The Act also redressed the balance in previous legislation towards a particular aspect of local government financial transparency: the ability of local electors to access details of local authority payrolls under s. 17(1) of the Local Government Finance Act 1982. Prompted by the 1985 case of *Oliver v. Northampton Borough Council*, the Act precluded public access to accounts or documents containing personal information about authority employees.

Since entering office the Lib-Con coalition has promoted greater financial transparency at local level: as of January 2011, authorities have had to proactively publish details online of every item of spending costing £500—  including salaries and expenses of senior staff, councillors' allowances, and software purchases, utility bills, and consultancy fees—as part of Mr Pickles' 'revolution in town-hall openness and accountability'. They must also publish invitations to tender and final contracts for all projects worth more than £500.

## ≣ Topical feature idea

Figure 12.3 features an extract from Tamworth Borough Council's 2009–10 Budget Report, in which various 'contingency budgets' were proposed for the three-year period to 2011–12 to insure the authority against financial 'uncertainties', including the ongoing aftermath of the **recession**, the unpredictability of **interest rates**, and the council's (at the time) unresolved RSG and housing subsidy settlements from central government. What are the most eye-catching items, and what potential stories do they indicate? Who would you approach to obtain more background information and for help decoding the data? Does the council appear to expect its overall balance sheet to be in surplus or deficit by the end of the three-year period?

**Figure 12.3** An extract from Tamworth Borough Council's 2009–10 Budget Report

| Significant items affecting the base budget are detailed below: | |
| --- | --- |
| **Key Areas** | 3 Years £000s |
| **Loss of income/economic downturn** | |
| Investment income—due to recent and further expected falls in interest rates resulting from global economic issues and potential recession in the UK (base rate reductions) | 1,093 |
| Investment income—effect of Icelandic banking situation | 1,718 |
| Land charges—revised/reduced income forecast | 150 |
| Market income | 150 |
| Car park fees | 159 |
| Industrial and commercial rents | 286 |
| Building control | 180 |
| Grass cutting service income | 150 |
| **Sub-total** | **3,886** |
| **External factors/legislative requirements** | |
| New national concessionary fares scheme | 834 |
| Waste mgt/recycling—revised estimates | 367 |
| Waste mgt contingency | 350 |
| **Sub-total** | **1,551** |
| **Growth areas** | |
| Members allowances—effect of approved increases | 87 |
| Service restructure (EHRS) | 75 |
| Cash collection payment cards—associated with increased usage following change in payment arrangements | 69 |
| Belgrave Sports Centre outdoor events/bonfire | 63 |
| Locality working/community development/interpersonal violence co-ordinator | 66 |
| Tree surveys, street scene, play area maintenance, graffiti removal service | 129 |

| | |
|---|---:|
| Waste management—equipment, vehicle tracking, hazardous waste, Christmas collections | 72 |
| **Sub-total** | **561** |
| ***Efficiency savings/additional income/reduced expenditure*** | |
| ICT operating costs—following review/alternative working arrangements | −111 |
| Decriminalised parking enforcement—revised estimates following experience from implementation elsewhere | −78 |
| Licensing Act income | −70 |
| Savings from review of existing budgets/service reviews | −90 |
| Staffs Connects/CRM—anticipated reduction in costs | −126 |
| HR and transformation staffing | −54 |
| Specific contingency savings 2008/09 | −90 |
| JE contingency saving | −450 |
| Concessionary travel grant—revised forecast 2011/12–2013/14 | −100 |
| Concessionary travel—reduced increase | −168 |
| Insurance/reserve | −300 |
| Charging for pest control/dogs | −51 |
| Housing and planning delivery grant estimate | −419 |
| Building control partnership | −96 |
| Economic development shared service LDC | −60 |
| Assembly rooms and TIC | −195 |
| NNDR on vacant commercial/industrial units—revised legislation | −130 |
| Charge for bulky waste | −70 |
| Reduce floral display budget | −100 |
| Market arrangements potential changes | −150 |
| Reverse inward investment in ind properties/commercial | −150 |
| Vacancy allowance revision (from 4.5% to 5%) | −154 |
| Equipment, printing and stationery budgets saving 10% | −67 |
| Efficiency savings from AES/procurement | −90 |
| Use of reserves | −581 |
| **Sub-total** | **−3,950** |

## ✳ Current issues

- **Return of general block grants:** after years of criticizing Labour's increasingly prescriptive approach to financing local government, the coalition has indicated it intends to hand back to councils the power to decide how to spend most of their revenue income, replacing specific grants with bigger revenue support grants.
- **Lowering Council Tax**: the Conservatives entered the May 2010 election pledging to freeze Council Tax in England for two years, and force councils to hold local

referendums before raising it above pre-determined thresholds set by the government in future. However, with the Department for Communities and Local Government facing a £780m cut in its first year, it remains unclear when this policy will be enacted.

■ **Greater accountability over council spending**: as of September 2010, local authorities have had to publish details of all items of spending of £500-plus in a standard format on their websites. Since January 2011, they have also had to publish invitations to tender and final contracts for all projects worth more than £500. Launching the policy, Communities Secretary Eric Pickles said he hoped to unleash an 'army of armchair auditors' to hold councils accountable for spending.

## ? Review questions

1. What is the difference between 'revenue' and 'capital' expenditure? Outline the main sources of each available to local councils.

2. How does the government determine how much money to give an individual local authority in grants each year, and how does it control how and where that money is spent?

3. How is the Council Tax calculated generally and how does this translate into bills sent to households? List some of the exemptions and reductions.

4. What are the arguments for and against a property-based local tax?

5. Who sets and collects the uniform business rate (national non-domestic rate) and why is it controversial?

## → Further reading

Challis, P. (2003) *Local Government Finance*, London: Local Government Information Unit. **Primarily aimed at local government professionals, but a thorough, detailed, generally accessible guide to the complexities of revenue and capital budgeting.**

Fischel, W. A. (2005) *The Homevoter Hypothesis: How Home Values Influence Local Government Taxation, School Finance, and Land-Use Policies*, Cambridge, MA: Harvard University Press. **Globe-spanning sociological text examining the impact of homeowners on the concentration and quality of local services, and the emergence of 'stakeholder-led localism'.**

Hollis, G., Davies, H., Plokker, K., and Sutherland, M. (1994) *Local Government Finance: An International Comparative Study*, London: LGcommunication. **Again targeted at local government professionals, this offers useful comparisons between Britain's system of local government finance and those applied elsewhere, primarily in mainland Europe.**

Midwinter, A. F. and Monaghan, C. (1993) *From Rates to the Poll Tax: Local Government Finance in the Thatcher Era*, Edinburgh: Edinburgh University Press. **Thoughtful exploration of turbulent Thatcherite reforms of local government finance, focusing on the replacement of rates by the Community Charge.**

## Online Resource Centre

www.oxfordtextbooks.co.uk/orc/Morrison2e/
Visit the Online Resource Centre that accompanies this book for web links and regular updates.

# 13

# Local government decision-making

The previous two chapters examined the nature of local authorities, how they evolved, and the funding systems underpinning them today. But how are councils structured *internally*? What form does their chain of command take, and how do they take decisions?

## ▌ Councillors and officers—who's who?

The work of local authorities is divided between two sets of individuals: *councillors* and *officers*. Like central government, local authorities are composed of a series of spending departments the duties of which spread across the range of services for which they are responsible. These departments—covering areas like education, housing, and social services—are each administered by paid civil servants who are expected to be politically neutral. *Appointed* to their posts on merit, like anyone else given a job, these are the *officers*.

While officers are concerned with process, decisions to put money into one service area rather than another—and precise choices about how those services are run—are based on political judgements taken by elected councillors, whose role is to 'govern' the authority in a manner akin to that in which decisions affecting the whole UK are taken by members of Parliament (MPs). Like MPs, councillors (also known as 'members') each represent their own equivalent of a *constituency*. In the case of county councillors these are known as *electoral divisions* (or 'county divisions'), while in unitary authorities and district and *borough councils* they are usually called *wards* (see p. 417).

# What kind of person becomes a councillor?

The seminal 1972 Bains Report defined the duties of local councillors as to:

- direct and control the affairs of the local authority;
- take key policy decisions defining the objectives of the council and allocating the resources required to attain them;
- keep under review the progress and performance of local services.

This vision of the operation of local government was echoed 14 years later by the 1986 Widdicombe Report, which stressed the importance of the 'complementary relationship' between 'part-time councillors' and 'full-time officers with professional expertise'. The issue was also tackled by a 1990 *Audit Commission* discussion paper, entitled *We Can't Go on Meeting Like This*, which outlined a threefold role for councillors. Four years later, a report by Robert Gifford, then leader of Milton Keynes District Council, identified four 'typical' profiles for councillors. The main conclusions of the latter two papers are listed in Table 13.1.

Although councillors may be likened to MPs in that they are elected (and therefore accountable to voters), there is a fundamental difference between the two: unlike MPs councillors are not paid a salary. The work they do on behalf of local people is therefore essentially voluntary and, for those trying to juggle it with their day jobs, necessarily 'part-time'.

**Table 13.1** Two models for effective councillors

| What all councillors should aspire to be* | The four different types of councillor** |
|---|---|
| *Politician*—an agent of both policy and social change | *Strategists*—those driven to initiate change in a particular policy area |
| *Representative*—a guarantor that the local authority is held to account for prioritizing services, allocating resources, and its overall performance | *Community activists*—those keen to combat a particular local problem |
| *Board member*—willing to share **collective responsibility** for the organization and activities of the local authority, accountable to the dual threat of:<br><br>1. being *voted out* at an election, once every four years;<br>2. being personally *surcharged* for making serious mistakes in major decisions involving public expenditure and/or other responsibilities | *The conscientious*—those eager to repay society for advantages that they have enjoyed |
|  | *Stragglers*—those who are 'last in the room when nominations are handed out' |

*Audit Commission (1990) *We Can't Go On Meeting Like This: The Changing Role of Local Authority Members*, Management Paper No. 8, September, London: HMSO.

**Robert Gifford (1994) in *Municipal Journal*, June, London: Institute for Fiscal Studies.

The fact that councillors are unsalaried has given rise to considerable controversy over the decades, not least because it leads to many councils being dominated politically by the retired and wealthy—those with the time and money to devote themselves to unpaid work for their local communities. Because most councils and their committees have traditionally met for business during normal working days, any employed person able to stand as a councillor has tended to be in a managerial post or running his or her own company—in other words, someone free to set his or her own hours or negotiate time off to attend meetings.

This combination of militating factors has also tended to discriminate against women, fewer of whom have historically held such senior posts and many of whom have been housewives, with all of the attendant childcare responsibilities. Ethnic minorities are also under-represented—even in areas with large immigrant populations. Hardly surprising that the media so often portrays town halls as the preserve of pushy pensioners and white, middle-aged, middle-class men. Recent moves to introduce more evening sittings in some areas—particularly around London, where many people work unsocial hours and commute long distances—have done something to address these issues, but not enough to satisfy critics.

In 1986, the government-appointed Widdicombe Committee found that 81 per cent of councillors were male and 59 per cent hailed from one of three socio-economic groups: professionals, employers and managers, and 'intermediate non-manual' jobs—together representative of only 23 per cent of the overall population. The average councillor at the time was aged 45, with none under the age of 24. The oldest was aged 85. The Committee made 88 recommendations for reform—although most concerned moves to democratize the *political* composition of councils and their committees. Many were implemented by the Local Government and Housing Act 1989.

A series of recent censuses by the Local Government Association and the Improvement and Development Agency (IDeA) suggest little has improved. Announcing the results of the 2008 census (the most recent to date) in January 2009, IDeA remarked that *'little has changed in the diversity of community representatives'*. While the proportion of women councillors had risen by half—from 19 per cent in 1986 to 31 per cent in 2008—the average age of councillors had *increased,* to 59. Just under 87 per cent of all councillors were over 45. Ethnic minorities also continued to fare poorly: only 3.4 per cent were non-white (compared to 8.4 per cent of the UK population). The findings came three years after then Communities Secretary Hazel Blears had used her Labour conference speech to promise a concerted attempt to 'recruit' a more youthful and diverse body of councillors.

Almost as contentious as the question of how to make councillors more representative of multicultural twenty-first-century Britain is the issue of how much work should be expected of them, given their 'unpaid' status. Various attempts have been made to quantify exactly how much time is spent by the average member on council duties both inside and outside 'official hours' (principally meetings). Widdicombe compared his own research with that contained in an earlier study, published in 1964. At that time the average number of hours councillors spent on their duties was 52 a month; by 1986 this had risen to 74. According to a 1998 *Green Paper*, it had increased to 97 by 1992.

The most comprehensive survey of councillors' hours to date, however, was undertaken by Ken Young and Nirmala Rao for the Joseph Rowntree Foundation in 1994. Covering a sample of 1,682 councillors in 53 local authority areas, *The Role of Local Government Councillors in 1993* found that:

- councillors spent 74 hours a month on average on council business (the same figure cited in the Widdicombe Report);
- a fifth of councillors felt their hours were 'about right';
- most felt their most rewarding duty was 'representing' their wards, with only a small minority preferring policymaking or 'carrying out their party's programme';
- councillors spent 56 per cent of their time in council itself, whether attending meetings or liaising with officers;
- most councillors were happy with the long-standing committee and full council decision-making system (see pp. 389–91);
- there was widespread scepticism about the idea of adopting Westminster-style *cabinets*, but considerable support for introducing scrutiny committees based on Commons-style select and standing committees (now *public Bill committees*).

The last two of these observations were ultimately to feed into the root-and-branch reorganization of the internal chains of command within councils instigated by Labour in the Local Government Act (LGA) 2000 (examined in detail later this chapter).

## Councillors' allowances and expenses

Introducing more 'flexible' working hours is not the only way in which local authorities have sought to increase participation by younger working people, women, and those from less affluent backgrounds. In a radical attempt to widen participation some councils are increasingly bending the rules to offer more generous allowances in lieu of formal 'wages'.

Although councillors are unsalaried, there has been a recognized system of allowances and expenses in place for some time. Allowances are designed to give elected members modest payments for attending meetings, while they may also claim expenses to reimburse themselves for the cost of return travel to meetings by car, bicycle, or public transport. Expenses are also available to cover other outgoings that arise out of their official duties, such as paying for overnight accommodation, meals bought during the course of such business, and subsidizing postal costs and domestic telephone bills for phone calls related to their pastoral work with local electors. Councillors aged under 70 are also now eligible to join the generous Local Government Pension Scheme.

The two main types of allowance are:

- the **basic allowance**—a flat-rate annual payment, usually paid—like a salary—on a monthly basis, for *all* councillors representing a specific authority, to which they each become entitled from the moment they are elected as members;

- the **special responsibility allowance**—an additional payment received by councillors who, as well as representing their electors, hold posts of greater responsibility. The size of allowances varies according to how much responsibility they have: council leaders (the most senior councillors) receive the biggest special responsibility allowances, while members of subcommittees and committees, other than their chairpersons, are paid much smaller ones.

Each English council is free to set its own allowance levels, subject to certain restrictions. Since the LGA 2000 every council has been required by law to establish an **independent remuneration panel** comprising at least three individuals—none of whom are themselves councillors. It is the panel's task to review (and adjudicate on) any application by the authority to increase or otherwise amend its allowances. In Scotland, Wales, and Northern Ireland, the system is administered more centrally, with councillors' allowances in each of the devolved countries set by a single independent panel.

Recent surveys point to wide disparities in the generosity of allowances paid by different local authorities—with certain councils offering payments at a level comparable to full-time salaries. According to LGA figures, the average basic allowance paid by English local authorities in 2008 was £6,099, rising to £9,739 for London councillors. Special responsibility allowances averaged £17,753 for council leaders, with those in London boroughs receiving an average of £37,486. Just over half of the 324 councils that replied (representing 84 per cent of the total) offered their members pension schemes similar to those to which their officers were entitled.

In general, councils paying more argue that they are trying to encourage a more representative cross-section of the community to stand. Others, such as Plymouth City Council, have argued that to perform their council work properly members need to treat it as a full-time job—and to be able to do this those without independent means require allowances comparable to a living wage. Devolved administrations have proved considerably more generous with allowance settlements: in 2010, the Independent Remuneration Panel for

Wales recommended a rise in basic allowances from the £11,000-plus many councillors had previously received to £13,868, with council leaders (many already 'earning' £40,000 or more) licensed to claim up to £57,785. Alive to public disquiet about the then recent MPs' expenses scandal—not to mention the pay cuts and freezes many workers endured in the *recession*—some authorities, including Cardiff City Council, refrained from claiming their full entitlements. Meanwhile, in January 2010 the Convention of Scottish Local Authorities (Cosla) voted to back a one-year freeze on basic allowances for councillors (which, in any case, already averaged £15,000—twice the level in England). In Northern Ireland, where by August 2010 around two-thirds of MLAs (each earning at least £42,000) also retained seats as local councillors, controversy has focused less on the size of members' allowances, which averaged £9,500 in 2009, than on their 'double-jobbing' status and the fact they have been able to continue claiming for council duties while sitting at Stormont. At time of writing, a *private member's Bill* aiming to force MLAs to give up their council seats had recently passed its second stage in the Northern Ireland Assembly.

## Meet the experts—the role of local government officers

The number of officers employed by councils varies widely and is ultimately decided by how many resources councillors allocate to finance them. In broad terms, however, every council is obliged to provide certain statutory services and its administration is therefore split, like Whitehall's, into different departments. Each department tends to be run by a qualified professional with expertise in that area.

There are two main types of council spending department: *service* and *central*. As the term implies, the former are concerned with delivering services to the public—housing, education, social services, etc. Central departments are those concerned with the *administration* of the council's functions—principally its legal and financial departments, and those devoted to corporate activities, such as public relations (PR) and marketing.

Officers, like Whitehall civil servants, must be *politically neutral*—whatever their levels of seniority. Those in senior grades are also *politically restricted* (see p. 119). Despite being required to avoid political bias, however, officers are expected to provide councillors with policy advice based on their knowledge and experience. Their roles are to:

- *advise*—defined by the Widdicombe Report as giving 'politically impartial' information and support to aid councillors in their decision-making;
- *support* the executive, non-executive, and scrutiny arms of the council—helping *all* councillors, not only the most senior ones—as outlined in 2000 by the then Department for Transport, Local Government, and the Regions (DTLR).

Each department is headed by its own equivalent of a Whitehall **permanent secretary**. Among the most influential of these are the leading civil servants in the biggest spending areas: the directors of social services and children's services, and the chief planning or housing officers.

Higher up still are three officials whose role is to oversee the workings of the council as a whole, as follows.

- The *chief executive*—also known as the *head of the paid service*, the chief executive is the council's main policy adviser, manager, and coordinator, and is expected to have the requisite experience and maturity to carry out this role effectively. Chief executives often perform the role of 'acting returning officer' at elections, on behalf of the official *returning officer*—normally, the council chairperson or *mayor* (see p. 421). They also have statutory duties to oversee local emergency procedures.

- The **monitoring officer**—the job of the monitoring officer is to report to members, in consultation with the chief executive, any acts of maladministration or breaches of good conduct by officers or councillors, and to uphold the council's **code of conduct** (see pp. 402–3). They are normally also their councils' chief legal officers and should be trained lawyers. It is also for monitoring officers to make sure councils act within their statutory remits at all times—that is, that they do not overreach the powers granted them.

- The *chief financial officer* (or *treasurer/director of finance*) is responsible for overseeing the administration of their council's finances, chief financial officers must be members of recognized accountancy bodies. They may also be referred to as 'directors of central services' or 'section 151 officers' (a reference to the statutory provision from which their authority derives).

Under the LGA 2000 chief executives are formally barred from being appointed as monitoring officers. In addition, like any other officer, chief executives, monitoring officers, and chief financial officers are all subject to a statutory disciplinary procedure that could ultimately lead to their dismissal in the case of misconduct.

To streamline administration of its affairs, improve efficiency, and avoid duplication, each council now has a chief officers' management team. This is a group of senior officers, headed by the chief executive, that meets weekly or fortnightly to discuss policy ideas that might be put forward for councillors' consideration at meetings and/or issues relevant to more than one department.

## New models for service delivery—the era of subcontracting

Until the 1980s the bulk of local authority services—from refuse collection and street cleaning through to building, equipping, and maintaining schools and care homes—were carried out directly by council employees. But over the past thirty years there has been a fundamental shift in the role of councils from being direct *providers* to *enablers*. Whereas everyone from local parking attendants to account clerks would all once have been local authority employees, today they are just as likely to be on the payroll of a private company, voluntary organization, or agency. Rather than delivering local services through the aegis of their own officers and departments, councils are charged with financing, coordinating, and 'commissioning' those services—and the private and voluntary sectors have as much chance of winning contracts to provide them as do local authorities themselves.

The system that ushered in this contract-based approach to local service delivery was known as 'compulsory competitive tendering' (CCT). Introduced in the Local Government, Planning, and Land Act 1980, this forced local authorities to put services out to tender—inviting competing bids from public, voluntary, and/or private sector organizations. The idea was that the most 'cost-effective' bid would be successful, cutting waste and bureaucracy and giving local taxpayers better value for money—while having the added benefit of curbing the influence of unions, following the mass strikes of the 1970s and early 1980s.

Compulsory competitive tendering initially applied largely to 'blue collar' areas of service provision, such as building maintenance and construction work, but it was extended by the Local Government Act 1988 to cover refuse collection, street cleaning, school catering, and other areas. A further extension was introduced by the Local Government Act 1992, which enabled councils to outsource 'professional' and/or 'support services', such as their information technology (IT), marketing, and PR roles. Councils wishing to continue providing services in-house were required to set up arm's-length 'companies' to compete for the contracts on an equal footing with the private and voluntary sectors. The name given to council-owned companies competing for building and/or maintenance contracts for things such as schools, care homes, and council housing was 'direct labour organizations' (DLOs). Those vying to provide services such as refuse collection and school catering were called 'direct service organizations' (DSOs).

In practice the CCT system was constrained by the following factors:

- exceptions to the need to tender for service provision were granted to smaller councils—notably shire districts—under the *de minimis* principle;
- contracting out of corporate and administrative services was eventually given a blanket exemption from CCT;
- following early complaints about service cutbacks after contracting out, ministers were eventually forced to accept advice that the ability to provide a service at a cheap price should *not* be the only criterion for awarding contracts.

Despite these restrictions, councils were soon complaining of being 'forced' to contract services out to private providers. Other criticisms of CTT are listed in the table entitled 'Criticisms of the compulsory competitive tendering (CCT) system', to be found on the Online Resource Centre that accompanies this book.

Although DLOs and DSOs struggled to fend off competition from the private sector, in practice CCT had some positive knock-on effects for them. Many councils decided to group together a number of DSOs and/or DLOs covering different services under a senior chief officer—known as 'contract services divisions'—giving them a more professional overall management structure and producing some of the economies of scale enjoyed by large private companies. When 'support services' like personnel (human resources), legal, and finance departments are run in-house by councils, they are regulated by a formal contractual arrangement called a 'service level agreement' (SLA).

When Labour returned to power in 1997, it scrapped the existing CTT framework. But anyone hoping for a wholesale reversal of the policy of forcing councils to put local services out to tender was to be disappointed, because it was simply replaced with a new system: Best Value (BV) (see also pp. 407–8). The party's 1998 local government Green Paper—*Modernizing Local Government: Improving Local Services through Best Value*—introduced a new statutory obligation for councils to hire the 'most suitable' provider (whether public, private, or voluntary).

Ministers spelt out four 'defining elements' of BV embracing the following aims:

- attaining 'economic, efficient, and effective' services (the '3 Es');
- regular service reviews within which they must demonstrate they had provided Best Value—by comparing their services to those of other providers, and consulting local businesses and residents;
- auditing and measuring their performance through a range of indicators, performance plans, and reviews;
- being prepared for government intervention if Best Value was not attained.

In theory, introducing Best Value meant less emphasis on the wisdom of contracting out services to the private sector for the sake of it—unless it demonstrably offered local people a better deal. There was a perception that, in the past, some councils had outsourced work purely to cut costs and what had often resulted was an inferior alternative delivered by a company, the first priority of which was to pay its shareholders, rather than to provide a high-quality service for local taxpayers. The 1998 Green Paper accused CTT of 'neglecting' service quality and producing 'uneven and uncertain' efficiency gains, 'antagonism' between rival providers, and 'significant costs for employees', including high staff turnover and demoralization. Despite such statements, councils were still expected (if not legally compelled) to put contracts out to tender and, although price was no longer the biggest factor in determining successful bids, many argue the use of 'Best Value' criteria to award (and remove) contracts amounted to CTT in all but name.

The various means by which central government has monitored whether councils are delivering value for money in practice and made this information publicly available are examined in the next chapter.

## Cameron's 'Big Society'—what role for councillors and officers now?

One of the central planks of the Conservatives' May 2010 election campaign—and an enduring slogan of the coalition's first few months in power—was that of the 'Big Society'. Although derided by critics for lacking tangibility, the underlying philosophy underpinning David Cameron's approach to government appeared to be an eagerness to devolve as much power as possible from Whitehall (and, indeed, local authorities) to citizens themselves. This delegation of power, and responsibility, to the grass roots manifested itself in a number of ways in the early days of the new government: the loosening of 'red tape' Mr Cameron saw as stymieing business investment and the planning process; the 'freeing' of schools and hospitals from direct government control (see pp. 442–3 and 176); and, perhaps most fundamentally, the invitation to ordinary members of the public, working alone, in groups, or in partnership with charities or private companies, to set up and run their own local services.

The idea of community-run bus services or road-sweeping patrols staffed by socially conscious pensioners may sound fanciful to some, but in a major speech in July 2010 Mr Cameron signalled his hope of returning to a (to some, imaginary) golden era of active 'volunteerism'. He talked of transforming the 'third sector' (charities and voluntary organizations) into the 'first', and 'turning government upside-down'. While Opposition MPs dismissed this vision as a smokescreen for further public spending cuts—Shadow Work and Pensions Secretary Yvette Cooper described the 'Big Society' as a 'big con', and even Mr Cameron's trusty Communities Secretary Eric Pickles conceded in a BBC interview that it was tied in with the government's wider drive to save money—  for now this new bottom-up approach to commissioning and delivering local services appears to be here to stay. In his first concrete steps towards empowering communities to take control of their own local services, Mr Cameron used his speech to launch a new Big Society Bank to which people could apply for start-up funding—financed by the money held in dormant British bank accounts. He also named four local authority areas as his trailblazing 'Big Society communities': Liverpool, Eden Valley in Cumbria, Windsor and Maidenhead, and Sutton.

## Politicization of council officers—the rise of political assistants

While local government officers are expected to be politically neutral, as early as the Widdicombe Report it was recognized that senior councillors might benefit from access to professional political advice from central government-style special advisers (see pp. 108–9). Widdicombe envisaged 'political assistants' being hired in the following circumstances:

- for councils the chief executives of which are 'by disposition' managers, rather than politicians;
- where a council is 'hung', with three parties all holding the balance of power.

The report emphasized that appointees must be *overt*—that is, that no council should employ officers who acted 'unofficially' as political advisers. Its ideas were further elaborated on by the 1989 Act, which allowed councils to employ political assistants under terms listed in the table entitled 'Conditions of employment for political assistants', to be found on the Online Resource Centre accompanying this book.

In addition, elected mayors under the new local government models introduced by the LGA 2000 would be entitled to appoint their own political assistants. As mayors of London, Ken Livingstone and his successor, Boris Johnson, hired several *spin doctors*, in addition to special policy gurus such as US public transport expert Bob Kiley, the former's adviser on part-privatization of London Underground, and Lord Rogers, his architecture guru. While both of these were effectively consultants, journalists should be wary when dealing with a local authority or its leadership through political advisers, rather than press officers. As political appointees, they are not expected to give as objective a view as their press office colleagues, who are essentially politically neutral administrators.

## ▌ The local government hierarchy under the pre-LGA 2000 system

Prior to the LGA 2000 one fundamental truth applied to all councillors, irrespective of whether the parties to which they were affiliated held overall power on their local authorities: they each had a *direct say* in at least some policy decisions taken by their councils. Policies were initially referred for debate to specialist subcommittees or committees of councillors covering the relevant areas, and had to be approved at that level before ever being presented for final approval to full council. If they were rejected at this first hurdle, the full council would never get to discuss them. If reworded, diluted, consolidated, or otherwise amended at this early stage, then the version of the policy voted on by the full council had usually been substantially shaped by the committee. Because every councillor—whether from the ruling political group, a minority party, or none at all ('independents')—sat on at least one such committee, they each had a direct input, however minor, into the policymaking process. Committee decisions were normally couched as 'recommendations'—that is, they were subject to final approval by full council. The council also reserved the right to reject their rulings, or *refer back* items for reconsideration. Committees did, however, constitute an important part of the day-to-day policymaking function of their local authorities. This 'bottom-up' approach to policymaking is illustrated by the flow chart in Figure 13.1.

In addition to giving all councillors a direct say in policy decisions—and treating them all as 'equals' when it came to voting in full council—the pre-LGA 2000 local authority set-up preserved a simple hierarchy of councillors not dissimilar to that seen among MPs in the House of Commons. A political party that won sufficient seats in a local election to secure an 'overall majority' on the council would become 'the government' in all but name, and its leader would automatically be appointed **leader of the council**—effectively, local 'prime minister'. But beyond this, there were no visible divisions in 'status' between members of the ruling party (or ruling group) and the other councillors on the authority.

There were three types of local authority committee under this pre-LGA 2000 model:

- *standing (statutory) permanent* committees set up to discharge a specific function (for example, to take decisions on planning, education, environmental services);

**Figure 13.1** A flow chart depicting the decision-making process in 'old-style' local authorities and district councils continuing to operate under 'alternative arrangements'

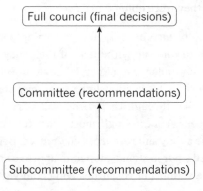

- *ad hoc* committees—often given briefs directly related to the above, but set up to consider specific issues in greater detail than was possible on standing committees;
- *area-based* committees—formed to look at policy governing specific geographical areas under a council's control. They sometimes contained members of the local community beside councillors and even had budgets delegated to them.

As in Parliament, the political composition of committees and subcommittees tended to reflect the balance of power in the main council chamber at any one time. If the Conservatives were in overall control of the council, a majority of committee chairpersons would hail from that party and overall membership of committees would be more or less proportionate to the distribution of seats between parties on the full council. Where no political group had overall control of the authority, standing committees sometimes had no permanent chair; instead, a different chairperson was elected to serve on a meeting-by-meeting basis.

Other conventions governing old-style committees included:

- an ability to 'co-opt' non-councillors to serve on them, either temporarily or on an ongoing basis. These de facto members did not have voting rights—unless they were church representatives sitting on an education-related committee;
- mayors, council chairpersons, and leaders were treated as *ex officio* members of *all* committees in addition to those of which they were normal members. Significantly, this gave them the right both to attend *and* to vote on these committees;
- councils had to avoid any perceived or real conflicts of interest by ensuring that committees with related functions had different memberships;
- in addition to committees, councils often set up working parties comprising both councillors and officers to consider policy options in detail. There has been some controversy about these de facto bodies, because they did not necessarily open their doors to the media and it was a moot point whether they were obliged to do so.

Despite the influence of committees, like governing parties at Westminster ruling groups tended to come up with many of the policy ideas debated at full council meetings, even under the 'old-style' system. Indeed, assuming they had big enough majorities after a local election, they could normally muster sufficient votes to drive through their proposals. The leader was also usually appointed chairperson of the single most powerful local authority committee on the council: the **policy and resources committee**. Because this committee controlled the council's purse strings, it had to approve any major policy decision likely to involve significant resources and could veto those it considered too costly. Most councils covering fewer than 85,000 inhabitants have now abolished this committee, although some have retained an equivalent 'board' or 'panel'.

But beyond these powers, the ruling group had little real 'executive power' in the sense that the government and prime minister do at national level. The leader could appoint a cabinet of senior colleagues, but it had no authority to make executive policy decisions behind closed doors, as commonly occurs at Westminster. Moreover, in practice, the limited majorities attained by ruling groups in many local elections meant coalitions were commonplace—forcing the largest party to compromise many of its policy ideas.

At present, the 'old-style' decision-making system is still used by certain councils. Some dragged their feet, preferring this model to the new ones introduced by the LGA 2000, but others—primarily district councils covering fewer than 85,000 people, and those, like Brighton and Hove City Council, that held unsuccessful ***referenda*** to introduce ***directly elected mayors*** (see p. 397)—were permitted to retain these 'alternative arrangements' indefinitely by the government. They have been allowed to bypass the new-style executive models for now, on condition that they adopt a committee-based system with sufficient scrutiny powers to carry out the same functions competently.

## Local government hierarchies since the LGA 2000

So exactly what form do the 'new' hierarchies introduced by the LGA 2000 take? The main difference between the 'old-style' decision-making system and its principal replacements is that, under the new structures, the balance of power between 'ordinary councillors' and those in ruling groups has shifted radically in favour of the latter. Whereas once all councillors were active participants in the local legislative process, today's council leaders—or, where adopted, elected mayors—hold disproportionate power. Their cabinets, too, have moved from being largely nominal entities to ones equipped to take executive decisions that the rest of the council has little chance of overturning.

The three types of executive management introduced by the LGA 2000 were:

- leader of the council and cabinet/executive;
- directly elected mayor and cabinet/executive;
- directly elected mayor and council manager.

Although actively encouraged by central government to adopt one of the LGA 2000-style models, councils must go through the following two-stage consultation process before introducing their chosen new system on the ground.

1. They must issue an explanation to the public of the three models of executive structure.
2. They must carry out a more detailed formal consultation among local people.

Once a decision has been taken to adopt one of the models, the council must agree the wording of a formal constitution with the Communities Secretary. Any subsequent attempt to change it requires the constitution to be rewritten in consultation with ministers.

Under all three of the LGA 2000 models, the position of leader or mayor is of paramount importance. All councils adopting one of these systems are further divided hierarchically into the following functions: *executive, non-executive*, and *scrutiny*. As is the case at national level, the term 'executive' refers to the powers exercised by senior councillors—members of the cabinet, plus the leader or mayor. Like the prime minister and his or her Cabinet, these individuals may meet and initiate policy in private—even taking final decisions on some matters—without the need first to consult committees and subcommittees, as was the case under the 'old-style' system.

The terms 'scrutiny' and 'non-executive' both apply to committees and subcommittees. Each describes one of the two roles undertaken by committees under the post-LGA regimes.

## Non-executive committees

These committees have *delegated powers* to take some decisions—that is, to reject or approve matters brought before them. The range of matters referred to non-executive committees is limited, however, compared to those deliberated over by committees under the 'old-style' model. A planning subcommittee or committee, for example, might take a decision to reject or approve an application brought before it—without the need for it to be referred on to the full council or cabinet for final approval—but this would only apply to *minor* applications (for example, relating to a small extension to someone's house). The outcome of such applications will already largely have been dictated by the local authority's existing planning rules, as previously agreed by the full council and set by higher tiers of government. More major applications—for example a bid by Tesco to open an out-of-town superstore—will have to go to the full council for final approval.

## Scrutiny committees

'Overview and scrutiny' (or simply 'scrutiny') refers to the function accorded to committees and subcommittees charged with focusing on specific council policy proposals and/or the workings of individual spending departments—for example, children's services, social services, or transport. Their powers, then, are more akin to those of Westminster-style select or public Bill committees (see p. 48) than 'old-style' local authority ones: like parliamentary committees, they can propose policy amendments, call witnesses, and publish reports, but have little power to reject or overturn executive decisions. All local authorities—including those operating under alternative arrangements—are required to establish an overarching **overview and scrutiny committee** comprising councillors drawn from parties in proportion to the distribution of seats on the council. In practice, the majority have split their scrutiny function among a number of subject-specific subcommittees or panels, with some even referring to these as 'select committees' in reference to their parliamentary antecedents.

## Criticisms of the new system

One of the Blair government's principal arguments for the new-style hierarchies was a desire to speed up the pace of council decision-making. By reducing the ability of committees and subcommittees to delay final policy decisions, it hoped to streamline council business. But the stark division between the influence on policymaking exerted today by cabinet members as against 'ordinary' councillors has sparked severe criticism of the Blair reforms—not least from veteran councillors who, after years of public service, have found themselves with less of a direct say than before in the running of their local authorities. The new-style models were widely viewed as introducing 'two tiers' of councillors, as at Westminster: a powerful 'front bench' and a sometimes vocal but ultimately toothless 'back bench'.

Some criticisms of the post-2000 committee changes are undoubtedly justified—not least those levelled by frustrated journalists who yearn for a return to the more knockabout meetings and policy standoffs of old. However, the dilution of 'ordinary' councillors' ability to block contentious proposals or table rebel amendments in the theatrical setting of a lively town-hall meeting has overshadowed the very tangible input many scrutiny committees have had into councils' policy initiatives. In July 2009 the London Borough of Hounslow's children and young people scrutiny panel was awarded £90,000 by the Department of Health to commission new services to tackle speech and language difficulties among poor children in its area. Its successful bid for 'pathfinder' funding came after it completed a review into the communication needs of local preschool children, which found that up to 50 per cent of those living in deprived wards had a language delay or disorder. A month earlier, a credit union was set up to provide low-cost loans to poor households across North Yorkshire after a scrutiny review launched by county councillors brokered a partnership between public, private, and voluntary organizations—bringing to an end a decade of campaigning by locals.

## Types and levels of council decision

Under the 'new-style' executive models, the full council (which used to have to approve virtually all policies before they were implemented) is now only concerned with the most significant decisions. These proposals—defined as those affecting two or more wards or electoral divisions of the authority, and being likely to incur 'significant' expenditure—are called **key decisions**. An example of a key decision might be for the approval of a *Council Tax* rise, or a planning application by developers keen to build a new road (which, by definition, is likely to affect several wards). Each month, in the interests of transparency to local electors, every authority is required to publish a **forward plan** of all key decisions it intends to take over the coming four weeks.

Whatever internal decision-making framework they favour, there are certain other terms common to all local authorities in relation to their proceedings:

- the specific roles and powers delegated by a council to its committees, subcommittees, and cabinet/executive are known as **prescribed functions;**
- whenever final decisions are taken on a matter before a committee, the full council, or cabinet/executive, these are known as **resolved items**. Scrutiny committees or panels may, however, 'call in' items resolved in cabinet and, if they wish, refer them back for a rethink (as with 'old-style' committees).

Figure 13.2 illustrates the top-down decision-making process that defines the chain of command in post-LGA councils. Table 13.2 gives an overview of arguments for and against the LGA 2000 hierarchical models.

**Figure 13.2** A flow chart depicting the decision-making process in post-LGA 2000 councils

**Table 13.2** Arguments for and against the LGA 2000 management models

| For | Against |
| --- | --- |
| Allowing leaders, elected mayors, and cabinets to take some executive decisions unilaterally makes local legislative process faster—and more effective—than when committees had to approve everything. | The new models have created 'two-tier' internal council structures, in which front-benchers not only have more influence on policymaking than **backbenchers**, but sometimes are the *only* councillors with obvious powers. |
| Introducing elected mayors engages the public more closely with local democ-racy—giving it a direct say in decisions over the leadership of its council. In this sense, it is more democratic and councils more accountable than under the old system. | By giving small groups of individuals execu-tive powers, we are replicating 'elective dic-tatorships' sometimes perceived at national level, and making councils *less* democrati-cally accountable now. |
| The LGA 2000 laid down a process by which local electorates could demand referenda on the introduction of elected mayors—an example of bottom-up local democracy in action. It also introduced local constitutions, allowing local authorities to change their leadership structures subject to ministerial agreement. | Introducing three alternative models for council leadership led to patchwork land-scape of local authority hierarchies across the UK. This confuses voters and can lead to inconsistent local representation. |

# The 'leader and cabinet' model

Of the three new executive management options introduced by the LGA 2000, that with the most similarities to the existing system is the 'leader and cabinet' model. As under the 'old-style' council hierarchy, the leader is normally the head of his or her party—usually that which secured the most seats in the pre-ceding local election. Like 'old-style' leaders, he or she heads a cabinet made up of close confidantes on the council, normally drawn from his or her own party or (where no single party has overall control) a coalition grouping.

But this is where the similarities between 'old-style' and 'new-style' leader-and-cabinet systems end. The new-style cabinets/executives are much more like those formed by prime ministers than the ones that preceded them. Until recently, it was left to the discretion of individual councils adopting this model to decide whether they wanted a 'weak' leader or a 'strong' one. Under the former approach, the council as a whole selects its leader and individual cabinet mem-bers, and all executive decisions must be taken *collectively* by that cabinet. The 'strong leader' approach, in contrast, allows the leader (once elected by his or her fellow councillors) to choose his or her own cabinet members, delegating Westminster-style policy portfolios to each. As of December 2010, this variant became mandatory for all councils with a leader and cabinet (other than those still using alternative arrangements)—with county councils, London boroughs and metropolitan districts, and finally non-metropolitan districts/boroughs and unitary authorities introducing them successively in a programme of phased reform under the Local Government and Public Involvement in Health Act 2007.

The 2007 Act also stipulated that executive leaders should serve automatic terms of four years—an approach dubbed 'strong leader plus'—whereas the 2000 changes had allowed councils to appoint them for one year at a time.

Controversially, although individual cabinet members are generally expected to consult with cabinet colleagues, in some cases they may take executive action with little input from any other councillors—either 'backbench' or 'frontbench'. The same applies to the leader. Of still greater concern to some critics of the post-2000 changes is the fact that, although most cabinets now meet in public at least some of the time, they are only obliged to do so in relation to policy matters they are due to resolve as a collective. In other words, matters delegated for a decision to individual cabinet members (or, in some cases, unelected officers) may be resolved in secret.

The committee system has therefore gone from being a *proactive* agent in policymaking to a largely *reactive* one. Meanwhile, meetings of the full council—which still nominally has the final say over whether policies are approved—are often portrayed as 'rubber stamps' for decisions already finalized behind closed doors in cabinet. Similar charges are made of the second of the three models. In July 2010 Mr Pickles revealed in an interview with Conservative blogger Iain Dale that he intended to include a provision in his then forthcoming Local Government Bill allowing councils keen to scrap cabinets and return to an old-style committee system to do so.

## The 'directly elected mayor and cabinet' model

As explained in Chapter 11, there is a long-standing tradition among district and borough councils and metropolitan district councils of appointing mayors. The office of mayor has customarily, however, been a ceremonial one—with elected councillors taking it in turns to spend a year in the role, before passing on their chain of office to a colleague. While serving as mayor, the individual will adopt the role of returning officer in the event of a local, general, or European election, and officiate over civic duties (opening fetes, visiting schools, etc.), as well as chairing meetings of full council. In this capacity, like the Commons *Speaker*, he or she will temporarily drop his or her party allegiances and right to take part in policy votes.

Directly elected mayors occupy a different position. First, unlike both council leaders and old-style mayors, they are not themselves councillors: instead they are voted in by their local electorates in separate ballots run *alongside* the main council elections in their areas. When the Conservative candidate for London Mayor, Boris Johnson, thwarted Ken Livingstone's bid to win a third term in May 2008, the separate election for members of the *Greater London Authority (GLA)* saw the Tories lose one seat to Labour (although they remained the biggest party, having eight seats to Labour's six). In this respect, the post of elected mayor bears more similarities to that of the US president than the

British prime minister. While no Labour prime minister could remain in post long after a general election in which the Tories won more seats, the same is not true of presidents: the 2006 US congressional elections returned narrow Democratic majorities in both the Senate and House of Representatives, but Republican president George W. Bush stayed in post for two more years. This mirrored the 2004 London mayoral contest, in which Mr Livingstone won his second term, despite Labour's losing control of the GLA (dropping to five seats against the Tories' nine).

Before being permitted to introduce elected mayors, local authorities are required to hold a referendum of the local electorate. Conversely, if 5 per cent of that electorate decides it favours the mayoral system, it may *demand* a referendum—whatever the council's own view. Where referenda are held, the question used adopts the following standard wording:

❝ Are you in favour of the proposal for [name of city/borough] to be run in a new way, which includes a mayor, who will be elected by the voters of [that place], to be in charge of the council's services and to lead [name of authority] and the community it serves? ❞

Labour's hope was that *all* councils would have initiated a consultation within six–nine months of the passage of the LGA 2000—with many favouring the mayoral option. In practice it took until February 2002 for most English councils to publish proposals, and when they did 80 per cent opted for the leader-and-cabinet model. At time of writing, only 13 councils had introduced elected mayors, with the Greater London Authority Act 1999 making the GLA the first  to adopt one and the London Borough of Tower Hamlets becoming the latest to do so, with its first mayoral election on 21 October 2010. The slow pace of reform elsewhere has been put down, in part, to the fact that whenever a referendum is lost another cannot be held by the same council for five years. Of the 37 such referenda held to date, 25 failed to secure a majority in favour of elected mayors. In addition, campaigns have been launched at various points in four local authority areas to abolish the post: Stoke-on-Trent (where it was subsequently scrapped—see p. 398), Doncaster, Lewisham, and Hartlepool (where, in 2009, Hartlepool United Football Club mascot 'H'Angus the Monkey'—alias Stuart Drummond—became the first elected mayor to win a third term). The 13 councils operating an elected mayoral system as of October 2010 are listed in the table entitled 'Local authorities with directly elected mayors', to be found on the Online Resource Centre accompanying this book.

To boost take-up of elected mayors, the Labour government published a raft of new proposals in July 2008, making it easier for local electors to trigger referenda, by enabling those campaigning for 'yes' votes to recruit supporters through online petitions. The plans were announced shortly after the failure of a campaign led by the *Birmingham Mail* newspaper to marshal the 36,000 electors required to kick-start a mayoral contest in Birmingham. In their May 2010

see p. 398

election manifesto, the Conservatives pledged to introduce directly elected mayors (subject to referendum approval) in Birmingham and the 11 other largest English cities outside London: Leeds, Sheffield, Bradford, Manchester, Liverpool, Bristol, Wakefield, Coventry, Leicester, Nottingham, and Newcastle. At time of writing, though, there was no firm timetable.

Labour's policy document also set out several proposals for boosting grass-roots localism by bringing council decision-making closer to electors. In particular, it emphasized the idea of 'double *devolution*'—devolving lower-level, day-to-day decisions on how to run amenities like parks and community centres from elected councils to community-based groups led by their users. In the event, this idea was to be usurped (and taken much further) by Mr Cameron's 'Big Society'.

## The 'mayor and council manager' model—and its demise

The most contentious illustration of the increased powers accrued by some individuals under the LGA 2000 was found in the third executive management option it proposed: the 'elected mayor and council manager' model. Under this system, executive decision-making powers would be vested in only one person other than the elected mayor: the council manager, who, as a senior officer, would be appointed (rather than elected) to the second most influential position in the authority.

That more has not been made of this questionably democratic set-up in the national media must largely be down to the lack of interest expressed in it by councils: by 2006 only one English authority—Stoke-on-Trent—had adopted it, and in October 2008 local electors voted to drop it in favour of the leader-and-cabinet model.

Following Stoke's abandonment of the mayor and council manager model, the 2007 Act abolished this option in England. Although it remains in Wales for the time being, the devolved Assembly is expected to scrap it by 2012.

### ☰ Topical feature idea

Since December 2010, all local authorities operating under post-2000 leader and cabinet executive arrangements have had to adopt a 'strong leader plus' approach to governance. Leaders are now elected by their fellow councillors for four-year terms (unless due to face a local election before the end of that period), and may only be removed by formal resolutions passed by those councillors. They may appoint their own cabinet members, delegating decision-making powers as they see fit. If they fall ill, quit, or are otherwise 'unable to act', their deputy leaders will assume their full leadership powers in their absence. The changes confer significant extra authority on many leaders, who up to now have generally only held office for a year at a time and have had to work with cabinets chosen by their councils. How have the post-2007 changes affected councils in your area, and how recently have they come into effect? What do backbench councillors (and members of the public) feel about them?

## ✳ Current issues

- **The future of directly elected mayors:** prior to regaining power in May 2010, the Conservatives committed themselves to rolling out Labour's drive to introduce US-style directly elected mayors in English towns and cities, but Communities Secretary Mr Pickles has since indicated the plans might be delayed for financial reasons.

- **Curbs on pay of senior council officers:** as he battles to find cuts of £780m, Mr Pickles has said that in future few senior officers (some of whose salaries 'would make a football manager blush') can expect to earn more than £100,000.

- **Greater transparency over allowances and expenses:** Mr Pickles wrote to all councils in June 2010 urging them to introduce 'greater clarity' over expenses and allowances claimable by councillors. Precise details of the extent to which these will need to be contemporaneously published in future remain as unclear, but since September 2010 all expenses incurred by councils over £500 have had to be published.

## ? Review questions

1. Outline the main difference between the responsibilities of 'officers' and 'councillors'. Who has most power and who is more accountable?

2. Describe the main changes to internal local authority hierarchies introduced under the Local Government Act 2000. Which model is most democratically accountable?

3. What are the differences between the traditional roles of mayors and those of directly elected mayors? How does a town or city go about introducing the latter?

4. Who has power to take executive action under the three forms of local authority leadership introduced by the LGA 2000? Why have the changes been so contentious?

5. How are councillors currently remunerated? What are the arguments for and against increasing their payments and/or introducing salaried councillors?

## → Further reading

Boynton, J. (1986) *Job at the Top: Chief Executive in Local Government*, London: Financial Times/Prentice Hall. **Concise, authoritative text examining the emergence and growing influence of local authority chief executives and other senior officers.**

Hodge, M., Leach, S., and Stoker, G. (1997) *Local Government Policy: More Than the Flower Show—Elected Mayors and Democracy*, London: Fabian Society. **Pamphlet arguing for the merits of directly elected mayors, prior to their introduction by the Blair government.**

Randle, A. (2004) *Mayors Mid-term: Lessons from the First Eighteen Months of Directly Elected Mayors*, London: New Local Government Network. **Impeccably researched booklet from NLGN think tank citing quantitative and qualitative data examining the impact of the introduction of directly elected mayors.**

Rogers, S. (1998) *Performance Management in Local Government: The Route to Best Value*, 2nd edn, London: Financial Times/Prentice Hall. **Second edition of the guide, principally aimed at local government professionals, focusing on new management standards introduced by Labour.**

## 🌐 Online Resource Centre

www.oxfordtextbooks.co.uk/orc/Morrison2e/

Visit the Online Resource Centre that accompanies this book for web links and regular updates.

# 14

# Local government accountability and elections

British local authorities are responsible for spending more than £65bn a year in taxpayers' money between them. Perhaps understandably, the decisions they make on behalf of those whose interests they represent are subject to increasing scrutiny.

Councils are accountable to local citizens by:

- publishing their own **standing orders**, *codes of conduct*, and constitutions;
- submitting their accounts to independent audits and publication of performance data;
- allowing press and public to attend their meetings and to access **agendas** and reports;
- giving local people a say through the ballot box at local authority elections.

This chapter focuses on the increasing array of ways in which today's councillors (and officers) are held to account.

## ▌ Local government post-Nolan—the new era of transparency

As with central government, local authorities have long been expected to adhere to systems, rules, and procedures in conducting their business. But the extent to which councils were required to *demonstrate* their integrity and openness underwent a profound shift following the succession of high-profile parliamentary scandals that led to the findings of the Nolan Inquiry (see pp. 53–4).

The immediate effect of Lord Nolan's recommendations, published in 1996, was to compel all public officials—starting with MPs, but extending down to local councillors and officers—to uphold the 'Seven Principles of Public Life': selflessness, integrity, objectivity, accountability, openness, honesty, and leadership (see p. 54). But he and the prime minister who commissioned his inquiry, John Major, had a desire to go further—an aspiration shared by the latter's successor, Tony Blair, who consolidated his reforms in the Local Government Act 2000. Today, the processes introduced to police the behaviour of MPs at national level also underpin accountability in local government.

## Emergence of council constitutions

As mentioned in the previous chapter, under the LGA 2000 every local authority is now obliged to draw up—and agree with the Communities Secretary—its own **council constitution**. Within reason, this constitution can take any number of forms—whether a broad mission statement or a more detailed breakdown of the council's responsibilities and services. The very fact that individual councils are free, in theory, to devise their own wording reflects an acknowledgement by government that the particular issues different councils face in running their affairs vary. Since 19 December 2000, however, *all* constitutions have had to contain all of the components listed in Table 14.1.

**Table 14.1** The compulsory components of a local authority constitution since 19 December 2000

| Component |
|---|
| 1.  Summary and explanation of purpose and content of constitution. |
| 2.  Description of composition of council, scheme of ordinary elections for members of council, and their terms of office. |
| 3.  Breakdown of principal roles and functions of councillors, including rights and duties of individual members. |
| 4.  Scheme of allowances for councillors. |
| 5.  Description of local inhabitants' rights and responsibilities, including their rights to vote in local elections, access information about local services, and access council, committee, subcommittee, and **cabinet**/executive meetings. |
| 6.  Description of council's roles. |
| 7.  Rules governing conduct and proceedings of meetings of authority. |
| 8.  Description of roles and functions of chairman of council (including **mayors**), leader/**directly elected mayor**, cabinet/executive, individual cabinet members, and individual officers with delegated executive powers. |
| 9.  Description of arrangements for operation of **overview and scrutiny committees**, their terms of reference, membership, and any rules governing them. |
| 10. Provisions in local authority's executive arrangements with respect to appointment of committees of executive. |

| | Component |
|---|---|
| 11. | Membership, terms of reference, and functions of committees and subcommittees, and any rules governing conduct of their meetings. |
| 12. | Description of roles of authority's **standards committee** and any parish council sub-committee of standards committee (plus details of membership). |
| 13. | Description of roles and membership of any area committees of authority. |
| 14. | Description of any joint arrangements made with other local authorities. |
| 15. | Description of officers' roles, including those of senior management. |
| 16. | Role and functions of **chief executive**, **monitoring officer**, and chief finance officer. |
| 17. | **Code of conduct** for local government employees issued under Act, plus any details governing their recruitment, disciplinary procedures, etc. |
| 18. | Any protocol established by authority in respect of relationships between its members and officers. |
| 19. | Description of arrangements the authority has in place for access of the public, members, and officers to meetings of full council, the cabinet/executive, committees, subcommittees, and joint committees. |
| 20. | Description of arrangements the authority has in place for access of public, members, and officers to information about decisions made—or to be made—by any of above meetings. |
| 21. | Register stating names and addresses of every member of local authority executive, **wards** or divisions they represent, and names of every member of each executive committee. |
| 22. | Description of rules and procedures for management of authority's financial, contractual, and legal affairs, including procedures for auditing. |
| 23. | Authority's financial rules and regulations, and those governing procedures regarding contracts and procurement (including authentication of documents). |
| 24. | Rules and procedures for legal proceedings brought by and against the authority. |
| 25. | Description of **register of members' interests** of all full and co-opted members of authority, and procedures for publicizing, maintaining, and updating it. |
| 26. | Description of rules and procedures for review and revision of authority's constitution, and its management structure. |
| 27. | Copy of authority's standing orders and code of conduct. |

Section 37 of the LGA 2000 specifies that copies of councils' constitutions must be available for inspection by the public 'at their principal offices' within 'all reasonable hours'. Personal copies must also be supplied by them to anyone on request—subject to the payment of a 'reasonable fee'.

# The foundation stones of council constitutions

What, then, of the various technical terms highlighted in the government's criteria for the content of constitutions? The concept of 'standing orders' is one that should be familiar to anyone who has worked for an organization of any size, whether in the public, private, or voluntary sector. It refers to the overall system of rules and guidelines governing the day-to-day conduct of local authority business. Like the constitution as a whole, individual councils set their own standing orders—meaning they can be as detailed or as vague as they wish. Some authorities may choose to incorporate into their standing orders rules governing the propriety of councillors and officers—for example, the requirement that those with financial interests in a matter due to be discussed by a committee in which they are involved declare this fact and remove themselves from its meetings. Others may confine their standing orders to mundane procedural issues (as a bare minimum, most contain a breakdown of the customary order of business at council, committee, and cabinet meetings).

The remaining terms singled out by the LGA 2000 in instructing councils how to frame their constitutions all refer to the post-Nolan preoccupation with enforcing national standards of ethical conduct by public officials. Most councils have long had agreed codes of conduct specifying lists of 'dos' and 'don'ts' by which their members must abide. In the wake of the sleaze allegations of the 1990s, however, a new onus was placed on those in public life at all levels to clean up their acts—in particular, keeping their 'outside interests' separate from the duties they performed on the public's behalf.

Given the unpaid nature of councillors' work and the fact that many are juggling their duties with earning livings elsewhere (not always in the same town or city), the potential conflicts of interest in local government are arguably more multifarious than those faced by MPs at Westminster. The councillor who is a member of his or her authority's planning committee and also sits on the board of a company with development interests in the area poses an all-too-familiar conundrum—and for this reason most authorities have long had in place clear rules compelling members to make a **declaration of interest** in relation to any outside pecuniary interest. There has also been some criticism that councillors in this position, particularly those who stand for election in the first place on 'independent' tickets related to particular causes, such as defending a local service from closure, are relegated to weaker positions than conventional party-political ones.

The Local Government Act 1972 was the first to introduce the idea of local registers of interests, but as these were voluntary, councils were under no legal obligation to comply. It was the LGA 2000 that finally standardized the process, requiring *every* council to publish a reworded constitution reflecting Lord Nolan's 'Seven Principles'. Declarations of interest, meanwhile, must now be made at the point at which someone first stands for election. As with MPs and peers they are required to enter all interests on a register of members' interests (see p. 52) within 28 days of being elected, which—given that new ones can emerge at any time—must be updated within 28 days of any such changes occurring. Councillors must also declare relevant interests at the start of any meeting in which they are due to participate should there be any agenda items in which they have a personal involvement. In such circumstances, they should remove themselves from the meeting—but only for the duration of that item. The main types of interest defined by law are:

- employment or business interests;
- contributions to election expenses;
- shareholdings of £25,000 or more or ownership of more than 1 per cent of issued share capital in a company with a place of business or land in the council's area;
- a business interest in contracts between the authority and any other;
- land owned, leased, or held under licence for more than 28 days in the authority's area;
- membership or management of a public authority, company, charity, trade union, or professional association.

Beyond this, it is the precise *nature and extent* of a councillor's interest that determines whether it falls into one of two categories that might affect their ability to carry out their duties in an impartial and/or trustworthy way. Where previously interests would have been seen as either 'pecuniary' or 'non-pecuniary', the LGA 2000 defines them as either:

- *personal*—any matter considered by the council the outcome of which might reasonably be regarded as affecting the 'wellbeing or financial position' of him or herself, a relative, friend, or organization in which he or she has an interest; or
- *prejudicial*—a matter which a member of the public with knowledge of the facts might reasonably regard as so significant that it is likely to prejudice the councillor's judgement of what is in the public interest.

The main powers of the National Standards Board are outlined in the table entitled 'The main powers of the National Standards Board for England', to be found on the Online Resource Centre that accompanies this book.

## Police authorities

The requirement to adopt a code of conduct under the LGA 2000 also applies to *police authorities*, the members of which are expected to observe their code whenever conducting business in its name or otherwise representing it. From time to time authority members are called on to sit on another authority or body in an official capacity, and when doing so they are bound not only by their own code, but also by that other body's. In addition to adhering to the code of conduct, police authority members are bound by the following 'general obligations':

- to promote equality by not discriminating unlawfully against anyone;
- to treat others with respect;

- to act in accordance with the authority's requirements when using or authorizing the use of its resources, ensuring that those resources are not used for political purposes;

- to have regard in reaching decisions to the advice of the authority's chief finance officer and monitoring officer.

Further, they must *not*:

- do anything likely to compromise the impartiality of a police officer or anyone who works on behalf of the authority;

- disclose information given to them in confidence, or information they believe to be confidential, without the consent of a person authorized to give it;

- prevent another person accessing information to which he or she is entitled by law;

- conduct themselves in their official capacity in ways that might bring their offices or authorities into disrepute.

# Regulating standards

So much for the rules: who polices them? As explained in the last chapter, each local authority has a designated monitoring officer whose job is to ensure that the council as a whole—and its constituent parts—act within the law and do not overreach their powers. The introduction of codes of conduct and registers of interests—coupled with the onus placed on officers, as well as councillors, to act accountably—has been accompanied by a new emphasis on objective scrutiny. To this end, each council must now appoint a standards committee, like that at Westminster, to monitor the actions of its officials and to raise concerns about unethical conduct. Its independence is theoretically assured by the fact that, in addition to two or more members of the council itself, it must include at least one individual who is neither a councillor nor an officer of that or 'any other relevant' authority.

The roles of standards committees are to:

- promote and maintain high standards of conduct by members and co-opted members;

- assist members and co-opted members of the authority to observe its code of conduct;

- advise the authority on the adoption or revision of a code of conduct;

- monitor the operation of the code of conduct;

- advise, train, or arrange to train members and co-opted members of the authority on matters relating to the code of conduct.

On a day-to-day basis, they often devolve many of their functions to a subcommittee of the authority, but the composition and precise remit of that subcommittee must be formally agreed with the involvement of local parish councils.

At the other end of the scale, the conduct of English local authorities, their councillors, and officers has, for more than a decade, been overseen by a *quango*, the *Standards for England* (formerly the Standards Board for England). Members of authorities made aware of any apparent misconduct by a colleague have been expected to make formal 'written allegations' to it. However, coalition Communities Secretary Eric Pickles announced its abolition in May 2010, so it remains to be seen how complaints relating to English local authorities will be handled in future. In Wales, allegations of code of conduct breaches are handled by its overarching *Public Services Ombudsman for Wales*, while errant members of Scottish authorities may be disciplined by the *Standards Commission for Scotland*. At time of writing, the Northern Ireland Assembly was finalizing plans for a new standards framework through the passage of its Local Government (Reorganization) Bill.

While the various standards regulators have only minimal legal powers, helpfully for the media they normally disclose the fact that a complaint has been made, issuing full details of their eventual decisions and any sanctions arising from them.

### From 'Beacon Councils' to the National Indicator Set—the growth of performance data

The growing emphasis placed on promoting high ethical standards among public officials emerged hand in hand with what critics decried as a spiralling government obsession with centrally directed performance targets, league tables, and ratings systems to grade the quality of their work. First up under New Labour were 'Beacon Councils'—authorities singled out as examples of best practice in particular areas of service delivery. Then came Best Value performance indicators (BVPIs), which defined four key 'dimensions of performance' (or criteria, to the layperson) against which the effectiveness of specific local services would in future be measured:

- *strategic objectives*—why the service existed and what it sought to achieve;
- *service delivery outcomes*—how well the service was run;
- *quality*—how well the services delivered, reflecting users' experience of them (that is, not only 'how many' or 'how quickly', but 'how good');
- *fair access*—the ease and equality with which the services could be accessed.

The early Blair years saw an explosion of BVPIs—some covering local services as a whole; others specific aspects of individual ones, ranging from local street cleaning to childcare provision. Early BVPIs focused on 'service delivery' (the actual standard of local services from the public's perspective) and 'corporate health' (a category itself containing a further 18 indicators, relating to everything from 'customers and the community' to 'partnership working'). Eventually there were more than ninety BVPIs.

But the advent of BV marked merely the beginning of a new era of monitoring, auditing, and evaluating local authorities' performance. In December 2002 a new system of service-by-service performance ratings was introduced: *comprehensive performance assessment (CPA)*. Overall responsibility for monitoring the effectiveness of individual local authorities in England and Wales (including police authorities)—and taking action when necessary—was handed to a central government quango, the **Audit Commission**, which has discharged this role through a network of **district auditors** (each overseeing a specific authority area). Scottish councils are held to account by Audit Scotland, while Northern Irish ones have their books pored over by designated officers from the Northern Ireland Audit Office (NIA).

Initially covering only 'top-tier' local authorities (county councils and unitaries), CPA was subsequently extended to encompass districts/boroughs, and fire and rescue authorities. One of the main differences between BV and CPA was that the new set of data was made public, allowing local taxpayers and the media to judge the performance of their councils in specific service areas against those of other authorities in much the same way that they might view hospital league tables or school exams performance data.

CPA used a four-star ratings system and broke each of its frameworks down into a list of service areas. Councils were rated on a department-by-department basis—meaning that, for example, the same county council might score highly in relation to its social care provision, but poorly in education—or vice versa. Star ratings were applied in the following four assessment categories:

- corporate efficiency;
- use of resources;
- quality of services;
- direction of travel—that is, whether they were improving and how rapidly.

The public could visit the Commission's website at any time to access their local council's CPA 'scorecard', while its annual reports would 'name and shame' the best and worst of the previous year, which judged them not only on their absolute star rating, but also a value-added basis, known as 'direction of travel'. But CPA was far from the last word in New Labour's quest to find the perfect rating system.

In April 2009, a modified version of CPA was introduced in the form of *comprehensive area assessment (CAA)*, which sought to focus not on the performances of individual local authorities but on the overall 'experience' of public services for people living and working in a given council area. The resulting dataset reflected a growing belief in government circles that taxpayers were more concerned about the standard of *services* than the notional 'performance' of the specific organizations that happened to deliver them.

Like CPA, CAA incorporated four key elements, placing particular emphasis on the 'direction of travel' of local services and how effectively local resources were being used. Shortly after Gordon Brown replaced Mr Blair in Downing Street, Labour finally began to rationalize the amount of local government data it was generating—bringing all existing datasets (principally CAA and BVPIs) together under a single banner, known as *National Indicator Sets (NIS)* and giving everyone instant online access to all of this information via a single website (oneplace.direct.gov.uk).

At time of writing, the future of publicly available performance data was in question, following Mr Pickles' decision to scrap CAA and introduce a new emphasis on individual local authority transparency. Both NIS and the Oneplace website were under review, and it appeared there would be a new onus on councils themselves to proactively publish their own performance data in an 'open and standardized manner'—reflecting the Conservatives' determination to promote 'localism' in all aspects of service commissioning and delivery. Everything from waste disposal and recycling rates to food hygiene reports and pub licensing decisions were due to be laid open for public inspection on councils' websites, alongside details of all items of expenditure of £500 or more (see p. 373). Mr Pickles also unexpectedly announced that the Audit Commission, set up by a previous Tory government in 1983, would be axed by 2012. Its research role would be scrapped, but its auditing function would become an arena for competition from private companies. A new, independent auditing framework would also be established specifically for local health services.

Other ways of assessing performance are outlined in the table entitled 'Other recent measures for assessing local authority performance', to be found on the Online Resource Centre that accompanies this book.

## The last resort—the role of Local Government Ombudsmen

Targets, league tables, and performance data can only take things so far. What can people do if they feel they are the victim of an injustice at the hands of their local authorities—or if they believe they have lost out because a council has, say, taken an incorrect decision on their eligibility for services to which they are entitled?

In relation to English local authorities, the answer is to lodge formal complaints with the *Local Government Ombudsman*—better known today as the **Commission for Local Administration** in England. The remit of the three ombudsmen employed by the service is to investigate allegations of maladministration—the negligent or incompetent running of local services. They are not there simply to investigate complaints relating to decisions about which people are unhappy, however, *unless* those decisions show evidence of maladministration. Since 1988 complainants have been able to take their cases direct to the ombudsmen without the need to use their local councillors as intermediaries (a principle enshrined in the Local Government Act 1974, which had first established it). This change had an immediate impact on the number of complaints made: in the first year alone they soared by 44 per cent.

England's three ombudsmen are each responsible for a specific geographical area:

- London, Buckinghamshire, Berkshire, Hertfordshire, Essex, Kent, Surrey, Suffolk, and Sussex;
- Birmingham City, Solihull MBC, Cheshire, Derbyshire, Nottinghamshire, Lincolnshire, Warwickshire and the north of England;
- the rest of the country.

In Wales, since 2006 local government maladministration has been policed by the overarching *Public Services Ombudsman for Wales*, while in Scotland a *Scottish Public Services Ombudsman* was introduced in 2003. The *Northern Ireland Ombudsman*, meanwhile, has been in place since 1969.

Complaints processes to these various bodies are subject to a range of conditions. The conditions applying in England are indicative of those in the devolved countries, and are as outlined in the table entitled 'The conditions for filing complaints with the Local Government Commissioner', to be found on the Online Resource Centre that accompanies this book.

As more people become aware of the remit of the ombudsmen, so the number of complaints investigated each year continues to rise. In 2008–09, the latest year at time of writing for which precise data was available, England's ombudsmen received 21,012 new complaints. A breakdown of the areas into which they fell is given in Figure 14.1.

Understandably, journalists are always keen to find out about cases being heard by the ombudsmen, because they tend to concern major complaints and to be highly newsworthy. At times, however, these stories can be frustrating: while ombudsmen's final adjudications are always made public, because the identities of those involved are usually kept anonymous, the resulting reports are rarely as revealing as the press (or public) might hope.

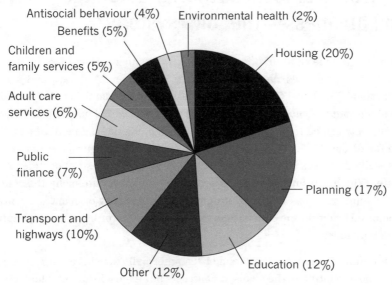

Figure 14.1  A breakdown of complaints to the Commissioner 2008–09

Source: Local Government Ombudsmen (2010) *Annual Report 2008–09*

## Punishing errant councillors and officers

In exceptional circumstances, individual councillors and senior officers found culpable of major financial or managerial irregularities have in the past been personally *surcharged* by the Audit Commission on behalf of their local authorities. The most infamous example of wilful misconduct of this kind was the so-called 'homes for votes' scandal of July 1987, which saw then leader of Westminster City Council Dame Shirley Porter and her colleague, David Weeks, conspire to sell off 500 council houses a year to potential Tory voters living in marginal wards, in an effort to engineer Conservative victories in forthcoming elections. The mass sell-off—dubbed 'Building Stable Communities'—was made possible by the Thatcher government's 'Right to Buy' scheme (see pp. 494–7), but Dame Shirley's motives were exposed after an investigation by district auditor John Magill, who condemned her actions as 'disgraceful and improper gerrymandering'. After a legal battle lasting for much of the 1990s, the Tesco heiress was ordered to repay £27m to the council, plus interest and legal costs. Having initially claimed she had little more than £300,000 to her name, in 2004 she finally relented—reimbursing £12m. The surcharging power was repealed by the LGA 2000 but, like MPs, councillors and officers can still be prosecuted for serious offences like fraud.

# ▶ Access to local authority meetings and business—the 'old' system

Until recently the rights of press and public to attend meetings of local authorities, their committees, and subcommittees were straightforward and widely understood. The Local Government (Access to Information) Act 1985—arising out of a **private member's Bill** introduced by Conservative **backbencher** Robin Squire—enshrined their right to attend *all* such meetings, unless information due for discussion was 'confidential' or 'exempt'. The former category refers to specified classes of information supplied by government departments, or matters the disclosure of which is prohibited under statute or by the courts. An example might be details relating to national security or crime prevention prohibited by either the Official Secrets Act or anti-terror laws. 'Exempt' information includes:

- details judged 'personal' and/or 'commercially sensitive'—for example, those relating to the terms of contracts public disclosure of which might have a negative impact on the authority's future ability to negotiate value for money for local taxpayers;
- matters 'in the process of being negotiated'—for example, details of contractual negotiations with competing companies the council is considering hiring to provide services;
- issues 'protected by legal privilege'—for example, when a council's members are discussing confidential legal advice given to it in relation to litigation by or against it, or contractual matters they are seeking to resolve through the courts.

Under these arrangements councils tended to use one of two methods for excluding the press and public from meetings—or more usually *sections* of meetings. Most commonly, local authorities divided their meetings into a 'part one' and 'part two'—with all confidential and/or exempt items (commonly known as 'below the line') held back until the second half. Alternatively, they might hold a vote to exclude the press and public for the duration of a single specified agenda item. The vote had to be formally proposed, seconded, and carried by members at the meeting—and a *reason* given to those excluded (usually citing the Schedule to the 1985 Act under which the exclusion was being sought). Should the motion fail, the matter concerned had to be heard publicly, and copies of supporting reports instantly circulated to members of the press and public present.

In addition to granting the press and public automatic access to its meetings, local authorities were also required to provide information in *advance* of the proceedings, and after the event to publicize the outcomes of any votes and debates. At the meetings themselves, clerks had to ensure that they went further, in the interests of accessibility, than simply unlocking the doors to the press and public galleries. The bulk of these access provisions, which apply to open meetings to this day, are listed in Table 14.2.

In the past councils were frequently accused of going against the spirit of these access requirements (if not the letter). The not uncommon practice of holding meetings on controversial issues in very small rooms—or barring entry on grounds of 'overcrowding'—was once famously condemned as 'bad faith' by then Lord Chief Justice Lord Widgery.

Other measures local authorities were encouraged to take to improve their communication with—and accountability to—press and public included the appointment of public relations (PR) and/or press officers (a move suggested in the Bains Report). The remit of such paid PR people would be strictly to promote council initiatives and policies in a broad sense, rather than to generate positive publicity for a specific political grouping. Councils were also expected

**Table 14.2** Access-to-meetings requirements expected of local authorities

| Requirement | What it means |
| --- | --- |
| Public registers | Each local authority must keep these, listing names and addresses of all elected councillors, and details of committees on which they serve. Any powers delegated to officers must be listed. |
| Copies of agenda papers | Orders of business and all reports prepared by officers for consideration at meetings—and submitted during open parts—must be made available on day. No matters must be heard at meetings unless listed on agendas *at least three days beforehand*. Only exception is when urgent issues arise that could not have been predicted. In such circumstances, they should be mentioned during 'matters arising', towards the end of the agenda. |
| Access to **background papers** | All reports presented for public inspection should list any background papers used to help to draft them. The press and public may also examine these (although they may be charged a 'reasonable fee' for doing so). |
| *Minutes* of previous meetings | Copies of minutes of open meetings should be made available automatically to press and local electors on request. Minutes are records of proceedings that *actually* take place at meetings—including items debated that were not on original agenda. They normally take the form of a detailed 'summing up' of what each person said, rather than a verbatim record. Minutes of local authority meetings will usually be sent to journalists, along with agendas for subsequent meetings. |
| 'Reasonable accommodation' | This must be provided for both press and public. This normally means there should be sufficient numbers of seats and, whenever possible, press benches. At meetings expected to be unusually popular (e.g. a planning committee or full council meeting at which a decision is due to be made about a major housing development) 'overflow rooms' should be provided. If it is oversubscribed, an audio and/or video feed of proceedings should be made available to those forced to sit or stand outside the meeting room, to enable them to see/hear proceedings. |

to give journalists access to individual councillors—particularly committee chairmen or cabinet members—to obtain quotes justifying political decisions, and even senior officers, should they require *technical* explanations for background to their articles.

In practice, by the mid-1990s many local authorities still had no press office, although more recently a common complaint levelled at them by the press has been that they place too much emphasis on proactive media management designed to deflect criticism of their actions and promote council policies, and too little on serving the needs of journalists. Controversy has also surrounded the plethora of taxpayer-funded newspapers, magazines, and newsletters published by councils, ostensibly to inform local residents about the services they provide. Editors and owners of commercial newspapers have accused some authorities of undercutting them by courting paid external advertising, and professionalizing their publications by recruiting experienced journalists on generous salaries to write them, while broadening their coverage to encompass non-council-related articles. By 2010 *East End Life*, a weekly published by the London Borough of Tower Hamlets, was being posted free of charge through the letterboxes of 81,000 homes, while its long-established independent rival, the *East London Advertiser*, was selling just 6,800 copies at a 50p cover price.

 In their defence, some councils have argued that they feel forced to publish their own news sheets because of the unwillingness of their local press to run positive stories, or ones concerning worthy but dull information they need to pass on to local people. However, mounting concern about the use of public money for such purposes has prompted successive Communities Secretaries to liken council publications to 'Pravda' and 'propaganda sheets', and in June 2010 Mr Pickles promised to clamp down on the practice.

# ▌ Access to local authority business— the 'new' system

 The LGA 2000 introduced significant new limitations on the extent to which press and public would be allowed access to local authority meetings in 'new-style' councils—those adopting one of the 'new' models of executive arrangement (see pp. 394–8). While full council, committee, and subcommittee meetings remain as open to the public as ever under these regimes, access to others has become more restricted. Because many final decisions are now effectively taken by cabinets and related bodies with *delegated powers*, critics argue that—contrary to the rhetoric—councils are now *less* transparent than previously. Initially cabinets were not obliged to meet in public at all, but the LGA 2000 was modified by government guidance issued in 2002 requiring them to convene publicly whenever discussing *key decisions* to be taken by their members as a collective. Controversially, however, key decisions delegated to individual cabinet members, or in some cases officers, may still be taken in private.

The main requirements for openness in council decision-making under the LGA 2000 (as modified by the later guidance and the Local Government and Public Involvement in Health Act 2007) are listed in Table 14.3.

The principal differences between the 'old-style' and 'new-style' systems in relation to openness to press and public scrutiny are twofold. Because many significant decisions about policy formulation and implementation are now taken in cabinet—or even individually, by elected mayors, leaders, or cabinet members (and sometimes officers) with delegated executive powers—by holding such meetings in private councils can prevent the public finding out about their plans until after the event. For example, in February 2010 Woking Borough Council finalized the £68m purchase of a local shopping centre in a closed meeting—only revealing the fact in a statement afterwards on its website. The buy-out is relying on a loan from the *Public Works Loan Board (PWLB)* that will take the borough's taxpayers 50 years to repay. Such practices are occurring, say critics, at a time when meetings that *are* still open to the public—those of subcommittees, committees, and even the full council—are being reduced to talking shops (see p. 396).

The new system has attracted influential critics. In February 2000, while the LGA was still being debated in Parliament, a critical briefing paper designed to mobilize opposition to the changes was jointly published by the Local Government Information Unit and two constitutional pressure groups, Charter 88 and the Campaign for Freedom of Information.

Criticisms aside, the press and public continue to have a right to the following:

- three days' notice of meetings open to the press;
- agendas and minutes of council meetings;

**Table 14.3** Changes to access-to-meetings criteria under the 'new-style' system

| | Change |
|---|---|
| 1. | Full council, committee, and subcommittee meetings to continue meeting in public, subject to 'access to information' requirements under the 1985 Act. |
| 2. | Executive or cabinet bodies *not* required to meet in public unless discussing key decisions they are due to resolve collectively. They must, however, publish more minor decisions after taking them, as well as monthly **forward plans** outlining all upcoming key decisions in advance. |
| 3. | Decisions of mayors or individual executive politicians are subject to the 1985 Act—but a 'record' of their decisions must be published after they are taken. |
| 4. | Overview and scrutiny committees—and other scrutiny bodies—to meet in public, subject to existing 'access to information' requirement. |

- registers of planning applications;
- records of payments to councillors;
- the council constitution, code of conduct, standing orders; and
- a statutory register of members' interests;
- copies of any reports into allegations of maladministration by the Local Government Commissioner (Local Government Ombudsman);
- the council's annual accounts, annual audit (including the rights to inspect certain items), performance indicators, and future performance plans;
- general financial information;
- the council's full annual report (including comparative data, indicating how well it has performed as against 'similar authorities').

## The order of business in local authority meetings

All meetings of local authority members—whether committee, full council, or executive—follow the same format as they did under the old system, as outlined in Table 14.4.

Table 14.4  Order of business in council, committee, and subcommittee meetings

| Order of business | What happens |
|---|---|
| Publication of agenda | Agenda—document outlining matters to be discussed at a meeting and the proposed order of business—prepared by council's chief executive, a secretary, or director of administration—and made available in advance. |
| Approval of minutes | Meeting opens with formal approval of minutes of previous meeting of same body. |
| Questions | Usually written down in advance by specific councillors, these are put to committee chairpersons. At full council meetings for local authorities that have adopted a post-LGA 2000 constitution, questions put to elected mayor, leader, or most relevant cabinet member. |
| Public questions | Observers on public benches are given chance to question committee chairpersons (optional). |
| Petitions | Any petitions from electors (e.g. in protest over proposed site of a new landfill site) are presented to full council by local councillors representing relevant ward or *electoral division*. Actual debates on these issues, however, will be held at relevant later committee meetings. |
| Consideration of reports | In full council, reports from committees are considered, while committees consider those of subcommittees. Debates often arise at this stage if matter raised is politically controversial. Councillors with strong objections to given proposal may ask for a matter to be amended or even 'referred back' to the committee (or cabinet, if related to a cabinet decision). |
| Notices of motion | Individual councillors should table these in advance if they wish them to be debated. These usually cover issues not formally listed on agenda. In LGA 2000-style councils, any notices that impinge on executive issues must be referred to the executive/cabinet for final decision. |

# ▌ Local elections

Until 1974 local elections were held throughout the first week in May, but the Local Government Act 1972 changed this, stipulating that they take place on the *first Thursday in May* (unless the Home Secretary fixed another day). The Act also clarified—for the first time—that *all* councillors must be directly elected. Up to this point archaic offices had remained in certain areas—for example, 'aldermen', who were elected only by other councillors.

All councillors are now elected for four years—except those voted in at by-elections caused by deaths of sitting councillors, or their resignation or dis-qualification from office in mid-term. Councillors elected in by-elections sit for the remainder of the term of the members they are replacing, before standing for re-election at the same time as their colleagues. If a councillor dies or other-wise leaves office after the September of a year preceding a local election, his or her seat remains vacant until polling day—that is, it is considered too near the general poll to bother with calling a by-election.

## Local authority constituencies

Councillors, like MPs, have their own constituencies (albeit covering far smaller geographical areas than parliamentary ones). Unlike Commons *constituencies*, however, those used in council elections are represented by up to three councillors at a time.

The terms used to refer to council constituencies differ from one type of local authority to another:

- 'county divisions' (or electoral divisions) are the constituencies in county council elections in England and Wales. Some unitaries also use electoral divisions. They tend to be geographically bigger, and represent more people, than those for other types of council;
- wards are the constituencies in district or borough, metropolitan bor-ough, London borough, and most unitary authority elections in England and Wales. All Scottish local authority constituencies are called wards.

In general, whether a ward or electoral division is represented by one, two, or three councillors is determined by the size of its population. Most urban wards contain roughly the same number of electors and, because they are based in towns, have fairly high populations. As a result they are generally represented by three councillors. In rural electoral divisions and wards in mixed rural/urban areas, population levels can be significantly more varied—meaning some have only one councillor, while others are designated 'multimember divisions or wards', with up to three.

There have been 10,661 wards and electoral divisions in the UK as a whole since 6 October 2004. The average population for a ward or electoral division is 5,500. The table entitled 'The numbers of wards and electoral divisions in the UK', which can be found on the Online Resource Centre that accompanies this book, gives an overview of the number of wards and electoral divisions in each of the four countries of England, Wales, Scotland, and Northern Ireland.

## Local authority election cycles

The precise election cycle followed by a local authority—that is, the years in which it holds its elections—depends on which type of council it is. Present cycles are listed in Table 14.5.

As illustrated above, local election cycles in the UK can be confusing for electors. This is especially true for those living in two-tier areas, who face elections more often than most, given that they are covered by not one but two councils: a district/borough and a county. In some areas, where district/borough and county elections are occasionally held in the same year, the process can be particularly confusing.

Among the many other changes it heralded, the LGA 2000 envisaged the patchwork election cycles of local authorities gradually being rationalized

**Table 14.5** The electoral cycles for the different types of English local authority

| Type of local authority | Electoral cycle |
| --- | --- |
| County council | Every four years, with whole council retiring at same time. Elections last held in 2009, and due in 2013, 2017, etc. |
| London **borough councils** | Every four years—with whole councils retiring at same time. To avoid conflicting with county polls, London boroughs hold elections in different years. Last were in 2010. |
| Metropolitan borough councils | Three out of every four years—a third of councillors retire each time (usually one councillor per ward). Elections never take place in these areas in same year as county council elections held elsewhere. Current cycle began in 2010. |
| District/borough councils | Choice of elections *either* in three out of every four years—third of council retires each time *or* all councillors in one go. If districts or boroughs opt for 'three-out-of-four-year' cycle, electoral calendar is same as that for metropolitan boroughs, but if they decide to stage 'Big Bang' polls every four years, these are held midway between those of counties—that is, in 2011, 2015, etc. |
| Unitary authorities | Choice of elections *either* in three out of every four years *or* all councillors in one go—special arrangements made in areas where there is a hybrid council structure (one or more unitary authorities coexisting with two-tier system—see p. 327). When new unitary authority is created from amalgamation of pre-existing district and county, a statutory order may be passed stating new council should initially sit for *less than four years*—to stop elections clashing with future county ones. |
| Parish, town, and community councils | Every four years—whole council retires at same time, as in 2011, 2015, etc. Each parish council has to have at least five councillors and actual numbers are fixed by local district council. Some parishes follow ward-based system (like their parent authorities). |

over time. The Act tried to facilitate this by recommending all councils adopt one of the following three models:

- whole-council elections *every four years* at the same time;
- half the council stands for election *every two years*;
- one-third of the council stands in *three out of four years*.

Because it was left up to individual councils to decide when (and whether) to reform, little has come of the Act's recommendations. In January 2004, following a lengthy consultation, the **Electoral Commission** warned in a report that public confusion about electoral cycles was contributing to the general malaise afflicting local democracy by further eroding turnouts already dwindling due to widespread political apathy. It cited research conducted on its behalf in April 2003 by MORI, which found that a quarter of British people did not know whether elections were due to be held in their areas that May. Only one in six were able to say how often elections were held locally. The findings prompted the Commission to make the following recommendations—yet to be acted on by the government:

- that all local authorities in England should hold whole-council elections every four years;
- that county councils and the **Greater London Authority (GLA)** should hold elections in different years from boroughs/districts, unitaries, metropolitan, and London boroughs.

Quite apart from their baffling nature, the present local electoral cycles have produced curious quirks. Because individual district and borough councils are permitted to choose whether to follow a whole-council election model or one in which votes are held in three out of every four years, there are some counties in which, in any one year, an election may be held for a borough, district, county, and potentially even neighbouring unitary authority. By the same token, two district or borough councils sitting side by side in the same county may choose to adopt different electoral cycles, meaning that—despite having the same council functions—they only hold elections on the same day as each other a maximum of once in four years.

## Who can stand as a councillor?

As at general elections (see Chapter 4), any citizen of the UK, Irish Republic, or a Commonwealth country who lives in Britain and is *over the age of 18 on the day he or she is nominated* may stand as a candidate—provided that he or she can prove one of a range of verifiable connections with the area in which he or she is standing and is not disqualified in law for any of the reasons listed in Table 14.6. There is no requirement for an *election deposit*.

**Table 14.6** Disqualifications for candidacy as a councillor

| Category of person | Details of disqualification |
|---|---|
| Some bankrupts | Prospective candidates barred if they are undischarged bankrupts subject to a bankruptcy restriction order made by the Insolvency Service (an **executive agency** of the Department of Business, Innovation, and Skills). This means they have been found to have acted dishonestly or in an otherwise 'blameworthy' way. In Northern Ireland anyone adjudged bankrupt is barred from standing, while in Scotland anyone whose estate has been sequestered is banned. |
| Certain recent convicts | Those convicted of a criminal offence with a minimum penalty of three months in prison during five years before election. |
| Electoral fraudster | Anyone convicted of corrupt or illegal election practice in previous five years. |
| Politically restricted officials | Those working for local authority for which they intend to stand or holding post with any other council that is politically restricted (e.g. a senior officer position in which they are expected to work closely with elected councillors and give dispassionate advice free from any personal political bias—see p. 119). Civil servants working for Whitehall departments above 'Grade 7' may only stand in local elections with permission of their employers. Most senior ones are banned. |

Unlike at general elections, candidature is also open to EU citizens who meet these criteria. To be nominated, a prospective councillor has to obtain the signatures of both *proposer* and *seconder*—both of whom must be registered to vote in the relevant local authority area. Candidates must also be able to prove that *at least one* of the following is true of them:

- he or she is a legitimate elector listed on the local *electoral register*—the list of registered voters kept by the local electoral registration officer;

- he or she has been resident in the area for the 12 months before the nomination process;

- he or she has had a 'principal or only place of work' for the whole preceding year in the area;

- he or she has owned property in the area for the whole of the preceding year.

The ability of EU citizens to stand as councillors and the rather fluid test of 'residency' within a council's area make the qualifications for local authority candidates seem rather less stringent than those for prospective MPs. Unlike in general elections, this liberal attitude extends to peers entitled to sit in the Lords, who, although barred from standing for the Commons, may become councillors. Labour peer and former minister Lord Bassam was, for a time, leader of Brighton and Hove Council in the 1990s.

# Who can vote in local elections?

Only those people whose names are on the electoral register for a given local authority area are entitled to vote. To be eligible for inclusion on the register, a person must be:

- aged at least 18 or due to turn 18 during the 12-month period covered by the register (*provided* that this is by the date of voting);
- a UK, Commonwealth, Irish Republic, or other EU citizen;
- qualified on the basis of normal residency, service in the Armed Forces or as a merchant seaman, or a declaration as a voluntary mental patient;
- not barred because he or she:
  - is a foreign national from outside the EU and Commonwealth;
  - is a convict detained in prison or a mental institution;
  - has been convicted within the previous five years of corrupt or illegal practices.

As with general elections, it is the electoral registration officer's responsibility to ensure that every household completes a *compulsory* electoral registration form. Anyone moving from one council area to another may have his or her name added to the electoral register at the start of a given month under a system of 'rolling registration' introduced in 2000.

# The local election process

The basic procedure governing local elections is summarized in Table 14.7.

**Table 14.7** Local election procedure in Britain

| Stage | Procedure |
| --- | --- |
| Notice of election | Must be published *at least 25 days before an election.* |
| Nomination papers submitted | To be handed in *by noon 19 days before the election.* |
| Publication of candidates' list | Must be published *by noon on the 17th day before the election.* |
| Candidate withdrawals | This can happen *no later than 16 days before the election.* |
| Appointment of officials | Each council appoints a **returning officer** to preside over the election count (normally the mayor or chairperson of council, but role taken on day by 'acting' or 'deputy returning officer', usually the chief executive—see p. 384). It is his or her responsibility to appoint presiding officers and poll clerks to attend polling stations during the day, supervise counting of votes, rule on whether any ballot papers have been 'spoiled', and publish the finished results. |

| Stage | Procedure |
|---|---|
| Polling stations open | Usually based at local schools and community centres, these open from 8 a.m. to 9 p.m. for local elections. |
| Votes cast | When electors (or their proxies) arrive at the polling station to vote, their names are checked against the register before the ballot paper is issued. If an elector has applied for a **postal vote**, he or she must send it to the designated place other than the polling station. |

Of the various other rules governing the legitimate conduct of local elections, most notable are those limiting the sums candidates are allowed to spend on campaigning. The spending cap was most recently raised in March 2005, by statutory instrument, at the Electoral Commission's request. Those standing as councillors are now allowed to spend £600 on campaign expenses, while mayoral candidates may spend up to £2,000 (both sums are broadly equivalent to 5p per elector). The decision to more than double spending limits (council candidates had previously been forced to keep their expenditure below £242) was in part a belated response to the impact of the Representation of the People Act 1983, which, for the first time, required candidates to declare the financial value of 'benefits in kind' such as free use of stationery, offices, or other facilities. To ensure that limits are not exceeded, agents must send inventories of their candidates' expenses to their returning officer after the poll.

## Moves towards improving local election turnout

Dwindling engagement in local elections has long been a concern for UK governments. Compared to many EU countries, the turnout in Britain's local polls is extremely poor: in a 2000 survey by the then Office of the Deputy Prime Minister (ODPM), it came bottom of the European league, with an average turnout of just two out of every five electors (a drop of 37 per cent since 1987). Between 2 million and 4 million people are estimated to be absent from the electoral register at any one time—whether intentionally (to avoid being charged *Council Tax*), or because of apathy towards the democratic process.

The Labour government, aided by the Commission, mooted several changes to boost local election turnout, but up to now they have only been implemented in a piecemeal way:

- introducing *anonymous registration* for those reluctant to have their names listed;
- opening polling stations at supermarkets, workplaces, colleges, doctors' surgeries, etc.;
- allowing voting over a period of a few days, rather than just one;
- introducing universal postal voting;

- electronic voting—that is, via email, Internet, text messaging, etc.;
- holding *annual* elections for at least a portion of each council, to make councils more accountable to electors by forcing them to campaign for votes continually.

The most 'successful' local elections—such as the 2008 vote for London mayor and the GLA—are often viewed through the prism of what is happening on the national and global political stages, rather than interpreted as true tests of public opinion about the merits of candidates and parties locally. The results of 'mid-term' local elections—those held partway through a Parliament, when voters are often disenchanted with the serving government—frequently send a shot across its bows, and are consequently styled 'protest votes' by political commentators and opinion pollsters. The 2008 local elections were an object lesson in protest voting. Barely a week after Mr Brown's government had meekly pledged to compensate low-earners hit by the abolition of the 10p  starting rate of Income Tax (many of them its own grass-roots voters), Labour polled its worst election result for more than forty years. It scored barely 24 per cent, coming one point behind the Lib Dems and 20 shy of the Tories—a share that would have sent it to a crushing defeat at a general election.

The task of reviewing the electoral arrangements of English local authorities—and overall structures and boundaries—was until recently the responsibility of a committee of the Commission, the Boundary Committee for England, but in 2010 it was a replaced by a new dedicated **Local Government Boundary Commission for England (LGBCE)**. The Committee is charged with carrying out electoral reviews of all local authorities every few years to ensure that the number of electors represented by each councillor is broadly the same nationwide. It may also undertake discrete reviews for individual councils, such as newly established unitary authorities. There are separate local government boundary commissions for Scotland and Wales, and a *Local Government Boundaries Commissioner for Northern Ireland*.

## ☰ Topical feature idea

Figure 14.2 is a summary of the official 2009 NIS assessment for Weymouth and Portland Borough Council, Dorset, taken from the government's Oneplace website. What are the most obvious potential angles for a background feature, and how would you develop them? What questions are raised by references to the council's past performance, and where would you go to find out more information about this? Whom would you approach for interviews?

**Figure 14.2** Summary of the official 2009 NIS assessment for Weymouth and Portland Borough Council, Dorset, taken from the government's Oneplace website

| | |
|---|---|
| Managing finances | 3 out of |
| Governing the business | 2 out of |
| Managing resources | 2 out of |

**Description of scores:**

1   An organisation that does not meet minimum requirements, performs poorly

2   An organisation that meets only minimum requirements, performs adequately

3   An organisation that exceeds minimum requirements, performs well

4   An organisation that significantly exceeds minimum requirements, performs excellently

**Summary**

Overall, Weymouth and Portland Borough Council performs adequately.

For many services the Council delivers good results for local people. It has awards for making sure that local people benefit from the Olympic Games after 2012, high quality green spaces and beach management. More household waste is recycled than any other Dorset council. And the Council ha helped local people and businesses to cope with the effects of the recession. Strong action has bee taken to better understand why local people have a low opinion of the Council, and do something about it. But, the Council still needs to improve some important things. It needs to do more work to deal with the gap between the good quality of many of its services, and local people's opinion of th Council. More work is needed with partners to reduce some types of crime.

The Council scored 2 out of 4 for its use of resources. Overall, its services offer adequate value for money for local people. It has adequate standards for the way the Council is run and managed, and makes adequate use of its staffing. It is good at planning how it will use its money, changing spending plans to fit with what is most important. It checks how it is doing against spending targets.

Performance is managed well and has scored 3 out of 4. But overall the Council has been assessed as performing adequately. This is because the Council still has much to do to deliver consistently good services that local people appreciate. It also has to make improvements to the way it runs its business.

The Council has strong leadership. The joining of its revenues and benefits service with a neighbour ing council is a great success. It is talking to two other councils to join more services to improve eff ciency and reduce costs. But an attempt to share more services across the whole of Dorset has not been as successful. The Council is also looking at other ways to reduce costs and improve perform ance. One layer of managers has been removed at the Council to save money and concentrate on its priorities. Despite recent changes in the Council, many staff remain optimistic and enjoy working there.

The Council understands what it needs to do to improve. In the past the Council took too little notice of issues outside the Borough, and some councillors behaved in a way that damaged the Council's reputation. Since then the Council has been determined to find ways to improve and show local people how good its services now are. The Council is helping to do this by getting to know its local communities better. And councillors now better represent the Council to other organisations.

## ✳ Current issues

- **The 'end' of target culture:** comprehensive area assessment (CAA), the latest of several systems introduced by Labour to rate the performance of service areas overseen by local authorities, is to be abolished by the Lib-Con coalition, generating an estimated annual saving to the taxpayer of £39m. Instead, councils must voluntarily 'throw open their books' by publishing details of all spending over £500.

- **Abolition of Standards for England:** as part of its strategy of moving away from national and regional oversight of local government to more localized regulation, the Lib-Con coalition is abolishing Labour's Standards for England. The board's annual cost to the taxpayer had been some £7.8m, although it handled only around 1,000 complaints a year. But as yet, there is no word on who will police standards in future.

- **Attempts to increase turnout at local elections:** the coalition showed early signs of wanting to move further and faster towards addressing the historical decline in voting in local elections than Labour, rolling out electronic voting (or e-voting) and postal ballots, and opening polling stations in supermarkets and shopping centres.

## ? Review questions

1. Outline the electoral cycles for district/borough councils, county councils, and unitary authorities. Why might a district council have an election in a year when a neighbouring borough council does not, and vice versa?

2. What are the qualifications for candidates and electors in local elections? Who oversees the running of local government elections and to whom besides this individual might one complain about the handling of electoral procedures?

3. In what ways besides elections can local councillors be held accountable for their actions? What mechanisms exist to punish them for misusing their positions?

4. Outline the main ways in which the performance of local authorities in service delivery is assessed, exposed, and regulated.

5. What rights do the press and public have to attend and access information from meetings of local authorities, and their committees and subcommittees? How were the access rights changed by the Local Government Act 2000?

## → Further reading

Johnston, R. and Pattie, C. (2006) *Putting Voters in Their Place: Geography and Elections in Great Britain*, Oxford: Oxford University Press. **Thoughtful examination of the geographical differences in voting and turnout patterns in local, national, and European elections. Examines the emergence of safe seats and the roles of marginal wards and constituencies in winning polls.**

Knowles, R. (1993) *Law and Practice of Local Authority Meetings*, 2nd edn, London: ICSA Publishing. **Updated second edition of an indispensable guide to statutory rules and regulations governing access for press and public to local authority meetings.**

Pratchett, L. (2000) *Renewing Local Democracy? The Modernisation Agenda in British Local Government*, London: Frank Cass. **Thoughtful assessment of the impact of 'New Labour' reform agenda in local government, focusing on its attempts to increase public participation in local democracy through mayoral elections and new forms of voting.**

Rogers, S. (1998) *Performance Management in Local Government: The Route to Best Value*, 2nd edn, London: Financial Times/Prentice Hall. **Second edition of the guide, principally aimed at local government professionals, focusing on new management standards introduced by Labour.**

 ## Online Resource Centre

www.oxfordtextbooks.co.uk/orc/Morrison2e/

Visit the Online Resource Centre that accompanies this book for web links and regular updates.

# 15

# Local authorities and education

In Chapter 6, the National Health Service was described as a subject with a near-unique ability to shape the news agenda. But if any other political issue has the capacity to rival it occasionally that issue is education. Whether it is local unrest over changes to school catchment areas, anger over disruption caused by striking teachers, reports about soaring undergraduate student debt, the annual rows over 'grade inflation' when General Certificate of Secondary Education (GCSE) and A level results are published, or the frantic scramble for university places through the clearing system each summer, the trials and tribulations of parents and pupils are seldom far from the media spotlight.

The involvement of British local authorities in this huge policy area stretches across all four 'phases' of the education process: primary, secondary, tertiary— or *further education (FE)*—and higher education (HE). These phases are explained in Table 15.1.

In addition, local authorities have a statutory responsibility to ensure that suitable preschool education is available across their areas, through nurseries, registered *childminders*, and other forms of recognized early years childcare. This chapter examines each layer of state education in detail, beginning with perhaps the most important and certainly the most controversial: the school system.

# ▌ The origins of state schools and rise of comprehensive education

Until Victorian times many British children had little or no formal education. The offspring of the aristocracy and the bourgeois middle classes that emerged during the Industrial Revolution fostered the growth of a burgeoning private

**Table 15.1** Structure of the British education system

| Phase | Structure |
|---|---|
| Primary phase | Education in subjects of 'primary' importance (e.g. English language, maths, basic history, and science). This takes place in **primary schools** (ages 5–11), or in two stages, at infant school (ages 5–7) and junior school (ages 7–11). In some areas of the UK, children attend first school (ages 5–8/9) then middle school (ages 8/9–12/13). |
| Secondary phase | Education for 11–16-year-olds (or 13–16-year-olds in some areas) in both core subjects like English and maths, and with increasing specialization in other areas after children take their 'options' at the age of 13 or 14. Compulsory secondary education in England, Wales, and Northern Ireland leads to final assessment between the ages of 14 and 16, through GCSEs and/or new vocational diplomas. GCSEs are awarded through a mix of exams and course-work across eight grade bands: A*–G. In Scotland, the GCSE equivalent is the Standard Grade (levels 1–7). Standard Grades take up the first half of a four-year National Qualification (NQ) programme, encompassing the Scottish equivalent of the gold standard pre-degree qualification in the rest of the UK, A levels (known as the Scottish Higher). School-age qualifications and most of those taught in sixth forms and at FE level in England are regulated by the Office of the Qualifications and Examinations Regulator (Ofqual), which also oversees vocational qualifications taught in Northern Ireland. These qualifications are accorded a 'level' on its *National Qualifications Framework (NQF)*— a form of 'credit transfer' system for accredited UK courses and exams. In Northern Ireland, school-age qualifica-tions are regulated by the *Council for the Curricu-lum, Examinations, and Assessment (CCEA)*, while in Wales it is handled in-house by its Department for Children, Education, Lifelong Learning, and Skills (DCELLS), and in Scotland by the *Scottish Qualifica-tions Authority (SQA)*. |
| Further education (FE) phase | 'Sixth-form' education in chosen subjects to A level in England, Wales, and Northern Ireland, Advanced Subsidiary (AS) Level (taken during the first year of a standard two-year A level course), vocational diploma, or International Baccalaureate (IB) (a qualification widely taught outside the UK). In Scot-land pupils study for intermediate-level certificates, followed by Scottish Highers. 'Catch-up' tuition for the less academic and/or those seeking to retake GCSEs/Standard Grades is also offered at this stage. BTEC National Diplomas, foundation degrees, and other practical, trade-based post-GCSE certificate are also often taught in school sixth forms, and at further education (FE), technical, or tertiary colleges. |

| Phase | Structure |
|---|---|
| Higher education (HE) phase | University education to degree—Bachelor of Arts (BA) and Bachelor of Science (BSc)—and postgraduate—Master of Arts (MA), Master of Science (MSc), Doctor of Philosophy (PhD)—level for those who gain the requisite A levels or equivalent qualifications. |

education system for those who could afford it. But for the large number of poorer households, paying the high fees they charged was out of the question. Poor parents were forced either to teach their children themselves or to rely on piecemeal philanthropy from any local churches, charities, or guilds—groups of wealthy merchants and tradesmen—prepared to fund local schools for the working classes. In the absence of a state system, the opportunity for children from many families to gain an education varied hugely from place to place—an early 'postcode lottery'.

By the late nineteenth century, however, there was a growing clamour for the government to provide some form of across-the-board schooling for the nation's children. Campaigns by civil rights movements like the Chartists and Radicals had brought social inequality into sharp focus. Morality aside, there was also a belated recognition that allowing 'the masses' to remain uneducated might be limiting Britain's potential to compete on the world stage economically.

The foundation stone of the modern 'state school' system—or 'maintained sector'—was the Elementary Education Act 1870, which introduced the first nationwide 'elementary schools'. The term 'elementary' is key here: even at this stage, poorer children were only to be offered the most basic level of teaching, and only up to the age of 13—what would later be termed secondary school level. Neither was even this limited schooling guaranteed to be within the financial grasp of all parents: local school boards elected to manage the system on the ground, setting up new schools in areas devoid of ones provided by a church or guild, charged families up to 9d a week to send their children. While boards had discretion to waive fees for the poorest households, they could only do so for a limited time. It was only with the Education Act 1891 that elementary education became free for most pupils and 1918 that every last fee was abolished. This reform was initiated by county councils, which, as of 1901, were designated *local education authorities (LEAs)*.

The path towards introducing secondary schools was even more protracted: not until after the Education Act 1944 did a nationwide system open to all children—regardless of their parents' ability to pay—come into being. When the 1870 Act had been passed, the compulsory school-leaving age for children was just 10 (despite the fact that elementary schools were prepared to teach them up to 13). The leaving age was increased incrementally—first to 11, then 13, then 14—by three subsequent Acts, in 1893, 1899, and 1918, respectively. But it was only Tory Education Minister Rab Butler's 1944 Act that introduced second-ary schooling for all in England and Wales (a provision extended to Northern Ireland in 1947).

Despite the widespread welcome given to the new universal free second-ary schools, the Butler Act was far from uncontentious. Its most controversial innovation was the introduction of not one, but three types of secondary school:

- **grammar schools**—for the most academically gifted;
- *secondary modern schools*—a more standard alternative for the less able;
- *technical schools*—offering practical, vocationally orientated education rather than academic.

Whether a child was admitted into one or other would depend on their per-formance in a new exam they would sit at normal elementary school leaving age—the '11 plus'. This system came to be known as *selection*. Table 15.2 offers a timeline charting major education reforms up to and including the 1944 Act.

The ideological divisions caused by the introduction of academic selec-tion and the repeated efforts of later Labour governments to scrap grammar schools (still unfulfilled in some areas) are discussed in detail later this chapter. One such government, however—Harold Wilson's first administration, elected in 1964—went further than most towards abolishing the tripartite secondary school framework ushered in by Butler in favour of a more egalitarian sys-tem. Under the Conservative governments of the late 1950s and early 1960s, the number of non-selective secondary schools had been gradually increased to cater for the post-war 'baby boom' generation. These schools—focusing on a broad-based academic education—came to be known as **comprehensive schools**. But it was under Labour Education Secretary Anthony Crosland that comprehensives truly earned their name, becoming the norm for the majority of British schoolchildren as the government fought to persuade LEAs to begin dismantling what they saw as the 'two-tier system' preserved by grammars. In time these schools came to be known variously as 'high schools', **community schools** (see p. 439), and in Scotland, 'academies' (not to be confused with their modern-day namesakes—see pp. 440–4).

The number of grammar schools has since fallen dramatically, thanks to a slow process of attrition that began in the late 1960s. Between then and the late 1970s, successive Labour and Conservative governments engaged in a game of educational ping-pong over the future of grammars, with Mr Wilson initially instructing LEAs to start dismantling the system only for his Tory successor, Ted Heath, and his Education Secretary (one Margaret Thatcher) to reverse this directive after winning the 1970 election. When Labour was re-elected in 1974, it swiftly overturned Mrs Thatcher's instructions, but a sluggish response in certain areas meant that, by the time she became prime minister in 1979, a number still remained.

**Table 15.2** Timeline of major UK school reforms

| Date | Reform | Effect |
| --- | --- | --- |
| 1841 | The School Sites Act | Introduced 'voluntary schools', principally in villages and rural areas. These taught basic English, maths, and other core subjects, and were built on land donated by local landowners or vicars. Covenants protected the ownership of the land, which generally remained with the donor. |
| 1870 | Elementary Education Act (also known as the 'Foster Act', after Foster) | Set up elected school boards to run voluntary schools as part of a universal 'elementary education' system in England and Wales, and introduced new schools where none existed before. Boards charged up to 9d a week for teaching, but could subsidize the poorest. |
| 1891 | Education Act | Made elementary schools free for most pupils. |
| 1901 | Education Act | Abolished school boards, transferring their responsibilities to newly established county councils—the first local education authorities (LEAs). Councils to offer financial help to these schools through local taxes. |
| 1918 | Education Act | Last remaining elementary school fees abolished. School leaving age raised to 14. First nursery schooling for preschool children introduced. |
| 1944 | Education Act (also known as the 'Butler Act') | Brought in comprehensive education in all but name, by raising school-leaving age to 15 and giving all children access to free secondary schooling. Three types of secondary introduced: grammar, secondary modern, and technical. The then three-tier education system—primary, secondary, and further education (FE)—was also formalized, and new measures introduced to support children with disabilities and learning difficulties. |
| 1960s/1970s | Wilson/Crosland reforms | Successive Labour governments attempt to persuade LEAs to scrap grammar schools, during a period of mass expansion of comprehensives. |
| 1988 | Education Reform Act | Introduction of **National Curriculum**, GCSEs to replace GCE O levels, school league tables, and grant-maintained (GM) schools, allowing primaries and secondaries to opt 'out of' local authority control for the first time. |
| 1992 | Education (Schools) Act | Creation of the **Office for Standards in Education (Ofsted)** and Chief Inspector of Schools. |
| 1998 | School Standards and Framework Act | GM schools become **foundation schools.** |

| Date | Reform | Effect |
|---|---|---|
| 2000 | Learning and Skills Act | Self-governing, partially selective, 'city academies' introduced to replace CTCs. Later renamed simply academies. |
| 2007 | Education and Inspections Act | Concept of **trust schools** introduced, allowing foundation schools to form charitable trusts to manage their assets and decide admissions policies. |
| 2008 | New qualifications launched | New vocational diplomas launched as alternative or complementary qualifications to GCSEs and A levels. |
| 2010 | Academies Bill | All state schools, including primaries, invited to apply for academy status. |
| 2010 | Education and Children's Bill | Proposed introduction of Swedish-style '**free schools**'—set up and run by parents, teachers, and/or charities. Proposals published to give schools greater freedom to vary the National Curriculum. |

In their mid-1960s heyday there had been several hundred grammar schools, including 179 'direct grant' schools—fee-paying grammars that agreed to take between a quarter and half of their pupils from poorer families in return for state subsidies. Today, there are but 164, spread over ten LEA areas, including Devon, Kent, and Lincolnshire. The Conservatives' traditional support for selection gave grammars a reprieve in the 1980s, but few new ones were established.

In recent years, however, the great selection debate has reared its head again. Mrs Thatcher (herself an ex-grammar school pupil) would do more to encourage selection than simply save the 11-plus. In 1980, she introduced the 'assisted places scheme'—a means by which pupils from lower-income families who passed entrance exams for private and public schools were entitled to state financial aid with tuition fees, according to a sliding scale.

Labour scrapped assisted places when it returned to power in 1997. Yet the 11-plus remains in many areas where it survived the axe in the 1970s, thanks to the more consensual way in which the party broached the issue of grammar schools under Tony Blair. Rather than abolishing them (and infuriating many of its new-found middle-class supporters), the School Standards and Framework Act 1998 instead gave local people in areas where they remained a direct say in whether the 166 then still standing should be kept or scrapped. To this end, two types of ballot (effectively local **referenda**) were held:

- *area ballots*—in areas where *most* secondary schools were grammars, *all* parents were balloted. One county in which this process was due to be used, Kent, was ultimately exempted from the ballot, due to what the government described as logistical problems;
- *feeder ballots*—in areas where *some* secondary schools were grammars, all parents of children attending 'feeder' primary schools—those in the

catchment areas of the grammars—were balloted. In Ripon, the first area to be balloted, two out of three parents voted to retain grammar schools.

Labour's failure to make good on its long-standing pledge to abolish grammars—despite its huge Commons majority—infuriated many of its *backbenchers*. These rumblings of unease grew louder when it emerged that ministers were planning to *introduce* a degree of selection in *academies* (see p. 440).

But it was not only Labour's leadership that had trouble containing its back-benchers over the grammar school question. In 2006, then newly elected Tory leader David Cameron provoked a fight with party traditionalists—portrayed in some parts of the media as his 'Clause 4 moment' (see pp. 146–9)—by announcing that a future Conservative government would not found any new grammars. The following May, after months of in-fighting over the issue, he accused his critics of 'clinging on to outdated mantras that bear no relation to the reality of life', adding that most parents did not 'want children divided into successes and failures at 11'. He was later forced to make a significant concession to rebels, however, after the party's Europe spokesman, Graham Brady, resigned over the issue. Mr Cameron reassured diehard '11-plus' supporters that a Tory government *would* consider building more grammars in areas where they already existed and there was enough demand. At time of writing the coalition was also understood to be planning to reintroduce technical schools for 14–19-years-olds less suited to academic subjects.

# ▌ The 1988 Act—and the birth of 'independent' state schools

Just as it turned its back on forty years of consensus over health policy by introducing the NHS 'internal market' (see pp. 162–6), in 1988 Mrs Thatcher's Conservative government initiated the most profound change in the state education system since comprehensive schools were first established. The Education Reform Act 1988 marked the culmination of the 'Great Debate' of the early Thatcher years, revolutionizing the way in which many primary and secondary schools were managed—by liberating them from LEAs and giving parents and teachers a greater say in their day-to-day running than ever before. It also polarized political opinion between those who viewed the transfer of power from councils to citizens as a triumph of full-blooded 'localism' over bureaucratic interference and defenders of the faith who saw in it a recipe for post-code lotteries and the fragmentation of the universal ideal. The debate over whether (and how far) to increase school autonomy continues to dominate the education agenda in England to this day (see pp. 438–45).

Until 1988 the designation 'independent schools' was used as an umbrella term for fee-paying schools in the private sector: 'private schools' and older, more expensive, 'public schools' like Eton (alma mater of Mr Cameron). What the 1988 Act did was apply the concept of independent *governance* for the first time to schools in the public sector. Schools would be offered the opportunity to 'opt out' of LEA control—in much the same way as GPs were invited to break away from district health authorities to become fundholders (see p. 164). Schools opting out would be renamed 'grant-maintained (GM) schools', and given autonomy to take their own decisions on admissions, staffing, and spending, funded by direct grants from central government. The Tories were effectively handing them de facto independent status (albeit without the freedom to charge fees) in the name of a new form of localism that would give direct power to ordinary citizens, rather than councillors elected to discharge it on their behalf. The underpinning philosophy was that decisions on the running of vital public services like education and, progressively, health and social care should be placed in the hands of the people who 'knew best'—those who *used* and/or staffed them—rather than politicians or civil servants. The main provisions of the 1988 Act are outlined in Table 15.3.

**Table 15.3** Main provisions of the Education Reform Act 1988

| Reform | Effect |
| --- | --- |
| Introduction of grant-maintained (GM) schools | Primary and secondary schools with at least 300 pupils allowed to 'opt out' of LEA control, becoming GM schools. Initially, entitlement was a 'reward' for high-performing schools (those with high numbers of pupils attaining five or more A–C GCSEs), but eventual aim was to extend it to most state schools. GM schools could set pay and conditions for staff and decide their own admissions policies (some began to select academically). They received direct government revenue grants towards their running costs, and could apply for capital funding for new equipment and buildings and repairs to existing ones. |
| Local Management of Schools (LMS) | Day-to-day financial decisions delegated to head teachers of GM schools working with their schools' boards of governors. |
| Introduction of National Curriculum (NC) | Dictated not only key subjects all schoolchildren must be taught (or offered) at various stages in schooling, but also the core skills and content that must be covered in them (e.g. basic spelling and punctuation in English language). The curriculum was to cover broadly same content throughout England and Wales, up to and including GCSE level, with exams at 'key stages' one, two, and three (ages 7, 11, and 14), through ***National Curriculum assessments (SATs).*** In Wales, the Welsh Assembly has authority to make slight adjustments—and has made teaching of the Welsh language compulsory in all state schools, alongside English. |

| Reform | Effect |
| --- | --- |
| Launch of key stages (KS) | Formal stages introduced by which each pupil expected to attain certain educational objectives. This is normally established through testing and/or continuous assessment. |
| Emergence of parent choice | First signs of 'choice' introduced in schools admissions process, with parents allowed to specify which local school they would like their children to attend. |
| First school league tables | Publication of school exam results—seen by ministers as means of providing objective information on performance of local schools to parents considering where to send their children. Attention today focuses on comparative data relating to truancy, exclusions, and performance in external exams—primarily GCSEs and benchmark of how many children achieve five 'good' passes (A*–C). Since 2007 the A*–C grades recorded by all schools for league table purposes— excluding academies—have had to include English language and maths, following criticism that many top grades are obtained by students studying 'easier' subjects. |
| Introduction of **city technology colleges (CTCs)** | New generation of **specialist schools** geared to needs of industry and technology sector established, with private companies invited to sponsor them. In time, most of these would become academies under Labour. |

The *Local Management of Schools (LMS)* scheme that supported grant-maintained schools proved hugely divisive. The element of selection introduced by some popular schools to simplify their admissions procedures and cherry-pick 'academic' applicants was seen to favour children with educated, professional parents, discriminating against those from disadvantaged backgrounds. Critics argued it would worsen existing inequalities between schools, leading to a gradual polarization between high-performing ones dominated by the affluent middle classes and 'sink schools' in poorer areas. The ability of head teachers and governors to set their own pay scales to attract the 'best' staff was seen to compound this problem: by headhunting high-performing teachers from LEA-run schools, or ones with poorer results, they would make their own schools yet more 'successful', while further impoverishing those already struggling. To top it all, government money followed the high-performing schools—rewarding them with funding bonuses and extra freedoms and fast-tracking grant allocations for GM head teachers by enabling them to bypass the cumbersome application procedures used by 'one-size-fits-all' LEAs.

Although it would adopt its own version of LMS after regaining power, Labour stood firmly opposed to the 1988 reforms. All the more embarrassing for Mr Blair, the party's leader, when in 1995 it emerged he was sending his eldest son, Euan, to the London Oratory, a Roman Catholic GM school—and for Harriet Harman, Labour's then health spokesperson, who was revealed to be sending one of her sons to the same school and her other to a grammar school.

To some opponents the idea of introducing 'parent choice' into the GM schools' equation set the final seal on an emerging 'two-tier' state education system. If parents were allowed to choose between rival schools in their area, who in their right mind would opt for the one with worse results and less money to spend on pupils? As these 'successful' schools became richer and still more successful, the less popular ones were likely to fall further behind and become 'poorer'. Moreover, successful schools would realistically have only limited ability to expand to take in growing numbers of applicants and, given their vested interest in favouring those most likely to succeed, they might be tempted to become increasingly selective. All the while, children forced to attend less popular and/or 'failing' schools were likely to suffer. Table 15.4 presents a summary of the main arguments for and against schools being allowed to opt out.

The first school to gain grant-maintained status was Skegness Grammar School, in 1988. By the time GM schools were finally abolished (in name at least) in 1998, there were nearly 1,100 nationwide—three out of five at secondary level.

**Table 15.4** Arguments for and against state schools being allowed to 'opt out'

| For | Against |
| --- | --- |
| Parents know what is best for their own children. Giving them a direct input into running their schools will enable them to customize teaching to suit individual children's needs, replacing a 'one size fits all' approach devised by bureaucrats. | Allowing schools to become self-governing worsens inequalities in state system. Given control of own budgets and teacher recruitment, they poach the 'best' from elsewhere—widening the gap between 'successful' and 'failing' schools. |
| Giving more power to head teachers and boards of governors (including parents, teachers, and members of the local community) gives them a sense of *ownership* of the school. Ownership increases determination to drive up standards. | Giving schools control of own disciplinary procedures, staff recruitment, and budget decisions will breed huge inconsistencies in nature and quality of provision across sector. It is also the thin end of wedge: how long before they demand the right to select the brightest pupils—or use 'social selection' to do so by back door? |
| LEAs are unwieldy and bureaucratic organizations, and slow to take decisions. Putting power in hands of governors and head teachers speeds up decision-making by 'cutting out the middle man'. | Local authorities are run by elected councillors and therefore accountable to all members of community at ballot box. School governors are accountable to no one but parents of children already attending those schools, and only have a responsibility to those families. Who will stop them taking decisions that adversely affect other schools? |

# City technology colleges and the rise of specialist schools

Although pedants might point towards the technical schools established in the 1950s and 1960s as early examples of secondaries specializing in specific disciplines—in their cases, practical subjects like carpentry—the birth of specialist schools per se came much later. Reviving the notion that some children are less predisposed towards academic subjects and more towards vocational ones—and that more needed to be done to tailor the skills and qualifications with which 16–18-year-olds left school to the demands of industry and the scientific community—the 1988 Act saw the Conservatives introduce a new generation of 'technical schools'.

From the outset these secondary schools-cum-sixth-form colleges—city technology colleges (CTCs)—were distinct from anything before them. Taking their inspiration from the US experience of involving business and industry sponsors through 'charter schools', CTCs saw private companies become involved not only in funding buildings and equipment, but, more controversially, in day-to-day decisions about how they were run. Rather than focusing entirely on teaching practical subjects, as an alternative to the National Curriculum, they still offered pre-16 children all of the usual subjects. In *addition* to this, however, they were equipped with particular specialisms in the sciences, maths, the emerging field of information technology (IT), and other related disciplines.

But the defining characteristic of CTCs was the extent of private sector involvement. In capital terms, private sponsors helped to finance up-front the expansion and refurbishment of existing schools—and the construction of brand new ones—in return for a long-term leaseback agreement that would make their investments profitable over time. This was one of the first tangible manifestations of the Tories' new 'big idea' for funding expensive public sector projects, the *private finance initiative (PFI)* (see p. 222). But the sponsorship arrangements went deeper than this: companies investing in CTCs were given seats on the governing boards of those schools. To the horror of some, certain schools went so far as to 'rebrand' themselves, incorporating the names of sponsoring companies into their official titles and logos. The first CTCs were set up at the tail end of the 1980s in Kingshurst, Birmingham, and Nottingham. But the most controversial early opening—and the first to incorporate the name of its sponsor so explicitly—was Dixons Bradford CTC, funded by the high-street electrical retailer. The college, which opened in 1990, has since converted into an academy. At time of writing, only three CTCs remained, the rest having done likewise, but Mr Gove was said to be planning a new generation of schools-cum-colleges along similar lines (see p. 432).

The purpose of CTCs was not solely to provide an education more geared to the changing demands of industry and the oncoming technological revolution. By granting them a degree of independence commensurate with that offered to GM schools, the government was giving head teachers a more decisive say in running their schools—but with the quid pro quo that under-performance would be questioned by their increasingly influential boards of governors. These boards—far from being the talking shops of old, there to be 'consulted' by LEAs but otherwise powerless—gave parents, teachers, local residents, and members of the business community a direct say in school man-agement for the first time.

## Foundation schools, academies, and the growth of school autonomy

Mr Blair's election in 1997 owed much to his rallying cry of 'education, educa-tion, education'—and his pledge to improve school standards and opportuni-ties for children from all backgrounds. Labour had opposed both CTCs and the whole principle of schools 'opting out' of LEA control in opposition, and sure enough set about ending both the LMS and CTC programmes within months of entering office. As with the health service, however, it was not long before Mr Blair and his ministers were converted into champions of specialist schools, PFI—which they renamed *public–private partnerships (PPPs)*—and the con-cept of school autonomy.

New Labour arguably left the state school landscape considerably more patchwork than it had found it. The School Standards and Framework Act 1998 converted all existing GM schools into foundation schools. Its immediate effect was to bring them back under a measure of LEA control—to the extent that, rather than continuing to be funded by direct government grant, they would have revenue funds channelled through their councils. In practice, however, the sums allocated to each foundation school would largely be determined by Whitehall, and in many respects, they would retain a degree of independence akin to that wielded by GM schools before them. The land and buildings occu-pied by foundation schools would be owned by their governing boards (unless ownership were handed, or had historically belonged, to a charitable founda-tion), and they would gain control over their own admissions policies; they would also be able to hire and fire their own staff, rather than rely on local authorities to recruit on their behalf.

The most controversial of these three extensions of autonomy was the sec-ond. If schools were to be allowed to decide which pupils to admit and exclude, critics argued, would this not reintroduce selection by the backdoor? How were LEAs and the government to prevent popular schools discriminating between applicants on the basis of their prior academic record, social backgrounds, or even appearance?

A layer of complication was added to the debate when, in Mr Blair's final weeks in office, the Education and Inspections Act 2007 introduced the term trust school into the equation. Trust status—a term borrowed, like 'foundation', from the health service—has since been offered to foundation schools choosing to set up a charitable trust to manage their affairs. Within a year 300 foundation schools had either converted into trusts or were in the process of doing so. A number have since been formed through the merger of two or more schools, or the takeover of 'failing' schools by more successful ones. Trust schools are not generally offered any additional funding as an incentive to convert—nor are they allowed to 'opt out' of local authority control to any greater extent than foundation schools—but in December 2007 then Schools Secretary Ed Balls offered several 'sweeteners' to encourage high-performing schools to team up with less successful ones, including the promise of £300,000 cash injections to smooth over the process. The idea of two or more schools 'clubbing together' under the same head teacher and governing board was extended further by Labour in later years through the introduction of *federation*—a form of shared governance, like trust status, open to both primaries and secondaries.

Alongside foundation schools, the 1998 Act retained two other principal types of secondary school: community schools and voluntary schools. Community school is the umbrella term for all 'ordinary' state primaries and comprehensives: local authorities continue to own and maintain their infrastructure, determine their admissions policies, and recruit their staff. Prior to the 1998 Act, standard primary and comprehensive (or 'high') schools had for some time been known as 'county schools'. Some community schools have since been renamed community *colleges*, reflecting the fact that, in addition to teaching the National Curriculum, they also offer adult education and training (normally through evening classes) like that provided elsewhere by FE and tertiary colleges.

'Voluntary schools' are (as their name suggests) stalwarts of earlier times normally linked to either the Church of England or Roman Catholic Church. They are divided into two types: **voluntary aided schools** and *voluntary controlled schools*. The former are schools the land and buildings of which are owned by either a church or charitable foundation, but which receive all of their revenue funding and up to 50 per cent of their capital outlay from the state in return for teaching the National Curriculum and offering school places free of charge. As with foundation schools, however, their governing boards may determine their admissions and staffing policies. The principal difference between voluntary aided and voluntary controlled schools is that, in the latter case, the LEA controls their admissions and staffing procedures in return for providing all of their funding.

Although the term 'voluntary school' is not generally used in Scotland, since the Education Act 1918 it has been commonplace for secondary schools to specify a denominational bias, with a number labelling themselves 'RC schools'.

# The emergence of academies—and the return of specialist schools

The most significant additional change to school designations under New Labour was its conversion to the twin ideas of specialization and independent management *within* the state sector. The Learning and Skills Act 2000 introduced 'city academies'—schools with state-of-the-art buildings and facilities, part-funded by commercial companies, which would be allowed both to specialize in key subjects geared to the demands of their local communities and to manage their own internal affairs (including admissions). Some traditionalists saw in the policy a direct contradiction of the party's initial opposition to CTCs, and a betrayal of the ideals of comprehensive education being entirely funded and managed both within and *by* the public sector—by local and central government. Labour modernizers like Mr Blair and then Education Secretary David Blunkett saw it as a way of pumping much-needed teaching resources into deprived areas more quickly than if the government were to finance the investment single-handedly, while equipping previously disadvantaged youngsters with the skills demanded by modern industry.

In their early years, academies (as they were later renamed) had much in common with CTCs. Buildings and amenities received significant boosts from private capital in return for complex PFI/PPP leaseback arrangements and often a stake for sponsoring companies in the running of the schools. For some this was to be an 'arm's-length' arrangement—a presence on the governing board and consultation over expansions or mergers—but for others it became more hands on. Towards the end of Labour's tenure, private investors often became directly involved in the day-to-day staffing of ancillary functions such as administration, security, maintenance, and/or catering at academies such as William Hulme's Grammar School in Manchester. Pupils attending academies (as with CTCs) often work slightly longer days than their peers in other types of school, and/or between different term dates. Unlike CTCs, however, they have not tended to specialize in scientific, business, or technological subjects: if the local communities in which they are based lack adequate sports facilities, or if there are specific demands for people with skills in the arts and media, these factors have generally determined their specialisms.

Perhaps the most controversial 'privilege' granted to academies under Labour was their qualified exemption from one of the sacred cornerstones of the party's traditional education policy: its opposition to selection. From the outset academies were permitted to select up to 10 per cent of their pupils on the basis of 'aptitude' in their specialist subjects. The choice of this word—pointedly distinguished from 'ability' by ministers—has been the cause of considerable controversy (not to mention semantic debate). Labour appeared to be walking a tightrope between offering some head teachers the autonomy they craved to introduce limited selection and distancing itself from the Conservatives' wholesale support for selective schools. In drawing what many saw as an artificial distinction between a pupil's 'potential' to do well in a subject (their 'aptitude') and their proven 'ability' in it, however, ministers left many head teachers nursing headaches. In 2003 the House of Commons Education and Skills *Select Committee* recommended that tests be scrapped, arguing that the government had failed to provide a convincing definition of 'aptitude'. Ministers countered that the aim of introducing limited selection was to identify pupils who 'would benefit from' accessing a specialism.

Arguments about autonomy aside, the rise and fall of CTCs, and their subsequent metamorphosis into academies, was in many ways just the latest manifestation of a decades-old debate about the wisdom of dividing pupils into 'academic' and 'practical', and gearing education towards the *needs* of industry as well as the *aspirations* of young people keen to develop their intellects in a wider sense. In earlier times, this debate led to the schism between left and right over grammar schools (see pp. 430–2); more recently, it has been played out in arguments over the introduction of new qualifications covering vocational disciplines. Since September 2008, 14–19-year-olds have had the option of studying for new vocational diplomas covering subjects as varied as health and social care, creative media, and engineering in addition to—or instead of—GCSEs and/or A levels.

Indeed, the specialization reintroduced under the academies programme is far from confined to those schools today. During the second and third Labour terms, in fact, it became so prevalent in the state sector that the majority of secondary schools now specialize in one or more subjects—meaning the oft-used label 'specialist school' is less a separate category than an umbrella term embracing all schools that do so (whatever other 'box' they fall into). A council-run community school is just as likely to specialize in something as one that is independently managed, and any secondary head teacher may apply for specialist status to the Department for Education.

Achieving specialist status usually earns a school a significant injection of capital and revenue funding to support the development of its new specialism. To date, the specialist schools programme has required those seeking to obtain specialist status first to raise around £50,000 in sponsorship. If granted their wish, they then qualify each year for an extra £100,000 or more in capital grant from government, plus around £130 per pupil, to help to put their specialist ambitions into practice. Applications are normally successful if the chosen specialism either:

- relates to a genuine area of outstanding achievement by pupils of the school; or
- fills a gap in provision of facilities for the local community in which the school is based (for example, playing fields or concert facilities).

In return for its funding boost, the school is normally expected to make its new, improved amenities available to neighbouring schools and community groups. Like academies, many specialist schools are permitted to select up to 10 per cent of their pupils on the basis of their aptitude in a relevant subject. Whether schools were allowed to select, however, depended on the nature of that specialism under Labour—only those specializing in languages, the performing and visual arts, and sport were permitted to do so. In 2007, then Shadow Education Secretary David Willetts committed the Tories to extending the 10 per cent selection principle to all specialist schools if the party were returned to power, but at time of writing it remained to be seen what Michael Gove had in store.

## The future of academies

Labour's original academies programme was intended to prioritize 'failing' comprehensives—principally those in deprived areas—by using public–private partnerships to funnel capital injections into rejuvenating their existing facilities, or in some cases building new schools from scratch. After a sluggish start, the number of academies began growing steadily—rising from 17 in the first year to 203 by the time the party lost the May 2010 election. In its third term, academies' greatest advocate, then Education Minister Lord Adonis, invited private schools struggling to meet recruitment targets in the face of growing competition in the 'true' independent sector to consider converting into them. Several, including Belvedere School in Liverpool and Bristol Cathedral School, subsequently did. Meanwhile, applications for academy status were increasingly being granted to less obviously 'struggling' schools and/or those in more affluent areas.

But the arrival of Conservative Education Secretary Mr Gove in May 2010 looked set to herald not only a dramatic acceleration in the rollout of academies but also a significantly more liberal attitude towards the kinds of school that would qualify. In the months preceding the election Mr Gove had made clear his determination to extend academy status to primary as well as secondary schools and, sure enough, within weeks of taking office he had written to the head teachers of every primary and secondary in England inviting them to take up his offer. Under the ensuing Academies Bill (over which the new government was subsequently criticized for rushing it through the Commons before the summer recess), schools rated 'outstanding' by Ofsted could be 'fast-tracked' by September 2010. In the event, only around 32 new academies opened ready for the autumn term.

Inevitably, the hyperactive approach to advancing the programme meant that, unlike their predecessors, many of this new breed of academies would be taking the leap shorn of commercial sponsorship and the up-front capital injections accompanying it. However, as a sweetener—and a symbolic fore-taste of the enhanced autonomy Mr Gove intended to offer them—the Bill unveiled plans to boost their revenue budgets by giving them direct access to the 10 per cent of central government funding for each state school (includ-ing academies) currently still spent by local authorities on their behalf. Mr Gove also promised to offer academies greater freedom to form partnerships with other public and private sector organizations, and allow them to devise their own curricula (in so doing abandoning the National Curriculum his own party had introduced!). Although the academies programme has fervent champions, a decade or more after its introduction the jury is still out about the extent to which it has enhanced academic performance across the board. In September 2009, at the end of his final academic year as Schools Secre-tary, Mr Balls announced that GCSE results for academies had improved by more than twice the national average rate in the preceding 12 months. Since becoming an academy, one of Labour's flagships, Harefield Academy in Hillingdon, west London, had seen a fivefold increase in GCSE A*–C pass rates—rising to 45 per cent from just 8 per cent when it was a floundering comprehensive. But critics point to less rosy examples, and to the fact that as academies are currently exempt from the Freedom of Information Act 2000 (see Chapter 20) it is impossible to judge whether they are performing more or less well than other secondary schools, as their pupils may be achieving top grades in 'easier' subjects.

Mr Gove was also criticized for placing so much initial emphasis on already high-performing schools, by fast-tracking their academy appli-cations. In his defence, he said that as a precondition for adopting academy status each applicant would have to be prepared to take a lower-performing one 'under its wing'. The coalition was also committed to intro-ducing a 'pupil premium'—an idea drawn from the Lib Dem manifesto—to provide additional funding per head for less academically able children from poorer backgrounds.

Table 15.5 outlines the main changes in school designations under Labour.

**Table 15.5** Changes in school designations under Labour

| School name pre-1997 | School name since 1997 |
| --- | --- |
| County | Community school/community college |
| Grant-maintained (GM) | Foundation/trust |
| Controlled | Voluntary controlled |
| Aided | Voluntary aided |
| City technology college (CTC) | Academy (formerly city academy) |
| Maintained special | Community special |
| GM special | Foundation/trust special |

## Specialist versus special schools—avoiding confusion

Despite the similarity in designation, specialist schools are not to be confused with **special schools**, which specialize not in particular disciplines but in teaching children with learning difficulties, such as dyslexia or autism, or mental or physical disabilities. Prior to the 1997 election, these were commonly known as 'special needs schools'.

To be judged eligible to attend a special school, a child must be 'statemented'—that is, awarded a 'statement of special education need'—by his or her LEA, following a diagnosis by a GP or specialist and (in some cases) a formal test of his or her academic ability. Recent years have seen a growing trend for such pupils to be integrated into mainstream schools, to avoid segregation from their peers and to help them to attain skills and qualifications that will give them career prospects comparable to those of other children. Some mainstream primaries and secondaries now have their own 'special units', while others integrate disabled children and those with learning difficulties into general classes. However, the disparate approach adopted by different LEAs has created a widening postcode lottery.

The question of 'integration versus segregation' continues to be politically sensitive, with many local authorities having closed down dedicated special schools in recent years, often for financial reasons rather than because they have a strong policy in favour of the former approach. During the May 2010 election campaign, Mr Cameron was barracked in front of television cameras by the father of a boy with spina bifida who accused the Tories of planning to 'segregate' disabled children by promoting a return to separate schools. Mr Cameron, whose late son, Ivan, suffered from cerebral palsy and epilepsy, had used his party's manifesto to condemn what he described as Labour's 'ideologically driven closure of special schools' and end the 'bias' towards pushing them into mainstream ones.

# ▶ The dwindling role of LEAs

As alluded to earlier in this chapter, LEAs have had their powers increasingly eroded over the past twenty years—caught between the pincer movement of growing self-determination for schools and direct intervention in cases of underperformance by the *Secretary of State* (see p. 45). But the single most significant recent reform of local education occurred in the Children Act 2004, passed in the wake of the Victoria Climbié child abuse case (see p. 514). The media inquest into this gruesome tragedy led to a sweeping reorganization, under the 'Every Child Matters' agenda. This saw old-style education departments hand their oversight of schools over to across-the-board 'children's services' departments and the post of chief education officer replaced by a new all-encompassing 'director of children's services' in each county council and unitary area. The aim was to join up a range of services affecting children that were seen to have become fragmented, in an effort to better safeguard child welfare and to make it less likely that warning signs of abuse would be missed in future.

Despite their overarching role in implementing the 2004 Act, local authorities have seen significant reductions in their powers in relation to schools. Today, they tend to be less the principal state education providers in their areas than enablers and coordinators, and in light of the coalition's determination to drive forward the academies programme and introduce a new breed of free schools run by parents and teachers (see pp. 445–8) their influence is only likely to diminish further. Table 15.6 details how councils' powers over local schooling have been reduced, alongside those they retain.

# ▶ Faith schools, free schools, and other recent trends in schooling

One debate that has bubbled consistently in recent years concerns the future of 'faith schools'—an umbrella term used to describe schools run by particular religious communities. The term 'faith school' has traditionally been used interchangeably with 'voluntary school', as discussed earlier in this chapter. In this context, however, it also denotes schools run by non-Christian faith groups, including the Muslim, Sikh, Hindu, and Jewish communities. There are around 7,000 faith schools in England, Wales, and Northern Ireland, and a growing number in Scotland. A breakdown of the split between different religions in England and Wales is given in the table entitled 'A breakdown of faith schools by religion/denomination in the UK', which can be found on the Online Resource Centre that accompanies this book.

Faith schools were championed by Mr Blair, whose eldest son, Euan, attended one. He and other advocates argue they have above-average attendance rates compared to standard primaries and comprehensives, and high achievement rates. They have also been praised for instilling firm discipline and respect among pupils. Mr Blunkett famously said he wanted to 'bottle' the essence of faith schools and use it as a template for reform elsewhere. Two *White Papers* advocating further integration of faith schools into the state sector followed: one in 2001, focusing on all denominations, and a second (in 2005) specifically aimed at Muslim schools, as part of the government's wider efforts to tackle the perceived cultural isolation of some localized Islamic communities.

Table 15.6 Powers retained and lost by local education authorities (LEAs)

| Retained | Lost |
|---|---|
| Provides and maintains premises for primary and secondary schools. | Until the Education Act 1993, LEAs had statutory duty to appoint education committees. Those operating in areas with voluntary schools included members of relevant churches alongside councillors. The obligation to convene committees has gone, but some councils still do so. Education committees remaining under John Major required to involve teachers and governors in decisions, as co-opted (non-voting) members. Labour extended this invitation to parents. |
| Has to ensure every school-aged child in their areas has access to formal state education. | 1993 Act gave Education Secretary formal responsibility for 'promoting the education of the people of England and Wales'. It made no mention of LEAs, and new *quangos*—Funding Agency for Schools and Schools Funding Council for Wales—were introduced. In areas with many GM schools, the agencies could share with the LEA—or take over—its schools planning and funding role. This centralizing agenda has arguably continued (despite rhetoric about localism), with Labour channelling direct funding to academies and allowing limited local authority involvement in foundation schools, and the coalition rolling out the academy programme and introducing free schools—with funds again bypassing LEAs and going straight to schools. |
| Channels funds to the governors of community, foundation/trust, voluntary, and special schools, and ensures all schools follow the National Curriculum. | School Standards and Frameworks Act 1998 introduced new requirement for LEAs to prepare education development plans (EDPs) for Secretary of State. This was seen as attack on council autonomy, transferring executive power to Whitehall. |
| Recommends reform of individual schools in response to Ofsted reports (see pp. 445–8). | Local authorities have no role in day-to-day running of academies, CTCs, or free schools. |
| Establishes an independent schools organization committee, comprising councillors and representatives of other interest groups, including boards of academies and CTCs. These met every three years to consider school organization plans, proposed by council, addressing prospective mergers, closures, and changes to catchment areas, until they were scrapped in May 2007 and their commissioning role taken in-house by LEAs. | |

Yet there has been much opposition. Although most faith schools are subsidized by the state, non fee-charging, and obliged to follow the National Curriculum, critics like the National Secular Society regard the idea of any child being educated from a young age at a school with a prescriptive underlying worldview as a form of brainwashing incompatible with one of state education's primary roles—to foster freedom of thought and expression. Others, including some politicians and teaching unions, have argued that maintaining single-faith schools—whether inside or outside the state system—promotes ghettoization and undermines efforts elsewhere to promote understanding between communities with contrasting beliefs. Some also object to their being allowed to exercise limited selection, albeit faith-based rather than academic, unlike any other state schools save academies and grammars. In March 2008, the National Union of Teachers (NUT) proposed a novel approach to paving the way for an end to single-faith schools: by requiring *all* state schools to become 'multi-faith' institutions, offering faith-based instruction, a choice of religious holidays, and varied prayer facilities.

Alleged self-segregation is not the only criticism to have been levelled against faith schools: in April 2006 it emerged the Emmanuel Schools Foundation (sponsored by Christian car dealer Sir Peter Vardy), which runs schools including the King's Academy in Middlesbrough, was teaching 'creationism' as an alternative view of the origins of the universe to Darwin's theory of evolution.

Where New Labour ministers were keen to emulate the models of governance embodied in many faith schools, the Tory-led coalition, keen to promote bottom-up localism, is investing its belief in a new form of school that can be set up and governed directly by parents: free schools. Shortly after inviting all state head teachers in England and Wales to apply for academy status, Mr Gove wrote a second letter (to LEA chief executives and children's services directors) setting out the process by which charities, universities, and other interested parties—including groups of teachers and/or parents—could found their own schools. Like academies, these would be run independently of LEAs and allowed to draw up their own curricula. They would, however, have to admit children of all abilities and be non-selective and non-fee-charging. The new approach, a hybrid of a profit-based 'free school' model that originated in Sweden and the US charter school approach, is intended to:

- respond to parental demand in areas where there is felt to be a lack of 'good quality' schools in place by making it easier and quicker for new ones to be established;
- promote hands-on involvement by parents, teachers, and local business-people in developing the ethos, teaching methods, and outcomes of their schools, as part of the Conservatives' 'Big Society' approach to fostering community involvement in place of what the party portrayed as intrusive and controlling state intervention.

Mindful of early scepticism about the logistical hurdles some parents might face with the nitty-gritty of setting up their own schools (particularly those with full-time day jobs), Mr Gove added that, as well as central government funding, ministers would offer project managers professional guidance through the

New Schools Network, an independent charity established to promote social mobility through flexible models of state education. He also revealed that local authority planning policies would be relaxed to enable school building programmes to be fast-tracked, with £50m immediately diverted from Labour's Harnessing Technology Grant fund to provide up-front capital finance for free schools, in the hope that the first would be ready to open by September 2011. But a year before the prospective 'launch date', Mr Gove was forced to concede only 16 were likely to open in year one.

While some critics predicted Mr Gove's offer would be met by a deathly silence, there were early takers. Among them was a 400-strong consortium of parents headed by journalist Toby Young (whose father, the eminent sociologist and Labour peer Lord Young, had ironically been one of the architects of the comprehensive system). Mr Young and his fellow West London Free School campaigners announced they were planning a free school open to children of all backgrounds and abilities. But opponents of the scheme, including Shadow Education Secretary Mr Balls, warned of the danger of creating a two-tier schooling system—with 'pushy middle-class parents' exploiting the new freedoms to set up schools dominated by children from similar households, while families in poorer areas (where new and better schools were more needed) might lack the skills and confidence to mobilize in the same way. Other argued it would be folly to establish free schools in areas where there was no shortage of 'good' schools already—simply because some people wanted them—when their introduction might generate surplus places, and jeopardize the viability of existing providers.

## Monitoring school standards—and the great 'parent choice' debate

Besides selection, the other great issue to have dominated debate about state schooling over the past 15 years is that of 'parent choice'. At the heart of this is the long-standing notion that families should be free to send their children to whichever local school they choose. Dividing lines were sharpened, however, in the Thatcher and Major years by the introduction of two key innovations designed to inform parents better about the relative academic merits of the various schools in their areas: school league tables and a national inspectorate, the Office for Standards in Education (Ofsted).

League tables of school exam results were introduced under the 1988 Act, but took a while to catch on with parents. The more decisive agent of parental choice was arguably the introduction of systematic school inspections. Until 1992, school standards were enforced by inspectors from two bodies: Her Majesty's Inspectorate of Education and LEAs themselves. But the Education (Schools) Act 1992 and the School Inspections Act 1996 established Ofsted in England and *Estyn* in Wales, providing more consistent nationwide frameworks. (In Scotland, school inspections remain the province of the HM Inspectorate, while Northern Ireland has an *Education and Training Inspectorate*.)

Ofsted is headed by a Chief Inspector of Schools, and tasked with inspecting all English state schools on a regular basis. Its first set of inspections were carried out within four years of its inception, but thereafter they became six-yearly until Labour decided to make them more frequent, and give schools shorter notice periods so as to allow them less scope to engineer positive reports by 'cleaning up their acts' at the last minute.

As of 1 April 2007, Ofsted was renamed the *Office for Standards in Education, Children's Services, and Skills*. Today, it inspects the following types of educational provider:

- nursery and primary schools;
- secondary schools;
- special schools;
- service children's education—for offspring of those in the Armed Forces;
- pupil referral units—schools set up for children 'who cannot attend' normal schools, such as pregnant teenagers, those with specific medical problems, and children excluded from mainstream schools for bad behaviour;
- some independent schools, excluding members of the Independent Schools Council (ISC) and Focus Learning Trust, which are inspected by the Independent Schools Inspectorate (ISI) and School Inspection Services (SIS).

Ofsted reports rate schools as 'outstanding', 'good', 'satisfactory', or 'inadequate', and are made public on its website. After an inspection, a school will be expected to act on any recommendations the report contains, according to the process outlined in Table 15.7 overleaf.

Perhaps unsurprisingly, the advent of league tables and Ofsted has intensified competition for places at high-performing schools. By effectively promoting 'the best' schools and naming and shaming 'the worst' they have helped to create a thriving market for places at successful ones and an exodus of middle-class families from those deemed 'failing'. There was no starker illustration of this pattern than the East Brighton Centre of Media Arts (COMART)—a 'failing' comprehensive that went through not one, but two, name changes, and a costly PFI building programme, before finally closing in summer 2005. Based in one of Brighton's most deprived areas, Whitehawk, the school consistently had the worst GCSE and truancy rates in Brighton and Hove. Better-off parents voted with their feet—reducing its social mix and overall pupil numbers, and sending its standards plummeting still further.

**Table 15.7** Process for responding to recommendations in an Ofsted report

| Stage | Process |
|-------|---------|
| School action plan | Initial summary report considered formally by school's governing body, which produces an action plan within 40 working days. Both report and school's response are open to public inspection. |
| Local authority report | If report contains significant recommendations, local LEA is required to produce its own report (even if the school is not council-run). |
| Special measures | Where report finds that school is *'failing to give its pupils an acceptable standard of education'*—a 'failing' school—it can be placed in 'special measures'. In such cases, an action plan must be submitted to Secretary of State, who will closely monitor school's progress over following two years. |
| Fresh Start | If no appreciable signs of improvement follow, school's management and teaching staff will normally be replaced and school reopened under the 'Fresh Start' scheme. Head teacher and all existing teaching staff are normally sacked and replaced. Often a 'super-head' is parachuted in from a 'successful' school, at request of LEA or Secretary of State. In 1999 Torsten Friedag was headhunted for a £70,000 salary (£20,000 above the then norm) from Croydon's BRIT School to take over Islington's George Orwell School (since reopened as Islington Arts and Media School). |

Critics argue the advent of 'parent choice' has parallels with the rise of 'patient choice' in the NHS, which has seen successful hospitals oversubscribed and failing ones avoided. While a growing number of 'failing' schools are closing, 'successful' ones gain greater financial rewards and freedoms—enabling them to headhunt the most experienced staff and improve further. Devoid of these privileges, underperforming schools can become locked in a downward spiral. Many fear this is a fate awaiting unpopular community schools in areas where the coalition's academy and free school programmes are soon to be rolled out.

From a journalistic viewpoint, particularly for local media outlets, Ofsted reports provide 'easy-hit', newsworthy stories that can usefully fill space or airtime. As Ofsted inspections have become more frequent and the process better understood, however, the regulator itself cannot be relied on to send out reports proactively to newspapers or television and radio stations, so it is usually up to journalists to chase them. Reporters should also be wary about relying on a school's own account of its inspection and Ofsted's findings: as with most things in journalism, it is best to go straight to the horse's mouth for the full story.

Another area of controversy related to the growing national obsession with school league tables is that of testing. Ministers have consistently come into conflict with head teachers and unions in recent years over the sheer volume of assessment with which schoolchildren are now faced—and the pressure this puts on both pupils and teachers. Opposition to the culture of testing intensified in summer 2008 when ETS Europe, the commercial company contracted to oversee marking of the Key Stage 2 and 3 tests for 11 and 14-year-olds, was responsible for a marking fiasco. Results for some schools suffered severe delays and there were reports of packages of exam papers lying uncollected (and unmarked) in head teachers' offices weeks after exams had been sat. The government launched an independent inquiry into the scandal, headed by Lord Sutherland, and in August ETS Europe had its £156m five-year contract terminated by the now-defunct QCA. It had been paid £39.6m for 2008 alone.

In a surprise olive branch to critics of school testing, in October 2008 Mr Balls scrapped National Curriculum assessments (SATs) for 14-year-olds. He said a new US-style 'report card' would be introduced in 2011 for each primary and secondary school child, giving an overall grade from A to F covering not only his or her exam results and performance, but also his or her attendance and/or truancy rate, behaviour, and health. In July 2010 Mr Gove announced a review of SATs after a quarter of primary schools boycotted the tests for 11-year-olds during a bout of industrial action during the previous month.

Other recent trends to monitor and improve standards have seen more direct state intervention to help struggling schools. Prior to leaving office, Mr Balls offered schools with fewer than 30 per cent of pupils achieving five GCSE A*–C passes extra money to channel into top-up tuition via a National Challenge for Schools programme. In a further sign of a shift towards 'carrots' and away from 'sticks', in April 2008 new *school improvement partners (SIPs)* were introduced in many areas of England—individuals or organizations with relevant expertise that provide an outside consultancy role to schools to help them to improve standards.

# ▶ The future of school catchment areas

The flipside of 'failing' schools becoming unpopular is that 'successful' ones become *over*-popular. The trends in school applications fostered by the extension of 'parent choice' have had an inevitable impact on *catchment areas*—the geographical patches within which families need to live to be eligible to send their children to a particular school. Pressure on popular schools to admit more pupils—potentially at the expense of maintaining the high standards for which they are renowned—has seen some councils take drastic steps to 'ration' places, to keep their numbers sustainable and improve the social mix and performance of other institutions.

In 2008 Brighton and Hove Council controversially began allocating places for oversubscribed secondary schools in the city's 'Golden Triangle' by lottery (or 'random allocation'). Many families living in this area had paid high prices for houses in the expectation of being automatically entitled to send their children to one of these popular schools. Under the lottery system, the schools' catchments were extended to cover areas until now devoid of comprehensives, and children from outlying districts became just as likely to be admitted as those living on their doorstep, as once applications to attend one of the affected schools exceed the number of places available, a lottery is used as a tie-breaker. Brighton's experiment was soon emulated elsewhere, and a new admissions code was introduced by the Labour government urging head teachers of oversubscribed schools to determine who should be offered places effectively by drawing names out of a hat. The guidelines—intended to stamp out 'selection by mortgage'—also banned schools from interviewing parents, considering their backgrounds, or excluding people financially by, for example, stipulating that they buy uniforms from expensive suppliers. However, a report published by the British Educational Research Association in September 2010 found that, contrary to expectations, the Brighton experiment had failed to produce any visible improvement in 'social mix' at the schools concerned. The report did not criticize the use of the lottery system per se, but rather the fact that the council had redrawn catchment boundaries in such a way that even the enlarged area from which applications had since been accepted principally embraced middle-class neighbourhoods, with poorer ones in peripheral parts of the city still excluded.

Until the *recession*, concern about the use of lotteries and rationing of state school places saw growing numbers of middle-class parents defecting to the independent sector, angry that their children were no longer guaranteed places in 'good' state schools nearby. Some fear that, by admitting more youngsters from deprived backgrounds, the high-performing schools to which they currently send their children risk compromising their academic standards. Furthermore, oversubscribed schools have, on occasion, reportedly rejected siblings of children already attending them because of pressure on spaces—making the 'school run' increasingly complicated for parents. This has further fuelled the flight to the private sector. According to a 'census' published in April 2008 by the Independent Schools Council (ISC), 50,000 more children were being sent to private school than in 1997—with parents paying up to £27,000 for the privilege. This was despite Labour's record investment in state schools and the fact the overall number of school-aged children in the UK had dropped since 1997. Neither were parents put off by the fact that independent school fees had risen by 6.2 per cent—twice the *inflation* rate—in the same period.

To bolster the state sector—and, ministers argue, break down a false divide between state and independent schools—Mr Brown's government instructed the Charity Commission to impose new conditions on private and public schools seeking to retain their charitable status (which entitles them, among other things, to significant tax breaks not enjoyed by companies). The biggest condition was a requirement to earn this privilege by opening up their playing fields and other facilities to state schools and community groups. These moves were denounced at a hearing of the Commons Children, Schools, and Families Select Committee by Chris Parry, short-lived head of the ISC, as provoking a new 'Cold War' between the independent and state school sectors. Undeterred, ministers pointed to other developments, including a recent invitation to independent schools to sponsor academies (accepted by the £18,000-a-year Wellington School, the headmaster of which was Mr Blair's biographer, Anthony Seldon), and to share amenities and expertise with the new trusts, as proof of their desire for partnership.

## Guaranteeing fairness—the role of schools adjudicators

Ofsted is not the only body to have been introduced in the 1990s to police the state school system. The 1998 Act saw the establishment of a second: the *Office of the Schools Adjudicator (OSA)*. Despite its title, like Ofsted (which employs a number of inspectors) the office has more than one adjudicator: in fact it has ten, led by a 'chief adjudicator'.

There are many misconceptions about the OSA—the most common being that it is there to rule on complaints by parents about their children's failure to get into their chosen school. In fact, that role is taken by independent appeals panels. The OSA, in contrast, has statutory duties to:

- determine objections to admission arrangements and appeals from schools against directions from the local authority to admit a particular pupil;
- resolve local disputes on statutory proposals for school reorganization, or on the transfer and disposal of non-playing field land and assets;
- decide on competitions to set up new schools where the local authority has entered the contest with its own proposals;
- decide on requests to vary already agreed admission arrangements.

## Intervention of last resort—the role of the Secretary of State

As the powers of local authorities to control state education in their areas has diminished with the emergence of new types of self-governing school, conversely Secretary of State's role has been resurgent. Direct intervention by the Education Secretary can now take any of the forms outlined in Table 15.8.

## Other issues affecting schools

Besides the customary slew of stories about damning Ofsted reports, catchment areas, and league tables, there has been significant coverage in recent months about public spending cuts in relation to schools. During Mr Brown's

**Table 15.8** Modern-day powers of the Schools Secretary

| Power | Effect |
| --- | --- |
| Intervention 'in default' | Prevents unreasonable uses of power by local authorities and 'acts in default' when they fail. |
| Managing the availability of school places | Directs LEAs to reduce surplus places in schools by merging and/or closing unpopular ones, or to increase provision where there is high demand. |
| Intervening in 'failing schools' | Places 'failing' schools under special measures, and instigates the Fresh Start should they fail to improve. In 2000, Mr Blunkett introduced 'fresh starts' for schools in which fewer than 15 per cent of pupils achieved five or more C or above GCSE passes. First up was Gillingham Community College in Kent, where not one pupil had achieved a C. When Labour left office, schools where fewer than 30 per cent of pupils achieved five A–Cs were judged to be 'underperforming', but Mr Gove raised the bar to 35 per cent. |
| Tackling inequalities of educational opportunity | Education Secretaries intervene, if necessary, to improve educational opportunities for poorer children; in 2007, Alan Johnson ordered local authorities to ensure a good social mix at schools in their areas. |

reign, the then DCSF teamed up with the Department of Culture, Media, and Sport (DCMS) to offer all state school pupils aged between 5 and 16 at least five hours of sport and five hours of 'quality culture' per week by 2010 through a scheme dubbed 'Find Your Talent'. But within weeks of taking office, the Lib-Con coalition axed the programme as part of its sweeping deficit reduction programme: as ever, it seemed as if culture was to be forced to the back of the queue at a time of scarce government handouts. Also scrapped was Labour's costly pre-election pledge to extend eligibility for free school meals to 500,000 additional low-income families, and to roll out an existing pilot offering free lunches to every primary school child.

More contentious still was Mr Gove's abandonment of Labour's £55bn programme for refurbishing or rebuilding every secondary school in England: 'Building Schools for the Future'. This initially saw £3bn devolved direct to local authorities to spend on improving and maintaining their school buildings, with the aim of renewing the school in greatest need in each locality with money from the fund by 2011. Every LEA was told to start work on  at least one major building project by 2016. To howls of protest, Mr Gove announced the cancellation of the bulk of the programme with immediate effect in July 2010, initially stating that 715 schools previously earmarked for redevelopment would no longer undergo work, and 123 prospective academy projects would be reviewed on a case-by-case basis. In an early embarrassment for the coalition, however, he had to revise the list of schools spared from the chop not once but five times—eventually admitting that of those he had earlier led to believe had been saved, at least 30 rebuilds would not now go ahead.

# ▶ The role of local authorities in further education

Councils have had an on–off relationship with the FE sector over the past twenty years. Like schools, FE colleges—at the time, generally known as 'technical colleges'—were both managed and financed by county councils up to 1988. But the sweeping education reforms under the 1988 Act included the removal of FE and sixth-form colleges from LEA control, giving them a 'semi-independent' status *within* the state sector analogous to that granted first to GM schools and CTCs, then foundation and trust schools, academies, and free schools.

Labour initially did little to challenge FE colleges' newfound autonomy. In 2001 it established the *Learning and Skills Council (LSC)*, administered through 47 satellite offices, to finance provision in the sector across England and Wales. This replaced the existing Further Education Funding Council (FEFC), set up by the Tories. In Scotland, the Scottish Further Education Funding Council was transformed into a joint body in 2005, charged with overseeing the funding of the country's 43 FE colleges and 19 HE institutions: the Scottish Further and Higher Education Funding Council (SFC).

The government also introduced the concept of 'centres of vocational excellence'—accolades linked to the reward of additional funding for individual colleges, departments, or practical courses, in recognition of high achievement.

By way of answering some of the criticisms levelled at FE colleges under the self-governing regime introduced by the Tories, in the Learning and Skills Act 2000 Labour extended Ofsted's scope to cover FE. Since September 2001 all FE and sixth-form colleges have been inspected on a four-year cycle. This decision was, in part, an attempt to address growing concerns about the lack of transparency in management of some colleges, shorn of direct LEA scrutiny. To cite an example, in 1998 Stoke-on-Trent College received a bottom grade for management from government inspectors, following a succession of scandals that led to an £8m deficit, and the dismissal of a principal accused of bullying staff and running a pub in Wales while on extended sick leave. Under Mr Brown's government, the tone of FE policy began shifting away from college autonomy. By the time Labour left office, ministers had drawn up plans to return the UK's 385 English and Welsh FE colleges to some form of LEA control, and the LSC had been wound up. Reflecting its enthusiasm for self-governing educational institutions, however, the coalition was expected to restore FE colleges' autonomy, with their governing bodies—'boards' or 'corporations'—regaining primary autonomy over their day-to-day management and local authorities providing only a *strategic* role, in much the same way as *strategic health authorities (SHAs)* for many years directed the work of other local NHS bodies (see p. 169). In a rare example of a real-terms spending increase at a time of swingeing cutbacks, in May 2010 Chancellor George Osborne also announced a modest £50m boost for investment in FE building projects. Shortly afterwards, Business Secretary Vince Cable used a speech at London South Bank University to call for an end to artificial distinctions between further and higher education—signalling his intention to increase funds for technical, part-time, and adult courses in FE.

# ▌ The role of LEAs in higher education

LEAs play an increasingly limited role in HE. For decades they were responsible for providing mandatory awards—or education maintenance grants—to students undertaking full-time degree courses at universities or other HE institutions. In 1997, however, after being 'frozen' for seven years, state grants were scrapped by Labour, in favour of a further roll-out of the Student Loans system introduced by the Tories in 1990. Following fierce opposition from many families, then Education Secretary Charles Clarke announced the return of grants in 2004—albeit only up to £1,000 a year initially and only then for students whose parents earned less than £10,000. The value of grants (and the number of people entitled to them) has twice increased since then. As of September 2010, students whose parents have a joint income of £25,000 or less are entitled to 'full' grants of £2,906 a year and to have their tuition fees paid for them. Those with parents earning up to £50,020 (down from £60,000 previously) still receive a partial grant.

Over and above the mandatory undergraduate grants for students from poorer backgrounds, LEAs also retain the power to make discretionary awards to those who follow courses that do not benefit from this system—for example, vocational postgraduate degrees.

## Funding and monitoring fairness in higher education

Higher education funding in England is the responsibility of the **Higher Education Funding Council for England (HEFCE)**. There is a separate *Higher Education Funding Council for Wales (HEFCW)*, while both further and higher education in Scotland is the province of the *Scottish Funding Council*. In Northern Ireland, funding comes direct from the Assembly's Department of Employment and Learning. The principal roles and purpose of HEFCE are to:

- distribute public money for teaching and research to universities and FE colleges delivering HE courses;
- promote high-quality education and research in a 'financially healthy' sector;
- play 'a key role' in ensuring accountability and promoting good practice.

To this end HEFCE has its own board and committees with the following remits:

- quality assessment, learning, and teaching;
- widening participation;
- research;
- business and the community;
- leadership, governance, and management.

The task of ensuring HE institutions operate 'fairly'—particularly in relation to the thorny issue of admissions policy—falls to the *Office for Fair Access (OFFA)*, led by a 'Director for Fair Access'.

The primary job of OFFA is to ensure institutions that opt to charge tuition fees above the 'standard level' produce an 'access agreement' detailing how they intend to ensure their courses do not exclude people from disadvantaged backgrounds. In practice many universities have sought to do this voluntarily, even before OFFA started work in 2006–07, by offering bursaries and scholarships targeted at high achievers from low-income households, those with disabilities, and people from under-represented minority groups.

The Office for Fair Access arose, in part, out of the perceived continuing bias of some 'top' universities towards children from independent school backgrounds. Concern about this issue has been rumbling since Mr Brown publicly condemned Magdalen College, Oxford, in 2000, for failing to offer Laura Spence, a pupil at Monkseaton Community High School in Whitley Bay, North Tyneside, a place to read medicine—despite the fact that she had achieved ten A* passes at GCSE and was predicted to gain five As at A level. In the event, Ms Spence (who secured straight As) won a £65,000 scholarship to Harvard. As recently as September 2007, however, it emerged that a third of all Oxbridge places were still being taken by pupils from 3 per cent of elite independent schools. One of England's foremost public schools, Westminster College, successfully groomed half of its sixth-formers to win places at either Oxford or Cambridge. The figures were criticized by the Sutton Trust, an educational charity formed to promote greater equality of opportunity in the British school system. Sir Peter Lampl, the Trust's chairman, urged universities to recognize the 'unevenness of the system' from which applicants are drawn and to ensure that they were 'nurturing and developing talent, not honing a finished product'.

The Office for Fair Access's job has become harder, argue critics, since the government's introduction of 'top-up fees' in England and Wales in 2006–07. In an effort to enable the HE sector to raise more income for investment to enable it to lure 50 per cent of British 18-year-olds into HE by 2015, ministers permitted individual institutions to charge additional fees over and above their basic tuition costs for students from families with combined incomes above a designated level. Opponents of this system—rejected in Scotland, and a long-time bête noire of the Lib Dems in opposition—say it favours youngsters from well-heeled backgrounds and will only worsen the social mix of universities, because those from low-income households just over this threshold will be deterred from applying. In a move that sparked a wave of mass student protests, however, once in government Lib Dem ministers unanimously backed Tory-led proposals permitting universities potentially to triple top-up fees as of 2012—from £3,290 a year to £9,000. The party's leader, Nick Clegg—who had signed a pledge opposing fees during the election campaign—was widely vilified for betraying his manifesto promises.

# ▶ The growth of free preschool education

LEAs today have limited direct involvement in providing preschool or nursery education in their areas. Prior to 1997 the Conservatives left it up to individual councils whether to fund free nursery education for children from lower-income backgrounds. Given the choice between squeezing more money out of already tight budgets and leaving it to 'the market' to provide where there was sufficient demand, many authorities voted with their feet. A 1986 audit found that free provision ranged from zero to a maximum of 27.5 places per 100 children—hardly a ringing endorsement of council investment. Many LEAs today run at least some nurseries themselves, but most are provided by the private and voluntary sectors. In addition, money directed to enable children from poorer backgrounds to access preschool education tends to come directly from central government, rather than via local authorities (as with many schools).

In the early 1990s, the Conservatives made limited inroads into funding free nursery care for preschool children. So-called 'nursery vouchers'—virtual money used to 'buy' access for children aged 4 and over to preschool education and/or childcare worth up to £1,100—were introduced in 1996, but abandoned by Labour. The voucher system had baffled many parents: although billed as an extension of 'parent choice', it could not compensate for the fact that—however willing families were to shop around for a desirable nursery—in many areas there simply were not enough places to go round.

Labour's solution was to launch its first National Childcare Strategy, focusing on two immediate priorities:

- increasing the number of childcare places available;
- guaranteeing all 4-year-olds a nursery place from April 1998 onwards.

Provision has been gradually extended. From April 2004 LEAs were obliged to guarantee free nursery places to all 3 and 4-year-olds for up to 12.5 hours a week (to be taken in up to five 2.5-hour sessions), for 33 weeks a year. As of September 2010 free weekly provision for 3-year-olds was extended to 15 hours. While Labour's pre-election plans to extend universal provision to 2-year-olds was indefinitely shelved, however, a Lib Dem policy to provide this for 12,000 children in poorer areas was set to go ahead.

## Improving access and accountability in preschool education

While responsibility for 'early years education' rests with the devolved administrations in Scotland, Wales, and Northern Ireland, in England, a new programme was established in 1999 to drive through the government's aims of guaranteeing high-quality provision for children from low-income households: **Sure Start**. Although its primary focus is on welfare and educational development, Sure Start has extended its support to the whole of a child's family.

The 'Sure Start' concept arose out of New Labour's conviction that early years education was crucial to a child's social and emotional well-being, and that families prevented from accessing it were missing out on a vital development tool. Ministers' decision that preschool teaching should be a core entitlement, rather than an optional 'add-on' accessible only to the middle classes, was based on a body of research into its impact in later life and the outcomes of experiments in similar schemes pioneered in Scandinavian countries.

Sure Start aims to:

- increase the availability of childcare for all children;
- improve health and emotional development for young children;
- support parents as parents and in their aspirations towards employment.

Sure Start operates through a network of children's centres, often based at the heart of deprived estates, in community centres and church halls. Staffed by multidisciplinary teams comprising health visitors, teachers, and social workers, they have become focal points for liaison between families and a whole range of support services over and above those concerned with childcare—from *Jobcentre Plus* to expert antenatal and postnatal advice for new parents.

Where Sure Start ensures that everyone has *access* to preschool education, Ofsted monitors the *standard* of that provision. Its remit was recently increased to cover nurseries, nursery schools, and also playgroups and childminders. At time of writing, the coalition was committed to retaining Sure Start, although Labour was warning of a U-turn after it emerged that its local authority funding would no longer be ring-fenced—meaning that some councils might choose to use it for other purposes.

## ☰ Topical feature idea

In July 2010 Mr Gove announced that more than 700 planned school refurbishments and rebuilds scheduled under Labour's 'Building Schools for the Future' programme would no longer proceed—and within days had to apologize after it emerged that at least 30 schools previously led to believe their projects were safe would not now benefit. Figure 15.1 is a story from the *Birmingham Mail* newspaper focusing on the revelation that nine school projects in a single West Midlands borough, Sandwell, were to be axed despite earlier assurances they were safe. How would you develop this as a news feature idea, widening it to focus on the scale of cutbacks across Birmingham and neighbouring areas as a whole?

**Figure 15.1** An article from the *Birmingham Mail*, 7 July 2010

# Gove sorry after Sandwell schools left off list of cancelled projects

No byline

*Birmingham Mail*

7 July 2010

Web link: http://www.birmingham-mail.net/news/black-country/black-country-news/2010/07/07/gove-sorry-after-sandwell-schools-left-off-list-of-cancelled-projects-65233-26805300/

Education Secretary Michael Gove has apologised 'unreservedly' for errors in information released about a cancelled school building programme, which saw nine Sandwell schools believing their building projects were safe.

There were 25 mistakes in a Department for Education (DfE) list that set out which building projects would be scrapped, reviewed, and protected following the axing of the Building Schools for the Future (BSF) programme.

It means several schools that thought their building projects were safe have now been told they will not go ahead. The affected schools in Sandwell were Bristnal Hall, Heathfield, Manor, Meadows, Menzies, Perryfields, Stuart Bathurst, Wood Green, and a new school.

Mr Gove announced in the Commons on Monday that the £55 billion BSF programme is to be abandoned, saying it had been beset by 'massive overspends, tragic delays, botched construction projects and needless bureaucracy'.

Mr Gove is due to send a letter to Speaker John Bercow on Wednesday, apologising for the errors.

A DfE spokesman said: 'We apologise unreservedly for these errors and lack of clarity for parents, teachers and parents in these areas.'

Under the original BSF scheme, set up by Labour in 2004, all 3,500 secondary schools in England were to be rebuilt or refurbished by 2023.

Following Mr Gove's announcement on Monday, the DfE published a list of 1,500 schools detailing how their building plans would be affected. It included 715 schools which were told their re-building projects had been cancelled.

But on Tuesday concerns were raised by former schools minister Vernon Coaker that the list contained a number of errors. He demanded that Mr Gove come to the Commons to explain to MPs 'what on earth has been going on'.

On Wednesday, the DfE admitted the errors, and published a corrected list. It means that an extra 10 schools—nine in Sandwell and one in Doncaster—have now been told their projects have been stopped. A further 11 schools' projects are now up for 'discussion'.

## ✳ Current issues

- **Mass expansion of academies programme:** Education Secretary Mr Gove is inviting all state school head teachers to apply for academy status. The coalition remains committed to extending the academies programme, in so doing freeing hundreds more schools from local authority control and giving them greater discretion over the extent to which they stick to teaching the National Curriculum.

- **Emergence of 'free schools':** one of the Conservatives' key manifesto commitments was to allow parents and teachers in areas devoid of good secondary schools to set up their own. The adoption of this 'free school' model, originating in Sweden, has received a lukewarm reception from teaching unions and Opposition MPs, but already several consortiums of parents have come forward to apply.

- **Introduction of 'pupil premiums':** in negotiating their coalition agreement with the Lib Dems, the Conservatives agreed to introduce the 'pupil premium' proposed in the former's election manifesto. This top-up funding will be used to cover the cost of enhanced tuition for low-achieving children from poorer backgrounds, ensuring that wherever they attend school they are given extra help to stop them falling behind.

## ❓ Review questions

1. Outline the structure of state education in Britain, identifying the main differences between England, Wales, Scotland, and Northern Ireland.

2. How have the designations of different types of state school changed since 1997?

3. Describe what is meant by 'localism'. What are the main types of self-governing state school and how do their levels of autonomy differ?

4. What are the main issues surrounding higher education in relation to student access? How has Labour sought to address them?

5. Outline the role of Ofsted and local league tables. What impact have they had on the relative popularity of different schools and the growth of the independent sector?

## → Further reading

Crook, D., Power, S., and Whitty, G. (2000) *The Grammar School Question: A Review of Research on Comprehensive and Selective Education*, London: Institute of Education. **Examination of comparative qualitative and quantitative data relating to selective and non-selective state schools.**

Jones, K. (2002) *Education in Britain: 1944 to the Present*, Cambridge: Polity Press. **Historical and sociological examination of the evolution of schooling in the maintained sector since the Second World War.**

Mansell, W. (2007) *Education by Numbers: The Tyranny of Testing*, London: Politico's Publishing. **Informed overview and critique of recent British governments' increasing reliance on targets, league tables, and academic testing.**

Phillips, R. and Furlong, J. (2001) *Education, Reform and the State: Twenty-Five Years of Politics, Policy and Practice*, London: Routledge Falmer. **Critical overview of the major trends and debates in educational reform in the UK over the past quarter-century.**

##  Online Resource Centre

www.oxfordtextbooks.co.uk/orc/Morrison2e/
Visit the Online Resource Centre that accompanies this book for web links and regular updates.

# 16

# Planning policy and environmental protection

Education and social care may be the local policy areas closest to the hearts of the British public, but if there is one subject (besides *Council Tax* rises) guaranteed to get them even more agitated it is planning. Local newspapers are crammed with stories about planning controversies on a daily basis: from rows about out-of-town superstores sucking the lifeblood from town centres to protests by 'not in my backyard' (NIMBY) residents about proposed sites for New Age traveller camps or drug treatment centres.

But away from the placard-waving and alarmist headlines, planning is a deeply serious issue. Without planning policy there would be no schools, hospitals, offices, care homes, supermarkets, or village shops. Before a developer can start work on a site, or a company, school, or hospital trust gets anywhere near opening new premises or altering existing ones, they need to obtain planning consent. And decisions by local authorities about whether to grant consent will be dictated by overarching guidelines—some set by central government, others by councils themselves—designed to make overall patterns of development as effective as possible, while limiting its impact on the natural environment.

Compared to other areas of local authority responsibility—particularly highways, transport, and public health—planning policy (traditionally known as 'town and country planning') has emerged relatively recently. Its three underlying principles are to:

- ensure that all development is supported by appropriate infrastructure—for example, roads, traffic crossings, bus routes, leisure facilities;
- make sure that any environmental impact it has is sustainable;
- ensure that it is located on land unlikely to be affected by factors such as flooding.

To this end there is a single Town and Country Planning Code governing all forms of development in England and Wales, which arose through nine principal Acts:

- Town and Country Planning Act 1947;
- Town and Country Planning Act 1968;
- four separate Acts passed in 1990;
- Planning and Compensation Act 1991;
- Planning and Compulsory Purchase Act 2004;
- Planning Act 2008.

The planning process itself is divided into two broad categories:

- *forward planning*—the drawing up of strategic development plans, by individual local planning authorities (district or **borough councils** and unitaries) at area level, until June 2010 subject to overarching guidelines set by *regional development agencies*. These map out long-term planning strategies for each area, acting as a guide to councils in their planning decisions;
- *development control*—authorities' decisions whether to approve individual planning applications to undertake material changes to existing land or buildings or carry out physical development, such as construction or demolition.

The role of the Communities Secretary in relation to planning is outlined in Table 16.1.

**Table 16.1** Role of the Communities Secretary in relation to planning procedures

| Role | Responsibilities |
| --- | --- |
| Guidance | Publishes guidelines on how planning authorities should discharge responsibilities by issuing *statutory instruments*, known until recently as 'planning policy guidance notes' (PPGs) but renamed 'planning policy statements' (PPSs). Under Labour these were supplemented by more specific *regional spatial strategies (RSSs)*—formerly regional planning guidance (RPGs)—produced by government Offices for the Regions. Planning is due to be delegated to a more local level by the coalition. |
| Setting ground rules | Draws up fixed rules about types of land suitable for development. |
| Arbitration | Acts as final arbiter in disputes between individuals and authorities appointing independent inspectors to convene planning inquiries to determine disputed applications. |
| Ruling in last resort | Can 'call in' controversial planning applications to give final ruling where **planning inquiry** has failed to resolve the issue. |

# ▍ Forward planning

Between 1991 and 2008 there were three varieties of local authority development plan, the names of which varied according to the types of council that drew them up. All three—structure plans for counties, local plans for districts and boroughs, and unitary plans for metropolitan and unitary areas—were eventually replaced by a more *regional* approach to development planning by Labour. As with most issues concerning local government, here and there the system produced exceptional quirks. In most hybrid counties—those in which **two-tier structures** sat alongside one or more unitary authorities—county-wide development plans, encompassing the elements of structure, local, and unitary plans, tended to be produced by joint strategic planning authorities. In London, in addition to unitary plans produced by individual boroughs, the **Greater London Authority (GLA)** continues to oversee a joint strategic planning authority for the whole city today.

The 2004 Act began the process of replacing all of the above with a simplified system, which the government claimed would speed up and harmonize development planning across the UK—giving a handful of regional bodies the power to take strategic decisions for huge swathes of the country. This system—and the one scheduled to replace it—are outlined below.

- *Regional spatial strategies (RSSs)* were overarching 20-year planning frameworks for each of England's eight regions and were produced by designated *regional planning bodies*. Until 2010, these were the eight regional assemblies, but RDAs briefly took over their duties before being served notice by the Lib-Con coalition that they would be abolished by the end of March 2012. The capital is (for the time being) still covered by an overarching London Spatial Development Strategy, while each of the three devolved countries has its own single spatial plan.

- **Local development documents** (LDDs, introduced at the same time as RSSs) remain the principal local planning strategies produced by individual local authorities. When RSSs were still in place, these were effectively 'watered-down' local and unitary plans because authorities were unable to deviate from the strict guidelines set at regional level. And they were further constrained by the terms of *local development schemes*—broad statements of intent by authorities about their long-term planning strategies, which dictated the terms within which specific plans were proposed. In scrapping RSSs, Communities Secretary Eric Pickles confirmed that LPDs would also be replaced—by a less-'bureaucratic', more bottom-up system more in keeping with the coalition's 'Big Society' agenda. In future, communities themselves would be able to propose new long-term *neighbourhood plans*, which, if approved in local referenda, would have to be implemented by their local authorities.

The coalition's objection to RSSs rested on its conviction that they amounted to 'Soviet-style top-down planning targets' that undermined local communities' ability to determine the most appropriate direction for development to take in their areas. Labour's 2008 Bill had arguably taken this trend further, by introducing the concept of centrally determined 'national policy statements' (NPSs). Opponents argued that ministers could impose unsympathetic and/or unsustainable development on local authorities in the interests of national targets. An example was the ongoing dispute between Whitehall and town halls over centrally determined 'housing quotas'—another policy scrapped by Mr Pickles (see pp. 500–1).

Criticism was also directed at the bodies responsible for determining regional planning policy, which lacked councils' accountability. In England the eight regional assemblies originally responsible for it had initially been set up by former Deputy Prime Minister John Prescott as a first step towards introducing directly elected regional chambers. But after the abandonment of plans for English regional *devolution*, following overwhelming rejection of the idea in a *referendum* in the north-east in November 2004 (see p. 36), all assemblies except London's simply trundled on under their previous memberships. Although 60 per cent of these were elected councillors seconded from relevant local authorities, they had no direct mandate in their regional role and the remainder of their colleagues were appointed. Critics argued that power had been seized from elected councils and handed to distant regional bodies with no obvious accountability to local people. RDAs, meanwhile, were wholly appointed. In abolishing them, Mr Pickles said they would be replaced by a new generation of *local enterprise partnerships (LEPs)*, which unlike their precursors would be staunchly 'local' (as opposed to regional) alliances of councils and businesses—bottom-up localism once again. However, if councils and business leaders in particular areas agreed that the interests of those areas would be best served by forming partnerships at regional level, they would not be precluded from doing so.

Finally, the past three years have also seen the birth and death of another government body introduced by Labour to preside over the planning process. The short-lived Infrastructure Planning Commission was established in April 2009 as a means of fast-tracking major construction programmes, including nuclear power stations, wind farms, and new A and M-roads—if necessary overruling regulations preventing building on **greenfield** and **greenbelt** sites (see pp. 475–7). Its members—although bound by NPSs devised by the Department for Communities and Local Government (DCLG)—were independent of government, and held their hearings in public. By taking the final say on infrastructural planning away from the *Secretary of State* it also theoretically replaced politically motivated judgements with decisions based on pragmatism and impartiality. No such selling points were sufficient to save it from the chop, however: in its maiden *Queen's Speech*, the coalition included a Devolution and Localism Bill confirming its impending abolition.

# ▌ Development control

Although long-term development plans impact significantly on British families and businesses, it is specific planning applications that tend to arouse the strongest emotions. This is invariably reflected in the nature of press coverage about planning issues: while most people would struggle to remember the last time there was a notable debate about their council's planning scheme, most  will be familiar with local disputes about the proposed locations of new sewage works and landfill sites. And how many can claim never to have been riled by a neighbour's plans to extend the size of his or her property, or the increase in traffic and parking problems caused by a new housing development?

As explained previously, the procedure used by local authorities to determine the success or otherwise of individual planning applications is known as 'development control'. The right to build on a site from scratch or make major structural alterations to an existing development, is known as **planning permission**. Minor material alterations to existing buildings may require no permission, or only a 'one-stop' decision from the planning authority to give consent. But most 'new-build' applications, however big or small, require permission in two stages.

1. **Outline planning permission**—consent 'in principle' for sites to be developed. Obtaining outline permission is often used by building developers to 'test the water' with a proposal they may not pursue once they have investigated further to decide its commercial viability—for example, a proposed shopping centre. Plots of land are often sold to prospective developers with outline permission already in place. Outline permission lasts five years from the date granted, but if developers have not proceeded to the next stage within three, it also lapses.

2. *Detailed (full) planning permission*—once outline permission is obtained and a developer decides to proceed with the prospective development, he or she will apply for detailed permission. With any major scheme, the outline planning process will usually have highlighted 'gaps' in detail the developer now has to fill—for example, a detailed proposal for an out-of-town retail park will need to address concerns about transport, access and environmental impact. It will also need to specify the exact location, dimensions, and make-up of the proposed development—including how many shops and parking spaces the retail park will include. Like outline permission, detailed permission lapses if not acted on within five years.

When deciding whether to grant planning permission, authorities have three options:

- *unconditional consent*—approving the application with no alterations;
- *conditional consent*—approving it subject to provisos (for example, better access to the site, improved or new traffic crossings, additional parking, environmental adaptations). A developer will often be given outline permission with attached conditions and he or she will be expected to satisfy these before being granted detailed consent;
- *refusal*—outright rejection of an application.

Before any planning authority can decide whether to grant permission for a proposed development, it is generally expected to follow a detailed process designed to give every 'interested party'—those likely to be most directly affected by its approval—the chance to air their views. This procedure is detailed in Table 16.2.

**Table 16.2** Stages of the development control planning process

| Stage | Process |
|---|---|
| Completing an application | Official forms obtained from local authority responsible for development control (district or borough council in two-tier areas, unitary authorities, or metropolitan/London borough councils). |
| Entering on the register | Application appears in formal register of applicants and immediate neighbours immediately notified by council. Parish and/or community councils are also fully consulted at this stage. |
| Advertising application | Certain kinds of application advertised in local press to enable others who 'may be affected by it' to make representations. |
| Public consultation and exhibition stage (major applications only) | Proposals for major developments see the authorities organize public exhibitions, often involving detailed plans and models, either at their own offices, local libraries, or other council-run venues. |
| Subcommittee, committee, and full council decisions | Routine/small-scale planning applications (e.g. extensions to a domestic garage) normally determined at subcommittee or committee level, purely on basis of existing regulations. Major applications treated as **key decisions** (see p. 394), to be determined by both **cabinet** and full council. |
| Appeal | If application turned down, applicant has six months to lodge appeal with Secretary of State. Each stage of application must be determined within two months (unless granted extension due to complexity). If not, application may apply for ruling from central government on 'non-determination' grounds. |
| 'Calling in' | Secretary of State may 'call in' controversial planning applications for final decision—normally when bid raises 'unusual issues' or ones of national or regional importance, arouses 'more than local opposition', or it becomes 'unreasonable' to expect local planning authority to adjudicate on it alone. |

As with so much of its approach to policymaking, the coalition announced proposals for a new element of bottom-up localism to development control in July 2010. Housing Minister Grant Shapps said rural communities would be allowed to bypass the traditional planning process entirely in relation to small-scale housing project developments. Instead of submitting formal applications and waiting for them to be approved by their local authorities, villages would be left to decide for themselves if building should go ahead by putting the plans to a local referendum. If a 'high' proportion of villagers—between 80 and 90 per cent—were to vote in favour, the development would proceed, and villagers would be able to collectively acquire the land on which building was taking place in trust, preserving it for future generations as an ongoing local asset. Mr Shapps said he hoped such developments would go some way towards addressing affordable housing shortages (see p. 486).

## Small-scale planning applications—and changes of use

While a tight rein is kept on more ambitious development plans, because of their potential to affect large numbers of people other than the applicants, it is not always necessary to obtain formal permission for minor material alterations to land or buildings. Under the Town and Country Planning (Use Classes) Order 1987 and the Town and Country Planning (Use Classes) Order 1995, various kinds of land and property are split into 'classes' and material changes of use 'within the same class' will normally not need planning consent; neither will certain changes between 'related' classes (provided that they entail no major building work).

For example, a greengrocer may be changed to a newsagent with no need for planning permission, because both are class A1 business premises, and therefore considered sufficiently similar not to require it. Restaurants, meanwhile, can be changed into shops without permission, because both are within the same overall 'class order' (the former A1 and the latter A3). The same is not always true in reverse, however—changing a shop into a restaurant may also involve making further applications, including obtaining a liquor licence. Neither is it possible to change from an A to a B-class establishment without permission. The table entitled 'Changes of use allowed without acquiring planning permission', which is found on the Online Resource Centre, outlines the changes currently allowed without planning permission.

In addition to the above permitted changes of commercial use, the 1995 Order allows home extensions to go ahead without the need for planning consent—provided that they comply with specified conditions. Local authorities have discretion, however, to pass an 'Article 4 Direction' removing some of these permitted development rights—particularly if the extension is likely to have a negative impact on the view and/or quality of light enjoyed by a neighbouring property.

Planning consent is not usually required to lop or cut down a tree—provided that it is not under a tree preservation order (TPO) or in a **conservation area**. If the former is violated, the local authority may prosecute.

Applications for planning permission are *always* required for material changes of use involving amusement centres, theatres, scrapyards, petrol filling stations, car showrooms, taxi firms, car hire businesses, and youth hostels—all of which are categorized as *sui generis*.

## Planning appeals and inquiries

It is possible for either an applicant or opponent to appeal against a council's approval or rejection of a planning application—provided that he or she does so within six months of the decision letter. If permission is refused, or only conditional consent granted, applicants may lodge appeals for free with a Planning Inspectorate in England and Wales (there is one for each of the two countries).

There are three ways in which appeals can be decided:

- planning inspector's consideration of written representations by both parties, alongside a brief site visit;
- formal hearing with both parties present;
- full planning inquiry—by far the lengthiest and most costly option.

At present, four-fifths of appeals are decided by the 'written method', 16 per cent by hearings, and 4 per cent after an inquiry.

In Scotland, the Planning (Scotland) Act 2006 altered the previous appeal system—which saw them referred directly to the *Scottish Government*'s Directorate for Environmental and Planning Appeals—to bring decision-making closer to the ground. Plans mooted by Labour for appeals about minor developments to be heard by panels of councillors, rather than inspectors, in England and Wales were eventually shelved, due to objections from members of Parliament (MPs) and peers. In Northern Ireland the planning appeal process remains the responsibility of the Planning Appeals Commission.

The most high-profile planning inquiries tend to be those called in response to objections to approved developments—rather than appeals by unsuccessful applicants. Stansted Airport has been the subject of two such inquiries in recent years, both related to the expansion plans of its owner, BAA. The first concerned its attempts to increase its current annual passenger limit of 25 million a year. The second, concluding in October 2007, centred on BAA's application to build a second terminal and runway (as recommended in both a 2003 and a 2006 **White Paper**). Plans for a further inquiry into the proposal (fiercely opposed by environmental groups) were eventually delayed until after the 2010 election—at which point the coalition made it clear it would not be approving the expansion. BAA has since withdrawn its application, while it continues to contest an order by the *Competition Commission* that it should sell Stansted—a parallel dispute that, at time of writing, was still being played out in the High Court. The company's plans for a fifth terminal at Heathrow—finally realized in 2008—were also subject to an inquiry that began in May 1995 and lasted nearly four years.

Even after an inquiry, the Secretary of State occasionally intervenes to make a final judgement, based on the recommendations included in an inspector's report. This was the case in the decade-long debacle over Brighton and Hove Albion Football Club's ultimately successful application to build a new 22,000-seater stadium near the village of Falmer in East Sussex, that prompted two separate planning inquiries.

The only way in which the Secretary of State's 'final decision' in these exceptional cases may be challenged is in the High Court, by a judicial review based on a point of law. Both appellant and planning authority may apply to the inspector for the other side to pay its costs should the judgment go their way. In the Brighton stadium case, then Secretary of State John Prescott's decision to back the proposal in October 2005 led to an immediate pledge by its main opponents—Lewes District Council, Falmer Parish Council, and the South Downs Joint Committee—to mount a challenge. But after his successor, Hazel Blears, reaffirmed his verdict in July 2007, they reluctantly dropped their plans.

The procedure surrounding planning inquiries is outlined in Table 16.3.

**Table 16.3** Procedure for planning inquiries

| Stage | Procedure |
|---|---|
| Advertisement | Inquiries to be publicized in advance—with invitations to address the hearings sent to any formal objectors to plans, anyone with legal interest in site, and local parish/community council. Independent inspector (in exceptional cases, two) appointed by Secretary of State to chair proceedings and make recommended judgement at end. |
| Convening hearings | Formal hearings held, often over period of weeks, with all above allowed to speak. At his or her discretion, inspector *may* allow individuals other than those 'with a right to be heard' to speak. |
| Presentations of evidence | Inspectors listen to evidence for and against, and visit site of proposed development. More than one site visit likely to occur. |
| Verdict | Often made by inspector a few weeks or more after completion of inquiry hearings. With some major inquiries, inspector may refer his or her recommendations to Secretary of State for final decision. |
| Appeal | Application for leave for judicial review may be filed with High Court—but only on 'point of law' or human rights issue. |

# ▌ Other issues affecting major developments

Although notionally highly rigorous, the convoluted consultation procedure surrounding planning applications has often been dismissed as no more than a paper exercise in local democracy. Despite its supposed transparency, councils (and developers acting under their instructions) have been criticized for doing too little to make the public aware a 'consultation' is actually taking place—sticking poorly photocopied notices to trees and lampposts, rather than proactively leafleting homes or knocking on doors. The planning process is memorably lampooned in Douglas Adams's novel, *The Hitchhiker's Guide to the Galaxy*, in which the hero, Arthur Dent, awakes to find a bulldozer about to demolish his house to make way for a bypass about which he knows nothing. On questioning the developers, while lying in front of the bulldozer, he reflects on the tortuous lengths to which he had to go to view the plans while they were 'on display'—by taking a torch into a disused toilet bearing a sign with the legend: 'Beware of the Leopard!'

In real life, if a proposed development is not in breach of the law, the odds have historically been stacked in favour of major developments—especially where they are likely to bring new jobs and other economic benefits—and councillors have frequently been criticized for being won over by grandiose gestures and promises of prestige. One recent example of this was Brighton and Hove Council's ultimately ill-fated decision to grant detailed planning permission to a consortium of developers and architects, including Frank Gehry, who designed Bilbao's world-famous Guggenheim museum, for an ambitious £290m residential block comprising two 'crumpled tin can' towers, a sports centre, a GP surgery, cafes, and restaurants directly overlooking the sea. Although toned down from earlier designs—including one that would have seen four towers, each up to 25 storeys high—the plan infuriated residents of the signature Regency townhouses and apartments that line Hove's seafront, many of whom argued it would blot out their views.

## Planning contribution (or planning gain)

Developers have increasingly sought to persuade local authorities to look kindly on their applications by offering them 'sweeteners', in the form of additional infrastructural improvements the councils would otherwise struggle to afford. For example, a company seeking permission to build a new luxury apartment complex might offer to build social housing elsewhere in the area at a reduced price in the hope of inducing councillors to back its principal project. This offer of a 'benefit in kind' is known as *planning contribution (or planning gain)*. Gain is also intended to avoid major new developments putting an unnecessary strain on existing infrastructure by ensuring that developers make the necessary changes needed to accommodate them.

Although it had operated informally for a number of years beforehand, the concept of planning gain was legally recognized in the Planning and Compensation Act 1991. Up to that point it had been the convention for developers only to provide the infrastructure—roads, crossings, and community amenities—*within* the bounds of the housing estate or business development they were building. All external roads, access points, traffic crossings, etc. tended to be financed by the council. But since 1991 it has become commonplace for developers to provide both *on-site* and any *off-site* gain required to enable the proposed development to function properly—for example, both to give people access to and from the site, and even to transport them there. Although this saves councils a lot of money and 'penalizes' developers in theory, the quid pro quo is that applicants are able to use the incentive of off-site planning gain as a 'carrot' to wave before councils more liberally than in the past. In this sense, planning contribution is arguably as much a 'gain' for the developer as for the authority.

Nonetheless, planning gain has undeniably helped to finance much that is worthwhile. Recent examples have included the £2.5m invested by London's Canary Wharf (a privately owned estate) in the Tower Hamlets Further and Higher Education Trust—a grant-giving body designed to provide educational opportunities for people from deprived backgrounds. And it is not only commercial businesses that get involved in negotiations over planning gain: in June 2008, then Environment Secretary Hilary Benn wrote to every local authority asking it to consider 'volunteering' to become the location of a deep geological disposal facility for waste from Britain's nuclear power stations. The prize should they agree? More local jobs and 'other benefits', including improved infrastructure and services.

Indeed, ministers have looked for even more imaginative ways of helping local authorities to profit from commercial development. In its 2006 White Paper (the first of two that formed the basis of the 2008 Bill), Labour proposed a new 'planning gain supplement'—a tax of up to 20 per cent on the profits made by landowners selling off land for development. The idea was that up to 70 per cent of the proceeds would be pumped back into the local area to help to finance the schools, roads, and community amenities needed to support the government's huge housebuilding programme. But, following extensive lobbying by the building industry, which argued that less land would be available for housing as a result, the plan was shelved. The 2008 Bill also promised a new tax on development land—the 'community infrastructure levy'—which failed to materialize.

Planning gain is not the only means by which local authorities enter into bilateral agreements with developers to secure additional benefits for communities. The 1990 Act (as amended by the 1991 Act) introduced 'section 106 agreements'—a means by which, having already granted outline permission for a site, councils may subsequently require developers to sign legally binding contracts obliging them to provide specified community infrastructure, avoid damaging existing facilities, and even transfer ownership of development land to the authority or another body for 'safekeeping'. Examples include:

- developers giving an area of woodland to the council, together with a suitable fee to cover its future maintenance;
- developers being required to plant specified numbers of trees and maintain them for a number of years—or only to use some of the land for a specified amenity purpose;
- a requirement for a developer to build a specified quantity of social housing in a particular location, provide funds for a school or other community facilities local to a housing estate it has constructed, or create a park, playground, or nature reserve.

Developers cannot be *forced* into signing section 106 agreements. In practice, however, they are often happy to do so—not least in relation to controversial developments otherwise likely to become the subject of appeals by disgruntled residents or businesses—because they offer as much legal protection to them as councils. The aforementioned proposal for a tower block in Hove was made subject to a section 106 agreement shortly before its backers pulled out in July 2008.

A related idea worth mentioning here is the concept of 'per cent for art'—a widely used device whereby local authorities can compel developers to set aside small percentages of their total project costs to fund public art. This can take the form of anything from a sculpture erected outside the development itself to a payment in kind to the council towards the cost of, for example, a local arts festival elsewhere in the locality.

## Greenfield versus brownfield sites—and the decline of the greenbelt

An enduring conflict facing planning authorities is their struggle to balance the perceived need for certain developments—housing estates, schools, hospitals, and shopping centres—with their legal and ethical obligations to protect the natural environment. At a basic level, councils have to take decisions almost daily about whether to approve applications to build on greenfield sites—plots of land that have either never been built on before or have remained 'natural' for prolonged periods. Obvious examples of greenfield land include agricultural fields, parks, and public gardens. The alternative to the greenfield site—and that favoured by New Labour, at least early on—is the **brownfield site.** This is a plot of land, normally in a town centre or suburb, that was previously the site of a development. It may be the location of an abandoned office block or car park, or a largely derelict scrap of land devoid of extant buildings.

Between the 1960s and 1980s successive governments liberalized the planning laws to make it easier for developers to build on 'out-of-town' or 'edge-of-town' greenfield sites, in recognition of the pressure on space in tightly developed town centres (many of which had originally developed in unplanned, organic ways). By the late 1990s, however, a backlash had begun against such developments, with town-centre businesses complaining of losing custom to the then new breed of out-of-town superstores, and growing social and infrastructural problems afflicting housing estates in outlying areas—many the preserve of benefit claimants and the unemployed.

In its first few years in office, Labour sought to redress the balance, introducing guidelines to encourage councils to lure developers into town centres. The aim was twofold: to regenerate eyesore urban sites while providing homes and amenities in the heart of the community (in so doing integrating previously marginalized groups, and making it easier for them to obtain work and contribute meaningfully to society).

But times change—and so do government priorities. The soaring house prices of the 1990s and 'Noughties' boom years saw many British people—including modestly paid 'key workers', like nurses and teachers—unable to climb onto even the lowest rung of the property ladder. The limited space offered by brownfield sites for development on the scale the government believed necessary to tackle the national shortage of affordable homes led to sweeping quotas being imposed on many regions and local authorities. This trend saw more developments targeted at rural areas, including the greenbelt—land formally designated by local authorities around towns and cities to be preserved from development to prevent urban sprawl and protect wildlife.

Introduced in 1935 by the then Greater London Regional Planning Committee, the notion of a ring of land indefinitely protected from urbanization quickly became fashionable in smaller centres. It was eventually formalized by central government—first in the Town and Country Planning Act 1947 and more recently in Planning Policy Guidance Note 2 (PPG2, introduced in 1995). As of the 1993 structure and local plans—in the event, the last to be drawn up—around 13 per cent of the English countryside has been designated greenbelt, covering 14 discrete areas in all.

Planning Policy Guidance Note 2 specifies that greenbelts should:

- check the unrestricted sprawl of large built-up areas;
- prevent neighbouring towns merging into one another;
- assist in safeguarding the countryside from encroachment;
- preserve the setting and special character of historic towns;
- assist in urban regeneration, by 'recycling' derelict and other urban land.

Once an area has been designated greenbelt, it is expected to safeguard:

- opportunities for access to the open countryside for the urban population;
- opportunities for outdoor sport and outdoor recreation near urban areas;
- attractive landscapes and enhanced landscape near where people live;
- improvement of damaged and derelict land around towns;
- secure nature conservation areas;
- retention of land in agricultural, forestry, and related uses.

For many years greenbelts were treated as sacrosanct by local authorities, but facing pressure to meet central government targets under Labour councils increasingly compromised their long-held resistance to expansion into these zones.

Since 1996 developers proposing to build new supermarkets on the outskirts of towns, or within relatively easy reach of a town, have been forced to satisfy both a 'needs test' and an 'impact test' to be eligible for planning permission. The former requires them to prove a new superstore is 'needed' in that location, given lack of choice for consumers elsewhere, while the latter is meant to ensure that there will be no negative impact on trade in the nearby town centre. A government consultation document under consideration towards the end of Gordon Brown's premiership proposed to relax this provision by combining the twin tests—a move that, according to the Association of Convenience Stores, led to a notable rise in the number of out-of-town stores when adopted in Scotland.

Greenbelts are not the only designation used to protect land from development. Some rural and coastal areas are regarded as so exceptional in terms of their beauty, and the richness and/or rarity of their flora and fauna, that they qualify for designation under the National Parks and Access to the Countryside Act 1949 as either:

- an **area of outstanding natural beauty (AONB)**—a locality recognized as being deserving of special protection to conserve and enhance the natural beauty of its landscape, to meet the need for quiet enjoyment of the countryside by the public, and to have regard for the interests of those who live and work there; or
- a *national park*—an area of countryside with additional statutory protection against development, commercial exploitation, and habitation.

Until recently both AONBs and national parks were designated by the Countryside Agency, but this job now falls to another *quango*, **Natural England.**

According to its mission statement, Natural England is committed to 'conserve, protect, and manage the natural environment for the benefit of current and future generations'. It seeks to promote:

- a healthy natural environment;
- enjoyment of the natural environment;

- sustainable use of the natural environment;
- a secure environmental future.

Natural England's remit is to protect AONBs, national parks, and green spaces more generally, but it has not been afraid to challenge some long-standing 'sacred cows' since its inception in October 2006. In 2007, then chairman Sir Martin Doughty used its first anniversary speech to argue that 'the sanctity of greenbelt land should be questioned' in light of the then government's drive to find space for 3 million more homes by 2020 (see p. 500).

There are currently 40 AONBs in England and Wales: 35 wholly in England, four entirely in Wales, and one straddling the border. Nine exist in Northern Ireland, with another two (Erne Lakeland and Fermenagh Caveland) proposed. The smallest AONB is the Isles of Scilly (designated in 1976), which is just 16 km², and the largest is the Cotswolds (covering 2,038 km²). Although they notionally qualify for greater protection than mere greenbelts, in practice councils are not required by law to preserve AONBs and have little power to do so, other than by applying standard planning controls more vigorously.

Perhaps because of this, significant development has continued on or alongside AONBs, leading to vociferous protests from countryside pressure groups, most notably the Campaign to Protect Rural England (CPRE), fronted by best-selling author Bill Bryson. In 2006 it highlighted the plight of three. Dorset AONB was threatened by major road plans, while the Kent Downs faced the encroachment of proposals by Imperial College, London, to build thousands of new homes and offices. The Brighton stadium debacle (see p. 471) was particularly sensitive because of the scheme's proximity to the Sussex Downs AONB (since designated a national park).

National parks are a higher form of designation afforded greater statutory protection than AONBs. To this end, they are protected by their own *national park authorities*. There are 15 in total—ten in England, three in Wales, and two in Scotland, where AONBs do not exist (the nearest equivalent being *national scenic areas, or NSAs*). The existing national parks are listed in Table 16.4.

**Table 16.4** National parks

| National park | Established | Area (km²) |
|---|---|---|
| Peak District | 1951 | 1,438 |
| Lake District | 1951 | 2,292 |
| Snowdonia (Welsh: *Eryri*) | 1951 | 2,142 |
| Dartmoor | 1951 | 956 |
| Pembrokeshire Coast (Welsh: *Arfordir Penfro*) | 1952 | 620 |

| National park | Established | Area (km²) |
|---|---|---|
| North York Moors | 1952 | 1,436 |
| Yorkshire Dales | 1954 | 1,769 |
| Exmoor | 1954 | 693 |
| Northumberland | 1956 | 1,049 |
| Brecon Beacons (Welsh: *Bannau Brycheiniog*) | 1957 | 1,351 |
| The Broads | 1988 | 303 |
| New Forest | 2005 | 580 |
| South Downs | 2008 | 1,641 |
| Cairngorms | 2003 | 3,800 |
| Loch Lomond and the Trossachs | 2002 | 1,865 |

In addition to AONBs, national parks, and greenbelts, successive governments have tried to conserve much of Britain's wooded areas in the teeth of ever-increasing demand for development land. The quango responsible for preserving woodland for public benefit is the Forestry Commission, headed by a chairman and up to ten regional commissioners.

## Land banks and the great supermarket stranglehold

A planning issue that has come to prominence recently is the growing practice by some big developers and their clients of accumulating 'land banks'. This term refers to the idea of purchasing pockets of land—and often obtaining outline planning permission to develop them—without actually doing so for prolonged or indefinite periods. The use of land banks is viewed as unscrupulous by its critics: although developers argue they are merely guaranteeing themselves 'first refusal' to build on a site, the fact they are 'sitting on it' without doing so is seen as an anti-competitive move primarily designed to stop anyone else getting in first. In some cases, land banks have proved even more controversial, with developers or their clients buying up land only to sell it on to third parties—in so doing, writing clauses into sales agreements preventing the sites being developed by rival companies.

Of all alleged 'land-bankers', the one most often cited is supermarket chain Tesco. In St Albans the company is believed to have purchased more than four acres of land that has lain undeveloped for more than seven years. Perceived threats to the town's historic marketplace prompted the formation of a media-savvy 'St Albans Stop Tesco Group' and captured national newspaper headlines, as well as being covered by several BBC reports.

## New Age traveller and gypsy sites

During the 1990s, a familiar staple of British local newspapers was the periodic dispute between 'New Age traveller' and/or gypsy communities looking for land on which to camp—often temporarily, but sometimes for longer periods—and sedentary households concerned about the mess, noise, and damage to their own property prices they alleged were caused (whether consciously or unwittingly) by such encampments. New Labour responded to the growing number of disputes by the time it entered office by introducing clear rules requiring local authorities to provide adequate land for camps. Over time, some £150m was paid to local authorities to facilitate the construction of designated traveller sites.

In May 2010, the coalition scrapped the £30m set aside by Labour to establish new sites during that year, and three months later it announced a major revision of the previous government's rules on establishing encampments. However, in describing most travellers as 'law-abiding', Mr Pickles said councils would be allowed to use some money from the New Homes Bonus scheme being introduced to encourage more affordable house-building to establish additional authorized traveller sites in suitable locations.

## Compulsory purchase orders and planning blight

Sometimes plans are approved for developments on such a mammoth scale—or with such a significant likely impact on surrounding environments—that it is necessary for land and buildings that might otherwise stand in their way to be 'cleared' before work can proceed. Examples of such projects include the building of new airport runways, such as those mentioned above, or roads, waterways, harbours, or new towns (see pp. 488–90). In such cases it is sometimes necessary for planning authorities to force homeowners and businesses to move, so their premises can be bulldozed to make way for the development. In this case, councils serve a **compulsory purchase order** *(CPO)*, in a process outlined in the table entitled 'The compulsory purchase order (CPO) process', which can be found on the Online Resource Centre that accompanies this book.

CPOs are not the only means by which local authorities sometimes find themselves having to pay compensation to the owners of property because of their planning decisions. Should a property's value drop due to a council's decision to approve a controversial application—for example, for a sewage works—the property might be regarded as 'blighted'. In such cases, the owners can effectively force the authority to buy their blighted homes from them—a type of 'CPO in reverse'. People owning property the value of which has been cut by a minimum threshold amount due to fumes from public works that began after 1971 may also claim compensation.

The process for lodging a planning blight claim is outlined in the table entitled 'The procedure for making a claim against planning blight', which can be found on the Online Resource Centre accompanying this book.

## Other quirks of the planning system

Authorities now have the power to decline to consider planning applications on the grounds that the Secretary of State has refused a 'similar' one, on appeal, within the preceding two years. In addition, there are various ways of *enforcing* planning controls, as well as monitoring to ensure developments granted are lawful, as listed in the table entitled 'Other forms of planning notice', to be found on the Online Resource Centre that accompanies this book.

# Other planning-related issues—building regulations

Even when formal planning permission is not required for a 'new build' or to adapt an existing building, **building permission** (under **building regulations**) invariably will be. The reason for such regulations is to ensure that buildings are structurally sound from a point of view of safety, health, and design. An inspector (normally from the local authority) will visit the property during work to ensure that it meets the specified regulations.

Other than in inner London (which has its own system), the standard of regulations is the same across the country. It derives from the Public Health Act 1961, which stopped councils making their own building **by-laws** and returned that power to ministers, and the Health and Safety at Work Act 1974. The process for applying is as follows:

- plans for the building work must be submitted to the planning authority;
- if they comply with the basic regulations and are not in any other way defective, prima facie, they must be approved; if not, they must be rejected.

Building regulation cases are usually overseen by trained inspectors, rather than councillors, because of their technical complexity. Local authorities can order buildings without regulation consent to be demolished or remedial work to be undertaken by the owner. Alternatively, they can carry out the work themselves—but at the owner's cost.

## Listed buildings and conservation areas

Although buildings of historic or architectural interest are not immune to being demolished if they fall into severe disrepair, their owners can obtain substantial help with their upkeep by getting them 'listed'. Local authorities may choose to pursue this route to protect premises that they fear might otherwise be unsympathetically altered, or knocked down by developers.

Buildings are listed—on the advice of **English Heritage**—because they are:

- of 'architectural interest'—for example, the recently renovated Grade II* Morecambe Bay Hotel in Lancashire, regarded as a classic example of Art Deco;

- of 'historical interest'—reflective of a particular period or movement (a criterion that might also apply to the above example);
- linked to nationally important people or events—Charleston, the Grade II listed country home of the Bloomsbury Set, near Lewes in East Sussex;
- have 'group value' as an architectural or historical unit, or a fine example of planning—for example, the Regency Brunswick Square in Hove.

There are three 'grades' of **listed building**:

- *Grade I*—buildings judged 'exceptional' (for example, the Royal Pavilion in Brighton);
- *Grade II\**—fractionally lower down the pecking order than Grade I, these include the Shakespeare Memorial Theatre in Stratford-upon-Avon;
- *Grade II*—buildings judged 'particularly important'.

A decision to list a building ultimately has to be approved by the Culture Secretary under the Listed Buildings Act 1990. Although there has traditionally been a reluctance to list post-war buildings, in 1988 a rolling '30-year rule' was introduced, stipulating that any structure deemed of sufficient interest for one of the above reasons and at least 30 years old could be listed.

When buildings are listed, the lists themselves must be published and notified to local planning authorities, their owners, and occupiers. Once listing has taken place, any alteration or addition to a building entails the owner obtaining listed building consent in addition to other forms of permission. Among the new constraints will be limitations on the types of material they are permitted to use—and an obligation to keep the property in a good and characteristic state of repair. Unauthorized work on a listed building will see the planning authority issue a listed building enforcement notice requiring it to be reversed.

If local authorities wish to protect 'non-listed' buildings threatened with demolition or serious alteration, they may place building protection notices on them—a process referred to as 'spot-listing'. This covers the building for six months, during which time the Culture Secretary must decide whether to list it formally.

One further way of protecting groups of buildings—or whole areas of a village, town, or city deemed to have 'special architectural or historic interest'— is for them to be designated conservation areas. Introduced by the Civic Amenities Act 1967, conservation areas offer particular protection for buildings from unsympathetic and/or inappropriate cosmetic alterations. Special attention is paid to conservation areas whenever a planning application arises within them. 'Permitted development rights' allow changes of use of buildings without the need for planning permission, but do not apply to those in conservation areas. Planning authorities can make 'Article 4 directives' to increase their control over issues such as the insertion of replacement doors and windows.

Councils must advertise in a local paper notice of any planning application in a conservation area that might affect its 'character or appearance'—and the public has 21 days in which to object. It is a criminal offence to lop or cut down trees in conservation areas.

## ▤ Topical feature idea

Reproduced in Figure 16.1 is a list of planning applications discussed at a meeting of Nottingham City Council's development control committee on 19 May 2010. Several proposals are highly newsworthy. Which of the items listed do you think might make a page lead for the *Nottingham Evening Post* paper? Which angles would you follow up, and how?

**Figure 16.1** A list of planning applications discussed at a meeting of Nottingham City Council's development control committee on 19 May 2010

**Planning Applications**

(a)  Victoria Leisure Centre, Gedling Street, St Anns

Partial demolition of existing buildings and construction of new leisure centre—applications fo planning permission and conservation area consent

(b)  County House and the Cock and Hoop Public House, 23 and rear of 25 High Pavement

Change of use of vacant offices to hotel, including partial demolition and erection of extensions—planning permission and listed building consent

(c)  Park and ride site, Gala Way, Bulwell

Erection of 12 food business units

(d)  Nottingham Academy, Ransom Road (former Elliott Durham School, Mapperley)

Refurbishment of existing school buildings incorporating some demolition and extension, re-cladding, extension to car park, revised access and erection of temporary classrooms

(e)  Nottingham Academy, Hereford Road (Site of Jesse Boot School), Bakersfield

Construction of new academy school buildings and associated works. Demolition of existing school buildings. Use of land south of Greenwood Road as sports pitches and erection of fencing

(f)  Bilborough Medical Centre, 48 Bracebridge Drive, Bilborough

Alterations and extensions to existing medical centre to create additional consulting rooms an pharmacy. Creation of additional car parking spaces. Diversion of public right of way

(g)  White Hart Public House, 54 Glasshouse Street

Conversion of first floor (part of) and second floor to two eight-bed student flats including new roof and roof lights

(h)  Units 3 and 4 Lenton House, Lenton Lane

Alterations and change of use from class B2 (general industrial) to class D1 for the purpose o youth training and education centre

(i)  The Fabric Warehouse, Huknall Lane, Bulwell

Use as retail store

(j)  Jolly Higglers Public House, 256 Ilkeston Road, Radford

Creation of car park with associated minor works

(k)  Oakdale Hotel, Oakdale Road, Bakersfield

Erection of extension to rear and ramped access and steps

(l)  Cow, 2A George Street

Change of use of ground floor from retail (Class A1) to restaurant (Class A3).

**Enforcement actions**
(a)  Nazareth Road and Nazareth Court, Priory Street, Dunkirk
     Alleged breach of condition restricting occupation of dwellings by students
(b)  16 Pearmain Drive, St Anns
     Alleged unauthorised raised decking
(c)  38 Bells Lane, Nottingham, Aspley
     Alleged unauthorised extension
(d)  15 Kings Court, Commerce Square
     Alleged unauthorised satellite dish
(e)  3 Yew Close, Mapperley
     Alleged breach of obscure glazing condition

## ✳ Current issues

- **Abolition of regional planning bodies:** regional spatial strategies and planning bodies are being phased out, to be replaced by a return to greater control by local authorities. The coalition has also abolished the Infrastructure Planning Commission, and is proposing to give local people the first say in drawing up future local strategic plans—a bottom-up approach known as 'collaborative planning'.

- **Ban on 'garden-grabbing':** the practice of developers buying up land on which there have previously been houses with gardens and concreting over them to provide room for high-density urban and suburban accommodation (known as 'garden-grabbing') was banned by Communities Secretary Eric Pickles in June 2010. He was able to block such development by withdrawing the brownfield site classification of domestic gardens, thereby allowing local authorities to preserve more green spaces.

- **Reduction in the number of planning inquiries:** in an effort to cut bureaucracy, the coalition announced plans in May 2010 to reduce the frequency of planning inquiries, introducing new rules to prevent them taking place unless there is evidence of abuse of process or failure to follow agreed local strategic plans.

## ? Review questions

1. Outline the application and decision-making process for standard planning proposals. What is the difference between 'outline' and 'detailed' consent?

2. What is 'planning contribution' (or 'planning gain')? Who benefits from the 'gain' concerned—local authority or developer? Give some examples.

3. What devices are available to local authorities and other public bodies to force property owners to comply with planning regulations?

4. What is the difference between building regulations and listed building consent?

5. Outline the planning appeals process, and explain to whom appeals should be made in England, Wales, Scotland, and Northern Ireland.

## → Further reading

Bryan, H. (1996) *Planning Applications and Appeals*, Oxford: Architectural Press. **Helpful guide to handling the complexities of the planning process.**

Cullingworth, J. B. and Nadin, V. (2006) *Town and Country Planning in the UK*, 14th edn, London: Routledge. **Fourteenth edition of the standard text giving a comprehensive overview of the planning process at a local level. Updates core sections to take into account the impact of recent government reforms.**

Hall, P. (2002) *Urban and Regional Planning*, 4th edn, London: Routledge. **Fourth edition of the classic text charting the history of town and country planning in Britain up to and including the New Labour years.**

Smart, G. and Holdaway, E. (2000) *Landscapes at Risk? The Future for Areas of Outstanding Natural Beauty in England and Wales*, London: Spon Press. **Insightful look at the challenges facing AONBs in an era in which land is in increasingly short supply. Examines the new economic pressures being tackled by AONB managers in effort to preserve them.**

## ◉ Online Resource Centre

www.oxfordtextbooks.co.uk/orc/Morrison2e/
Visit the Online Resource Centre that accompanies this book for web links and regular updates.

# 17

# Local authorities and housing policy

One of the most politically sensitive issues in Britain is housing—particularly the lack of 'affordable' homes for those on low incomes and others without the means to clamber onto the property ladder. Local authorities have traditionally been responsible for the following aspects of housing policy:

- building and maintaining their own council housing stock;
- liaising with **housing associations**, other voluntary bodies, and private companies to promote developments that bring low-cost or social housing to their local rented sector, and affordable homes to the ownership market;
- granting *planning permission* for appropriate public, private, and voluntary sector housing schemes in locations best suited to meet demand;
- providing night shelters, temporary accommodation, and, where necessary, longer-term support for the homeless;
- assessing claims for *Housing Benefit* and administering it locally.

Until the mid-1980s local authorities played a more direct role in providing social housing for the poor and unemployed, by building council flats and houses and making them available for rent at subsidized rates. But during Margaret Thatcher's premiership, the stock of council housing began steadily to diminish, as long-term tenants were given the right to buy their homes at discounted prices and councils' ability to build more to replace them was curbed, in favour of an expanded role for the voluntary and private sectors in social housing provision.

Today, 2 million homes remain in local authority ownership nationwide and about the same number are managed by voluntary housing associations (see pp. 498–9). But perhaps ironically, in September 2009 the National Housing

Federation predicted that by 2011 around 2 million families would be on waiting lists for rented social homes.

The amount of 'capacity' available in the social housing sector varies widely from area to area. In some areas the number of 'council homes' surviving is piecemeal; in others, non-existent. Much of the rented accommodation currently available to low-income tenants is today owned by private agencies, professional and semi-professional landlords, and a new generation of amateur 'buy-to-let' developers. Meanwhile, as successive governments have asserted the public's 'right' to aspire to own their homes, the political focus has switched, at least in part, away from 'social' and towards 'affordable' housing: making houses and flats on the private property market more accessible to for ordinary working people.

# ▶ From prefab to new town—a potted history of social housing

Providing fit and proper public housing has been one of the prime purposes of local government since embryonic council services emerged in the nineteenth century (see Chapter 11). Eliminating overcrowding and poorly constructed housing—in so doing, integrating proper sanitation and sewerage systems, and improving hygiene—was a vital part of the fight against diseases such as cholera, dysentery, and typhoid fever undertaken by early public health authorities.

But it was partway through the twentieth century, between the First and Second World Wars, before any large-scale investment occurred in the provision of social housing: houses and flats built on a mass scale for families previously unable to afford roofs over their heads, or deprived of their homes during the 1914–18 bombing raids.

## Public housing and the prefab

Between the world wars there was a period of major public housing activity. A campaign dubbed 'Homes Fit for Heroes' arose out of concern about the poor physical health of many young servicemen from lowly backgrounds recruited to bolster the ranks in the trenches and, under the Housing Act 1919, a start was made on clearing the worst slums. New planned estates were constructed in their place, largely in existing urban areas. But it was not until after the Second World War that a proper house-building boom began, as the struggle to provide shelter for people rendered homeless by Hitler's bombing campaigns became a national emergency.

Ironically, the Blitz (although it could hardly be described as a blessing) helped to clear the way for development. The large areas of wasteland created by the bombings of Britain's major cities offered ample scope for extensive housing projects and it was not long before the new spirit of collectivism channelled into the 'war effort' was being harnessed to build cheap, functional homes for those returning from the fighting, and the many families left dispossessed by its impact on their homeland.

Displaced families needed housing at a time when materials were in short supply, so the 'prefab' was developed—literally, a prefabricated, single-storey compact house, made not from conventional bricks and mortar but anything from shipping containers to surplus aluminium aircraft parts. Prefabs could be manufactured off-site and erected quickly. Their lifespan was intended to be limited, but they fared so well that they survived into the 1970s and can be viewed in building museums to this day.

Prefabs were not the only weapon in the post-war Labour government's bid to provide new housing. In October 1945, Lord Reith was appointed chairman of a 'new town housing committee' charged with devising a workable solution to the growing problem of city overspill. His suggested solution was to draw inspiration from the British New Town movement of Victorian philanthropist Ebenezer Howard, who created the garden cities of Letchworth and Welwyn, both in Hertfordshire: government-backed development corporations would acquire land for construction within 'designated areas'. The resulting New Town Act 1946 designated Stevenage (again in Hertfordshire) as Britain's first official 'new town', and within a decade there were ten more.

## The rise of high-rise living

Population growth during the 1950s' 'baby boom' inevitably led to increasing demand for housing and, by the end of the decade, ministers had empowered councils to clear away many of the jerry-built prefabs, demolish the last inner-city slums, and commence a mammoth house-building programme.

Under a series of Acts, beginning with the Housing Act 1957, local authorities (LHAs) embarked on extensive slum clearance schemes, using *compulsory purchase orders (CPOs)* (see p. 479) to obtain enough land sufficiently quickly to facilitate the construction of suitable alternative housing. But no sooner had they done so than they faced an immediate dilemma that echoes to this day in the decision-making of urban planners: how were they to accommodate a rapidly rising population without resorting to a similar tactic to their forebears, namely cramming homes together in high-density Victorian-style terraces or overcrowded estates? Their solution was to build upwards, rather than laterally, as in the past—in so doing, creating the first generation of high-rise tower blocks.

Although a number of multistorey blocks still exist in and around major towns, there has been a growing backlash against them since the 1970s by town planners, politicians, and public. Tight terraces and sink estates might have been shoddily built and poorly served by infrastructure, but at least many of those homes had their own backyards or small gardens, facilitating interaction and cooperation between neighbours. Neither were residents forced to share the entrances into their blocks, or to take a temperamental lift up ten or twenty floors before reaching their own flats. Many tower blocks were initially of sturdier construction than the social housing that preceded them, but over time their sheer height and overall scale engendered major long-term structural weaknesses. The lack of accessible shared social spaces and amenities—especially for those living on higher levels—contributed to serious social problems like drug-taking, vandalism, violent crime, and general isolation. Today, like the sprawling slums before them, tower blocks are viewed by many as ghettoes for a forgotten 'underclass', cut off from mainstream society.

Tower blocks have also witnessed ugly scenes. Broadwater Farm in Tottenham, north London, was depicted as one of the worst places to live in Britain in Alice Coleman's influential 1985 book about the perils of one-size-fits-all urban planning, *Utopia on Trial*. Later the same year, it witnessed one of the most notorious riots of the 1980s. The Aylesbury estate in Walworth, south-east London—these days a favourite backdrop to everything from party-political broadcasts to rap videos and episodes of ITV1's *The Bill*—has one of the UK's lowest ACORN (A Classification of Residential Neighbourhoods) demographic classifications, principally due to its infamous crime rate. By May 2005, a crime was being reported there every four hours. Less than a year later, Southwark Council issued a demolition notice on residents of the estate's main tower block, arguing (against stiff local opposition) that knocking it down was necessary if the area was to be regenerated. The first of four phases of the estate's planned 15–20-year, £2.4bn redevelopment finally got under way in March 2009.

## The great 'new town' boom

Given the limited capacity of tower blocks to cater for rapidly rising population levels and the social deprivation increasingly associated with them, by the 1960s it was perhaps unsurprising that both central and local government were looking for an alternative solution to providing low-cost housing on a mass scale for those unable to buy homes on the open market.

A consensus quickly emerged that there should be a further rollout of new towns and, in the decade from 1960, ten more were founded. By far the most famous centre to emerge from the ensuing English new town programme was Milton Keynes in the Midlands—a new-build city founded from scratch in 1967. In other cases, the term 'new town' proved a misnomer: the ancient cathedral city of Peterborough in Cambridgeshire was designated one in 1967, with

Northampton acquiring the status a year later. In effect, these designations gave the towns—along with nearby Warrington—a licence to expand, boosted by government capital investment, on a scale out of step with elsewhere.

The advantages of new towns over other housing solutions were manifold. By effectively starting out with a blank slate, urban planners had free rein to design roads, estates, and other infrastructure in a more ergonomic, 'human-centred' way, making the maximum use of space and integrating vital community facilities to enhance the quality of life of those who would be living there. The housing itself tended to be built on a more domestic scale, with two to three-storey homes arranged along clear street patterns, backed and/or fronted by individual gardens and focal spaces.

But new towns had their downsides: established urban areas rarely provided enough building space for them, so they tended to be developed in largely rural locations, becoming satellite or dormitory towns from which residents had to commute, often considerable distances, to the established urban centres in which they worked. Efforts were, however, made to ensure that new towns were as self-sufficient as possible, with their own shops, sports and leisure centres, cinemas, and, in time, employment opportunities. In some cases, new towns became so populated that new local authorities were set up to cater for their services.

Despite the demonstrable benefits of new towns for families on modest incomes previously excluded from the property market, in practice they brought limited gains for those at the bottom of the heap. During the 1970s and 1980s, a growing divide opened between poorer households fortunate enough to live in new towns in which there had been sufficient investment in new council housing and the large number of council tenants in older towns still confined to tower blocks.

Between 1947 and 1970 21 new towns were established in England, and the new town experiment has been extended over time to the rest of Britain, with Scotland acquiring six, and Wales and Northern Ireland two each. Table 17.1 lists all 32 existing new towns, together with their populations.

Table 17.1 A list of new towns currently designated in Britain

| New town | Population |
| --- | --- |
| Basildon | 102,400 |
| Bracknell | 52,243 |
| Central Lancashire (Preston, Chorley, and Leyland) | 365,000 |
| Corby | 53,000 |
| Craigavon | 57,685 |
| Crawley | 99,727 |

| New town | Population |
|---|---|
| Cumbernauld | 51,300 |
| Cwmbran | 47,254 |
| Dawley | 11,399 |
| Derry | 107,300 |
| East Kilbride | 73,820 |
| Glenrothes | 38,927 |
| Harlow | 80,600 |
| Hemel Hempstead | 83,000 |
| Irvine | 33,090 |
| Letchworth | 33,600 |
| Livingston | 50,826 |
| Londonderry | 83,652 |
| Milton Keynes | 230,000 |
| Newton Aycliffe | 25,504 |
| Newtown | 12,783 |
| Northampton | 194,400 |
| Peterborough | 161,800 |
| Peterlee | 30,093 |
| Redditch | 79,216 |
| Runcorn | 61,252 |
| Skelmersdale | 38,813 |
| Stevenage | 79,790 |
| Telford | 138,241 |
| Warrington | 158,195 |
| Washington | 60,000 |
| Welwyn Garden City and Hatfield | 97,546 |

# ▌ The Housing Revenue Account (HRA)

Every local authority maintaining its own stock of social housing is required by law to record all income and expenditure relating to it on a separate balance sheet to that used for its general revenue funds (see Chapter 12). This discrete balance sheet is called the *Housing Revenue Account (HRA)*. The HRA is split into two halves: one covering revenue income and spending; the other, capital payments. Most income generated by the HRA takes the form of rent, but councils may also charge one-off fees for arrears or damage to property, and the account can accrue interest. The primary purpose of the capital component of the HRA is to record all income generated from house and flat sales under 'Right to Buy' (see pp. 494–7). The way in which HRAs operate is currently the subject of a government review.

# Council tenants' rights and how they qualify

Council tenancies have traditionally boasted significant advantages over the standard shorthold tenancies available when renting in the private sector, including:

- security of tenure;
- no deposit;
- rent set at a level that is substantially below the market average;
- the right to buy their home at a discount (see pp. 494–7).

Unsurprisingly, social housing is much prized among those on low incomes. To ensure that they allocated their limited social housing stock as fairly and equitably as possible, councils traditionally kept a *housing register* (or 'housing waiting-list'). Anyone over the age of 16 who met certain eligibility criteria could apply to enter the register, with certain types of applicant prioritized—for example, minors, the elderly, the vulnerable, and those with long-standing connections to a local area. This system was changed by the Homelessness Act 2002, which introduced a 'points system' to prioritize applicants. It stipulated that 'reasonable preference' should be given to anyone falling into a set of specified categories, although other long-standing factors favouring certain households over others must also be taken into account. These are outlined in Table 17.2. Those granted council homes normally begin with an 'introductory tenancy' for a year. Assuming they 'pass' this de facto probation period, they are usually then awarded a 'secure tenancy' lasting for life, *unless* they are evicted for:

- not paying their rent;
- causing nuisance to neighbours;

**Table 17.2** Criteria for prioritizing social housing applicants

| 'Reasonable preference' under the Homelessness Act 2002 | General criteria |
| --- | --- |
| The 'unintentionally' homeless (see p. 502) | Residency—does the applicant live in the area where they wish to be housed? |
| People living in unsanitary, overcrowded, or unsatisfactory housing | Financial circumstances—benefit claimants and low earners are normally treated as priority cases |
| Those needing to move on medical or welfare grounds | Tenancy record—councils are wary of those who have previously defaulted on rent payments |
| People needing to move to a particular locality in the district of the authority where failure to meet that need would cause hardship to themselves or others (e.g. a parent with a child in a local school) | Time on register—applicants may gain extra points if they have been on the housing register for some time |

- using the property for illegal activities such as drug dealing;
- moving out of their homes or sub-letting them to someone else.

The continuation of tenancies 'for life', although for many years seen as a justified perk of council housing, has become increasingly controversial as home short-ages have worsened, particularly in oversubscribed areas of the south-east, where the cost of private accommodation is disproportionately high. Recent governments have faced growing pressure to prioritize Britain's limited social housing stock, if necessary by terminating tenancies for people whose financial positions significantly improve during their occupancy (enabling lower-income households to replace them) In October 2010, George Osbourne confirmed he would be scrapping secure tenancies for new social housing tenants in favour of fixed-term contracts. This followed David Cameron's earlier pledge to intro-

duce. greater 'flexibility' to encourage unemployed tenants to move to other areas in pursuit of work, and to move those whose incomes increased over time across to the private rented sector—freeing up housing for the most needy. Ministers have also launched a 'Freedom Pass' scheme, allowing English social housing tenants to swap homes with those in other areas, to facilitate economic mobility. How these reforms play out in practice remains to be seen, particu-larly in light of Mr Osborne's further announcement that social rents will in future rise to up to 80 per cent of levels charged in the private sector—all at a time when Housing Benefit is being capped. Confirming these changes in his October 2010 *Comprehensive Spending Review (CSR)*, Mr Osborne further added that the budget set aside by Labour for building more affordable housing would be slashed by 60 per cent, piling further pressure on an already squeezed social housing sector. In the wake of the CSR, charities such as Citizens Advice and Shelter warned of an impending rise in homelessness.

Some councils use their discretion to explicitly *disqualify* certain people from applying for social housing (making the job of finding homes for 'qualify-ing' applicants easier). Alnwick District Council, Hampshire, bars anyone who has previously left a social housing tenancy owing £250 or more, or who lived in a council home locally at a time when 'nuisance to neighbours' or damage to the property occurred. Burnley Borough Council, Lancashire, writes into its tenancy agreements a clause allowing the social housing provider to evict ten-ants for antisocial behaviour (a sanction authorized by the Housing Act 1996). Recent governments have also clambered onto this conditional tenancy band-wagon: in spring 2008, then Housing Minister Caroline Flint mooted the idea of requiring new council tenants to sign 'commitment contracts' promising to look for work. Her proposal was prompted by several studies, including a report by Professor John Hills of the London School of Economics, published in February 2007, which found that people living in council housing were twice as likely to be unemployed as the average person—largely because of the 'neigh-bourhood effects' of living in deprived areas.

Once their home is secured, occupants of social housing have recourse to a number of measures should they have grievances about the way in which it is managed, or its overall quality. These are outlined in the table entitled 'The safeguards for social housing tenants', to be found on the Online Resource Centre.

## Other local authority housing responsibilities

Local authorities not only have to provide *new* houses and flats for rent, but are required to maintain and improve existing social housing—as well as to monitor the state of private sector accommodation in their areas. Many councils have now combined their housing and environmental health departments, following a series of court actions brought against landlords under various Public Health Acts. The 1990 Act outlined councils' duty to inspect existing buildings in their area to detect 'statutory nuisances'—defined as including premises prejudicial to health, as well as menaces like smoke, dust, fumes, rubbish, and noise pollution. The Act gave local authorities powers to 'eliminate' the statutory nuisance.

Councils may also take action over houses deemed 'unfit for human habitation'. Most of this work relates to the private sector. When assessing if a house is 'unfit', housing authorities look at its state of repair, freedom from damp, natural lighting, ventilation, water supply, drainage, and sanitation. The Housing Act 1985 gave councils the power to serve 'repair notices' on the owners of individual unfit homes. Alternatively, they may carry out specified repairs to bring dwellings up to a habitable standard themselves, charging the owner afterwards. In exceptional circumstances, they are allowed to serve 'closure notices' (ordering owners to cease using a dwelling for that purpose) or 'demolition notices' (requiring them to demolish the dwelling). Today, they can go further—buying unfit houses outright and taking them into their own housing stock. Before any demolition or closure order is agreed, the council must give the owner the opportunity to carry out any remedial work. It must also re-house occupiers and potentially pay them compensation.

Councils may occasionally take action against an entire 'area', requiring or undertaking improvements or demolition. Demolished areas are known as 'clearance areas'. Before a clearance order can be made, the authority must arrange rehousing for all tenants and finance the work. The Housing, Grants, Construction, and Regeneration Act 1996 enables councils to pay discretionary relocation grants to displaced people to help them to buy at least a part-share in a new home in the same area.

In addition to the above, the Local Government and Housing Act 1989 empowered local authorities to declare whole districts 'renewal areas' for up to ten years. These normally encompass a minimum of 300 dwellings, at least 75 per cent privately owned, and a third of the inhabitants of which are receiving benefits. Once a renewal area is designated, the authority may acquire the land by agreement or through a CPO, providing new housing, improving existing stock, and disposing of property to a suitable third party for future management.

Privately owned accommodation can also benefit from council help. Under the Housing 1996 Act, means-tested, mostly discretionary, grants were introduced to help private homeowners unable to afford essential adaptations themselves. More recently, various new 'green' grants—funded by central government—have also been introduced to help tenants and homeowners to improve their energy efficiency to reduce both their fuel bills and carbon footprints. The main types of grant are listed in the table entitled 'Local authority grants available to private home owners', to be found on the Online Resource Centre.

# ▌ Thatcherite housing policy and the decline of the council home

As with many areas of policy, such as health, education, and the utilities, the Thatcher government had a profound effect on the availability of social housing in Britain. Less than a year after gaining office in 1979, the Conservative prime minister embarked on a radical overhaul of the extant council house framework—giving long-standing tenants the chance to buy their homes at knock-down prices and compelling local authorities to sell to them. Within the decade, responsibility for building and maintaining social housing had moved decisively away from local authorities, towards new not-for-profit organizations independent of direct democratic control—housing associations—overseen by a similarly unaccountable national *quango*: the Housing Corporation.

Things would never be the same again.

## 'Right to Buy' and the privatization of council housing

One of the defining election-winning policies of the Thatcher era—and in many ways the death knell for traditional council housing—was the 'Right to Buy' programme ushered in by the Housing Act 1980 in England and Wales, and the Tenants' Rights (Scotland) Act 1980 north of the border. Under this scheme, some 5 million 'long-term' council tenants were offered the chance to purchase their homes at a discount on the price they were estimated to be worth on the open market.

Tenants eligible for 'Right to Buy' could initially claim the following discounts:

- households who had occupied their homes for at least three years were allowed to buy at a 33 per cent discount for a house or 44 per cent discount for a flat;

- those who had rented from a council for more than 20 years received a 50 per cent discount on either a house or a flat.

The Housing Act 1985 increased the value of discounts significantly, as follows:

- tenants living in houses for more than two years could claim a 32 per cent discount plus 1 per cent for each complete year by which the qualifying period exceeded two years (up to a 60 per cent maximum);
- those resident for two years or more could claim 44 per cent plus 2 per cent for each complete year by which the qualifying period exceeded two years (up to a maximum of 70 per cent).

Between 1980 and 1995, 2.1 million homes previously in the local authority, housing association, or new town social sectors were transferred to private ownership. Since then social housing has continued being sold off at a rate of around 60,000 a year—with the result that some areas, including Leicester and parts of Argyll and Bute in Scotland, now have little or no council-owned stock left.

'Right to Buy'—lauded by Mrs Thatcher in the Tories' 1983 election manifesto as the 'the biggest single step towards a homeowning democracy ever taken' and 'the transfer of property from the State to the individual'—was understandably popular with aspirational working-class voters. By the time of the party's 1987 general election victory even Labour had dropped its formal opposition. On the face of it, the policy also provided a welcome boon to hard-pressed councils, liberating them from responsibility for financing the upkeep of often aged and creaky accommodation, and raising millions of pounds in capital receipts that (at least theoretically) could be spent in other areas of need. According to social policy think tank the Joseph Rowntree Foundation, proceeds from council home sales between 1987–88 and 1989–90 generated £33bn—more than the windfalls from privatizing BP, British Telecom, British Gas, British Airways, and Rolls Royce put together.

But critics maintain 'Right to Buy' has had a devastating impact on the ability of local authorities and housing associations to provide homes for future generations devoid of the financial means to rent or buy in the private sector. Perhaps its most controversial feature was the strict controls imposed by the government on councils' ability to spend the capital receipts generated by sales on improving or increasing their remaining social housing stock. Initially, they were limited to spending only 20 per cent of this income on housing, rising to 25 per cent following the Housing Act 1989. But what the 1989 Act gave with one hand, it took away with the other: it stated that the 75 per cent of receipts remaining must be spent not on building new schools, care homes, or roads, but on paying off their debts. These rules have since been modified (see p. 370), but there continues to be criticism of the strictures they place on councils.

The mass sell-off of council homes has been blamed by some for the transformation of picturesque villages and coastal towns in areas like the West Country and Wales into 'ghost towns'. The lack of social housing in such areas has priced many locals out of the property market, with buy-to-let and absentee holiday home-buyers pushing up both private rents and sale prices way beyond the means of native people employed in traditional rural and seaside jobs. In Tenby, Pembrokeshire, the price of the average house had risen to £200,000 by 2010, and 40 per cent were second homes. But help may be at hand: as of July that year, the **Welsh Assembly Government** was granted devolved powers to ban 'Right to Buy' purchases in situations in which allowing them would have a detrimental effect on housing stock. At a wider national level, the coalition's favoured solution to shortages of affordable housing is for local communities to take it into their own hands to promote development—by allowing them to fast-track applications for small-scale housing projects without the need to go through the whole local authority planning process (see p. 469).

Between 1997 and 2010 Labour took incremental steps towards restoring local authorities' ability to build new housing stock—with, for example, ministers giving the go-ahead to the construction of 2,000 new council homes across England in September 2009, in the face of warnings that a further 200,000 families were heading for housing waiting lists. Nevertheless, with the ONS predicting Britain's population is likely to top 65 million by 2020, the country continues to lack the sustained investment in new social housing some say is needed. Arguments for and against 'Right to Buy' are explored in Table 17.3.

**Table 17.3** Arguments for and against 'Right to Buy'

| For | Against |
| --- | --- |
| 'Right to Buy' offers low-income households who would never otherwise be able to afford their own home a chance to buy one. It is a progressive policy promoting opportunity, aspiration, and ownership among the poor. | Under 'Right to Buy', councils have generally only been allowed to spend a fraction of capital receipts from council house sales on building more. This leaves fewer available for poor people who need them in future. |
| Council tenants have traditionally had to rely on local authorities for repairs and essential maintenance—often waiting months, or even years. Enabling them to buy their homes liberates them from shackles of local bureaucracy—giving them flexibility to pay for repairs as and when needed, and motivating them to maintain their properties to high standards. | Distribution of local authority housing has historically been unequal and some councils are more proactive about promoting 'Right to Buy' than others. Council tenants' ability to buy their homes is therefore subject to a 'postcode lottery'—with those on low incomes forced to rent from private landlords because of lack of rentable social housing. |
| 'Right to Buy' raises significant revenue for local government that can be used to pay off debt run up elsewhere. Less debt means healthier finances, as more money will be left to pay for essential services—and savings may feed through into lower **Council Tax**. | Selling off council housing enables local authorities to offload the punitive cost of repairs and maintenance onto former tenants. While initial sale prices may be attractive, the poor state of repair of some former council homes leaves those purchasing them with high ongoing depreciation costs. |

Despite its manifest attractions for aspiring homeowners of limited means, the 'Right to Buy' scheme contained caveats designed to deter people from cashing in on the policy. If a house was sold within three years of being bought by a tenant, part of the discount had to be repaid—pro rata the time that had elapsed since its purchase. The general thrust of the government's approach, however, was to do everything possible to persuade tenants to purchase their council housing and local authorities to part with it. If councils appeared to be doing too little to promote the scheme, the *Secretary of State* could appoint a commissioner to investigate and, if necessary, enforce it. Some Labour authorities, like Norwich City Council, actively tried to sabotage it and ended up footing the legal bill for their unsuccessful fight to preserve their housing stock.

Ministers also introduced 'Right to Buy mortgages', administered by local authorities—although in time these were replaced by 'rent-to-mortgage' schemes introduced under the Leasehold Reform, Housing, and Urban Development Act 1993. The price fixed for a house or flat comprised two elements:

- *initial capital payment*—a form of partial mortgage paid in regular instalments at the same or a similar level to the rent for which they would previously have been liable;
- *deferred financial commitment*—a lump sum that accrued no interest but was repayable on the sale of the property, the death of the purchaser, or by a voluntary payment that could be made at any time.

These models were the forerunners of the shared ownership schemes commonplace today, under which 'tenants' buy shares in a property from a housing association, with the help of a normal home loan, paying rent on the remainder. A cash incentive scheme was also launched in time, enabling tenants to borrow cash at a low interest rate to help them to buy property in the private sector.

## From housing associations to social landlords

The 1957 Act had formalized local authorities' responsibilities as the primary providers of social housing in their communities. But when the 1985 Act supplanted it as the 'principal' housing law on the statute book, this mantle was passed to the new not-for-profit housing associations. Coming at the same time as Mrs Thatcher's government was waging war on the Greater London Council, metropolitan *borough councils*, and so-called 'loony lefty' authorities elsewhere, the decision to dilute the powers of local housing departments was viewed by some as another assault on the autonomy of elected councillors. Local authorities, it seemed, were caught in a carefully orchestrated pincer movement—between individuals and families keen to buy up their council homes on the one hand and the newly emancipated housing associations (backed by Whitehall) on the other.

Sometimes called the 'third arm of housing', Britain's 1,800 housing associations—today known as *registered providers* (until recently *registered social landlords*), along with certain other types of social home provider—are regulated by the *Tenant Services Authority (TSA)* and receive funding from the *Homes and Communities Agency (HCA)* (although the former is due to be scrapped by the coalition, and the latter downsized). Together these replaced the long-running quango, the Housing Corporation, in November 2008. In Scotland, HAs are regulated directly by the **Scottish Government**, in Wales by the Welsh Assembly, and in Northern Ireland by the *Northern Ireland Housing Executive*. Most housing associations are registered as industrial and provi-dent societies. All have volunteer management committees elected by their membership. Some have no professional staff, while others are large—formed from amalgamation or takeover—with substantial workforces.

Local authorities may loan money or provide guarantees to registered hous-ing associations, in return for interest income. They normally have the right to nominate 50 per cent of council home tenants in their areas to housing associa-tion schemes.

The primacy of housing associations was cemented by the introduction of 'Tenants' Choice' in the Housing Act 1988, under which local authorities came under pressure to promote them as alternative social housing providers. But rather than simply giving tenants the right to move into a housing associa-tion property, the Act sought to facilitate the transfer of housing stock itself into association hands. In truth even some Labour-run authorities (whatever their ideological objections) were attracted by the prospect of offloading their homes, given the high running costs and other complexities associated with repairs and maintenance. By July 1996 51 local authorities had transferred their entire council home stocks to housing associations—totalling 220,000 properties.

Further undermining of local authorities' status as the pre-eminent pro-vider of social housing was to follow. The 1993 Act and the detailed regulations flowing from it introduced the concept of 'tenant management organizations' (TMOs). Groups of council tenants living in a designated area were permitted to set up a TMO to take over the day-to-day management of their housing and its associated finances—effectively *replacing* the local authority and forming their own de facto housing associations. Formation of a TMO was subject to approval of its competence by a recognized development agency and a ballot of local tenants. The National Federation of Tenant Management Organizations had more than 100 member TMOs by September 2010.

A further development came with the passage of the Housing Act 1996, which introduced the label 'social landlord'—an umbrella term used to define a vari-ety of different models of shared social housing management. Whatever pre-cise form they take, social landlords are overseen, like housing associations, by the TSA. They include a new type of not-for-profit 'housing company'—often partnered with, but not directly controlled by, local authorities and tenants themselves—and 'housing co-ops' (a variation on TMOs).

The outcome of this flurry of reforms was precisely what the Conservatives had set out to foster—in their own words, 'a more pluralist and more market-oriented system'. A symbolic final seal was set on the logical direction of the party's policies when the Local Government and Housing Act 1989 explicitly freed local authorities from any obligation to retain their own social housing stock.

## The rise of owner-occupancy and the 'affordable housing' debate

Recent surveys suggest that, despite years of spiralling house prices and the well-reported financial obstacles faced by first-time buyers, Britain has indeed gone some way towards becoming that great 'homeowning democracy' heralded by Mrs Thatcher back in 1983. Figures 17.1 and 17.2 provide a comparison between the breakdown of dwelling types in 1961 (the year in which records began) and 2009 (the most recent year for which UK-wide data is available). Information from the census of 31 March 1961 revealed that, of the 13.83 million dwellings in which UK inhabitants were then living, 6.1m (44 per cent) were owner-occupied houses and flats, while 4.4m (32 per cent) were rented from private landlords or as part of a job or business for which the residents worked, and 3.38m (24 per cent) were rented from local authorities (council housing). Forty-eight years later, in the ONS's second-quarter housing tenure survey for 2009, out of a total of 25.8m dwellings, the number of owner-occupied properties had soared to 68 per cent of the total (17.5m), with

**Figure 17.1** Where UK residents were living as of 31 March 1961

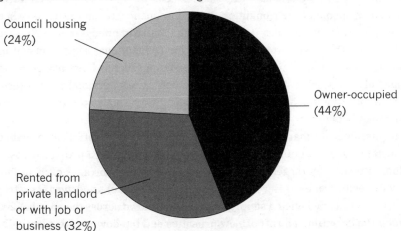

Council housing (24%)

Owner-occupied (44%)

Rented from private landlord or with job or business (32%)

Source: Department for Communities and Local Government (DCLG)

**Figure 17.2** Where UK residents were living as of second quarter 2009

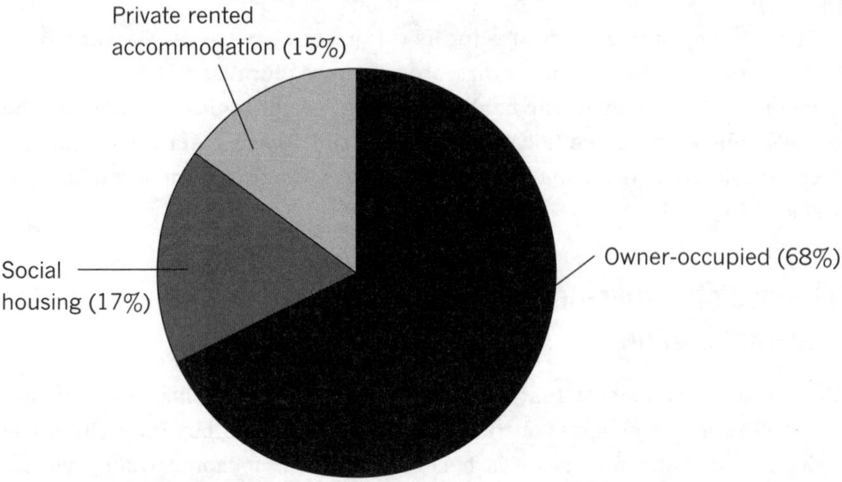

Private rented
accommodation (15%)

Social
housing (17%)

Owner-occupied (68%)

Source: Department for Communities and Local Government (DCLG)

the number rented from private landlords having fallen by more than a half,
to just 15 per cent (3.8m). The amount of social housing had dropped nearly
a third to nearly 17 per cent (4.5m), with fewer than one in ten of these being
traditional council houses or flats. The rest were properties rented from the
various other types of social landlord. The statistics therefore demonstrate
two trends: a decisive shift in the number of people living in owner-occupied
accommodation, and the steady decline of local authorities as the principal
providers of rented housing.

Despite the growth in home ownership, however, many people—particularly
those on low incomes and single public sector professionals living in south-
east England—found it next to impossible to enter the property market during
the housing boom of the Noughties. As a consequence, recent years have seen
much government rhetoric—and significant chunks of policy—geared towards
helping out those who would not qualify for conventional social housing but
cannot afford their own homes. Particular emphasis has been placed on the
plight of 'key workers'—public servants such as teachers and nurses (especially those living in areas like inner London, where house prices are disproportionately high).

To guarantee the market provided more houses that were 'affordable', Labour
ministers aimed to build 3 million new homes by 2020, at a projected cost of
£8bn. In theory, by targeting the homes at areas with shortages of affordable
private sector homes, this would have both provided bricks and mortar up front
and, by increasing housing supply, forced prices down across the board. A 2007
*Green Paper* outlined a raft of new priorities and top-down targets, including

a pledge to build 70,000 new homes a year (45,000 in the social housing sector) and speed up the planning process to prevent local authorities stalling.

The sheer scale of development proposed for some areas generated fierce opposition. In the south-east, where 200,000 new houses were due to be built, councils and local residents alike objected to the 'quotas' they were presented with by ministers. The newly designated South Downs National Park looked set to be the location of thousands of new homes (many in flood plains) to the fury of local parish councils and environmental campaigners. There was also considerable controversy over the government's pledge to give prefer-ential planning permission to sustainable housing developments—so-called 'eco-towns'. Criticisms have included the fact that, in order to establish these supposed paragons of environmental friendliness, large tracts of as-yet-undeveloped countryside would need to be surrendered to house-building. Green campaigners also argued that some of the sites earmarked for such developments were in rural areas where there was little or no existing public transport infrastructure—a factor likely to lead to higher than average levels of car ownership among those who ended up living there, in so doing making a mockery of their 'eco' credentials. Protests about the mass house-building programme have been held from the south-west to the north-east.

In contrast, some experts claimed the government's house-building plans were too modest. In October 2007 the National Housing and Planning Advice Unit quango predicted that typical house prices in the UK would spiral to nine-and-a-half times the average salary by 2026 unless the government increased supply even more dramatically. By 2016, it argued, 270,000 new homes would need to be built each year to avert a crisis in home ownership among people on low and middle incomes—as opposed to the 240,000 a year planned by ministers at the time.

Whatever the true picture, by autumn 2008 the arguments for and against the onset of a fresh 'new town' era were looking increasingly academic: the severe economic downturn, coupled with a collapse in the housing market, saw many developers involved in the government's plans on the brink of collapse or voluntarily bringing their house-building programmes to a standstill. Although the mortgage market has since stabilized, the number of approvals in the year to June 2008 slumped by 70 per cent, according to the British Bankers' Associa-tion. To jump-start the housing market Labour unveiled a range of measures designed to help first-time buyers in September that year. These included a one-year 'stamp duty holiday' for homes sold for less than £175,000, a shared equity plan offering low and middle-income families free loans worth up to a third of a property's value, and a Homeowner Mortgage Support Scheme designed to stave off repossession for those experiencing short-term difficulties with repay-ments (see p. 194). Chancellor Alistair Darling also made it a condition of the £50bn rescue package offered to Britain's major high-street banks and building societies after the October 2008 stock market crash that they use some of the money pumped into the system by the government to approve more mortgage loans.

As for top-down housing targets, they were finally abandoned in July 2010 (to wails of protest from opposition MPs and the House-Builders' Federation) by coalition Communities Secretary Eric Pickles. In future, he said, it would be up to individual councils to determine 'the right level of local housing provision in their area'. To allay fears that the abolition of quotas and regional spatial strategies might leave behind a policy vacuum in the short run, while councils worked out their ongoing approaches to strategic planning, Mr Pickles urged them to decide swiftly whether to abandon or retain the housing targets previously imposed on them so 'communities and landowners know where they stand'. As critics pointed to the fact that, even before the scrapping of targets, house-building in England had fallen to its lowest levels since the 1920s, in August 2010 Grant Shapps unveiled a New Homes Bonus scheme, designed to incentivize local authorities to build affordable housing by offering them extra funding for doing so. For every new home built, the government would match the Council Tax raised on the premises for the following six years. But Mr Shapps' Labour  opposite, John Healey, said the devil would be in the detail, and in practice existing government grants to councils were likely to be raided to finance it—meaning that ministers would be 'robbing Peterborough to pay Poole'.

## Housing policy and the homeless

Local authorities have a statutory duty to house the 'unintentionally homeless' and those threatened with homelessness *within 28 days of being made aware of their predicament* under the Housing (Homeless Persons) Act 1977 and the Homelessness Act 2002. Under the Housing Act 1996, however, the ambit of 'homelessness' was narrowed to allow councils to take into account available accommodation across the UK and even 'elsewhere'. The aim of this reform was to help out local authorities presented with disproportionately high numbers of homeless people (particularly asylum seekers), because it would be unreasonable for them to be expected to house all applicants in their own areas. Ensuing regulations also tightened the law regarding the eligibility of asylum seekers for help with housing: anyone who did not claim asylum-seeker status at the port of their arrival was rendered ineligible (barring refugees and those granted 'exceptional or unconditional leave to remain in the UK'). The Act also introduced a two-year limit on the provision of accommodation in certain cases and a review of all cases after that.

The following categories of homeless people are treated as priority cases:

- people with dependent children;
- people made homeless by an emergency and disaster (flood, fire, etc.);

- people vulnerable because of old age, or mental or physical disability;
- pregnant women and their households.

When assessing applications from homeless people for permanent housing and while waiting for flats to become available, local authorities often use short-stay, hostel, and/or so-called 'bed and breakfast' accommodation (in reality, often little more than dingy bedsits or studio flats within multi-occupancy dwellings).

The overriding controversy over local authorities' responsibilities towards the homeless, however, relates to the Act's rather wide-ranging definition of 'unintentional homelessness'. Under the law, the 'intentionally homeless' include people evicted from private sector accommodation for falling behind with rent and even those fleeing their home 'voluntarily' to escape domestic abuse. Nonetheless, if an intentionally homeless person fits into a priority category, the authority must provide them with advice, assistance, and temporary accommodation.

The coalition has gone even further in lessening the responsibility of local authorities towards the homeless—by allowing them to abandon their 'duty of care' once they have successfully steered people into private-sector accommodation for a year or more.

Tony Blair's government made a high-profile effort to tackle the problem of street homelessness during its first term. Under a Rough Sleepers Unit headed by bullish 'Homelessness Tsar' Louise Casey, he launched the Rough Sleepers Initiative, initially in central London but then across several other cities with high levels of homelessness, including Bristol and Brighton. Its stated aim was initially to provide places in short-term hostels and leased spaces in 'move-on' accommodation, before re-routing street sleepers to permanent homes, high-dependency specialist care homes, and special accommodation for people with drink and/or drug problems. The initiative officially ended in March 2002, having (according to the government) more or less achieved its aims.

But not everyone was convinced by the figures officials produced to demonstrate the reduction in street homelessness. 'Spot counts' of rough sleepers were periodically carried out on the streets of target towns and cities—but controversy erupted when several charities and support groups accused those conducting them of massaging their figures by using questionable criteria. In December 2002 volunteers working with the homeless in Waterloo and West-minster alleged that rough sleepers had been moved out of the London boroughs two nights before a count to gerrymander their figures downwards, while a Bristol-based volunteer wrote to a national newspaper alleging that the previous Christmas street sleepers had been moved prematurely into a temporary night shelter just ahead of a count there. This had the effect of taking 19 sleepers off the streets on that night—artificially slashing the headcount as a result.

## Local authorities and Housing Benefit (Local Housing Allowance)

In addition to providing social housing and shelter for the unintentionally homeless, local authorities administer Housing Benefit (since April 2008, Local Housing Allowance for new claimants or those claiming HB who move to a new home) on behalf of the Department for Work and Pensions (DWP). Housing Benefit (HB) is a payment equivalent to all or part of the rent charged to low-income tenants living in private, public, or voluntary sector accommodation.

There are two types of HB, depending on individuals' circumstances:

- *standard Housing Benefit*—paid to employed people on low earnings;
- *certificated Housing Benefit*—for those on **Jobseeker's Allowance (JSA)**, **Income Support**, Incapacity Benefit, and other benefits related to an inability to work.

The principal difference between HB and LHA—rolled out nationwide after a long-running pilot in nine 'pathfinder' areas—relates to the method used to assess how much eligible claimants receive. Housing Benefit involved individual properties being inspected by council employees to determine their (notional) rental values, with successful claimants then receiving payments commensurate with what their council felt the accommodation was worth. LHA has simplified this process, by offering claimants blanket rates for different levels of property (from one-bedroom flats to four-bedroom houses) based on 'middle-of-the-range' market rents for each category in their neighbourhoods (known as *broad market rental areas*).

Anti-poverty campaigners argue that the new calculation method means the sums received by even those granted 'full' help with rental costs, and living in modest properties, often fall well short of what they are actually charged by landlords. Disability groups, meanwhile, have complained that LHA discriminates against severely disabled people who require two-bedroom homes because of their need to accommodate live-in carers. In November 2009 a benefits tribunal found against Walsall Council in a case brought by the mother of a severely disabled woman who argued the new regulations had unfairly left her with a weekly £70–£75 rent shortfall on the two-bedroom home they shared. Discontent over cutbacks to HB was gathering momentum at time of writing, with the announcement in George Osborne's maiden Budget that he was capping it (see p. 233) at £280 a week for a one-bedroom flat and £400 a week for a four-bedroom house—putting paid to the type of story, beloved of the *Daily Mail*, about welfare-dependent families being paid HB worth tens of thousands of pounds a year to live in palatial homes in central London that most waged households could never dream of affording. Mr Osborne's subsequent CSR included plans to save another £2bn a year by cutting the amount of HB claimable by single people under the age of 35 to the cost of a room in a shared property, rather than their own flat. In a further blow to jobless households living in costly (but often far from salubrious) parts of London and the south-east, he said claimants who spent more than a year on JSA would in future have their HB/LHA cut by 10 per cent—forcing jobseekers still without work to either dig into their £65-a-week living expenses to continue covering their rent or uproot themselves and their families and move elsewhere.

→
see also
central
govern-
ment,
p. 233

As some London local authorities revealed they were already seeking out 'bed and breakfast' accommodation in cheaper outlying suburbs in anticipation of a rise in evictions, Labour frontbencher Chris Bryant condemned the government's reforms as a form of 'social cleansing' that risked turning the capital's central boroughs into replicas of the more exclusive areas of Paris, while influential *backbencher* John Cruddas likened them to a latter-day 'clearances'—a reference to moves to corral paupers and the unemployed in the eighteenth and nineteenth centuries. Meanwhile, in an article in *Inside Housing*, the trade journal of the social housing sector, Helen Williams, assistant director of the National Housing Federation, made the point that, far from being a mass of feckless, workshy scroungers, three-quarters of the 4.7 million households claiming HB/LHA are either retired, disabled, or full-time carers. Of the remaining 24 per cent, half are in employment.

Local authorities are paid subsidies by central government to cover the cost of assessing claimants' eligibility and administering the benefit on the ground (although, as this equates to just 95 per cent of the actual cost, councils have often complained that this role places an unfair burden on them—one reason for the introduction of LHA, which is cheaper to administer).

Alongside HB and LHA, local authorities also administer Council Tax Benefit, which normally equates to a full Council Tax rebate for those qualifying for HB/LHA. However, in his 2010 Comprehensive Spending Review Mr Osborne ordered local authorities to cut the amounts they pay out in this benefit by 10 per cent. It remains to be seen how this cut will be implemented on the ground by individual councils, and whether they will find ways of insulating the poorest from its impact. At the time of Mr Osborne's announcement, Andy Sawford, chief executive of the Local Government Information Unit, predicted some authorities might choose to scrap the benefit for specific groups, such as the long-term unemployed, in order to protect others.

## ☰ Topical feature idea

Figure 17.3 is an article taken from the *Western Morning News* on 16 January 2010. It focuses on the counter-argument to campaign groups protesting at the imposition of unsympathetic housing developments on areas of countryside—namely, that many existing villages and communities may end up unsustainable unless more affordable homes are built for local young people otherwise priced out of the market. How would you develop this story into a detailed backgrounder, representing both sides of this fiercely argued debate?

**Figure 17.3** Article from the *Western Morning News*, 16 January 2010

# Homes crisis 'could kill villages'

No byline

*Western Morning News*

16 January 2010

Web link: http://www.thisiswesternmorningnews.co.uk/news/Affordable-homes-crisis-kill-West-villages/article-1717695-detail/article.html

WORKING Westcountry villages will 'die' unless small communities are given the power to build homes for local people, the region's housing industry has been told.

Matthew Taylor, Lib-Dem MP for Truro and St Austell, told planners, developers and elected officials that the prohibitive costs of buying a home across large swathes of the West country was forcing the working population to live miles away from the community it served.

Mr Taylor, a key adviser to the Government on the country's rural affordability crisis, was a keynote speaker at the region's first regional housing summit, held in Exeter yesterday.

Organized by the South West Housing Initiative, which represents housebuilders, housing associations and employers, the summit was designed to show how there is a pressing need to provide affordable homes for key workers to enable sustainable and vibrant communities.

More than 100 delegates heard how some villages 'did not have a sustainable future by anyone's definition of the word' because amenities were forced to shut.

He said that in St Agnes, a village popular with second home owners on the north Cornwall coast, the shop and post office had closed and the pub was considering opening only in the summer season.

The people running the shop had been forced to live in a Transit van because they could not afford to live in the village, Mr Taylor said.

The MP, also chairman of the National Housing Federation, told the audience: 'We have to deliver housing for the needs of those living and working in support of those communities, and those that are living on rural wages'.

Echoing the report he prepared for the Prime Minister last year, he said opposition to any plans for new houses from so-called Nimbys ('Not in my back yard') could be overcome by adopting a policy of 'localism'.

He argued as few as 10 to 12 houses kept in local ownership, in perpetuity, would make a difference, and that community support for a housing scheme could be determined at parish rather district or county level.

Mr Taylor insisted the 'community needs to make the decision'.

He said: 'By imposing a decision, some former barrister will lead the campaign against you.'

'But if you were to say "do you want to keep the school and the shop?", the answer you would likely get is <e>.... (we'll build) a terrace of houses. The solution comes from the community itself.'

Other speakers at the day-long summit included Stuart Whitfield, South West chairman of the Confederation of British Industry, who told delegates that a lack of affordable housing risked damaging business's capacity to recruit staff.

Henley MP John Howell, a Conservative front-bencher on planning and local government, told how local people had become "disenfranchised" by housebuilding targets handed down by the Labour Government, and repeated his party's commitment to scrap them if it came to power.

## ✳ Current issues

- **Housing targets replaced by New Homes Bonus scheme:** one of Communities Secretary Eric Pickles' earliest actions was to write to all councils telling them Labour's centrally dictated house-building targets introduced were to be abandoned. Gordon Brown's government had been committed to building 3 million new homes in England by 2020—principally affordable houses and flats aimed at key workers and those on low-to-middle incomes. The decision to scrap targets came as a relief to local authorities struggling to find suitable development land, but was criticized by housing campaigners, who said many households would continue being priced out of the property market. Housing Minister Grant Shapps later announced a New Homes Bonus Scheme to incentivize councils to build homes.

- **Expansion of eco-friendly homebuilding schemes:** the coalition wants to ensure that by 2016 all new homes built in Britain are carbon-neutral. Its definition of 'zero carbon' is based on the outcome of a four-year consultation instigated by Labour. Appropriate housing schemes are now being offered grant support from a range of government bodies, including the Homes and Communities Agency.

- **Bottom-up social housing development:** in place of Labour's top-down house-building targets, the coalition has introduced local housing trusts to consult with local residents on where and in what form to provide new low-cost housing. In an echo of Mrs Thatcher's 'Right to Buy' policy, Mr Shapps has also revived the term 'aspiration', promoting shared ownership housing schemes and offering social housing tenants more opportunities to buy or part-purchase their homes.

## ? Review questions

1. What is the difference between 'social housing' and 'affordable housing'?
2. Who are the main providers of social housing in Britain today and how did this multi-agency system come about?
3. Explain what is meant by the term 'Right to Buy'. How and when was it introduced, and what are its benefits for council tenants?
4. What is the Housing Revenue Account (HRA)? Outline how it works.
5. What is meant by 'unintentional homelessness' and what responsibilities do local authorities have to house the unintentionally homeless?

## → Further reading

Bramley, G., Munro, M., and Pawson, H. (2004) *Key Issues in Housing: Policies and Markets in 21st-Century Britain*, London: Palgrave Macmillan. **Examination of the most burning contemporary housing issues in Britain, including the supply of social and affordable homes, new demographic pressures, and the threats to greenbelt sites.**

Jones, C. and Murie, A. (2006) *The Right to Buy: Analysis and Evaluation of a Housing Policy*, London: Wiley-Blackwell. **Thorough and balanced evaluation of the legacy of Thatcher government's 'Right to Buy' policy. Policies set in the context of New Labour's housing reforms.**

Lund, B. (2006) *Understanding Housing Policy*, Cambridge: Policy Press. **Up-to-date appraisal of issues in social and low-cost housing, focusing on the decline of local authority housing, and the growth in involvement of housing associations, co-ops, and other providers.**

Malpass, P. (2005) *Housing and the Welfare State: The Development of Housing Policy in Britain*, London: Palgrave Macmillan. **In-depth historical critique of the evolution of housing policy in Britain since the Second World War.**

## ⓦ Online Resource Centre

www.oxfordtextbooks.co.uk/orc/Morrison2e/
Visit the Online Resource Centre that accompanies this book for web links and regular updates.

# 18

# Children's services and adult social care

One of the most intricate (and occasionally explosive) aspects of local authority policy delivery is 'social services'—an umbrella term referring to the provision of everything from foster care and adoptive parents for vulnerable children to residential and nursing homes for the elderly and disabled. Today, 1.5 million people in England rely on support from social services, including 400,000 children.

Although the term 'social services' may not be used as often in the media as 'NHS' or 'health service', stories relating to its work—and, more often than not, scandals arising from its failings—are seldom far from the news agenda. Controversies have ranged from complaints about errant social workers failing to identify cases of domestic child abuse until it is too late (Victoria Climbié's death at the hands of her **foster parents** and the 2008 'Baby Peter' case), to screaming headlines about discharged mental patients running amok during the era of the now notorious 'Care in the Community' drive (for example, the 1992 murder of musician Jonathan Zito by schizophrenic Christopher Clunis).

Most of these stories, however, have arisen out of atypical circumstances and, with the exception of specialist sections such as *Society Guardian*, the British media is often accused of neglecting the complexities of this 'difficult' policy area in favour of sensationalism. But given some of the current demographic and social trends in the UK—the liberalization of the **adoption** laws, rising diagnoses of mental illness, and a rapidly ageing population—only a foolish editor would be unwilling to engage with the underlying issues that determine the direction of policy (and occasionally give rise to some of the more dramatic situations about which we so often hear).

Until the early twentieth century, such social welfare services as existed were provided on an ad hoc basis by charities and voluntary foundations, or in workhouses or infirmaries funded by parishes under the Poor Law. But social reform under the modernizing governments of David Lloyd George and Clement Attlee saw the introduction of more widespread and coordinated social care provision, paralleling the nationwide establishment of the National Health Service (NHS) and welfare state. The main landmarks included a seminal report by the 1968 Inter-Departmental Committee on Local Authority and Allied Personal Services (the 'Seebohm Report'), which led to the decision, two years later, to form discrete social services departments from the merger of the pre-existing health and welfare and children's departments under the Local Authorities Social Services Act 1970. The new departments, run by county councils, worked closely with existing housing departments (part of a district or borough) and the NHS.

Until 2004, when children were given their own dedicated department following the Climbié case, social services departments were responsible for three broad policy areas:

- child protection (often known as 'children and families');
- domiciliary and residential care for the elderly and disabled;
- care for those with mental health problems.

# ▶ Child protection

Until recently child protection was overseen collaboratively by social services departments, in partnership with various other organizations:

- local education departments (normally within the same local authority);
- police child protection units;
- *NHS trusts* and *primary care trusts (PCTs)*;
- the National Society for the Prevention of Cruelty to Children (NSPCC);
- registered adoption agencies.

These various agencies liaised through an area review committee (ARC), which determined the child protection procedures each of them should follow and conducted reviews of cases when those processes had failed to prevent 'non-accidental injury' from taking place. Information on vulnerable children was shared between them through a local child protection register maintained by the ARC.

The Children Act 2004—passed in the wake of the Climbié case—moved to scrap ARCs in favour of a new breed of **children's trusts**: all-in-one bodies bringing together representatives of every statutory agency involved in promoting child welfare and comprising multidisciplinary teams of experts, including social workers, health visitors, paediatricians, and child psychologists. Local child protection registers have also been replaced by **child protection plans**, to be drawn up by professionals following an initial child protection conference to assess the child's degree of risk.

The sweeping changes, ushered in under the 'Every Child Matters' banner (see pp. 514–18), saw all services relating to children—from schooling to social care—combined under the discrete heading 'children's services', under a director of children's services. Adult social care remains within the remit of social services, albeit under new directors of adult services.

Children's social services are required to:

- promote the general welfare of children;
- encourage the upbringing of children by their families (wherever possible);
- pay regard to the wishes and feelings of the child;
- work in partnership with parents in the best interests of the child;
- provide accommodation for children over whom no one has 'parental responsibility' (see pp. 511–14), if the child is lost or abandoned, or if the person responsible is unable to provide care;
- advise, assist, and befriend any child who leaves local authority care—and provide financial assistance and support to find accommodation.

The following two sections primarily focus on the web of regulations and guidelines currently governing child protection policy in England and Wales, as derived from two key Acts:

- the Children Act 1989;
- the Children Act 2004.

## The 1989 Act and the definition of 'parental responsibility'

The Children Act 1989 sought to harmonize the existing body of public and private law on the care, protection, and safe upbringing of children, giving it a more cohesive focus than previously. It came into force in England and Wales in 1991 and Northern Ireland in 1996, after minor alterations.

As had long been the case, the Act's presumption was that the best place for children to be brought up was at home with their parents or guardians—unless there was serious concern for their welfare should they remain there. To this end, councils were given a 'general duty' to 'keep a child safe and well', and to provide suitable support services to help them to remain with their families. The Act's definition of 'family' is quite fluid, however—referring to any adult(s) who have 'parental responsibility' for a child in law. It defines 'parental responsibility' as meaning 'all the rights, duties, powers, responsibilities and authority which by law a parent of a child has in relation to the child and his property'.

The main categories of 'children in need' defined in the Act are those who are:

- disabled—blind, deaf, dumb, or with a mental disorder or physical handicap;
- unlikely to have—or have the opportunity to have—'a reasonable standard of health or development' without the help of services from a local authority;
- unlikely to progress in terms of health or development;
- unlikely to progress in health or development without the help of local authority services.

The Act entitles any parent, guardian, or carer who feels his or her child might be eligible for services to contact the relevant department for a 'needs assessment'. This assessment, carried out by a qualified social worker, should take into account not only the child's needs, but also those of his or her parent(s) or guardian(s). For example, the child might need remedial educational support or therapy, but the adult with parental responsibility might qualify for financial assistance, counselling, or (depending on circumstances) respite care—a short break from caring, perhaps involving a stay away from home, while the child is looked after by professionals. Since 2000 assessments have been conducted in a 'multi-agency' way, under the Department of Health's Framework for the Assessment for Children in Need and their Families. This means that, in addition to providing for a child's immediate physical, mental, and emotional needs, a more holistic plan must also be put in place—catering for any ongoing specialist social, financial, or educational requirements.

The range of services available under the 1989 Act includes:

- short break services;
- holiday play schemes;
- care at home—including help with washing, dressing, and mobility;
- some aids and adaptations—for example, stair lifts, hoists, wheelchairs;
- financial help—for example, to pay for fares to hospital visits.

Services can be arranged by councils on behalf of children and families, with social services providing some and outside agencies and charities usually contracted to deliver others. Alternatively, the parent or guardian may request the use of a *direct payment* scheme. This involves cash payments being made directly to the family, giving them the freedom to 'shop around' for the services of their choice rather than being left to make do with the 'one-size-fits-all' approach traditionally used by councils. Direct payments (also known as *self-directed support*)—based on a similar principle to that fuelling current proposals to extend 'patient choice' in the NHS—was piloted in the context of care packages for the elderly as early as 1996, but recently extended, controversially, to severely mentally impaired adults and the elderly (see pp. 531–2).

→
see also
central
government,
p. 171

In addition to setting out the range of day-to-day services available for children in need, the 1989 Act addressed the thorny issue of local authorities' role in the wider question of child welfare. In particular, it defined the circumstances in which social services should intervene to ask the family courts to decide where (and with whom) a child felt to be 'at risk' of neglect or abuse at the hands of his or her parents, guardians, or other relations should live. The Act set out four types of court order—collectively known as 'section 8 orders' (see Table 18.1).

From time to time, the level of intervention by social services departments permissible under the above orders is insufficient to deal with the care needs of a child; at other times, the terms of an order may be breached, again putting the child at unacceptable risk. In these circumstances, it may be necessary for the local authority to consider taking children 'into care'—away from the adult(s) with parental responsibility for them. The procedure for doing this and the range of care options available to children once removed from their own homes is discussed in the section on **care orders**, fostering, and adoption later in this chapter.

The 1989 Act only applies to England and Wales, although most of its provisions are reflected in the Children (Scotland) Act 1995. The one significant difference is that under Scottish law legal proceedings surrounding child welfare follow a distinct process, known as the 'children's hearings system', first established in the early 1970s, which determines any compulsory measures

**Table 18.1** Types of 'section 8 order' under the Children Act 1989

| Order | Effect |
|---|---|
| Contact order | Requires person with whom the child is to live to allow him or her to visit or stay with another named person (e.g. another parent) or for that person and the child to have other specified contact. |
| Prohibited steps order | Prohibits certain 'steps' related to role of person with parental responsibility for the child to be taken without express prior agreement of the court (e.g. to prevent parent with whom the child does not live taking him or her away on holiday in circumstances in which there is thought to be danger of parent absconding with the child). During some family proceedings (particularly those relating to serious custody disputes between separated couples), the court may make the child a *ward of court*. This is where the court itself, rather than social services, takes the child into care temporarily. Again, this is normally used to prevent one parent leaving the country with the child unlawfully. |
| Residence order | Specifies that the child must live with a named person, often outlining other specific arrangements. |
| Specific issue order | Determines 'specific question' that has arisen, or may arise, in relation to care of the child (e.g. where the child should go to school, if parents or guardians disputing custody each want him or her to attend one near their homes). |

of supervision a minor may need. The 1995 Act's one notable strengthening of existing procedures was in its emphasis on the role of 'safeguarders'—that is, individuals with relevant professional backgrounds (normally lawyers, social workers, or teachers) appointed to act as the 'voice of the child'.

## The 2004 Act and the 'Every Child Matters' agenda

The 2004 Act focused less on introducing additional duties of care or legal powers for local authorities and the courts than on radically shaking up the *culture* of child protection. Its main emphasis was on improving communication between professionals and early intervention, following the horrific case of Victoria Climbié.

In 2000, 8-year-old Victoria died of hypothermia, with 128 separate injuries to her body, after two years of systematic torture and abuse at the hands of her great aunt, Marie Thérèse Kouao, and the latter's boyfriend, Carl Manning, at their London bedsit. She had been sent to Britain in the hope of a better life by her parents, who both live on the Ivory Coast. During the months before her death Victoria was systematically beaten, burnt with cigarettes and scalding water, tied up, and forced to sleep in a bath with only a bin liner over her naked body. Police, social workers, and even the NSPCC failed to treat the warning signs sufficiently seriously—closing a child protection investigation that was opened at one stage on the basis of a paediatrician's mistaken diagnosis that scars on her skin were caused by scabies.

After Victoria's treatment was finally exposed, both Kouao and Manning were jailed for murder at the Old Bailey, a number of social workers at Haringey Council were sacked, and three major investigations were prompted—one by the local authority, another by the *Independent Police Complaints Commission (IPCC)*, and the third a public inquiry chaired by senior social worker and former Chief Inspector of Social Services Lord Laming. The last, which reported in January 2003, made a series of 17 recommendations for the reform of child protection procedures. The most significant are explained in Table 18.2.

The government's response was to publish a now famous *Green Paper, Every Child Matters*. It dwelt on four key 'themes' in relation to the issue of child protection:

- increasing the focus on supporting families and carers—described as 'the most critical influence on children's lives';
- ensuring that necessary intervention takes place before children reach crisis point and protecting children from falling through the net;
- addressing underlying problems identified in the report into the death of Victoria Climbié—weak accountability and poor integration;
- ensuring that people working with children are valued, rewarded, and trained.

**Table 18.2** Main recommendations of the Laming Inquiry

| Recommendation | Details |
| --- | --- |
| Government to take lead with new ministerial board | Children and Families Board to be established at heart of government, chaired by *Cabinet* minister. Like *Cabinet committees*, it should be made up of ministers or other senior representatives from all departments concerned with child and family welfare. |
| New regulator | **Children's Commissioner** for England (Children's Commissioner) should be established, who would also be chief executive of National Agency for Children and Families. He or she would report directly to the Board.<br><br>Agency would be responsible for:<br><br>(a) assessing and advising the board about impact of proposed policies;<br>(b) scrutinizing relevant new legislation and guidance;<br>(c) advising on implementation of **United Nations (UN)** Convention on the Rights of the Child;<br>(d) advising on setting 'nationally agreed outcomes' for children, and how best to monitor and achieve these;<br>(e) ensuring policies are implemented at local level and monitoring this process through regional offices;<br>(f) reporting annually to Parliament on quality and effectiveness of children and family services. |
| Major case reviews by government | Agency to conduct 'serious case reviews' in the event of death or serious deliberate injury of child. |
| New local authority committees | Each local authority responsible for social services to establish its own committee of members for children and families, to include lay members of management committees of key services. |
| Proper coordination of local services | Local authority *chief executives* to chair management boards for services to children and families, and report to above committees. |
| Full inspection of delivery and support services | Government inspectorates responsible for monitoring children and family services must in future inspect not only service delivery on ground, but also effectiveness of inter-agency arrangements surrounding those services. |
| Tighter fostering procedures | Ministers should review law regarding registration of private foster carers. |
| Full recording and information-sharing between partner agencies | Every individual agency involved in a child's care should record basic information about him or her—including name, address, age, name of primary carer, GP, and name of his or her school. |
| Stripping away jargon | Department of Health to establish new 'common language' for effective identification of, and intervention in, child protection issues, to be disseminated to all agencies involved in area. Existing child protection register system to be replaced by 'more effective system' (child protection plans). |
| National database | Government should hold feasibility study with view to setting up national children's database containing details of all children under the age of 16. |
| Improved training for professionals | Local management boards to ensure proper training in child protection—on 'inter-agency' basis—to be monitored by government inspectorates. |

Following a widespread public consultation and a further paper, *Every Child Matters: The Next Steps*, many of Lord Laming's recommendations came into effect under the 2004 Act. They revolved around five 'Every Child Matters' outcomes, which set out to enable all children to:

- be healthy;
- stay safe;
- enjoy and achieve;
- make a positive contribution;
- achieve economic well-being.

To drive forward these outcomes, the government created children's trusts—multidisciplinary teams comprising professionals of all types involved in promoting the 'well-being' of children. To improve the coordination of children's services on the ground, the idea was that these trusts should bring together various professionals at a single location in the local community, such as a children's centre or school. Between them they would be expected to carry out the following:

- joint needs assessments for a child in need;
- shared decisions on priorities relating to a child's well-being;
- identification of all available resources suited to improving a child's well-being;
- joint plans to deploy those resources, to avoid duplication or overlap.

Even before trusts were in place everywhere, plans were unveiled in June 2008 for their remit to be widened to encompass aspects of youth justice previously overseen by the Police Service and Prisons Service Agency. Then Children's Secretary Ed Balls increased collaboration over the care of the 2,900 under-18s in young offender institutions, privately run secure training centres, and local authority secure units between the Youth Justice Board established earlier by Labour and children's trusts. His stated aim was to replace the pre-existing, more punitive approach to youth justice with an early-intervention strategy designed to 'catch' potential career criminals early and prevent repeat offending. The policy—branded *Integrated Resettlement Support (IRS)*—arguably marked a return to the 'tough on crime, tough on the causes of crime' view espoused by Tony Blair in his days as Shadow Home Secretary.

To steer Labour's changes to child protection policy, an independent Children's Commissioner was appointed in March 2005, in the shape of Professor Al Aynsley-Green, a former national clinical director for children in the Department of Health (since succeeded by Maggie Atkinson, a former head of children's services at Gateshead Council). The Commissioner's remit is to:

- promote awareness of the views and interests of children among all sectors;

- work closely with organizations that take decisions affecting all aspects of children's lives, including the police, schools, hospitals, and voluntary groups;
- have regard to the framework of the five 'Every Child Matters' outcomes and the rights of children under the 1989 UN Convention on the Rights of the Child.

In the run-up to the Commissioner's appointment, consultation among children found that their main concerns included bullying, personal safety, and pressure in education (especially from exams). Many also stressed the problems they faced coming from deprived and minority social backgrounds.

A further significant reform instigated in the wake of *Every Child Matters* was the introduction of discrete children's services departments, and the requirement for them to develop an integrated children's system to coordinate needs assessments, planning, early intervention, and periodic reviews of service provision. As of April 2006 social care services for under-16s were removed from the general social services arena and combined with education provision under this new all-embracing umbrella. The Act also stipulated that every county council or unitary authority—except those with an 'excellent' rating under comprehensive area assessment (see p. 409)—must publish a periodic *children and young people's plan (CYPP)*, to which every agency should contribute. These should detail all services for children and young people in their area, and the shared objectives of partner organizations for improving them.

The local authority-run boards demanded by Lord Laming were introduced under the 2004 Act in the guise of **local safeguarding children's boards (LSCBs)**. These are charged with coordinating the various agencies involved in delivering services and monitoring the effectiveness of their work. The Act defined three levels of action to be taken by boards, as outlined in Table 18.3 overleaf.

**Table 18.3** Three levels of responsibility of local safeguarding children's boards

| Type of responsibility | Meaning |
|---|---|
| Activities | Preventing maltreatment—or 'impairment of health or development'—by introducing better mechanisms to identify cases of abuse or neglect, and providing clear, accessible contact points for children seeking to report them. |
| Proactive work | Offering outreach activities for specific groups—e.g. children identified as 'in need' but not suffering abuse or neglect. |
| Reactive work | Responding more quickly and effectively where children are suffering neglect or abuse by family members, other adults known to them, other young people, professional carers, or strangers. |

To further facilitate a more joined-up approach to providing care and support to children in need, a new database, ContactPoint, was launched in 2009 enabling communication and expertise to be exchanged between different agencies involved in an individual child's care. Controversially, its aim was to record the following basic details for each child in England up to his or her 18th birthday:

- name, address, gender, date of birth, and a unique identifying number;
- name and contact details of the child's parent or carer;
- contact details for services working with the child, including educational setting (for example, school) and GP practice, but also other services, where appropriate;
- a means of indicating whether a practitioner is a lead professional and if he or she has undertaken an assessment under a new common assessment framework (CAF).

see also central government, p. 106

Months before the £224m database had even been launched, it was already generating controversy. Despite reassurances from the government that only professionals involved in the care of children would be able to access it—and then only subject to passing advanced Criminal Records Bureau (CRB) checks to ensure that they had no convictions for offences involving children—the Conservatives and several charities expressed concern about potential security breaches. They cited the experience of the succession of then recent data leaks by government departments relating to everything from the personal details of Child Benefit claimants to the domestic arrangements of military personnel. Eyebrows were also raised about the fact young people's details would remain on the database until they reached the age of 25. The Tories accused the government of hiding a sinister agenda—a 'Big Brother' obsession with keeping tabs on the every move of British citizens—behind the more respectable cloak of 'child protection'. In the event, the Lib-Con coalition is expected to scrap ContactPoint. However, ministers have also ordered a further, 'fundamental', review of child protection, in the hope of identifying ways in which social workers can be freed up to spend more time working directly with children. The inquiry, headed by Eileen Munro, professor of social policy at the London School of Economics, was due to publish an initial report in September 2010 and full interim findings by January 2011.

## Care orders

The reforms described so far illustrate the extent to which social services and the various agencies working to promote child protection have become increasingly interventionist, due in part to pressure from the media, the general public, and families themselves. But sometimes they are required to be more proactive still, in the interests of a child whom they believe to be at serious risk of abuse or neglect if he or she remains in the care of a parent or guardian. The Climbié case highlighted what can happen if early warning signs are not noted or acted upon by professionals. Similar allegations were levelled at the authorities more recently over the death of 17-month-old Peter Connolly (known as 'Baby P') after eight months of abuse at the hands of his stepfather and a family lodger in Haringey—just streets away from where Climbié had died. The scandal led to the sacking of Haringey's director of children's services, Sharon Shoesmith, and the resignation of the council leader and cabinet member for children and young people.

While it lambasts the system for any failure to identify abuse, the media is equally quick to criticize conscientious social workers who, fearing a child is living in an abusive environment, intervene overzealously to remove them.

Perhaps the most infamous example of heavy-handed intervention by the authorities occurred in Cleveland in 1987, when 121 cases of suspected child abuse were diagnosed by two Middlesbrough-based paediatricians, Dr Marietta Higgs and  Dr Geoffrey Wyatt. Several children were removed from their families by social services in the ensuing investigation using a power introduced under the Children and Young Persons' Act 1969, known as a 'place of safety order'. In the end, 26 children from 12 families were found by judges to have been wrongly diagnosed and cases involving another 96 alleged victims were dismissed by the courts.

More recently, several newspapers—notably the *Daily Mail*—castigated Portsmouth City Council for being too ready to take children into care following the death of a 17-month-old girl, Anna Hider, who drowned in her foster parents' swimming pool, allegedly while they were entertaining guests. But the pendulum swung back the other way yet again when news broke in April 2009 of a vicious  attack by two brothers, aged 10 and 11, on two other boys in Edlington, south Yorkshire. A serious case review concluded the violent sexual assault might have been prevented had some 31 chances to intervene with the families not been missed by nine different agencies over a 14-year period. The case review launched by Doncaster Council marked the tipping point in a five-year period during which seven children had died in and around the town—despite being on the 'at risk' register.

Recent Acts have seen successive governments attempt to walk the tightrope between guaranteeing high standards of child protection and preventing cavalier intervention by social services and other agencies. Since the 1989 Act the principal means by which local authorities have been able to take children into care for an indefinite period—often against the will of their parent or guardian—is by applying to a family court for a care order. Under these circumstances the parent or guardian must still be allowed 'reasonable access' to the child (unless the court explicitly prohibits it) but the local authority assumes parental responsibility in law and has the power to determine the *degree* of any contact. Occasionally, the need to safeguard a child's welfare is perceived to be so urgent that a local authority can apply to a court for a 'fast-tracked' care order to remove him or her from a threat at home. This is known as an *interim care order* or **emergency protection order**. Initially granted for up to eight days, but renewable for a further week, emergency protection orders may only be granted if a court judges there to be 'reasonable cause to believe that the child is likely to suffer considerable harm' if left in situ. Since the Family Law Act 1996 the emphasis has been on removing 'the source of danger', rather than the child (for example, applying for a non-molestation order against a named individual will lead to his or her removal—not the child's).

Local authorities also have the power to apply for a lesser action known as a 'supervision order'—a device enabling them to 'supervise' parents or guardians in a closer way than normal to ensure that children potentially at risk are properly cared for. Under the 1989 Act a court may only make a supervision order if it is satisfied:

- a child is suffering, or likely to suffer, significant harm if one is not granted;
- the harm, or likelihood of harm, is attributable to the care given to the child (or likely to be given if the order is not made) not being what it is 'reasonable to expect a parent to give' or the child's being 'beyond parental control'—likely to be persistently truant from school, and/or to commit crime.

Under supervision orders it is the council's duty to 'advise, assist, and befriend' the child and approach the court for a variation of the order—converting it into a care order—if it is felt to be insufficient in practice. Likewise, the authority may apply to the court for the order to be lifted should it feel it is no longer necessary. Where the request for an order is specifically in relation to a child's non-attendance at school or his or her parents' refusal to send him or her, a local education authority may apply for a specific 'education supervision order'.

## Fostering and other forms of local authority care

So, there are various ways in which children can be removed from their home environments, should professionals and the courts be sufficiently concerned for their welfare. But where do these children—known as 'looked-after children'—actually *live* while under council protection?

Whether a child is under an emergency protection order or a full care order, he or she will normally be accommodated by social services in one of two ways:

- in a registered community children's home;
- with foster parents (sometimes known as a 'foster home').

### Children's homes

As with other forms of residential accommodation for vulnerable groups (see the sections on nursing and care homes for the elderly and mentally infirm later this chapter), today's children's homes may either be run directly by local authorities or any number of other registered providers, from private companies to specialist charities like Barnardo's. Although far removed from the grim Victorian orphanages and children's homes of yesteryear, many of those operating today still contain shared dormitories, as well as individual rooms. They tend to take both boys and girls, rather than being single sex, and house up to a hundred or more children at any one time (although most tend to limit their intake to double figures).

The roles of children's homes are to:

- keep young people safe;
- give them consistent boundaries and routines;
- give them assistance in accessing education;
- promote their health and well-being;
- provide quality of life—for example, games, leisure activities, external trips.

Children's homes—like adult care homes—used to be inspected by their local authorities, but in 2000 this role was taken over in England by a nationwide *quango*: the National Care Standards Commission. This was abolished in April 2004 and, after a brief interval during which inspections were carried out by the (also now defunct) *Commission for Social Care Inspection (CSCI)*, these responsibilities were handed to Ofsted (see pp. 448–51), in line with the widening of its remit to reflect that of the recently established council children's services departments. In Scotland all social care, including that for children, is regulated by the *Scottish Commission for the Regulation of Care (SCRC)*, while the *Scottish Social Services Council (SSSC)* is charged with raising standards in social work in both adult and child social care. In Wales these functions are discharged by the *Care and Social Services Inspectorate Wales (CSSIW)* and the *Care Council for Wales* respectively, while all health and social care is regulated by a single body: the *Regulation and Quality Improvement Authority (RQIA)*.

## Foster parents

Fostering can be arranged on a long-term or short-term basis by children's services, often with the help of an independent foster agency. It is usually seen by councils as preferable to keeping a child in a community children's home because the involvement of designated foster parents places them in a familiar, domestic-style setting, rather than an impersonal institution. Children placed in long-term foster care will normally be located with 'parents' who have at least one child of their own. They may continue living in this environment for a number of years, although (unless formally adopted) if they leave home at the age of 16 their foster carers will no longer have any legal rights over them. If their stay proves to be very long-term, however, their foster parents may apply at some stage to adopt them. Assuming this application is successful, the foster parents will then become their legal parents.

There are various forms of foster arrangement, the main ones of which are explained in Table 18.4. The strict vetting procedure for prospective foster parents is outlined in Table 18.5.

The number of children in foster care in Britain has risen by almost a third in recent years—from 32,300 in 1995 to 41,700 a decade later. Yet, in light of the growing preference for foster care over traditional children's homes, there is a national shortage of eligible carers, with some estimates suggesting that at least 10,000 more are needed to provide for all of the youngsters waiting to be placed. Some campaigners have blamed the shortfall on the financial burdens of fostering. In 2007 the charity Fostering Network called for foster carers to be paid a professional salary. A survey published at the start of its campaign found that 75 per cent of foster carers received less than the minimum wage and 40 per cent nothing at all.

Despite this, all foster carers qualify for an allowance to cover the basic cost of clothing, feeding, and otherwise providing for them. If a fostering

**Table 18.4** Different types of fostering arrangement

| Arrangement | How it works |
| --- | --- |
| Emergency | Where children need somewhere safe to stay for few nights—normally after emergency protection order granted. |
| Short-term | Carers look after children for few weeks or months, while plans are made for their long-term future (with interim care order in place). |
| Short breaks | Disabled children or children with special needs or behavioural difficulties enjoy short stay on pre-planned and/or regular basis with another family, and their parents or usual foster carers have short break. |
| Remand fostering | Young people in England or Wales can be 'remanded' by court to care of specially trained foster carer in relation to criminal conviction. Scotland does not use remand fostering because young people usually attend children's hearings, rather than court. Hearings might, however, send young person to secure unit and some Scottish schemes hope to develop fostering as an alternative to secure accommodation. |
| Long-term | For children choosing to live with long-term foster carers until they reach adulthood and are ready to live independently. |
| 'Family and friends' or 'kinship' fostering | Children looked after by local authority are put into care of relatives, friends, or other people they already know. |
| Private fostering | Where parents arrange for child to stay with someone who is not close relative and has no parental responsibilities, and child may stay with that person ('private foster carer') for more than 27 days. Although this is private arrangement, special rules exist to determine how child is cared for. Councils must be told about arrangements and visit to check on child. |

**Table 18.5** Vetting procedure for foster parents

| Procedure | What happens |
|---|---|
| Background investigation | Children's social services staff provisionally approve prospective foster parents following an investigation into their family lives, and medical and criminal backgrounds. Anyone convicted of causing or permitting bodily harm to child barred from fostering. Anybody living in same house as someone with such background is usually prohibited, as are those who have had orders made against them to remove child from their care. |
| Regular spot checks | Social workers retain right to see foster children on request at regular intervals and can remove them from care without notice if they believe this is in child's interests. Such actions can, however, prompt foster parents to apply to court for residence order, asserting their right to keep child with them. |
| Training for foster parents | Prospective foster parents required to attend classes on statutory responsibilities of foster carers. Although this is not yet compulsory, many also study for formal qualifications: in England and Wales, National Vocational Qualification (NVQ) Level 3 in Caring for Children and Young People; in Scotland, Scottish Vocational Qualification (SVQ) can be pursued. |

arrangement has been negotiated through an agency, the level of this allowance will be set by that agency and is usually dependent on the child's age, with carers of older children qualifying for more. As of April 2007, in recognition of the wide disparities in foster allowances from agency to agency, the government introduced guaranteed minimum levels for the first time in relation to different age groups—as outlined in the table entitled 'The national minimum weekly fostering allowance for England (2007–08)', to be found on the Online Resource  Centre that accompanies this book.

In addition, in 2003 the government introduced a new Income Tax allowance for foster parents, allowing them to 'earn' up to £10,000 a year from foster allowances tax-free. At the same time, a new *National Insurance*-backed scheme called 'Home Responsibility Protection' was introduced to ensure that long-term foster parents would not retire on anything less than the state retirement pension—a *contributory benefit*—even if they had made too few NI contributions to qualify for it under normal rules.

see also central government, p. 239

## The adoption process

The distinction between fostering and adoption is that, while the former is theoretically a finite arrangement, the latter is permanent. At any point up to 4,000 children across the UK are looking for adoptive parents. By law children can only be adopted through an adoption agency—either a children's services authority or a government-approved registered adoption society (a voluntary adoption agency). Most agencies cover a radius of around 50 miles from their offices. Not all agencies actually arrange placements themselves, but all may carry out adoption assessments to ensure that prospective adoptive parents are suitable.

So, who is entitled to adopt? Until very recently, the right was largely restricted to married heterosexual couples, with those under the age of 40 more likely to be successful than older applicants (who would be of mature age by the time their adopted children had grown up). But much of this changed with the passage of the Adoption and Children Act 2002, which opened adoption up to single people, as well as one partner in an unmarried couple (whether straight or gay). The law was further tweaked in 2005 to enable unmarried couples to apply to adopt jointly—effectively giving them the same rights as married ones. For gay couples, the procedure is usually quicker if they are in a civil partnership, but provided that they live together they will normally stand as much chance of success as straight couples. Qualifying conditions for adopters are listed in Table 18.6.

There are two different types of adoption process, depending on whether the natural parent(s) of the child have given their consent for him or her to be adopted:

- *single-stage adoption*—a placement made with the full cooperation of the child's natural parents. This is the procedure followed when, for example, the child was conceived during rape or by a girl below the age of consent (16) who feels unable to take on the responsibility of bringing him or her up. In such cases a straightforward adoption order will be made by the court, without any opposition, because the mother fully endorses the procedure;

**Table 18.6** Criteria for prospective adopters

| Criterion | Meaning |
|---|---|
| Age | Must be over age of 21 and able to prove they are happy to make space in their life and home for child, and are patient, flexible, energetic, and determined to make difference to child's life. There is no official upper age limit, although agencies may sometimes favour younger couples. |
| Criminal checks | Must not have been convicted of any serious offence against child. More minor offences will have to be looked into, but may not exclude them. |
| Relationship status | Single person, or one partner in unmarried couple (heterosexual, lesbian, or gay) may adopt. Unmarried couples may apply to adopt jointly. |
| Good health | Prospective adopters must have medical examinations and health issues (including hereditary conditions) need to be explored. |
| Ethnic/cultural background | People of all ethnic backgrounds may adopt. Preferential treatment often given to prospective parents of same racial and/or religious identity as child. This follows research into well-being of minority-adopted adults who grew up with families who did not match their ethnic identity. |
| Disability access | People with disabilities may adopt, subject to conditions set down on case-by-case basis. |

- *two-stage adoption*—when a child's natural parent(s) object to his or her (or their) child being adopted, an adoption agency will have to apply to a court for a *freeing order*—an order removing the child from his or her parents' custody against their will. At this stage, the parents of the child are often not identified in court.

The usual adoption procedure for applicants follows a similar, if slightly more rigorous, route to that for fostering, as explained in Table 18.7.

# Childminding

'Childminding' is the term used to describe a type of day care provided for children, usually under school age, outside of nursery or preschool. A registered *childminder* will look after the child in his or her own home, normally while the parents or guardians are at work. Since the passage of the Care Standards Act 2000, regulation of childminding has been overseen by the *Office for Standards in Education, Children's Services, and Skills (Ofsted)*, rather than local authorities, as in the past.

Ofsted's role is to:

- provide a register of professionals paid for looking after children under the age of 5, on an area-by-area basis;
- inspect the homes of anyone applying to be registered as a childminder to ensure that there are adequate facilities, including toilets and play equipment.

**Table 18.7** The adoption process

| Procedure | What happens |
| --- | --- |
| Initial meeting(s) | Following application through adoption agency, prospective adopter(s) will meet with a social worker, together and individually (if in a couple), on several separate occasions. |
| Background investigation | Prospective adoptive parents' personal backgrounds investigated and they are asked why they want to adopt. Confidential enquiries made through their local social services department and police. |
| Personal references | These must be supplied by at least two friends of adopter(s), and they will have a GP medical examination. |
| Independent adoption panel | Hearing by panel linked to agency through which prospective adopter(s) have applied will consider their case and decide if they should progress to final stage: opportunity to meet panel in person. |
| Provisional care agreed | Once adopters approved in principle, child put into their provisional care (children's services authorities or adoption panels must be notified if done through approved adoption society, rather than local authority). |
| Adoption order confirmed | Decision made by family proceedings court, sitting in private, three months after notification to authority. |

Registration, when granted, is subject to various conditions covering the facilities to be provided; the number of staff, and their qualifications/experience of working with children; and the maximum number of children who may be minded at one time (particularly babies and those aged under 12 months).

Following initial inspections, further ones can take place at any time. If registration conditions are breached at any point, registration can be revoked or modified to reduce the maximum number of children to be minded.

## The Protection of Children Act 1999

Introduced following a series of high-profile scandals about the abuse of children in residential care homes, the Protection of Children Act 1999 saw the launch of a statutory list of all people considered unsuitable to work with children. The Consultancy Service Index, a list along these lines, had been kept by the *Secretary of State* since 1993, but the 1999 Act (in Scotland, the Protection of Children (Scotland) Act 2003) formalized the process by enforcing it as a statutory list, to which all existing names were added.

It requires childcare organizations to inform the government if:

- they transfer or dismiss someone who has harmed a child, or put a child at risk;
- an individual evades disciplinary action along these lines by resigning or retiring.

# ▶ Adult social services and the rise of community-based care

Although children's services account for the bulk of local authorities' social care budgets—and attract by far the most media coverage—councils retain significant responsibilities in relation to both the elderly and adults of working age with enduring physical and mental illnesses or disabilities.

Until relatively recently, much of the care provided for people falling into these categories was delivered in institutional environments—long-stay residential care homes (like adult versions of children's homes) or nursing homes for those who had reached a stage at which they could no longer wash or dress themselves or perform other basic functions without assistance.

People with mental disorders severe enough to prevent them continuing to live at home were often transferred for prolonged periods into NHS-run mental hospitals or specialist secure asylums managed by their local authorities. The oldest of these asylum facilities had been established in the early 1800s and many continued in more or less uninterrupted use for the best part of 200 years.

But under Margaret Thatcher and John Major, a revolution occurred that was to transform the culture of social care for both the mentally ill and all other categories of adult 'service user'.

This transformation came in the form of the National Health Service and Community Care Act 1990, which restyled patients as 'clients' and ushered in the now-notorious policy of 'Care in the Community'. In simple terms its aims were to:

- place greater emphasis on **community care**—providing support services for elderly people and those with mental and physical illnesses and disabilities in their homes, with a view to enabling them to remain in a community setting for longer periods, while reducing the pressure in acute wards and residential facilities;

- make the delivery of social care more cost-effective and increase choice for service users through the greater involvement of providers from the private and voluntary sectors, including charities.

Although few opposed the idea of empowering the vulnerable to continue living in their own homes in *theory*, many were alarmed by the way in which the NHS and local authorities began implementing the Act in practice. Long starved of funding for the so-called 'Cinderella service' of mental health, and with many of their homes and asylums severely underoccupied and therefore uneconomical to maintain, a number of councils and trusts used the freedom granted by the Act to shut down half-empty units—discharging inpatients to return to 'the community' irrespective of the strength of their personal support networks or ability to fend for themselves.

Tabloid newspapers reported a slew of scare stories about assaults, and even killings, by prematurely discharged mental patients. Perhaps the most infamous case was the 1992 murder of musician Jonathan Zito by a paranoid schizophrenic released from mental hospital just weeks earlier under 'Care in the Community'. Mr Zito's death prompted the establishment of the Zito Trust by his  wife, Jayne, which continues to campaign for changes to mental health policy in the best interests of both patients and public. Other high-profile cases included the 1996 murders of Lin Russell and her 6-year-old daughter, Megan, by Michael Stone on a country lane in Kent. Stone, who had a severe personality disorder, had been out of prison and receiving a package of community care since 1992.

At the time of the murders, it was not only the 1990 Act that was criticized in the media but also the Mental Health Act 1983, which, opponents claimed, contained a loophole preventing mental health professionals providing care for  people suffering from untreatable conditions, such as Stone's, even when they asked for help (Stone had repeatedly pleaded to be admitted to Broadmoor). The *British Medical Journal* subsequently cast doubt on this suggestion, yet criticisms of Stone's case remain. Much more recently, in July 2010, it emerged that the fugitive gunman Raoul Moat, who led police on a week-long manhunt after murdering his ex-partner's boyfriend and shooting both her and a police constable, had asked Newcastle City Council social workers to refer him to a psychiatrist just months before his rampage. But not every aspect of the renewed emphasis on community care has proved negative. For many elderly and disabled people the channelling of social services funding into care packages tailored to their individual needs, and home adaptations designed to make their domestic environments more comfortable and user-friendly, has proved liberating—enabling them to spend crucial extra years living near friends and family that would have been 'lost' had they been prematurely admitted to residential homes.

The responsibilities with which social services authorities are charged under the 1990 Act in relation to community care are as listed in Table 18.8.

The scale of the 'Care in the Community' controversy proved so damaging and long-lasting that when Labour returned to power in 1997 it swiftly scrapped the initiative (although, in practice, the 1990 Act remains the main legal basis underpinning social care provision). Community care is still the government's preferred option for caring for the elderly and disabled, at least until such time as they require full-time nursing, although the balance has been redressed somewhat between domiciliary and residential care arrangements.

New Labour's biggest reforms included:

- the Health Act 1999—introduced new forms of NHS structure and, with them, new partnerships with the private healthcare sector, formally abolishing the joint consultative committees established in 1977;

**Table 18.8** Main provisions of the Community Care Act 1990

| Measure | Meaning |
| --- | --- |
| Emphasis on 'Care in the Community', rather than residential care | Local authorities to promote domiciliary (home care), day care (attendance at day centres and activity groups), and respite services (short breaks for both carers and cared for), to allow people to live in own homes. |
| Emphasis on practical support to promote self-reliance | Ensuring all agencies and authorities involved in providing services prioritize practical support. |
| Detailed needs assessment | Carrying out 'proper assessment' of individuals' needs, followed by good case management by appointed key workers (normally social workers or occupational therapists). |
| Promoting partnerships | Developing flourishing independent/private sector alongside good public services. |
| Long-term care planning | Preparing strategic plans for community care arrangements, working with NHS authorities, publishing them, and keeping them under review, in consultation with bodies in public and voluntary sectors. Collaboration between NHS and local government to improve non-hospital services had first been introduced under the National Health Service Act 1977, when joint consultative committees (JCCs) were set up, consisting of representatives from all relevant statutory agencies. |

- the National Carers' Strategy—built on the Carers (Recognition and Services) Act 1996, which gave statutory recognition to the work of unpaid relatives or friends looking after people receiving community care in their homes. It enabled these informal carers to access their own support.

## Community care—what the state provides

Social services authorities have a duty to assess the needs of people requiring care due to their age, infirmity, or disability. If an assessment indicates someone requires services, the authority must determine the services required and inform them of the details of their assessment and their right to appeal. Some authorities have been accused of raising the bar in relation to 'eligibility criteria' because of budgetary concerns, and the courts have ruled it appropriate for councils to take their financial resources into account when setting those criteria.

The principal community care services provided by social services departments, whether delivered by them, a voluntary organization, or a private agency, include:

- home help (help with washing, dressing, and sometimes cleaning the home);
- hot meals ('meals on wheels');
- help with shopping and financial management;
- advocacy (advice and support with accessing other services, paying bills, etc.);
- telephone access;
- cheap travel (disabled and OAP bus passes, free transport to appointments);
- free and accessible parking, through the 'disabled badge holder' scheme;
- day care (access to day centres for structured activities, day trips etc.);
- respite care;
- home modifications and aids to daily living (stair lifts and hoists are usually provided by housing departments on social services' advice; wheelchairs and other mobility aids are often accessed through the NHS or charities).

In addition, training and employment can be provided for disabled people in sheltered workshops, while day nurseries and centres are available for their children.

These days, 'packages' of community care are put together by a client's key worker (or case worker). Because most social care professionals now work in multidisciplinary teams designed to improve coordination between social services, the health service, and the other agencies by bringing them together under one roof, this may be a social worker, community psychiatric nurse (CPN), or occupational therapist (OT). The latter's expertise lies in assessing individuals' capacity to perform basic tasks for themselves and providing support in carrying them out where needed.

Key workers have a statutory duty to produce—and regularly update—a care plan individually tailored to each client's needs. This should be made available in writing to the client and/or his or her carer, on request, and cover the following ground:

- the services to be provided (and by whom), when and where this will happen, and what is intended to be achieved by providing them;
- a contact point at which to deal with problems about service delivery;
- information on how to ask for a review of services provided if the client's and/or carer's circumstances change.

Specific concern about the plight of people with serious mental health issues led to the introduction, in 1991, of a more rigorous care plan procedure, known as the 'care programme approach' (or 'care plan approach'). This is broken down into four stages:

1. initial assessment of the client's needs;
2. consultation with all professionals involved, any informal carer, and (depending on their degree of mental capacity) the client themselves;
3. appointment of a key worker;
4. coordination of services agreed on the basis of the initial assessment by that key worker.

## The role of home carers

Britain's rapidly ageing population, coupled with the growing emphasis on community-based care over residential arrangements, has led to a huge rise in the number of carers—defined as people who spend at least part of their lives looking after elderly and/or disabled relatives or friends in their or the other person's home. Some 6 million Britons identified themselves as carers in the 2001 census.

Long-running campaigns by support groups set up to help home carers have led to belated recognition of their work, initially through the 1996 Act (which entitled them to limited respite care), and the National Carers' Strategy established by Mr Blair in 1999. This ten-year strategy, renewed by Gordon Brown in 2008, made the commitments listed in the table entitled 'The main points  of Labour's ten-year "National Carers' Strategy"', to be found on the Online Resource Centre that accompanies this book.

In practice, although it has undeniably improved the situation for some, the strategy was just that. Recent studies suggest that carers still feel isolated, undervalued, and bewildered by the often labyrinthine network of services and providers theoretically available to them, and the bureaucratic, jargon-laden processes involved in accessing them. Of the 400 carers interviewed in a survey of carers' views in summer 2006 for the Princess Royal Trust for Carers' 'Duty to Care' campaign, more than half confessed to having felt like walking out on the person for whom they cared. Fifty-six per cent said they felt 'depressed', 71 per cent 'stressed', and 86 per cent 'frustrated'. Towards the end of its tenure, Mr Brown's government began to pressurize strategic health authorities to do more in their areas to identify and support the needs of isolated home carers. Despite making emollient noises towards carers early on, the coalition had yet to unveil any firm proposals to improve their lot at time of writing.

## Choice in community care—the rise of direct payments

As if negotiating the maze of options available to those in community care—and the mountains of paperwork that accompany them—was not already mind-boggling enough, recent governments have put service users and carers more directly in the driving seat as part of their 'choice' agenda (see p. 160). The Tories introduced this concept, in the Community Care (Direct Payments) Act 1996. This enabled cash payments to be made by local authorities to dependent individuals, enabling them to 'buy' their own care services from the providers of their choice. This approach was not mandatory and authorities were required to ensure that any individual to whom they paid money had the capacity to take informed decisions about their needs and locate and access suitable services. In some cases—when there was evidence that the money had been spent on things other than services related to the client's needs (for example, alcohol or gambling)—councils could halt direct payments and even require that the money paid thus far be refunded.

In 'policy and practice guidance' issued in 2000, Labour made it clear it intended to retain some form of direct payment system, stating it wanted to see 'more extensive use made' of it. In January 2006 a *White Paper* entitled *Our Health, Our Care, Our Say* outlined plans to roll it out further, taking in groups of clients who, until then, had been seen as having insufficient capacity to make decisions for themselves due to the nature of their conditions. These included:

- young disabled people whose parents have managed a direct payment on their behalf and whose payments may have to stop when they reach 18;
- people with dementia, where the use of direct payments is not set out in a power of attorney (PoA) agreement—a legally binding document detailing the individual(s) authorized to handle the affairs of their estate;
- people with more profound learning disabilities.

Variously known as 'individual budgets', 'personal budgets', and now once again direct payments, this approach has divided campaigners for the elderly and mentally ill. While some have welcomed the flexibility it allows capable service users to seek out the medical and psychological support (not to mention social and leisure opportunities) best suited to them, others argue that vulnerable individuals in dire need of care and/or treatment may end up losing out on help to which they are entitled because of the complexity of negotiating the system and managing their own accounts. An in-depth 2008 evaluation of the impact of individual budgets (as they were then known) in 13 pilots areas found that, while working-age people with mental health difficulties had responded positively to them on the whole, they were causing 'anxiety and stress' to elderly service users—many of them concerned that, after a lifetime spent under a top-down NHS and social services model, they were suddenly being expected to shop around for their own support.

→
see also
central
govern-
ment,
p. 171

## Care homes, nursing homes, and the rise of the private sector

When it is agreed that a person is no longer well and/or capable enough to continue living in his or her own home or that of a carer, arrangements will normally be made for him or her to move into either a long-term residential care home or one with nursing provision (a 'nursing home'). The former is usually a 'low dependency' environment, in which residents can enjoy a relatively independent lifestyle in the company of other people of similar age or with comparable physical and/or mental health needs. A nursing home, in contrast, is targeted at individuals with more severe physical and/or mental impairments—often the very old or those at an advanced stage in the progression of their conditions—who require care provided or supervised by a registered nurse.

Broadly speaking, the process followed when an elderly person reaches the point of requiring residential accommodation is as follows:

- they are assessed by a key worker in a multidisciplinary team and placed in a home that best suits their needs (local authority, voluntary, or private);
- where a private home is chosen, the ability of the person to pay 'the full economic cost' of their care is assessed—taking into account the value of property in their name, which might be sold to contribute to care home fees.

Since the late 1980s there has been a marked increase in the amount of residential care provided by private companies, rather than social services themselves.

In many local authority areas, there are no longer any homes maintained by the council directly: all are owned and managed by the private or voluntary sectors. Under the Tories' 'mixed economy of care', residents in private homes could claim a 'social security residential care allowance', which they had to pass to the owner, and a small 'personal allowance', which they could keep for themselves.

But those in local authority homes were not entitled to the former—a fact that meant the final 'bill' presented for the care of individuals admitted to them often appeared superficially higher. This was used by the government as leverage to argue that councils were being 'excessive' with their charges. Opposition leaders at the time accused ministers of making it a pretext to expand the private sector and undermine councils, particularly when a special transitional grant (STG) was made available to them, on condition that they spent 85 per cent of the money provided on arranging private sector residential placements.

In tandem with the expansion of private sector provision and the rising fees that followed, Mr Major's government risked infuriating the 'grey vote' with new moves to divide the cost of residential care between state and individual. Under the 1990 Act, anyone with assets of £16,000 or more—including the homes in which they lived until being admitted into residential care—was expected to pay for themselves up to the point at which that money was exhausted (at which stage the state would take over). In practice this meant that many people—particularly widows and widowers whose homes were entirely in their possession—ended up being 'forced' to sell the houses and flats for which they had spent much of their working lives paying. The 'capital/assets limit' remains in place, but was raised to £18,500 in 2001 and £22,250 in 2008.

So politically combustible had this issue become by the end of New Labour's reign, with increasing diagnoses of age-related conditions requiring long-term care, such as Alzheimer's disease and dementia, that then Health Secretary Andy Burnham announced plans for a new 'National Care Service'—to improve homecare provision and stop individuals forced to move into residential/ nursing care from having to sell their homes to pay the fees. His unrealized  plans (which he touted as a legacy for Labour in this century comparable to the NHS it bequeathed in the last) were lambasted by the Tories, who used a high-profile poster campaign to accuse him of planning a 'death tax' on grieving families. They were referring to Mr Burnham's favoured option—revived during his subsequent Labour leadership bid—which was to finance the proposed new service using a 10 per cent levy on all estates (paid after death). At the time, the Tories' proposed alternative was to charge people a one-off 'voluntary' payment of £8,000 at age 65—a fee critics pointed out would be beyond the means of many. In July 2010, the *coalition government* launched an independent commission to consider all options for funding long-term care, including its preferred voluntary insurance scheme and a compulsory levy.

Another source of tension that emerged around the same time was that between social services departments and the NHS over how to provide for people not yet considered in need of residential care but who experienced frequent, sometimes prolonged, periods of ill health necessitating hospital treatment. Hard-pressed acute hospitals—already struggling with long waiting lists—increasingly became the subject of newspaper and television news reports as they combated 'bed blockage' ('bed-blocking'): the need to cater for vulnerable patients too sick to be sent home, but for whom a residential care space was either not yet felt to be necessary or not available.

Given that more than half of people aged over 65 now have a disabling condition requiring long-term care and that the British population is ageing fast, it is no wonder bed-blocking remains a serious issue as councils struggle to find enough care home places to meet demand—particularly for those with unusual and/or debilitating ailments. Yet critics argue the government's answer has merely been to intensify the pressure, by getting tough with local authorities found 'guilty' of contributing to bed-blocking, rather than concentrating on boosting the number of residential care places. Under the Community Care (Delayed Discharges etc.) Act 2003, NHS hospitals may fine their local councils up to £120 a day for every 'blocked' bed—a rule condemned by the Local Government Association. The Act was motivated, in part, by a 2001 *Audit Commission* report that found two out of three patients in English hospitals at any one time were aged over 65—with around 5,000 people on any given day unnecessarily stuck on acute wards. To discourage hospitals from discharging patients prematurely, Health Secretary Andrew Lansley announced in June 2010 that those having to readmit the same individuals within a month of sending them 'home' would receive no extra funding if they were to have to treat them again for the same condition.

→ see also central government, p. 178

## Regulation of social care

→ see also central government, p. 180

The regulator charged with ensuring high-quality care standards are provided throughout England is the *Care Quality Commission (CQC)*. In the social care field, it is responsible for inspecting day centres, care homes, domiciliary care agencies, nurses' agencies, children's homes, and residential *special schools*.

All residential care and nursing homes must be formally registered under the Registered Homes (Amendment) Act 1991 (previously the Registered Homes Act 1984), but since 2004 the 18,500 listed homes have also had to register separately with the Commission. On inspection, all care organizations (including agencies) are rated under a star system. The meanings of these classifications are as follows:

- no stars—poor;
- one star—adequate;

- two stars—good;
- three stars—excellent.

Following an inspection, or subsequent investigation, the Commission may use its statutory powers either to demand that an organization meets specified 'conditions to improve', to bring it up to the agreed national minimum standards, or in extreme cases to force its immediate closure. In addition, instances of abuse or neglect may be referred to the police and/or Crown Prosecution Service (CPS). The Commission is especially vigilant in relation to adults with serious mental or physical disabilities or impairments that are seen to put them at greater risk of abuse—in line with the 'Protection of Vulnerable Adults' (POVA) scheme introduced in July 2004. As with children in social care, anyone directly involved in caring for vulnerable adults must undergo periodic Criminal Records Bureau (CRB) checks and there are bans on those who have harmed such people in the past from continuing to work with them.

Although the Commission has theoretically tightened up regulation of the increasingly disparate social care 'market', serious concerns have been raised on more than one occasion about the rigour with which its inspections are carried out. In June 2008 an investigation by Radio 4's *Today* programme found that many of the Commission's own inspectors were unhappy with the frequency and quality of its care home inspections. More than 200 employees of the then CSCI—now absorbed into the CQC—participated in an anonymous questionnaire, with one commenting: 'I wouldn't leave my dog in 90 per cent of our care homes.'

## 'Sectioning' the mentally ill

Since the Mental Health Act 1983 councils have had limited powers in relation to mentally infirm adults not in residential care, as outlined in Table 18.9.

## The Mental Health Act 2007

Before it finally received *royal assent* in July 2007, Labour's Mental Health Bill (originally published more than four years earlier) endured one of the rockiest rides of any approved piece of legislation in recent memory. At the heart of the Bill were two key proposals that provoked fury among mental health and human rights campaigners and a high-profile campaign by *The Independent on Sunday*:

- new powers to enable doctors to detain people with serious mental health conditions who might pose a potential risk to themselves or others primarily for the protection of the public—rather than to receive treatment;

**Table 18.9** Powers of social services in relation to the mentally infirm

| Power | Effect |
|---|---|
| Application for compulsory observation | Approved mental health practitioners (AMHPs)—formerly approved social workers (ASWs)—may apply for person to be admitted to hospital for up to 72 hours for compulsory observation, under s. 136 of the Mental Health Act 1983. AMHPs may either be social workers, nurses, occupational therapists (OTs), or psychologists. Their application must be supported by two *responsible clinicians*—formerly responsible medical officers (RMOs). These may be social workers, nurses, OTs, or psychologists—not only GPs and/or psychiatrists, as was the case previously. In 'emergencies', applications may go ahead with only one RMO's endorsement. |
| Appointment of 'nearest relatives' | Applications for people to be admitted to mental hospital normally subject to consent by nearest relative. If AMHP believes consent is being withheld 'unreasonably', he or she can apply to courts for order appointing someone else to assume 'nearest relative' rights. |
| Application to extend observation | Observation order may be granted for up to 28 days if hospital psychiatrist sees fit under s. 2 of the Act. Following this (or sometimes from outset), six-month renewable treatment period may be agreed under s. 3 of Act. This may be renewed after initial six months, subject to approval by mental health review tribunal (MHRT) and with patient and/or nearest relative given right to appeal against decision. Further renewal may be made after 12 months and thereafter at yearly intervals. |
| Application for warrants | If AMHP believes mentally disordered person is being ill-treated or neglected on private property, he or she may make application to magistrate for warrant to search premises. |
| Assumption of the role of 'guardian' | Social services authorities can be appointed 'guardians' to mentally ill people unlikely to respond to hospital treatment, but needing protection. Private individuals can be appointed, too—but only with council's consent. |

- that clinicians (doctors and psychiatrists) were to be given authority to 'impose' treatment on the severely mentally ill, regardless of their wishes and even if judged to have the mental capacity to make their own decisions.

At various stages the Bill was opposed by campaign groups across the gamut—most notably the Mental Health Alliance, a coalition of 78 organizations, including Mind, the King's Fund, and various bodies representing practitioners in the field. In the end it was watered down, although the ability of doctors to prescribe enforced medication remained in the final version.

The Act's other main features are listed in Table 18.10.

Prior to the final passage of the 2007 Act, Labour introduced a marginally less controversial reform in the guise of the Mental Capacity Act 2005, which sought to enshrine the rights of people with severe mental health issues to exercise power over their own care that legally had previously only existed in

**Table 18.10** Main provisions of the Mental Health Act 2007

| Provision | Effect |
| --- | --- |
| New definition of 'mental disorder' | Rationalized system by abolishing references to different types of condition. |
| Detention only if relevant treatment available | Introduced new 'appropriate medical treatment' test preventing patients being compulsorily detained unless medical treatment appropriate to their disorder and all other circumstances of case is available to them. Pre-existing 'treatability test' abolished. |
| Extension of 'sectioning' powers to wider range of professionals | Broadened group of professional practitioners allowed to perform functions previously undertaken by ASWs and RMOs (now AMHPs and responsible clinicians). |
| New rights for patients to challenge 'nearest relatives' | Gave patients right to apply to displace nearest relative, with county courts also allowed to do so on 'reasonable grounds'. Awarded civil partners nearest relative status in same way as husbands and wives. |
| More community supervision of discharged patients | Introduced supervised community treatment (SCT) for patients following periods of hospital detention. Aim is to allow 'small number' of patients with mental disorders to live in community while subject to certain conditions under 1983 Act (as amended by 2007 Act), to ensure that they continue with required medical treatment. Intention is to address 'revolving door' whereby some patients discontinue medication in community and end up being detained again. |
| Fast-track mental health review process to safeguard patient and 'nearest relative' rights | Reduced amount of time before cases must be referred to Mental Health Review Tribunal, and introduced single MHRT for England, modelled on existing single one for Wales. |
| Services customized more to different age groups | Improved 'age-appropriate services'—ensuring people under age of 18 are accommodated suitably, rather than on adult wards. |
| Professional advocacy for all patients | Entitled every detained patient to independent mental health advocate. |
| More emphasis on therapy and non-invasive treatments | Introduced new safeguards limiting use of electro-convulsive therapy (ECT). |

common law. The Act covered only England and Wales, but similar provisions had earlier been made north of the border under the Adults with Incapacity (Scotland) Act 2000.

The Act also introduced:

- a new *Independent Mental Capacity Advocate Service (IMCAS)* for England and another for Wales from 2007;
- new criminal offences of 'wilful neglect' and 'ill treatment';
- ability of service users to nominate 'substitute decision-makers' to their nearest relatives under a new lasting power of attorney (LPA);
- a new *Court of Protection* with extended powers.

Figure 18.1 is a human interest news story from the *Oxford Mail* newspaper focusing on the topical issue of the rising costs of home care for the elderly and disabled. Your news editor asks you to use this couple's experience as the peg for an in-depth feature looking at the dilemmas and difficulties service users face in fighting for the right to continue living in their own homes. How would you expand on the Thompsons' story, who else would you approach for interviews, and what questions would you ask (and of whom) to add context?

**Figure 18.1** A human interest news story from the *Oxford Mail*, 30 April 2010

# Family's alarm at care costs

Amanda Williams

*Oxford Mail*
30 April 2010

Web link: http://www.oxfordmail.co.uk/sport/omboysleague/archive/2009_2010/2010/04/30/Other+news+%28hs_other_news%29/8129332.Family_s_alarm_at_care_costs/

A woman fears her husband may be forced into a home because of the rising cost of care in Oxfordshire.

It comes after consumer watchdog Which? revealed the county has one of the highest rates for home care in the country.

Oxfordshire County Council charges up to £17.68 per hour for help with care such as getting washed, dressed, and fed.

It means the county is the second most expensive local authority after Cheshire East at £17.76. In some parts of London care is free.

About 2,600 people qualify for carers, most of them over 65, although it is available to all disabled residents.

Ken Thompson, 70, from Goring, was diagnosed with vascular dementia almost ten years ago.

His round-the-clock home care was paid for by NHS Oxfordshire, but this month his wife, Glynne, 62, discovered responsibility is being handed to Oxfordshire County Council's social care team.

She said a cloud hung over how much they will have to pay, adding: 'I have no idea what is going to happen now.

'Ken needs care from 8 a.m. to 8 p.m., which if I have to pay for I simply can't afford.

'All I want is for Ken to spend his last precious days at home. If they decide it would be cheaper for him to be in a nursing home I will fight them all the way.

'I would rather he died at home, with me, in dignity, than in a nursing home.'

Oxfordshire County Council said it received less money than many other councils.

A spokesman added: 'Some of those with higher resources choose to use them not to charge for adult social care.

'We are not in a position to do that without increasing council tax.'

County Hall said people's financial circumstances were assessed and they were asked to contribute what they could afford.

The spokesman added: 'In practice this means approximately half of all people receiving home care in Oxfordshire are assessed to pay nothing towards the cost of their care, and very few pay the full amount quoted.'

NHS Oxfordshire declined to comment.

But Paul Cann, Chief Executive of Age Concern Oxfordshire, called for an overhaul of the system. He said: 'Many older people and their families are bewildered and distressed by the care system.'

Which? chief executive Peter Vicary-Smith said: 'Everyone should have comparable access to the care and support they need to remain independent and in their own home, regardless of where they live.'

Which? gathered the figures by carrying out a Freedom of Information request on 212 councils.

## ✳ Current issues

- **Expansion of self-directed support:** Labour began a large-scale move away from the traditional means by which social care in the community had been funded (a top-down approach, with professionals applying for funds on behalf of the service-users for whom they were responsible). It introduced a system of 'self-directed support', which gave service users themselves and/or their carers direct control of their own budgets—leaving them to 'shop around' for suitable services. The coalition plans to move further and faster in this direction, giving direct payments to carers to ensure that they are able to seek out and apply for their own respite care more easily.

- **Review of long-term care:** one of the most heated election issues was the question of how to fund future long-term care for the elderly and/or seriously ill or disabled. For 20 years or more, individuals moving into long-term care have been expected to sell their homes to pay for it (unless there is someone else still living there), but in its manifesto Labour proposed introducing a National Care Service, funded by some form of estate levy that was likely to take account of individuals' ability to pay. The Conservatives have launched a review into future funding of long-term residential care.

- **Review of child social work:** a 'fundamental review' of child protection practices was launched by the coalition on entering office, in an effort to identify and recommend ways of ensuring that child social workers can spend more time dealing directly with children. Following the scandals in local authority areas such as Doncaster, where a series of serious case reviews remained hidden from councillors and the public until a local newspaper exposed them, all local safeguarding children's boards have also been told they must publish the overview reports and executive summaries of all future serious case reviews.

## ❓ Review questions

1. What is the definition of 'children in need'? Outline the main responsibilities of local authority social services departments in relation to such children.

2. What were the main reforms arising from the Victoria Climbié Inquiry and the 'Every Child Matters' agenda? What are 'children's trusts'?

3. What is the difference between adoption and fostering? Outline the processes for adopting or fostering, and the range and types of people entitled to adopt or foster under British law.

4. What is meant by the term 'community care'? What are the main types of support available to the elderly and mentally ill under this policy?

5. Outline the purpose and powers of the Care Quality Commission.

## → Further reading

Blackman, T., Brody, S., and Convery, J. (eds) (2001) *Social Care and Social Exclusion: A Comparative Study of Older People's Care in Europe*, London: Palgrave Macmillan. **Thoughtful and informative comparisons between different approaches taken by six states—including Britain—to providing social care for elderly.**

Leff, J. (1997) *Care in the Community: Illusion or Practice?* London: Wiley-Blackwell. **Critical evaluation of the impact of the Conservative Party's 'Care in the Community' policies on the mentally ill and those who treat them.**

Philpot, T. (2007) *Adoption: Changing Families, Changing Times*, London: Routledge. **Examination of British adoption laws, focusing on real-life stories and recent changes to open up the process to same-sex and unmarried couples.**

Stanley, J. and Goddard, C. (2002) *In the Firing Line: Violence and Power in Child Protection Work*, London: Wiley-Blackwell. **Thoughtful insight into the pressures faced by child social workers and other professionals in identifying and protecting children in need, containing recent case studies.**

##  Online Resource Centre

www.oxfordtextbooks.co.uk/orc/Morrison2e/
Visit the Online Resource Centre that accompanies this book for web links and regular updates.

# 19

# Transport, environment, and 'quality of life' issues

As we have seen from previous chapters, the bulk of local authorities' time and money is spent raising and allocating funds, administering the planning process, and managing (if not always directly delivering) core services like schools, housing, and social care. But beyond these complex and costly policy areas, councils are responsible for a range of other things: maintaining roads and arranging them into bus routes; licensing pubs and nightclubs; inspecting hotels and restaurants; and running museums, theatres, and libraries. This broad sweep of service areas—covering everything from public transport to environmental health and trading standards—is where the basic utilitarian needs represented by the core spending areas listed above make way for those that might broadly be described as about 'quality of life'. It is these that are the focus of this penultimate chapter.

## ▌ Highways and public transport

One of the prime motivators behind the emergence of local government in the UK was the promotion of production and trade, and the need to service the rapidly evolving agricultural and manufacturing economy ushered in by the Industrial Revolution. To this end, the embryonic councils of the nineteenth century became preoccupied with two broad areas of policy designed to facilitate the expansion of this new economy:

- *highways and transport*—specifically, the movement of workers and goods from country to town and between markets, and the maintenance of proper roads;

→
see also
central
govern-
ment,
p. 176

- *Public health*—the provision of housing and sanitation of sufficiently high quality to cater for the workers on whose labour the new economy was founded. Today, this is split between local authorities' housing functions (see Chapter 17), environmental health and waste management services, and local authorities' recently boosted scrutiny role in relation to the National Health Service.

For hundreds of years the only public highways of a decent navigable standard were the remains of Roman roads and others built from the Tudor period onwards by local parish councils. But the growth of commerce and long-distance trade in the eighteenth century meant industrialists and merchants soon woke up to the need for their goods to be transported as speedily and safely as possible. This led to an increase in the level of private investment in highways.

The main developments early on in the history of highways and public transport are outlined in Table 19.1.

## Types of road and the highways authorities responsible for them

The construction and maintenance of Britain's labyrinthine road network is today divided between multiple authorities. Minor roads and more major ones linking two or more towns together are usually maintained by the relevant local

**Table 19.1** Timeline of emergence of road-building in Britain

| Date | Development |
| --- | --- |
| Eighteenth century | Emergence of 'Turnpike trusts' (an early form of public–private partnership), with locally based companies given parliamentary powers to build and maintain specific sections of road. This was financed by levying tolls on road-users—a system now being revisited in some areas of UK. |
| 1816 | Convex road-building technique pioneered in Bristol by John Macadam to improve drainage and the camber for transporting heavy loads. This is subsequently adopted nationwide. |
| 1888 | Responsibility for maintaining public roads in each area handed to newly emerging county councils. |
| 1959 | First section of M1, Britain's first major national **trunk road**, opened between Berrygrove, Hertfordshire, and Crick, Northamptonshire. |
| 1968 | Final stretch of M1 completed after being extended several times into Yorkshire. |
| 1973 | First section of London orbital motorway, the M16 (later renamed M25), built between South Mimms and Potters Bar, Hertfordshire. |
| 1986 | M25 officially opened by Margaret Thatcher on completion of section between junctions 22 and 23 (London Colney and South Mimms). |

authorities (county councils, unitary authorities, or metropolitan *borough councils*), but the longest and widest (A-roads and M-roads, or motorways) are normally the direct responsibility of the *Secretary of State* for Transport. Upkeep of these primary roads falls to the *Highways Agency*, an *executive agency* of the Department of Transport (DoT). While highway maintenance may sound like the dullest possible subject for a news story, inadequate street lighting, potholes, and general road disrepair are among the most common causes of complaints to local authorities (which in itself is arguably newsworthy). The main road designations and authorities responsible for them are outlined in Table 19.2.

New highways are usually either the result of deliberate local and/or central government road-building schemes—in which case they are automatically 'adopted' as the responsibility of the relevant authority once built—or an incidental effect of the laying out of a new housebuilding programme. In the latter case, the developer behind the scheme will normally enter a formal agreement

**Table 19.2** Types of road and the authorities responsible for them

| Road type | Definition | Authority |
|---|---|---|
| Trunk roads (M and major A-roads) | Major roads linking one town or city with another and/or connecting them to ports and airports. Normally divided into at least dual carriageway layout, the biggest are multi-lane motorways. M25 will shortly become an eight-lane motorway, with one stretch (between junctions 12 and 14) boasting ten. | Secretary of State for Transport and Highways Agency |
| **County roads** (A roads) | Major arterial roads (almost all A-roads) linking smaller towns together and normally falling within boundaries of single county. | County councils, unitary authorities, metropolitan borough councils, and individual London boroughs |
| Secondary roads (B roads), and public bridleways and footpaths | B-roads and smaller roads in both rural and urban areas, particularly those linking villages, hamlets, and smaller settlements. Bridleways and footpaths often little more than dirt tracks, following lines of medieval or more ancient routes and paths through fields and woodland. | Local authorities (as above) |
| Private roads | Highways contained within boundaries of private estate like Canary Wharf, east London, or City of London. | Private estates and related businesses (e.g. Canary Wharf)—unless road has been formally adopted by relevant local authority under Private Street Works Act 1892 |

with the planning authority to ensure that it can hand over responsibility for the roads as soon as the development is complete. Such agreements are backed with 'bonds' issued by banks or building societies to ensure that, if the developer enters receivership or defaults, the roads will be finished without expense to local taxpayers.

In some circumstances, however, highways—normally footpaths or bridleways—may be closed or diverted to enable development. There are two main ways in which this is done:

- if a highway is being closed because it is no longer used, the authority must apply to magistrates for an 'extinguishment order' under the Highways Acts (this will not be granted if there is a proven objection on the basis that the highway *is* still used);
- a highway can sometimes be *realigned* to run around a development, rather than through it, by the granting of a 'public path diversion order' under the terms of various Town and Country Planning Acts.

Developers must carry out detailed research before embarking on their plans to ensure that they have applied for any necessary extinguishment or diversion orders. This is done by consulting a 'definitive rights of way map' maintained by the highways authority.

## The role of the Secretary of State and the Highways Agency

Because of their major infrastructural significance, motorways are designated 'special roads' by the government. In relation to both motorways and trunk roads (other major roads), the Secretary of State is ultimately responsible for:

- *overall policy*—whether and where to build new motorways and A-roads, the use of tolls and other forms of road pricing, and the balance between road-building and investment in public passenger transport via the rail network and airports;
- *planning, improvement, and maintenance*—the logistics of building, repairing, and maintaining major roads, and the implementation of policies on the ground;
- *financing and controlling* the trunk road and motorway programme through taxation.

In practice many important decisions have traditionally been taken in the (soon to be abolished) regional government offices, and much of the maintenance and improvement is overseen by the Highways Agency, which, in turn, subcontracts hands-on engineering work to other companies—for example, UK Highways. In addition, although county councils have long undertaken road maintenance on behalf of the Secretary of State, this, too, is franchised out to private contractors.

There is also an increasingly complex system by which primary, secondary, and unclassified roads can be 'designated' to lower-tier authorities to take control of their day-to-day maintenance to ensure the smooth flow of traffic, and tackle issues like congestion and pollution from noise and petrol fumes. In this way the Secretary of State can 'designate' responsibility for maintaining motorways and major A-roads to London boroughs, while county councils can 'designate' to their local borough and/or district councils. When a road is designated downwards for good this is known as 'de-trunking'.

The Highways Agency, established in 1994, is overseen by its own board, under a chief executive earning £180,000 a year. It boasts seven regional control centres and another 28 outstations from which its traffic officers operate. According to its website, its official statutory responsibility is to oversee the 'operation and stewardship of the strategic road network in England on behalf of the Secretary of State'. The more specific roles of the Highways Agency include:

- managing traffic;
- tackling congestion;
- providing information to road users;
- improving journey times, road safety, and reliability;
- minimizing the impact of the road network on the environment.

The agency, working with the Secretary of State and individual local authorities, is responsible for organizing wide-ranging consultations when major road projects are planned. The main stages in this process are outlined in Table 19.3.

In practice, even at this late stage in the process, road projects often go far from smoothly. A number of high-profile protests have occurred in recent years against major projects, the most famous being the campaign against the 'Newbury Bypass'—a nine-mile stretch of dual carriageway built around the market town of Newbury, Berkshire. From January to April 1996 some 7,000 protestors—ranging from hardcore environmentalists, based at a series of 20 roadside camps along the route, to middle-aged professionals and pensioners—picketed a 360-acre site in an effort to thwart the building programme, which involved the felling of 120 acres of ancient woodland. In the end the work went ahead, but not before the cost of policing the protest (dubbed 'Operation Prospect') had topped £5m, and that of hiring private security firms to erect fences and patrol the perimeter had reached £24m.

Other notable protests include those over the construction of the A30 between Exeter and Honiton in Devon, which saw a network of tunnels and tree houses built at a road camp near Fairmile. These protests made a media celebrity out  of 'Swampy' (aka self-proclaimed eco-warrior Daniel Hooper), whose later antics included a one-off stint as a panellist on BBC1's current affairs comedy quiz show, *Have I Got News for You*.

**Table 19.3** Main stages in the consultation process for major road projects

| Stage | Procedure |
| --- | --- |
| Consultation document published | Document must cover following criteria:<br>1. description of potential alternative routes;<br>2. project's predicted cost, including explanation of differences between various alternative options;<br>3. environmental impact assessment (EIA) disclosing details of any potential environmental issues arising from project, as stipulated by EU Directives;<br>4. other relevant factors (e.g. potential impact on historical sites). |
| Comments invited on proposal | Copy of consultation document sent to all local authorities affected by proposals. Public exhibition arranged at which proposal explained and alternative solutions discussed. |
| Invitation for alternative schemes | Opponents offered chance to submit objections formally to Secretary of State. |
| Assessment of objections | Views of objectors examined in detail following consultation period. |
| Approval or rejection of proposal | Secretary of State publishes final decision on plan in statement, giving reasons for advocating project and benefits it will bring. |
| Detailed plans for implementation of proposal drafted | Draft orders covering proposed route drawn up—including any **compulsory purchase orders (CPOs)** necessary for it to go ahead. |
| Public inquiry | Discusses in detail any objections to draft order, with directly affected parties invited to speak. Will focus solely on questions about viability of route, its design, and case for it. |
| Final decision | Final say given by Secretary of State once inquiry inspector has heard cases for and against plans and produced report. |

# Recent national reforms of traffic policy

Road-building continues to be an issue of huge controversy across Britain, not least because there is little evidence continuing expansion of the network has done much to ease congestion. In some cases studies suggest the funnelling of government spending away from public transport and into major building programmes is *increasing* the likelihood of traffic jams—by encouraging more people to drive. An independent study by transport consultant Halliburton  published in 2002 predicted an increase in congestion in the M25 corridor of a third by 2016 unless radical steps were taken to persuade people to use public transport. It recommended charging tolls and introducing a luxury bus service around the motorway to lure people out of their cars.

Concern about road policy is arguably one of the rare issues to unite supporters and opponents, albeit from different perspectives: to environmental campaigners, road congestion represents a cause of serious pollution and long-term ecological damage, while motorists and long-distance hauliers view traffic jams as a huge source of discomfort and frustration. Perhaps unsurprisingly, the government has launched a number of initiatives in recent years to address congestion and pollution, as listed in Table 19.4.

**Table 19.4** Major government traffic and transport initiatives since 1997

| Initiative | Effect |
|---|---|
| Traffic Reduction Act 1997 | Required future highway design to take account of need to cut traffic by adding bus lanes and park-and-ride schemes to encourage more people to travel by passenger transport. |
| *A New Deal for Transport: Better for Everyone* (1999) | **White Paper** outlining need for 'integrated transport policy' to increase use of trains and buses. |
| Transport Act 2000 | Created new Commission for Integrated Transport to: <br> 1. advise ministers how to implement integrated transport policy; <br> 2. monitor developments across transport, environment, health, and other areas; <br> 3. review progress towards government objectives. |
| *Transport 2010: The Ten-Year Plan* | Published in July 2000, this gave effect to many ideas in 1999 White Paper. It enshrined following proposals: <br> 1. target to cut traffic congestion by 5 per cent by 2010; <br> 2. local highways authorities allowed to levy charges to ease congestion (see pp. 548–51); <br> 3. Highways Agency to change from being 'road-builder' to 'road network operator' (effectively, road equivalent of **Network Rail**), charged with improving and operating the trunk road network using outside contractors; <br> 4. 60 per cent of trunk roads to be retained as 'core' network of nationally important routes, with others 'de-trunked'; <br> 5. future trunk road planning to be overseen by regional planning guidance (RPG); <br> 6. Highways Agency to work closely with rail companies to improve 'interchanges' between public and private transport; <br> 7. local authorities required to formulate five-year local transport plans to coordinate and improve public transport, promote walking and cycling and green transport plans for journeys to work, school, and elsewhere, and reduce social exclusion (especially in rural areas) by improving bus routes; <br> 8. by end of 1999, councils expected to publish draft transport plans covering 2000–05 (these replaced the existing transport policies and programmes (TPP) system). |
| *The Future of Transport* | This 2004 White Paper introduced the Transport Innovation Fund (TIF), offering financial backing to local authorities and other bodies keen to invest in innovative transport projects. It had two strands: Congestion TIF, offering councils money to invest in congestion charging and related initiatives; and Productivity TIF, which would support projects earmarked by the DfT as 'of national importance'. Beginning in 2008–09, the TIF was to have invested more than £9.5bn in projects by 2014–15, but in June 2010 it was suspended by the Lib-Con coalition. |

Despite this, many road and rail users agree that Britain has some way to go before it can boast anything like the 'integrated transport policy' first promised by then Deputy Prime Minister John Prescott in 1999.

## Local traffic management, road-pricing, and congestion charging

The term 'traffic management' was, for long years, synonymous with little more than road crossings, signs, signals, and diversions—in short, the bread-and-butter mechanisms used to direct traffic from A to B, help pedestrians cross it, and 'warn' motorists about everything from changes in speed limits to steep slopes, sharp bends, and bumpy road surfaces. To a large extent, the day-to-day work of highways authorities remains preoccupied with these and other humdrum concerns—many of which continue to excite the attention of local newspapers and television news outlets. The more workaday responsibilities of highways departments include planning, installing, and monitoring the effectiveness of:

- traffic lights;
- major and mini-roundabouts;
- sleeping policemen (speed bumps) and other forms of 'traffic calming' measures;
- zebra crossings, pelican crossings, and crossings manned by 'lollipop ladies';
- road signage;
- one-way systems;
- 'park and ride' schemes—free bus services to and from town centres;
- dedicated bus and taxi lanes and cycle lanes/paths.

In recent years traffic management has entered a new phase, as pedestrians' and motorists' frustration with mounting congestion has sparked growing calls from both the environmental lobby and the business community for radical action to address what is widely perceived as an unsustainable growth in private car ownership. The prime concern of environmentalists remains the pollution caused by carbon monoxide exhaust fumes and the noise generated by heavy traffic. Business leaders, meanwhile, are increasingly alarmed by the impact of lengthy traffic delays on the smooth running of the economy. A 2005 survey by the Institution of Civil Engineers (ICE) estimated that road traffic was costing UK businesses up to £20bn a year because so many employees were arriving late for work. Similar figures have been quoted by the Confederation of British Industry (CBI).

Faced with the prospect of roads becoming even more clogged, with all of the associated negative impacts on people's quality of life, successive governments have looked to other countries for inspiration in an effort to find a way of luring people out of their cars and onto passenger transport. Given the high cost of travelling by rail and the severe congestion experienced by train commuters on many routes—particularly in south-east England—the 'carrot' of public transport has historically failed to persuade sufficient numbers to leave their cars at home. As a result, during the New Labour era policymaking gradually shifted towards adopting more of a 'stick' approach, focusing on mechanisms borrowed from overseas, like congestion charging and road-pricing (tolls).

## Congestion charging

Originating in Singapore, where it was introduced in 1975, congestion charging is the system by which flat-rate fees are charged to drivers of vehicles entering a specified 'congestion charge zone' (usually in or around a town or city) between specific hours on a given day. In Britain the most famous example of congestion charging to date was introduced by former London Mayor Ken Livingstone in February 2003, initially within a limited central zone broadly defined by the capital's inner ring road. It was extended to cover much of west London in February 2007, although in May 2010 his successor, Conservative Mayor Boris Johnson, outlined plans to scrap this extension by Christmas that year. The charge operates between 7 a.m. and 6 p.m., Monday to Friday, and was initially set at £5 a day. It is currently £8 a day for most qualifying vehicles (£7 for fleet lorries). Drivers may now pay by credit or debit card over the phone, by mobile phone text message, via a dedicated website, or over the counter in shops equipped with a PayPoint facility. Those who fail to pay are fined £120 (or £60 if they make payment within 14 days of receiving the fine).

The congestion charge has won praise from both business leaders and green lobbyists, with various reports suggesting it has significantly cut traffic jams in central London by anything from 8 to 20 per cent. It has won fans in the medical community, too: according to a 2008 study in *Occupational and Environmental Medicine* magazine, its impact on pollution may have already 'saved' up to 1,888 extra 'years of life' among London's 7 million residents. Perhaps unsurprisingly, however, it has infuriated many motorists—including shift workers required to arrive at (or leave) work in central London at unsocial hours, when little or no public transport is available.

On its launch, the charge became the subject of a high-profile campaign by stage actors, including Tom Conti and Samantha Bond ('Miss Moneypenny' in the Pierce Brosnan James Bond films), who cited the plight of low-paid shift workers, but also argued that the timings of the daily charge period would adversely affect the size of audiences for West End performances by penalizing theatregoers for entering the zone in early evening.

Nonetheless, the perceived success of the policy has seen major international cities from New York to Stockholm racing to imitate it, and the before leaving office the Labour government (initially sceptical of Mr Livingstone's plans) had committed itself to rolling it out elsewhere. In June 2008 then Transport Secretary Ruth Kelly approved what would have been the biggest congestion charge scheme introduced anywhere in the world, in the form of a dual-ring zone around Greater Manchester covering an area 12 times bigger than the original London zone. The zone, intended to be introduced in 2013, would have operated at peak times only (from 7–9.30 a.m. and 4–6 p.m.), and Ms Kelly vowed it would be accompanied by a 'world-class public transport system'—funded by £2.8m in public investment, £1.5m of which would come from central government and the remainder from the Association of Greater Manchester Authorities (AGMA). However, in December 2008 the plan was thrown into disarray when local residents rejected it by 79 to 21 per cent in a *referendum*. While Norwich and Edinburgh (whose voters previously rejected the charge) have also shelved their plans indefinitely, by early 2010 Bristol and Bath were still planning a joint application for congestion zone funding to the DfT's Transport Innovation Fund. However, the advent of the Tory-led coalition threw this into question after new Transport Secretary Philip Hammond announced in June that the fund would be suspended with immediate effect as part of his drive to find departmental savings of 25–40 per cent.

In addition to congestion charging itself, in February 2008 Mr Livingstone introduced a 'low-emission zone' encompassing all of Greater London—an area covering 610 square miles (1,580 km$^2$). The worst polluting lorries, buses, and coaches were fined £200 per day for entering the capital. On entering office, Mr Johnson, who had condemned the charge as 'the most punitive, draconian fining regime in the whole of Europe', suspended it, although he was later rumoured to be considering its reintroduction. Meanwhile, individual local authorities—including some in the capital—have experimented with even more novel ways of penalizing the most 'gas-guzzling' vehicles. In January 2007, Richmond became the first of nine London boroughs to introduce higher-rate residents' parking permits for owners of 'Chelsea tractors' and other cars with larger engines. Although the scheme was replicated elsewhere in the UK, after years of protest from residents and motoring organizations like the AA the council finally scrapped the scheme in July 2010.

## Road-pricing

Congestion charging may be flavour of the month among highways authorities seeking to battle traffic problems (while raising a million or two to invest in other local services), but the idea of forcing motorists to pay up-front to use roads is hardly new. In Britain 'road-pricing' was first mooted by John Major's Conservative government, which outlined proposals to introduce a network of privately financed toll roads on major routes, modelled on the system used in

France and other mainland European countries. To date the UK has only one private toll motorway—a 27–mile stretch of the M6 between Coleshill, Warwickshire, and Cannock, Staffordshire, which opened in December 2003. In July 2004, then Transport Secretary Mr Darling announced plans for two 50-mile 'pay-as-you-go' expressways between Wolverhampton and Manchester. But these remain unrealized, and could well remain so in light of figures published by the Campaign for Better Transport in August 2010, which revealed that the private company operating the route, Midland Expressway Ltd, had been running it at an annual loss of £25m.

The Labour government remained ambivalent about private toll roads overall, in light of research into the so-so impact of road-pricing. In January 2005 an answer to a parliamentary question to the DoT revealed that congestion on and around the M6 had actually *increased* since the opening of the existing toll road. Junctions to the south had seen traffic levels rise daily by up to 10,000 vehicles, with those to the north seeing 5,000 extra a day. Altogether, 38,000 additional cars and lorries a day were using both the toll route and the free M6. Ministers' focus has been sharpened by the scale of apparent public opposition to increased road-pricing. In February 2007, 1.7 million people signed an online petition objecting to more tolls—prompting outgoing Prime Minister Tony Blair to write to them collectively, stressing the government's mind had not yet been decided. It never was.

### 'Speed' cameras

The days of roadside safety cameras—used to photograph the number plates of vehicles exceeding official speed limits on major roads, and to award their drivers with fixed penalties for speeding—appeared to be numbered at time of writing, following the coalition's decision to withdraw central government financial support for them. In July 2010, Oxfordshire County Council became the first major local authority to vote to stop funding them. Its decision to end its contributions to the collaborative Thames Valley Safer Roads Partnership, which encompasses several counties, led to speed camera enforcement in Oxfordshire ceasing with immediate effect (although the partnership said it would continue funding cameras elsewhere). There were early indications that other authorities, including Warwickshire County Council, were minded to follow suit.

## Other aspects of highways and transport policy

### Street lighting

Street lighting tends primarily to be the preserve of local highways authorities. As with parking policy (see pp. 555–6), however, district and borough councils often have responsibility for maintaining and repairing roads and pathways delegated to them, along with the budgets required to contract out the necessary work. *Quality parish councils* (see pp. 331–2) are also increasingly taking over the maintenance of individual roads in smaller towns, villages, and other rural settlements.

## Public transport

Since the 1980s privatization of the National Bus Company (Britain's nation-wide bus service provider), the subsequent deregulation of local routes, and the introduction of dedicated passenger transport authorities in metropolitan areas, local authorities have played a diminishing role in providing public transport. As in many policy areas they have largely been reduced to the status of 'enablers'—monitoring the provision of bus, tram, underground, and river boat services by the free market, and stepping in to act as 'providers of last resort' where unacceptable gaps and/or inconsistencies in services emerge.

Under the Local Government Act 1972, the then newly established metropolitan county councils were charged with providing bus services through 'passenger transport executives' designed to promote 'integrated' local transport. But in 1985, this changed when Margaret Thatcher's government replaced the metropolitan counties with metropolitan boroughs and scrapped the GLC, introducing independent passenger transport authorities in these areas. The most famous of these was London Transport—now *Transport for London (TfL)* (see p. 335). At the same time, local authorities' responsibility for providing transport links to and from airports and docks was transferred to new joint boards. The one abiding legacy of the 1972 Act was the transfer of highways and transport responsibilities from borough and district councils to county councils. This remains the case to this day, except in unitary areas.

The effective privatization of local transport was formalized in the Transport Act 1985, with councils expected to provide directly only 'socially necessary' services—for example, those linking villages and smaller towns—and only then when the market had failed to do so. A year later the system was formally deregulated, allowing any number of bus companies to compete on a specific route—known as a 'registered bus route'—provided that they first obtained a 'public service operator's licence' from the **Traffic Commissioners**. Trams, like those operating in urban centres from Manchester to Croydon, had to be similarly licensed.

Under the present licensing regime, there are seven regional Commissioners. Their main responsibilities are to:

- license operators of delivery lorries, or heavy goods vehicles (HGVs), and the operators of buses and coaches—known as 'public service vehicles' (PSVs);
- register local bus services;
- grant vocational licences, and take action against drivers of HGVs and PSVs.

The Traffic Commissioner for Scotland has additional powers that in England and Wales are exercised individually by officers in local authority highways departments. These include determining appeals against taxi fares and charging, and removing improperly parked vehicles in Edinburgh and Glasgow.

One effect of deregulating local bus services was to undermine councils' ability to subsidize public transport. While in some areas the introduction of competition did improve services by pushing down fares, in others the loss of council-run buses deprived residents of heavily subsidized tickets that found no replacement in the privatized marketplace. Among the most celebrated local services were the cut-price buses ushered in by Mr Livingstone in the days of the Greater London Council and the record-breaking 2p fares introduced by future Home Secretary David Blunkett while leader of Sheffield City Council in the 1970s.

Contracting out bus services has also been blamed for the increasing isolation of some local communities, particularly those based in remote villages and hamlets, because—shorn of state subsidies—private companies have been reluctant to maintain, let alone initiate, unprofitable routes. On occasion, poorer suburbs of towns and cities have also been left isolated by private operators' refusal to continue running services there—normally in response to outbreaks of vandalism, or verbal and/or physical violence towards drivers. In June 2006 one of Britain's biggest private bus operators, Stagecoach, briefly suspended services to Hull's Orchard Park estate after receiving 16 separate reports of missiles being thrown at buses in just four days.

While bus service licensing has long since passed to the Commissioners, county councils, unitary authorities, and metropolitan boroughs retain responsibility for issuing licences to the operators of taxi services and minicab firms, including Hackney carriages outside London (where they are licensed by the Commissioner of the Metropolitan Police).

Although deregulation of the buses may have produced a patchy service in many areas, with some now very poorly served, recent years have seen the introduction of generous **concessionary fare schemes** for those who meet certain criteria, such as students, the disabled, and old-age pensioners (OAPs). Local authorities fund the schemes by subsidizing local bus operators the equivalent of the full fares they are 'losing' by implementing them. As of April 2006, all local authorities have had to provide a bare minimum of free off-peak bus fares for pass-holders. And since April 2008 registered OAPs and the disabled have been entitled to free off-peak travel anywhere in England and Wales, rather than simply in their local authority area, as had been the case before. 'Off-peak' is defined as between 9.30 a.m. and 11 p.m. (that is, not the morning rush hour). Both Scotland and Northern Ireland recently introduced equivalent schemes.,

While major public transport infrastructural projects have traditionally been overseen by central government, in recent years there has been a trend towards devolving autonomy for this to local and regional authorities, particularly in metropolitan areas. However, by June 2010 this short-lived era appeared to be nearing an end following the *coalition government*'s abolition of regional development agencies (see pp. 464–6) and its decision to individually review all transport projects yet to secure full *planning permission* and funding. Among the initiatives facing the axe at time of writing (together worth £5.2bn) were phase one of an oft-delayed Tees Valley Metro system linking Teesside to Darlington and a proposed Leeds 'trolleybus' network of electric buses powered by overhead cables.

## Transport for London (TfL)

Transport for London (TfL) is a *quango* charged with managing (if not directly running) the following:

- London buses, Croydon Tramlink, and the Docklands Light Railway;
- the London Underground (the 'Tube') network;
- the Transport for London Road Network (TLRN);
- London River Services—that is, licensed passenger ferries along and across the Thames.

It is also responsible for:

- delivering the Integrated Transport Strategy published by the mayor in July 2001, and revised in 2004 and 2006, in consultation with the Greater London Assembly (GLA);
- regulating taxis and minicabs;
- helping to coordinate the Dial-a-Ride and Taxicard schemes for door-to-door services for transport users with mobility problems;
- installing and maintaining traffic lights across London;
- promoting the safe use of the Thames for passenger and freight movement.

To help to deliver the strategy for London, in 1998 a Transport Committee for London was set up by the GLA to replace the four pre-existing bodies in charge of overseeing the Underground, buses, taxis, most main roads running into and through the capital, and the Docklands Light Railway (a privately owned company).

While all this may sound very cooperative and harmonious, at times in the past few years the process of taking decisions about the future of London's transport network has been far from that. Between 1997 and 2001 Mr Blair's government was locked in a tortuous stalemate with Mr Livingstone and London Transport Commissioner Bob Kiley over ministers' insistence on the 'part-privatization' of the underground. Despite widespread criticism about the shambolic selloff of the national rail network, the government went to huge lengths to persuade the mayor to accept a *public–private partnership (PPP)* arrangement (see p. 222), which saw a near-identical model adopted for the Underground, with franchises to run services on individual lines contracted out to competing private companies, while the tracks, signals, stations, and even rolling stock remained in the hands of a separate authority (in this case, TfL). With the Underground, the proposed management/ownership split was actually three-way, rather than two-way, as with the railways—with companies contracted to carry out the £13bn, 15-year programme of improvements on the Underground infrastructure given a stake in it, too. But under an 11th-hour compromise agreed between Mr Blair and Mr Kiley, the Commissioner was ultimately offered a 'golden share' in the infrastructure companies—giving him the power to sack their chief executives, appoint his own representatives to their boards, intervene in their maintenance programmes, and even challenge their internal budgets and share policies.

More recently, TfL was involved in the protracted negotiations over Crossrail—the proposed new £16bn overland train link bringing 24 overland rail services an hour through the heart of London from Maidenhead, Berkshire, in the west, eastwards to Essex. The project was finally approved in September 2007, after a decade of deliberation, and despite fears to the contrary the coalition has committed to pursuing it.

## Car parking

Responsibility for administering and policing car parking is broadly divided between local authorities as outlined in Table 19.5.

Until relatively recently, car-parking responsibilities were split fairly clearly in two-tier areas between borough/district councils and counties, with the former managing off-road car parks and the latter on-street parking. In many areas these distinctions are blurred today, with some district councils entering into agency agreements with neighbouring counties, and vice versa, effectively to contract out these functions to the other. To confuse the public further, while the fixed-penalty fines system tends to be administered by county councils or unitary authorities, the actual issuing of penalty notices—the action of placing them on parked vehicles—has traditionally been performed by traffic wardens

**Table 19.5** Types of local authority responsible car-parking services

| Type of parking | Local authority |
| --- | --- |
| On-street and residents' parking schemes | Traditionally county councils and unitary authorities, but now administered by all types of council (subject to local arrangements) |
| Open-air car parks on public or council-owned land | Traditionally district/borough councils and unitary authorities, but now depends on local arrangements |
| Multi-storey car parks | Private firms like National Car Parks Ltd (NCP) |
| Car parks at hospitals, colleges, universities, and business premises | Run by organizations themselves, increasingly using private contractors |

employed by local police forces. This recently changed, with council-employed parking attendants taking over the role in most areas—and themselves being redesignated 'civil enforcement officers' in 2009.

As with traffic management, parking issues have a habit of raising the blood pressure of motorists—and, as a result, provide the raw material for frequent news stories. A common misconception—fuelled by countless local newspaper reports to this effect—is that wardens and attendants are paid commissions or 'bonuses' related to the number or value of the fixed-penalty notices that they issue. In fact, the government legislated to prevent this happening in the Traffic Wardens and Parking Attendants Act 2005. So combustible has the car-parking issue become in recent years, nonetheless, that ticket recipients may now appeal to a National Parking Adjudication Service (NPAS).

# ▌ Waste management and environmental health

Public health has been on the local authority agenda for longer than almost anything else. A chronology of major Public Health Acts and other relevant legislation is given in Table 19.6.

**Table 19.6** Chronology of public health legislation in the UK

| Law | Reform |
| --- | --- |
| Public Health Acts 1872 and 1875 | Local boards of health and sanitary authorities set up |
| Public Health Act 1936 | Public health responsibilities transferred to new local authorities |
| Public Health Acts 1948–74 | Public health responsibilities—other than environmental health—gradually transferred from local authorities to NHS |
| Environmental Protection Act 1990 | Earlier Acts consolidated to summarize councils' responsibilities, creating new environmental services departments |
| Food Safety Act 1990 (adapted for Scotland and Northern Ireland) | New powers of inspection and criminal prosecution given to **environmental health officers** |
| Food Safety Act 1999 | Food Standards Agency (FSA) established, roles of local inspectors clarified, and more all-encompassing environmental services departments introduced |
| Public Health White Paper 2010 | Proposed transfer of FSA's control of nutrition policy to Department of Health and food labelling to Department for Environment, Food, and Rural Affairs (Defra), with FSA retaining charge of vetting food safety |

The task of ensuring that housing, businesses, and local amenities in a given area conform to basic hygiene and safety standards today falls to district/borough council and unitary authority environmental health departments. Of their myriad responsibilities by far the most costly and complex are those related to the effective organization of waste management services—an area so broad it requires the active involvement of every type of council.

# Waste collection, recycling, and waste disposal

There are two overriding aspects to waste management, each handled by a different type of local authority in two-tier areas:

- *waste collection*—district or borough councils, unitaries, and metropolitan boroughs;
- *waste disposal*—county councils, unitaries, and metropolitan boroughs.

### Waste collection

Throughout the UK household and business waste collection has traditionally been carried out in the form of weekly door-to-door services. In recent years, however, a growing number of local authorities have introduced fortnightly collections to save money, while the nature of 'rubbish collecting' itself has changed, with a growing emphasis on recycling, rather than the simple disposal of refuse at 'tips' (landfill sites).

As with most areas of local service delivery, waste collection is periodically put out to tender (see pp. 384–7), with the result that many 'bin men and women' are now employed not by councils directly but private contractors hired on their behalf. Having started out with kerbside recycling points at supermarkets, parks, and other public amenities, many collection authorities in England and Wales now operate at least a fortnightly door-to-door recycling service. The operator contracted to collect the normal, non-recyclable household and/or business waste (food waste, plastics, etc.) may not be the same one picking up the recycling.

Despite dramatically increasing its levels of recycling in recent years, Britain was slow to embrace it compared to most European countries. As a result, Labour ministers considered increasingly fiendish ways of cajoling or forcing householders and businesses to recycle more waste. The most controversial of these was the mooted introduction of 'pay-as-you-throw' fines for people who chuck away too much 'black bin waste', with commensurate 'rebates' for those who disproportionately use their green bins. Then Environment Secretary David Miliband announced plans to give councils the power to charge for excessive black bin waste in May 2007 as part of the government's drive to force councils to recycle at least 40 per cent of waste by 2010 and 50 per cent by 2020. Under the Climate Change Act 2008, trials of bin taxes began in 2009 in five pilot areas, policed by a new breed of unelected quangos, known as 'joint waste authorities', which in future would potentially have the power to set new taxes. Not content to wait for the outcome of the government's pilots, some local authorities launched the pay-as-you-throw concept off their own backs: in September 2006, Woking Borough Council was accused of snooping on households after installing electronic chips capable of weighing 'residual' (non-recyclable) waste in its wheelie bins. But on entering office, coalition Communities Secretary Eric Pickles abandoned the concept—announcing plans to 'incentivize' households to recycle, rather than punish those that did not, by rewarding the diligent with vouchers to be used in their local shops, restaurants, or leisure centres. This idea was based on a popular pilot run by Windsor and Maidenhead Council, Berkshire—earmarked by David Cameron as a potential standard-bearer for his volunteer-led 'Big Society' approach to running local services (see p. 387).

Whether carrot or stick wins out in the end, British councils are facing an uphill struggle to meet European Union recycling targets over the coming decade: a 1999 directive specified that the amount of biodegradable waste dumped at UK landfill sites—equivalent to 18.1m tonnes in 2003–04—should be cut to 13.7m tonnes by 2010, 9.2m tonnes in 2013, and 6.3m in 2020. Failure to meet these targets would see the government fined £180m a year by the *European Commission*. At time of writing, Britain was on course to meet its first target by the end of the 2010.

## Waste disposal

The Environmental Protection Act 1990 required all waste disposal authorities to form arm's-length waste disposal companies (LAWDCs) to dispose of refuse on their behalf—a form of direct service organization (DSO) (see p. 385). In turn, these were required to 'hire' waste disposal contractors (in practice, either the company itself or another franchisee) to:

- provide the waste transfer and landfill sites to which householders can take large items of waste (for example, electrical goods) for landfill or destruction;
- dispose of items collected from local people's homes by collection operators;
- recycle waste or sell it for scrap.

Contractors running waste disposal sites on behalf of local authorities must obtain waste management licences (WML) from the *Environment Agency* in England and Wales. In Scotland applications must be made to the Scottish Environmental Protection Agency (SEPA), and in Northern Ireland to the Department of the Environment (Environment and Heritage Service).

Because the EU has stepped up its use of targets to promote recycling, the issue of straightforward rubbish dumping has become acutely politically sensitive in Britain over the past 15 years. Faced with rapidly dwindling capacity at the country's existing landfill sites, successive governments have sought to deter local authorities from continuing to dump waste in the age-old tradition. Perhaps the most contentious mechanism they have used is the Landfill Tax. Introduced under the Conservatives in the Finance Act 1996, this was initially levied on councils, waste disposal companies, and other organizations involved in dumping rubbish at a standard rate of £7 a tonne and a reduced rate of £2 a tonne. In its 1999 Budget, Labour raised the standard rate to £10 a tonne and introduced a 'Landfill Tax accelerator' designed to increase it by a further £1 a tonne each year until 2004. In his 2002 Pre-Budget Report, then Chancellor Mr Brown announced further stepped rises, with the medium to long-term aim of charging £35 a tonne. For 2010–11, the two rates were as follows:

- *standard rate*—£48 a tonne (rising by a further £8 a tonne each year until at least 2014) for household waste that may decay and/or contaminate land;
- *reduced rate*—£2.50 a tonne for rocks and soils, ceramics and concrete, unused minerals, furnace slag, ash, low-activity inorganic compounds, and water.

To ameliorate the impact of the Landfill Tax on site operators, Mr Major's Environment Secretary, John Gummer, introduced a Landfill Tax credit scheme designed to reward them with a 90 per cent tax credits against any donations made to an environmental body registered with the scheme's regulator, Entrust. This was, however, capped at 20 per cent of their Landfill Tax liability. Labour later introduced a Landfill Allowance Trading Scheme (LATS), overseen by Defra (under the Waste and Emissions Trading Act 2003), to allow individual waste disposal authorities with surplus landfill space to 'sell' it to those in 'deficit' in the manner of carbon trading. Rows over the Landfill Tax and recycling targets are not the only reasons the issue of waste disposal is so constantly in the news. In 2005 an investigation for BBC1's *Real Story* programme found that 500 tonnes of supposedly recycled waste from UK households had actually been dumped by contractors in Indonesia—raising concerns that British citizens might be salving their consciences over recycling at the expense of developing countries. Around the same time, EA figures revealed that half the 8m tonnes of green waste generated each year in Britain finished up overseas.

## Air quality, noise pollution, fly-tipping, and dog fouling

The local authority officials charged with inspecting domestic and business premises to ensure that they meet statutory environmental health standards are environmental health officers. One of their main duties is to investigate complaints relating to waste collection and disposal—or, rather, *lack* of collection and disposal in cases when, for example, a property owner or occupier fails to leave out his or her rubbish or place it in the correct place for removal by the collection authority. They also investigate incidents of 'fly-tipping'—the practice of dumping rubbish on someone else's doorstep or in their backyard, often used by residents or businesses to offload refuse on a neighbouring street after missing their own collection day. Complaints will often arise through a neighbour who reports an unpleasant smell or the unsightly presence of overloaded bin bags days before they are (or were) due to be collected. In extreme cases, rotting waste that has been inadequately stored in bags or dustbins or left out for days before the next collection is due may attract mice or other forms of vermin, necessitating direct intervention by environmental health 'pest controllers' to remove them. The cost of doing so and of ridding the area of vermin will normally be passed straight on to the offending party—and the council may also choose to prosecute them under environmental health legislation. Conviction usually leads to a fine.

Another menace accorded greater priority in recent years has been dog fouling. After years of campaigning by environmental groups and others concerned about the potential danger contact with dog mess poses to young children, so-called 'poop scoops' and dog litter bins have become a common feature of most parks and public rights of way. Yet many areas remain blighted by it today—prompting some local authorities to go so far as to use CCTV cameras to spy on errant dog owners who failed to clean up after their pets. Councils' ability to do this (using anti-terror legislation) sparked a media outcry when it emerged in June 2008, and it is expected to be curbed by coalition Home Secretary Theresa May as part of her wider review of Labour's 'Big Brother' legislation.

→
see also
central
govern-
ment,
pp.
249–51

Other menaces continue to be the subject of strict statutory powers, though. In response to growing pressure on the UK to conform to EU directives, the Pollution Prevention and Control Act 1999 made councils responsible for exercising 'local authority pollution prevention and control' (LAPPC) in relation to so-called 'Part B' industrial installations in their areas. These include smaller power plants, glassworks, waste disposal sites, sewerage works, and municipal and hospital incinerators. More major polluting installations—for example, oil refineries, nuclear power stations, steelworks, and large chemical plants—were designated as 'Part A1' and placed under 'integrated pollution prevention and control' (IPPC) orders overseen by the EA, SEPA, or the Northern Irish Department of the Environment. There is also a third category of process ('Part A2'), which relates to medium-range installations. This, like Part B, is policed by local authorities in the following way:

- applications for a process to be carried out must be made to the relevant authority (if refused, appeals can be lodged with the Environment Secretary);
- if an enforcing authority believes an operator has breached an authorization, it can serve an enforcement notice specifying the nature of the

breach, the steps that need to be taken to rectify it, and a deadline for that work to be completed;

- if the authority feels external factors are creating an imminent risk of serious pollution (even if unconnected with the process itself), it can serve a prohibition notice.

Another newsworthy issue in recent years has been the growing intolerance of 'noise pollution'. In certain circumstances authorities may now seize offending equipment, such as stereos or drills. The Noise Act 1996 empowered them to send in officers to investigate the sources of excessive noise at night and to 'measure' noise levels. Wherever it exceeds statutory limits, warning notices may immediately be served on those responsible. Failure to comply is a criminal offence and officers may subsequently enter properties without a warrant to seize offending equipment. Prosecution often also follows—a fact that, when the first round of cases emerged in the late 1990s, provided endless amusement for local newspaper editors (and presumably readers).

Noise pollution has also been a notable target of government crackdowns on 'antisocial behaviour' (see pp. 340–1). The use of *antisocial behaviour orders (ASBOs)* to tackle it has generated highly newsworthy, occasionally outlandish, outcomes. In March 2005 Andrew Gordon and his 18-year-old son, Phillip, were banned from their own home in Dunfermline for three months under the Anti-Social Behaviour (Scotland) Act 2004 because of severe noise and disruption caused due to drinking, cursing, fighting, and drug-taking at the house at times when Mr Gordon was away.

Action taken against 'unpleasant' smells has also made plenty of headlines. One contentious case involved an award-winning vegetarian cafe in Greenwich, which was ordered to stop serving cooked food in June 2008 after neighbours complained about the smells it produced.

Environmental health officers also oversee various other areas, as listed in Table 19.7.

## Environmental health and food safety

One of the most widely understood duties of environmental health officers (or 'inspectors') is the role they play in promoting food safety by ensuring that restaurants, cafes, pubs, and shops serving food to the public are preparing, cooking, and storing meat and other food items of suitable quality and under appropriate conditions. This role—memorably satirized in the classic 'Basil the Rat' episode of BBC1 sitcom *Fawlty Towers*—covers all aspects of food hygiene, including its sale, importation, preparation, transportation, storing, packing, wrapping, displaying, serving, and delivery.

The Food Standards Act 1999 set up a *Food Standards Agency (FSA)* to oversee food hygiene and animal husbandry issues at a national level, while

**Table 19.7** Additional responsibilities of environmental health officers

| Responsibility | Definition |
| --- | --- |
| Litter | Local authorities, 'statutory undertakers' (companies contracted by councils to run services on their behalf), and other public landowners legally bound to keep their land free of litter. If council designates a specific 'litter control area', it becomes offence for anyone to throw, drop, or dispose of litter on land owned by public body in that area. |
| General health risks | If measures for preserving public health fail and diseases like dysentery, smallpox, typhoid—or, more recently, foot and mouth—break out, authority must inform NHS and local community physician or Director of Public Health. |
| Maintaining public areas | These range from public parks and playgrounds to cemeteries. |
| Vermin control | Taking action to tackle infestations of rodents, insects, etc.—if necessary charging private individuals after the event, should infestation relate to privately owned land or property. |
| Contaminated land | Management of land contaminated by industrial processes or military tests involving radiation is still covered by the 1990 Act. Borough/district councils or unitary authorities responsible for identifying and registering contaminated land in their areas. If serious problem noted, authority must designate a 'special site' and notify EA/SEPA, which will take responsibility for enforcing any action taken. Enforcing authority serves remediation notice on person or business responsible, specifying action needed to remedy problem. In Northern Ireland, contaminated land issues overseen by country's Department of Health under Radioactive Contaminated Land Regulations (Northern Ireland) 2006. |
| Air quality | Following types of emission prohibited under Clean Air Act 1993 (which built on provisions of Clean Air Act 1956, introduced to eliminate winter smog): <br>1. dark smoke' issuing from chimneys; <br>2. excessive smoke, grit, dust, and fumes from chimneys; <br>3. excessively high chimneys; <br>4. excessive exhaust emissions; <br>5. smoke emissions in designated 'smoke control areas'. <br><br>Environment Act 1995 required councils to review present and likely future air quality in their areas. Where air not meeting desired standard, councils given powers to designate 'air quality management areas' covered by air quality action plans. |
| Statutory nuisances | 1990 Act empowers local authorities to serve 'abatement notices' on those responsible for statutory nuisances prejudicial to health. In addition to vermin and noise pollution generated by premises, vehicles, machinery, or equipment in street (e.g. by road workers), these include smoke, gas, fumes, dust, steam, or effluvia, and accumulations of rubbish. |
| Public lavatories | Providing sufficient public conveniences to hygienic standard, including accessible toilets, baby-changing facilities, etc. |

building on existing legislation to introduce two criminal offences for businesses failing to meet minimum standards: those of rendering food 'injurious to health' and selling food 'unfit for human consumption'. The Act also introduced new, all-encompassing local authority environmental services departments, specifying that environmental health officers had the responsibility for:

- inspecting and seizing suspicious food;
- issuing improvement notices to owners of food businesses;
- serving emergency prohibition notices to close down businesses in the case of perceived serious health risks;
- liaising with the National Health Service (NHS) whenever they feel it necessary to take action in relation to potentially communicable disease risks;
- issuing additional enforcement notices dictated by central government in instances of sudden crisis—for example, the ban on the sale of beef on the bone as a consequence of the bovine spongiform encephalopathy (BSE), or 'mad cow disease', crisis in the late 1980s and early 1990s.

The aforementioned 'outbreak' of BSE presented one of the biggest instances in recent memory of environmental health issues breaking into the wider public health arena. The alarm generated by the first diagnoses of BSE in cattle, in November 1986, and subsequent identification of symptoms of Creutzfeldt–Jakob disease (CJD) in several British people became of international concern—  leading to a ten-year ban on the export of UK beef to EU countries, from 1996 to 2006.

Other examples of recent environmental health scares have included a succession of outbreaks of foot-and-mouth disease in British livestock. The major one occurred in 2001, leading to a mass cull of sheep and cattle—including tens of thousands of healthy animals—in what was widely portrayed in the media as a panicky, botched, unnecessarily costly reaction. Two localized outbreaks occurred in 2007, attracting more measured responses. Under the law, where a landowner suspects an outbreak of a communicable (infectious or conta-  gious) disease among his or her animals, he or she must inform the police, local authority, and Defra. Once an outbreak has been confirmed, the movement of animals 'from the land' or 'within and beyond the local area' is prohibited, other than through a licence granted by an inspector.

More usually, environmental health officers are called in to individual business premises to remove samples of food for laboratory analysis on receiving public complaints about food poisoning, unpleasant tastes or odours, or outdated food labels. Among the more commonplace—if potentially dangerous—food safety issues arising is the identification of bacteria such as *E. coli* or salmonella. In one of the most notorious examples of overreaction by government to the latter, in 1988 Junior Health Minister Edwina Currie provoked widespread alarm by erroneously telling reporters:

   66 Most of the egg production in this country, sadly, is now affected with salmonella. 99

Food safety authorities also oversee the regulation of slaughterhouses in accordance with EU rules and inspect the quality of meat bought from them. They are also authorized to provide their own public slaughterhouses, cold stores, and refrigerators.

Environmental health officers are not the only officials involved in policing outbreaks of diseases like foot-and-mouth, *E. coli*, and salmonella: *trading standards officers* (employed by unitary authorities and county councils) and other Defra-approved contractors also have duties in such instances, albeit primarily in relation to animal welfare. Trading standards departments (the wider role of which is discussed in the next section) inspect livestock for signs of illness or poor treatment, and help to enforce UK and EU legislation relating to safe and humane animal transportation. Meanwhile, a 2007 EU Directive introduced a requirement for formal 'competence assessments' to be carried out by agencies appointed by Defra on anyone intending to transport livestock, horses, or poultry over distances of more than 65 km.

# ▌ Trading standards and the new licensing laws

While environmental health officers are responsible for verifying the *safety* of food sold to the public, wider consumer protection issues relating to its sale and presentation fall to trading standards officers to police. Under the Food Safety Act 1990 there are two main criminal offences relating to trading standards:

- selling food 'not of the nature or substance or quality demanded by the purchaser';
- 'falsely describing or presenting food'—usually without advertisement or labelling.

In addition to these food-related responsibilities, trading standards officers are responsible for ensuring businesses comply with government policy in several other areas.

## General consumer protection

General consumer protection involves monitoring the accurate description of goods, the use of credit, and product safety for items such as household tools, appliances, and children's toys. Trading standards departments are also responsible for ensuring that trade is carried out 'fairly' in their areas, under terms set out by the *Office of Fair Trading (OFT)* (see pp. 203–5). So time-consuming and costly can general consumer protection work be that some authorities have even established dedicated consumer advice departments to pool resources with their local Citizens Advice Bureaux (CABs) and the Consumers Association.

The Fair Trading Act 1973 introduced a Director General of Fair Trading, who has the authority to ask anyone in the course of business 'acting in a way detrimental to the interests of consumers' to give assurances as to his or her future conduct. If he or she fails to do so, the Director General can take the individual to a county court or the Restrictive Practices Court, which has the power to accept an assurance that he or she will not repeat the offence—or make an order. Civil claims under the Sale of Goods Act 1979 must be brought by individuals through county courts.

## Weights and measures

Each authority must appoint a 'chief inspector of weights and measures' to ensure that all traders in its area are complying with authorized weights and measures (the 'metric system' of metres and litres used throughout the EU, rather than the previously familiar 'imperial system' of yards and ounces, dating back to the Middle Ages).

The history of Britain's reluctant conversion to metric standards is almost as long and tangled as its relationship with the EU itself. It began in earnest with the passage of the Weights and Measures Act 1963, which formally redefined yards and pounds in terms of metres and kilograms, and abolished a number of archaic imperial measurements, such as 'scruples', 'rods', and 'minims'. In 1965, under pressure from industry, the then President of the Board of Trade committed the state to adopting the metric system fully within a decade and by 1968 a Metrication Board had been established to promote it. The pledge was reaffirmed on Britain's entry into the European Economic Community (EEC) in 1973.

Despite several concrete moves, such as the decimalization of the UK's currency in 1971, subsequent governments further delayed full implementation of metrication and it was only with the advent of two EU directives—in 1995 and 2000 respectively—that Britain was finally ordered to introduce the metric system across the board, first for packaged goods and then bulk-sold goods (for example, fresh fruit and vegetables sold on market stalls).

This diktat did not stop some traditionalists resisting. The first few years after the introduction of metrication in fruit and vegetable markets was marked by a succession of high-profile court cases that captured the imagination of the popular press—with so-called 'metric martyrs' continuing to label their goods in pounds and ounces in defiance of EU law. In September 2007, in the face of continuing widespread defiance, the resistance finally scored a pyrrhic victory when the EU Commissioner responsible for the single market, Gunther Verheugen, announced they would be permitted to continue labelling their items in imperial measures after all—provided that they also did so in metric measurements. The EU subsequently relaxed its stance even more, allowing most traders to continue using only imperial measures, but some local authorities still insisted on prosecuting those who did so. Victory for the metric martyrs finally came when, in October 2008, the then Department for Innovation, Universities, and Skills (DIUS) issued new guidelines to councils urging them to take only 'proportionate' action against refuseniks in future.

In addition to checking that goods are itemized in metric measures, inspectors regularly vet market stalls and shops to ensure that food is not sold in 'short weight'—that is, that scales are being used correctly and that consumers are being sold the correct quantities of goods. Short weight is a criminal offence. Weights of manufactured goods are checked at factories, while those of loose food, fuel, and beer are checked at the point of sale.

## Sunday trading

The Deregulation and Contracting Out Act 1994 marked the first major liberalization of Britain's retail laws, which up to that point had been among the strictest in Europe—with most shops commonly opening only between 9.30 a.m. and 5.30 p.m., and few allowed to trade on Sundays out of respect for Christian worshippers. The 1994 Act gave, for the first time, individual traders freedom to decide their own shop-opening hours and other employment practices on weekdays and Saturdays. A Bill introduced by the Tories to remove all remaining restrictions—particularly those relating to Sunday opening—initially collapsed on its *second reading* in the early 1990s, but change was finally introduced in the Sunday Trading Act 1994, which stipulated that:

- 'large shops'—those with internal sales areas of 280 m² or more—could open for up to six hours between 10 a.m. and 6 p.m., but must remain closed on Easter Sunday and Christmas Day (if the latter falls on a Sunday);
- smaller shops could open as and when they chose to;
- certain measures were introduced to protect the rights of shop workers who did not wish to work on a Sunday—especially those who wished to attend church.

## Trade descriptions

It is a criminal offence under the Trade Descriptions Acts of 1968 and 1972 for 'false descriptions' to be ascribed to goods or 'false indications' given of their sale prices—for example, for labelling not to include VAT as part of the cover price.

# Licensing of pubs and clubs, and drinking by-laws

The Licensing Act 2003, which finally came into force in February 2005, ushered in so-called '24-hour drinking' by allowing pubs and bars to apply to vary their existing liquor licences so they could open until later than the customary 11 p.m. closing time on weekdays and Saturdays and 10.30 p.m. on Sundays. At the same time nightclubs and restaurants were given the option of applying for 'late licences' allowing them to stay open beyond their usual 2 a.m. shutdown. In liberalizing the drinking laws, the Labour government's stated aim was to tackle Britain's rising epidemic of 'binge-drinking' by ending the frantic 'last orders' culture, which often saw drinkers racing to buy two or more drinks just before closing time to get the most out of the limited time available to them. The hope was that this more relaxed approach to buying and drinking alcohol would foster a Continental-style 'cafe culture', with a steadier stream of drinkers drifting in and out of bars at different times and fewer of the sudden explosions of violence and rowdy behaviour traditionally witnessed at 'chucking out' times.

The 2003 Act also introduced significant changes in terms of the way in which licences were issued and policed. Until 2005, local magistrates' courts were responsible for awarding and varying liquor licences, but the Act transferred this duty to local authorities. Councils would henceforth work together with the police to ensure that the terms of licences were adhered to, obtaining formal orders from magistrates to revoke them in the event of a breach.

The new licensing laws had a mixed reception from licensees, public, and police alike. One of the main complaints made by pub landlords and nightclub owners in the early days related to the complexity of the revised system. Rather than having to apply simply for a personal licence to serve alcohol between stated hours on stated days and a single public entertainment licence giving them the freedom to stage occasional events, such as concerts or stand-up comedy, they were now required to apply for both the former and a separate premises licence or temporary event notice for each occasion when they planned to stage any entertainment—whether a live acoustic band or a karaoke competition.

Following a high-profile run-in between the Musicians' Union, various other groups representing performers, and the Department of Culture, Media, and Sport (DCMS), the ministry charged with implementing the reforms, the wording of the Act was tweaked to avoid any unintended consequences, such as  deterring pubs from putting on shows or plays. In rationalizing this aspect of the law, however, ministers unwittingly made it easier for licensed premises to put on all manner of other performances: lap dancing, for example, was re-categorized alongside other forms of more innocuous public entertainment, meaning premises no longer needed to apply for separate 'sexual encounter' licences, as before, to stage it. Perhaps unsurprisingly, there has since been a huge increase in the number of clubs and bars offering shows involving at least partial nudity—with the pressure group Object identifying some 300 in Britain today, compared to a handful in the late 1990s. The Licensing Act has also been criticized by police forces and residents in some towns and cities for alleg-edly turning their centres into 'no-go areas' for older residents, particularly on Friday and Saturday nights. In 2008, in its submission to a government review of the impact of the 2003 Act, the LGA described it as 'a mistake', and its chair-man, Sir Simon Milton, told an interviewer from the *Daily Telegraph* it had 'failed miserably'. The policy has also been openly condemned by everyone from the Archbishop of Canterbury, Rowan Williams, to former Labour Health  Secretary Frank Dobson. A Freedom of Information Act 2000 request by the *Daily Telegraph* to all 43 police forces in England and Wales, made just ahead of the publication of the Home Office's official review in February 2008, appeared to support their reservations, by uncovering official statistics confirming 12 forces had seen a 46 per cent rise in the number of antisocial incidents with which they dealt since the Act was enforced—with 16 reporting an increase of 5 per cent in alcohol-related assaults, harassment, and criminal damage. Nationwide, serious violent offences in the early hours of the morning had risen by a quarter.

In the end, buoyed by reports from a number of individual police forces that pointed towards no significant increase in criminal offences—and, in some cases, suggested crime rates had fallen—the government's review recom-mended retaining the 'new' licensing regime when it was finally published in March 2008. Ministers did, however, introduce a new 'two-strikes rule' designed to deter off-licences from selling alcohol to underage drinkers.

As for the '24-hour' aspect of the legislation, despite the initial expectation that all-night drinking would become a feature of most town centres, statistics obtained from 86 per cent of licensing authorities in November 2007 found that fewer than 500 pubs and clubs in England and Wales had ever been granted 24-hour licences. Most 'late licences' have tended to cover only an additional hour or two of business, and only then at weekends in many cases. Of the 5,100 venues operating 24-hour licences between April 2006 and March 2007, 3,300 were hotels, 910 supermarkets, and 460 pubs and clubs. Nonetheless, concern about the links between late night drinking and unruly behaviour remain—prompting the coalition government to announce a 'complete review' of the policy in May 2010.

On a related note, local authorities have long had powers under statute to curb public drinking. In the early 1990s Plymouth and Bristol City Councils were among the first to invoke *by-laws* forbidding public consumption of alcohol in specified locations within their areas of jurisdiction and similar measures have since been widely implemented. Additional powers were introduced under the Criminal Justice and Police Act 2001, enabling councils to pass alcohol-free zone orders—or, to use their official title, 'alcohol consumption in designated public places orders'—again related to specified locations. Once such a zone is in place, police officers may require individuals spotted drinking there to stop immediately and, where necessary, confiscate their alcohol. In the last resort, those failing to comply may be prosecuted and, if convicted, fined up to £500. Some authorities have gone still further: within weeks of his election as London Mayor, Mr Johnson banned all drinking from London Underground and other public transport throughout the capital.

Shortly after, then Communities Secretary Hazel Blears launched a nation-wide crackdown on problem drinking and related antisocial behaviour, in the guise of **alcohol disorder zones (ADZs)**. Ministers gave individual local authorities the power to designate specific areas as needing extra policing to curb drink-related crime and disorder. The cost of the additional patrols would be met by pubs, bars, and other licensees themselves, in the form of a £100-a-head fee. At time of writing the coalition was preparing to go further, by empowering local authorities to charge licensed premises that chose to open late at night additional 'law and order levies' to help with the cost of policing any resulting disorder.

Such measures notwithstanding, unlike smoking (banned in all workplaces and enclosed public spaces, including bars and pubs, from 1 July 2007), Labour's attitude towards licensing has been seen as highly liberal. This liberalism also extended for a time towards another popular British pastime—gambling—which former premier Mr Blair and Culture Secretary Tessa Jowell planned to popularize still further by giving the go-ahead to at least one 'super-casino' in a major city and a network of smaller ones in other towns. The government's stated aim was to use the casinos as engines to attract industry, jobs, and private sector investment into deprived areas of the competing cities.

In January 2007 Manchester became the surprise choice of location for the super-casino project—beating off competition from, among others, Blackpool and London's former Millennium Dome. But within a short time of entering Downing Street, Mr Brown lived up to his puritanical image by scrapping the plans.

# ▌ Leisure and cultural services

Providing for citizens' quality of life arguably means more than managing public transport, clearing up refuse, and maintaining a social environment relatively free of crime and disorder. Among the 'softer services' traditionally offered by local authorities—directly or indirectly—are those falling beneath the broad umbrellas of leisure and/or cultural services. These terms—increasingly fused together by some councils—cover everything from the maintenance of local swimming pools and sports centres to the provision of theatres, museums, and galleries, and the financing of local festivals, such as the Edinburgh International Festival or England's largest equivalent, the Brighton Festival.

# Swimming pools, leisure centres, parks, and playgrounds

Under the Local Government (Miscellaneous Provisions) Act 1972 local authorities were given discretion—and ability to raise finance through local taxation—to provide 'such recreational facilities as they think fit'. These included:

- sports centres;
- pitches for team games and athletic events;
- swimming pools;
- tennis courts;
- stadiums, and premises for athletic and other sporting clubs;
- golf courses and bowling greens;
- riding schools;
- campsites;
- facilities for gliding, boating, and water-skiing;
- staff (including instructors) for any of the above.

As in most other areas of local service provision, compulsory competitive tendering was introduced under Mrs Thatcher to force local authorities to compete with private contractors for franchises to run leisure centres. Wearing another 'hat', however, councils still have responsibility for ensuring that *standards* of service meet statutory requirements, not least in terms of health and safety, and disabled access.

# Libraries, museums, galleries, and the performing arts

Under the Public Libraries Act 1850, emerging local authorities were empowered to *provide* libraries, but not actually to stock them with books. This changed under the Public Libraries 1919 Act, which allowed them to 'spend more than a rating limit of one penny in the pound on books'. Today there is no statutory limit and authorities are charged with 'providing a comprehensive and efficient library service' covering everything from books, newspapers, periodicals, to records, CDs, and DVDs. Public libraries have also been required to provide free Internet access to the public since 2002, funded by the New Opportunities Fund 'Community Access to Lifelong Learning' (CALL) programme.

There were fears that libraries might become the latest of a long line of 'added value' local services to fall prey to the coalition's public spending squeeze when the Department for Culture, Media, and Sport announced plans to shake up local library services in August 2010.

With recent figures showing that only 29 per cent of British people now regularly visited their libraries, and that many local branches were home to dwindling and outdated stocks of books, Culture Minister Ed Vaizey launched a Future Libraries Programme in an effort to both generate cost savings and attract more users by reorganizing library services in a way better suited to the pressures and routines of modern living. Among the ideas floated by Mr Vaizey was that of relocating some libraries to premises other than conventional library buildings, such as local shops and pubs. He revealed he had received 51 submissions for support from the programme, representing 100-plus local authorities. Ten—involving 36 councils—are being pursued in the initial phase. These cover the following areas:

- Northumberland with Durham;
- Bolton, with Bury, Manchester, Oldham, Rochdale, Salford, Stockport, Tameside, Trafford, Wigan;
- Bradford;
- Lincolnshire, with Rutland, Cambridgeshire, North East Lincolnshire, Peterborough;
- Suffolk;
- Oxfordshire with Kent;
- Herefordshire with Shropshire;
- Cornwall with Devon, Plymouth, Torbay;
- Lewisham with Bexley, Bromley, Croydon, Greenwich, Lambeth, and Southwark;
- Kensington and Chelsea with Hammersmith and Fulham.

Although the statutory requirements are less stringent, local authorities are also 'allowed' to provide museums and galleries, and require neighbouring councils to contribute towards the expense of doing so. Museum 'activities' over and above collecting, maintaining, and displaying objects—for example, public events such as readings or classes—were until recently coordinated through area museum councils. This role was taken on by new 'hubs' (larger museums) set up by the Museums, Libraries, and Archives Council (MLA) and now assumed by Arts Council England (ACE) following the MLA's recent abolition. The Local Government Act 1972 also gave councils the power to establish theatres, concert halls, and other places of entertainment, maintain their own bands or orchestras, and foster arts and crafts.

The use of the broad-brush term 'cultural services' to encapsulate these many and varied 'quality of life' provisions has been increasingly criticized—not least by those directly employed by the organizations concerned. Whenever central government offers local authorities a less-than-generous financial settlement—forcing them to tighten their belts, as at the present time—'non-essential' services like libraries, museums, and theatres are usually the first to suffer, as councils move to protect 'core' areas such as education and social services from serious cutbacks. The museums sector for one has suffered, as long-serving curators have retired without being replaced, while councils have sought to make economies by introducing job shares and substituting specialist curatorial jobs with generalist managerial positions.

Hard-pressed local authorities have often also been 'forced' to withdraw funding from theatres and other performance venues. In 1990 Derby Playhouse faced closure after its annual £130,000 revenue grant from Derbyshire County Council was withdrawn overnight, following the authority's decision to scrap its entire arts budget to save money. Although thrown a lifeline at the time by Arts Council England, the playhouse again narrowly avoided permanent closure in 2007, after Derby City Council withdrew a £40,000 grant, criticizing the theatre's poor management and what it described as 'unsustainable' losses.

In addition to their overarching role in promoting cultural venues and events for the benefit of local people, councils play a part in encouraging tourism and monitoring its effects on their local economies. Towards the end of Labour's tenure the DCMS began formulating a new nationwide 'Tourism Prospectus' intended to define the future role of local authorities in promoting tourism alongside regional tourist boards, RDAs, and the national quango Visit Britain (formed from the merger of the British Tourist Authority and English Tourism Council in April 2003).

## ☰ Topical feature idea

Figure 19.1 is the *agenda* for a Cambridgeshire County Council *cabinet* meeting on 5 July 2010. With four hours until your deadline, your news editor on the *Cambridgeshire Evening News* has sent you to the meeting in pursuit of a page lead story for tonight's final edition. He has specified he would like a story relating to one of the areas discussed in this chapter. Which are the most promising leads on this agenda, and how would you follow them up?

**Figure 19.1** The agenda for a Cambridgeshire County Council cabinet meeting on 5 July 2010

| | Monday 5th July 2010<br>(Note day of meeting)<br>10.00 a.m.<br>KV Room, Shire Hall, CAMBRIDGE |
|---|---|
| | **CONSTITUTIONAL MATTERS** |
| 1 | Minutes—15 June 2010—*to follow* |
| 2 | Apologies and Declarations of Interests |
| 3 | Petitions |
| 4 | None at first despatch. Deadline 9.00 a.m. Thursday 1 July |
| 5 | Member Led Review—Local Government Shared Services Business Case |
| | **COUNCIL DECISIONS** |
| 6 | Local Government Shared Services Detailed Business Case and Joint Committee Structure |

**KEY DECISIONS**

7    Street Lighting Private Finance Initiative Selection of Preferred Bidder

8    Integrated Resources and Performance Report—May 2010

9    East Cambridgeshire Local Development Framework—
     Implications for Planning Secondary School Provision

10   Investigation into the choice of Single or Multi-Storey Design Solutions for
     New-Build Primary Schools and the implications for the Quality and Delivery
     of Education

11   Library Service Review

12   Section 106 Deferral—Development at Papworth Everard

**OTHER DECISIONS**

13   End of Year Performance Report 2009/10 and Annual Report 2009/10

14   Great Ouse Catchment Flood Management Plan—Consultation by the
     Environment Agency

**MONITORING REPORTS**

15   Quarterly Update Report on Key Partnerships

16   Annual Performance Assessment of Social Care Services for Adults Services for Cam-
     bridgeshire Action Plan—Six Monthly Update Report

17   Cambridgeshire Guided Busway Update

18   Draft Cabinet Forward Agenda Tuesday 7 September 2010

19   Delegations from Cabinet to Cabinet Members/Officers

## ✳ Current issues

- **Increased enforcement powers for Environment Agency and *Natural England*:**
  the statutory bodies charged with protecting the natural environment from
  unsympathetic development and pollution were awarded enhanced regulatory
  powers in 2010, including the ability to impose spot fines on businesses in breach
  of environmental protection legislation.

- **Carrot rather than stick approach to recycling:** Labour proposals to introduce a
  'pay-as-you-throw' policy to encourage households and businesses to recycle more
  waste by fining them if they do not were abandoned by the Lib-Con coalition soon
  after taking power. Instead, Communities Secretary Eric Pickles is aiming to place
  the emphasis on incentives—taking his cue from Conservative-run Windsor and
  Maidenhead Council, which rewards households who increase their recycling with
  vouchers they can use in local shops.

- **Cuts to local transport projects:** an early casualty of the public sector cuts
  announced by the coalition was a tranche of local and regional transport projects that
  had been approved (and, in some cases, part-funded) by the previous government.
  These have so far included plans to improve the Midland Metro tram system, linking
  South Yorkshire to Bristol and Tyne and Wear, and the Mersey Gateway Bridge
  Scheme, which was to include a toll bridge between Widnes and Runcorn.

## ? Review questions

1. Which are the main highways authorities and how are their responsibilities divided up?

2. What are the main weapons available to local authorities and central government to tackle traffic congestion? Give some recent policy examples.

3. Explain the distinction between 'waste collection' and 'waste disposal'. What policies are being used to promote greener waste management in Britain?

4. What are the main duties of environmental health officers? How are their responsibilities in relation to food distinct from those of trading standards officers?

5. Outline the range of leisure and cultural services provided by local authorities.

## → Further reading

Docherty, I. and Shaw, J. (2003) *A New Deal for Transport: The UK's Struggle with the Sustainable Transport Agenda*, London: Wiley-Blackwell. **Critical overview of the Blair government's sustainable transport policy, evaluating the impacts against professed aspirations, by experts on transport and highways.**

Gumpert, B. and Kirk, J. (2001) *Trading Standards: Law and Practice*, Bristol: Jordans. **Comprehensive overview of statutory trading standards regulations, and how they work in theory and practice. Aimed at professionals, companies, and public.**

Lane, K. (2006) *National Bus Company: The Road to Privatisation*, Shepperton: Ian Allen. **Affectionate account of the last years of the National Bus Company monopoly, and the revolution in public passenger transport ushered in by the Thatcher government's privatization and deregulation reforms.**

Lang, C., Reeve, J., and Woolard, V. (eds) (2006) *The Responsive Museum: Working with Audiences in the Twenty-First Century*, Aldershot: Ashgate. **Thoughtful examination of the present-day challenges facing public museums in light of diminishing support from the state and local government, and increasing competition from other attractions and leisure pursuits.**

Morgan, S. (2005) *Waste, Recycling and Reuse*, London: Evans Brothers. **Practical evaluation of the West's mounting waste management problem, with suggested solutions, focusing on the 'three R's'—reducing, reusing, and recycling.**

Waters, I. and Duffield, B. (1994) *Entertainment, Arts, and Cultural Services*, London: Financial Times/Prentice Hall. **Informative look at the changes in provision and funding of arts, entertainment, and other aspects of cultural services during the 1990s, emphasizing the tensions between different parts of the sector.**

## Online Resource Centre

www.oxfordtextbooks.co.uk/orc/Morrison2e/
Visit the Online Resource Centre that accompanies this book for web links and regular updates.

# 20

# Freedom of information

The bulk of this book has been concerned with explaining *how* Britain is governed—both politically and through the nuts and bolts of public administration. We began with an examination of the UK constitution and the place within it of core institutions: Parliament, the government, and the monarchy. We went on to explore the concept of *devolution*, the place of individual spending departments, executive agencies, and *quangos*, and the role local authorities play in delivering day-to-day services to citizens.

This final chapter focuses not on who wields power, what that power amounts to, and how it is broadly exercised, but on the means by which journalists (and taxpayers) can find out more about individual decisions taken on their behalf and hold the institutions responsible to account. Where can citizens go to obtain information about the precise composition and remit of the (often unelected) bodies that hold sway over their lives? What rights, if any, do they have to question or challenge them, and how can they exercise those rights? In a way, this is a chapter to which the rest of the book has been leading. We now know how government in Britain works (at least in theory)—but how can it be made to work *better*?

## ▌ The origins of the Freedom of Information Act 2000—what is 'FoI'?

The concept of 'freedom of information' rests on the notion that, in a democracy, taxpayers and voters should be entitled to know as much as possible about the actions and decisions of the politicians elected to represent them, and the officials appointed by decision-makers to implement their policies. More important still, to many, is the principle that participating citizens should be able to find out how public money—largely derived from the taxes they pay on their earnings—is spent on their behalf.

Freedom of information was a long time coming in the UK. At least seventy other states had legislation in place enshrining the rights of their citizens to access details about how their money was being spent by the 'powers that be' long before the Freedom of Information Act 2000 (in Scotland, the Freedom of Information (Scotland) Act 2002) received *royal assent* at Westminster. It was not until Tony Blair's election in 1997 that Britain gained a government committed to implementing such reforms. Even then it was several years into New Labour's first term before the party put its manifesto pledge into action—and in somewhat watered-down form at that. Not until 1 January 2005, towards the end of its second term, did the full force of the new law come into effect, under the then Department of Constitutional Affairs (now the Ministry of Justice).

The concept of freedom of information has long been celebrated in the USA, which has a nationwide Freedom of Information Act based on the principle of democratic accountability, as well as numerous state-specific laws governing access to public documentation and the records of tax-levying entities. These Acts are collectively known as 'sunshine laws'. Elsewhere in Europe, where freedom of information legislation is also commonplace, FoI Acts are generally known as 'open records'. The European Union (EU) as a whole, meanwhile, is governed by Regulation 1049/2001, passed by the *European Parliament (EP)* and Council of Ministers on 30 May 2001. This sets out a detailed system of rules regarding public access to the main EU institutions, including the *European Commission* and the Council and EP themselves.

Lest blinkered constitutional historians try to convince us Britain is the seat of democracy, as so often purported, it is worth noting that the earliest known 'open record' was passed in Sweden back in the late eighteenth century, in the form of the Freedom of the Press Act 1766. And while some might scoff at the idea of openness and accountability operating under dictatorships it is intriguing to note that, since 1 January 2008, even China has had a freedom of information in law in place (at least notionally), in the form of the Regulations of the People's Republic of China on Open Government Information.

Given the huge number of FoI laws in force around the world, perhaps unsurprisingly there is little conformity in their exact wording or provisions. With some exceptions, however, most of these laws share some general traits—in particular, the principle that the 'burden of proof' falls on the institution from which information is being sought, rather than the individual seeking it. In other words, the person making a request is not normally required to explain why he or she is asking for the information, whereas the organization questioned must give a valid reason should it fail to supply the details requested. What constitutes a 'valid reason' is, of course, open to debate. The next section seeks to answer this question in relation to Britain.

# Information the Act covers—and information that is exempt

The FoI legislation operating in the UK applies to more than 100,000 'public authorities', ranging from individual schools and hospitals to local councils, quangos, and entire government departments. If a legitimate FoI request is made under either Act, the authority asked must first tell the questioner whether it holds the relevant information and, assuming it does, supply it *within 20 working days* of the request.

The authority may, however, *refuse* to confirm or deny the existence of information—and/or provide it—if any of the following conditions apply:

- it is exempt;
- the request is vexatious or similar to a previous request;
- the cost of compliance exceeds an 'appropriate limit'.

The term 'exemption' might invite the idea that an authority possessing information has free rein to refuse to disclose it, but according to the Acts even exempt material should sometimes be made available.

There are two broad classes of exemption: 'absolute' and 'qualified'. While the former may not be disclosed under any circumstances, the latter may be if the 'public interest' in disclosing it outweighs that in keeping it secret. For example, a public authority involved in security policy might legitimately refuse to disclose exempt information that could compromise public safety by jeopardizing counter-terrorism operations, but it would be hard pressed to do so if the information it was withholding were likely to *improve* safety—by, for example, revealing the expected time and location of an impending attack.

In addition to absolute and qualified exemptions, several entire categories of information are exempt. Authorities may also refuse requests they consider 'likely to prejudice' law enforcement or the UK's interests abroad. The three categories of exemption are listed in Table 20.1.

In addition, even when none of the above exemptions applies, it is wise for journalists to proceed with caution before reproducing certain kinds of 'information' wholesale in the media. Under the Re-use of Public Information Regulations, introduced in July 2005, some details disclosed by public authorities under FoI remain subject to their legal copyright. This means that, while the requester is entitled to answers, he or she does not necessarily have an 'automatic right' to re-use the information, other than for the purposes for which it was originally produced by the authority concerned. Although theoretically these regulations could be used by disingenuous authorities to delay or prevent media disclosure of perfectly 'free' information, in practice they tend to be invoked to protect the intellectual property rights of third parties whose work is included in the disclosed material: for example, freelance photographers, architects, or designers.

**Table 20.1** Exemptions under the Freedom of Information Act 2000

| Absolute | Qualified | Categories |
|---|---|---|
| Information supplied by, or relating to, bodies dealing with security matters | Intended for future publication | Information relating to investigations and proceedings conducted by public authorities |
| Court records and information related to impending prosecution | Related to national security (other than information supplied by or relating to named security organizations, in which case duty to consider disclosure in public interest does not arise) | Court records |
| Information that would infringe **parliamentary privilege** | Which might limit defence of British Isles, or 'capability, effectiveness, or security' of armed forces | Formulation of government policy |
| Personal information of *either* of following kinds:<br>1. that relating to person making request, which could be obtained under Data Protection Act 1998;<br>2. about another individual, if it would breach data protection principles. | Potentially prejudicial to international relations between UK and any other state, international organization, or court, or UK's interests abroad | |
| Information held by Commons or Lords that may be prejudicial to effective conduct of public affairs | Information that might prejudice relations between administrations within UK | |
| Information provided in confidence | Information likely to prejudice financial and/or economic interests of UK | |
| Prohibitions on disclosure where disclosure is prohibited by enactment or would constitute contempt of court | Information relating to investigations and proceedings conducted by public authorities | |
| | Information likely to prejudice law enforcement—defined as prevention or detection of crime, prosecution of offenders, assessment of taxes, etc. | |
| | Information relating to public authority with audit functions in relation to another public body (e.g. **Audit Commission**) | |
| | Information relating to formulation of government policy, communications between ministers, or operations of ministerial office | |

| Absolute | Qualified | Categories |
|---|---|---|
| | Information held by public authorities other than House of Commons or House of Lords that may be prejudicial to effective conduct of public affairs | |
| | Information relating to communications between Queen, her ministers, and/or other public bodies, including those in relation to honours system | |
| | Information likely to endanger health and/or safety of any individual | |
| | Environmental information authority is obliged to make public under s. 74 of the Act | |
| | Personal information believed by institution not to breach data protection principles, but in relation to which individual who is subject of request serves notice that disclosure would cause *'unwarranted substantial damage or distress'* | |
| | Subject to legal professional privilege | |
| | 'Trade secrets' or information liable to prejudice commercial interests of any person (including authority holding it) | |

These, then, are the categories of information that carry exemptions, but what of the Acts' definitions of 'public authority'? Are any organizations or individuals that might be considered to fall under this umbrella term exempted from FoI requests per se?

In short, 'yes'.

## The Queen and Royal Household

The Royal Family's website defines the status of the Queen and Royal Household thus:

❝ The Royal Household is not a public authority within the meaning of the FOI Acts, and is therefore exempt from their provisions. ❞

It goes on to cite the *'fundamental constitutional principle'* that communications between the reigning sovereign and ministers or other public bodies remains confidential—not least to ensure that the royals do not compromise their 'political neutrality'. As the site stresses, however, the fact the Royal

Household is not bound by the FoI Acts does *not* mean it is unwilling to make certain information available voluntarily.

To this end it is happy to '*account openly for all its use of public money*'. It does this by posting online every June a consolidated report, including a full annual account and breakdown of the *Civil List* and grants-in-aid. In addition, the Prince of Wales voluntarily publishes details of his income from the Duchy of Cornwall estate—both before and after tax—on his own website.

→
see also
central
govern-
ment,
pp. 22–3

What the sites fail to emphasize is the fact that no information about the Royal Household's funding was made public by it until 2001, when it was persuaded to agree to greater openness as part of its negotiation with HM Treasury over a new ten-year financial settlement from the government. Perhaps even more remarkable is the amount of detail about its dealings the Royal Family still will *not* disclose. For example, nowhere will British taxpayers find details of the size of the Privy Purse (see p. 25)—that mysterious treasure trove, derived from the Duchy of Lancaster estate and reserved for the personal expenditure of the reigning monarch. Nor will they be able to access details about other aspects of the royals' personal finances, such as the incomes derived by several members of the family from service in the Armed Forces, the Duchess of York's royalties for her series of *Budgie the Little Helicopter* children's books, or the dividends and profits derived from family members' numerous shareholdings and other investments. Soon after the May 2010 election, the coalition pledged to give the National Audit Office greater access to the Queen's accounts, but it remains to be seen what exactly this will entail.

The list of specific FoI exemptions for the Queen and the Royal Household are detailed in Table 20.2.

Despite this array of exemptions, which place the Royal Family in a significantly more privileged position than any other, recent annual disclosures of their public accounts have shed light on the huge lengths to which members appear to go to defend FoI applications. According to the Royal Household's 2006–07 accounts, it spent £180,000 of taxpayers' money in that one year shielding itself from FoI requests. Buckingham Palace explained at the time the sum was spent reminding government departments of the exemption to prevent them releasing details of communications with the household.

In addition, it is normally possible for resourceful journalists to find ways of circumventing the royals' exemption. In June 2008 an FoI request to the Ministry of Defence unearthed the cost of Prince William's controversial flight in an RAF Chinook helicopter to an exclusive stag party on the Isle of Wight. The trip—one of five 'familiarization exercises' undertaken by the prince, which saw him stop off en route to pick up his brother, Prince Harry, in London—set taxpayers back £8,716.

**Table 20.2** Specific FoI exemptions relating to the Royal Household

| Exemption | Details |
|---|---|
| Financial and other personal matters | Information relating to personal affairs of sovereign and members of Royal Family—including private finances and activities in personal capacity—exempt under s. 40 of FoI Act and s. 38 of the Scottish FoI Act (Data Protection Act provisions) |
| Correspondences with deceased family members | Personal information on recently deceased members of Royal Family relating to communications with Queen, other members of family, or Royal Household. If contained in records less than 30 years old, this may be exempt under s. 37 of the UK FoI Act (s. 41 of the Scottish FoI Act) |
| Other information relating to deceased royals | Information relating to recently deceased members of Royal Family disclosure of which would damage 'right to family life' of deceased's relatives may be exempt under s. 44 of the UK FoI Act and s. 26 of the Scottish FoI Act and art 8—'Private Life and Family'—of Human Rights Act 1998 |

## Utilities, train companies, and other passenger transport operators

To widespread dismay among journalists and supporters of open government, including the Campaign for Freedom of Information, the privatized utilities— water, electricity, gas and telecommunications providers, and rail-operating companies—were excluded from automatic coverage by the FoI Acts when they entered their final draft stages. After they were included in the remit of the government's 1997 *White Paper, Your Right to Know*, hopes were high that they would be subject to scrutiny under the Act when it was finally passed. But after intensive lobbying by the companies concerned—many of which argued that being subject to FoI could jeopardize commercially sensitive operations— they were eventually omitted.

The decision to exclude companies involved in supplying British taxpayers with such vital 'natural monopolies' as energy and water was enough to infu- riate many, but more baffling still for some was the fact that even *Network Rail*—the not-for-dividend company set up by the government to take over the maintenance of the railway infrastructure after the collapse of private firm Railtrack in 2001—was also exempted. In a test case ruling in January 2007, the *Information Commissioner*—the individual appointed to hear FoI appeals (see pp. 588–60)—clarified that Network Rail was a 'private company' and therefore not a 'public authority' under the Act's terms. His ruling came in response to an appeal against the company's refusal to answer a request made in May 2005, under the Data Protection Act 1998, regarding information about a flood beside a railway line.

Although utility companies themselves are not subject to FoI, the regula- tors set up by the government to monitor them—such as the *Office of Gas and Electricity Markets (Ofgem)* and the *Office of Communications (Ofcom)* (see p. 217)—*are*. This fact has been used as an argument by organizations such as the Confederation of British Industry (CBI) for retaining the 'light-touch' approach to the utilities, which currently remains—despite repeated hints from the Labour government that it was 'attracted to' extending the scope of the Acts to cover them.

## Academies

One of the most contentious examples of an organization exempt from current FoI legislation is that of *academies*—the new generation of 'independent' secondary schools operating within the state sector (see pp. 438–43). Their exemption—granted because of the involvement of private companies in financing them and, in some cases, running their ancillary services, such as catering and cleaning—is widely viewed as a double standard, given that it exempts them from having to reveal performance data that all other state schools are expected to publish. Some have even suggested the exemption is a convenient way of masking the relatively sluggish academic performance of these schools, which, when introduced in 2002, were trumpeted as a way of turning round 'failing' comprehensives by pumping in private capital. Academies' quasi-independent status in law enables them to present information on their exam results in a different way from other schools—omitting details of the subjects in which GCSE A*–C grades have been obtained, and making it difficult for parents to make informed decisions about whether they are performing better (or worse) than their rivals.

Some critics of the academies exemption have also pointed to a clear contradiction between the government's public insistence that, despite being largely privately financed, they are in the public sector—and not the start of a creeping privatization of the state schooling system. At time of writing, academies finally looked set to be brought within the scope of the Act after a House of Lords committee amended the Academies Bill introduced by the coalition to this effect.

## The Security Service, MI6, and other intelligence agencies

Just as most security-related material is exempt from the provisions of the FoI Acts, there is a blanket exemption for any information relating to the work of the Security Service (MI5), MI6, and all other British intelligence agencies. Similar exemptions apply to Special Forces, such as the Special Air Squadron (SAS).

## The Trades Union Congress (TUC), individual unions, CBI, and public limited companies

Neither trades unions nor employers' organizations, like the CBI or Institute of Directors (IoD), are required to divulge information under FoI rules. Similarly, exemptions apply to all businesses, including *public limited companies (plcs)*. The latter fact—and the qualified exemption for sensitive information defined as being of 'commercial interest'—pose a frequent source of frustration for journalists seeking to hold public authorities like councils and government departments accountable for their use of taxpayers' money. With more and more public sector work being carried out by private sector companies contracted to do so on the authorities' behalf, rather than directly, some reporters see the 'commercial interest' exemption as being open to abuse by organizations seeking to cover up waste and inefficiency—particularly in cases of contractual negotiations that have given the public purse poor value for money.

## How to make an FoI request—and how not to

Around 120,000 FoI requests are made each year in the UK—six out of ten by members of the public, one-fifth businesses, and only around 10 per cent journalists. That said, the exhaustive nature of some journalistic enquiries has taken its toll on public authorities' time and resources. Media-related requests reportedly take up significantly more time than those from private individuals and companies between them. The overall cost of complying with FoI requests was estimated at £35.5m in 2005 alone.

So, how does one make a request? Although the exact procedure varies from one public authority to another, it entails writing to the organization either by email or post, detailing the specific question(s) to which an answer(s) is requested. If there is any ambiguity in the wording of a request, the authority is encouraged to enter into a proactive dialogue with the requester to clarify the question(s) and to supply the information as quickly as possible—provided that it is not exempt. Authorities are also expected, where relevant or necessary, to supply additional explanatory material if it is likely to elucidate otherwise complex or confusing information, and avoid the necessity for a prolonged correspondence with the questioner. As in other states, the questioner must give his or her name and contact details when filing the request, but he or she is not expected to divulge a 'reason' for doing so. In principle, FoI requests are free and it is highly unusual for organizations to charge for answering them.

In addition to the aforementioned exemptions, authorities may refuse to respond to requests in certain other circumstances. If a single request to a government department or other body is likely to cost more than £600 in terms of the time and staffing needed to locate the information (£450 in the case of other public authorities) it may be refused. Alternatively, the authority concerned may levy a charge to the requester. There is also provision in law for authorities to decline to respond to 'vexatious' requests. The definition of this term was clarified by the Information Commissioner's Office (ICO) in a guidance note issued in July 2007. It ruled a request to be 'vexatious' if it imposed a 'significant burden' on the public authority in terms of expense or distraction, *and* met one or more of the following criteria. That it:

- clearly does not have any serious purpose or value;
- is designed to cause disruption or annoyance;
- has the effect of harassing the public authority;
- can otherwise fairly be characterized as obsessive or manifestly unreasonable.

Examples of 'vexatious' enquiries cited by the ICO included the case of an individual refused information by Birmingham City Council after making more than 70 previous requests. Their final one consisted of multiple questions and would have cost £3,500 to answer. In another case, West Midlands Transport Executive estimated it had spent 175 hours responding to one person's enquiries. TfL, meanwhile, reported it had received so many letters from a single enquirer it had had to devise a new internal management strategy to cope with them. But perhaps the most burdensome FoI addict to date was the individual who sent no fewer than 347 requests to police forces, 412 to the Ministry of Defence, and 22 to the Cabinet Office. In a joint decision notice, the individual was judged by the Commissioner to be 'vexatious' because:

    ❝ It is entirely appropriate to consider the aggregated effect of dealing with all the requests known to have been made across the public sector. ❞

Just as authorities may reject vexatious requests, they may also refuse to answer 'repeated' ones—those that are identical to others to which they have previously responded in full (or refused to respond), particularly if they originate from the same individual or organization.

## The Environmental Information Regulations 2004

The FoI Act was not the only new legislation designed to promote greater government openness to take effect in 2005. Under EU law, the Environmental Information Regulations (EIR) 2004—in Scotland, the Environmental Information (Scotland) Regulations 2004—came in at the same time, giving the British public access to information about the state of their natural environment, particularly in relation to potential hazards like pollution.

Unlike the FoI Acts, EIR requests—also generally made by post or email and subject to a 20-day maximum delay in response times—do not need to be made in writing and may be lodged verbally. They also cover various private sector organizations currently outside the remit of general FoI legislation. For example, EIR requests may be made to privatized utilities, such as water and electricity companies, responsible for activities with a direct impact on the environment.

Environmental information covered by the Regulations falls into six categories:

- the state of the 'elements of the environment'—air, water, soil, land, fauna (including human beings);
- emissions and discharges, noise, energy, radiation, waste, and other such substances;
- measures and activities such as policies, plans, and agreements affecting, or likely to affect, the state of the environment;
- reports, cost-benefit, and economic analyses;
- the state of human health and safety, and contamination of the food chain;
- cultural sites and built structures—to the extent that they may be affected by the state of the elements of the environment.

As with the FoI Acts, there are certain 'absolute' and 'qualified' exemptions to the provisions of the EIR. These are outlined in Table 20.3.

Unlike FoI requests enquiries made under the EIR tend to incur a charge to the questioner, provided that it is set at a 'reasonable' level and the authority publishes a schedule of all of its charges. It may not, however, refuse a request on grounds of cost alone.

**Table 20.3** Exemptions under the Environmental Information Regulations 2004

| Absolute | Qualified |
| --- | --- |
| Information not held by the authority (if so, it has 'duty' to refer request to relevant body) | Information's release would breach confidentiality of legal proceedings |
| Request is 'manifestly unreasonable' | Information might prejudice international relations between Britain and other states or international bodies, public security, or national defence |
| Request is 'too general' (although the authority should still fulfil duty to advise and assist) | Information might jeopardize course of justice and right of citizens to fair trial |
| Request is for unfinished documents or data (in which case, estimated time for completion must be given) | Commercially confidential information |
| Request is for internal communications | Certain information related to intellectual property rights |
| | Information related to personal and/or voluntary data |
| | Information related to work of environmental protection |

# FoI versus data protection

The Data Protection Act 1984 (as amended by the Data Protection Act 1998) relates to the notion of protecting individuals' privacy, as its name suggests. On the face of it, this may appear to conflict with the more 'free-for-all' aspects of information disclosure ushered in by the FoI Acts. In practice, however, the two Acts largely complement and build on each other—a fact assured by the government's decision to give the task of policing both of them to the Information Commissioner in 2005 (see pp. 588–90).

The 1998 Act applies to 'personal data'. This is defined as 'any data which can be used to identify a living person'—including names, addresses, telephone, fax, and mobile phone numbers, email addresses, and birthdays. It applies, however, only to data that is (or is intended to be) held on computer or in another 'relevant filing system'. The Act's scope is fairly broad in this latter context: an individual's paper diary may be considered a 'relevant filing system' if used for commercial purposes. The Act is underpinned by seven 'key principles' relating to the handling of personal data by public authorities, private sector companies, and other organizations as outlined in Table 20.4.

Table 20.4 Conditions relating to the use of personal data under the Data Protection Act 1998

| Condition | Details |
| --- | --- |
| Focus | Data may only be used for specific purposes for which it was collected. |
| Privacy | Information must not be disclosed to other parties without consent of individual to whom it relates, unless there is legislation or other overriding legitimate reason to share information (e.g. the prevention or detection of crime). It is an offence for other parties to obtain this personal data without authorization. |
| Accessibility | Individuals have right of access to information held about them, subject to certain exceptions (e.g. information held for prevention or detection of crime). |
| Time-sensitivity | Personal information may be kept for no longer than necessary. |
| Protection | Personal information may not be transmitted outside European Economic Area (EEA) unless individual to whom it relates consents, or adequate protection is in place (e.g. by the use of a prescribed form of contract). Entities holding personal information required to have adequate security measures in place. Those include technical measures (such as computer firewalls) and organizational measures (e.g. staff training). |
| Regulation | All entities that process personal information, with one or two exceptions, must register with Information Commissioner. |

The Act gives anyone whose personal data is processed the right to:

- view any data held by an organization for a small fee (known as 'subject access');
- request that incorrect information be corrected—if the organization ignores his or her plea, a court may order the data to be corrected or destroyed, and compensation may be paid;
- require that data is not used in a way that causes 'damage or distress';
- require that his or her data is not used for direct marketing.

So how do the two Acts—governing 'data protection' on the one hand, and 'freedom of information' on the other—work together in practice?

The first point to be made is that many enquiries that individuals might think of making under the FoI Act in relation to information specifically relating to them will be exempt under it. This is, however, only because the correct procedure for accessing that information actually falls under the 1998 Act. If, however, an individual seeks to make a request relating to themselves that will also disclose information about a third party, the correct Act to use is likely to be the 2000 Act. Confusingly, however, the authority asked to supply this information must consider 'data protection principles' applicable under FoI before deciding whether to release the details. Because many FoI requests tend to concern what might be termed 'corporate' information—procedural, statistical, and/or constitutional matters—rather than personal data, in practice the number of serious conflicts between the 2000 and 1998 Acts is relatively limited. There have, however, been notable altercations between the media and local authorities—particularly in relation to the salaries and perks of *chief executives* and other senior officers. Councils have often tried to hide behind 'data protection' legislation when asked for such details under FoI, arguing that—because officers are not elected representatives—such details constitute information of a personal nature, which should therefore be treated as confidential. The Commissioner has sought to clarify the legal position surrounding this, by making a distinction between information relating to the private lives of public officials (which should be exempt) and that relating to the discharge of their public duties. Sections 34 and 35 of the 1998 Act exempt individuals from data protection if the data requested consists of information the authority handling the request is obliged to make public by law or if a court order or other '*rule of law*' has required its disclosure. Either of these can override personal data protections otherwise guaranteed by s. 40 of the 2000 Act.

In March 2008, MPs played the data protection card, too, in an effort to limit disclosures about the generous expenses packages for which they were eligible in relation to their London homes (see pp. 54–5). Details of the so-called 'John Lewis list' had been obtained under an FoI request by the Press Association, but the House of Commons challenged the publication of a full run-down first in an Information Tribunal hearing and then in the High Court—arguing it would compromise data protection principles by potentially revealing personal details such as their *constituency* addresses. Their efforts failed and the rest is history.

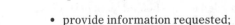

→    see also central government, pp. 10 and 57–8

## FoI appeals and the Information Commissioner

Anyone refused information under the FoI Acts has a right to appeal, initially through the authority's own internal review procedures but ultimately to the Information Commissioner's Office (ICO)—the regulator that replaced the Data Protection Commissioner's Office in 2005, following the passage of the FoI Act. In addition to its central London office, the ICO has three offices based in the capitals of the devolved regions: Edinburgh, Cardiff, and Belfast.

It is the job of the ICO, among other things, to make sure the 23 exemptions contained in the Act are not abused by authorities seeking to keep secret information they regard as embarrassing but which is not actually exempt in law. In Scotland complaints are made to the Scottish Information Commissioner. By way of underlining the importance of disclosure wherever possible, the public also has a further right to appeal over and above the Commissioners themselves, via the Information Tribunal.

To aid designated public authorities in complying with the FoI Acts, the ICO has published 'Ten Top Tips' for them to follow. These are listed in the table entitled 'The Information Commissioner's Office's "Ten Top Tips" for handling  requests', to be found on the Online Resource Centre that accompanies this book.

Complaints may be made to the ICO if a public authority fails to:

- provide information requested;
- respond to a request within 20 working days (or explain why longer is needed);
- give proper advice and help;
- give information in the form requested;
- properly explain any reasons for refusing the request;
- correctly apply an exemption under the Act.

Complainants must provide the following material:

- covering letter, giving details of their complaint;
- details of their initial request;
- copy of the authority's initial response (the 'refusal notice');
- copy of the complaint they made to the authority's internal review or complaints procedure;

- copy of the public authority's response;
- any other information they think relevant;
- their contact details.

The stories in which the Commissioner has played a prominent role in recent times have, ironically, had more to do with data protection than FoI. In June 2008 he confirmed he would be serving formal enforcement notices—the toughest sanction available to him—against both HM Revenue and Customs (HMRC) and the Ministry of Defence over 'deplorable failures' leading to 'serious data breaches'.

The Commissioner was referring to two major data protection fiascos that embarrassed the government during Mr Brown's early months in Downing Street. On the first occasion, in November 2007, HMRC confessed to losing two unencrypted data discs containing personal details of 25 million Child Benefit recipients—effectively every family in Britain with a child under the age of 16. The information—including names, addresses, birthdates, *National Insurance (NI)* numbers, and bank details—had been en route from the HMRC offices at Waterview Park, Sunderland, to the NAO in London.

The second breach, revealed in January 2008, concerned the theft of an MoD laptop containing confidential details of 600,000 service personnel. In reporting the crime to the Commons in a statement, then Defence Secretary Des Browne revealed two further thefts of departmental laptops had also occurred since 2005.

Table 20.5 Priority types of information covered by the FoI 'public interest test'

| Category | Definition |
| --- | --- |
| Matters of public debate | Covers issues in relation to which public debate has been generated and debate cannot properly take place without disclosure of information, issue affects wide range of individuals and/or companies, government has put its views on record, and issue may affect legislative process |
| Public participation in political debate | Covers situations in which local interest groups need sufficient information to be able to represent those interests, and requests relate to facts behind major policy decision—particularly one of 'unprecedented importance' |
| Accountability for public funds | Matters relating to government accountability for sale of public assets, or legal aid spending, need for openness relating to tender processes and prices relating to public spending and services, misappropriation of public funds, when accountability of elected officials whose propriety has been called into question, and need for public bodies to obtain value for money in spending receipts from taxpayers |
| Public safety | Information relating to air safety, nuclear plant security, and public health, contingency plans in an emergency, and potential damage to the environment |

There is a welter of guidance on the ICO's website about the rights of public and media to access information under the Acts it administers. One of the most useful for journalists is the guidance notice—based on specified precedents set by both British and international FoI authorities—explaining how public authorities should weigh the 'public interest' of a request against any potential qualified exemptions (see Table 20.5 on page 589).

# ▌ Freedom of information and the headlines—some case studies

Perhaps unsurprisingly, news reporters working on everything from local weekly free sheets to national dailies have been quick to embrace the FoI Acts as a source of potential stories—not least because they enable a modicum of what might loosely be termed 'investigative journalism' to be carried out within the increasingly restrictive parameters of the modern newsroom environment. Widespread cutbacks—from the offices of regional publishers to those of major national newspapers—have seen the size of many papers' reporting staff dwindle in recent years. Papers are facing growing competition from the Internet and other forms of new media, and as a result new recruits are expected to 'multitask' as everything from video journalists and photographers to designers, sub-editors, and bloggers. At the same time, the ever-tighter economies imposed on newsrooms means that what conventional  reporting is still being done is increasingly being carried out over the telephone and/or email, rather than in the face-to-face, hands-on fashion of days gone by.

The FoI Acts, therefore, offer a means by which journalists with suitably forensic minds can target their questions at the relevant public authorities and hold them to account 'on the cheap'. Whereas once they might have had to invest significant amounts of time (and money) in rooting out information organizations were keen to keep out of the public domain, much of this can now be obtained (at least theoretically) by sending a simple email. Freedom of information legislation has also spawned several 'amateur' journalism websites almost entirely dedicated to using it as an investigative tool (notably http://helpmeinvestigate.com and www.opendemocracy.net).

The FoI bonanza did not begin in earnest until January 2005. Within days of the 2000 Act coming fully into force, the *Observer* ran a story listing a 'who's  who' of celebrities and businesspeople who had been wined and dined by then Prime Minister Mr Blair at his country retreat, Chequers, since 2001. The luminaries—whose names it had obtained under the new FoI rules—included entertainer Des O'Connor, former Spice Girl Geri Halliwell, television presenter

Esther Rantzen, Lord Lloyd Webber, Olympic champion rower Sir Steve Red-grave, and Tesco chief executive Sir Terry Leahy.

That August, BBC2's *Newsnight* used an FoI request to expose the fact that Harold Macmillan's British government sold Israel sufficient quantities of uranium 235 and heavy water to enable it to develop its nuclear weapons programme. In a statement to the International Atomic Energy Agency (IAEA), then Foreign Office Minister Kim Howells denied Britain had been a party to any such sale, but in March 2006 *Newsnight* used a further FoI request to expose sales of plutonium to Israel during Harold Wilson's first term.

Perhaps even more shocking was the disclosure, in December 2005, of a hushed-up report by a Scotland Yard detective, Inspector Tom Hayward, into a brutal torture camp operated by British forces in post-war Germany. *The Guardian* used an FoI request to obtain a copy of the document, which detailed the outcome of interrogations of 372 men and 44 women at the Bad Nenndorf camp, near Hanover. Among the grisly details included was an account of how two men suspected of being Communists were starved to death, another was beaten to a pulp, and numerous others suffered serious injuries or lost toes to frostbite. Four months later, the paper published images of emaciated prisoners after winning an appeal against the MoD's refusal to release photographs of the victims contained in the report.

In July 2006, under its FoI Act obligations to publish proactively information in the public interest, the Foreign Office released an alarming gazetteer of allegations against foreign diplomats showing that, between 1999 and 2004, they had been accused of 122 separate criminal offences—including murder, child abuse, rape, and sexual assault. No charges had been brought against any of them because under international law officials on diplomatic business have immunity from prosecution. Criminality seemed to be catching around that time: in the same month statistics published by 13 UK police forces revealed that at least 174 serving officers had convictions, ranging from drink-driving to criminal damage and public order offences. Some had committed crimes while employed by the police.

But FoI requests do not always produce such sensational outcomes. In most cases they 'unearth' humdrum information—much of it unexciting and lacking in any obvious news value. Indeed, there is a feeling in some quarters—not least in the offices of the less well-staffed public authorities—that journalists have come to rely on the Acts a little too heavily. Before the concept of 'freedom of information' had passed into British law, reporters were forced to rely on those timeworn qualities—guile, ingenuity, and perseverance—to tease out material organizations wanted to keep under their belts. If they received tip-offs that councillors were fiddling their expenses or public officials taking overseas flights using taxpayers' money, they would often have to confront the relevant authority's press office head on, citing phrases like 'public interest' and 'public domain' to remind them of their obligation to confirm or deny such activities, and where necessary supply details. Reluctant though authorities invariably were to expose themselves to criticism by admitting such abuses, more often than not they grudgingly put their hands up. Today, able to hide behind the cloak of having to 'dig out the information' or 'go through all of the files', the same authorities can cheerfully take far longer to make disclosures—using the cover of the statutory 20-day time limit to craft polished excuses and put off answering questions until any newsworthiness derived from them has dwindled or passed entirely.

Seasoned FoI users—particularly those experienced enough to know the difference between a story requiring the Act and one that can be stood up using more conventional tactics—cite the counter-argument that, given the relative ease and effectiveness of the legislation, far too few journalists are taking advantage of it. Used in a targeted way it is certainly true that FoI provides an excellent source of off-diary stories (gold dust for news editors).

# ▌ The future of freedom of information— and moves to restrict it

Labour made a big noise about its commitment to FoI during its first term, but by its third it appeared to be regretting laying itself open to quite so much scrutiny. Ministers' discomfort with some of the outcomes of FoI began emerging in May 2007, when Conservative *backbencher* David Maclean introduced a *private member's Bill (PMB)* into the House of Commons—the Freedom of Information (Amendment) Bill—which effectively proposed exempting MPs from the 2000 Act (ostensibly to protect details contained in their personal correspondences, including the addresses of private individuals). It also proposed incorporating the cost of the time officials spend 'thinking' about whether (and how) to disclose information within the £600 limit above which requests become chargeable. Around the same time, it was reported that then Lord Chancellor, Lord Falconer, was privately drawing up his own proposals to curb FoI requests relating to MPs' affairs—so it came as little surprise when Mr Blair declined to condemn Mr Maclean's Bill when challenged to do so publicly.

The issue came to a head in June that year after the Bill was provisionally approved by the Commons and passed to the Lords, where it appeared ministers were seeking a sympathetic peer to 'sponsor' it. When no one came forward, and the Bill was roundly condemned by both the Commons Constitutional Affairs *Select Committee* and the Lords Constitution Committee, it finally fell—but not before then *Leader of the House* Jack Straw had announced he would be issuing new guidelines to public authorities to ensure that MPs' personal details were not compromised by releasing correspondences between them and their constituents.

It is not only public authorities themselves that occasionally gripe about the FoI Acts. In May 2007, the Commissioner himself used his address to the annual Freedom of Information Conference to urge people to act with 'restraint' when making requests. He cited an enquiry about how much the Foreign Office spent on Ferrero Rocher chocolates and another asking about the number of eligible bachelors in the Hampshire Police Force as examples of frivolous, time-wasting queries. Mr Thomas went on to announce plans to produce a new 'charter' for 'responsible' FoI requests.

Beyond measures to *restrict*—or otherwise qualify—the Act's application, its scope is expected to be extended in coming months, through the inclusion of as yet unspecified new guarantees of 'transparency' in the upcoming 'Freedom' or Great Repeal Bill. This will supersede an earlier Ministry of Justice consultation paper that mooted rolling out the Act to cover not only bona fide public authorities, but also private companies providing services on behalf of the public sector and those carrying out 'public' functions, including utility companies and independently run care homes with residents funded by social services departments, or private sector providers involved in treating NHS patients or running prisons.

## ☰ Topical feature idea

Figure 20.1 is the top section of a lengthy news story from the award-winning *Computer Weekly* magazine based on an FoI request by investigative journalist Mark Ballard. It focuses on the highly topical concern about the vulnerability of personal data held electronically by law enforcement agencies, and the danger that confidential information held on government computer systems could be open to misuse by errant employees of the state. You work on a national broadsheet newspaper, and your editor has requested a detailed background feature on the wider subject of data protection (or lack thereof). How would you develop the information contained in this extract to paint a fuller picture of the scale of the problem identified, and whom would you approach for interview to give weight to the concerns aired—and to offer the government's defence? How would you humanize the story?

**Figure 20.1** Article from *Computer Weekly*, 16 July 2010

# HM Courts Service staff breached government database of personal information

Mark Ballard

*Computer Weekly*

16 July 2010

Web link: http://www.computerweekly.com/
Articles/2010/07/16/241990/HM-Courts-Serv-
ice-staff-breached-government-database-
of-personal.htm

Staff working for Her Majesty's Courts Service have breached security on the government
database that stores personal data about everyone in the UK.

Also, local authorities sacked 26 employees
last year for snooping on personal data stored
on the Department for Work and Pensions
(DWP) Customer Information System (CIS),
which, with 90 million records, is one of the
largest databases in Europe.

Freedom of Information (FoI) requests by
*Computer Weekly* revealed that the DWP
caught 124 council workers breaching database security in the year to April 2010.

E-mail exchanges by IT security staff at the
DWP and the Ministry of Justice (MoJ), and
obtained by *Computer Weekly*, also expose the
weak grip the DWP had on the security of the
five-year-old CIS database.

Public sector workers have been repeatedly
caught snooping on personal data stored
by the DWP since the department gave other
government agencies access to the database
in 2005.

The MoJ said HM Courts Service staff had
been caught looking at CIS personal data
on 23 occasions since April 2008 and the
breaches had continued through 2010.

The DWP was regularly catching staff
snooping on CIS even while it drew up plans
in 2007 for the citizen database to become a
spine for sharing personal data across the
whole of government. The security breaches
continued as ministers approved plans for
the CIS-Cross Government (CIS-X) scheme
to become the biographical core of the now-
defunct ID cards programme.

So far, 180 CIS users are known to have
breached its security by looking up personal
data about or on behalf of friends, relatives,
colleagues, celebrities, and themselves. At
least 35 public sector workers have been
sacked. The MoJ said it had not retained
records of breaches committed by Courts
Service staff before 2008.

About 200,000 public sector staff have regular access to the CIS.

## ✳ Current issues

- **Widening the scope of the FoIA:** the coalition agreement specifies that the 'scope'
  of the FoIA will be widened to 'provide greater transparency', but fails to go further.
  Among the possible changes could be a wider overall remit for the Act, perhaps
  encompassing academies and privatized utilities.

- **Extension of Information Commissioner's powers to police data protection**: both
  the Lib Dems and the Tories proposed in their 2010 election manifestoes to extend
  the powers of the Information Commissioner to audit public sector bodies accused
  of violating data protection principles to the private sector. It is unclear how far they
  intend to go in office, but several external organizations, including the European
  Union Agency for Fundamental Rights, have previously criticized Britain for not
  doing enough to ensure that individuals' data is properly protected.

- **Relaxation of '30-Year Rule':** for decades, there has been a rule (still present under the FoIA) preventing British governments having to make public **Cabinet** papers and other official documents until 30 years after they were written. However, in February 2010, Justice Secretary Jack Straw announced this would shortly be changed to 20. The reform—which fell short of a 15-year limit for secrecy proposed by an inquiry set up by Gordon Brown and headed by *Daily Mail* editor Paul Dacre—is due to be phased in gradually over ten years (assuming it goes ahead), allowing 2 million additional documents to be transferred to the National Archives at Kew, east London.

## ? Review questions

1. What are the main stated aims of the Freedom of Information Act 2000 and Freedom of Information (Scotland) Act 2002?

2. Outline the main types of exemption from the FoI Acts and give some examples of how these exemptions apply in practice.

3. How and to whom does an individual make a formal complaint about a refusal by a public authority to disclose information under the FoI Acts?

4. How do the FoI Acts relate to the Data Protection Act 1998? Do they complement or contradict each other?

5. Give some examples of news stories to have been unearthed by FoI requests.

## → Further reading

Brooke, H. (2006) *Your Right to Know: New Edition—A Citizen's Guide to the Freedom of Information Act*, London: Pluto Press. **Step-by-step guide to making effective Freedom of Information Act requests by the journalist who exposed the MPs' expenses scandal. Includes an introduction by Ian Hislop, editor of *Private Eye,* on his magazine's prolific use of the FoIA.**

Carey, P. (2004) *Data Protection: A Practical Guide to UK and EU Law*, Oxford: Oxford University Press. **This handy jargon-busting guide, now in its second edition, offers succinct explanations of UK's data protection laws and EU rules from which much of their content is derived—including the Directive on Privacy and Electronic Communication, which came into force in December 2003 and governs the potential for electronic privacy infringement arising from the abuse of the Internet, telecommunications, and CCTV.**

Macdonald, J., Crail, R., and Jones, C. (eds) (forthcoming) *The Law of Freedom of Information*, 2nd edn, Oxford: Oxford University Press. **Second edition of the acclaimed legal handbook, which offers a forensic breakdown of law and how it applies in practice to public authorities in UK.**

Wadham, J., Griffiths, J., and Harris, K. (2007) *Blackstone's Guide to the Freedom of Information Act 2000*, 3rd edn, Oxford: Oxford University Press. **Revised third edition of the popular, user-friendly FoI guide, which contains clear pointers to making worthwhile FoI requests, what not to bother requesting under the Acts, and full explanation of various exemptions.**

## @ Online Resource Centre

**www.oxfordtextbooks.co.uk/orc/Morrison2e/**
> Visit the Online Resource Centre that accompanies this book for web links and
> regular updates.

# Glossary

## A

**academy** Labour's successor to the Conservatives' **city technology colleges (CTCs)**, these are semi-independent state secondary schools (many funded by injections of private capital), which are allowed to specialize, but must also teach the **National Curriculum**. Initially targeted at 'failing' comprehensives, academy status has since been offered to more successful ones, and the coalition is extending the programme to include primary, as well as secondary, schools. Up to 10 per cent of pupils may be selected on the basis of aptitude in their specialism.

**acceptable behaviour contracts (ABCs)** written agreements that young people identified as having caused a public nuisance in their area are required to sign, with the consent of their parents or guardians, as part of the government's 'Respect' agenda. They are a form of pledge that the signatories will refrain from future antisocial behaviour.

**adoption** the process by which registered 'children in need' are taken into the permanent care of a family other than their biological one. Their adopters become their legal parents; recent reforms have extended this right to gay and unmarried heterosexual couples, as well as those that are married. (cf. **foster parent**)

**Advisory, Conciliation and Arbitration Service (ACAS)** a **quango** charged with mediating between employers and employees in industrial disputes. It is often asked to intervene by one of the two parties to prevent industrial action, such as strikes, being taken in the first place, but can be called in later on to bring the opposing sides back to the negotiating table in pursuit of a peaceful settlement.

**agenda** an outline of the timetable for a meeting of a subcommittee, committee, full council, **cabinet**/executive, or other body.

**alcohol disorder zone (ADZ)** a locality that has traditionally been the scene of alcohol-related public disorder, often adjacent to at least one licensed premises, this can be formally designated by a local authority as requiring more intensive policing. Local licensees will be charged a £100 fee to help to finance the additional patrols.

**alternative vote (AV)** an electoral system used in Australia and proposed by the Lib-Con coalition as a potential replacement for the first-past-the-post (FPTP) procedure used to elect British MPs. Like FPTP, AV returns only one member per **constituency**, but rather than casting a single vote, electors place candidates in order of preference. If no one candidate wins 50 per cent or more of votes cast on the first count, the lowest-placed contender is struck off the ballot paper and his or her second-preference votes distributed among the remainder. This process is repeated until someone finally achieves a simple majority.

**antisocial behaviour order (ASBO)** a form of punishment issued by the police and local authorities for 'antisocial behaviour' that falls short of a criminal offence (e.g. shouting and swearing in the street). An ASBO can be used to impose restrictions on an individual's movements or actions, and its breach can result in prosecution.

**area of outstanding natural beauty (AONB)** a geographical area designated for special legal protection from development and commercial exploitation because of its natural beauty, and/or rare or unique flora and fauna.

**Audit Commission** the national **quango**, due to be abolished in 2012, which employs the **district auditors** who awarded local authorities their star ratings under comprehensive area assessment (CAA). Individual councils' CAA 'scorecards' can be accessed via the Commission's 'Oneplace' website.

## B

**backbencher** term referring to the majority of members of Parliament in the House of Commons, who represent a **constituency** but have no additional job title or responsibilities within the government or opposition, and therefore tend to sit on the 'back benches' (the seats behind the front row on either side of the house).

**background paper** a document or file produced by a local government officer for consideration as support for a policy proposal to be considered at a subcommittee, committee, **cabinet/executive**, or full council meeting.

**balance of payments** the difference in value between imports to and exports from the UK in a given financial year, *including* all types of payment. It encompasses both 'visible' items (such as cars and refrigerators) and 'invisible' ones (such as legal and financial services), as well as the value of financial transfers and debt payments to foreigners. If the value of imports exceeds that of exports, Britain is in a 'balance of payments deficit'; if the reverse is true, it is in a 'balance of payment surplus'. (cf. **balance of trade**)

**balance of trade** the difference in value between import to and exports from the UK in a given financial year, excluding financial transfers and debt repayments to foreigners. If Britain is importing consumer goods and services worth more than those it is exporting, it is in a 'balance of trade deficit'; if the reverse is true, it is in a 'balance of trade surplus'.

**Bank of England** Britain's central bank, based at Threadneedle Street in the City of London. It has its own governor and was given independence from government by then Chancellor Gordon Brown within days of Tony Blair's 1997 election victory.

**basic allowance** a standard fee (usually modest) paid to all councillors out of the revenue budgets of their local authorities. It can vary from one area to another.

**billing authority** the local authority that sends out **Council Tax** bills to local households, collects the money, and keeps a register of who has and who has not paid. This is the responsibility of district councils or **borough councils** and unitary authorities. (cf. **precepting authority**)

**borough council** a type of local authority with exactly the same powers as a district council, but which has the right to call itself a 'borough' because of a historical connection to the Crown.

**Boundary Commission for England** a national **quango** responsible for periodically reviewing the sizes and boundaries of English parliamentary **constituencies** to ensure that they cover approximately the same number of voters.

brownfield site an area of land (usually in a built-up area) that has previously been used for development and may still have extant buildings on it. (cf. **greenfield site**)

building permission/building regulations additional consent required by private individuals or developers on top of **planning permission** in relation to work on extant buildings, normally relating to internal structural alterations. To attain *building permission*, developers must meet a series of *building regulations*, relating to health and safety, energy efficiency, etc.

by-law a form of **delegated legislation** that may be invoked by a local authority to combat a specific problem. For example, many councils have invoked by-laws allowing them to ban the drinking of alcohol in the street in order to improve public order. (cf. **statutory instrument**)

## C

Cabinet the committee of senior government ministers, which meets at least once a week in Downing Street. (cf. **cabinet**)

cabinet a form of executive arrangement introduced under the Local Government Act 2000, which mimics the Westminster **Cabinet** system. Most members of the local government cabinet will be drawn from the party with the greatest number of seats on the council and each will be handed a specific portfolio, or brief (e.g. housing).

Cabinet committees subsets of the **Cabinet**, usually made up of groups of three or more senior ministers whose departmental responsibilities are related in some way. There are three types: standing (permanent); ad hoc (temporary); ministerial (permanent, but made up not of ministers, but of senior civil servants from related spending departments).

capital expenditure the share of a local authority's annual budget spent on building and repairing infrastructure, such as roads, schools, care homes, and libraries. (cf. **revenue expenditure**)

capping the process by which central government (particularly under the Conservative Party) has sometimes stopped local authorities raising **Council Tax** above a certain level. It has also occasionally been used to cap spending in particular areas.

care order an umbrella term for a type of court order, for which a local authority must apply in order to take a child away from his or her parents and into protective care. This can be a temporary arrangement (e.g. with a **foster parent**), or a permanent one (**adoption**).

Care Quality Commission (CQC) regulator established in April 2009 from the amalgamation of the Healthcare Commission and the Commission for Social Care Inspection. It handles complaints about National Health Service treatment, and carries out regular inspections of social care services in England and Wales, including residential homes and day-care facilities.

Chairman of the Conservative Party the title held by an official (often a member of Parliament) whose responsibility is to mastermind the public image of the party as a whole, and to coordinate its national fund-raising operation and membership recruitment.

chief constable the most senior officer in a local police force, responsible for hiring and firing junior officers and ensuring that resources are spread effectively across the area that the force covers. He or she is held accountable by his or her local **police authority**.

chief executive (also known as the **head of the paid service)** the most senior officer working for a local authority. The chief executive will frequently take the role of 'acting **returning officer'** for his or her area at local, general, and European elections.

child protection plan  formerly known as the 'child protection register', this is a list of all recognized 'children in need' in each local authority area, which is shared between the various public, private, and voluntary organizations involved in protecting them.

Children's Commissioner  a government regulator appointed under the 'Every Child Matters' agenda to ensure that all professionals and organizations involved in protecting recognized children in need are discharging their duties effectively.

children's trust  an all-in-one body, formed in 2008, comprising multidisciplinary teams of professionals involved in the care of recognized children in need, including social workers, paediatricians, and child psychologists.

city council  a purely honorary title bestowed on certain district councils, **borough councils,** unitary authorities, and metropolitan borough councils that have been granted Royal Charter status.

city technology college (CTC)  a type of semi-independent state secondary school, introduced by the last Conservative government to specialize in maths, sciences, and information technology (IT), often with hands-on involvement from the private sector. (cf. **academy)**

Civil List  one of two sources of taxpayers' money that are used to finance the monarchy. Until recently, all members of the Royal Household (that is, the immediate Royal Family), other than the Prince of Wales, received annuities from the Civil List, but this now only applies to the Queen and the Duke of Edinburgh. Seventy per cent of Civil List money is used to pay the salaries of royal servants and 30 per cent is used to fund annual royal garden parties.

coalition government  a form of Westminster government comprising ministers drawn from two or more parties that is formed in the event that no single party wins a working majority at a general election. Britain's long-standing first-past-the-post electoral system tends to return majority governments, because of the 'winner takes all' outcomes it produces in each **constituency,** but the May 2010 poll resulted in a Liberal Democrat-Conservative coalition—the UK's first since 1945.

code of conduct  a system of rules governing the behaviour of councillors and officers that, since the Local Government Act 2000, has had to be formally adopted by each local authority. It must set out details of unacceptable conduct and any penalties incurred.

collective responsibility  the principle that all members of a parliamentary party's front bench (and especially of the government) should either 'sing from the same hymn sheet' publicly, whatever their personal views on some of their party's policies, or be prepared to resign. The late Labour **Leader of the House** Robin Cook resigned in 2003 in protest at the UK's impending invasion of Iraq. (cf. **individual ministerial responsibility)**

**Commission for Equality and Human Rights (CEHR)** a **quango** formed as a result of the amalgamation of the Commission for Racial Equality (CRE) and the Equal Opportunities Commission (ECO), to ensure the equal treatment of employees in the workplace, regardless of their gender, race, or age.

**Commission for Local Administration** (also known as the **Local Government Ombudsmen**) there are three of these independent officials, each covering a different region, who investigate complaints from the public, businesses, and other organizations about alleged incompetence by local government officials.

**Commission of the European Union** (also known as the **European Commission**) the European Union's Civil Service, spread over 27 departments known as 'Directorates-General'. Unlike the British Civil Service, however, it *initiates* policy as well as implements it on behalf of elected politicians. Each Directorate-General is headed by a commissioner.

**committee stage** the third stage of a Bill's passage through Parliament, this gives a committee of **backbenchers** the chance to scrutinize it line by line and to suggest amendments. The type of committee that examines Bills is known as a **'public Bill committee'** (formerly 'standing committee') and normally sits in a room outside the main Commons chamber. Emergency legislation, however, and committee stages of international treaties due to be incorporated into British law tend to be heard on the floor of the Commons itself—a so-called 'Committee of the Whole House'. (cf. **report stage**)

**community care** an umbrella term for social care provided to the elderly and adults with mental health issues in their own homes, or in the home of a friend or relative. Examples of help available under community care include 'meals on wheels'.

**community school** the term used for LEA-controlled state secondary schools under 'New Labour'. Some community schools are known as 'community colleges', because they provide adult education and evening classes on top of their primary role as day schools.

**Competition Commission** formerly the 'Monopolies and Mergers Commission' (MMC), this regulatory **quango** vets prospective company mergers and takeovers to ensure that they are not likely to have the effect of compromising free market competition.

**comprehensive school** a colloquial term used to refer to all types of LEA-run maintained secondary school other than **grammar schools**.

**Comprehensive Spending Review (CSR)** a method used by the Treasury to encourage individual spending departments to plan strategically for the future by announcing how much money it intends to allocate to them on a three-yearly basis, rather than annually through the Budget. Three spending reviews—in 1998, 2007, and 2010—have been dubbed 'comprehensive' because of their more detailed nature.

**compulsory purchase order (CPO)** an enforceable statutory order used by local authorities to force homeowners and businesses to sell up and move out of their properties, so that they can be demolished to make way for a new development.

**concessionary fare schemes** types of discount bus fare scheme, often operated by individual councils and passenger transport authorities, to allow qualifying individuals—such as children, pensioners, or students—to travel at a reduced rate. The government launched a nationwide concessionary fare scheme in April 2008, allowing all pensioners to travel free of charge on local buses anywhere in the UK.

conservation area  a district of a city, town, or village that is characterized by buildings of a particular historical and/or architectural vintage, and offered statutory protection from unsympathetic alteration (particularly to exterior appearance).

Conservative Campaign Headquarters (Conservative Central Office)  the national headquarters of the Conservative Party and the building that it occupies at Victoria Street, Westminster.

constituency  the geographical area represented by a member of Parliament. There are 650 constituencies in the present House of Commons and all members (including ministers) must stand for re-election when a general election is called.

Consumer Council for Water  the consumer watchdog focusing on the water industry.

consumer price index (CPI)  the government's preferred measure of inflation, this charts the movement in a notional 'basket' of goods regularly bought by a typical British household. Unlike the retail price index (RPI), it does not include mortgage payments and its readings therefore tend to be lower.

contributory benefits  an umbrella term for more generous social security benefits to which British people are entitled (subject to meeting other criteria) if they have made sufficient National Insurance contributions during previous periods in employment. For example, Incapacity Benefit is a contributory benefit that is related to illness and disability. (cf. non-contributory benefits)

council constitution  each local authority has been obliged to adopt its own constitution since the Local Government Act 2000, outlining its chosen form of executive decision-making arrangements and other procedural matters.

Council of Europe  an alliance of 47 European member states formed in 1949, prior to the European Union. It aims to promote common legal and ethical standards in all member states, and its most celebrated achievement is the European Convention on Human Rights (ECHR).

Council of Ministers of the European Union (also known as the Council of the European Union)  the European Union's supreme decision-making body. It is composed of senior ministers from each member state and its precise composition varies according to the issue being debated. For example, if health policy is on the agenda, each state will send its most senior health minister. The Council is chaired by a leading politician from the country holding the EU presidency, which rotates on a six-monthly basis.

Council Tax  a form of local taxation currently paid by UK residents. It is charged to households and is predominantly property-based (under a banding system from A–H, related to the capital values of the home), but with elements of a 'head tax'. It was introduced in 2003 to replace the unpopular Community Charge (or 'Poll Tax').

county road a major arterial road—
normally an 'A' road linking one town
or city to another—the whole length of
which falls within the boundaries of a
single county. (cf. **trunk road**)

# D

debt charge the money that local authorities must set aside each year in their
revenue budgets to pay back the interest on outstanding loans taken out for
capital projects.

declaration of interest an admission made
by a councillor on being elected or at
the beginning of business in full council, committee, subcommittee, or **cabinet** that he or she has an outside vested
interest in an issue due to be discussed
and/or voted on. He or she will be
expected to leave the meeting for the
duration of that item.

Dedicated Schools Grant (DSG) a **ring-
fenced grant** from central government paid to local authorities on the
proviso that it is spent only on school
staffing and maintenance.

delegated legislation (also known as **secondary
legislation**) a 'lower-tier law', derived
from a parent Act of Parliament,
which may be implemented by
ministers without the need to pass
further Bills. There are three main
types: **statutory instruments**; **by-laws**;
Orders in Council.

designated public places order (DPPO) applied
by local authorities to specified 'public
places' (e.g. streets and parks) that
have become trouble spots for drink-
related antisocial behaviour, this gives
local police the authority to remove
alcohol forcibly from people in those
areas and, if necessary, charge them
with an offence.

devolution the constitutional concept of
delegating a degree of power from a
central parliament to regional and/or
local assemblies. In the UK, Scotland,
Wales, and Northern Ireland were all
granted devolution in 1998—with the
first of these gaining the most power,
including the right to vary Income Tax
by up to 3p in the pound. Devolution is
distinct from independence, which is
the handover of full sovereignty.

direct taxes an umbrella term for taxes,
such as Income Tax and Corporation
Tax, that are taken directly from the individual or company on whom they are
levied, normally at a progressive rate
determined by their income levels in a
given financial year. (cf. **indirect taxes**)

directly elected mayor the most senior
and powerful local politician in towns
and cities that have voted in a local
**referendum** to adopt one of the three
new forms of executive arrangement
outlined in the Local Government Act
2000. They can run their administrations either with the aid of a **cabinet**,
or a council manager (senior officer).
Ken Livingstone, the inaugural **mayor**
of London, was Britain's first elected
mayor.

dispersal order applied by local authorities to antisocial behaviour 'black
spots' in which groups of two or more
people alleged to be causing 'harassment, alarm, or distress' may be
forcibly broken up by **neighbourhood
wardens** or police officers.

dissolution the procedure by which
Parliament is formally 'dissolved'
following the resignation of a government and before a general election.

district auditor the official employed by the
**Audit Commission** to monitor the performance of local authorities in a given
geographical area using the comprehensive area assessment (CAA) system.

district valuer See valuation officer

## E

**elected hereditary peerage** peerages that are passed from one generation to the next. Until 1999, every hereditary peer was entitled by birthright to sit in the House of Lords, but all except 92 (who have since been elected to remain by their colleagues) had this privilege removed in the House of Lords Act 1999. (cf. **life peerage**)

**election deposit** a £500 deposit paid by each candidate who stands in a general election. The payment is lost if they fail to poll votes from more than 5 per cent of the registered electorate in the **constituency**. It was introduced in 1929 as a deterrent to 'frivolous candidates', but has been criticized recently for being too affordable.

**Electoral Commission** the **quango** responsible for ensuring that the correct procedures are followed in parliamentary, local, and European elections, and for enforcing rules on party finance. Its responsibilities include keeping campaign spending by election candidates within agreed statutory limits, and it may refer cases to the Crown Prosecution Service if it feels that electoral law has been broken.

**electoral division** the term used for the **constituencies** represented by county councillors and some unitary authority councillors. Each has between one and three councillors, depending on the size of its population.

**electoral register** the official list of all electors registered to vote in local, general, and European elections in a given local authority area. It is compiled by an electoral registration officer employed by a district council or **borough council**, or unitary authority.

**emergency planning officer** an officer employed by a county council or unitary authority to oversee strategic planning for civil emergencies, such as floods.

**emergency protection order** (also known as an interim care order) a type of **care order** allowing a local authority to take a child into care immediately, because of a perceived threat to his or her well-being. It initially applies for eight days, but may be renewed for up to a further week.

**English Heritage** a national **quango** responsible for managing heritage monuments and properties, such as Stonehenge, on behalf of the government. English Heritage administers the **listed buildings** programme.

**enlargement** a term referring to the expansion of the European Union. It has been enlarged twice in the past decade, with a number of former Soviet countries joining for the first time: ten new states joined in 2004, and a further two—Bulgaria and Romania—in 2007.

**Environment Agency** the **executive agency** of the Department of the Environment, Food, and Rural Affairs (Defra), responsible for regulating the quality and safety of water in rivers and streams, and for strategic planning for flood protection.

**environmental health officer** an officer employed by a district council or **borough council**, or unitary authority, to investigate complaints about environmental health hazards, such as vermin infestation, rotting waste, and noise pollution, and to inspect business premises serving food for their hygiene.

**euro (€)** the single European currency, introduced in all European Union member states bar the UK, Denmark, and Sweden as of 1 January 2002. The Labour government pledged to hold a **referendum** before joining the euro, but Gordon Brown, when Chancellor, said it would not do so until 'five economic tests' were met.

European Central Bank (ECB) based in Frankfurt, the central bank of the European Union, which issues the **euro**.

European Commission See Commission of the European Union

European Court of Human Rights (ECtHR) based in Strasbourg, the ultimate court of appeal for citizens of states that have signed up to the European Convention on Human Rights (ECHR) and passed it into their own domestic law. Britain belatedly ratified the convention by passing the Human Rights Act 1998. The Court was established by the **Council of Europe** and has no link to the European Union.

European Court of Justice (ECJ) the European Union's main legal body, this ensures that EU law is correctly implemented in member states. Each state contributes one judge—making 27 in all—although only 13 ever sit in session together. Only major cases go to the full ECJ, with others being heard by the General Court (formerly the Court of First Instance). Warring parties have their cases presented to the judges by one of 11 advocates-general.

European Parliament (EP) based primarily in Brussels, but moving to Strasbourg for one week in every month, this Parliament is elected every five years. Members of the European Parliament (MEPs) sit in political groupings, rather than along national lines. For example, the British Labour Party sits with the Socialist Group.

executive agency a subset of a large government spending department, staffed by civil servants, charged with delivering a particular area or areas of its policy. Examples include the **Health and Safety Executive**, within the Department of Health, and the **Highways Agency**, in the Department for Transport.

## F

federalism the flipside of **subsidiarity**, this is the idea promoted by Eurosceptics that further extension of the powers of the European Union will lead to individual member states surrendering autonomy for their internal affairs to centralized institutions, turning the Union into a 'United States of Europe', or 'European super-state'.

first reading the formal introduction of a proposed Bill to the House of Commons. The reading usually consists solely of the full title of the Bill being read out by a minister. (cf. **second reading**; **third reading**)

free schools a key plank of Conservative education policy and its 'Big Society' vision of government, these are a planned new generation of publicly funded secondary schools that parents, teachers, and other members of their community will be able to set up and run for themselves. Based on a model devised in Sweden.

forward plan a list of upcoming **key decisions** due to be taken by a local authority that must be made public at least a month in advance.

foster parent an adult who is registered to look after children in need in his or her own home, often for a short period of time, while a more permanent situation is sought. (cf. **adoption**)

**foundation school** like the Conservative Party's grant-maintained (GM) school, this is a self-governing state secondary school, permitted to spend its budgets as it pleases, within certain conditions set by central government. Money is allocated to it via its local education authority (LEA), but it may hire and fire its own staff, and set its own admissions and disciplinary policies distinct from those of LEA-run schools.

**foundation trust** the most successful hospital trusts (those with the highest star ratings) may apply for 'foundation' status, allowing them greater autonomy over running their own internal finances, setting their own pay scales, etc.

**FT100 Share Index (FOOTSIE)** the *Financial Times* Stock Exchange 100 Share Index (to use its full title) is the most famous of a number of 'indices', or lists, of major companies listed on the London Stock Exchange. It lists the hundred highest valued companies at any one time, in order of their share value.

**further education (FE)** an umbrella term for education and training provided by tertiary colleges and school sixth forms. It can encompass resits of A levels and other qualifications aimed at those of school age, but primarily focuses on vocational courses and diplomas.

## G

**general block grant** a generic term for revenue grants paid by central government to local authorities that may be used for any service area, according to local needs and priorities. It is often used as a synonym for the **revenue support grant (RSG)**.

**globalization** a term describing the gradual convergence of national economies into a bigger international whole. It is used increasingly in relation to the idea of free trade and the free movement of labour between countries, and the expansion of the Internet.

**grammar (selective) school** a type of maintained secondary school, phased out in much of the UK, which admits only pupils who have passed an academic test known as the '11 plus'. Those who fail it are admitted to standard **comprehensive schools**.

**Greater London Authority (GLA)** London's overarching 'council', which came into being in 2000 at the same time as the city gained its first **directly elected mayor**. Individual London boroughs retain their own councils to run local services at ground level, but the GLA is responsible for taking strategic decisions for the whole capital.

**Green Paper** a consultation document on a tentative government policy proposal that may, in time, evolve into a **White Paper**, and from there into a proposed Bill. All government Bills (other than emergency legislation) will go through at least one Green Paper stage, although if the public and/or interest groups react strongly against a proposal, it is unlikely to go much further.

**greenbelt** a term used for designated zones around towns and cities that have deliberately been kept free of development to prevent urban sprawl and to protect wildlife.

**greenfield site** an area of land on which there has been little, or no, prior development. (cf. **brownfield site**)

**gross domestic product (GDP)** the total profit from all goods and services generated in Britain in a given financial year, irrespective of which state benefits from them. (cf. **gross national product (GNP)**) gross national product (GNP) the total profit from all goods and services generated by British-based companies in a given financial year, irrespective of where they are physically produced. For example, Far Eastern call centres owned by UK companies such as BT or Virgin would still count towards the state's GNP. (cf. **gross domestic product (GDP)**)

G8 (Group of 8) a loose organization, or forum, devoted to promoting economic free trade and **globalization**, made up of the world's eight leading industrial nations—currently the USA, the UK, Japan, France, Germany, Italy, Canada, and Russia.

# H

Hansard the official record of all parliamentary business in both Houses. Protected by legal privilege and now available to read online, it is nonetheless not an entirely verbatim record of proceedings (except for the words used by the serving prime minister).

head of the paid service See chief executive

Health and Safety Executive (HSE) an **executive agency** of the Department of Health, which is charged with setting and enforcing health and safety legislation in the workplace across the UK. It recently merged with the Health and Safety Commission (HSC), which had previously drawn up health and safety rules.

health service scrutiny committee a statutory body set up by a county council or unitary authority to monitor the quality of health service provision in its area. Each committee is composed of 15 members, including a chairperson, local councillors, and representatives from relevant voluntary sector organizations.

High Representative for Foreign Affairs and Security Policy influential new permanent **European Commission** post created under the terms of the 2007 Treaty of Lisbon. The first holder of the post, due to be backed from 2010 by a diplomatic corps known as the European External Action Service, was Britain's former EU trade commissioner Baroness Ashton of Upholland.

Higher Education Funding Council for England (HEFCE) a **quango** that channels public money for teaching and research into universities.

Highways Agency the **executive agency** of the Department for Transport responsible for building and maintaining Britain's major roads.

honours list a generic term used for two annual lists of individuals chosen to be honoured with ceremonial titles by the Queen in recognition of their worldly achievements. The lists are compiled by ministers and shadow ministers, and honours are awarded in the Queen's Birthday Honours List and the New Year's Honours List.

House of Lords Appointments Commission a **quango** that vets potential candidates for **life peerages** after they have been nominated by a political party leader. It may have an enhanced role as and when the last hereditary peers are finally removed from the House after the next general election.

housing association a not-for-profit organization formerly overseen by the Housing Corporation **quango**. Housing associations are the principal providers of social housing in Britain today, often working with, or on behalf of, local authorities.

**Housing Benefit (Local Housing Allowance)**
a means-tested benefit for the unemployed and low earners, ultimately paid by **Jobcentre Plus**, but administered by district councils or **borough councils** and unitary authority housing offices. Since April 2008, new claimants hoping for help with their rent and existing claimants who move home have been offered local housing allowance, which is pegged at a lower level than Housing Benefit.

**hung parliament** an outcome of a general election that leaves no single party with an overall majority, and the largest one facing the prospect of either ruling as a minority administration or forging a coalition with one or more other parties. The May 2010 election produced Britain's first hung parliament since 1974.

**hybrid structure** a type of local government structure that exists in some counties in England and Wales, in which a **two-tier structure** remains in certain areas while others have adopted the newer **unitary structure**. East Sussex is an example of a hybrid county: Lewes is covered by both a district and a county council, while neighbouring Brighton and Hove has a **city council**, which is a unitary authority.

**I**

**Income Support** a basic level of benefit paid to a range of people who satisfy certain needs-based criteria, but have paid insufficient prior **National Insurance** contributions to qualify for **contributory benefits**. It is available to certain people between the ages of 16 and 60 who are not in full-time work, such as carers or single parents.

**Independent Parliamentary Standards Authority (IPSA)** new regulator created in 2009 to police MPs' and peers' allowance claims and pay their salaries. The **quango**, which began work in earnest only after the May 2010 election, was introduced as a replacement for the in-house Fees Office following the long-running scandal over parliamentary expenses, which led to a number of members standing down prematurely from Parliament and several being prosecuted for fraud.

**Independent Police Complaints Commission (IPCC)** a national **quango** responsible for investigating complaints against **chief constables** and/or their forces. The Commission will automatically launch an investigation whenever a civilian is killed by a police officer.

**independent remuneration panel** a body comprising at least three non-councillors, which was set up in each local authority area under the Local Government Act 2000 to adjudicate independently on any application by the council to increase its member allowances.

**indirect taxes** often referred to as 'hidden' or 'stealth' taxes, these are embedded in the cost of items bought by individuals or companies. Value added tax (VAT) and excise duties on tobacco and alcohol are examples of indirect taxes. Because they are charged at a flat rate on relevant items, they are seen as regressive—that is, they do not take account of an individual or company's ability to pay. (cf. **direct taxes**)

**individual ministerial responsibility** the principle that a **secretary of state** should be prepared to 'fall on his or her sword' and resign if a major failing is exposed in his or her department. In practice, ministers often have to be pushed by their prime minister (as happened in the case of then Chancellor of the Exchequer Norman Lamont after 'Black Wednesday' in 1992). (cf. **collective responsibility**)

inflation  changes in the prices of goods and services from one month to the next. This is calculated using either the **consumer price index (CPI)** or **retail price index (RPI)**, which monitor fluctuations in the values of a notional 'basket' of goods containing items regularly bought by a typical British household.

Information Commissioner  a statutory official appointed to police the implementation of the Freedom of Information (FoI) Act 2000, adjudicating on complaints from individuals and organizations of lack of transparency by public authorities in response to legitimate FoI requests.

interest rates  an instrument of monetary policy used to promote saving and investment, and reduce consumer spending. Since the 1980s, raising interest rates has been the preferred method of controlling **inflation**. The **Bank of England**'s **Monetary Policy Committee (MPC)** meets monthly to decide whether or not to raise or lower interest rates.

interim care order  See emergency protection order

## J

Jobcentre Plus  this replaced the Benefits Agency in 2002 as the main body responsible for administering benefits of all kind, from **Jobseeker's Allowance (JSA)** and **Income Support**, to sickness and disability-related benefits, and maternity benefits.

Jobseeker's Allowance (JSA)  a benefit paid to people over the age of 16 who are registered as unemployed and actively seeking work. There are two types of allowance: contributions-based (which is related to prior **National Insurance** payments) and income-based.

## K

key decision  a policy decision affecting two or more **wards** or **electoral divisions** in a local authority area, and likely to involve 'significant expenditure' if approved. They are judged to be so significant that they must be presented for a final say to the full council and cannot be taken solely in **cabinet** unless delegated to an individual portfolio holder.

## L

leader of the council  the most senior and powerful local politician in authorities that have either adopted the third new executive arrangement outlined in the Local Government Act 2000, or retained their pre-existing one. Like the prime minister at Westminster, they are normally the leader of the party with the greatest number of seats on the council.

Leader of the House  the government minister responsible for organizing the weekly House of Commons timetable, and for proposing changes to its working hours and orders of business.

life peerage  honorary peerages conferred on individuals for life in one of the two annual **honours lists**. As their name suggests, these titles die with their recipient and therefore cannot be passed on to his or her children. (cf. **elected hereditary peerage**)

listed building  an individual building, or small group of buildings (e.g. a Georgian crescent), offered statutory protection against alteration or demolition because of its link to specific historical personalities, events, or architectural movements. There are three levels of listing: grades I, II*, and II.

**local development documents (LDDs)** strategic plans produced by individual local planning authorities outlining the projected nature and scale of development in their area over the following few years. The schedule of publication for LDDs is outlined in a publicly available local development scheme (LDS).

**local government association** the regional coalitions of local authorities that lobby Parliament and central government on their behalf. There is also a national Local Government Association (LGA).

**Local Government Boundary Commission for England (LGBCE)** national **quango** tasked with periodically reviewing boundaries between **wards** and **electoral divisions** to ensure each is represented by the correct number of councillors relative to its population size. It replaced the *Boundary Committee for England* in 2010.

**Local Government Ombudsmen** See Commission for Local Administration

**local involvement networks (LINks)** the replacement for patients' forums in the National Health Service, these are groups of local service users, working together with voluntary sector professionals, who channel complaints and feedback on local health service bodies and social services care providers to those organizations.

**local safeguarding children's board (LSCB)** the committees set up by every county council and unitary authority under the Children Act 2004 to coordinate the efforts of all organizations involved in looking after recognized children in need.

**Lord Speaker** a recently introduced post designed to mimic that of the Commons **Speaker**, this title is given to a peer elected by his or her colleagues in the House of Lords to chair debate in the chamber.

**Lords Spiritual** a collective term for the 26 senior Church of England bishops, led by the Archbishop of Canterbury, who remain entitled to sit in the House of Lords.

# M

**mayor** a ceremonial title that has traditionally been rotated between councillors on local authorities on a year-by-year basis. Its recipient spends 12 months chairing full council meetings on a non-partisan basis and attending civic events.

**member of the European Parliament (MEP)** an elected representative who sits in the **European Parliament**, of which there are 754, elected every five years. Each state contributes a number of members that reflects its population size.

**minister of state** an umbrella term for all ministers in government departments, including junior ministers.

**minutes** the written record of the proceedings of a meeting of a subcommittee, committee, full council, **cabinet/ executive**, or other body.

**Monetary Policy Committee (MPC)** a committee of the **Bank of England** that meets once a month to decide whether or not to raise or lower **interest rates**, on the basis of the previous month's **inflation** figures.

**monitoring officer** a senior local authority officer responsible for monitoring councillors' and officers' compliance with their council's **code of**

**conduct**, and recording and reporting to members any cases of suspected maladministration.

## N

**National Assembly for Wales** the full title of Wales's devolved assembly, which is based in a purpose-built chamber in Cardiff Bay.

**National Curriculum** the compulsory content that must be taught in maintained (state) schools in Britain in certain core subjects, such as English language and maths.

**National Curriculum assessments (SATs)** academic tests taken by state school pupils at three key stages in their **National Curriculum** learning. Key stages 1, 2, and 3 take place at the ages of 7, 11, and 14, respectively.

**National Executive Committee of the Labour Party (NEC)** often referred to as 'Labour's ruling NEC', a senior policy committee composed of representatives of all of the main branches of the Labour Party, including members of Parliament, **constituency** party members, and trade unionists. Major changes to the party's constitution must be approved by this committee.

**National Institute for Health and Clinical Excellence (NICE)** a **quango** set up to vet medication before it is made available on the National Health Service, and to carry out its own research into potential cures and treatments. It is headed by a chief medical officer.

**National Insurance (NI)** a system of contributory payments deducted from employees' wages and topped up by employers, to finance entitlement to future benefits should they be needed. The system was originally set up in 1911 to protect workers from poverty should they become unable to work through sickness or injury.

**national non-domestic rates (NNDR)** (also known as the **uniform business rates (UBR)**) the local taxation paid by companies, the bills of which are calculated according to the **rateable values** of business premises and a national multiplier set each year by the government (e.g. 50p in the pound). The money is collected locally, but then funnelled through the Treasury and redistributed around the country according to need.

**National Offender Management Service (NOMS)** an **executive agency** of the Ministry of Justice responsible for recruiting and employing the UK's 48,000 prison staff, and overall policy regarding the day-to-day running of its 135 jails. The Prisons Service is now a part of NOMS and is responsible only for publicly funded jails.

**national park** one of the 14 geographical areas of Britain designated for the highest degree of protection from development or commercial exploitation possible under UK law.

**Natural England** a **quango** responsible for conserving, protecting, and managing the natural environment in England for current and future generations.

**neighbourhood policing teams** community-based teams made up of serving police officers, **police community support officers (PCSOs)**, and volunteers, which are intended to increase the visibility of patrols on the streets. Since April 2005, 3,600 neighbourhood policing teams have been set up across the UK.

**neighbourhood warden** a salaried, community-based official, based in a local authority area, whose job is to patrol areas with reputations for anti-social behaviour, graffiti, and criminal activity. The warden is employed by the Department for Communities and Local Government's Neighbourhood Renewal Unit.

**Network Rail** the not-for-dividend company set up by the government in 2001 to take over repairs and maintenance of the UK overland rail network (tracks, signals, and stations) from Railtrack, the private monopoly initially given those responsibilities following the privatization of British Rail in the early 1990s.

**NHS trust** an umbrella term referring to hospitals, ambulance services, and mental health services provided on the National Health Service. The term 'trust' was coined in the early 1990s and relates to the new levels of autonomy given to these bodies to run their own affairs. Each has its own board, like a company, and is designated a service 'provider'—rather than a 'commissioner', like **primary care trusts (PCTs)**.

**1922 Committee** often referred to as 'the influential 1922 Committee', this is made up of all of the backbench Conservative members of Parliament at any one time. The 'mood' of the Committee is a crucial test of the likely lifespan of its leadership and it was widely credited with delivering the knockout blow to Margaret Thatcher's premiership after she was challenged by Michael Heseltine in 1990.

**non-contributory benefits** an umbrella term for lower-level social security benefits to which British people are entitled (subject to meeting other criteria) irrespective of their previous **National Insurance** contributions. **Income Support** is an example of a purely 'needs-based', non-contributory benefit that is paid to people in lieu of a higher level entitlement. (cf. **contributory benefits**)

**North Atlantic Treaty Organization (NATO)** a military alliance made up of 26 predominantly Western powers, NATO was formed with the signing of the North Atlantic Treaty in Washington DC in 1949. It was initially designed to act as a bulwark during the Cold War against the expansion of the Soviet Union and the Warsaw Pact.

# O

**Office for Budget Responsibility (OBR)** a **quango** set up by the **coalition government** to produce independent economic forecasts and comment on the likely impact on jobs and inflation of the government's budgetary decisions. For its first three months it was overseen by Sir Alan Budd, a former economic adviser to Margaret Thatcher and founder member of the **Bank of England**'s **Monetary Policy Committee (MPC)**.

**Office of Communications (Ofcom)** a **quango** dubbed a 'super-regulator' because of its all-embracing responsibilities for overseeing the telecommunications and broadcast media industries (radio, television, and the Internet). Ofcom may fine broadcasters, including the British Broadcasting Corporation (BBC), for breaking the rules governing taste and decency, and it monitors their public service content (such as current affairs and news output).

**Office of Fair Trading (OFT)** a national regulatory **quango** established to ensure that free and fair competition operates in a given market for the benefit of the consumer on a day-to-day basis. The OFT investigates complaints about restrictive practices, cartels, and other anti-competitive behaviour.

**Office of Gas and Electricity Markets (Ofgem)** a regulatory **quango** that oversees Britain's privatized energy market to ensure that there is free and fair competition between suppliers, and that bills are kept within acceptable bounds. It is headed by a Director General of Gas and Electricity Markets.

**Office for Standards in Education, Children's Services, and Skills (Ofsted)** a central government inspectorate, headed by a Chief Inspector of Schools, which visits maintained schools, preschools education providers, and **further education** colleges on a rolling basis to monitor standards of teaching and administration, and awards grades from '1' to '4'.

**Office of the Qualifications and Examinations Regulator (Ofqual)** a new national regulator established in 2008 to monitor the standard of qualifications, exams, and tests in England. Ofqual is headed by a ruling committee. It is part of the Qualifications and Curriculum Authority (QCA).

**Office of Water Regulation (OFWAT)** (also known as the **Water Services Regulatory Authority**) one of three statutory regulators of the privatized water industry, OFWAT monitors the transparency of individual water companies' accounts and share policies.

**outline planning permission** the first stage of obtaining consent to develop a site, during which permission is granted 'in principle', subject to the submission of a more detailed plan. (cf. **planning permission**)

**overview and scrutiny committee** an overarching 'super-committee' adopted by some local authorities under the Local Government Act 2000, which scrutinizes the workings of council departments, and decisions taken by

**cabinet** and senior officers. There will normally be several scrutiny subcommittees that focus on more specific policy areas.

## P

**parish meeting** the lowest form of local authority, this is a de facto parish council that convenes once a year in small villages to discuss the provision of local services and to make representations to the statutory authorities on behalf of local people.

**Parliamentary Commissioner for Administration** (also known as the **Parliamentary and Health Service Ombudsman**) also responsible for overseeing administration in the National Health Service, the Commissioner hears complaints from members of the public and organizations about alleged maladministration by Parliament, rather than corruption.

**Parliamentary Commissioner for Standards** a post created on the recommendation of the Nolan Inquiry, which was prompted by a series of 'sleaze' scandals involving Conservative members of Parliament in the early 1990s, including the 'cash for questions' affair, when Neil Hamilton was accused of taking payments from Harrods owner Mohamed Al Fayed to ask parliamentary questions on his behalf. The Commissioner polices the rigorous system of disclosure of outside interests that was introduced after these scandals.

**Parliamentary Labour Party (PLP)** Labour's equivalent of the **1922 Committee** in the Conservative Party, this is the collective term for all Labour **backbenchers**.

**Parliamentary and Health Service Ombudsman** See **Parliamentary Commissioner for Administration**

**parliamentary private secretary (PPS)** a very junior government post often offered to an upcoming member of Parliament judged to have ministerial potential. PPSs are the 'link' between senior ministers and the ordinary **backbenchers** in their party, and are often used to float potential policy ideas to 'test the water' among their parliamentary colleagues.

**parliamentary privilege** the constitutional convention allowing members of Parliament and peers to speak freely within their respective chambers, even criticizing named individuals without fear of being prosecuted for defamation. Even under parliamentary privilege, certain terms are banned in reference to their fellow MPs or peers, including the word 'liar'.

**parliamentary sovereignty** the constitutional principle derived from the 1689 Bill of Rights that elevated Parliament to a position of supremacy over the sovereign in governing England and Wales (and, in due course, the whole of the UK).

**parliamentary under-secretary** the lowest form of government minister, this is a junior minister below the level of **minister of state** and **secretary of state**.

**parole** the procedure by which prisoners are released early from their sentences for 'good behaviour'. Those convicted of more minor offences are usually granted automatic early release after serving half the length of their sentences, but serious offenders, such as rapists and serial murderers, will usually serve at least 20 years.

**Passenger Focus** (also known as the **Rail Passengers' Council**) a consumer watchdog representing the interests of overland rail commuters and passengers.

**permanent secretary** the most senior civil servant in a government department. He or she will offer day-to-day advice to the **secretary of state** and other ministers, and therefore occupies a **politically restricted post**.

**planning contribution** (or **planning gain**) an offer by a developer of added value for a local authority in exchange for being granted **planning permission** for a major project. For example, the developer may offer to finance a new playground for children in a deprived **ward** as a form of 'sweetener' to help its bid to build a new supermarket.

**planning inquiry** a public inquiry held into a contentious development proposal to which there is strong opposition. It will be chaired by an independent inspector appointed by the Secretary of State for Communities and Local Government, and those immediately affected by the proposal will be allowed to speak at it.

**planning permission** consent given to an individual, company, or other organization to build new premises, or to extend or adapt an existing one. (cf. **outline planning permission**)

**police authority** the local authorities of the UK police service, these are composed of a mix of local councillors and laypeople, and are charged with hiring and firing **chief constables** and their deputies, and holding them to account for their policies.

**police community support officers (PCSOs)** these semi-trained officers are employed as auxiliary police officers, with the power to arrest and issue some minor punishments, such as fixed penalty fines for antisocial behaviour.

policy and resources committee  traditionally the most powerful local authority
committee, because it is in charge of
the council's overall budget, this committee must be consulted on major
decisions (e.g. to build a new road),
because it will have to approve the
funding.

political sovereignty  the constitutional
concept of an institution or individual
holding political supremacy (or 'sovereignty') over the citizens of a nation. In Britain, political sovereignty
originally rested with the reigning
monarch (or 'sovereign'), but passed
to Parliament after the 1689 Bill of
Rights.

politically restricted post  the contractual
position held by senior public officials
(civil servants and local government
officers) who are barred from canvassing openly for a political party at
elections, or standing for office, due
to their close day-to-day working relationship with politicians.

Postal Services Commission (Postcomm)  the
regulatory quango monitoring the
quality and reliability of postal delivery services in the UK.

postal vote  a means of casting a vote
in an election by post, rather than in
person. The British government is
committed to extending rights to vote
by post across the country, following
several recent pilots, but this has provoked criticism from some quarters
because of the perceived risk of fraud
in multi-occupancy households.

Postwatch  a consumer watchdog with no
statutory recognition, which channels
complaints from the public and businesses to the government.

precepting authority  all local authorities
that receive some of their revenue
funding through the Council Tax are

precepting authorities. The term
'precept' refers to the 'invoice' that
such authorities present to the billing
authority, outlining the sum that they
wish to raise through the Council Tax
in the coming financial year.

prescribed function  a role and responsibility formally delegated by a council to
its committees, subcommittees, cabi-
net/executive, and individual cabinet
members. These will normally be
spelt out in the council's constitution.

President of the European Council  newly
created permanent post at the helm
of the European Council, a powerful body comprising the most senior
politicians from each European Union
member state. Introduced under the
2007 Treaty of Lisbon, its inaugural
holder is former Belgian Prime Minister Herman van Rompuy.

Press Complaints Commission (PCC)  the
independent, self-regulatory industry body responsible for handling
complaints from the public about
newspapers and magazines. It has
17 members, including editors, and
representatives of the public relations
(PR) and marketing industries, and
enforces a code of practice to which
all print journalists must adhere. This
prohibits practices such as major in-
trusions into personal privacy.

primary care trust (PCT)  a body headed
by general practitioners (GPs), community nurses, and other primary
care professionals based in a given
area, and responsible for 'commissioning' the vast majority of National
Health Service care on behalf of
local people. Primary care trusts, responsible for 80 per cent of the NHS
revenue budget and covering populations of up to 600,000, are due to be
abolished by 2013.

primary schools  maintained schools that deliver primary teaching to pupils in core subjects such as English, maths, and science between the ages of 4 (reception class) and 11.

private finance initiative (PFI)  the main way in which major capital projects are now funded, this is an arrangement between a public authority (e.g. a council or government department) and a private company, under which the latter foots most of the initial bill and the former pays it back (with interest) over a period of years. (cf. **public–private partnership (PPP)**)

private member's Bill (PMB)  a Bill proposed by an individual **backbencher**, normally on an issue dear to his or her heart, and/or one that concerns his or her constituents. While they may cast the media's spotlight onto an issue, most PMBs are never allotted sufficient parliamentary time to pass into law, but there have been exceptions, including the 1967 Abortion Bill, introduced by future Liberal leader David Steel.

Privy Council  an ancient committee of state, originally formed as a group of close confidantes for the reigning monarch to counteract the power of the Great Council or *Magnum Concilium*, composed of peers of the realm. Today, all serving and past **Cabinet** ministers and leaders of the Opposition are appointed members for life, and advise the monarch on matters such as the use of the Privy Purse (their personal pot of money, derived from the Duchy of Lancaster estate) and the making of Orders in Council.

proportional representation (PR)  an umbrella term for alternative electoral systems to the 'first past the post' (FPTP) process used in British general elections. Most Western countries use PR, including Ireland, which uses the single transferable vote (STV). The Liberal Democrats have been campaigning for STV to be adopted in Britain, arguing that is fairer than the UK system, because the number of seats won by a party tends to bear more of a relationship to the votes cast for them than does FPTP.

prorogation  a term that denotes the procedure by which Parliament is temporarily suspended (or 'prorogued') at the end of a parliamentary session.

public Bill committee  a temporary parliamentary committee convened to scrutinize and debate a Bill or another prospective Act of Parliament. They were formerly known as 'standing committees' because, being only temporary, their members are notionally not in their positions for long enough to warrant permanent seats at the committee table.

public limited company (plc)  a type of larger registered company in the UK that makes its shares available to the general public to buy by 'floating' itself on the London Stock Exchange. It has a legal obligation to maximize profits for its shareholders. Most household-name companies in Britain are plcs (e.g. BP).

public–private partnership (PPP)  a financial arrangement used to fund major capital projects, such as roads and prisons, whereby a government department or other public authority will share the cost of the initial outlay with a private company or companies. The bulk of the up-front investment is usually made by the private sector and the public sector will pay it off (with interest) over a period of years. PPP is 'New Labour's' successor to the Conservatives' **private finance initiative (PFI)**.

public sector net cash requirement (PSNCR) formerly the 'public sector borrowing requirement' (PSBR), this is the sum of money that the British government will need to borrow through commercial loans or from the public in a given financial year to meet its public spending commitments—that is, it is the difference between the total taxation that the Exchequer expects to raise in a year and its actual outgoings.

Public Works Loan Board (PWLB) a body that can lend money to local authorities for major capital projects at a lower rate of interest than those offered by the banking sector. The PWLB is part of the UK Debt Management Office, a Treasury **executive agency**.

# Q

qualified majority voting (QMV) a system of voting in the **Council of Ministers of the European Union** that enables certain issues to be decided by a majority vote in favour or against, rather than unanimously. Under QMV, each member state is allocated a certain number of votes in proportion to its population, meaning that some have substantially more say in matters than others and that decisions are taken on a 'qualified' majority basis. The UK, for example, has 29 votes, while Malta has just three.

quality parish council a form of parish council made up of elected councillors from a village or small town that has performed its limited duties (e.g. maintaining local play facilities) so efficiently that it has been rewarded with additional responsibilities—and resources to act on them—by the statutory local authorities.

quango (quasi-autonomous non-government organization) a non-departmental body set up by a government department, and partly funded by the taxpayer, to regulate, monitor, or otherwise oversee a particular area of policy delivery. UK quangos have their own executive boards, like companies, and include the Arts Council England and the **Commission for Equality and Human Rights (CEHR)**.

Queen's Speech an annual address given by the Queen at the State Opening of Parliament in October or November. The speech is actually a list of legislation to be proposed by the government during the coming parliamentary session (year) and is written not by the monarch herself, but by the prime minister and the **Cabinet**.

Question Time sessions of parliamentary business during which **backbenchers** and/or peers on all sides have the opportunity of questioning individual departmental ministers on the conduct of their ministerial business. Major spending departments each have a question time session at least once a fortnight, while the most famous is 'Prime Minister's Questions', held every Wednesday lunchtime.

# R

Rail Passengers' Council See **Passenger Focus**

rateable value the sum of money that a business premises would be able bring in on the rental market. Both **national non-domestic rates (NNDR)** and the rates—that is, the property-based domestic tax that preceded the Community Charge—are (or were) based on rateable values.

recession an economic term used to describe a rapid slowdown or negative growth. Technically, it refers to a period of two successive economic quarters during which the economy has 'shrunk'—that is, consumers have stopped spending, sales of goods and services have dwindled, and manufacturers have reduced production.

referendum  a public vote on a single issue. In Britain, referenda are rare, but a national referendum was held in 1975 on the question of whether the country should remain in the European Community, and the people of Scotland, Wales, and Northern Ireland were consulted in referenda about whether they wanted devolved government.

register of members' interests  under the Local Government Act 2000, each local authority must keep a register listing the outside business and other interests of all of its councillors. The register was adapted from the parliamentary register used for members of Parliament, following the Nolan Inquiry.

report stage  the stage immediately after the **committee stage**, when the **public Bill committee's** chairperson will 'report back' to the Commons with its recommendations.

resolved items  the matters concluded at the end of a committee, full council, or **cabinet**/executive meeting. A vote will normally be taken to make the final decision.

retail price index (RPI)  the measure of **inflation** (changes in prices of goods and services) preferred by most economists to the **consumer price index (CPI)**, this charts the movement in the value of a notional 'basket' of goods regularly bought by typical British households. Because it includes mortgage payments, it is usually higher than the CPI.

returning officer  the official responsible for overseeing local and general election procedures on the day of a poll, ordering recounts where necessary, and announcing the result. Officially, this post is held by the chairperson or **mayor** of a neighbouring or coterminous local authority, but a senior council officer will usually perform the duties in practice—often a **chief executive** or electoral registration officer.

revenue expenditure  the share of a local authority's annual budget spent on the day-to-day running costs of schools, libraries, offices, and other local services. (cf. **capital expenditure**)

revenue support grant (RSG)  one of three types of formula grant allocated to local authorities by central government for their revenue spending, this was traditionally the biggest single chunk of money that they receive. It is calculated on the basis of a formula relating to the demographic make-up of the local area and it may be used by the council in any area of revenue spending.

ring-fenced grant  one of two types of **specific grant** for local authority revenue spending (cf. **unfenced grants**), which must be used for a purpose stipulated by central government. The **Dedicated Schools Grant (DSG)** is the most famous.

royal assent  the 'rubber stamp' given to a Bill by the reigning sovereign to make it an Act of Parliament. In practice, the royal assent is a formality today and no monarch has refused to give it since Queen Anne attempted to do so in 1707.

royal prerogative  a constitutional term used to refer to the (now largely notional) idea that power in the UK derives from the authority of the reigning sovereign. In practice, today the majority of prerogative powers (e.g. the ability to declare war, and to appoint ministers) rests with the elected prime minister of the day.

rule of law  a constitutional principle, derived from 1215's Magna Carta, stipulating that no one is 'above the law of the land', including (in theory) the sovereign.

# S

Schengen Agreement  the collective term for two European Union treaties—signed in 1985 and 1990, respectively—which formally abolished systematic border controls between member states.

Scottish Government (Scottish Executive)  the title used by the devolved administration in Scotland.

Scottish Parliament  Scotland's devolved assembly, which is based in a purpose-built parliamentary building at Holyrood, at the foot of the Royal Mile in Edinburgh.

second reading  the first stage at which the main principles of a Bill are formally read out to the House and debated. This normally takes place within a few weeks of the **first reading** and may lead to an early vote on some aspects of the Bill. (cf. **third reading**)

secondary legislation  See **delegated legislation**

secretary of state  an umbrella term for the most senior government minister in a spending department (e.g. the Secretary of State for Health).

select committee  a permanent parliamentary committee charged with scrutinizing the day-to-day workings of a government department, and other public authorities related to the responsibilities of that department. For example, the Culture, Media and Sport Select Committee examines the work of the Department for Culture, Media and Sport, as well as that of the British Broadcasting Corporation (BBC).

separation of powers  a principle stipulating that the three main seats of constitutional authority in the UK—the executive, legislature, and judiciary—should be kept separate to avoid concentrating power in too few hands. In practice, there are overlaps, with the prime minister and **Cabinet** (executive) also sitting in Parliament (legislature).

Speaker  a member of Parliament elected by his or her peers, traditionally on a motion moved by the Father of the House (the member with the longest unbroken service to the chamber) following a general election, to serve as chairperson of debates and maintain discipline in the Commons.

special responsibility allowance  a top-up fee added to the **basic allowance** for a councillor in recognition of additional responsibilities, such as sitting on, or chairing, a local authority committee. The allowance can vary according to the level of responsibility.

special school  a state school dedicated to teaching children with learning difficulties and/or mental or physical disabilities.

specialist school  a generic term for all state schools that are permitted to specialize in one or more subjects over and above teaching the **National Curriculum**. **Academies** are, by nature, specialist schools—but, in practice, most **community schools** also have subject specialisms, enabling them to draw down extra funds to improve facilities.

specific grant one of two different categories of non-formula grant given to local authorities each year to help with revenue spending (cf. **area-based grants**). Specific grants can either be **ring-fenced grants** or **unfenced grants**.

spin doctor a layperson's term for a type of special adviser usually employed by a senior figure in a political party to put a positive 'spin' on their policies to the public and the media. Alastair Campbell, the former Downing Street director of communications, became one of Britain's most infamous spin doctors during Tony Blair's ten years in power.

standards committee a committee set up by each local authority under the Local Government Act 2000 to monitor councillors' and officers' compliance with the council's **registers of members' interests** and **code of conduct**. The committee must have at least one lay member.

standing order the system of rules adopted by individual local authorities to govern the day-to-day conduct of business in the full council, and its committees, subcommittees, and/or **cabinet**.

subsidiarity a loose constitutional principle underpinning the European Union, which holds that member states retain primary sovereignty over their internal affairs, with the EU acting as a 'subsidiary' institution and the last port of call if individual self-determination falters.

supplementary estimate when a local authority is calculating the level of revenue funding that it will need in the next financial year, it will ask each department to make an estimate of its projected spending. Occasionally, departments underestimate their needs and, at a later date, ask for an additional sum—the supplementary estimate.

Supreme Court Britain's final court of appeal for civil cases, and the highest for criminal matters in England, Wales, and Northern Ireland, this was established in October 2009 in an effort to emulate the constitutional **separation of powers** in the USA. It replaced the Appellate Committee of the House of Lords—previously the UK's ultimate court—which had been the seat of the 'Law Lords' for centuries. There are 12 Justices of the Supreme Court, all currently former Law Lords.

Sure Start a government programme launched in 1999 to improve access for low-income families to early years teaching and other support services.

# T

tactical voting a type of strategic voting by electors voting in 'first past the post' (FPTP) elections, which sees them vote for a candidate other than their 'sincere preference' in the knowledge that to do so would be 'wasted vote'. Tactical voters instead opt for their 'least worst option'— choosing a 'bearable' third party, in order to stop the candidate they most oppose winning.

ten-minute rule one of three ways in which **private member's Bills (PMBs)** may be introduced into Parliament and the one that most often grabs headlines. A member of Parliament must have their idea for a Bill proposed and seconded by colleagues, and obtain a further eight members' signatures, and they will then be given ten minutes in which to introduce their proposals to the Commons. A MP who opposes the Bill will then have the same amount of time to make a speech outlining his or her objections.

**third reading** the final stage of a Bill's passage through the House of Commons. It is at the third reading that members of Parliament are confronted with the final version of the Bill's wording, so it is an occasion for any major disagreements to be fought out in a formal vote. (cf. **first reading**; **second reading**)

**trading standards officer** an officer employed by a county council or unitary authority to ensure that local businesses are adhering to regulations regarding issues such as product labelling, and weights and measures.

**Traffic Commissioner** one of seven regional commissioners, who are employed to license public transport routes and operators, and long-distance haulage companies.

**Transport for London (TfL)** the **quango** responsible for strategic planning and day-to-day running of London's transport network, including the London Underground, Docklands Light Railway, city bus services, and river ferries.

**trunk road** a major arterial road—an 'A' road or a motorway—linking towns and cities, and sometimes crossing the boundaries between counties. (cf. **county road**)

**trust schools** a new form of **foundation school** introduced under the Education and Inspections Act 2006. These are primary and secondary schools supported by charitable trusts that employ their staff, manage assets, and set admissions policies.

**two-tier structure** a type of local government structure established under the 1974 reorganization of local authorities, in which there are two levels of council operating in the same area: district councils and/or **borough councils** responsible for services such as waste collection, housing, and environmental health; and an overarching county council providing countywide services, such as education and highways (roads).

# U

**unfenced grant** one of two types of **specific grant** for local authority revenue spending (cf. **ring-fenced grant**), it may be spent in whatever way a council sees fit, subject to certain conditions. For example, the Housing and Planning Delivery Grant (HPDG) must be used for planning, but councils may choose precisely how to spend it.

**uniform business rates (UBR)** See **national non-domestic rates (NNDR)**

**UNISON** the main local government trade union, it counts among its members many departmental officers, social workers, and health professionals.

**unitary structure** a type of local government structure that has replaced the **two-tier structure** in many areas, in which a single—unitary—local authority is responsible for all local services, from waste collection, to education and social care.

**United Nations (UN)** a global peacemaking body formed in 1945, as a successor to the defunct League of Nations established after the First World War. The UN is headquartered in New York. Its main constitutional bodies include the UN General Assembly and the UN Security Council (which debates international conflict).

## V

**virement** a process allowing local authorities limited discretion to transfer money from one spending area to another during a given financial year, if the former is showing a surplus and the latter a deficit. Councils' ability to use virement has been severely curtailed in recent years, as the government has issued more **ring-fenced grants**.

**voluntary aided school** a type of school in the state sector, the land and buildings of which are owned by a charity or local church. Although such schools receive some funding through the local authority, they are more autonomous than voluntary controlled schools, employing their own staff and setting their own admission policies.

## W

**ward** a term used to describe a **constituency** represented by district council, **borough council**, and some unitary authority councillors. Each has between one and three councillors, depending on its population size.

**Water Services Regulatory Authority** See **Office of Water Regulation (OFWAT)**

**Welsh Assembly Government (Welsh Executive)** the title adopted by the elected **devolved** administration in Wales.

**whip** members of Parliament and peers with the job of 'whipping into line' their parliamentary colleagues, by making sure that they attend important debates and votes, and that they 'toe the line' by supporting their party.

**White Paper** a crystallized version of a **Green Paper**, containing more concrete proposals. If a proposed government Bill has got this far, it will normally proceed further into a formal draft Bill, and may well subsequently become an Act of Parliament.

# Bibliography

## A

Atkinson, H. and Wilks-Heeg, S. (2000) *Local Government from Thatcher to Blair*, Cambridge: Polity Press.

## B

Bartholomew, J. (2006) *The Welfare State We're In*, London: Politico's Publishing.

Blackman, T., Brody, S., and Convery, J. (eds) (2001) *Social Care and Social Exclusion: A Comparative Study of Older People's Care in Europe*, London: Palgrave Macmillan.

Bomberg, E. and Stubb, A. (eds) (2008) *The European Union: How Does it Work?* Oxford: Oxford University Press.

Boynton, J. (1986) *Job at the Top: Chief Executive in Local Government*, London: Financial Times/Prentice Hall.

Bramley, G., Munro, M., and Pawson, H. (2004) *Key Issues in Housing: Policies and Markets in 21st-Century Britain*, London: Palgrave Macmillan.

Brooke, H. (2006) *Your Right to Know: New Edition—A Citizen's Guide to the Freedom of Information Act*, London: Pluto Press.

Brown, C. and Ainley, K. (2005) *Understanding International Relations*, London: Palgrave Macmillan.

Bryan, H. (1996) *Planning Applications and Appeals*, Oxford: Architectural Press.

Budge, I., Crewe, I., McKay, D., and Newton, K. (2007) *The New British Politics*, 4th edn, London: Longman.

Burnham, J. and Pyper, R. (2008) *Britain's Modernised Civil Service*, London: Palgrave Macmillan.

## C

Campbell, A. (2007) *The Blair Years: Extracts from the Alastair Campbell Diaries*, London: Hutchinson.

Cannon, J. and Griffiths, R. (1998) *The Oxford Illustrated History of the British Monarchy*, Oxford: Oxford Paperbacks.

Carey, P. (2004) *Data Protection: A Practical Guide to UK and EU Law*, Oxford: Oxford University Press.

Challis, P. (2003) *Local Government Finance*, London: Local Government Information Unit.

Crewe, I. (ed.) (1998) *Why Labour Won the General Election of 1997*, London: Frank Cass.

Crook, D., Power, S., and Whitty, G. (2000) *The Grammar School Question: A Review of Research on Comprehensive and Selective Education*, London: Institute of Education.

Crossman, R. (1979) *The Crossman Diaries: Selections from the Diaries of a Cabinet Minister, 1964–1970*, London: Book Club Associates.

Cullingworth, J. B. and Nadin, V. (2006) *Town and Country Planning in the UK*, 14th edn, London: Routledge.

## D

Daniels, P. and Ritchie, E. (1996) *EU: Britain and the European Union*, London: Palgrave Macmillan.

Denver, D. (2006) *Elections and Voters in Britain*, 2nd edn, London: Palgrave Macmillan.

Docherty, I. and Shaw, J. (2003) *A New Deal for Transport: The UK's Struggle with the Sustainable Transport Agenda*, London: Wiley-Blackwell.

## E

Edwards, P. (2003) *Industrial Relations: Theory and Practice in Britain*, 2nd edn, London: Wiley-Blackwell.

Evans. G. and Newnham, R. (1998) *The Penguin Dictionary of International Relations*, London: Penguin.

## F

Fischel, W. A. (2005) *The Homevoter Hypothesis: How Home Values Influence*

*Local Government Taxation, School Finance and Land-Use Policies*, Cambridge, MA: Harvard University Press.

### G

Gallagher, M. and Mitchell, P. (2008) *The Politics of Electoral Systems*, Oxford: Oxford University Press.

Glendinning, C. and Kemp, P. (2006) *Cash and Care: Policy Challenges in the Welfare State*, Bristol: Policy Press.

Grimsey, D. and Lewis, M. (2007) *Public Private Partnerships: The Worldwide Revolution in Infrastructure Provision and Project Finance*, London: Edward Elgar.

Gumpert, B. and Kirk, J. (2001) *Trading Standards: Law and Practice*, Bristol: Jordans.

### H

Hall, P. (2002) *Urban and Regional Planning*, 4th edn, London: Routledge.

Ham, C. (2004) *Health Policy in Britain: The Politics and Organisation of The National Health Service*, 5th edn, London: Palgrave Macmillan.

Hansen, R. S. (2001) *Citizenship and Immigration in Post-war Britain: The Institutional Origins of a Multicultural Nation*, Oxford: Oxford University Press.

Hardman, R. (2007) *Monarchy: The Royal Family at Work*, London: Ebury Press.

Harrison, K. and Boyd, T. (2006) *The Changing Constitution*, Edinburgh: Edinburgh University Press.

Hazell, R. and Rawlings, R. (2007) *Devolution, Law Making and the Constitution*, Exeter: Imprint Academic.

Hennessey, P. (2001) *The Prime Minister: The Job and Its Holders Since 1945*, London: Penguin.

Hodge, M., Leach, S., and Stoker, G. (1997) *Local Government Policy: More Than the Flower Show—Elected Mayors and Democracy*, London: Fabian Society.

Hollis, G., Davies, H., Plokker, K., and Sutherland, M. (1994) *Local Government Finance: An International Comparative Study*, London: LGcommunication.

### J

Jackson, R. and Sorensen, G. (2003) *An Introduction to International Relations: Theories and Approaches*, Oxford: Oxford University Press.

Johnston, R. and Pattie, C. (2006) *Putting Voters in Their Place: Geography and Elections in Great Britain*, Oxford: Oxford University Press.

Jones, A. (2007) *Britain and the European Union*, Edinburgh: Edinburgh University Press.

Jones, B. (2004) *Dictionary of British Politics*, Manchester: Manchester University Press.

Jones, B., Kavanagh, D., Moran, M., and Norton, P. (2006) *Politics UK*, 6th edn, London: Longman.

Jones, C. and Murie, A. (2006) *The Right to Buy: Analysis and Evaluation of a Housing Policy*, London: Wiley-Blackwell.

Jones, K. (2002) *Education in Britain: 1944 to the Present*, Cambridge: Polity Press.

Jones, N. (2002) *The Control Freaks: How New Labour Gets Its Way*, London: Politico's Publishing.

### K

Klein, R. (2006) *The New Politics of the NHS: From Creation to Reinvention*, Abingdon: Radcliffe Publishing.

Knowles, R. (1993) *Law and Practice of Local Authority Meetings*, 2nd edn, London: ICSA Publishing.

### L

Lane, K. (2006) *National Bus Company: The Road to Privatisation*, Shepperton: Ian Allen.

Lang, C., Reeve, J., and Woolard, V. (eds) (2006) *The Responsive Museum: Working with Audiences in the Twenty-First Century*, Aldershot: Ashgate.

Leach, R., Coxall, B., and Robins, L. (2006) *British Politics*, London: Palgrave Macmillan.

Leff, J. (1997) *Care in the Community: Illusion or Practice?* London: Wiley-Blackwell.

Lowe, R. (2004) *Welfare State in Britain Since 1945*, 3rd edn, London: Palgrave Macmillan.

Lund, B. (2006) *Understanding Housing Policy*, Cambridge: Policy Press.

## M

Macdonald, J., Crail, R., and Jones, C. (eds) (2009) *The Law of Freedom of Information*, 2nd edn, Oxford: Oxford University Press.

Malpass, P. (2005) *Housing and the Welfare State: The Development of Housing Policy in Britain*, London: Palgrave Macmillan.

Mansell, W. (2007) *Education by Numbers: The Tyranny of Testing*, London: Politico's Publishing.

Marr, A. (2008) *A History of Modern Britain*, London: Pan Books.

McCormick, J. (2008) *Understanding the European Union: A Concise Introduction*, London: Palgrave Macmillan.

Michie, R. C. (2001) *The London Stock Exchange: A History*, Oxford: Oxford University Press.

Midwinter, A. F. and Monaghan, C. (1993) *From Rates to the Poll Tax: Local Government Finance in the Thatcher Era*, Edinburgh: Edinburgh University Press.

Monbiot, G. (2001) *Captive State: The Corporate Takeover of Britain*, London: Pan Books.

Moran, M. (2006) *Politics and Governance in the UK*, London: Palgrave Macmillan.

Morgan, S. (2005) *Waste, Recycling and Reuse*, London: Evans Brothers.

## N

Norton, P. (2005) *Parliament in British Politics*, London: Palgrave Macmillan.

## P

Phillips, R. and Furlong, J. (2001) *Education, Reform and the State: Twenty-Five Years of Politics, Policy and Practice*, London: Routledge Falmer.

Philpot, T. (2007) *Adoption: Changing Families, Changing Times*, London: Routledge.

Pollock, A. M. (2006) *NHS plc: The Privatisation of Our Health Care*, London: Verso Books.

Pollock, A. M. and Talbot-Smith, A. (2006) *The New NHS: A Guide to Its Funding, Organisation and Accountability*, London: Routledge.

Pratchett, L. (2000) *Renewing Local Democracy? The Modernisation Agenda in British Local Government*, London: Frank Cass.

## R

Randle, A. (2004) *Mayors Mid-term: Lessons from the First Eighteen Months of Directly Elected Mayors*, London: New Local Government Network.

Reiner, R. (2000) *The Politics of the Police*, 3rd edn, Oxford: Oxford University Press.

Rogers, R. and Walters, R. (2006) *How Parliament Works*, 6th edn, London: Longman.

Rogers, S. (1998) *Performance Management in Local Government: The Route to Best Value*, 2nd edn, London: Financial Times/Prentice Hall.

Roy, D. (2005) *Liberals: A History of the Liberal and Liberal Democratic Parties*, London: Hambledon Continuum.

## S

Sanders, A. (2006) *Criminal Justice*, London: LexisNexis UK.

Seldon, A. and Snowdon, P. (2004) *The Conservative Party*, Stroud: The History Press.

Smart, G. and Holdaway, E. (2000) *Landscapes at Risk? The Future for Areas of Outstanding Natural Beauty in England and Wales*, London: Spon Press.

Stallion, M. and Wall, D. S. (2000) *The British Police: Police Forces and Chief Officers 1829–2000*, London: M. R. Stallion.

Stanley, J. and Goddard, C. (2002) *In the Firing Line: Violence and Power in Child Protection Work*, London: Wiley-Blackwell.

Stevens, A. (2006) *Politico's Guide to Local Government*, 2nd edn, London: Politico's Publishing.

Stewart, J. (2003) *Modernising British Local Government: An Assessment of Labour's Reform Programme*, London: Palgrave Macmillan.

Swann, D. (1988) *Retreat of the State: Deregulation and Privatisation in the*

*United Kingdom and the United States of America*, London: Prentice-Hall.

**T**

Thorpe, A. (2001) *A History of the British Labour Party*, 2nd edn, London: Palgrave Macmillan.

**W**

Wadham, J., Griffiths, J., and Harris, K. (2007) *Blackstone's Guide to the Freedom of Information Act 2000*, 3rd edn, Oxford: Oxford University Press.

Waters, I. and Duffield, B. (1994) *Entertainment, Arts and Cultural Services*, London: Financial Times/Prentice Hall.

Wilson, D. and Game, C. (2006) *Local Government in the United Kingdom*, London: Palgrave Macmillan.

Wilson, D., Ashton, J., and Sharpe, D. (2001) *What Everyone in Britain Should Know about the Police*, London: Blackstone Press.

Wrigley, C. (2002) *British Trade Unions Since 1933*, Cambridge: Cambridge University Press.

**Y**

Young, J. and Kent, J. (2003) *International Relations Since 1945: A Global History*, Oxford: Oxford University Press.

# Index